PURPOSIVE INTERPRETATION
IN LAW

PURPOSIVE INTERPRETATION
IN LAW

Aharon Barak

Translated from the Hebrew by Sari Bashi

PRINCETON UNIVERSITY PRESS   PRINCETON AND OXFORD

Second printing, and first paperback printing, 2007
Paperback ISBN: 978-0-691-13374-4

The Library of Congress has cataloged the cloth edition
of this book as follows
Barak, Aharon.
Purposive interpretation in law / Aharon Barak.
p.   cm.
Includes bibliographical references and index.
ISBN 0-691-12007-2 (cloth : acid-free paper)
1. Law—Interpretation and construction. 2. Law—Philosophy.
3. Semantics (Law) I. Title.
K290.B37 2005
340′.1—dc22   2004042067

British Library Cataloging-in-Publication Data is available

This book has been composed in Galliard

Printed on acid-free paper. ∞

press.princeton.edu

Printed in the United States of America

3   5   7   9   10   8   6   4   2

For Elika, the love of my life

Contents

Introduction

IT IS THE well-known saying of one judge that books on spirituality and books on legal interpretation are two kinds of books he does not read.[1] That view is unfortunate. In recent years, legal scholars have written numerous books and hundreds of articles on legal interpretation, many of them valuable and worth reading. Indeed, the question is not whether books on interpretation in law should be read, but rather whether there is room for another book on the topic. How does this book differ from its predecessors? What makes it worth reading?

The question is apt, and I hope my answer will satisfy. This book differs from other books on legal interpretation for two primary reasons: *First*, this book is an original attempt to construct a comprehensive theory of interpretation applicable to all legal texts (will, contract, statute, constitution, and everything in between). Currently, the field of legal interpretation is divided among systems of interpretation that apply to different kinds of legal texts. One system applies to constitutional interpretation, while another addresses statutory interpretation. One system applies to the interpretation of contracts, while another tells how to interpret wills. Experts in legal interpretation are generally experts in the interpretation of, at most, one or two kinds of texts (i.e., constitutions and statutes), and they make no real attempt to learn from the way other legal texts are interpreted. This book, on the other hand, presents purposive interpretation as a general system of interpretation to be used for all legal texts. It creates a general, unified approach to interpretation that recognizes the uniqueness of each kind of text and the interpretive emphases characteristic of it. This unified approach, however, exists in tension with the uniqueness of each legal text. Purposive interpretation resolves the tension with a *second* innovation: the concept of purpose. The system views purpose as a legal construction that the interpreter shapes, guided by the rules of purposive interpretation. *Purpose* is an expression of the internal relationship (which changes according to the type of text) between the intent of the specific author of the text (subjective intent) and the intent of the reasonable author (objective purpose). Purposive interpretation thus differs from the purposivism that a number of scholars advocate, which is really just authorial intent at a high level of abstraction. My goal is to convince the reader that purposive interpretation—employed by Israel with great success—is superior to other systems of interpretation used in common law countries. I hope that even

[1] J. Landis, "A Note on Statutory Interpretation," 43 *Harv. L. Rev.* 886 (1929–30).

the reader who does not agree with the idea of a unified, comprehensive system of interpretation for all legal texts will nonetheless find this system of interpretation to be best for each particular type of legal text—constitution, statute, contract, and will.

In addition to introducing these two innovations, purposive interpretation—as presented in this book—has at least four unique characteristics. The *first* aspect of its uniqueness relates to the very concept of interpretation. Few scholars who deal with legal interpretation have defined the concept. For one thing, some are concerned with issues that probably fall outside the concept of interpretation (narrowly defined). This book seeks to define the concept of interpretation and to determine its boundaries. It delimits the field in which the various systems of interpretation operate, and it delimits the non-interpretive fields of non-interpretive doctrines, such as the doctrine of filling in a gap (lacuna) in a legal text, the doctrine of correcting a mistake, or the doctrine of altering a text to avoid an absurdity.

The *second* aspect of the system's uniqueness is its interpretive perspective. Purposive interpretation is holistic. It views each text being interpreted as part of the legal system as a whole. Whoever interprets one text, interprets all texts. Each individual text is connected to the totality of texts in the legal system. Furthermore, there are no barriers between interpreter and text—neither time nor admissibility divide them. There is free movement between text and interpreter, and between interpreter and text. There is no vital distinction between a plain text and a text whose meaning is not plain. No text is plain until it is interpreted, and every text is plain—for purposes of the interpretive problem in question—at the conclusion of the interpretive process.

The *third* aspect of purposive interpretation's uniqueness is the structure of its interpretive "laws." Most of the laws of purposive interpretation are based on neither rules nor canons, but rather on presumptions that apply immediately and always. These presumptions reflect both the intent of the specific author of the text and the intent of the reasonable author who, at the highest level of abstraction, stands in for the fundamental values of the legal system. The interpretive process aspires to unity and agreement among the relevant presumptions and resolution of any conflicts among them. Unlike Professor Llewellyn's image of pairs upon pairs of conflicting rules, purposive interpretation is based on presumptions of purpose that reflect the intent of the text's author and the values of the legal system. Resolving the conflicts among these presumptions lies at the core of purposive interpretation. It is the driving force behind the distinctions in interpreting different kinds of legal texts. Resolution of these conflicts sometimes requires a judge to exercise interpretive discretion.

Indeed, the *fourth* unique aspect of purposive interpretation is its open acknowledgment of the role of judicial discretion. Many existing systems of interpretation—most notably intentionalism and textualism—assume that the rules of interpretation inexorably direct the interpreter toward resolution of every interpretive problem, without the need for him or her to exercise discretion. I find these systems to be fundamentally flawed. It is impossible to construct a valid system of interpretation without recognizing judicial discretion as a critical component. The drawback of most existing systems of interpretation is that they use judicial discretion without admitting it. Purposive interpretation tells the truth. It acknowledges the existence of judicial discretion, regarding it, along with language and purpose, as a critical component of the system. However, in contrast to free systems of interpretation that are based entirely on the interpreter's discretion, purposive interpretation restricts discretion by establishing a framework for its operation.

Now to the heart of the matter: What is the system of purposive interpretation at the core of this book, how does it differ from other systems of interpretation, and why is it superior to them?

Purposive interpretation begins with the idea that interpretation is about pinpointing the legal meaning of a text along the spectrum of its semantic meanings. Semantic meaning sets the limits of interpretation. The interpreter may not give the text a meaning that its language cannot bear. A system of interpretation establishes criteria for determining the legal meaning of the text, within its semantic boundaries. In purposive interpretation, that criterion is the purpose of the text. It is the context according to which the text is interpreted. Purpose is the goals, interests, and values that the text seeks to actualize. It is a legal concept. The interpreter determines purpose according to the criteria that purposive interpretation establishes. That purpose has two components: subjective and objective.

The subjective component is the goals, interests, and values—at various levels of abstraction—that the author of the text sought to actualize. It is the intent of the testator; the joint intent of the parties to a contract; the intent of the members of a legislative body; and the intent of the founders and amenders of a constitution. This subjective aspect reflects what the author or authors of the text actually intended its purpose to be, at the time they created it. Purposive interpretation translates that aspect into presumptions about the purpose of the legal text. The interpreter learns about subjective purpose from the text itself and from the circumstances surrounding its creation. The movement from text to the circumstances of its creation is free and free of technical restrictions. The interpreter need not determine that the text is unclear in order to justify consulting its context.

The objective component of purpose is the goals, interests, and values—at various levels of abstraction—that a text of the type being interpreted is designed to actualize. It is not related to the actual intent of the author. Rather, the author's hypothetical intent determines objective purpose. It reflects the social values prevalent at the time the text is interpreted, including values of morality and justice, social goals (like the public interest), proper modes of behavior (like reasonableness and fairness), and human rights. These values appear before the interpreter in the form of presumptions of purpose. The interpreter gets information about this purpose from the text itself and from the legal system's values. Comparative law assists in this process.

The ultimate purpose of the text—which the interpreter uses to pinpoint its legal meaning along the spectrum of its semantic meanings—depends on the relationship between subjective and objective purpose. This relationship is easy to determine when the two purposes, and their presumptions, point in the same direction. When the two purposes—and the presumptions derived from them—conflict, purposive interpretation expresses its uniqueness by establishing the relationship between subjective and objective purpose according to the type of text in question.

For a will, the only interest worthy of protection is the intent of the testator. Therefore, the interpreter gives decisive weight to subjective purpose, which he or she learns from the language of the will and the circumstances surrounding its making. Objective purpose continues to exist, however, and it is of assistance in the many cases in which there is no credible information about subjective purpose.

For a contract, the primary interest worthy of protection is the joint intent of the parties. It is therefore decisive in formulating the purpose of the contract. However, as is the case for a will, sometimes there is no reliable information about the joint intent of the parties, and sometimes that joint intent is not relevant to resolving the interpretive problem that the judge faces. For the many instances in which there is no way of accessing the joint intent of the parties, objective purpose determines the purpose of the contract. Objective purpose also gains strength when a third party has a reliance interest, or when the type of contract warrants paying special attention to objective purpose. The interpreter of a relational contract or adhesion contract, for example, accords significant weight to objective purpose.

Matters become more complicated in statutory interpretation. Considerations of legislative supremacy would cut in favor of making subjective purpose the decisive factor. Considerations of the supremacy of values and human rights would argue in favor of objective purpose. Purposive interpretation takes both these considerations into account by conditioning the relationship between subjective and objective purpose on the type of statute in question. For example, the interpreter of the following types of statutes accords substantial weight to subjective purpose: a young statute; a specific statute; and a statute expressed in the form of rules. In contrast, the interpreter of an old statute, a general statute or codification, and a statute expressed in the form of standards, accords significant weight to objective purpose. The list of distinctions among types of legislation continues to expand. When there is insufficient guidance about which purpose is dominant, the interpreter uses discretion to decide.

For a constitution, objective purpose has decisive weight. The nature and character of a constitution warrant it. Having said that, an interpreter should always take subjective purpose into account, and it may be useful in selecting among conflicting objective purposes.

According to purposive interpretation, you cannot know how to interpret unless you know what the goal of interpreting is. In my opinion, the goal of interpreting is to achieve the purpose of law, in general, and of the individual legal text as part of it, in particular. Law has a purpose. It is a social device. The goal of interpretation is to achieve the social goal of law. That is the theoretical basis for the centrality of purpose in purposive interpretation. The relationship between the subjective and objective aspects of purposive interpretation depends on constitutional considerations about the roles of the various branches of government, including the judicial branch, and on constitutional considerations of human rights. For private law texts, the decisive factor is the autonomy of the private will. Hence the centrality of subjective purpose in interpreting these texts. Statutory interpretation, in contrast, must take a number of constitutional considerations into account, including legislative supremacy and the supremacy of fundamental values, in general, and human rights, in particular. These considerations, which constitute the core justification for judicial review of the constitutionality of statutes, also constitute the core justification for purposive interpretation of statutes. The conflict between these considerations determines the relationship between subjective and objective purpose, as well as the scope of interpretive discretion. In constitutional interpretation, considerations relating to the essence of the constitution and its role in social life prevail. This role—of guiding public behavior over the course of generations—warrants preferring objective purpose in constitutional interpretation.

Of course, none of the above propositions is self-evident. In this book, I analyze each of them.[2] I discuss the pros and cons of each proposition and express my opinion about which is proper. My approach depends on three fundamental assumptions: *First*, that there is no true interpretation, because the reader accesses a text only after interpreting it. All understanding results from interpretation. Pre-interpretive understanding does not exist. The search, therefore, is not for the true system of interpretation, but rather for the best and most proper system of interpretation. That is the system which, more than any other, within a democracy—and I will

---

[2] The appendix tables present the general argument in visual form for those who might, in the course of the analysis, find a quick reminder helpful.

discuss the relationship between the regime and its system of interpretation—interprets the individual text so that it achieves its goal, and in doing so, helps achieve the goals of the system as a whole.

The *second* fundamental assumption is that human beings are complicated creatures, and that no one explanation, no one theory, and no one system can encompass the full complexity of the human condition. My theory is eclectic. It culls what is best from every legal and social philosophy, balancing the different considerations properly and recognizing the need for interpretive discretion when the balancing scales come out even.

The *third* fundamental assumption is that the selection of a proper system of interpretation—a task usually assigned to the judiciary—should express the role of the judge in a democratic regime. That role includes bridging the gap between law and society's changing reality and protecting the democratic constitution.

This book discusses the advantages and disadvantages of the various systems of interpretation. I extensively analyze intentionalist systems of interpretation, which are based on authorial intent, and the critique of them. I also discuss various textualist approaches—new and old—and their advantages and disadvantages. I address the system of interpretation of Justice Scalia—a standard-bearer of new textualism—and its strengths and weaknesses. I also discuss Professor Dworkin's approach to interpretation and that of other pragmatists, most notably Judge Posner. Purposive interpretation shares many fundamentals with Dworkin's system of interpretation. Like the systems of Posner and other pragmatists, purposive interpretation uses interpretive discretion pragmatically. Purposive interpretation also shares common elements with Professor Eskridge's dynamic approach. Because objective purpose is so important to purposive interpretation, the system achieves dynamic results. This dynamism, however, is not a system of interpretation by itself, but rather an occasional result of purposive interpretation. After comparing purposive interpretation to the other systems of interpretation, I claim that, on balance, purposive interpretation is superior.

Recognizing purposive interpretation as the proper system of interpretation is not the end of the interpretive journey but rather its beginning. Purposive interpretation opens new avenues of thought and presents new difficulties that must be addressed. Different purposive interpreters will disagree with me over one or another aspect of my interpretive approach. Indeed, in some sense, there are many different purposive-interpretive approaches—or, more precisely, sub-approaches. The attempt to formulate a unified, comprehensive theory for all legal texts, on the one hand, and the desire to express the individuality of each legal text, on the other hand, naturally creates different purposive approaches, the examination of which will, in the future, enrich legal thinking and advance the goals of law.

I divide this book into three parts. In Part 1, I examine the essence of interpretation and its limits. I define interpretive activity in chapter 1, distinguishing between it and activities that resemble interpretation but are distinct from it, like filling in a gap in a legal text or correcting a mistake in it. I see these latter activities as non-interpretive, based on non-interpretive doctrines that I analyze. I analyze the fundamental perspectives of legal interpretation, including the relationship between text and context and the essence of the relevant context. I survey the major systems of legal interpretation, the primary hermeneutic perspectives relevant to law, and the extent to which the latter are relevant. I address the sources of interpretive rules, their legal status, and the possibility of deviating from them. I analyze the role of the judge as interpreter, the relationship between his or her interpretation and that of others in society (whether they be other branches of government or private parties). I discuss the importance of interpretive rules and the critique of them. I acknowledge the merit of some criticism of interpretive rules. That does not, however, negate the role of interpretive rules as rules that guide the interpreter and impart the necessary legitimacy to his or her activities. I include all legal texts in my analysis, whatever the type. In chapter 2, I discuss non-interpretive doctrines, which are related to interpretation but distinct from it. Readers who are mainly interested in the normative core of the argument may wish to skim this first part in favor of a more careful reading of the second and third parts, which outline my theory of purposive interpretation and how it is implemented.

I dedicate the *second* and primary part of the book to analyzing the purposive interpretation of all types of legal texts introduced in chapter 3. I discuss and analyze in depth the three components of purposive interpretation: language, purpose, and interpretive discretion. Regarding the first component, in chapter 4, I analyze the communicative nature of language and its limitations (ambiguity, vagueness). I discuss the different kinds of language relevant to legal interpretation, notably the distinction between public and private language, explicit and implicit language, and ordinary and exceptional language. I discuss the canons of interpretation (such as *expressio unius est exclusio alterius*), regarding them as rules of language and not of law.

The bulk of Part 2 is dedicated to the concept of purpose. In chapter 5, I discuss the subjective and objective purpose at the core of every legal text. In chapter 6, I emphasize the actual, static nature of subjective purpose, note the distinction between abstract purpose and concrete purpose (consequentialist or interpretive purpose), and explain why we should only take abstract purpose into account. I dedicate section 3 to the problem of multiple authors (such as the members of a legislative body or constitutional assembly) in formulating subjective purpose. I acknowledge how difficult it is to identify the subjective intent of an entity with a large number of authors. The difficulty is not insurmountable, however, and it does not justify ignoring the intent of the creators (such as the members of a legislative body) in interpreting the creation (the statute). I dedicate a substantial part of the analysis of subjective purpose in section 4 to the sources from which an interpreter may learn about it. The primary source is, of course, the text itself, examined in its entirety. However, the interpreter may also consult the circumstances surrounding the text's creation as a source of subjective purpose. The interpreter may always consult those circumstances, regardless of whether special conditions, such as the text being unclear, are met.

I devote a substantial chapter (chapter 7) to objective purpose, reflecting the intent of the reasonable author and the fundamental values of the legal system. I emphasize the dynamic aspect of this purpose. Most of my analysis focuses on the sources from which the interpreter may learn about objective purpose. These sources include the text in its entirety, the text's natural environment, generic law, the text's history, the text's general social and historical background, case law, jurisprudence and the legal culture, the system's fundamental values (analyzed in depth), and comparative law. I discuss at length the presumptions derived from objective purpose. Here, I address a number of presumptions common to all legal texts, like the presumption that a text is designed to actualize human rights and values of morality, justice, and the public interest. I analyze the essence of the presumptions of purpose, their status, and the relationship between conflicting presumptions. This relationship is determined by the weight of the presumptions, which reflects their relative social importance, and by the balance among them. In this context, I discuss the theory of balancing and its advantages and disadvantages.

After examining subjective purpose and objective purpose, in chapter 8 I discuss the formulation of ultimate purpose, which balances the two. The interpreter achieves this balance by seeking synthesis and integration. When that is impossible, the interpreter must decide which purpose prevails. Here, I develop the inner core of purposive interpretation. Rather than establish rigid rules of superiority, purposive interpretation evaluates each type of legal text, its characteristics, and the justifications for preferring its subjective or objective purpose. Based on the identity of the author, the system distinguishes among types of text: will, contract, statute, and constitution. Purposive interpretation in effect creates a spectrum of situations. On one extreme are wills, for which subjective purpose is the decisive factor, while on the other extreme are constitutions, for which objective purpose is decisive. Contracts and statutes fall in the middle. The interpreter evaluates the different types of contracts and statutes and assigns each type its own status vis-à-vis the balance between subjective and objective purpose.

In chapter 9, I continue with an analysis of the third component of purposive interpretation, judicial discretion. In my view, it is impossible to build a system of interpretation without recognizing the existence of judicial discretion. Such discretion must, however, be restricted. I discuss these restrictions, including procedural restrictions (fairness and objectivity) and substantive restrictions (rationality, consistency, coherence, and reasonableness). Within the range where judicial discretion exists, the purposive interpreter must adopt a pragmatic stance, with the goal of achieving what he or she believes to be the purpose of the text. In this context, I recommend exercising discretion according to considerations of justice.

I devote chapter 10 of Part 2 to the theoretical basis of purposive interpretation. I note that the goal of interpretation must be to give expression to the objective at the core of the legal text. For this purpose, I refer to various societal considerations that emphasize the nature of law as a social device. I bolster this approach with an analysis of the primary philosophical theories in law, including realism, positivism, legal process, law and economics, and the theory of Dworkin and the pragmatists. I seek to show that each of these theories contains core elements of purpose. I also turn to hermeneutic scholars outside the field of law (like Gadamer) in an attempt to ground various elements of purposive interpretation—primarily its search for normative unity and its holistic approach—in general hermeneutics. Finally, I address the constitutional considerations at the core of purposive interpretation. I analyze the concept of democracy and point out that democracy is a delicate balance between majority will, on one hand, and fundamental values and human rights, on the other. Subjective purpose reflects majority will. Objective purpose reflects fundamental values and human rights. The balance between the different elements of purpose mirrors the balance between the different elements of democracy. In this context, I discuss rule of law, separation of powers, and the role of the judge in a democracy. These principles, in my view, point to purposive interpretation as the most appropriate system of interpretation.

In chapter 11, I conclude Part 2 with a debate between purposive interpretation and conflicting systems of interpretation. I analyze systems of interpretation based on authorial intent (intentionalism), on the understanding of the text (new and old textualism), and on the approach of Professor Dworkin and various pragmatists. I note that, while some similarities exist between purposive interpretation and the other systems, there are substantial differences. I discuss these differences and claim that purposive interpretation is superior.

Finally, Part 3 evaluates how purposive interpretation acts upon the primary types of legal texts. Separate chapters address the interpretation of wills (chapter 12), contracts (chapter 13), statutes (chapter 14), and constitutions (chapter 15). I divide each of these types into subcategories that outline a more nuanced relationship between subjective and objective purpose.

I am not a legal philosopher. I am a judge, interested in the theoretical foundations of judicial activity, who seeks to formulate a judicial philosophy for himself. This book expresses my judicial philosophy. It does not belong to the lofty heights of philosophical study, though it is based on philosophical writing and occasionally critiques it. This book is intended primarily for judges and lawyers, teachers of law and its students. It does not attempt to describe specific discussions of specific issues, but rather to offer a general theory that provides the reader with tools for independent thought. Although most of my experience is with judicial work in Israel, this book is not a book on Israeli legal interpretation. It is a book on purposive interpretation in every legal system. I do, however, rely primarily on sources from common law systems (England, the United States, Canada, and Australia).

This book is a translation of major sections of the Hebrew text, *Parshanut Tachlitit Bimishpat*. It reflects the status of the law and the literature as of 2002.

I wish to thank my good friend Owen Fiss, who encouraged me to publish this book, and Dean Tony Kronman and Yale Law School, who helped with its translation into English. I also thank Meir Dan Cohen, Meni Mautner, Yigal Mersel, Andrei Marmor, Nir Keidar, and Roy Kreitner, who read the manuscript and offered useful and important comments. I am grateful to Yael Ilan for her excellent work typing the Hebrew version of this book, and to Sari Bashi, who gave of her time and talents as translator and editor to transform the Hebrew version into an English text. Finally, I am grateful to Elika, who, in her wisdom, helped me complete this book.

Part One

INTERPRETATION

CHAPTER ONE

What Is Legal Interpretation?

1. DEFINITION OF LEGAL INTERPRETATION

On the Concept of Interpretation in Law

"Interpretation" in law has different meanings.[1] Indeed, the word "interpretation" itself must be interpreted.[2] I define legal interpretation as follows: Legal interpretation is a rational activity that gives meaning to a legal text.[3] The requirement of rationality is key—a coin toss is not interpretive activity. Interpretation is an intellectual activity,[4] concerned with determining the normative message that arises from the text.[5] What the text is and whether it is valid are questions related to interpretation, but they are distinct from it. I assume the existence of a valid legal text. The question is what meaning to attach to that text. According to my definition, then, interpretation shapes the content of the norm "trapped" inside the text. The text that is the object of interpretation may be general (as in a constitution, statute, case law, or custom) or individual (as in a contract or will). It may be written (as in a written constitution or judicial opinion) or oral (as in an oral will or a contract implied-in-fact). The word "text" is not limited to a written text. For purposes of interpretation, any behavior that creates a legal norm is a "text."

---

[1] See A. Barak, *Parshanut B'mishpat* [*Interpretation in Law*] 29 (1992) and citations therein. *See also* W. Twinning and D. Miers, *How to Do Things with Rules* 166 (4th ed. 1999); G. Gottlieb, *The Logic of Choice* 95 (1968); A. Barnes, *On Interpretation* 7 (1988); A. Marmor, *Interpretation and Legal Theory* 13 (1992); A. Marmor, *Positive Law and Objective Values* 71 (2001).

[2] See M.S. Moore, "Legal Interpretation," 18 *Iyunei Mishpat* 359 (1994), and G.L. Williams, "Language and Law," 61 *Law Q. Rev.* 71, 392 (1945).

[3] See C. Ogden and I. Richards, *The Meaning of Meaning* (10th ed. 1956); M.S. Moore, "The Semantics of Judging," 54 *S. Cal. L. Rev.* 151 (1981); R. Cross, *Statutory Interpretation* (J. Bell and G. Engle eds., 3d ed. 1995); H. Hart and A. Sachs, *The Legal Process: Basic Problems in the Making and Application of Law* 1374 (W. Eskridge and P. Frickey eds., 1994); A. Dickerson, *The Interpretation and Application of Statutes* 34 (1975).

[4] See H. Kelsen, *Pure Theory of Law* 348 (Knight trans. from German, 2d ed. 1967).

[5] See K. Larenz, *Methodenlehre der Rechtswissenschaft* (5th ed. 1983); R. Zippelius, *Einführung in die Juristische Methodenlehre* (1971).

Constrictive Definitions of Legal Interpretation

The definition of legal interpretation at the core of this book is not the only possible definition. Some theorists define interpretation more narrowly, others, more broadly. Under a narrower or constrictive definition, there is room for interpretation only in places where the text is unclear, such that there are differences of opinion over it.[6] Similarly, a constrictive definition might restrict legal interpretation to finding the meaning that realizes the intent of the legal text's author.[7] I do not adopt these definitions. According to my theory, every legal text requires interpretation. The plainness of a text does not obviate the need for interpretation, because such plainness is itself a result of interpretation. Even a text whose meaning is undisputed requires interpretation, for the absence of dispute is a product of interpretation. Realizing the intent of the author is the goal of one kind of system of interpretation (subjective interpretation[8]). Interpretation, however, can also give the legal text a meaning that actualizes objective standards (objective interpretation[9]). The definition of interpretation (in contrast to systems of interpretation within that definition) cannot be reduced to merely giving meaning that realizes authorial intent.

Expansive Definitions of Legal Interpretation

Legal interpretation may also be conceptualized more expansively than my definition permits. For example, Dworkin defines law itself as an interpretive process:

> Legal practice is an exercise in interpretation not just when lawyers interpret documents or statutes but also generally. Propositions of law are not simply descriptive of legal history, in a straightforward way, nor are they simply evaluative in some way divorced from legal history. They are interpretive of legal history, which combines elements of both description and evaluation, but is different from both.[10]

While Dworkin's approach has been the subject of criticism,[11] an evaluation of his definition and the critique of it are beyond the scope of this

---

[6] *See* J. Wróblewski, *The Judicial Application of Law* 88 (1992).

[7] *See* F.V. Hawkins, "On the Principles of Legal Interpretation," 2 *Jurid. Soc'y Papers* 298, 307 (1860).

[8] *See* p. 32, *infra*.

[9] *See* p. 33, *infra*.

[10] R. Dworkin, "Law as Interpretation," 60 *Tex. L. Rev.* 529 (1982).

[11] *See* M.S. Moore, "The Interpretive Turn in Modern Theory: A Turn for the Worse?" 41 *Stan. L. Rev.* 871 (1989); D. Patterson, "The Poverty of Interpretive Universalism: To-

book. Dworkin's definition lies at the foundation of his philosophic project, and I respect it. My definition, however, is narrower. It lies at the foundation of a different project, whose concern is giving meaning to a legal text. The two projects are distinct but interrelated. From Dworkin's definition of interpretation, one can derive a system of understanding a legal text such as a constitution or statute. In that sense, Dworkin's (expansive) theory of interpretation becomes one of a variety of systems of interpretation (as defined above).

The Limits of Interpretation in Law

My definition of interpretation raises a number of questions of classification. The answers to these questions determine if the standards for interpreting a text can apply to additional legal activities. *First*, does resolving (antinomic) contradictions in a given legal text constitute interpretive activity? In my view, the answer to that question is yes. Imparting meaning to a given text requires resolving internal contradictions within the text itself. *Second*, does resolving contradiction between different legal texts on the same normative plane (two statutes, two contracts, two wills), or on different normative planes (constitution and statute, statute and contract, contract and will), constitute interpretive activity? Of course, giving meaning to *each* of those texts constitutes interpretive activity, but does resolving the *contradiction*—based on the meaning given—constitute an inherently interpretive activity? The question has no clear answer, other than saying that it depends on the tradition of a given legal system. In my view, however—and depending on the particularities of the legal traditions in question—resolving contradiction between norms arising from different texts is a non-interpretive activity. True, in resolving contradictions between different texts, we give meaning to a legal system. But this giving of meaning constitutes interpretive activity only in Dworkin's broad sense. It does not constitute interpretation in the sense I give to the word. For example, the rule of constitutional supremacy—that a statute which violates a constitutional provision is invalid—is a rule that resolves contradictions, but it is not a rule of interpretation. *Third*, does filling in a lacuna or gap in a legal text constitute interpretive activity? The German legal tradition distinguishes between ordinary interpretation (*einfache Auslegung*) and supplementary interpretation (*ergänzende Auslegung*). Indeed, the answer to this (third) question also depends on the legal tradition in question. I personally distinguish between interpretation in the narrow sense—the in-

---

ward the Reconstruction of Legal Theory", 72 *Tex. L. Rev.* 1 (1993). *See also* C.A. 3798/94 *Anonymous v. Anonymous*, 50(3) P.D. 133, 174.

terpretation that gives meaning to a legal text—and interpretation in the broad sense, which includes filling gaps in an incomplete text. The justification in calling the second activity interpretive—if only in the broad sense—stems from the fact that it does ultimately give meaning to a text, determining the normative message arising from it. Referring to the addition of an implied term to a contract, Hoffman writes: "It may seem odd to speak of interpretation when, by definition, the term has not been expressed in words, but the only difference is that when we imply a term, we are engaged in interpreting the meaning of the contract as a whole."[12] For this reason, I include correcting the language of the text, as in fixing a mistake, as part of interpretation in the broad sense.

Why do I insist on distinguishing between interpretation in its broad and narrow sense? The standards governing these two activities are different. Two separate and distinct systems govern the interpretation of an existing text and the completion of an incomplete text. Sometimes, a judge is allowed to interpret a text but is not allowed to fill a gap in it, as in the case of a criminal statute. Of course, so long as we remain sensitive to the distinctions I note, there is nothing wrong with generally referring to both kinds of activities as interpretive. The point is to avoid loading interpretation (in the narrow sense) with a burden it cannot bear. As we shall see, I take the limits of interpretation (in the narrow sense) to be the limits of language. An attempt to give the text a meaning that its language cannot bear is a non-interpretive project. Trying to cram that project into interpretation in its narrow sense distorts interpretation and undermines the legitimacy of judicial activity.

Legal Meaning and Semantic Meaning

Interpretation in law is a rational process by which we understand a text. Through interpretation, we come to know the normative message of a text. It is a process that "extracts" the legal meaning of the text from its semantic meaning.[13] Interpreters translate the "human" language into "legal" language. They turn "static law" into "dynamic law." They carry out the legal norm in practice. Legal interpretation turns a semantic "text" into a legal

---

[12] L.H. Hoffman, "The Intolerable Wrestle with Words and Meanings," 114 *S.A.L.J.* 656, 662 (1997).

[13] *C.A. 708/88 Shefes & Sons, Ltd. v. Ben Yaka Gat, Engineering and Building Co., Ltd.,* 40(2) P.D. 743, 747: "The basic rule of interpretation in contracts is that the interpreter must choose the legal interpretation that realizes the intentions of the parties from among the semantic meanings of the contractual 'text'" (Barak, J.). *See also* F.A.R. Bennion, *Statutory Interpretation* 14 (3d ed. 1997) (distinguishing between the grammatical meaning and the legal meaning).

norm—hence the distinction between the semantic meaning of a text and its legal (or normative) meaning. The semantic meaning of a text is the totality of all meanings that may be attached to the language of the text, in the ideal lexicon of those who speak the language in question (the public language) or in the private lexicon of the text's author (the private code). To interpret a text is to choose its legal meaning from among a number of semantic possibilities—to decide which of the text's semantic meanings constitutes its proper legal meaning. The semantic meaning of the text determines its semantic potential or semantic range of activity (the *Bedeutungsspielraum*).[14] The legal meaning carries this potential into practice. Usually, a text has a single, unique semantic meaning in the context of a given event, and that meaning also serves as the text's legal meaning. In these typical cases, there is complete identity between the text's semantic and legal meanings. All systems of interpretation will arrive at the same meaning of the text. Because language can be vague and ambiguous, however, a text sometimes has a number of semantic meanings in the context of a given event. Only one of these semantic meanings can serve as the text's legal meaning. The rules of interpretation become critical in these "hard" cases.

Interpretation and Semantics

Semantics determines the totality of meanings that a text may have in its language (public and private) for various potential fact patterns. We comprehend this totality through language. We understand the text because the language in which it was created is a language we know. Indeed, the linguist inquires into what meanings the text can "tolerate" in its language, in light of the totality of potential contexts. In principle, there is no difference between determining the semantic meaning of a legal text and determining the semantic meaning of any other (nonlegal) text. Linguists examine the range of semantic possibilities for texts. They need to know the rules of grammar and syntax customary in that language. They consult the canons, based in logic, which help them understand the language.

Legal interpreters build on the work of the linguists who determine linguistic range. Interpreters translate the language into law by pinpointing or extricating a single, unique legal meaning. We may therefore conclude that every interpreter of law is also a linguist,[15] but that not every linguist is an interpreter of law. I took this position in one case when I noted that

---

[14] Zippelius, *supra* p. 3, note 5 at 25. *See also* Bydlinsky, discussing the "courtyard of the expression" (*Begriffshot*): F. Bydlinsky, *Juristische Methodenlehre und Rechtsbegriff* 438 (1982).

[15] *See* L.M. Solan, *The Language of Judges* (1993).

interpretation is more than mere linguistics, but rather requires us to find the normative message arising from the text.[16] The linguist ascertains the meaning that the text is capable of bearing, in light of the range of possible contexts. In doing so, he or she sets the boundaries of interpretation. The legal interpreter determines the meaning that the text *must* bear, in the context relevant to legal interpretation. Many rules of interpretation are simply linguistic rules, designed to ascertain the (linguistic) meaning that may be given to the text. They in no way help to determine the text's legal meaning. Thus, for example, the interpretive principle that to express or include one thing implies the exclusion of the other (*expressio unius est exclusio alterius*) is merely a linguistic rule. It teaches us that from the "yes" of the text, we can infer the "no" of another matter. This is a possible, but not a necessary, linguistic inference. It does not establish an "interpretive" principle. It establishes a "linguistic" principle.[17]

Interpretation, Systems of Interpretation, and Principles of Interpretation in Law

The systems of interpretation in law determine the standards by which interpreters extract the legal meaning of a text from a variety of semantic meanings. Principles of interpretation, which are simply principles of "extraction" or "extrication," thus derive from systems of interpretation. Principles of interpretation are partly principles of language that establish the range of semantic possibilities. They are also—and this is important for our purposes—principles that govern how to determine a text's legal meaning. Interpretation in law determines the meaning of a legal text, and that meaning varies according to the system of interpretation. A system of interpretation based on authorial intent produces a different meaning than a system that asks how a reasonable reader would understand the text. Each system of interpretation produces its own principles of interpretation. These principles are—in the words of Professor Hart[18]—secondary rules. As secondary rules, they determine the scope or range of deployment of the norm extracted from the (primary) text. Note that we have not yet taken a position on the question of how to determine the text's meaning. That question depends on the system of interpretation and the principles of interpretation derived therefrom. The system of interpretation may vary from time to time and from legal system to legal system. We have so far ascertained only the definition of interpretation. We have not yet addressed what the proper system of interpretation is, and what principles of inter-

[16] H.C. 846/93, Barak v. National Labor Court, 51(1) P.D. 3, 10.
[17] *See* p. 108, *infra.*
[18] *See* H.L.A. Hart, *The Concept of Law* 94 (2d ed. 1994).

pretation derive from it. For example, I do not define interpretation as an inquiry into the intent of the text's author.[19] That inquiry constitutes a specific system of interpretation, one way of extracting the legal meaning from its textual receptacle, but it does not define interpretation itself. We must distinguish between the concept of interpretation, on the one hand, and systems of interpretation, including the principles that derive from them, on the other. There is only one definition of interpretation—rationally giving meaning to a text[20]—while there are many different systems of interpretation and derivative principles.

"True" Interpretation and "Proper" Interpretation

Many jurists embark on a futile[21] search to discover what the legal meaning of a text "truly" is. A text has no "true" meaning. We have no ability to compare the meaning of a text before and after its interpretation by focusing on its "true" meaning. All understanding results from interpretation, because we can access a text only after it has been interpreted. There is no pre-exegetic understanding. At best, we can compare different interpretations of a given text.[22] The most to which we can aspire is the "proper" meaning—not the "true" meaning. I therefore do not contend that purposive interpretation is the true interpretation. My claim is that among the various systems of interpretation in a democracy, purposive interpretation is the best. In no way do I negate the interpretive character of the other systems of interpretation. I claim that there is no "true" meaning, but, unlike Fish,[23] I

[19] For a definition in this vein, see B. Rüthers, *Rechtstheorie* (1999). *See also* P.S. Atiyah, *Essays on Contract* 272 (1988).

[20] *See* A. Corbin, 2 *Corbin on Contracts: A Comprehensive Treatise on the Rules of Contract Law* (1960): "Interpretation is the process whereby one person gives meaning to the symbols of expression used by another person." *See also* E.W. Patterson, "The Interpretation and Construction of Contracts," 64 *Colum. L. Rev.* 833 (1964).

[21] *See* H. Kelsen, *General Theory of Norms* 130 (M. Hartney trans., 1991): "In terms of the positive law, there is simply no method according to which only one of the several readings of a norm could be distinguished as 'correct.'" *See also* J. Wróblewski, "Outline of a General Theory of Legal Interpretation and Constitutional Interpretation," 32 *Folia Iuridica* 33, 71 (1987).

[22] *See* P.G. Monateri, "Legal Doctrine as a Source of Law: A Transitional Factor and a Historical Paradox," *Rapporti Italiani, Academie Internationale de Droit Compare* 19, 25 (1986): "The process is formed by the application of the various interpretative rules. . . . Because without this process the *interpretandum* is unknown, it follows that at the end we can compare or oppose only different results derived by the application of different rules of construction. . . . It is impossible to compare or oppose the result with the *interpretandum* itself. It's possible only to compare many interpretative results." *See also* B. Bix, *Law, Language and Legal Determinacy* (1993).

[23] *See* S. Fish, *Is There a Text in the Class? The Authority of Interpretive Communities*, 330, 338 (1980).

do not contend that there is no text. Nor do I claim that the text does not determine the boundaries of its interpretation. Quite the opposite: My claim is that the limits of the text set the limits of interpretation.[24] Within the limits of a text, the normative message that arises is ascertained through interpretation of the text, which cannot be proven "true" or "false."

Interpretation and Validity

In order to narrow the focus on interpretation, let me distinguish questions of meaning from questions of validity, the former of which are the subject of this book.[25] The validity of a norm refers to the force of that norm in law.[26] Thus, for example, when the author of a text fails to meet the requirements for establishing a norm in the legal system (like the proper form of a contract or will), the norm does not enter into force. Similarly, when an inferior norm contradicts a superior norm (like a statute contradicting a constitution, or a contract contrary to public policy), the inferior norm loses its force. The same applies to a later (and specific) norm that contradicts an earlier (and general) norm. In situations like these, we evaluate the power of the norm in the legal world. We assume a norm of a given scope, and we inquire into its validity.

A question about the text's meaning, in contrast, inquires into the normative content of the text. Questions of content address the meaning that the text should bear, while questions of validity deal with the status of the norm extricated from the text that has been interpreted. Judges decide both validity and interpretation, but the activity they undertake in each case differs in character, because each activity answers different questions. Rules of validity focus on the norm, responding to the question, "Is norm X valid in this system?" Rules of meaning focus on the text, responding to the question, "What is the content (range of deployment) of text X?" These two inquiries are related, however, and it is not always easy to distinguish between them. For example, one interpretive presumption requires that a text be given a meaning that preserves the validity of the norm it contains (presumption of validity[27]). Furthermore, every text requires interpretation, and its interpretation is a precondition for inquiring into the validity of the norm to be extracted from the text. The inquiry as to whether or not the norm is valid takes place against the backdrop of the given scope of the text from

---

[24] See p. 18, infra.

[25] See W. Twining and D. Miers, How to Do Things with Rules: A Primer of Interpretation 186 (4th ed. 1999) 155.

[26] See Kelsen, supra p. 3, note 4 at 7,10.

[27] Infra p. 173.

which it is extricated—and such scope is the product of interpretive activity. Every question of validity must deal with questions of meaning, but not every question of meaning raises issues of validity. As an empirical matter, most legal traditions conflate questions of validity with questions of interpretation. Thus, for example, Anglo-American judges treat contradictions between norms of equal status—like the rule that a later norm trumps an earlier norm (*lex posterior derogat priori*)—as questions of interpretation. There is no reason to challenge that approach, so long as it is clear that once a judge establishes the meaning of each of the two norms, the rules for resolving the contradiction between them are rules of validity, not meaning.

Interpretation and Political Regime

There is no "true" interpretation. We must seek, rather, proper interpretation. Hence, the interpretative system that is proper in a democratic regime is not necessarily the proper system of interpretation in a totalitarian regime.[28] Each type of regime has a system of interpretation that suits it. For example, when I assert that purposive interpretation is the most proper system of interpretation, I limit this assertion to the context of a democratic regime. Dissenters in a totalitarian regime might rightly prefer a literal system of interpretation to purposive interpretation. The system of interpretation depends on the constitutional requirements in force, and both elements are integrally related to the type of regime. In a given legal system, when the regime type changes, the system of interpretation changes accordingly.

The Object of Interpretation

The object of interpretation is the text. The text is the *interpretandum*. This is true of constitution and statute, case law and custom, contract and

[28] In my view, in a totalitarian regime, one should not use interpretation to express the fundamental totalitarian principles of the regime. One should also avoid interpreting a law according to the will of its totalitarian creator. In such a regime, the interpreter should privilege textual interpretation. There has been substantial criticism of German judges in the Nazi era who looked to the regime's fundamental totalitarian values in interpreting laws. See I. Müller, *Hitler's Justice* (D. Schneider trans., 1991); B. Rüthers, *Die unbegrenzte Auslegung: Zum Wandel der Privatrechtsordnung im Nationalsozialismus* (1973); M. Stolleis, *The Law under the Swastika* (T. Dunlop trans., 1998). Similarly, apartheid-era South African judges have been criticized for giving expression to legislative intent (which favored Apartheid), instead of the fundamental values of the system, which reflected the fundamental values of the common law. See D. Dyzenhaus, *Judging the Judges, Judging Ourselves: Truth, Reconciliation and the Apartheid Legal Order* (1998); D. Dyzenhaus, *Hard Cases in Wicked Legal Systems: South African Law in the Perspective of Legal Philosophy* (1991). See also C. Sunstein, "Must Formalism Be Defended Empirically? 6 *U. Chi. L. Rev.* 636 (1999).

will. Interpretive activity extracts or extricates the legal (constitutional, case-law, contractual, etc.) norm from its semantic vessel. We should, however, distinguish between the language that anchors the legal norm and the legal norm extracted from the language.[29] The norm extracted from the text is the product of interpretation. It is not the object of interpretation. The text is the object of interpretation. Consider, for example, a contract between Rueben and Simon for the sale of an asset that does not specify the time of delivery. A few norms might arise from the text: the legal obligation to deliver the asset immediately, within a year, or within a reasonable time. Through interpretation, we determine that the norm arising from the text is the legal obligation to deliver the asset within a reasonable time. The contract (as a text) and the contract (as a norm) are not the same thing. Interpretation engages the text, producing the norm. The norm presents itself to the interpreter after he or she has interpreted the text. In their role as interpreters, judges are not concerned with the status of the norm, its validity, or its relationship to other norms. For example, interpretive rules do not regulate the relationship between a superior norm (like a constitution) and an inferior norm (like a statute). The object of interpretation is the text of the constitution and the text of the statute. Once an interpreter extracts the norm from them, the interpretive work ends, and the non-interpretive work, establishing the norm's validity and status, begins. More precisely, in order to interpret each text, one must consider other relevant texts and the norms extracted from them. A judge's interpretation of the text of a constitution affects judicial interpretation of the text of a statute. Once judges have interpreted the different texts and extracted the legal norms from them, however, they face additional questions—like the validity of the statute and its relationship to the constitution—that are not questions of interpretation. Although a given legal tradition may treat these questions as interpretive, we ought to distinguish between these different types of questions. Henceforth, when I refer to legal interpretation, I refer to the interpretation of a legal text.

"A Plain Text Needs No Interpretation"

Every text requires interpretation. A text cannot be understood without being interpreted. As Professor Wigmore put it, "The process of interpretation, then, though it is commonly simple and often unobserved, is always present, being inherently indispensable."[30] We access a legal text only after

---

[29] *See* G. Hassold, "Strukturen der Gesetzesauslegung," *Festschrift für Karl Larenz* 214 (1983).

[30] *See* J.H. Wigmore, *Evidence* §2459 (Chadbourn Rev., 1981).

we have interpreted it, consciously or unconsciously. A text has no pre-interpretive meaning.[31] Professor Tedeschi was quite right in noting that

> *In claris non fit interpretatio* (clear rules do not require interpretation): That saying may not be classical Roman, but it is held sacred because of its long tradition, and it is well known by jurists everywhere. However, contemporary scholars increasingly realize the naiveté of the conception it implies—namely that the rule, if not the "clear" rule, can speak for itself. Another person's thought cannot act upon us unless we comprehend it. It is our very cooperation in that comprehension that constitutes the interpretive process, whether the interpretation is tiresome and difficult or done easily and without our noticing. And here, in this last instance, the interpretation will come, and it is precisely the ease and confidence with which it is done that allows us to conclude that the text or behavior in question is indeed clear.[32]

Indeed, the determination that a text's instructions are plain, and thus do not require interpretation, is an interpretive determination that succeeds, rather than precedes, the interpretive act. Characterizing a text as "unclear" is a result of the interpretive process, not an occasion to begin it.[33] In some cases, judges unconsciously determine the text's degree of clarity through interpretation, ironically thus concluding that the text has a plain meaning and need not be interpreted.[34] For other texts, the process takes place consciously—hence the conclusion that the text is unclear and must be interpreted. The assertion that a "plain" text does not require interpretation is not only incorrect, it is also dangerous, because it masks an unconscious act of interpretation. Indeed, the real question is not whether a plain text requires interpretation. The real question is what rules of interpretation are needed to arrive at the text's plain meaning.

While some trends in case law and legal literature insist that not every text requires interpretation, their proponents define interpretation more narrowly than I do. Those who believe that not all texts need be interpreted

---

[31] *See* C. Sunstein, "Interpreting Statutes in the Regulatory State," 103 *Harv. L. Rev.* 405, 411 (1989).

[32] G. Tedeschi, *Masot B'mishpat [Essays in Law]* 1 (1978). *See also* H.C. 47/83 *Air Tour (Israel) Ltd. v. Chair of the Council for Antitrust Oversight*, 39(1) P.D. 169, 176: "Every statute, including one whose language is 'clear,' requires interpretation. The statute is 'clear' only once the interpretation has clarified it. It is not clear without interpretation. Words are not 'clear' in themselves. Indeed, there is nothing less clear than the assertion that the words are 'clear'" (Barak, J.). *See also* Cr.A. 928/80 *Gov Ari Ltd. v. Netanya Local Planning and Construction Council*, 35(4) P.D. 764, 769: "Even the simplest and clearest instruction appears before us in its simplicity only after we have transferred it, consciously or unconsciously, through the melting pot of our interpretive grasp" (Barak, J.).

[33] *See* R. Dworkin, *Law's Empire* 352 (1986): "The description 'unclear' is the *result* rather than the *occasion* of Hercules' method of interpreting statutory texts."

[34] *See* F. Schauer, *Playing by the Rules* 207 (1991).

define interpretation as "deciphering an unclear text by selecting from among a number of possibilities that may be consistent with it."[35] If they define interpretation as such, my disagreement with them is a matter of semantics. I may disagree with the appropriateness of their definition, but that debate is secondary.

Does a Plain Text Exist?

Even a plain text requires interpretation, and only interpretation allows us to conclude that its meaning is plain. That does not, however, mean that no text is plain.[36] To the contrary: The vast majority of legal texts have plain meanings in the vast majority of cases. Only in a minority of cases is a text unclear—in other words, after a preliminary interpretive process (conscious or unconscious), the text still allows for more than one correct solution. Most cases that come before a court fall into this latter category. Indeed, it is impossible to formulate a text that will be clear in every circumstance. We have yet to find a linguistic formulation that covers every possible situation. We can, however, formulate a text that is likely to be unclear only in a tiny number of circumstances. By insisting that all texts, including "plain" texts, must be interpreted, I do not mean to take the pressure off drafters of texts to strive for precision. I agree with Friedmann's assertion that

> While no drafter can anticipate and address every potential development, deviant, unexpected developments are the exception, not the rule. In the absence of such development, parties should turn to a drafter who knows his or her work and who can express their intentions clearly. Parties have a right to expect that, should their document come before a judge, the judge will understand their intentions.[37]

Interpreting an Existing Text and Creating a New Text

Most legal systems say that a judge is "authorized" to interpret an existing text, but not to create a new text (nor to alter an old text). The judge's job

[35] Friedmann, "On the Interpretation of the Phrase 'Interpretation,' and Notes on the Apropim Decision," 6 *Hamishpat* 21 (2002).

[36] Friedmann understands me to say that "No contract is clear, and contracts are distinguishable only by their varying levels of lack of clarity." Friedmann, *supra* p. 14, note 35 at 21. That is not my approach. That would be the case only if I shared Friedmann's definition of interpretation, i.e., as the deciphering of an unclear text. Indeed, if interpretation were the deciphering of an unclear text, and every text required interpretation, then it would follow that every text is unclear. I disagree, however, with Friedmann's definition of interpretation.

[37] Friedmann, *supra* p. 14, note 35 at 22.

is to interpret a constitution or statute, not to invent (or change) it. The judge is "authorized" to interpret a contract created by the parties. He or she is not "authorized" to draft a new contract. The judge interprets a will made by the testator. The judge is not authorized to make a new will for the testator. At its core, this approach is correct. "Authorization" to alter a text belongs to its author, not its interpreter. Statements in the literature to the effect that court decisions or changes in court decisions brought about change in the text itself are just metaphors.[38] The law delineates the various ways that a text may be altered, but judicial interpretation is not one of them. However, in their non-interpretive capacities, judges do go beyond just interpreting the text to create a new one. In the case of contracts, parties may conduct negotiations, and because of one party's lack of good faith, the negotiations fail to produce a contract. In some of these cases, the court has authority to decide that because a party violated the principle of negotiating in good faith, the court will treat the parties as though they entered into the contract they were to have created. Judges filling in gaps in contracts engage in similar activity. Filling in a gap involves creating a new text. When a judge corrects a mistake in the contract, he or she changes the contract. As Professor Atiyah noted:

> That courts do not make contracts for the parties is an oft-repeated dogma. But . . . this is misleading. In practice, many contracts are held to exist by the courts in circumstances in which the parties did not intend to create one, or did not realize that they were creating one.[39]

The same is true for wills. Judges sometimes are "authorized" to deviate from the language of the will, as when they fill in a gap in the will[40] or correct it. In that case and in others, the will that is executed differs from that written by the testator. The judge has "made" a will for the testator. Judges engage in a similar creative activity in the field of statutes. Judges have the authority to fill in gaps in statutes[41] or to correct mistakes, and in doing so, they create new texts. Nevertheless, there is a distinction between interpreting the text and creating it. In each case in which a judge is authorized to create a new text or to correct an existing text, he or she does engages in non-interpretive activity, relying on non-interpretive doctrines.[42]

---

[38] See L. Tribe, *American Constitutional Law* 90 (3d ed. 2000).

[39] See P.S. Atiyah, *An Introduction to the Law of Contract* 96 (4th ed. 1989). *See also* E. Zamir, *Perush V'Hashlama Shel Chozim [Interpretation and Completion of Contracts]* 57 (1996).

[40] On filling gaps in wills, *see* Barak, 5 *Parshanut B'mishpat [Interpretation in Law]* 386 (2001).

[41] *See id.* at 352.

[42] *See* p. 69, *infra*.

2. THE LIMITS OF INTERPRETATION

The Importance of the Problem

What are the limits of interpretation? When is an activity "interpretive," and when does it cease to be "interpretive"? When is it possible to reach a particular result by interpreting the text—either through an original interpretation, or through a new interpretation that alters a prior one—and when is it necessary to change the text, in order to reach the same result? For example, when must the constitution be changed—something that interpretation cannot do—and when does it suffice to reinterpret existing text?[43] Take an example considered by Peczenik:[44] The articles of association of a nonprofit organization declare that "every chess player is eligible to be a member of the organization." To say that anyone who has played chess is eligible to be a member is an interpretive conclusion. We could also interpret the organization's directive constrictively—that membership is limited to those who are formally ranked in chess competitions. Barring the unranked chess player from membership is a constrictive interpretation, but it is still interpretation. Similarly, we can expand the definition to include all candidates who know the rules of the game, even if they themselves have never played. Such definition is expansive but still within the bounds of interpretation. However, does limiting membership to champions constitute a (constrictive) interpretive decision? Does allowing bridge players to join constitute an (expansive) interpretive decision?

The answer to these questions is important[45] for two reasons: *First,* the boundaries of interpretation establish the legitimacy of the interpretive activity. Judges have authority to interpret legal texts. Indeed, by creating a legal text, an author delegates power to a judge to interpret it. The principle of separation of powers—which authorizes judges to adjudicate disputes—legitimates this delegation. In order to adjudicate, judges must interpret the text at the center of a dispute.[46] In their role as interpreters, judges may not create a new legal text. When they finish their interpretive activity, the legitimacy of judicial activity—derived from the principle of

---

[43] *See Responding to Imperfection: The Theory and Practice of Constitutional Amendment* 3 (S. Levinson ed., 1995).

[44] A. Peczenik, *On Law and Reason* 388 (1989).

[45] *See* R. Pound, "Spurious Interpretation," 7 *Colum. L. Rev.* 379, 380 (1907).

[46] Hart and Sachs, *supra* p. 3, note 3 at 1375. Such is the rule in contracts and wills. The judge must respect the autonomy of the parties. Referring to interpretation of wills, Lord Mustill writes, in *Charter Reinsurance Co. Ltd. v. Fagen* (1997) A.C. 313, 318: "There comes a point at which the court should remind itself . . . that to force upon the words a meaning which they cannot fairly bear is to substitute for the bargain actually made one which the court believes could better have been made. This is an illegitimate role for a court."

separation of powers and delegation of authority from author to judge—
ends too. Judges who act outside the boundaries of interpretation must
find an alternative source of legitimacy for their actions; the system of interpretation does not provide it. Thus, for example, judges are authorized
to interpret criminal statutes. They are not authorized to fill in gaps in ways
that define new crimes. It is therefore important to know when judges
(properly) interpret criminal statutes and when they (improperly) fill gaps
in criminal statutes. The *second* reason we should differentiate between interpretive and non-interpretive activities is inherent to the different criteria that guide each activity. Interpreting a statute, contract, or will implicates different criteria than filling in a gap in each.

Difficulties in Determining the Limits of Interpretation

It is not easy to determine the limits of interpretation.[47] The line between
interpretive and non-interpretive activity is blurred, and dependent on the
given legal tradition and the legal system's culture. Thus, for example, the
common law considers resolving contradictions between two norms of
equal status to be an act of interpretation. By contrast, resolving a contradiction between two norms of unequal status is considered to be part of
constitutional or administrative law, not interpretive activity. Furthermore,
some legal doctrines apply to both interpretive and non-interpretive activity. For example, the common law employs a doctrine of good faith in interpreting a contract and in filling in a contractual gap. Judges contribute
to this confusion with their tendency to present all their actions as interpretive. They presume that, in doing so, they will enjoy the legitimacy that
interpretation confers on judicial activity. Judges sometimes "cram" non-
interpretive activities into interpretative limits, blurring the distinction between giving meaning to a text and acting beyond it. When a statute forbids dogs from entering a municipal park, determining that the ban extends
to lions, too, is non-interpretive activity. Conferring a meaning to the word
"dog" to include a lion blurs the distinction between interpretive activity—
according to which the word "dog" does not extend to lion—and non-
interpretive activity, which may extend the ban on dogs in the park to
include lions, as well. To make things even more confusing, judges sometimes exhibit the opposite tendency, namely to exempt themselves from the
rules of interpretation by characterizing essentially interpretive activity as

---

[47] This is a general problem in hermeneutics, not unique to legal interpretation: *See* E.D.
Hirsch, Jr., *Validity in Interpretation* (1967); E.D. Hirsch, Jr., *The Aims of Interpretation*
(1978); *The Politics of Interpretation*, (W.J.T. Mitchell ed., 1982); S. Fish, *Is There a Text in
This Class? The Authority of Interpretive Communities* (1980).

non-interpretive. This occurs, for example, in interpreting principles that appear in legislation, like "morality" or "justice." Some view interpreting these principles as non-interpretive activity, to be governed by the legal system's general directions on how to fill in a gap in legislation. In doing so, they blur the distinction between interpreting a statute and filling in its gaps.

Language and the Limits of Interpretation

What, then, are the boundaries of interpretation? Tribe says that, because of the multiplicity of systems of interpretation, all that can be said is that the boundary of interpretation is set by the good faith of the interpretive process.[48] In his opinion, there are no additional standards, because we have no standards with which to select among the various systems of interpretation. I accept that there are numerous systems of interpretation, most of which I cannot disqualify as illegitimate. When I claim that most, if not all—except for purposive interpretation—are improper, I do not claim that they exceed the bounds of interpretation. From my point of view, in order for a system to be interpretive—to belong to the interpretive family of law—it must adhere to one critical principle: Interpretation is a rational activity that gives a legal text a meaning that it can bear in its language (public or private). This condition is both necessary and sufficient for the existence of a system of interpretation. The good faith of the interpretive process and the way it is applied within a legal community—the very existence of which restricts the character of the interpretive answer—operate internally within a particular system of interpretation. They do not define the outer limits of interpretation. Indeed, my position is that the limits of the text set the limits of interpretation in law, and the limits of language set the limits of the text. An activity is interpretive if it confers meaning on a text that is consistent with one of its (explicit or implicit) meanings, in the (public or private) language of the text. Giving a text meaning beyond its semantic meaning is not an act of interpretation, and it must rely on non-interpretive doctrines. Interpretation ends at the point at which language ends.[49] Furthermore, interpretation can give a text an expansive or a constrictive meaning; the meaning may be natural to the language or innovative. But we must insist that interpretation confer upon the text a meaning that it is capable of bearing in the language in which it is expressed.

---

[48] Tribe, *supra* p. 15, note 38 at 92.

[49] J. Steyn, "Interpretation: Legal Texts and Their Landscape," in *The Coming Together of the Common Law and the Civil Law* 73, 81 (B. Markesinis ed., 2000): "The judge must concentrate on the different meaning which the text is capable of letting in. What falls beyond that range of possible meanings will not be a result attainable by interpretation. Principles of institutional integrity which bind all judges set those limits for judges."

Every meaning that an interpreter gives a legal text must have an Archimedean foothold in the language of the text. True, the interpreter is not a linguist. But linguistics sets the boundaries of legal interpretation. An interpreter may not give a text a meaning that a linguist could not give it. Justice Frankfurter said as much, noting that "While courts are no longer confined to the language, they are still confined by it."[50] I accept the view that language is not the most important thing. I begin with language, but I do not end with it. Nevertheless, the end of every interpretive process must remain within the bounds of language. The statement that language sets the limits of interpretation is not a statement about hermeneutics. I do not claim that the interpretation of every text is limited to the language of the text. In some disciplines, like literature, the interpreter may give the text a meaning that it cannot bear in its language. It is for each discipline to decide whether the interpretation is "legitimate." Hermeneutic theory does not require one or another solution. My claim that language sets the limits of interpretation is a constitutional claim, and I limit it to legal texts.

According to the principle of separation of powers, a judge's constitutional role as interpreter is to interpret a text created by those authorized to do so. In their capacity as interpreters, judges do not have the authority to create new texts. Any such authority lies outside the rules of interpretation. Judges are not authorized to create a will for a testator, but rather to interpret an existing will. The language of the will (private or public) sets the boundaries of the judge's role in interpreting the will. This conclusion derives from the constitutional principle of the autonomy of the private will. Judges who create wills must ground their authority in noninterpretive rules, such as the rule allowing a judge to correct a mistake in a will by recognizing the will that the testator wanted to make, but failed to create because of the mistake. Such is the case, also, in interpreting contracts. Giving a contract a meaning that it cannot bear (in its private code or public language) offends the autonomy of the parties to the contract and violates the constitutional role of the court as the interpreter of an existing text, not the author of a new text. Judges seeking to create new contractual texts must ground their activities in non-interpretive doctrines, like filling in contractual gaps or correcting a contract. A similar approach applies to statutory interpretation. Judges have no authority to give a statute a meaning that its language cannot bear. Lord Reid took this stance, saying that

> It is a cardinal principle applicable to all kinds of statutes that one may not for any reason attach to a statutory provision a meaning which the words of that provision cannot reasonably bear. If they are capable of more than one mean-

[50] F. Frankfurter, "Some Reflections on the Reading of Statutes," 47 *Colum. L. Rev.* 527, 543 (1947).

ing then one can choose between those meanings, but beyond that one must not go.[51]

Constitutional considerations of democracy, rule of law, and separation of powers bar judges from conferring on the language of a statute a meaning that it cannot bear. As Hart and Sachs said:

> The proposition that a court ought never to give the words of a statute a meaning they will not bear is a corollary of the proposition that courts are bound to respect the constitutional position of the legislature and the constitutional procedures for the enactment of legislation.[52]

The legislature enacts a statute using particular language. That language sets the outer limits of any possible interpretation. The democratic legislature enacts a statute using particular tools of expression. Those tools of expression must be given meaning. One cannot read into them what they do not contain. Judges as interpreters are not authorized to write the statute anew. They must interpret the statute that the legislature created. If they change the text of the statute—either add or delete—they must rely on non-interpretive doctrines, like the rule for filling in a gap in a statute.

These principles also apply to constitutional texts. A constitution is not a metaphor. Constitutional principles of separation of powers, democracy, and rule of law restrict interpreters from giving the language of the constitution any meaning they desire. True, constitutions are characterized by a high frequency of vague terms and phrases that can mean a number of things, acting as air valves that can open in different directions. Language, however, continues to restrict constitutional texts. Open-ended language is not infinitely malleable. Even vague phrases have semantic boundaries. The language of a constitutional text sets the boundaries of constitutional interpretation. Constitutional texts have no special interpretive status. There must be at least a minimal semantic connection between the semantic meaning of a constitutional text and its legal meaning. Interpretive activity in law is shackled to the language of the text—it ends where the language of the text ends.

Kelsen aptly compared the language of the text to the frame of a picture.[53] As we have noted, interpretive activity gives meaning to the picture inside the frame. It cannot operate outside the frame.[54] A meaning not se-

[51] *Jones v. Director of Public Prosecutions* [1962] A.C. 635, 662.

[52] Hart and Sachs, *supra* p. 3, note 3 at 1375.

[53] Kelsen, *supra* p. 3, note 4 at 348.

[54] *See* C.A. 6339/97, *Roker v. Solomon*, 55(1) P.D. 199, 283: "I accept, of course, that in interpreting a statute (in the narrow sense), one can only actualize the purpose of the legislation using its language. The language must be capable of actualizing the purpose . . . words are a means of communication, and those who use them must give them a meaning that is acceptable in the language in which they are written" (Barak, P.).

mantically grounded in the explicit or implicit language of the legal text is a meaning that an interpreter cannot reach through interpretation and thus he or she must rely on non-interpretive doctrines. When a will states that, at the testator's death, his property will pass to "my wife, Dina," it is an act of interpretation for the judge to decide if Dina is eligible for the inheritance, despite the fact that the couple separated between the time the testator made the will and the time he died. However, the judge would act outside the bounds of interpretation if he or she ruled that the heir designated by the will is Nancy, whom the testator married after divorcing Dina. There is no interpretive way of reading the words "to my wife, Dina," as meaning, "to my wife, Nancy." Of course, things would be different if the testator designated his heir as "my wife." In that situation, the conclusion that the heir is Dina (his wife at the time the will was made) or Nancy (his wife at the time the testator died) is an interpretive conclusion, and the outcome will vary, depending on the system of interpretation used. All systems of interpretation must respect language for its role in establishing a framework beyond which the judge, as interpreter, may not act.[55]

The Text's Language and Structure

By allowing the language of the text to set the boundaries of its interpretation, we focus on more than just the express meaning of the text. We also take into account the implied language.[56] This "implicit" meaning may be inferred from an individual provision or from the structure of the text and the totality of its provisions.[57] As Tribe wrote, referring to the United States Constitution,

> The Constitution's "structure" is (borrowing Wittgenstein's famous distinction) that which the text *shows* but does not directly *say*. Diction, word repetitions, and documentary organizing form (e.g., the division of the text into articles, or the separate status of the preamble and the amendments), for example, all contribute to a sense of what the Constitution is about that is obviously "constitutional" as are the Constitution's words as such.[58]

[55] G.H. Taylor, "Structural Textualism," 75 *B.U. L. Rev.* 321, 325 (1995). A judge may, of course, operate beyond the language of the text using non-interpretive doctrines. *Infra* p. 61.

[56] On implied language, *see infra* p. 104. *See also* Bennion, *supra* p. 6, note 13 at 381.

[57] Sunstein, *supra* p. 13, note 31; C.L. Black, *Structure and Relationship in Constitutional Law* (1969). *See also* M.O. Chibundu, "Structure and Structuralism in the Interpretation of Statutes," 62 *U. Cin. L. Rev.* 1439 (1994); A. Amar, "Intratextualism," 112 *Harv. L. Rev.* 747 (1999); A. Amar, "Foreword: The Document and the Doctrine," 114 *Harv. L. Rev.* 26 (2000).

[58] Tribe, *supra* p. 15, note 38 at 40 (emphases in original).

These words are true of all legal texts. The language of the text is not just words that can be looked up in a dictionary. The language of the text includes what we can infer from the text, its structure, organization, and the relationship among its different provisions. Tribe writes:

> The text of the Constitution is not just words but also spaces, often gaps arranged in telling ways, not simply ambiguities around the edges—spaces which, it may truly be said, structures fill and whose patterns structure defines.[59]

But what is the semantic border that even structural considerations cannot cross? We should not use structural arguments as a green light to introduce into the text things that it does not contain. Sometimes, we can tell from the structure of the text that a lacuna or gap exists. The structure of the text cannot fill in this gap, so we need to rely on non-interpretive doctrines.[60] Structural arguments cannot exceed the implied meaning of the text,[61] and there is a distinction between implied meaning and a textual gap. By analyzing the structure of a text, we can extract what is written between the lines, but we cannot add lines that are missing. For that, we need non-interpretive doctrines.

Language and "Non-Interpretive" Doctrines

In the 1970s and 1980s, U.S. constitutional scholars developed a theory of interpretation that allowed the words of a constitution to be given a meaning that does not take the semantic meaning of the words into account. In their view, the language of a constitution is only presumptively binding. Professor Brest championed the idea of "noninterpretivism"[62]— the constitutional text is so "open" that nothing in it sets the boundaries of interpretation. This theory misunderstands that even an open text has limits. As for "non-interpretive" techniques, in truth, they are in every way interpretive. As Grey writes, "We are all interpretivists; the real arguments are not over whether judges should stick to interpreting, but over what they should interpret and what interpretive attitude they should adopt."[63]

[59] Tribe, *supra* p. 15, note 38 at 47.

[60] *See infra* p. 61.

[61] *Infra* p. 104.

[62] P. Brest, "The Misconceived Quest for the Original Understanding," 60 *B.U. L. Rev.* 204 (1980).

[63] T. Grey, "The Constitution as Scripture," 37 *Stan. L. Rev.* 1 (1984). *See also* R. Dworkin, *A Matter of Principle* 35 (1985): "The theories that are generally classed as 'noninterpretive' are plainly interpretivist in any plausible sense"; G. Leedes, "Critique of Illegitimate Noninterpretivism," 8 *U. Dayton L. Rev.* 533 (1982–83); L. Alexander, "Painting without Numbers: Noninterpretive Judicial Review," 8 *U. Dayton L. Rev.* 447 (1982–83).

Language sets the boundaries and limits of every interpretive technique. No interpretation is without semantic restrictions, set by language. The phrase "non-interpretive technique of interpretation" is a contradiction in terms.[64] The binding nature of a text is not presumptive but rather mandatory.

Additional Limits of Interpretation: Rationality

Is language the only determinant of interpretive limits? Is it a necessary and sufficient condition? Is every one of a text's potential semantic meanings also an interpretive meaning? Does flipping a coin to choose among those meanings constitute an act of interpretation? Can we say that a coin toss is interpretive, even if it is a clumsy and flawed act of interpretation? The question is apt. Some would say that clumsy and flawed interpretation— even if barred by a particular legal system—is nonetheless interpretation. Others would reject that idea, holding that interpretation is limited to a rational-intellectual attempt to understand a text. I belong to the second school of thought. There is a distinction between the rational activity of interpretation and its result. An interpreter must assume a cognitive-intellectual stance toward the text. A coin toss is not just clumsy or flawed interpretation—it is not interpretation at all. We cannot reconcile its arbitrariness with a normative understanding of the interpretive process.

Does all rational activity that attempts to understand a text fall within the bounds of legal interpretation? Don't the conventions of the legal community set the limits of interpretation? Can't we say that any interpretative system not accepted by a given interpretive community falls outside the limits of interpretation? In my opinion, we should distinguish between the interpretative project on the theoretical level (the theoretical essence of interpretation) and a system of interpretation in force within a particular legal system (the legitimacy of a particular system of interpretation). When I say that language sets the limits of interpretation, I refer to the essence of interpretation, not the legitimacy of one or another system of interpretation within a legal system. A judge who interprets a law using a system of interpretation not valid in his or her legal system engages in interpretive activity, even if it is illegitimate.

Does Language Have Limits?

If interpretation is bounded by language, what, if anything, binds language? Semantic theory teaches us that language is not a precision instru-

---

[64] P. Hogg, "The Charter of Rights and American Theories of Interpretation," in *Canadian Perspectives of Legal Theory* 376 (R. Devlin ed., 1991): "Noninterpretivism is nonsense."

ment. Learned Hand said that "words are temperamental."[65] Language does not take on a single, unique meaning in the consciousness of every listener. As Justice Holmes noted, "A word is not a crystal, transparent and unchanged, it is the skin of a living thought and may vary greatly in color and content according to the circumstances and the time in which it is used."[66] Language is not, however, infinitely malleable. It may be vague, ambiguous, and capable of meaning different things in different contexts. But language cannot take on any meaning an interpreter wishes. If it did, the principle would collapse unto itself.[67] If language has no meaning, then there is no meaning to the statement that language has no meaning.[68] As Justice Scalia aptly said about words, "They have meaning enough, as the scholarly critics themselves must surely believe when they choose to express their views in text rather than in music."[69]

Life experience teaches us that people communicate. They understand each other. When the law sets the speed limit at 55 miles per hour, it issues an instruction that is usually clear. We do not think that a speed limit of 55 miles per hour means that parliamentary elections are governed by the principle of equality. If every instruction, in every context, were ambiguous or vague, it would be impossible to conduct normal life in either society or law. The words we use communicate a clear message at least some of the time.[70] The fact that the message is not always clear does not mean there are no circumstances in which words communicate a clear meaning. If an ordinance bans "vehicles" from a public park, it may not be clear to me whether a Ford with no wheels is a "vehicle." I know, however, that a Ford with wheels is a "vehicle"—and that its driver is not. It is meaningless to say that language has no bounds, or, in the well-known words of Humpty Dumpty:

> 'When I use a word,' Humpty Dumpty said, in rather a scornful tone, 'it means just what I choose it to mean—neither more nor less.' 'The question is,' said Alice, 'whether you can make words mean so many different things.' 'The question is,' said Humpty Dumpty, 'which is to be master—that's all.'[71]

Humpty Dumpty can use words as he pleases and make up his own words. But if Humpty Dumpty wants to rely on language as a means of commu-

---

[65] L. Hand, *The Spirit of Liberty* 173 (I. Dilliard ed., 3d ed., 1960).

[66] *Towne v. Eisner*, 245 U.S. 418, 425 (1918).

[67] M.S. Moore, "The Semantics of Judging," 54 *S. Cal. L. Rev.* 151, 310 (1981).

[68] H. Putnam, *Reason, Truth and History* 119 (1981).

[69] A. Scalia, "Originalism: The Lesser Evil," 57 *Cin. L. Rev.* 849, 856 (1989).

[70] F. Schauer, "Easy Cases," 58 *S. Cal. L. Rev.* 399, 408 (1985).

[71] L. Carroll, *Alice's Adventures in Wonderland and Through the Looking Glass* 169 (Bantam Classic ed. 1981, quoted by Justice Cheshin in C.A. 6339/97, *supra* p. 20, note 54 at 254).

nication, he must use words according to their accepted meaning in the given language. Hart and Sachs have this to say about Humpty Dumpty's system:

> In the world of nonsense he may have been right. But in the world of sense he was wrong. Language is a social institution. Its successful functioning depends upon commonly accepted responses to particular verbal symbols used in particular kinds of contexts. These responses are social facts. A particular user of the language may play tricks with it and assign his own private meaning to particular symbols in it. But he cannot unilaterally alter the social facts of other people's responses. He can affect those responses, if at all, only as people generally come to understand and accept his own originally private meanings.[72]

Language is neither infinite nor boundless.[73] It may contain a range of possibilities, but that range is finite. Language has a maximum and minimum.[74] It has limits like, in Justice Cheshin's words, a casing that, if stretched too far, will tear.[75] An interpreter cannot give a text any meaning he or she wishes. The limits of language set the limits of interpretation. A number of systems of interpretation operate within the limits of language, and we must choose the best among them. We therefore reject free systems "of interpretation" that allow an interpreter to give a text any meaning he or she desires. There is nothing interpretive about those systems—they replace basic linguistic and jurisprudential principles with nihilism.

[72] Hart and Sachs, *supra* p. 3, note 3 at 1188.

[73] There is some debate in American legal literature over whether the constitutional requirement that the president be at least 35 years of age permits the election of a 24-year-old president. *See* G. Spann, "Deconstructing the Legislative Veto," 68 *Minn. L. Rev.* 437, 532 (1984); G. Peller, "The Metaphysics of American Law," 73 *Cal. L. Rev.* 1151, 1174 (1985); M. Tushnet, "A Note on the Revival of Textualism in Constitutional Theory," 58 *S. Cal. L. Rev.* 683, 686; A. D'Amato, "Aspects of Deconstruction: The 'Easy Case' of the Under-Aged President," 84 *Nw. U. L. Rev.* 250 (1989); J. Soiker, S. Levinson, and J.M. Balkin, "Taking Text and Structure Really Seriously: Constitutional Interpretation and the Crisis of Presidential Eligibility," 74 *Tex. L. Rev.* 237 (1995); M.B.W. Sinclair, "Postmodern Argumentation: Deconstructing the Presidential Age Limitation," 43 *N.Y.L. Sch. L. Rev.* 451 (1999). This pointless debate is regrettable. *See* K. Hegland, "Goodbye to Deconstruction," 58 *S. Cal. L. Rev.* 1203, 1207 (1985); S. Levinson, "Law as Literature," 60 *Tex. L. Rev.* 373 (1982); D. Farber, "Statutory Interpretation and Legislative Supremacy," 78 *Geo. L.J.* 281, 288 (1989).

[74] M. Radin, "Statutory Interpretation," 43 *Harv. L. Rev.* 863, 866, 879 (1929–30).

[75] C.A. 6339/97 *supra* p. 20, note 54 at 253.

3. BASIC PROBLEMS IN INTERPRETATION

The Relationship between the "Form" of a Text and Its "Substance"

What accounts for the existence of different systems of interpretation? Why isn't the semantic meaning of a text identical to its legal meaning? The limits of language[76] and of the text's author account for these characteristics of interpretation. The author of a text establishes a general rule that, by its nature, deals with typical situations. The interpreter must decide how the rule applies to a specific instance. The generalization always applies to more situations than the author anticipated; otherwise, he or she would have listed each specific situation. This is the challenge of interpretation—to decide what the general rule means in specific factual situations. As Aristotle noted,

> [A]ll law is universal but about some things it is not possible to make a universal statement which shall be correct. In those cases, then, in which it is necessary to speak universally, but not possible to do so correctly, the law takes the usual case, though it is not ignorant of the possibility of error. And it is none the less correct; for the error is not in the law nor in the legislator but in the nature of the thing, since the matter of practical affairs is of this kind from the start . . . for when the thing is indefinite the rule also is indefinite.[77]

As human beings, we depend on interpretation.[78] The shortcomings of language and of the author make it impossible for a text to mean the same thing in every circumstance. Those shortcomings compel the interpreter to look beyond the text for criteria by which to understand it. They necessitate consideration of a text's environment, in order to understand it.[79] It is not hard to see that they also necessitate a search for the substance of the text as a device for understanding the text. The foundational problem in interpretation—the hallmark of every theory of interpretation of every legal text—is the appropriate relationship between the text and its envi-

---

[76] *See* H.W. Jones, "Statutory Doubts and Legislative Intention," 40 *Colum. L. Rev.* 957, 961 (1940).

[77] Aristotle, *Ethica Nicomachea*, bk. 5, ch. 10 (W.D. Ross trans., 1925).

[78] H.L.A. Hart, *The Concept of Law* 128 (2d. ed. 1994). Hart emphasizes that language has an open texture that imparts discretion to interpreters. In accounting for the rationale behind freedom of choice, he says, "[T]he reason is that the necessity for such choice is thrust upon us because we are men, not gods."

[79] Sunstein, *supra* p. 13, note 31 at 416 (The central problem is that the meaning of words [whether 'plain' or not] depends on both *context* and *culture*").

ronment,[80] between the text and the context, between the "form" and the "substance,"[81] between the *verba* and the *voluntas*.[82]

Some scholars assume that primitive legal systems tend to prefer form (language, text) over substance, while more modern legal systems tend to prefer substance over form.[83] In reality, older legal systems sometimes expressed the substance, not just the form (language), of a text, and modern systems sometimes tend to emphasize form (language) over substance.[84] Most perspectives on interpretation lie somewhere along the spectrum between those two points, trying to strike the proper balance between "form" and "substance." This dichotomy, while important to interpretive theory, also exists in other areas of law and has been part of law from its inception:[85] the distinction between "formalism" or "literalism" and "realism" or "substantivism"; between "form" and "content"; between "formal justice" and "substantive justice." In interpretation, shall we adopt a "formal-formalist" approach, deriving the meaning of the text internally, exclusively from within, or a "realistic-substantive" approach, deriving the text's meaning not only from within but also from the context surrounding it— and if so, which context? The philosophical perspective that stands for "formal justice," "form," and "formalism" usually translates into a system of interpretation that focuses on the text and language. The philosophical perspective that stands for "substantive justice," "substance," and "realism" usually translates into a system of interpretation that focuses on the "substance" of the text, or the spirit encompassing it. Most modern[86] inter-

---

[80] W. Blatt, "The History of Statutory Interpretation: A Study in Form and Substance," 6 *Cardozo L. Rev.* 799 (1985).

[81] F.E. Horack, "Statutory Interpretation—Light from Plowden Reports," 19 *Ky. L.J.* 211 (1932).

[82] J.F. Perrin, "Pour une Théorie d'Interprétation Judiciale des Lois," in *Les Règles d'Interprétation: Principes Communement Admis par les Jurisdictions* (J.F. Perrin ed., 1989).

[83] For example, Roman law required merchants to use specific language in executing a valid transaction, in contrast to the modern trend of allowing a valid contract to take any form.

[84] Under Jewish law, one of the oldest systems of law, a marriage contract can be formed in a number of ways, including through a written contract, the bridegroom giving the bride an object worth at least a penny, or consummation of marital relations. *See, generally,* Babylonian Talmud, Tractate *Kidushin* [Marriage], ch. 1 (c. third to fifth centuries C.E.). In contrast, the modern doctrine of the statute of frauds requires a writing for certain contracts to be valid.

[85] For a discussion of these questions, *see* R. Posner, *The Problems of Jurisprudence* (1990).

[86] Interestingly, Blackstone clearly supported the spirit of the law. *See* W. Blackstone, 1 *Commentaries on the Laws of England* 59 (3d ed. 1884): "The most universal and effective way of discovering the true meaning of a law when the words are dubious, is by considering the reason and spirit of it; or the cause which moved the legislature to enact it. For when this reason ceases the law itself ought likewise to cease with it." *See also* L.H. LaRue, "Statutory Interpretation: Lord Coke Revisited," 48 *U. Pitt. L. Rev.* 733 (1986–87).

pretive theories fall somewhere in between, just as most philosophical schools of thought fall somewhere in between. In this book, I do not seek only form or only substance, but rather a way to understand the form, and to develop it in light of its substance. The interpreter does not deal with form alone, because divorced from its substance, form has no vitality. The interpreter does not deal with substance alone, because divorced from form, the substance cannot be actualized. The interpreter works with the form of the text, guided by its substance. "To know the laws," according to a Roman saying, "is to grasp not just the words but the divine power" (*scire leges non hoc est verba earum tenere sed vim ac potestatem*). The foundational question in interpretation is how much form controls substance, or vice versa. To answer that question, we must first ask three secondary questions, discussed below.

(Subjective) Intent or (Objective) Goal

The *first* secondary question: What is the substance that gives meaning to the form? Is it the subjective intent of the text's author or the objective goal of a reasonable author? If it is the latter, then what is that goal? Do we interpret a constitution according to the intent of the framers, or according to modern values? Do we interpret a statute according to the intent of the legislators, or according to contemporary needs? Do we interpret a contract according to the joint intent of the parties, or according to its reasonable goal? Do we interpret a will according to the intent of the testator, or according to the (objective) values of the legal system? Generally, subjective and objective substance overlap, such that the intent of the author and the objective goal of the text point in the same direction. In the rare instances of contradiction between subjective intent and objective need, however, which one trumps? How do we resolve this schizophrenia in the substance of the legal text? Is there a single, unique formula that decides which substance takes precedence? Does that order of preference hold with equal force for every legal text? Or does the internal relationship between the subjective and objective substance vary by category of text and by individual text? What categories of texts are relevant? If we assume that the joint intent of the parties to a contract takes precedence over the objective purpose of the contract, must we then conclude that the intent of the constitutional founders trumps the contemporary needs of members of society? And if we say that the results need not be consistent across individual texts or categories of texts, which rules apply to each case, and what justifies the inconsistency?

"True" Intent or "Expressed" Intent

The *second* secondary question assumes that the intent of the author is relevant to understanding the text he or she has created. It asks: Is the (subjective) intent of the text's author his or her "true" intent, which an interpreter may learn from any source? Or is it the author's "expressed" intent, which an interpreter learns from the legal text itself. The scholarly literature divides between supporters of the will theory (*Willenstheorie*) and the expression theory (*Erklärungstheorie*). True intent is the psychological-historical intent of the legal text's author: the founders of the constitution, the legislators of a statute, the parties to a contract,[87] and the testator of a will. According to will theory, in each case the interpreter must consider the "true" intent of the text's author, which he or she may learn from the text or from sources external to it. Such intent may be realized through the text. The interpreter understands the language of the text against the backdrop of its author's "true" intent, not what he or she might infer the intent to be just from reading the text. The issue is not the intent that emerges from reading the text, but rather the message that the text's author (subjectively) intended to send through the text. Deciphering this latter message becomes more complicated when the intent we seek to honor is that of a multi-member body, like a constitutional assembly or legislative house.

Followers of the will theory offer various answers to these questions, which we will discuss.[88] In contrast, followers of the expression theory are not concerned with intentions unexpressed in the legal text, but only with the intent that the author expressed in the language of the text. The question is not what the text's author wanted, but rather what the text says: *non quod voluit sed quod dixit*. Of course, followers of the expression theory must deal with circumstances in which the intent of the author is not clear from the text. May an interpreter go beyond the four corners of the text, and if so, under what circumstances? Most expression theory scholars would permit an interpreter to consult related legal texts, like statutes passed by the same legislature. But does expression theory also permit an interpreter to consider legislative and constitutional history? When may an interpreter consider the circumstances under which the contract or will was made? Again, both theories operate within the limits of language, based on

---

[87] *See* A. Gordley, "Contract in Pre-Commercial Societies and in Western History," *Contracts in General: International Encyclopedia of Comparative Law* 30 (A. Van Mehren ed., 1997); D. Kennedy, "Form and Substance in Private Law Adjudication," 89 *Harv. L. Rev.* 1685 (1976).

[88] *Infra* p. 121.

the (positive) approach that language should be interpreted according to intent, and the (negative) approach that words should not be given a meaning they cannot bear in their language. The theories differ, however, in the sources from which the interpreter may infer the intent of the legal text's author. One theory allows the interpreter to infer intent from any source but uses a credibility test to limit the universe of sources. The other theory generally limits the interpreter to the language of the text but allows the interpreter to consult related legal texts (like statutes on the same issue). In the interstices of these two theories is an intermediate zone that illustrates the difference between them.

The Text's Objective Purpose

The *third* secondary question addresses the objective aspect of the legal text's substance. What is the "objective substance" of the text, and how is it determined? What are the values, interests, and objective purposes according to which a legal text is interpreted? How does the interpreter determine them? What does he or she do when constitutional values, interests, and purposes contradict each other? According to which values does a judge interpret a constitution? Do constitutional values exist outside the constitution? What happens when those values contradict each other? Interpreting a statute, contract, or will raises similar questions. Is it possible to formulate presumptions about these values, interests, and purposes? What is the status of those presumptions, and how much weight should we give them?

4. SYSTEMS OF INTERPRETATION IN LAW

A Multiplicity of Systems of Interpretation in Law

Because systems of interpretation go to the core of law and its place in society, it is inevitable that they will be numerous. Legal history is also the history of the rise and fall of different systems of legal interpretation. For example, we have learned[89] that in ancient legal systems, the primary interpretive emphasis was on the text's semantic meaning, at the expense of its substance. As legal systems modernized, they placed increasing importance on the substance of the norm in the text's interpretation. Recently, we witnessed a "new" trend in the United States—a return to the "textualist" approach to interpretation. Late-nineteenth-century Europe offers

---

[89] *See* Wigmore, *supra* p. 12, note 30, § 2405.

another example of the rise and fall of various systems of interpretation, in the development of systems of interpretation that gave the interpreter free reign. These systems, which extolled "free legal studies,"[90] eventually fell out of favor. In the 1960s, "critical legal studies"[91] developed in the United States, a return to what had already been accepted and rejected decades earlier. And the pendulum has yet to rest. What we sometimes view as a new or modern system of interpretation is simply an old method dressed up in new clothing whose time has suddenly returned—but will surely expire once again.

It is natural to have multiple systems of interpretation at any given time and place. Law is a human creation. The complexity of the human condition permeates the way we understand our environment, including the way we understand legal texts. Furthermore, because interpretation derives from and reflects a particular legal system, a multiplicity of legal systems necessarily creates a multiplicity of systems of interpretation. Systems of interpretation in common law countries differ from systems of interpretation in civil law countries.[92] Beyond that, each system of interpretation reflects a philosophical perspective on the role of law, and a constitutional perspective on both the proper role of a legal text (constitution, statute, contract, and will) in the legal system and the role of the judge as an interpreter within that system. A system of interpretation reflects the reciprocal relationship between judiciary-legislature-executive and the will of the individual within that system. Other factors in the choice of an interpretive technique include the systems of proof used in the legal system and the relationship between form and substance in that system. All these factors necessarily lead to a multiplicity of systems of interpretation. Nevertheless, in most instances, all systems of interpretation and all legal systems reach the same interpretive result.[93] Only in rare cases are the differences in systems of interpretation reflected through different results. I will now present three kinds of interpretive theory. Later, I will try to convince the reader that purposive interpretation is the most proper system of all.

---

[90] See J. Stone, *The Province and Function of Law: Law as Logic, Justice, and Social Control—A Study in Jurisprudence* 158 (1961).

[91] M. Kelman, *A Guide to Critical Legal Studies* (1987); *Critical Legal Studies* (A.C. Hutchinson ed., 1989); *The Politics of Law: A Progressive Critique* (D. Kairys ed., 3d ed., 1998).

[92] For a comparative survey of statutory interpretive methods, *see* D.N. MacCormick and R.S. Summers (eds.), *Interpreting Statutes: A Comparative Study* (1991); K. Zweigert and H. Kötz, *Introduction to Comparative Law* 400 (T. Weir trans., 3d ed. 1998).

[93] D. Farber, "Do Theories of Statutory Interpretation Matter? A Case Study," 94 *Nw. U. L. Rev.* 1409 (2000).

Subjective Systems of Interpretation in Law

The *first* kind of interpretive technique comprises subjective systems of interpretation. According to these systems, the psychological-historical intent of the text's author (the subjective purpose) confers meaning on a legal text. The goal of interpretation is to give the text the meaning that realizes the intent of its author. These systems of interpretation are operative for all legal texts. According to them, the interpreter must follow the same path as the text's author, only backwards. The author began with intent and ended with language. The interpreter begins with language and ends with intent. The author of the norm and the interpreter move along the same track, but in opposite directions. Subjective systems of interpretation seek to give a legal text the same meaning it had at the time it was drafted (*ex tunc*). There is no consideration of the reality in existence at the time of interpretation. The passage of time cannot change the intent of the author. It is fixed in time.

SURVEY OF SUBJECTIVE SYSTEMS OF INTERPRETATION IN LAW

There are numerous subjective systems of interpretation. *One* means of distinguishing between them is by the way they characterize subjective intent. Some try to realize the concrete ("legal" or "consequential") intent of the text's author, the (legal) meaning that the author gave the language and the solution that the author envisioned for the legal problem before the interpreter. Others try to realize the abstract ("general") intent of the text's author, meaning the (general) purposes that the author of the norm envisioned.[94] A *second* distinction concerns the sources that the judge may use in order to learn the intent of the text's author. Some theories restrict the judge to learning about the intent of the text's author only from the text itself. That is an extreme version of the subjective-literal system, barring the judge from going beyond the four corners of the text in order to grasp the (historical) intent of the text's author.[95] Other theories hold that if the intent of the text's author can be inferred from the text itself, the interpreter should not go beyond the text, unless the result would be absurd.[96] We can call this system a moderate version of the subjective-literal system. This moderate version recognizes an additional situation in which the in-

[94] *Infra* p. 121.

[95] *See, e.g.*, Lord Wensleydale, in *Abbot v. Middleton*, 7 H.L.C. 68, 114 (1858).

[96] This is England's golden rule, applicable not just to interpreting statutes, but rather to interpreting all legal texts: *see Grey v. Pearson*, 10 E.R. 1216, 1234 (1857). In the United States, the rule is known as the "plain meaning rule." In Continental Europe it is known as the doctrine of "sens clair."

terpreter may go beyond the text in order to discover the intent of the author: If the language of the text is vague or ambiguous, the interpreter may look beyond the text in order to understand the intent of the text's author.[97] At the other end of the spectrum, we find a comprehensive subjective system that allows an interpreter to learn the intent of the text's author from any credible source. This appears to be[98] the approach of members of the "legal process" movement. We will discuss this approach when we address the text's subjective purpose, which is a component of purposive interpretation. A *third* distinction relates to the time at which the author formulates his or her subjective intent. This generally happens at the time the text is created, but sometimes we might take changes in the author's intent into consideration. The intent of a testator, for example, may change between the time he or she makes the will and the time of death. The intent of contracting parties may change throughout the life of a (long-term) contract. The timing is more complicated for a statute, for which we might want to consider both the intent of the historical legislature that enacted the statute and that of the contemporary legislature. The problem is that the flesh-and-blood people whose intent creates legislative intent have changed over the years. A subjective system of interpretation must adopt a stance on these issues.

Objective Systems of Interpretation in Law

The *second* kind of system of interpretation comprises objective systems. They are objective in the sense that they attempt to understand the meaning of the text without reference to the intent of the text's author. They are distinct in their view that the connection between the text and its author is severed once the text is written. The author has completed his or her task, and his or her intent is of no further assistance.[99] The text stands on its own two feet, and interpreting it does not involve an inquiry into the intent of its author. The author's intent forms no part of the legal text and has no interpretive status. The judge may understand the text differently than its author does. He or she is even likely to understand the text better than its author. The judge does not retrace the steps of the text's author, and interpretation is not rethinking what was considered in the past. Rather, interpretation is new thinking about what has yet to be thought

[97] This is the "mischief rule" customary in England, the United States, and countries in Continental Europe.

[98] The doubt stems from the equivocal formulation of their position. *See* Hart and Sachs, *supra* p. 3, note 3 at 1378. It is not clear if their approach is subjective or objective.

[99] *See* Barak, *supra* p. 3, note 1 at 143; Steyn, *supra* p. 18, note 49 at 81. *See also* C. Curtis, "A Better Theory of Interpretation," 3 *Vand. L. Rev.* 407 (1950).

about.[100] According to scholars of objective systems of interpretation, the text, once written, takes its own path, like a bullet fired from a gun, an arrow shot from a bow and continuing in flight,[101] or a boat that lifts anchor, leaves port, and sails into the stormy sea.[102]

SURVEY OF OBJECTIVE SYSTEMS OF INTERPRETATION IN LAW

There are numerous objective systems of interpretation. Sometimes the gaps between them are greater than the gap between an objective system and a subjective system. The point of contention for proponents of objective systems of interpretation is the text's objective meaning, and how the interpreter should ascertain it. According to *one* approach, the goal of interpretation is to give the text a meaning that realizes the intent of its author. However, in contrast to the "true" subjective systems, the interpreter does not seek the true intent of the text's author, but rather his or her intent as a reasonable person would understand it. The interpreter supplants the true intent of the text's author with a hypothetical intent, which he or she then attributes to the author. The English golden rule—applicable to wills, contracts, and statutes alike—is used in such a fashion. A similar principle applies to the American plain meaning rule. This approach appears subjective but in actuality objectifies authorial intent.[103] Some call this approach "old textualism."[104]

Taking an additional step away from subjectivity, a *second* objective system discards the internal aspect of interpretation by ignoring the intent of the text's author. According to this technique, the (objective) meaning of a text is the meaning that a typical, reasonable reader would ascribe to the language of the text, reading it at the time it was drafted. This technique is "new textualism,"[105] and it derives from the system referred to as originalism.[106] According to new textualism, a judge should interpret a text according to the ordinary and natural meaning that the words would have to an ordinary person reading the text at the time it was created. Proponents

---

[100] This is Radbruch's metaphor, as cited by M. Hayoz, 1 *Berner Kommentar* 137 (Vol. I, part 1, 1966).

[101] Cowen, "Prolegomenon to a Restatement of the Principles of Statutory Interpretation," 1976 *T.S.A.R.* 131, 137.

[102] A. Aleinikoff, "Updating Statutory Interpretation," 87 *Mich. L. Rev.* 20 (1983).

[103] Scalia correctly points this out. *See* A. Scalia, *A Matter of Interpretation: Federal Courts and the Law* 17 (1997).

[104] For an analysis of this approach, see p. 270, *infra*.

[105] For an analysis of this approach, see p. 277, *infra*.

[106] For a discussion of this approach, see p. 277, *infra*. Some originalists are also intentionalists—they adhere either to subjective systems of interpretation or to old textualism. Our discussion here, however, is of originalists who are not intentionalists.

of this system are willing to go beyond the four corners of the text in order to comprehend its natural and ordinary meaning, by referring to dictionaries or to texts that address similar issues.

According to a *third* objective approach, the objective meaning of a text derives from the objective purpose that the text is intended to achieve. This purpose may exist at varying levels of abstraction, the highest of which is the intent to actualize the legal system's fundamental values, as they exist at the time of interpretation. On this view, the will of the legal system supplants the will of the text's author. We will expand the discussion of this approach when we address the objective purpose of a text, which constitutes a component of purposive interpretation.

A *fourth* objective approach disavows any search for purpose (objective or subjective) and allows the interpreter to give the language the meaning he or she thinks the text should actualize. The interpreter ascertains this meaning neither from the text itself nor from the intent of its author, but rather from the interpreter's own grasp of what the text should mean. The subjectivity of the interpreter supplants the subjectivity of the author. According to this genre of "free" approaches, textual language is always vague and ambiguous; understanding is always a function of context, but because even context is vague and ambiguous, language does not pose an obstacle to the interpreter who seeks to realize his or her ideas. The rules of interpretation do not constrain judges, because the rules themselves require judges' interpretation. At the end of the day, law becomes politics, and there are no objective criteria to guide judges. Free interpretation views any attempt to present objective legal doctrine as masking the reality that the judge interprets the text according to his or her political views. I categorize this approach as objective because while it focuses on the subjectivity of the interpreter, it ignores the subjective intent of the author, which is the focal point of subjective systems of interpretation.

Subjective-Objective Systems of Interpretation in Law

The *third* kind of system of interpretation is an intermediate type: subjective-objective systems of interpretation. Their unifying feature is that each, in various ways, combines subjective and objective aspects. There is, however, no attempt to synthesize or integrate the different principles. We will discuss three such non-integrative systems. Another type is based on a "compound" of objective and subjective principles, created by a new synthesis and integration of those principles. We will discuss two of these integrative systems.

Non-Integrative Subjective-Objective Systems
of Interpretation in Law

One subjective-objective approach is a two-stage process that the interpreter begins by using one of the subjective systems of interpretation. If one of these systems produces an unequivocal interpretation, the interpretive process ends. If the resulting interpretation is ambiguous, however, the interpreter turns to one of the objective systems of interpretation. These systems are popular in Continental law[107] and have also surfaced in common law practice. Posner's[108] "imaginative reconstruction," for example, takes this approach and shares historical roots with this two-stage process.[109] According to Posner, the interpreter must interpret the text according to the intent of its author. The interpreter acts as the author's agent ("the agency model").[110] On this view, a judge interpreting a legal text is like a subordinate who must interpret an order given by a superior officer. The subordinate must execute the order as the superior officer intended it to be done, but cannot ask questions of the senior officer because a malfunction in the communications system has severed contact between them. Posner recognizes, however, that this interpretive standard does not provide enough guidance for all situations. Often, there is insufficient information about the author's intent; sometimes his or her intent is ambiguous. For these and other reasons, at some point, the intent of the text's author ceases to control the meaning of the norm, and the interpreter must move to the second stage of the interpretive process. At this stage, the judge should give the text the meaning that its author would have wanted it to be given, had he or she thought about the matter—in other words, the intent of the reasonable author.

In a *second* subjective-objective approach, the interpreter interprets the text in order to realize the (abstract) intent of the author. Where the text's author intended the text to be given an objective meaning, however, the interpreter must switch to an objective system of interpretation. Some proponents of this approach rely on the presumption that typically, the text's author intends an objective interpretation. Those wishing to rebut the presumption—and it *is* rebuttable—must point to credible historical sources to show that the text's author wanted his or her (abstract) intent to guide the interpreter. A number of American scholars[111] adapt this approach as

[107] Larenz, *supra* p. 3, note 5 at 192; K. Engisch, *Einführung in das Juristische Denken* 85 (7th ed. 1977).

[108] Posner, *supra* p. 27, note 85 at 273.

[109] W. Lehman, "How to Interpret a Difficult Statute," 1979 *Wis. L. Rev.* 489.

[110] For a discussion of the agency model, see p. 248, *infra*.

[111] H.J. Powell, "The Original Understanding of Original Intent," 98 *Harv. L. Rev.* 885 (1985).

part of their attempt to show that the founders of the United States Constitution intended it to be given an objective meaning.

Professor Perlman developed a *third* subjective-objective approach for interpreting legislation.[112] His starting point is subjective—the interpreter must interpret a statute according to the intent of the legislature. However, it is difficult for the interpreter to comprehend the intent of the legislature, which enacted the statute many years before. Furthermore, freezing the meaning of a statute at its past intent renders law static and prevents it from offering solutions to contemporary problems. According to Perlman, as times change, so too does the meaning of a statute. Perlman's solution is for the interpreter to interpret the statute according to the intent, not of the legislature who passed the law, but rather of the modern legislature in power at the time the interpreter gives meaning to the text. In justifying this approach, Perlman writes:

> The judge can only guess as to what the ancient legislature would really have wanted, as that legislature cannot express its disagreement with the interpretation attributed to it. That attribution of intent may be mere fiction, used by the judge to disguise his own personal interpretation of a statute, offered as though it is in accord with the intent of the legislature that passed it. On the other hand, when the judge refers to the intent of the contemporary legislature, he expresses a conjecture that can be tested, because if the contemporary legislature disagrees, it can express its opinion and enact a statute governing the way statutes should be interpreted.[113]

Integrative Subjective-Objective Systems of Interpretation in Law

In integrative subjective-objective systems of interpretation, the interpreter may move freely between subjectivity (authorial intent) and objectivity (the intent of the reasonable author or of the system), in an attempt to integrate the two. Pragmatic interpretation, Dworkin's system of interpretation, and purposive interpretation all fall into this category. We will discuss these systems later.[114]

---

[112] Ch. Perelman, *Legal Logic* 131 (1984).

[113] *Id.* at 131. In France, Ballot-Beauque, President of the Cour de Cassation, takes a similar view. *See* R. David, "Sources of Law," in 2 *International Encyclopedia of Comparative Law* 92 (Int'l Assoc. of Legal Science ed., 1984).

[114] *Infra* p. 286 (pragmatic interpretation); *infra* p. 290 (Dworkin's interpretation); *infra* p. 182 (purposive interpretation).

5. ADVANTAGES AND DISADVANTAGES
OF INTERPRETIVE RULES

The Importance of Interpretation and Its Rules

Every text requires interpretation. To understand is to interpret. We understand a legal text only after it has been interpreted. But do interpretive rules have an impact on law? Can't we say that the judge reaches his or her conclusion about the meaning of a text in his or her own way, without the guidance of interpretive rules? Do rules of interpretation simply provide a cover for the conclusion the judge reaches without them? Rather than guiding principles, are interpretive rules simply rules of justification?

This kind of skepticism is unjustified. Interpretive rules are important. They guide judges. They direct them in their interpretive work and educate them to think like jurists. They are the key to solving unsolved questions. While interpretive rules themselves require interpretation, they nevertheless are a guiding force. It is true that discretion sometimes plays a role in interpretation. Indeed, without judicial discretion, judges could not resolve all the problems that demand interpretation.[115] Discretion does not, however, render interpretive rules superfluous. Judicial discretion operates within the framework of interpretive rules, not outside it. It expresses the perspectives of the legal community within which the judge operates,[116] a legal community that shares common perspectives and approaches to interpreting legal texts.

INTERPRETIVE RULES AND THE LEGAL COMMUNITY

I reject the view that law is politics, that interpretive activity is simply political activity, and that the interpreter acts according to his or her political whims, unguided by interpretive rules.[117] Legal language has the power to guide people's behavior. If it didn't, social life would be impossible. The existence of an organized, stable society and the observance of legal rules demonstrate that legal language is clear enough to guide human behavior

---

[115] R. Alexy, *A Theory of Legal Argumentation: The Theory of Discourse as Theory of Legal Justification* 4 (R. Adler and D.N. MacCormick trans., 1989).

[116] *See* O. Fiss, "Objectivity and Interpretation," 34 *Stan. L. Rev.* 739 (1981–82).

[117] Scholars of the critical legal studies take this view. *See* G. Peller, "The Metaphysics of American Law," 73 *Cal. L. Rev.* 1151 (1985); J.W. Singer, "The Player and the Cards: Nihilism and Legal Theory," 94 *Yale L.J.* 1 (1984). Note that Kelsen, the positivist, argues that while interpretation does not direct the interpreter to a single, unique solution, interpretive rules create a framework from which the interpreter may not deviate. From this viewpoint, interpretive rules do play a guiding role, not just in the "negative" sense. H. Kelsen, "On the Theory of Interpretation," 10 *Legal Stud.* 127 (1990).

in the overwhelming majority of cases. Despite the multiplicity of values and principles, there is no legal Tower of Babel. Every legal community has its own views on how to balance conflicting values. In cases of doubt, designated institutions resolve the conflict. The legal community derives its legal viewpoints from its social culture and legal tradition, and rules for interpreting legal texts constitute part of this culture and tradition. If those rules are strong enough to distinguish one legal community from another, then they are strong enough to guide the interpreter working within the community itself.[118] We must admit, however, that those rules do not always lead to a unique solution. Judicial discretion exists, but it does not undermine the foundations of the interpretive project. It is, rather, part of that project. Interpretive rules are critical to law. In the absence of interpretive rules, a legal text in the hands of the judge becomes an ax to grind as he or she chooses. The judge's intent supplants the intent of the author of the text. The text loses its independent character, and jurisprudence is reduced to an exercise in the psychology or sociology of the interpreter. Law becomes a caricature of itself. Anyone who recognizes the existence of law must also recognize the existence of legal rules that bind the interpretation of legal texts.

INTERPRETATION AND INTUITION

Empirically, it is clear that interpretive rules matter. First of all, an author usually creates a text against the backdrop of the rules for interpreting the text, with the knowledge that, down the line, the judge will act according to those rules. Such is the case in writing a constitution or statute, or making a contract or will. While it is true that an interpreter sometimes reaches his or her interpretive conclusion by intuition, it would be a mistake to view the entire interpretive process as merely intuitive, for two reasons: *First*, in many instances, intuition does not operate at all.[119] *Second*, the interpreter tests the validity of his or her intuition. Intuition must be rationalized.[120] Left unchecked, it leads to arbitrariness. I have yet to meet the judge who believes that intuition is a necessary and sufficient tool for judicial activity. Every judge seeks to challenge his or her own intuition,[121] and to modify it if it runs contrary to the interpretive rules.[122]

---

[118] O. Fiss, "Conventionalism," 58 *S. Cal. L. Rev.* 177 (1985).

[119] W. Parent, "Interpretation and Justification in Hard Cases," 15 *Ga. L. Rev.* 99 (1980–81).

[120] R. Wasserstrom, *The Judicial Decision: Toward a Theory of Legal Justification* 22 (1961); H.J. Friendly, "Reactions of a Lawyer–Newly Become Judge," 71 *Yale L.J.* 218, 230 (1961–62).

[121] I. Kaufman, "The Anatomy of Decisionmaking," 53 *Fordham L. Rev.* 1, 16 (1984–85).

[122] W. Schaefer, "Precedent and Policy," 34 *U. Chi. L. Rev.* 3 (1966).

The rules of interpretation guarantee rationality in the interpreter's thinking. They set cognitive boundaries that the interpreter may not cross. They introduce order to legal thinking. They facilitate critical evaluation of the interpreter's moves. They create accepted channels for legal argument. A lawyer appearing before a judge tries to persuade him or her with proper arguments, expressed through the vessel of interpretive rules. Without them, what would the lawyer argue before the judge? How would he or she know which arguments will or should persuade a judge? Interpretive rules are a legal community's rules of argument. They are the vessel for arguments considered to be appropriate. They even influence the intuition judges sometimes use. Intuition is the product of a judge's character, makeup, and legal and judicial worldview—products of education, study, thinking, life experience, and historical tradition. A judge's basic interpretive perceptions shape his or her worldview. Interpretive rules, then, do not simply justify the result that an interpreter reaches without them. They are the compass by which an interpreter navigates through the law's complexities.[123]

INTERPRETIVE RULES AS RULES OF LEGITIMACY

In addition to their practical value, interpretive rules serve an important theoretical function. They legitimize interpretive activity, even if, "historically," the judge made his or her decision based on intuition. Even those who disagree with the result nevertheless recognize its legitimacy, because the judicial decision came about through the observance of known and accepted rules. Resolution of a dispute in accordance with accepted rules of interpretation appears legitimate even to those who think the resolution is wrong. This legitimacy is particularly important for situations in which the interpretation does not just declare law but also creates it. In those instances, there is always a fear that the judiciary will be accused of trespassing on the terrain of the text's author. Interpretive rules assuage this fear by legitimating judicial activity. Interpretive rules help retain public confidence in judges. They also guarantee the "objectivity" necessary for the judicial process. They guarantee that the judge will not appear to impose his or her subjective opinions on the public. They preserve the independence and autonomy of the judicial process. Interpretation by the rules secures the equal application of law, guaranteeing not just public confidence in the judiciary but also the just application of law. Beyond that, interpretation by the rules makes it easier for reviewing courts to critique the interpretation, obligating the interpreter to explain his or her decision by reference to the interpretive rules within his or her system. Interpretive rules are the lan-

---

[123] D. Harris, "The Politics of Statutory Construction," (1985) *BYU L. Rev.* 745.

guage that jurists speak, through which they persuade each other. They serve as a vessel for the arguments that the legal community views as persuasive, bringing security and certainty to the law.

In order to adhere to the text being interpreted, the interpreter must follow the rules of interpretation. The rule of law and the principle of constitutional supremacy depend on the existence and application of interpretive rules. Without interpretive rules binding on the state as well as individuals, a nation of law and rule of law would be impossible. How is it possible to guarantee the observance of a constitution and statutes, if everyone is free to interpret them as he or she chooses? Adherence to a fixed system of interpretive rules is vital to a democratic society.

INTERPRETIVE RULES AS A TOOL FOR LEGAL DEVELOPMENT

Interpretive rules also play the important role of aiding in the development of law.[124] A legal norm applies to the (unknown) future, creating an inevitable gap between law and society's changing reality. Too great a gap between law and society tarnishes the law and public confidence in it. It does members of society a disservice. The legislature is the primary tool for bridging the gap, but legislative action is not always possible or advisable. Interpretive rules—along with other doctrines like good faith—constitute an additional tool through which a judge can develop law, thereby bridging the gap between law and social reality. Through interpretation, a judge gives a legal norm, created in the past, the breadth and content it needs to respond to contemporary needs. As Professor Pound puts it, interpretation is important for its role as an agent of growth.[125] Take the metaphor of a "living constitution." Life's changing needs create a gap between an old constitution and contemporary needs. Interpretation can narrow the gap without amending the constitution. Or, consider the theory of dynamic interpretation,[126] according to which law is "always speaking."[127] A judge gives a piece of legislation a modern interpretation to suit modern needs. The language of the statute remains as before, but its meaning has changed to adapt the law to contemporary conditions. An example is a law passed by a nondemocratic regime. When the regime changes and democracy

---

[124] J. Raz, "On the Authority and Interpretation of Constitutions: Some Preliminaries," in L. Alexander (ed.), *Constitutionalism: Philosophical Foundations* 152, 177 (1998) ("[L]egal interpretation is also a tool for developing the law, changing and reforming it").

[125] R. Pound, 3 *Jurisprudence* 467 (1959).

[126] W. Eskridge, *Dynamic Statutory Interpretation* (1994).

[127] *See* Bennion, *supra* p. 6, note 13 at 686; *Fitzpatrick v. Sterling Housing Association Ltd* [1999] 4 All E.R. 705, 711; *R. v. Hammersmith and Fulham London Borough Council, ex p. M* (1997) Times 19 February; *Victor Chandler International v. Customs and Excise Commissioners and Others* [2000] 2 All E.R. 315, 322.

reigns, a judge interprets the law according to democratic values, narrowing the gap between law and society. Understanding the text's (objective)
purpose infuses new foundational principles into the legal system. A parallel process takes place in private law, in which judges use interpretive rules
to develop default rules in contract law.[128] Doctrines like frustration,
waiver, and mistake similarly help judges infuse contract law with the legal
system's fundamental values. As Professor Atiyah said:

> Construction has become by far the most popular technique for the solution
> of practically all problems in the law of contract which do not depend on un-
> yielding rules of positive law, such as capacity, illegality, and the requirement
> of consideration.[129]

Lewison referred to this phenomenon as manipulation.[130] It is, however,
constructive manipulation, allowing the interpreter to advance the law and
bridge the gap between law and the needs of society. There is no reason to
hide it. It is a natural phenomenon. Law must be stable, but it cannot stand
still.[131] Change is necessary, and interpretation is a legitimate and crucial
tool to achieve it.

Critique of Interpretation

Scholars have recently expressed renewed interest in legal interpretation.
In the past, particularly in Anglo-American legal literature, the prevailing
view was that interpretation as a subject is obsolete. Lord Wilberforce
called interpretation a "non-subject."[132] It has been alleged that what little there is to say about interpretation has already been said—and even that

[128] See Lord Denning, in *Mitchell (George) (Chesterhall) Ltd. v. Finney Lock Seeds Ltd.*
[1983] 1 All E.R. 108, 113: "Faced with this abuse of power by the strong against the weak,
by the use of the small print of the conditions, the judges did what they could to put a curb
on it. They still had before them the idol, 'freedom of contract'. They still knelt down and
worshipped it, but they concealed under their cloaks a secret weapon. They used to stab the
idol in the back. This weapon was called 'the true construction of the contract'. They used it
with great skill and ingenuity."

[129] Atiyah, *supra* p. 9, note 19 at 267.

[130] K. Lewison, *The Interpretation of Contracts* 21 (2d ed. 1997).

[131] R. Pound, *Interpretations of Legal History* 1 (1923) ("Law must be stable and yet it
cannot stand still. Hence all thinking about law has struggled to reconcile the conflicting demands of the need of stability and of the need of change.")

[132] See his comments made in the House of Lords: 274 H.L. Deb. Ser. 5 Col. 1294, 16
November 1968. In a lecture given a number of years later, Lord Wilberforce explained what
he meant by his comments: "That it is really about life and human nature itself—too broad
and deep and variegated to be encapsulated in any theory, or, really to be taught." *Symposium
on Statutory Interpretation* 6 (Attorney General's Department ed., 1983).

is not worthy of scientific discussion.[133] Those assuming a benevolent attitude toward interpretation have called it an art, to be sensed rather than understood, and implemented by feel rather than according to rules. On this view, rules of interpretation are not legal rules but just advice for the interpreter.

This view of interpretation developed for a number of reasons. On the philosophical level, legal theories that attributed no significance to interpretive rules began to hold sway. Thus, for example, both Kelsen,[134] the positivist, and Grey,[135] the realist, thought that the principles governing the interpretive choice between meanings have nothing to do with law. The critical legal studies movement criticizes interpretive approaches and glorifies non-interpretive legal viewpoints. The pragmatists argued that interpretive rules do not lead the interpreter to a single, unique outcome, and that every issue is subject to conflicting interpretive rules. Professor Llewellyn said that "there are two opposing canons on almost every point."[136] Interpretive rules, on this view, are ineffectual and pointless. At most, they justify a conclusion that the judge reaches on his or her own ("rules of justification").

THE CRITIQUE IS PARTLY JUSTIFIED

This critique has some merit. The field of interpretation in both Continental[137] and Anglo-American law suffers from a lack of clarity. One gets the feeling that neither system has been able to construct a proper interpretive point of view.[138] Professor Gottlieb put it well in saying that

> The history of the interpretation of rules is a record of the successive misconceptions about the nature of law and language which have swept the juristic schools of the continent of Europe and the Anglo-Saxon countries. They are by no means at an end.[139]

Referring to statutory interpretation in the United States in the 1950s, Hart and Sachs noted that "The hard truth of the matter is that American

---

[133] R. Weisberg, "The Calabresian Judicial Artist: Statutes and the New Legal Process," 35 *Stan. L. Rev.* 213 (1982–83).

[134] Kelsen, *supra* p. 3, note 4 at 348.

[135] J. Gray, *The Nature and Sources of the Law* 170 (3d ed. 1921).

[136] Llewellyn, "Remarks on the Theory of Appellate Decision and the Rules or Canons about How Statutes Are to be Construed," 3 *Vand. L. Rev.* 395, 401 (1950).

[137] *See* P.O. Ekelof, "Teleological Construction of Statutes," 2 *Scandinavian Studies in Law* 75, 78 (1958); K. Zweigert and H.J. Puttfarken, "Statutory Interpretation—Civilian Style," 44 *Tul. L. Rev.* 704, 714 (1969–70).

[138] J. Witherspoon, "Administrative Discretion to Determine Statutory Meaning: The Low Road," 38 *Tex. L. Rev.* 392, 397 (1959–60).

[139] Gottlieb, *supra* p. 3, note 1 at 91.

courts have no intelligible, generally accepted, and consistently applied theory of statutory interpretation."[140] Interpretive theory is particularly muddled in the field of constitutional law. On this issue, the United States Supreme Court is divided between those who believe that the intent of the founders, or original intent, is the basis for interpreting the U.S. Constitution and those who would interpret it according to society's modern needs.[141] The split seems irreparable.

Even in interpretation of contracts and wills, there are no clear interpretive theories. Thus, for example, English law requires "objective" interpretation of contracts. The question is not what the parties to the contract subjectively wanted, but rather how a reasonable reader would understand their (objective) intentions.[142] In contrast, Continental law attempts to honor subjective intent in interpreting a contract.[143] American law employs both objective and subjective approaches.[144]

No system attempts to create a general theory of interpretation that would apply to all legal texts. Despite many years of significant engagement with interpretation, we know little about it. This is partly because interpretation has been approached as an "art," to be sensed. Also, scholars have tended to focus on the specifics of each situation, contributing to the feeling that each interpretive problem stands alone, and that the rules of interpretation lack significance. Our paucity of knowledge is also attributable to the overwhelming number of systems of interpretation and disappointment with their inability to create rules that provide an unequivocal answer in every case. The common law's precedential technique played a role insofar as it strayed from abstraction and was drawn into casuistry—frustrating the development of a general theory of interpretation.[145] Ignorance of linguistic philosophy and its lessons also contributed to the gloomy state of legal interpretation. Llewellyn's theory of the uselessness of interpretive rules is a natural outgrowth of a system of interpretation based entirely on formal and technical rules that are sometimes internally contradictory and that do not help the interpreter resolve his or her problem.

[140] Hart and Sachs, *supra* p. 3, note 3 at 1168.

[141] *See infra* p. 388.

[142] *Reardon-Smith Line Ltd. v. Hansen-Tangen* [1976] 3 All E.R. 570; *McCutcheon v. David MacBrayne Ltd.* [1964] 1 W.L.R. 125.

[143] *See* section 1156 of the Code Civile; section 133 of the B.G.B.; section 1362 of the Italian civil code; section 1425 of the Quebec code.

[144] *Restatement (Second) of Contracts* §201 (1981) (based on a subjective approach). There are, however, clear signs of an objective approach in the case law. *See* C. Goetz and R. Scott, "The Limits of Expanded Choice: An Analysis of the Interactions Between Express and Implied Contract Terms," 73 *Cal. L. Rev.* 261, 306 (1985).

[145] F. Pollock, *Essays in Jurisprudence and Ethics* 85 (1882).

The Need to Revitalize Interpretation

Where does this gloomy situation leave us? Instead of throwing up our hands in disappointment, we should reconsider interpretation and its role in society. We should revitalize, not abandon, interpretation. Indeed, scholars have expressed renewed interest in interpretation over the last few decades, to the point where today, they recognize its central role in law. A number of factors explain this development.

First, general hermeneutics took off, sparking interest in interpretation in literature, religion, and other branches of human creation,[146] including law. Theorists began asking if general hermeneutic philosophy could produce rules that would be useful to legal interpretation. As general hermeneutics flourished, legal hermeneutics followed suit. Furthermore, scholars have revitalized semantic theory in recent years, improving our understanding of jurisprudence and its connections to semantic theory. These developments have directly affected interpretation, whose foundation is in semantic theory.

The *second* factor is the recent development of certain legal theories that cannot be understood without paying a certain amount of attention to interpretation. Dworkin's theory and critical legal studies are prominent examples. Dworkin believes that law is nothing but a process of interpretation, and that to understand law, one must understand interpretation. Interpretive rules thus direct the interpreter to the single, unique legal solution that emerges from the system. According to critical legal studies, in contrast, law is politics, and interpretive rules do not constitute objective rules to guide a judge. These approaches clash over the proper treatment of interpretation, but the polemics surrounding each have bolstered interest in interpretation and its rules.

Third, "judicial lawmaking" is becoming increasingly well understood. No longer do people believe that judges declare law but do not create it; that idea has been discredited as "childish" and unrealistic.[147] Many people recognize and even encourage the creative power of judicial activity.[148] Nonetheless, jurists perceive a need to limit judicial lawmaking, to preserve the boundary between interpreting an existing text and creating a new one. Because interpretive rules preserve that boundary, people are expressing renewed interest in understanding them.

---

[146] D. Bell, "The Turn to Interpretation: An Introduction," 51 *Partisan Review* 215 (1984).

[147] L. Reid, "The Judge as Law Maker," 12 *J. Soc'y Pub. Teachs. L* 22 (1972); B. Laskin, "The Role and Function of Final Appellate Courts: The Supreme Court of Canada," 53 *Can. Bar. Rev.* 469 (1975); A. Lester, "English Judges as Law Makers," (1993) *Public Law* 269; T. Bingham, *The Business of Judging: Selected Essays and Speeches* 25 (2000).

[148] G. Calabresi, *A Common Law for the Age of Statutes* (1982).

Fourth, the creation or recreation of political systems in the wake of World War II, decolonization, and later, the collapse of the Soviet Union, has renewed interest in constitutions, their role in society, and in particular, their treatment of human rights. People now want to know how to interpret a constitution and how to make sure that judicial review of a law's constitutionality does not become a dictatorship of constitutional judges. Understanding interpretive rules—those that apply to the interpretation of both constitutions and statutes—has now become an issue of primary importance. Similarly, since World War II, there has been and continues to be increased interest in standardizing private law in general, and contract law in particular.[149] Attempts to standardize the laws of interpretation are part of this effort, which has been magnified by the growing strength of European Community law and the victory of globalization.[150] These factors and others helped revitalize interpretation and have fostered interest in studying it.

The Need for a Proper Theory of Interpretation

Renewed scholarly interest in interpretation has produced many opposing essays, few of which, however, have attempted to construct a general theory.[151] Most works have discussed the interpretation of constitutions and statutes, not contracts and wills. General hermeneutic theory has influenced these essays to a large extent. Courts in various countries have also begun paying special attention to interpretive theory. The result has been an extensive literature on the specific aspects of interpretation, without significant progress on overarching issues. We still lack a theory that is general enough to apply to all legal texts (constitution, statute, contract, and will) yet flexible enough to distinguish among the different texts, in order to interpret them. Is this task feasible? Are the unifying elements within the totality of legal texts strong enough to construct a general theory of interpretation? Can a unified theory permit the independent expression of each of these legal texts? My answer is yes. We need a theory of interpretation that is not based on contradiction and dyads of contrasting rules. We need a theory of interpretation that reflects the complexity of the interpretive

---

[149] *See* the proposed Principles of European Contract Law. On the proposal and its interpretation, see O. Lando and H. Beale, *Principles of European Contract Law* (2000).

[150] W. Twining, *Globalisation and Legal Theory* (2000).

[151] Betti made a valuable contribution to the attempt to construct a general theory. E. Betti, *Teoria Generale della Interpretazione* (1955); E. Betti, "On a General Theory of Interpretation: The *Raison d'Etre* of Hermeneutics," 32 *Am. J. of Jur.* 245 (1987); G. Wright, "On a General Theory of Interpretation: The Betti-Gadamer Dispute in Legal Hermeneutics," 32 *Am. J. of Jur.* 191 (1987).

process, on the one hand, and its operation in daily life, on the other. We need principles instead of rules, and presumptions instead of mandatory laws. We need a better understanding of semantic theory, and of the text in context. Purposive legal interpretation—the foundation of this book—attempts to take all of these into account.

6. THE STATUS AND SOURCES OF INTERPRETIVE RULES

Legal Rules

According to some strands of legal literature, interpretive rules are nothing more than advice for the interpreter.[152] Such approaches are fundamentally mistaken. Interpretive rules are part of the system of law by which interpreters must abide. They are not just options; they are, as Professor Hart[153] put it, secondary rules. The fact that they sometimes require artistry or craftsmanship and always require sensitivity, understanding, and experience does not detract from their legal, binding character. Interpretation goes to the heart of the social structure, social stability, and distribution of power in a given society. It is part of the operative jurisprudence of every legal system and constitutes a central component of constitutional law. Rules of interpretation are the laws of the laws. They constitute the "general component" of the laws of the system. Their jurisprudential character gives them a cosmopolitan quality, but every legal system has its own "local" rules of interpretation. Setting interpretive rules must take into account constitutional considerations like democracy, separation of powers, and the rule of law. Those who create rules of interpretation must consider these factors to ensure that the means of interpretation are not personal but institutional, and that the system of interpretation is a matter not of sentiment but of law.[154]

Implications of the Legal Character of Interpretive Rules

The legal character of interpretive rules leads to at least three practical conclusions. The *first* is that interpretive rules themselves require interpreta-

---

[152] Simlar, "Contracts et Obligations: Interpretation des Contracts," In *Juris Classeur*, Art 1156a, 1164 (1984); F.E. Horack, "The Disintegration of Statutory Construction," 24 *Ind. L.J.* 335, 337, 349 (1948–49).

[153] Hart, *supra* p. 26, note 78 at 94.

[154] Q. Johnstone, "An Evaluation of the Rules of Statutory Interpretation," 3 *U. Kan. L. Rev.* 1, 5 (1954–55).

tion. Even the interpretive norm grounded in a text must be inter-preted.[155] Sometimes, uncertainty over a text being interpreted reflects, to a lesser extent, uncertainty over the interpreting text. As Professor Hart put it:

> Canons of "interpretation" cannot eliminate, though they can diminish, these uncertainties; for these canons are themselves general rules for the use of lan-guage, and make use of general terms which themselves require interpreta-tion. They cannot, any more than other rules, provide for their own inter-pretation.[156]

Second, like other legal rules, the rules of interpretation actually consist of both principles and rules.[157] Most interpretive laws are principles rather than rules. As principles, interpretive norms do not provide details for each situation to which they apply. Similarly, as principles, interpretive norms do not become void if contradicted by other interpretive norms. Many prin-ciples express themselves through legal presumptions. In a given situation, a number of presumptions may apply, some of them contradictory. Judges resolve this contradiction by weighing the values underlying each pre-sumption. Of course, every system of interpretation has a number of basic, governing rules. For example, the prohibition against giving a legal text a meaning that it cannot tolerate in its language is a "rule" and not a "prin-ciple," as is the dictum that a legal text be interpreted according to its purpose, and that such purpose has subjective and objective aspects. The combination of "rules" and "principles" in interpretive laws guarantees se-curity, stability, and certainty while expressing the uniqueness of each text and bridging the gap between law and society.

Third, the interpretive norm is a matter of law, not fact; because it is part of substantive law, it is subject to the legal system's principle of *stare deci-sis*. Lower courts are therefore bound by supreme court decisions on in-terpretive rules.

Mandatory and Default Rules of Interpretation

Most interpretive norms are default rules. To the extent that the author of a text is free to decide its content, he or she is also free to set his or her own

---

[155] S. Fish, *Doing What Comes Naturally* 121 (1989); S. Fish, "Fish v. Fiss," 36 *Stan. L. Rev.* 1325 (1984).

[156] Hart, *supra* p. 26, note 78 at 126.

[157] For a discussion of this distinction, *see* R. Dworkin, *Taking Rights Seriously* 22 (1977); M. Bayles, *Principles of Law: A Normative Analysis* 11 (1987); K. Sullivan, "Foreword: The Justices of Rules and Standards," 106 *Harv. L. Rev.* 22 (1992). For a critique of this distinc-tion, *see* A. Marmor, *Positive Law and Objective Values* 81 (2001).

rules for interpreting the text. The constitution may therefore set rules for its own interpretation. However, constitutional supremacy prohibits a statute from setting rules for how to interpret the constitution.[158] The legislature may set rules for interpreting statutes, so long as those provisions do not conflict with the constitution. For example, a statutory provision declaring that the statute containing it or any others will be interpreted according to a particular person or authority—the president, the legislature, a legislative committee, or any other entity—is unconstitutional, violating the principle of separation of powers, under which courts have authority to interpret. Along these lines, parties to a contract may set their own rules for interpreting the contract; a testator is free to establish his or her own rules for interpreting his or her will. When a text's author is not free to decide the content of the text—as in the case of a problem subject to a mandatory rule (constitutional or otherwise)—he or she may not get around the prohibition by creating his or her own rules of interpretation.[159] Furthermore, an interpretive provision commanding deviation from the ordinary rules of interpretation will itself be interpreted according to those ordinary interpretive rules.[160] For example, a contractual provision saying that the contract should be interpreted according to the intent of one party alone must itself be interpreted according to the intent of both parties, because only the joint intent can be the basis for the special interpretive rule that the parties created. One must always find the Archimedean foothold outside the text, in order to interpret the text.

Legal Sources of the Laws of Interpretation

The legal source of the laws of interpretation is the same as that of other laws: constitution, statute, precedent, case law, custom, and the autonomy of the private will. Constitutions generally do not contain interpretive laws. Legislation in each legal system contains interpretive laws. Most civil codes contain instructions on how to interpret statutes,[161] contracts,[162] and wills.[163] In countries governed by Anglo-Saxon law, legislation commonly

[158] A statute governing interpretation, like Israel's Law of Interpretation, 1981, cannot, therefore, apply to constitutional interpretation.

[159] N.Q. Rosenkranz, "Federal Rules of Statutory Interpretation," 115 *Harv. L. Rev.* 2085 (2002).

[160] D. Charny, "Hypothetical Bargains: The Normative Structure of Contract Interpretation," 89 *Mich. L. Rev.* 1815, 1819 (1991).

[161] *See, e.g.,* section 12 of the Italian civil code; section 6 of the Austrian civil code; section 19 of the Chilean civil code.

[162] *See* sections 1156–64 of the French civil code; sections 1362–71 of the Italian civil code; sections 133 and 157 of the B.G.B.

[163] Sections 2064–86 of the B.G.B.; sections 908 and 1022 of the French civil code.

includes statutes (interpretation acts) that define terms without determining the general principle governing the meaning of a term. These statutes are concerned not with the laws of interpretation but rather with the results of interpretation. Of course, the laws of interpretation themselves must be interpreted, and sometimes interpretive statutes do contain interpretive laws (beyond the results-oriented definition of a term).[164] In most legal systems, however, whether they are civil law systems or common law systems, case law is the primary source of interpretive rules. Some systems favor the legislature's creation of statutory rules of interpretation.[165] I have doubts about the wisdom of that idea. Experience teaches that statutes setting laws of interpretation have little impact on the way judges actually interpret legal texts, in most cases because the guidelines are too general to be practically useful. Only in exceptional cases should statutory provisions govern interpretation—for example, to resolve a deep interpretive divide over whether legislative history should be used to interpret statutes.

Interpretation and Judging

All of us engage in interpretation all of the time.[166] The individual and the state conduct their affairs according to the interpretation they give (consciously or unconsciously) to legal texts. We live in a normative world in which every one of our actions is conceptualized according to our understanding of our world. The meaning of this understanding is—interpretation. Interpretation is not unique to judging. Every person and every entity—state and individual—interprets. Judicial interpretation, however, is special in that it is legally binding, not just on the parties, but also, through the principle of *stare decisis*, on the public as a whole. In creating a normative text, the author delegates authority to a judge to give the text a binding interpretation. A court's classic role is to adjudicate disputes brought before it. The court must find the facts, formulate for itself a position on the law, and apply the law to the facts. Determining the law is an incidental activity that necessitates interpretation of the law. Interpretation, then, is an incidental activity that is vital to judging. A court cannot judge without interpreting. Indeed, according to the principle of separation of

---

[164] *See, e.g.*, section 5 of New Zealand's 1924 Interpretation Act; section 15AB(3) of Australia's 1901 Interpretation Act; sections 10 and 11 of Canada's 1967–68 Interpretation Act.

[165] *See* Rosenkranz, *supra* p. 49, note 159.

[166] Some distinguish between interpretation, with which everybody deals, and construction, with which only judges deal, in order to give their decisions a binding force: *see* P.M. Tiersma, "The Ambiguity of Interpretation: Distinguishing Interpretation from Construction," 73 *Wash. U. L.Q.* 1095 (1995). I do not make this distinction, and I do not distinguish between these two expressions.

powers, interpretation is the constitutionally assigned responsibility of the court.[167] Any attempt to strip courts of their interpretive role would violate the principle of separation of powers. A statutory provision ordering the statute to be interpreted according to any entity other than a court is therefore unconstitutional.[168] Furthermore, a court should not privilege the constitutional assembly's interpretation of a constitution, the legislative body's interpretation of a constitution[169] or statute,[170] or, in administrative matters, the interpretation of the executive, whose power derives from the laws that must be interpreted.[171] In each of these cases, the question the court must ask is not whether the interpretation of the founders, the legislature, or the executive is reasonable or permissible, but rather whether it is the court's interpretation.

The court has no monopoly on interpretation.[172] The court interprets the text, but so do the other branches of government and so do individuals in the state. As we noted, however, judicial interpretation is unique in that it is binding. The executive, for example, cannot refuse to conform its behavior to the supreme court's interpretation of a constitutional or statutory provision, arguing that it believes the interpretation to be mistaken.

Having said that, in areas in which the court has not yet ruled, or in areas

[167] The source of this approach is found in *Marbury v. Madison*, 5 U.S. (1 Cranch) 137, 177 (1803) ("It is emphatically the province and duty of the judicial department to say what the law is"). *See also* Sunstein, *supra* p. 13, note 31.

[168] Rosenkranz, *supra* p. 49, note 159.

[169] This issue is far from resolved in American law. The literature is wide and comprehensive. For recent work, see S. Gant, "Judicial Supremacy and Nonjudicial Interpretation of the Constitution," 24 *Hastings Const. L.Q.* 359 (1997); L. Alexander and F. Schauer, "On Extrajudicial Constitutional Interpretation," 110 *Harv. L. Rev.* 1359 (1997); A. Ides, "Judicial Supremacy and the Law of the Constitution," 47 *UCLA L. Rev.* 491 (1999); E. Hartnett, "A Matter of Judgment, Not a Matter of Opinion," 74 *NYU L. Rev.* 123 (1999); N. Katyal, "Legislative Constitutional Interpretation," 50 *Duke L.J.* 1335 (2001); T. Merrill and K. Hickman, "*Chevron's* Domain," 89 *Geo. L.J.* 833 (2001); K. Whittington, "Extrajudicial Constitutional Interpretation: Three Objections and Responses," 80 *N.C. L. Rev.* 773 (2002).

[170] W. Popkin, "Foreword: Nonjudicial Statutory Interpretation," 66 *Chi. Kent L. Rev.* 301 (1990).

[171] *Black-Clawson International Ltd. v. Papierwerke Waldhof-Aschaffenberg A.G.* [1975] 1 All E.R. 810, 828; *Director of Investigation and Research (Competition) v. Southam Inc* [1997] 1 S.C.R. 748; J. Corry, "Administrative Law and the Interpretation of Statutes," 1 *U. Toronto L.J.* 286 (1936). The approach in the United States is different. *See Chevron U.S.A. v. Natural Resources Defense Council*, 467 U.S. 837 (1984). Extensive literature has developed around the *Chevron* doctrine. *See* K.C. Davis and R.J. Pierce, 1 *Administrative Law Treatise* 109 (3d ed., 1994); C. Sunstein, "Law and Administration After *Chevron*," 90 *Colum. L. Rev.* 2071 (1990); T. Merrill, "Judicial Deference to Executive Precedent," 101 *Yale L.J.* 969 (1992); R.J. Pierce, "*Chevron* and Its Aftermath: Judicial Review of Agency Interpretation of Statutory Provisions," 41 *Va. L. Rev.* 301 (1988).

[172] Tribe, *supra* p. 15, note 38 at 264.

in which other branches of government give an interpretation that differs from the court's but does not contradict it—for example by providing greater individual rights protection than is required by the supreme court's interpretation—other branches of government may act according to their own interpretations. Still, it is inappropriate within a legal system for each of the different branches of government to adopt its own system of interpretation. Any given legal system should have a single system of interpretation by which all branches of government and all individuals abide. For reasons of principle, the court's interpretation must be binding in order to maintain legislative supremacy as well as the supremacy of values and principles, particularly human rights. Because judges are not accountable in the same way as politicians are, they can express the legal system's fundamental values, central to which are human rights. For reasons of practicality, the court's interpretation must be binding to avoid wreaking havoc with the system.[173] Everyone is an interpreter, but the judge is the final, authorized interpreter. This book therefore focuses on the judge as interpreter. Note, however, that everything that will be said about judges as interpreters applies to every member of the public and every branch of government, because interpretive thinking must be consistent. Not that we all must agree with judicial interpretation. To the contrary—judges make mistakes, and, in any case, within a given system of interpretation, there may be disagreement about the application of the rule to a given instance. We are trying to reach agreement on the system of interpretation, not on the results of the interpretation.

Judicial Interpretation: Declaring Law and Creating Law

Legal scholarship contains a broad spectrum of opinions on the creativity of the judicial process of interpretation, particularly in the field of statutory interpretation. On one end of the spectrum is the opinion that, through interpretation, a judge just repeats the language of the statute. The judge is, in Montesquieu's words, the "mouth" of the legislator.[174] Judicial interpretation does not create a new norm. It simply declares what already exists in the system. This is the "phonograph theory,"[175] expressed by the Latin maxim that interpretation must extract the meaning of the instruction from the legal norm—not insert it (*sensus est efferendus non inferendus*). On this theory, legitimate interpretation requires judicial obedience,

---

[173] For an argument warning of this havoc, see Alexander and Schauer, *supra* p. 51, note 169. *Cf.* Wittington, *supra* p. 51, note 169 at 786.

[174] C. Montesquieu, *The Spirit of the Laws* 209 (Eng. trans., 1977).

[175] M. Cohen, *Law and Social Order: Essays in Legal Philosophy* 112, 113 (1933).

albeit "thoughtful obedience."[176] Interpretation is concerned with "discovering" the meaning hidden in the text.

On the other end of the spectrum is the belief that all interpretation is creation[177] or lawmaking. The meaning of the text is whatever meaning the interpreter gives it. The interpreter holds the power. Quoting Bishop Hoadly, Professor Grey noted that "Whoever hath an absolute authority to interpret any . . . laws, it is he who is truly the law-giver . . . and not the person who first wrote . . . them."[178] Radbruch expressed this position with two different sayings: "[J]udicial interpretation does not think again what has been thought before, but thinks through what has been thought of,"[179] and "The interpreter may understand the law better than its creators understood it; the law may be wiser than its authors—indeed, it *must* be wiser than its authors."[180]

Declaring Law and Creating Law

I think the truth lies somewhere between these two extremes. Montesquieu's approach does not reflect the fullness of judicial experience. Interpretation is not just declaring law. When the laws of interpretation do not lead to a single unique meaning, and the judge has judicial discretion to choose the proper outcome, the judicial act of interpretation is creative, not just declarative (*interpretatio praeter legem*).[181] A statute before and after an act of judicial interpretation is not the same statute. Limited judicial discretion is indeed part of interpretation.[182] Bishop Hoadly's pronouncement is mistaken for assuming that there is absolute license within interpretation. The presence of discretion does turn the interpretive act into a declaration of law that also creates law. Not every act of interpretation, however, involves discretion. When the laws of interpretation within the system mandate that the legal text being interpreted—without any use of judicial discretion—has a single, unique legal outcome, we have a declaration of law that does not create law (*interpretatio secundum legem*).[183]

---

[176] "Thoughtful obedience" (*denkender Gehorsam*) is a standard recognized by the interest jurisprudence (*Interessenjurisprudenz*), championed by Heck. *See* Larenz, *supra* p. 3, note 5 at 9.

[177] This is the approach attributed to the American realists and supporters of critical legal studies. *See* C. Curtis, *It's Your Law* 65 (1954).

[178] Grey, *supra* p. 43, note 135 at 172.

[179] G. Radbruch, "Legal Philosophy," in *The Legal Philosophies of Lask Radbruch and Dabin* 142 (K. Wilk trans., 1950).

[180] Radbruch, *supra* p. 53, note 179 at 141.

[181] Peczenik, *supra* p. 16, note 44 at 373.

[182] *See infra* p. 210; M. Cappelletti, "The Law-Making Power of the Judge and Its Limits: A Comparative Analysis," 8 *Monash U. L. Rev.* 15 (1981).

[183] Schauer, *supra* p. 13, note 34 at 408.

7. LAWS OF INTERPRETATION, JURISPRUDENCE, AND GENERAL HERMENEUTICS

Laws of Interpretation and Jurisprudence

The laws of interpretation are part of operational jurisprudence.[184] Philosophical theories and interpretive theories are interrelated. Often, a legal philosophy expresses its distinctiveness "practically" through its treatment of interpretation. For example, realists or neorealists emphasize a judge's freedom of choice in interpretation.[185] On the other hand, naturalists, who reject judicial discretion, put their trust in the laws of interpretation, which they view as laws to guide the act of judging.[186] Positivists are in the middle, as they recognize limited judicial discretion and the existence of "hard cases." In their view, interpretive rules guide a judge in the interpretation of a legal text up to a certain point, beyond which interpretive guidance ceases,[187] and the judge is left "with himself" to choose the interpretation that he or she deems best.[188] This last approach comports with judicial experience.[189] A judge does not have a free hand in the interpretation of a legal text. Like every wielder of power, a judge is limited in what he or she may do. This is the meaning of the rule of law, as opposed to the rule of judges. The neorealist perspective is an anti-legal perspective. The view that law is politics, and judicial interpretation is just judicial politics, is a nihilistic view whose conclusion means the end of law.[190] If judges do not have a free hand, however, neither are they completely bound. Interpretive laws cannot remove all uncertainty from a legal text. Sometimes, but not often, a judge retains discretion in interpretation.[191] Most of the time, however,

---

[184] They are part of what is called, in the Continental tradition, *Methodenlehre*, as opposed to *Rechtsphilosophie*. *See* Rüthers, *supra* p. 11, note 28 at 310. *See also* J.W. Harris, *Legal Philosophies* 140 (1980); W. Friedmann, "Legal Philosophy and Judicial Law Making," 61 *Colum. L. Rev.* 821 (1961).

[185] M. Radin, "Realism in Statutory Interpretation and Elsewhere," 23 *Cal. L. Rev.* 156 (1935); J. Frank, "Words and Music: Some Remarks on Statutory Interpretation," 47 *Colum. L. Rev.* 1259 (1947); M. Tushnet, "Following the Rules Laid Down: A Critique of Interpretivism and Neutral Principles," 96 *Harv. L. Rev.* 781 (1982); P. Brest, "Interpretation and Interest," 34 *Stan. L. Rev.* 765 (1982).

[186] With some reservations, Dworkin can be placed in this category. *See* R. Dworkin, "The Forum of Principles," 56 *NYU L. Rev.* 469 (1981); R. Dworkin, "Law as Interpretation," 60 *Tex. L. Rev.* 527 (1982). *See also* M.S. Moore, "A Natural Law Theory of Interpretation," 58 *S. Cal. L. Rev.* 277 (1985).

[187] Hart, *supra* p. 26, note 78 at 126. *See also* Fiss, *supra* p. 38, note 116.

[188] J. Raz, *The Authority of Law: Essays in Law and Morality* 197 (1979).

[189] A. Barak, *Judicial Discretion* (1989).

[190] Fiss, *supra* p. 38, note 116.

[191] It is hard to estimate the frequency of these instances. Justice Cardozo estimated them

interpretive laws do their job, removing uncertainty from the text without the need for discretion. Purposive interpretation honors this relationship between jurisprudence and legal interpretation. This book's theory of interpretation is based on an eclectic grasp of jurisprudence. Human experience is complicated, and jurisprudence should reflect that complexity.

Laws of Interpretation and General Hermeneutic Theory

Legal interpretation is part of the science of hermeneutics.[192] The historical roots of hermeneutics date back to such great thinkers as Maimonides[193] and Spinoza.[194] Modern hermeneutics has continued to develop with the theories of Schleiermacher[195] and Betti[196] (theoretical hermeneutics), Heidegger[197] and Gadamer[198] (philosophical hermeneutics), Habermas[199] and Hirsch[200] (critical hermeneutics), Ricoeur[201] (phenomenological hermeneutics), Baratta[202] and Lévi-Strauss[203] (structural hermeneutics), and Derrida[204] (deconstruction). Each of these the-

---

to be 10 percent of all cases that came before him. *See* Barak, *supra* p. 54, note 189 at 66, and B. Cardozo, *The Law* 60 (1924). For additional estimates, see A. Tate, "The Law-Making Function of the Judge," 28 *La. L. Rev.* 211 (1968); K. Llewellyn, *The Common Law Tradition: Deciding Appeals* 25 (1960); A. Patterson, *The Law Lords* 190 (1982); H. Edwards, "The Appellate Adjudication," 32 *Cleveland State L. Rev.* 385 (1984).

[192] The literature on hermeneutics is extensive. Levy summarizes it clearly in *Hermeneutics* (1986). *See also* J. Bleicher, *Contemporary Hermeneutics: Hermeneutics as Method, Philosophy and Critique* (1980); R.E. Palmer, *Hermeneutics: Interpretation Theory in Schleiermacher, Dilthey, Heidegger and Gadamer* (1969).

[193] *See* discussion in Levy, *supra* p. 55, note 192 at 43.

[194] B. Spinoza, *Theological-Political Treatise* (S. Shirley trans., 2d. ed. 2001).

[195] F. Schleiermacher, *Hermeneutik und Kritik* (1977).

[196] Betti, *supra* p. 46, note 151; J. Buttigieg, "The Growing Labours of the Lengthened Way: The Hermeneutics of Emilio Betti," 34 *Union Seminary Q. Rev.* 97 (vol. 2, 1979). For the relationship between Betti's theory and Gadamer's, see Wright, *supra* p. 46, note 151.

[197] M. Heidegger, *Being and Time* (J. MacDuome and E. Robinson trans., 1962).

[198] H.G. Gadamer, *Truth and Method* (J. Weinsheimer and D. Marshall trans., 2d rev. ed. 1989) (1960); H.G. Gadamer, *Philosophical Hermeneutics* (D. Linge ed. and trans., University of California Press, 1976). For an analysis of Gadamer's approach, see Levy, *supra* p. 55, note 192.

[199] Levy, *supra* p. 55, note 192 at 137; H. Baxter, "System and Lifeworld in Habermas's Theory of Law," 23 *Cardozo L. Rev.* 473 (2002); H. Baxter, "Habermas's Discourse Theory of Law and Democracy," 50 *Buff. L. Rev.* 1 (2002).

[200] E.D. Hirsch, Jr., *Validity in Interpretation* (1967); E.D. Hirsch, Jr., *The Aims of Interpretation* (1978).

[201] For an analysis of his theory, *see* Levy, *supra* p. 55, note 192 at 155.

[202] Levy, *supra* p. 55, note 192 at 212.

[203] *Id.* at 179.

[204] *Id.* at 264.

ories addresses how a text is given meaning and analyzes the triangular relationship between the author of the text, the text, and its reader.[205] They
investigate whether a text has an "objective" meaning that can be understood from within the text, or whether it has no independent meaning
apart from that given it by the interpreter, such that meaning varies with
different interpreters. Perhaps the meaning of a text is the subjective meaning that its author intended. Indeed, authorial intent is a central concept
in various hermeneutic theories. Some say this intent is the key to all interpretive theories;[206] others believe that it has no place in interpretation
("failure of intent"[207]). Others use the intent of the author as one among
many factors to be considered in interpretation.

At the heart of the various hermeneutic theories is the question of
whether hermeneutics has rules of its own that restrict an interpreter and
direct him or her toward the proper interpretation. Some scholars think
such rules exist and should be obeyed; others think there is neither room
nor need for rules, and that an interpreter's membership in his or her interpretive community is sufficient to carve out his or her interpretive maneuvering space. Some say an interpreter understands the text "better"
than its author; others, that an interpreter's understanding is different but
not better than the author's. The various hermeneutic theories emphasize
the problem created by the gap in time between understanding at the time
of creation and understanding at the time of interpretation. An interpreter's horizons are in the present, making it difficult for him or her to
understand a text whose horizons existed in the past. Various hermeneutic
theories address the importance of context in interpreting a text and the
need to interpret a text in order to understand it. Hence, the paradox of
the "hermeneutic circle," in which the whole cannot be understood without understanding the parts, but the parts cannot be understood without
understanding the whole.

The Relevance of General Hermeneutics to Legal Interpretation

I believe that these hermeneutic theories are relevant to legal interpretation.[208] Law is a human phenomenon, grounded in texts intended to guide

---

[205] D. Miers, "Legal Theory and Interpretation of Statutes," *Legal Theory and Common
Law* 254 (W. Twining ed., 1986).

[206] See Hirsch, *supra* p. 55, note 200.

[207] E. Margalit, "Al Pi Hacavana [According to Intent]," 27 *Iyun* 216 (1986).

[208] *See* Hassold, *supra* p. 12, note 29 at 213. *See also* Patterson, *supra* p. 54, note 191; K.
Abraham, "Statutory Interpretation and Literary Theory: Some Common Concerns of an
Unlikely Pair," 32 *Rutgers L. Rev.* 676 (1979); D. Hermann, "Phenomenology, Structural-
ism, Hermeneutics and Legal Study: Applications of Contemporary Continental Thought to

present and future behavior. It is only natural that hermeneutic philoso-phies, which also deal with influential texts, would be relevant to legal in-terpretation. It seems to me that studying hermeneutic theories teaches the following lessons, which are important to legal interpretation.

First, interpretation requires the interpreter to adopt an objective atti-tude toward the text. Even if interpretation is creative, it is distinct from the activity of the text's author. The interpreter must respect this distinc-tion. Even if a created work cannot be understood without being inter-preted, and even if it may be interpreted in different ways, interpreting a work is not the same thing as creating it. The interpreter's job is to extract from the work all that it contains, but avoid introducing things that the language of the work cannot absorb. The language of a text sets its inter-pretive limits: giving it a meaning it cannot support semantically is not in-terpretive activity but rather the creation of a new text.

Second, understanding a text requires its comprehension as a whole. Un-derstanding the whole requires understanding its parts, by finding the in-ternal connections between the parts, as well as the connections between the parts and the whole. To understand the parts, interpreters piece to-gether a preliminary understanding or fore-meaning[209] of the whole. This fore-meaning is the product of the way the interpreter grasps the reality in which he or she lives and the fundamental conceptions of the community to which he or she belongs, including its values and principles. Similarly, this fore-meaning includes an understanding of the circumstances sur-rounding the creation of the text, its history, and the tradition to which it belongs. Interpreters can never step into the shoes of the author—they live in a different era and belong to a different interpretive community. The in-terpreters' fore-meanings, however, must incorporate the rules for textual interpretation accepted in their legal community. Interpreters approach the text with these fore-meanings. As they interpret, they revise their fore-meanings and create new understandings that reflect their understanding of their environment. Any preliminary understanding—whether it comes early or late—is limited by the interpretive community's social concep-tions. Interpretation is a dialogue between the interpreter and the text, part of an attempt to forge a connection between present and past. Although the text was created in the past, the questions to which it responds are in

---

Legal Phenomena," 36 *U. Miami L. Rev.* 379 (1982); S. McIntosh, "Legal Hermeneutics: A Philosophical Critique," 35 *Okla. L. Rev.* 1 (1982); T.J. Phelps and J.A. Pitts, "Question-ing the Text: The Significance of Phenomenological Hermeneutics for Legal Interpretation," 29 *St. L.U.L.J.* 353 (1985); P. Goodrich, *Reading the Law* 140 (1986); *Law, Interpretation and Reality: Essays in Epistemology, Hermeneutics and Jurisprudence* (P. Nerhot ed., 1990). Scholars tried to introduce general hermeneutics to the field of law as early as the nineteenth century: *See* F. Lieber, *Legal and Political Hermeneutics* (1839).

[209] *Infra* p. 136.

the present. It is a dialogue that has both static and dynamic aspects. Some-times, a text carries meanings that its author did not anticipate and of which he or she was not aware. The dialogue between the text and the interpreter is never-ending. The interpreter's subjectivity necessarily leaves its imprint on the dialogue. Interpreters cannot disconnect themselves from either their environments or their own personalities. All interpretation is the product of a social, structural, and personal context. Even when inter-preters use "objective" interpretive standards, they work against the back-drop of the "subjective" facts that surround them. The text does not speak for itself. It responds to the questions that the interpreter asks of it. Such questions are external to the text. They are products of the present, and they are linked to our ability to understand the text in the present, against the backdrop of the past.

Third, no single system of interpretation emerges from hermeneutic studies. There is no hermeneutic litmus test to determine which system of interpretation is "correct" or "incorrect." A text contains no "internal" cri-terion to answer that question. There are a variety of approaches and per-spectives that can be compared. Hermeneutic study teaches that interpre-tive phenomena are extremely complicated, and that different systems of interpretation are—more than expressions of opposition and contradic-tion—different points of view on the same complicated phenomenon, or different components of a single totality. Eskridge's point about the lessons of hermeneutics for statutory interpretation is apt:

> Hermeneutics stresses the multidimensional complexity of statutory interpre-tation and, even more, the importance of an interpreter's attitude rather than her method. The hermeneutical attitude is open rather than dogmatic, criti-cal rather than docile, inquiring rather than accepting.[210]

Interpreters therefore interpret a literary text differently from a legal text. They are likely to adopt different approaches to interpreting a constitution, statute, contract, or will; and even for each kind of legal text, there are likely to be different interpretive approaches. In the end, the hermeneutic proj-ect demonstrates that an interpreter has discretion. Hermeneutic consid-erations create a number of options among which the interpreter must choose, at his or her discretion. Interpretation is choice, but not unre-stricted choice. Judges find their choices restrained by a system of her-meneutic considerations, central to which are the text itself and the legal community's perceptions of how to understand it.[211]

---

[210] W. Eskridge, "Gadamer/Statutory Interpretation," 90 *Colum. L. Rev.* 609, 633 (1990).

[211] W. Eskridge and P. Frickey, "Statutory Interpretation and Practical Reasoning," 42 *Stan. L. Rev.* 321, 383 (1990).

The Distinctiveness of Legal Hermeneutics

General hermeneutics, a field which has developed around the interpretation of literary and historical texts, can make only a limited contribution to legal hermeneutics[212] because of the nature of law.[213] Law is distinct for its power to coerce. A legal norm imposes an obligation, the violation of which entails a sanction. The interpretation of a legal text is "normative" interpretation. It establishes what is permitted and what is prohibited.[214] Rules of legal interpretation reflect this unique character of law.[215] No one claims that an interpretation given a literary text in the past is binding. In contrast, through the principle of *stare decisis*, the past interpretation of a legal text is binding on the future. In law, we cannot accept interpretive theories that give a reader the freedom to understand the text according to his or her subjective perception. We cannot recognize the interpretive freedom of every judge. In order to maintain normal life in society, we must recognize binding interpretive rules and a normative hierarchy that orders them.[216] Complete interpretive freedom would pervert law and render it irrational. As Professor Fiss noted, the judge is "a combination of literary critic and moral philosopher. But that is only part of the picture. The judge also speaks with the authority of the Pope."[217] An interpretation of *Hamlet*, even if correct, is not binding. In contrast, there must be a binding interpretation of a constitution, statute, contract, or will. The interpreter of *Hamlet* seeks to uncover the text's many meanings. The interpreter of a legal text must resolve the ambiguity of those meanings.[218] The literary text and the legal text fill different roles and perform different functions in society,[219] and the results of interpretation have different consequences. We do not look to a legal text for aesthetics, mystery, beauty, or inspiration. The interpreter of a literary text does not impose his or her opinion

---

[212] Twining and Miers, *supra* p. 3, note 1 at 375; Posner, *supra* p. 27, note 85 at 297.

[213] R. Posner, *Law and Literature* 211 (rev. and enlarged ed. 1998).

[214] S. Levinson, "Law as Literature," 60 *Tex. L. Rev.* 373, 386 (1982); S. Strömholm, "Legal Hermeneutics—Notes on the Early Modern Development," 22 *Scan. Studies in Law* 213, 219 (1978).

[215] Fiss, *supra* p. 38, note 116 at 755.

[216] J. Kohler, "Judicial Interpretation of Enacted Law," *Science of Legal Method* 190 (E. Brunken and L.B. Register trans., 1917).

[217] Fiss, *supra* p. 38, note 116 at 755.

[218] W.J. Brennan, "Construing the Constitution," 19 *U.C. Davis L. Rev.* 2 (1985) ("Unlike literary critics, judges cannot merely savor the tensions or revel in the ambiguities inhering in the text—judges must resolve them"); Brest, *supra* p. 54, note 185 at 152; Posner, *supra* p. 59, note 213 at 273.

[219] Gray, *supra* p. 43, note 135 at 2; W. Michaels, "Against Formalism: The Autonomous Text in Legal and Literary Interpretation," 1 *Poetics Today* 23 (1979). *See also* Farber, *supra* p. 31, note 93 at 291.

on us, but the interpreter of a legal text does exactly that. He or she coerces us. The interpretive freedom accorded the first cannot, therefore, be accorded the second.[220]

Interpretation in law fulfills two roles: declaring existing law and creating new law that articulates the rights and responsibilities of members of society. We cannot recognize a system of interpretation that ignores existing rights. Legal interpretation operates within an existing normative world, and it must be integrated into that world. Of course, interpreters face "hard cases" in which they must use judicial discretion. Interpretation, in those cases, creates law. While this type of judicial lawmaking is legitimate for hard cases, as a whole, judicial acts of interpretation do not create. Interpretive activity mostly declares existing law and only rarely deals with creating new law. Of course, even when judicial acts of interpretation involve creating new law, they cannot leave such creation to the absolute, personal freedom of the interpreter. Social and constitutional principles, not personal considerations or aesthetic preferences, must shape legal interpretation.

---

[220] R. Posner, "Law and Literature: A Relation Reargued," 72 *Va. L. Rev.* 1351, 1370 (1986); West, "Adjudication Is Not Interpretation: Some Reservations about the Law-as-Literature Movement," 54 *Tenn. L. Rev.* 203, 277 (1987). For a different approach, see S. Levinson and J. Balkin, "Law, Music and Other Performing Arts," 139 *U. Pa. L. Rev.* 1597 (1991); J. Balkin and S. Levinson, "Interpreting Law and Music: Performance Notes on 'The Banjo Serenader' and 'The Lying Crowd of Jews,' " 20 *Cardozo L. Rev.* 1513 (1999).

CHAPTER TWO

Non-Interpretive Doctrines

1. THE ESSENCE OF NON-INTERPRETIVE DOCTRINES IN LAW

Beyond the Limits of Language

Interpretation operates within the limits of language. It imparts to the text a meaning that its (public or private) language can bear. Non-interpretive doctrines operate beyond the language of the text. They impart a right according to the text, even though that right is not grounded in the language of the text. Consider a will naming Richard and Linda as the heirs, where Richard and Linda are the testator's son and daughter. After the making of the will, but before the death of the testator, a third child, Luke, is born. The facts show that the testator wanted Luke to inherit also, but he failed to modify the will. Does the will permit Luke to inherit?

Interpreting the will cannot make Luke an heir. The interpretation is not "capable" of "cramming" Luke within the limits of "Richard and Linda." We need a non-interpretive doctrine, like the doctrine about filling in a gap in a will, which can, according to the will, add Luke as an additional heir. I said as much in one opinion:

> There are situations in which the law permits the testator's intent to be realized, even if such intent is not grounded in the text. These are special cases in which the law allows the will to take on a meaning . . . that does not even have a minimal literal connection to the language of the will. These cases deviate from the interpretation of the will in its narrow sense. These cases, however, are within the limits of the will's interpretation in its broad sense.[1]

The same holds true for interpreting contracts. Consider a contract in which Richard sells Simon a horse. The parties have no special lexicon of their own. A judge acting within the limits of interpretation cannot decide that the property sold is a cow. Similarly, a judge cannot interpret a statute mandating a particular outcome for a horse to decide the fate of a cow. To decide what to do with the cow, a judge must have access to a non-interpretive doctrine. For example, perhaps the author made a mistake in

---

[1] C.A. 1900/96, *Talmachio v. General Guardian*, 53(2) P.D. 817, 829.

using the word "horse." A court is authorized to correct a mistake (in a contract or statute). Perhaps the word "horse" leads to an absurd result. To avoid the absurdity, the court may give the words of the contract or statute a meaning that is not accepted in the language of the text. In this and other instances, the judge deviates from his or her interpretive role. Authorized by a non-interpretive doctrine, he or she adds or subtracts from the language of the contract or statute.

The Legitimacy of Non-Interpretive Activity

A judge may use a non-interpretive doctrine only if the legal system authorizes it, generally through statutes and case law. A number of Continental codifications explicitly authorize a judge to fill in a gap in legislation.[2] The principle of good faith in a number of codifications permits a judge to fill in a gap in a contract, too.[3] Case law supplements the statutory authorization for non-interpretive activity. Anglo-American precedent, for example, recognizes the power of the judge to add to or subtract from the language of a statute in order to avoid an absurdity.[4]

How far may case law go in authorizing non-interpretive activity? Judge Calabresi has suggested that a judge is authorized to invalidate a statute that has become obsolete.[5] That is certainly not an act of interpretation, and judges should not be allowed to do it without legislative authorization. Calabresi himself was aware of the constitutionally problematic nature of his proposition, and he did not imply that such authority for judges should originate in a common law rule. All we may say is that the tradition of each legal system sets the boundaries of non-interpretive judicial creativity and the extent to which it belongs to the realm of interpretive activity. The Continental tradition (in Germany and France), for example, easily decided that judges may fill in a gap in legislation, while the common law tradition has yet to authorize it. As a general matter, however, judges enjoy less freedom to engage in non-interpretive activity, relative to interpretive activity. The reason is clear: in the latter case, the judges play their classical role of giving meaning to a text that someone else created; in the former kind of activity, judges depart from that role, creating a new text to correct a text that someone else created. Non-interpretive activity by judges raises constitutional questions of separation of powers (in the case of a constitution or legislation) and the autonomy of the private will (in the

---

[2] *Infra* p. 69.
[3] *Infra* p. 73.
[4] *Infra* p. 80.
[5] G. Calabresi, *A Common Law for the Age of Statutes* (1982).

case of a contract or will). We justify judicial engagement in the above kinds of non-interpretive activity because they are so closely related to interpretive activity. Taking an expansive view, we can consider such activity to be part of the interpretation of a text. I therefore consider non-interpretive activity to be interpretive in the broad sense, in contrast to ordinary interpretive activity, which is interpretive in the narrow sense.[6]

The Importance of Non-Interpretive Doctrines: "The Murderous Heir"

Non-interpretive doctrines are important both practically and theoretically. On the practical level, they allow a judge to reach the proper solution without the need for interpretive rules. This is important for cases in which interpretive rules, used in the ordinary way, fail to reach the proper solution. On the theoretical level, the doctrines impart legitimacy to judicial activity without the need to try to force the proper solution into the framework of interpretive rules—an attempt that will ultimately break the rules.

Take the familiar example of the heir who murders his father and then tries to inherit his father's property.[7] Our sense of justice tells us that the murderer should not inherit, as the Bible says: "Hast thou killed and also taken possession?"[8] But the murderer is the victim's son, and according to the law of succession, he is the heir. The law does not specify an exception for the murderous heir. Interpretive laws do not seem to provide a satisfactory answer. Professor Dworkin claims that one can deny the murderous son his inheritance by way of interpretation. Professor Pound—who was in no way a formalist—thought that interpretive laws cannot deny the murderer his inheritance. Interpretation that invalidates the murderous son's inheritance is "spurious interpretation."[9] Non-interpretive doctrines can lead to the proper solution without getting stuck on interpretive difficulties. The relevant doctrine is that of a lacuna or gap.[10] The inheritance

---

[6] *Supra* p. 64.

[7] Hart and Sachs discuss this dilemma. *Supra* p. 3, note 3 at 68. *See also* D. Farber, "Courts, Statutes, and Public Policy: The Case of the Murderous Heir," 53 *SMU L. Rev.* 31 (2000).

[8] "And the word of the Lord came to Elijah the Tishbite, saying, Arise, go down to meet Ahab king of Israel, which is in Samaria: behold, he is in the vineyard of Naboth, whither he is gone down to possess it. And thou shalt speak unto him, saying, Thus saith the Lord, Hast thou killed, and also taken possession? And thou shalt speak unto him, saying, Thus saith the Lord, In the place where dogs licked the blood of Naboth shall dogs lick thy blood, even thine." 1 Kings 21:17–19.

[9] Pound, *supra* p. 16, note 45.

[10] This also appears to be Posner's approach: "What the court did was to graft an exception onto the statute, the better to carry out in proper Aristotelian fashion . . . the desires the

law has a gap regarding an exception for the murderous heir. Filling in this gap creates a new rule that disposes of the case of the murderous heir. Skeptics will argue that it doesn't matter whether the path is interpretive or non-interpretive—only the result matters. They are mistaken. The result is important, but judges must reach it by reason and not by fiat. They must reach the result methodically, without breaking existing interpretive rules, so that similar cases will be resolved similarly.

Interpretation in the Narrow and Broad Sense: Interpretation and Construction

Non-interpretive doctrines, as their name suggests, go beyond the limits of interpretation, although a legal system's tradition may view them as part of the interpretive project. In the English system, for example, a judge's authority to change a text in order to avoid absurdity is part of the laws of interpretation. The Anglo-American tradition treats laws resolving a contradiction between two legal texts of equal stature—like the contradiction between two statutes or two contracts—as part of the laws of interpretation. In the German interpretive tradition, filling in a gap constitutes interpretive activity in the broad sense (*ergänzende Auslegung*, "supplementary interpretation"). The English tradition views implied terms that fill in a gap as part of the content of a contract, and sometimes even as a problem of interpretation. Of course, each system has its own tradition; there is no scientific "truth." Nevertheless, it is important to distinguish between ordinary interpretation (or interpretation in the narrow sense) and special interpretation (or interpretation in the broad sense, authorized by non-interpretive doctrines). Interpretation in the narrow sense gives meaning to what "is." Interpretation in the broad sense adds what "is" to what "isn't" (by filling in a gap) or corrects the "is" (by correcting a mistake).

Interpretation in the narrow and broad sense rely on different criteria. For example, the civil code's provisions regarding the interpretation of a contract or will do not apply to filling in a gap or correcting a mistake. Similarly, common law practice regarding implied terms differs from ordinary interpretive rules. Judges giving meaning to criminal statutes must limit themselves to interpretation in the narrow sense. They may not give meaning by filling gaps in criminal statutes. Nor are judges likely to be authorized to fill a gap in the constitution. A judge who uses non-interpretive

---

legislators would have had regarding the question if they had foreseen it." Posner, *supra* p. 27, note 85 at 106–7. *See also* R. Posner, *The Problematics of Moral and Legal Theory* 140 (1999).

doctrines gives meaning to a (new) text. That is why, in the American system, there is such a strong connection between interpretation (interpretation in the narrow sense) and construction (interpretation in the broad sense).[11] Professor Corbin said as much about contracts:

> [T]he word interpretation is commonly used with respect to *language* itself—
> to the symbols (the words and acts) of expression. In about the same degree,
> we speak of the construction of a *contract*. . . . By "interpretation of lan-
> guage" we determine what ideas that language induces in other persons. By
> "construction of the contract" . . . we determine its legal operation—its ef-
> fect upon the action of courts and administrative officials.[12]

Of course, interpretation in the broad sense, using non-interpretive doctrines, relies on interpretation in the narrow sense. In order to make use of non-interpretive doctrines, a judge must first use "ordinary" interpretation to determine the preconditions for their applicability. Take the case of two statutes that appear to contradict each other. Interpretation in the narrow sense decides the meaning of each statute. Interpretation in the broad sense decides the resolution of the contradiction between the two statutes, to the extent that there is a contradiction. Because of the close relationship between interpretation in its broad and narrow senses, I will briefly discuss interpretation in its broad sense. A more comprehensive discussion is beyond the scope of this book.

The Diversity of Non-Interpretive Doctrines

The list of non-interpretive doctrines is ever-expanding. Their source is mostly in case law, as opposed to statutory law. We will discuss five such doctrines: (1) filling in a gap in a text; (2) resolving a contradiction between two separate texts; (3) correcting a mistake in a text; (4) changing the language of the text in order to prevent an absurdity; and (5) fulfilling the purpose of the text by making a change ("doctrine of approximation" [*cy pres*]).

Is There a General Non-Interpretive Principle?

Every non-interpretive principle has its own rules, but is there a general non-interpretive principle? For example, may judges read into a legal text

---

[11] For another distinction between these two expressions, see Tiersma, *supra* p. 50, note 166.

[12] Corbin, *supra* p. 9, note 20 at 8. *See also* S. Williston, *A Treatise on the Law of Contracts* §602 (3d ed. 1961); Hoffman, *supra* p. 6, note 12 at 662.

a provision that it does not contain, subtract from the provisions it does contain, or give it a meaning different from the one that arises from its language? May they do so to realize the intent of the text's author, the purpose of the text, or for any other reason? I think the answer is no. Such a general and comprehensive non-interpretive doctrine is rare in modern legal systems. The guiding principle is that judges must work within the limits of language. Non-interpretive judicial activity that deviates from the framework of language is an exception that requires special doctrines to justify it. Without these doctrines, judges may not give a text a meaning that it cannot bear in its language. To do so would violate constitutional principles about the role of a judge in a democracy. If we gave judges broad authorization to change every legal text in order to realize the intent of its author or the purpose of the text, we would excessively infringe on the principle of separation of powers (for public legislation) and on the autonomy of the private will (for private texts).

2. FILLING IN A GAP IN A LEGAL TEXT

Interpretation and Filling in a Gap

Interpreting a normative text (interpretation in the narrow sense) and filling in a gap (*Lücke*, lacuna) in a text (interpretation in the broad sense) are separate and distinct normative activities.[13] Interpretation gives a text meaning, even if the meaning expands the language of the text to the outer edge of its semantic limits. In contrast, filling in a gap *adds* language to a text. As Merryman said, "The problem of interpretation is to supply meaning to the norm; that of lacunae is to supply the norm."[14] Hence the important distinction between interpretation—even expansive interpretation—and filling in a gap. For example, in order to understand a norm in criminal law, judges may engage in expansive interpretation, but they may not fill in a gap.[15] The distinction between the two is sometimes fine, but it remains intact. In interpretation, there is a text to which a judge gives meaning. In gap-filling, the text is missing, and the judge creates a new text.

---

[13] W. Canaris, *Die Feststellung von Lücken im Gesetz: Eine Methodologische Studie über Voraussetzungen und Grenzen der Richterlicheu Rechtsfortbildung Praeter Legem* (1983); Ch. Perelman, *Le Probleme des Lacunes en Droit* (1968); A. Von Overbeck, "Some Observations on the Role of the Judge under the Swiss Civil Code," 37 *La. L. Rev.* 681 (1977).

[14] J.H. Merryman, "The Italian Legal Style III: Interpretation," 18 *Stan. L. Rev.* 583 (1966).

[15] Analogy or parallel reasoning to fill in a gap in a criminal statute (and thus to create a new crime) is prohibited. Interpretive analogy is, however, permitted. Cr.A. 3622/96, *Chacham v. Kupat Cholim Macabi*, 52(2) P.D. 638, 650.

Consider a legal system whose statutes mandate that, when two contractual obligations to sell an asset conflict, the prior obligation trumps. The statutes do not address the relationship between the statutory duty to make restitution and the contractual obligation to sell. This is an apparent gap in the legal system's statutes.[16] Or take an agency statute stating that an agent breaches the duty of loyalty if he or she conducts business with his or her principal. The statute says nothing about a gift that an agent may try to give the principal. That is a (hidden) gap in the agency statute.[17] A contract mandates the return of a cash deposit at the end of a period of time, but fails to specify whether the deposit will be returned at its real or nominal value. That is a gap in the contract. A will does not specify what to do if there is a change in the composition of the heirs or assets after it is written. That is a gap in the will. These situations spark three central questions:[18] *First*, when does a normative text's silence on a particular issue constitute a gap regarding the resolution of that issue? *Second*, does the legal system permit a judge to fill in the gap? *Third*, what criteria should be used to fill in the gap? We will briefly examine each of these questions.

When a Text's Silence Constitutes a Gap

A normative text's silence may mean many things, and may speak in different voices.[19] Only one of these voices is the voice of a gap. A judge should exercise caution in deciding, through his or her interpretation of a text, that its silence constitutes a gap. In principle, a text's silence on a particu-

---

[16] The standard example is the following: Richard contracts to sell an item of chattel to Simon and delivers it to him. Simon enters into an obligation to sell the chattel to Luke but does not yet deliver it to him. Richard terminates the contract legally, because of a flaw in its formation. Simon faces two conflicting rights: Richard's right to have his property returned, and Luke's contractual right to buy the chattel. Whose right trumps?

[17] Canaris uses this example, *supra* p. 66, note 13 at 82. Another example is an inheritance law that does not include an exception for an heir who murders the legator. *See supra* p. 63. A hidden gap exists when the text appears to apply to the situations awaiting resolution, but once the text is interpreted, it becomes clear that it would have been appropriate to recognize an exception or limitation that is missing.

[18] The problem of a gap in law was a subject of considerable discussion in the nineteenth and twentieth centuries. *See, e.g.,* J. Stone, *Legal System and Lawyer's Reasonings* 188, 536 (1964). The literature addressed two questions: *First*, can a given normative text contain a gap, or can every legal question be resolved by reference to a general principle, positive or negative, that negates the existence of the gap? E. Zitelmann, *Lücken im Recht* (1903); F. Atria, *On Law and Legal Reasoning* 76 (2002). *Second*, can a legal system contain a question that has no answer (a *non liquet*)? M. Eisenberg, *The Nature of the Common Law* 159 (1988).

[19] *See* Barak, *supra* p. 3, note 1 at 465; G. Tedeschi, "B'aayot Halekuim Bachok (Lacunae) Visief 46 Lidivrei Hamelech Bimoatzato [The Problem of Lacunae]," *Mehkarim B'Mishpat Artzeinu*, 132 (2d. expanded ed. 1959).

lar issue can be interpreted in one of four ways: *First*, the text does not explicitly provide a solution for a particular issue, but interpreting the text implicitly resolves the issue. For example, the Canadian Charter contains explicit provisions on the structure of government and human rights. Canada's Supreme Court decided that those provisions imply that judges enjoy independence.[20] The Australian High Court found an implied right to freedom of expression from the constitutional provision governing the structure of the regime.[21] In cases like these, there is a (positive) provision, if an implied one. *Second*, the text is silent about a particular issue because it concerns a type of situation that the text does not address at all. Take a contract that is silent on the issue of remedy for its breach. The contract is not lacking. The remedy is laid out in the (default) rules regarding remedies for breach of contract. *Third*, the text's provisions for the issues it explicitly addresses do not apply to issues that it does not address. This is a "speaking silence" or a "conscious silence." The silence implies, and the implication is that the text's provisions do not apply to issues it does not address. Take a contract in which Richard rents Simon two apartments, one of which is specified as being furnished. The implication is that the second apartment rented is unfurnished. *Fourth*—and this is the meaning that interests us—the provision in the normative text is incomplete. The text implicitly or explicitly settles certain issues, but fails to regulate other issues that it is supposed to address, and that it does not exclude by conscious silence. There is a gap in the text regarding these issues. A gap in the text, then, exists when the text aspires to a comprehensive provision, but the provision is incomplete.[22] One can imagine the text as a wall with a missing brick.[23] We can call this gap an omission or an "empty space." The text is supposed to settle the issue, but it is incomplete, disabled. Note, however, that a provision that is unreasonable or unjust is a flawed provision but not a missing provision. An uncertain provision is not a missing provision, because the process of interpretation will eventually resolve the uncertainty. We can decide that a text contains a gap only at the conclusion of the process of interpretation (in the narrow sense). A text that uses expressions like justice, integrity, and reasonableness does not necessarily contain a gap. Interpretation will determine the meaning of those concepts.[24] Similarly, a text granting discretion to someone does not necessarily contain a gap. A text that includes instructions for filling in its own

---

[20] *Beauregard v. Canada* [1986] 2 S.C.R. 56; *Provincial Judges Reference* [1997] 3 S.C.R. 3.

[21] See the opinions cited on p. 69, note 31, *infra*.

[22] *See* C.A. 3622/96, *supra* p. 66, note 15 at 648: "A gap means that the statutory arrangement is incomplete in a way that contravenes its purpose" (Barak, J.). The aspiration toward wholeness is a condition for the existence of a gap. *See* Schauer, *supra* p. 13, note 34 at 225.

[23] The image belongs to Canaris, *supra* p. 66, note 13 at 25.

[24] Engisch, *supra* p. 36, note 107 at 141; Canris, *supra* p. 66, note 13 at 26.

gaps is not incomplete, because the text completes itself on its own, without the need for outside help.

May a Judge Fill in a Gap?

If the interpretation of a legal text reveals a gap, may a judge fill it in? The various legal systems agree that judges may fill in contractual gaps,[25] but the consensus ends there. As for legislation, the prevailing opinion in civil law is that a judge is authorized to fill in a statutory gap. Most civil law countries explicitly address the issue in their civil codes.[26] Section 12 of the Italian Civil Code is a typical example: "If a controversy cannot be decided by a precise provision, consideration is given to provisions that regulate similar cases or analogous matters; if the case still remains in doubt, it is decided according to the general principles of the legal order of the state."[27] In other civil law countries (like Germany and France), the codification is silent on this point. Those systems do not necessarily view textual silence as the deliberate absence of an arrangement (conscious silence), and they recognize the judge's authority to fill in a gap in legislation.[28] Anglo-Saxon legal systems adopt a less clear stance. Under the doctrine of equity of the statute,[29] which prevailed into the nineteenth century, judges were authorized to fill in a gap in legislation. Today, when the language of a statute is inadequate to achieve its purpose (when there is *casus omissus*), a court is not authorized to fill in the gap.[30] In that case, the judge resorts to the "safety net" of the common law.[31] In the context of wills, the German tra-

[25] *Supra* p. 72.

[26] Sec. 4 of the Venezuelan Civil Code (1942); sec. 7 of the Austrian Civil Code (1811); sec. 1 of the Swiss Civil Code (1911).

[27] The Italian Civil Code 2 (M. Beltramo et al. trans., 1969).

[28] S. Herman, "*Quot judices tot sententiae*: A Study of the English Reaction to Continental Interpretive Techniques," 1 *Legal Studies* 165, 180 (1981). In Continental law, a statute projects its rules and principles into the legal system. One can draw analogies from one piece of legislation in order to complete a gap in another piece of legislation. *See* I. Zajtay, "Reasoning by Analogy as a Method of Law Interpretation," 13 *Comp. Int. L.J. S. Afr.* 324 (1980).

[29] For a discussion of equity of the statute, *see* F.J. de Sloovere, "The Equity and Reason of a Statute," 21 *Cornell L.Q.* 591 (1936); R. Marcin, "Epieikeia: Equitable Lawmaking in the Construction of Statutes," 10 *Conn. L. Rev.* 337 (1978); J. Manning, "Textualism and the Equity of the Statute," 101 *Colum. L. Rev.* 1 (2001).

[30] The ban on filling in a gap need not lead to a ban on narrow interpretation or broad interpretation. The equity of the statute doctrine was unique for its authorization of a court to give a statute a meaning that it could not bear in its language. With the fall of the doctrine, this authority has disappeared, as well. However, another aspect of the doctrine—permitting a text to be read in a broad or narrow sense—remains valid. It is not related to filling in a gap but rather to interpretation.

[31] Herman, *supra* p. 69, note 28 at 179. *See also* N. Marsh, *Interpretation in a National*

dition permits gap-filling,[32] but the Anglo-American system fails to address it, apparently leaving judges to resort to the general laws of succession to resolve the issue. Israeli courts have explicitly held that a court may fill in a gap in a will.

There is little scholarly treatment of filling in gaps in constitutions. The Swiss legal system permits it,[33] and the Australian High Court has recognized an implied bill of rights[34] that in turn recognizes, among other things, freedom of political expression. The power of courts to fill in a constitutional gap is one way—although not the only way—of understanding implied rights. In American constitutional law, there is a trend toward recognizing human rights implied or created in the penumbra of existing rights. That is how the United States Supreme Court recognized the right to privacy as part of the penumbras of the First, Fourth, Fifth, and Fourteenth Amendments to the United States Constitution.[35] Can a theory of

---

and *International Context* 67 (1974); Cross, *supra* p. 3, note 3 at 95; E. Driedger, *On the Construction of Statutes* 122 (R. Sullivan ed., 3d ed. 1994); 2B Sutherland, *Statutes and Statutory Construction* 273 (N. Singer ed., 5th ed. 1992); R. Pound, "Common Law and Legislation," 21 *Harv. L. Rev.* 383 (1907); J. Landis, "Statutes and the Sources of Law," in *Harvard Legal Essays* 213 (1934); W. Page, "Statutes as Common Law Principles," 1944 *Wis. L. Rev.* 175; R. Traynor, "Statutes Revolving in Common Law Orbits," 17 *Catholic U. L. Rev.* 401 (1968); R.F. Williams, "Statutes as Sources of Law beyond Their Terms in Common-Law Cases," 50 *Geo. Wash. L. Rev.* 554 (1982); G. Calabresi, *A Common Law for the Age of Statutes* (1982); P.S. Atiyah, "Common Law and Statutes Law," 48 *Mod. L. Rev.* 1 (1985). The common law obfuscates the issue by using the word "gap" loosely. For example, in *Magor v. Newport Corp.* [1950] 2 All E.R. 1226, 1236, Lord Denning recognized the authority of an English judge to fill in a gap. The ruling changed, however, on appeal to the House of Lords: *Magor v. Newport Corp.* [1952] A.C. 189. I doubt that the term "gap" used by Lord Denning and the judges of the House of Lords is the same "gap" that I discuss in this chapter. In *Western Bank Ltd. v. Schindler* [1977] ch. 1, 18, Judge Scarman (L.J.) recognized a judge's limited power to complete *casus omissus* in legislation. The judge there emphasized, however, that an English court does not have the same authority as that granted to Swiss courts by Section 1 of the Swiss civil code. *See also* Bennion, *supra* p. 6, note 13 at 682.

[32] A. Gerhards, *Ergänzende Testamentsauslegung wegen postmortaler Ereignisse* (1996); D. Leipold, *Erbrecht* 271 (10th ed. 1993).

[33] 1 J.F. Aubert, *Traite de Droit Constitutionnel Suisse* 126 (1967); J.P. Müller, *Grundrechte: Besonderer Teil* 287 (1985).

[34] *Nationwide News Pty Limited. v. Wills* (1992) 177 C.L.R. 1; *Australian Capital Television Pty Limited v. Commonwealth* (1992) 177 C.L.R. 106; *Theophanous v. Herald & Weekly Times Limited* (1994) 182 C.L.R. 104; *Stephens v. West Australian Newspapers Limited* (1994) 182 C.L.R. 211; *Cunliffe v. Commonwealth* (1994) 182 C.L.R. 272; *McGinty v. Western Australia* (1996) 186 C.L.R. 140; *Lange v. Australian Broadcasting Corp.* (1997) 189 C.L.R. 520; *Kruger v. Commonwealth* (1997) 190 C.L.R. 1; *Levy v. Victoria* (1997) 189 C.L.R. 579.

[35] See Douglas's opinion in *Griswold v. Connecticut*, 381 U.S. 479 (1965). *See also* G. Reynolds, "Penumbral Reasoning on the Right," 140 *U. Pa. L. Rev.* 1333 (1992). *Roe v. Wade*, 410 U.S. 113 (1973) also belongs in this category. *See also* J. Rubenfeld, "The New Unwritten Constitution," 51 *Duke L.J.* 289 (2001).

gap-filling explain these cases? Legal systems whose analytic discussions do not address gaps and filling them in examine the issue through the lens of interpretation. This approach puts heavy pressure on interpretation, extending it to areas beyond its proper scope. Might it be better for those legal systems to recognize the non-interpretive doctrine of filling in a gap and to hold the socio-legal discussion within the framework of that doctrine?

Criteria for Filling in Gaps: Statutory Gaps

By which criteria does a judge fill in a gap in a legal text? As we saw, civil law countries discuss the issue extensively as it pertains to statutes and contracts, and Anglo-American law discusses it only in the context of contracts. We will focus on these issues, beginning with statutory gaps. Judges who would fill in gaps in statutes may be subject to homogenous or heterogeneous rules. According to homogenous supplementary rules, judges must fill in the gap in a way that preserves internal harmony between the incomplete statute and the supplementary rule. In applying homogenous supplementary rules, judges resort to analogy[36] and the legal system's general principles[37] as tools for developing the law and carrying out its potential in practice. One example is the Italian Civil Code's provision that judges should fill gaps in legislation using analogy, and where no appropriate analogy exists, they should resort to the state's general principles governing legal arrangements.[38] Heterogeneous supplementary rules, on the other hand, use principles external to the system to fill in gaps. There

---

[36] Most of the Continental literature discusses analogy: N. Bobbio, "Lacuna del Diritto," in 9 *Novissimo Digesto Italiano* 419 (1963); A. Peczenik, "Analogie Legis, Analogy from Statutes in Continental Law," in *Legal Reasoning* 329 (H. Hubien ed., 1977); I. Zajtay, "Reasoning by Analogy as a Method of Law Interpretation," 13 *C.I.L.S.A.* 325 (1980); C. Sunstein, "On Analogical Reasoning," 106 *Harv. L. Rev.* 741 (1993); J. Murray, "The Role of Analogy in Legal Reasoning," 29 *UCLA L. Rev.* 833 (1982); C. Sunstein, *Legal Reasoning and Political Conflict* 62 (1996); S. Brewer, "Exemplary Reasoning: Semantics, Pragmatics and Rational Force of Legal Argument by Analogy," 109 *Harv. L. Rev.* 923 (1998); L. Alexander, "Bad Beginnings," 145 *U. Pa. L. Rev.* 57 (1996). For a list of articles on analogy, *see Legal Knowledge and Analogy: Fragments of Legal Epistemology, Hermeneutics, and Linguistics* (P. Nerhot ed., 1991). The principle of equality underlies analogy: like cases should be treated alike. *See* Peczenik, *supra* p. 16, note 44 at 394. The similarity between cases must be material. Also, a distinction must be drawn between gap-filling analogy and interpretive analogy. *See* R. Schlesinger, H. Baade, M. Damaska, P. Herzog, *Comparative Law* 578 (5th ed. 1988) The distinction is important in criminal law, where interpretive analogy is permitted but gap-filling analogy that defines new crimes is barred. *See* W. Naucke, "Interpretation and Analogy in Criminal Law," 1986 *B.Y.U. L. Rev.* 535.

[37] *Supra* p. 69.

[38] Art. 12 of the Italian Civil Code, *supra* p. 69.

is, therefore, no internal harmony between existing statutes and the new supplementary rules. In the past, most English Commonwealth legal systems used heterogeneous supplementary rules. Commonwealth judges were to fill in gaps by reference to English law,[39] at least for issues involving certain kinds of general principles. Often, supplementary rules took on a "mixed" character, relying on both homogenous foundations (analogy) and heterogeneous foundations (justice, natural law, comparative law). The Swiss created an original version of supplementary rules which they still use:[40] If neither statute nor custom provides a solution to the problem before a judge—and the legal literature supports the use of analogy—the judge must decide the question as if he or she were the legislature, relying on jurisprudence and the given legal tradition.

Criteria for Filling in Gaps: Gaps in Contracts

A gap exists in a contract when the absence of an arrangement creates an incompletion that contravenes the purpose of the contract. We become aware of the gap when interpretation of the contract reveals that the contract is incomplete: because it is truncated; because it "cries out for completion"; or because the parties did not complete the formation of the contract. How can a judge fill in a gap in a contract? Everyone agrees that a contractual gap can be filled in using default rules, custom, and usage. Of course, these supplementary sources are not always effective, because supplementary rules relevant to the issue in question do not always exist. Even when relevant supplementary rules are available, the internal hierarchy of those supplementary sources is not always clear.[41] There is also a question of the relationship between the abovementioned type of supplementary sources and additional, second-order supplementary sources that may apply when there are no available default rules, usage, or custom as guides. In the English system, this second kind of supplementary rule takes the form of "implied terms." Courts read an "implied term"[42] into a contract when filling in a gap is necessary for the business efficacy of the contractual duties that the parties have taken on.[43] The courts, however, apply the officious bystander test[44]—whether a passerby glancing at the contract would say, "Of course, that's what the parties meant." In the past, Amer-

---

[39] W. Burge, *Commentaries on Colonial and Foreign Laws* (1907).
[40] Sec. 1 of the Swiss Civil Code (1902). See Hayoz, *supra* p. 34, note 100 at 144.
[41] Zamir, *supra* p. 15, note 39.
[42] Lewison, *supra* p. 42, note 130 at 119.
[43] *The Moorcock* (1889) 14 P.D. 64; *Luxor (Eastbourne) Ltd v. Cooper [1941]* A.C. 108.
[44] *Shirlaw v. Southern Foundries* [1939] 2 All E.R. 113.

ican law frequently made use of the theory of implied terms, but over the last few decades it has replaced that theory[45] with the "supplementary formulation" it uses today, as set forth in the Restatement:

> When the parties to a bargain sufficiently defined to be a contract have not agreed with respect to a term which is essential to a determination of their rights and duties, a term which is reasonable in the circumstances is supplied by the court.[46]

The Restatement's test is reasonableness.[47] Some judicial opinions use good faith as the criterion for filling in a gap in a contract.[48] Some Continental legal systems, like those of Germany[49] and Portugal,[50] also use the principle of good faith to fill in gaps. In France, judges can use principles of honesty to fill in contractual gaps,[51] based on the Code Civile's principle of good faith.[52] The Swiss system authorizes a judge to fill in a gap according to the (objective) purpose to which honest and fair parties, operating according to principles of justice, would agree.[53] International agreements use a similar approach. For example, according to the principles of Unidroit,[54] if the parties do not agree on a term important to their rights and duties, the court supplements the contract with a term that suits the relevant circumstances. The intent of the parties, the nature of the contract, fairness, honesty, and reasonableness all play a role in determining the term. Similarly, in European contract law, a contract may include implied terms based on the parties' intent, the nature of the contract and its purpose, good faith, and fairness. In recent years, numerous articles— mostly by American legal scholars—have addressed the use of "default rules" to fill in gaps in contracts. Only in some of those cases is the gap that these articles discuss a "lacuna" in the sense that I mean. Often, the gap is a silence of one of the other kinds, such as silence about an issue that the text is not designed to resolve. Thus, the default rules that these scholars

---

[45] Farnsworth has contributed to the change. *See* E.A. Farnsworth, "Disputes over Omission in Contracts," 68 *Colum. L. Rev.* 860 (1968); E.A. Farnsworth, "Some Considerations in the Drafting of Agreements: Problems in Interpretation and Gap-Filling," 23 *Record of N.Y. City B. Ass'n* 105 (1968).

[46] *Restatement (Second) of Contracts* § 204 (1981).

[47] R. Speidel, *Restatement Second*: Omitted Terms and Contract Method," 67 *Cornell L. Rev.* 785 (1982).

[48] M. Van Alstine, "Of Textualism, Party Autonomy, and Good Faith," 40 *Wm. & Mary L. Rev.* 1223, 1224 (1999).

[49] § 157 B.G.B.

[50] Section 239 of the Portuguese Civil Code.

[51] 1 H. et L. Mazeaud, J. Mazeaud, F. Chabas, *Leçons de Droit Civil* 320 (8th ed. 1991).

[52] C. Civ. § 1134–35.

[53] E. Bucher et al., *Schweizerisches Obligationenrecht* 160 (1979).

[54] Article 4.8 of Unidroit, *Principles of International Commercial Contracts* 284 (1994).

discuss also apply to situations in which there is no contractual gap in my sense of the word.

3. RESOLVING CONTRADICTIONS NORMATIVELY

(Antinomic) Contradiction between Legal Norms

Normative harmony requires, among other things, that norms within the same legal system do not contradict each other. Conflicting norms offend and contradict the principle of rule of law. They are inconsistent with a legal system's methodical structure. A legal system saying that X is both permitted and forbidden undermines its own stability and public confidence in it. That is why every legal system must establish rules for resolving contradictions between norms. The Continental system pays special attention to the problems of conflicting norms.[55] This is the problem of antinomy—a contradiction between two norms, where each norm is valid by itself, but both norms cannot apply simultaneously, together, to the same issue. Anglo-American law has also recognized the phenomenon of conflicting norms, but it has yet to give the issue the scientific attention it deserves.[56]

When Do Legal Norms Conflict?

A contradiction among legal norms occurs when two or more norms cannot be accommodated. Such is the case when one norm permits or mandates an action that another norm forbids,[57] creating a conflict between two legal rules. Resolution of the conflict usually invalidates one of the norms. No similarly absolute contradiction can exist between principles or values, because the conflict can be resolved while maintaining the validity of each principle or value in the system. Contradiction among competing values and principles is inevitable, reflecting the ordinary and proper state of affairs. Contradiction between rules, on the other hand, reveals a mistake in the legal system.

A "real" contradiction among rules exists only at the end of the interpretive process. Before that stage, the contradiction may be "imaginary." With the help of interpretive rules—including the presumption against the

---

[55] *See* Kelsen, *supra* p. 3, note 4 at 205; Radbruch, *supra* p. 53, note 179 at 43; *Les Antinomies en Droit* (Ch. Perelman ed., 1965); A. Baratta, *Antinomie Giuridiche e Confitti di Coscienza* (1963).

[56] *But see* I. Tammelo, *Modern Logic in the Service of Law* 126 (1978).

[57] Peczenik, *supra* p. 16, note 44 at 418.

existence of a contradiction—the court generally manages to resolve the contradiction. We witness a real contradiction only after exhausting every interpretive possibility of solving it. Of course, a given legal system can treat the rules for resolving a "real" contradiction as interpretive rules. However, we should distinguish between an (interpretive) process that determines the validity of each norm and a different process that determines the (normative) relationship between one norm and another. I personally view rules for resolving contradictions between norms embedded in separate texts as non-interpretive rules.

Contradiction between Norms Embedded in a Single Text

The first type of (real) contradiction occurs when two rules in a single text conflict with each other. The contradiction may be original, meaning that it existed when the text was created. It may be later, meaning that it came about due to changes made to the text after it was created. In both cases, the question is, which norm trumps? Every legal system has its own answers. For example, in English common law, when two provisions within the same piece of legislation conflict, the later provision takes priority.[58] On the other hand, when two provisions within a contract conflict, the earlier provision trumps.[59] This approach seems mechanical and unpersuasive.[60] Priority should be given to the instruction that more fully achieves the purpose at the heart of the text (constitution, statute, contract, will). Interpreters should prefer a primary norm over a secondary or subordinate norm and a specific norm over a general norm.

Contradiction between Norms of the Same Status Embedded in Different Texts

What happens when two norms of equal normative status, embedded in different texts, contradict each other? The typical example is a contradiction between provisions in two statutes or two regulations, but it can also happen with two contracts between the same parties, or two wills of a single testator. Of course, judges should first exhaust every interpretive possibility of showing the contradiction to be "imaginary." But what happens if the contradiction is real? The generally accepted rule is that the later norm trumps the earlier norm: *lex posterior derogat priori*. A later statute trumps an earlier

[58] Bennion, *supra* p. 6, note 13 at 902.
[59] Lewison, *supra* p. 42, note 130 at 245.
[60] *In Re Marr (A Bankrupt)* [1990] 2 All E.R. 880, 886.

statute; a later contract trumps an earlier contract; a later will trumps an ear-lier will. This rule reflects the autonomy of the creator of the norm. Just as he or she is authorized to create a norm, so is he or she authorized to create a contradictory norm that (implicitly or explicitly) nullifies the original norm. This rule, however, has one important exception: a later, general norm does not trump an earlier, particular norm: *generalia specialibus non derogant*. The earlier, particular norm trumps: *specialis derogat generali*. This rule creates no difficulty if it is merely an interpretive rule, stating that the scope of the later, general norm does not extend to the area covered by the earlier, par-ticular norm. In that case, the contradiction is imaginary, and the resolution is interpretive. What happens, though, when the contradiction is real? How do we justify the preference for an earlier, particular norm?[61]

Contradiction between Superior and Inferior Norms

What happens when a superior norm contradicts an inferior norm? The rule is that the superior norm trumps: *lex superior derogat inferiori*. The con-siderations used to determine which norm is superior are external to this rule. Once norm X is declared superior, it trumps a norm of lesser status, be it general or specific. Thus, when a constitution contradicts an ordinary statute, the constitution trumps. When a statute contradicts secondary leg-islation, the statute trumps.

Isn't this mere tautology? Aren't we just saying that a superior norm is superior? The answer is no, because there are circumstances under which a superior norm (a constitution) does not invalidate a conflicting inferior norm (a statute). Such is the case in the Netherlands, for example, whose constitution—the highest norm in the legal system—bars judges from re-viewing the constitutionality of statutes.[62] For systems like the Dutch legal system, the superiority of the norm is political, not legal, requiring the leg-islature to keep its actions in conformity with the norm. For systems that provide for judicial review of the constitutionality of statutes, when we say that a superior norm trumps an inferior norm, we mean that the superior-ity of the norm has practical legal consequences. The superiority is not just political but also legal, and it has the power to invalidate an inferior norm.[63] We see, then, that preferring a superior norm to an inferior norm is not a question of interpretation. Anyone who doubts the distinction between in-

---

[61] Whatever the explanation, it does not apply to wills, because a later, general will trumps an earlier, particular will.

[62] Art. 2 of the Dutch Constitution states that "The constitutionality of Acts of Parliament and treaties shall not be reviewed by the courts."

[63] This is the basis of the holding in *Marbury v. Madison*, 5 U.S. (1 Cranch) 137 (1803).

terpretive and non-interpretive activity must admit that the criteria for deciding the relationship between a constitution and statute or between a statute and secondary legislation are not interpretive criteria. Judges do not give meaning to the different texts, but rather determine their validity. To do so, they do not use interpretive rules—rules for understanding the text—but rather rules of validity, originating in constitutional law.

4. CORRECTING MISTAKES IN THE LANGUAGE OF A TEXT

Is a Judge Authorized to Correct Mistakes in a Text?

The author of a text is generally "authorized" to correct a mistake in it. The legislature may correct a mistake in a statute; the parties to a contract may correct a mistake in the formation of a contract; testators may correct their wills. May judges, however, correct mistakes in texts they did not write, like statutes, contracts, or wills?[64] Answering in the affirmative is uncontroversial as long as judges are permitted to make the correction within the framework of the text's language, without having to add to it or subtract from it. Such activity is just ordinary interpretation, in which judges consider the correct reality surrounding the text, rather than the mistaken one. Of course, a given legal system may not allow judges to treat the text as mistaken. That question is an internal one, and each legal system has its own answer.

What happens, however, when judges must change the text in order to fix the mistake? May judges make the changes? Take an example from French law: A statutory provision states that "It is forbidden to embark or disembark while the train is not in motion."[65] Must interpreters determine the legal meaning of the text according to its semantic meaning, or may they change the language of the statute by eliminating the word, "not"? Take a second example: A state of the United States bars the use of weapons on a public highway, "except for the purpose of killing some noxious or dangerous animal or an officer in pursuit of his duty."[66] Should a judge determine that the use of weapons in public highways is permitted for the purpose of killing an officer in pursuit of his duty, or may the court correct the mistake and decide that the word "by" comes after the word "or"?

These may be extreme examples, but the issue arises in moderate cases, too. The question is whether a judge may correct the language of a text. We might say that judicial alteration of a text that someone else created in-

---

[64] F.A.R. Bennion, *Statute Law* 14 (2d ed. 1983).

[65] P.A. Côté uses this example, among others, in *The Interpretation of Legislation in Canada* 326 (2d ed. 1991).

[66] Dickerson cites this example, *supra* p. 3, note 3 at 231, n. 43.

fringes on the autonomy of private actors (in the case of a contract or will) and on separation of powers (in the case of a constitution or statute). Lord Esher, M.R., had this to say about correcting a mistake in a statute: "If the words of an Act are clear, you must follow them, even though they lead to a manifest absurdity. The Court has nothing to do with the question whether the legislator has committed an absurdity."[67]

Esher's approach is harsh. Take a will in which the testator by mistake wrote Simon's name instead of Richard's. Correcting the mistake allows the judge to realize the testator's intent. The same is true of a mistake in a contract. Its correction realizes the parties' joint intent. Similar explanations would seem to apply to a mistake in a statute. The mistake frustrates the legislature's intent or the statute's purpose. Why should the judge not have the power to correct the statute and realize the legislative intent or statutory purpose? Correcting the mistake would not interfere with reasonable expectations, because most people who read the text realize that it contains a mistake. In any case, the damage done to reasonable expectations, if any exist, from correcting the mistake is no greater than the damage to reasonable expectations wreaked by any act of interpretation. With that in mind, we discuss correcting mistakes.

Correcting Mistakes in Statutes

The English legal tradition authorizes a judge to correct blatant errors in a text that has been enacted. The legislature is presumed to have wanted judges to correct blatant errors in statutes, particularly in order to realize its intent.[68] As Lord Reid said:

> Cases where it has properly been held that a word can be struck out of a deed or statute and another substituted can as far as I am aware be grouped under three heads: where without such substitution the provision is unintelligible or absurd or totally unreasonable; where it is unworkable; and where it is totally irreconcilable with the plain intention shewn by the rest of the deed or statute.[69]

American law adopts a similar approach.[70]

---

[67] *R. v. Judge of City of London Court* [1892] 1 Q.B. 273, 290.

[68] *See* Bennion, *supra* p. 6, note 13 at 676, claiming that a judge may give a text "a rectifying construction." Bennion includes the following categories in that phrase: "(1) the *garbled* text (which is grammatically incomplete or otherwise corrupt); (2) the text containing an *error of meaning*; (3) the text containing a *casus omissus*; (4) the text containing a *casus male inclusus*; and (5) the case where there is *textual conflict*." *See also* Cross, *supra* p. 3, note 3 at 36; A. Samuels, "Errors in Bills and Acts," [1982] *Statute L. Rev.* 94.

[69] *Federal Steam Navigation Co. Ltd. v. Department of Trade and Industry* [1974] 2 All E.R. 97, 100. *See also* Western *Bank Ltd. v. Schindler* [1977] ch. 1, 18.

[70] 2A Sutherland, *Statutes and Statutory Construction* 284 (N. Singer ed., 5th ed. 1992).

Correcting Mistakes in Contracts

Most legal systems allow a judge to correct a mistake in a contract.[71] Mistake, for these purposes,[72] is the gap between the "real" agreement reached by the parties, reflecting their joint subjective intent, and the agreement they actually put into writing. In order to prove the mistake, the judge may go beyond the four corners of the text (via the parole evidence rule, for example).

Correcting Mistakes in Wills

May a judge correct a mistake in a will? Mistake, for these purposes,[73] is the gap between the testator's subjective reality and the way he or she expresses it in the language of the will. Most legal systems allow judges to correct this kind of mistake:[74] *falsa demonstratio non nocet*. According to the rule, if a will describes a person or thing with enough specificity to allow it to be certainly identified, according to the testator's intent, then a judge can ignore (and correct) the will's incorrect descriptions of the person or thing. Take a will bequeathing property to "my cousin, Rachel," when Rachel is really the cousin of the testator's wife. Rachel inherits the property, because the court is authorized to correct the will. Similarly, assume the testator bequeaths property to his nephew, Richard—but he has no nephew named Richard. His nephew's name is Simon. A judge may correct the error, and Simon inherits. Israeli law explicitly grants this authority to judges: "Where a will contains a clerical error or an error in the description of a person or asset, in a date, number, calculation or the like and it is possible to determine clearly the true intention of the testator, the Court shall correct the error."[75] The court may correct a mistake when the

[71] Lewison, *supra* p. 42, note 130 at 227.

[72] Another type of mistake occurs when there is a gap between the language of the contract and the subjective intent of one of the parties, but that issue is beyond the scope of this book.

[73] Another type of mistake occurs when there is a gap between the objective reality and the testator's subjective viewpoint. In most legal systems, this kind of mistake nullifies the will. The Israeli system, however, authorizes judges to correct the will: *see* Succession Law, 1965, 19 L.S.I. 58, 63, sec. 30. American law has shifted on this issue, and it now recognizes the power of courts to correct a will. *See Restatement (Second) of Property* § 34.7 (1983). Australia follows a similar rule. *See* M.B. Voyce, "Statutory Reform of Rectification of Wills in New South Wales," 8 *Austl. Bar Rev.* 49 (1991).

[74] U. von Lübtow, *Erbrecht: Eine systematische Darstellung* 270 (1971); T. Feeney, *The Canadian Law of Wills* vol. 2, 103 (3d ed. 1987); P. Piotet, *Erbrecht* 208 (1978); *Restatement (Third) of Property* § 12.1 (Tentative Draft no. 1, 1995).

[75] Succession Law, 1965, 19 L.S.I. 58, 63, sec. 32.

true intention of the testator is clear from the language of the will and the surrounding circumstances. If there is ambiguity about his or her true intent, the court cannot correct the mistake and generally must discard the provision.

5. DEVIATING FROM THE LANGUAGE OF THE TEXT TO AVOID ABSURDITY

Absurdity plays two roles in the common law: *First*, it permits a court to deviate from the natural and ordinary meaning of the language if such meaning would lead to an absurd result.[76] The plain meaning rule or literal rule,[77] which applies to all legal texts, says that interpreters should understand the language of a text in its natural and ordinary meaning. The "golden rule,"[78] however, is an important exception that allows deviation from the natural and ordinary meaning, in order to avoid an absurdity. This aspect of absurdity is interpretive. It guides the interpreter's choice of the text's legal meaning from among the few semantic meanings that the text can tolerate in its language. It tells the interpreter to select a semantic meaning that is not absurd. The *second* aspect of absurdity operates beyond the limits of language, allowing a judge to correct language, add to it, or subtract from it, in order to avoid an absurdity.[79]

6. CY PRES PERFORMANCE

The Substantive Doctrine

The common law recognizes the doctrine of cy pres performance[80] in contract and estate law. If a contract or a unilateral legal action (trust or will) dedicates assets for a public purpose, and that purpose cannot be fulfilled,

---

[76] Bennion, *supra* p. 6, note 13 at 751; Cross, *supra* p. 3, note 3 at 16; Lewison, *supra* p. 42, note 130 at 85.

[77] *Supra* p. 34.

[78] Lord Wensleydale coined this phrase in *Grey v. Pearson* (1857) 10 E.R. 1216, 1234.

[79] Cross, *supra* p. 3, note 3 at 16: "The usual consequence of applying the golden rule is that words which are in the statute are ignored or words which are not there are read in."

[80] *See* E. Fry, *A Treatise on the Specific Performance of Contracts* (6th ed. 1921); J. McGhee, *Snell's Equity* (30th ed. 2000); R. Sharpe, *Injunctions and Specific Performance* 420 (1983); E. Fisch, *Cy Pres Doctrine in the United States* (1950); C.R. Chester, "Cy Pres: A Promise Unfulfilled," 54 *Ind. L.J.* 406 (1979); F. Schrag, "Cy Pres Inexpediency and the Buck Trust," 20 *U.S.F.L. Rev.* 577 (1986); R. Sisson, "Relaxing the Dead Hand's Grip: Charitable Efficiency and the Doctrine of Cy Pres," 74 *Va. L. Rev.* 635 (1988); A.M. Johnson and R.D. Taylor, "Revolutionizing Judicial Interpretation of Charitable Trusts: Applying Relational Con-

a court may order that the assets be used for an alternative and substantially similar purpose. Some legal systems have expanded the doctrine to the field of specific performance, applying cy pres generically to all contracts and wills. Today's version of the doctrine incorporates elements of the principle of good faith. What, then, is the relationship between cy pres and textual interpretation?

The following example will clarify: Richard creates a trust designating funds to a hospital to be used for the treatment of disease X. Years pass, and scientists eradicate the disease. May the hospital use the funds to treat disease Y? No interpretation of the text creating the trust can lead to this result; no interpretation of "disease X" can extend to "disease Y." Interpretive activity cannot change the mission of the trust, but cy pres, a non-interpretive doctrine, can. A judge may decide that the original trust allows the funds to be used for the treatment of another disease. Interpretation of the text cannot lead him or her to that outcome—the interpretation has reached its limits, and must stop. There is no need to try to cram into interpretive activity what it cannot bear. Pretending that disease X somehow includes disease Y is a fiction that violates the rules of interpretation. Instead, cy pres allows a court to change the destination of the assets, as long as the new purpose is close to the original. The original goal of the trust can thus be achieved without resort to interpretive rules and without "tearing" the text's semantic casing.

Cy Pres in Legislation

Can courts apply the doctrine of cy pres to legislation? The Latin maxim that a statute becomes invalid when the reasons behind it become obsolete (*cessante ratione cessat ipsa lex*) is not part of the modern perspective on law. Customary failure to abide by a statute does not invalidate the statute (desuetude),[81] but may the statute be used to carry out purposes similar to the original? Can courts thus revitalize obsolete statutes?

The governing jurisprudence does not allow such a result. Calabresi's suggestion that courts be permitted to invalidate obsolete statutes[82] would require explicit statutory authorization. Courts may not seize that authority for themselves, nor did Calabresi suggest that they should.

---

tracts and Dynamic Interpretation to Cy Pres and America's Cup Legislation," 74 *Iowa L. Rev.* 545 (1989); R. Atkinson, "Reforming Cy Pres Reform," 44 *Hastings L.J.* 1112 (1993).

[81] Bennion, *supra* p. 6, note 13 at 232.

[82] G. Calabresi, *A Common Law for the Age of Statutes* (1982). For a critique of Calabresi's approach, see R. Weisberg, "The Calabresian Judicial Artist: Statutes and the New Legal Process," 33 *Stan. L. Rev.* 213 (1983); S. Estreicher, "Judicial Nullification: Guido Calabresi's Uncommon Law for a Statutory Age," 57 *N.Y.U. L. Rev.* 1126 (1982).

7. FROM INTERPRETIVE THEORY TO PURPOSIVE INTERPRETATION

In this part, I have defined interpretation in law. I distinguished between interpretive and non-interpretive activity. In the course of doing so, I discussed different systems of interpretation without expressing preference for one over the other. I will now take the next step and answer the question, What is the most proper system of interpretation? I will do more than just survey all systems of interpretation and their treatment of non-interpretive activity. I will examine the system of interpretation that I think is best: purposive interpretation. Part Two will discuss its essence and components.

Part Two

PURPOSIVE INTERPRETATION

CHAPTER THREE

The Essence of Purposive Interpretation

1. "PURPOSIVE INTERPRETATION": TERMINOLOGY

Sources of the Term

The word "purpose" in the interpretation of legal texts is not new to common law tradition.[1] It often appears alongside or instead of the word "intent." In contrast, the phrase "purposive interpretation" (or "purposive construction") is relatively new, apparently surfacing in common law traditions at the end of the 1960s and beginning of the 1970s. It appeared simultaneously in American,[2] English,[3] Canadian,[4] Australian,[5] and New Zealand[6] common law. "Purposive interpretation" cropped up in Israeli

[1] For a discussion of "purpose," *see* J. Corry, "Administrative Law and the Interpretation of Statutes," 1 *U. Toronto L.J.* 286, 292 (1936); M. Radin, "A Short Way with Statutes," 56 *Harv. L. Rev.* 388, 400 (1942). For a historical analysis, *see* W.D. Popkin, *Statutes in Court* 131 (1991). Popkin identifies Judge Hand and Justice Frankfurter as the central figures in the United States who adopted the purposive approach. Substantively—as opposed to semantically—*Heydon's Case* (1584) 3 Co. Rep. 7a; 76 E.R. 637 may be the historical source of purposive interpretation. *See* Cross, *supra* p. 3, note 3 at 17. *See also* Viscount Delhorne's opinion in *Stock v. Frank Jones (Tipton) Ltd.* [1978] 1 W.L.R. 231, 234.

[2] *See, e.g., People v. Rodney,* 21 N.Y. 2d 1, 4 (1967); *Commonwealth v. Valentine,* 419 A.2d 193 (Pa. Super.) (1979). Justice Holmes used the term purpose as early as the beginning of the twentieth century. *U.S. v. Whitridge,* 197 U.S. 135, 143 (1904) (Holmes, J.) ("The general purpose is a more important aid to the meaning than any rule which grammar or formal logic may lay down"). The American realists also advocated using purpose as a criterion for interpretation, *infra* p. 225, as did legal process scholars, *infra* p. 227.

[3] *See, e.g., Kammins Ballrooms Co. Ltd. v. Zenith Investments (Torquay) Ltd.* [1971] A.C. 850, 879; *Kennedy v. Spratt* [1972] A.C. 83; *Carter v. Bradbeer* [1975] 3 All E.R. 158, 161; *Notham v. Barnet Council* [1978] 1 W.L.R. 220, 228; *Jones v. Wrotham Park Settled Estates* [1980] A.C. 74, 105; *Gold Star Publications Ltd. v. Director of Public Prosecution* [1981] 2 All E.R. 257.

[4] *See* Driedger, *supra* p. 69, note 31 at 35; Côté, *supra* p. 77, note 65 at 313. Similarly, then-Justice Dixon used the phrase "purposive analysis" in *Hunter v. Southern Inc.* (1984) 11 D.L.R. (4th) 641, 649. *See also* sR. *v. Big M Drug Mart* [1985] 1 S.C.R. 295, 344; *Re B.C. Motor Vehicle Act* [1985] 2 S.C.R. 486, 499; L. Walton, "Making Sense of Canadian Constitutional Interpretation," 12 *Nat'l J.Const.L.* 315, 340 (2000–2001).

[5] *Mayne Nickless Ltd. v. Federal Comm'n of Taxation* [1984] VR 863. *See also Kingston and Anor v. Keprose Pty Ltd.* (1987) 11 NSWLR 404.

[6] *Donselaar v. Donselaar* [1982] 1 NZLR 97, 114. *See also* J. Allan, "Statutory Interpretation and the Courts," 18 *New Zealand U. L. Rev.* 439 (1999).

law during this period, too.[7] The new phrase, developed primarily in the context of statutory interpretation, but it was also used in the interpretation of other texts.[8] The English Law Commission on the Interpretation of Statutes[9] may have helped popularize the phrase[10] by proposing the purposive approach to statutory interpretation. Anglo-American legal scholars also began writing about purposive interpretation in law in their theoretical literature.[11] Since von Savigny's work,[12] and under the influence of von-Ihering,[13] Continental law has recognized teleological interpretation[14] as a criterion, if not the primary criterion, for legal interpretation.[15]

What Is Purposive Interpretation?

The phrase "purposive interpretation" occurs frequently in court decisions and legal literature alike. The common thread running through most references to purposive interpretation is the understanding that "purpose" is

---

[7] C.A. 277/82 *Nirosta Ltd. v. State of Israel*, 37(1) P.D. 826, 832; C.A. 65/82 *Land Betterment Tax Administrator v. Hirshkowitz*, 39(4) P.D. 281, 288.

[8] *See, e.g., Antaios Cia. Naviera S.A. v. Salen Rederierna* A.B. [1985] A.C. 191.

[9] Law Comm'n, *The Interpretation of Statutes* (1969). The influence may also originate from England's being a party to the European Convention for the Protection of Human Rights and Fundamental Freedoms and a member of the European Community, both of which employ "teleological interpretation." *See* Steyn, *supra* p. 18, note 49 at 85.

[10] Cross takes this view. *Supra* p. 3, note 3 at 18.

[11] *See* Driedger, *supra* p. 69, note 31 at 35; Côté, *supra* p. 77, note 65 at 313; Cross, *supra* p. 3, note 3 at 17; Bennion, *supra* p. 6, note 13 at 731; Eskridge, *supra* p. 41, note 126 at 25.

[12] F.C. von Savigny, *System des heutigen römischen Rechts* 213 (vol. 1, 1840).

[13] R. von-Ihering, *Der Zweck in Recht* (vol. 1, 1877; vol. 2, 1883). The first volume is available in translation: R. von-Ihering, *Law as Means to an End* (I. Husik trans., 1913).

[14] For a discussion of teleological interpretation, *see* Côté, *supra* p. 77, note 65 at 313; Larenz, *supra* p. 3, note 5; Zippelius, *supra* p. 3, note 5. For a discussion of purposive interpretation in Scandinavia, *see* F. Schmidt, "Construction of Statutes," 1 *Scandinavian Studies in Law* 157 (1957); P.O. Ekelof, "Teleological Construction of Statutes," 2 *Scandinavian Studies in Law* 77 (1958); H. Thornstedt, "The Principle of Legality and Teleological Constructions of Statutes in Criminal Law," 4 *Scandinavian Studies in Law* 211 (1960); S. Strömholm, "Legislative Material and the Construction of Statutes: Notes on the Continental Approach," 10 *Scandinavian Studies in Law* 175 (1966); A. Peczenik and G. Bergholz, "Statutory Interpretation in Sweden," in *Interpreting Statutes* 311 (D.N. MacCormick and R.S. Summers eds., 1991). In *James Buchanan & Co. Ltd. v. Babco Forwarding & Shipping (UK) Ltd.* [1977] 2 W.L.R. 107, 112, Lord Denning writes that European judges "adopt a method which they call in English by strange words—at any rate they were strange to me—the 'schematic and teleological' method of interpretation. It is not really so alarming as it sounds. All it means is that the judges do not go by the literal meaning of the words or by the grammatical structure of the sentence. They go by the design or purpose . . . behind it."

[15] Zippelius, *supra* p. 3, note 5. *See also* K. Zweigert and H.J. Puttfarken, "Statutory Interpretation—Civilian Style," 44 *Tul. L. Rev.* 704 (1970).

a subjective term.[16] It reflects, at various levels of abstraction, but particularly at the highest levels of abstraction,[17] the intention of the text's creator(s). Bennion—who devotes a lengthy chapter to purposive interpretation[18]—notes that the historical source of purposive interpretation is the mischief rule established in *Heydon's Case*.[19] Eskridge analyzes purposivism in the context of "archaeological" systems of interpretation that are based on the will of the legislature.[20] Driedger,[21] Cross,[22] and Twining and Miers[23] take a similar approach. Hart and Sachs also appear to treat "purpose" as a subjective concept.[24] I say "appear" because, although Hart and Sachs claim that the interpreter should imagine himself or herself in the legislature's shoes, they introduce two elements of objectivity: *First*, the interpreter should assume that the legislature is composed of reasonable people seeking to achieve reasonable goals in a reasonable manner; and *second*, the interpreter should accept the non-rebuttable presumption that members of the legislative body sought to fulfill their constitutional duties in good faith.[25] This formulation allows the interpreter to inquire not into the subjective intent of the author, but rather the intent the author would have had, had he or she acted reasonably. In other places, literature on the common law formulates purpose in objective terms.[26] The addition of an "objective intent" arising from the language of the text creates uncertainty. Are we interested in subjective psycho-biological intent, or objective purposes? Why use the subjective language of "intent" to connote the objective concept of "purpose?" Continental law is not immune from this confusion. It distinguishes between a subjective teleological approach and an objective teleological approach without fully clarifying the relationship between the two.

[16] *See* Lord Diplock, one of the first to use the phrase, "purposive interpretation," in *Sweet v. Parsley* [1970] A.C. 132, 165 ("'Purpose' connotes an intention by some person to achieve a result desired by him").

[17] Dickerson, *supra* p. 3, note 3 at 88: "Lawyers tend to identify the immediate legislative purpose with 'legislative intent' and to reserve the term 'legislative purpose' for any broader or remote ('ulterior') legislative purpose." *See also* Sunstein, *supra* p. 13, note 31 at 428; M. Redish and T. Chung, "Democratic Theory and the Legislative Process: Mourning the Death of Originalism in Statutory Interpretation," 68 *Tul. L. Rev.* 803, 815 (1994).

[18] Bennion, *supra* p. 6, note 13 at 731–50.

[19] *Id.* at 732, *citing to Heydon's Case* (1854) 3 Co. Rep. 7a, 7b.

[20] Eskridge, *supra* p. 41, note 126 at 25.

[21] Driedger, *supra* p. 69, note 31 at 36.

[22] Cross, *supra* p. 3, note 3 at 20, 33.

[23] W. Twining and D. Miers, *How to Do Things with Rules: A Primer of Interpretation* 186 (4th ed. 1999).

[24] Hart and Sachs, *supra* p. 3, note 3 at 1378.

[25] *Id.*

[26] *See* Scalia, *supra* p. 34, note 103 at 17; p. 265, *infra*.

Definition of Purposive Interpretation

Against the backdrop of these issues, I wish to clarify my stance on purposive interpretation. My formulation of purposive interpretation differs from the standard use of the phrase in the Anglo-American or Continental literature in that it is neither entirely subjective nor entirely objective. I see purpose as a legal construction, like concepts of ownership, right, and duty. It combines subjective elements (subjective purpose; author's intent; subjective teleology) with objective elements (objective intent; the intent of the reasonable author and the legal system's fundamental values; objective teleology) so that they work simultaneously, rather than in different phases of the interpretive process. Although the content I give to the phrase "purposive interpretation" differs from its ordinary and accepted meaning, I have decided to stick with it—and not to replace it with alternatives like functional interpretation[27]—because it best expresses my stance. I will now describe my theory of purposive interpretation.

2. FUNDAMENTALS OF PURPOSIVE INTERPRETATION

Purposive Interpretation's Basic Approach

The key question in any interpretive study is: What is the goal of the interpretation? What is it designed to accomplish? In the field of law, my answer is that the goal of interpretation is to realize the goal that the legal text is designed to realize. This is the starting point of purposive interpretation. The interpretation is purposive because its goal is to achieve the purpose that the legal text is designed to achieve. What is this purpose? What kind of relationship do we create between the intention of the text's author and the "intention" of the legal system? The answer lies in constitutional principles. Constitutional considerations of the autonomy of the private will and its relationship to the social fabric are the primary determinants of the purpose of a private legal text. Constitutional considerations of democracy, separation of powers, rule of law, and the role of a judge in a democracy are the primary determinants of the purpose of a public legal text. Purposive interpretation uses this set of considerations—which shapes a legal text's purpose—to solve the fundamental problems of legal interpretation.

---

[27] This phrase has also been used already. *See* MacCormick and Summers, *supra* p. 31, note 92 at 187.

The Semantic Component

Purposive interpretation is based on three components: language, purpose, and discretion. Language shapes the range of semantic possibilities within which the interpreter acts as a linguist. Once the interpreter defines the range, he or she chooses the legal meaning of the text from among the (express or implied) semantic possibilities. The semantic component thus sets the limits of interpretation by restricting the interpreter to a legal meaning that the text can bear in its (public or private) language.

The Purposive Component

The second and core component of purposive interpretation is the element of purpose (the *telos*).[28] This is the *ratio juris*, the purpose at the core of the text (will, contract, statute, and constitution). This purpose is the values, goals, interests, policies, and aims that the text is designed to actualize. It is the function that the text is designed to fulfill.[29] The purpose of the text is a normative concept. It is a legal construction, like a right or a legal personality, which the interpreter formulates. It is not a psychological or metaphysical concept, and it is not a fact. The author of the text formulated the text. The interpreter of the text formulates its purpose.

Foundations of Purpose

The purpose of a norm has two foundations: subjective and objective purpose. The subjective purpose constitutes the values, goals, interests, policies, aims, and function that the text's author sought to actualize. This is authorial intent—the intent of the founders (constitutional interpretation); legislative intent (statutory interpretation); the joint intention of the parties to a contract (contractual interpretation); and the testator's intent (interpretation of a will). It is their psycho-biological intent, not the intent of a reasonable person. It is the subjective intent of the author, operating at different levels of abstraction.

An interpreter learns the intent through the language of the text as a whole and the circumstances external to it, like the history of its creation.

---

[28] *Supra* p. 86. Purposive interpretation belongs to the family of teleological interpretation. *Infra* p. 110.

[29] *See* L. Fuller, *The Morality of Law* (2nd ed. 1969); G. Gottlieb, *The Logic of Choice* 105 (1968); J. Wróblewski, *The Judicial Application of Law* 103 (1992); Moore, *supra* p. 24, note 67 at 265.

The interpreter may always look to extrinsic circumstances in his or her search for a text's meaning. Often, the information from different sources about the subjective purpose points in one clear direction, but sometimes the sources conflict. In those instances, the interpreter seeks the meaning that best realizes the intent of the author. The more credible the information, the more weight the interpreter should give it.

The objective purpose constitutes the values, goals, interests, policies, aims, and function that the text should actualize in a democracy. This purpose, too, operates at different levels of abstraction. At the lowest level, it is what the specific author would have wanted to carry out had he or she thought about it. At the intermediate level, it is what the reasonable author would have wanted to carry out. At the high level, it depends on the type of legal arrangement in question and its characteristics. At the supreme level, it actualizes the fundamental values of the legal system. I call these types of objective purpose the "intention" or will of the system.

An interpreter learns the objective purpose from "objective" data. Some data are unique to each specific text (individual objective purpose) and are derived from the language of the text, its character, and its type. The interpreter can also study similar texts to discover objective data. Other data are general (general objective purpose) and apply to all texts. They constitute the normative umbrella for all the texts, reflecting the legal system's fundamental values. When these values clash, an interpreter determines objective purpose by striking the right balance between the competing values, a balance that reflects their relative weight in the legal system. The balance depends on the relative significance and status of the different values at the point of decision.

The purpose of a norm is an abstract concept, composed of both its subjective and objective purpose. The first reflects the intention of the text's author; the second, the intention of a reasonable author and the fundamental values of the legal system. The first reflects, at varying levels of abstraction, an actual intention; the second reflects, at varying levels of abstraction, a hypothetical intention. The first reflects a historical-subjective intention; the second reflects a social-objective intention. The first is a fact established in the past; the second constitutes a legal norm that reflects the present.

The Centrality of Presumptions of Purpose

A unique feature of purposive interpretation is that the interpreter encounters the different data on the subjective purpose (authorial intent) and objective purpose (the legal system's intent) in the form of rebuttable presumptions. The presumptions reflect the author's intent (at varying levels of abstraction) and the intent of the legal system (at varying levels of abstraction). The main task of interpretation is to balance the different presumptions when they conflict. Indeed, presumptions of purpose are the foundation of purposive interpretation.[30] They replace rigid interpretive rules with flexible interpretive presumptions. They help bring the intent of the author and the intent of the legal system into sharp focus at every point of the interpretive process. They help express the idea that every text is a creature of its environment. Purposive presumptions apply always and immediately.

Constructing the Ultimate Purpose

The synthesis between a norm's objective and subjective purposes establishes its ultimate purpose. Interpreters view these two kinds of purposes as presumptions. On the one hand, interpreters presume that the purpose of the norm is to realize the author's intent. On the other, they presume that the norm's purpose is to realize the intent of the legal system. To arrive at the ultimate purpose, interpreters consider the presumptions together, assigning each a status according to its significance or weight. The significance varies from text to text and from type of text to type of text. For example, in a will, subjective intent is weighted so heavily as to be the determining factor, whereas in a constitution, the intent of the legal system carries the day. In a contract, the intention of the parties weighs in respectably, but the intention of the system is also given weight. In a statute, the author's intention (legislative intent) and the systemic intention (the intent of the statute) are both significant, and their relative weight depends on secondary distinctions between types of legislation (old or new, specialized or general, based on rules or principles, etc.). Regardless of its relative weight, each presumption, subjective or objective, remains in effect through the duration of the interpretive process.

The Discretionary Component

Discretion is the third component of purposive interpretation. It is the choice that purposive interpretation gives the judge from among a few interpretive possibilities, all of which are legal. While this discretion is narrowly bounded by a limited number of interpretive possibilities, it does help the judge formulate the purpose at the core of the text. Purposive interpretation thus recognizes the indispensability of interpretive discretion

---

[30] *Infra* p. 170.

in determining the ultimate purpose of the norm. This discretion operates at different junctions of the process of purposive interpretation. For example, an interpreter may need to exercise discretion in determining the limits of language; evaluating the reliability of sources of information about the author's intent; and determining the relevance of such intent to resolving the interpretive problem. Similarly, an interpreter may need to use discretion to resolve conflicts among the values and principles that formulate the objective purpose. The primary role for discretion, however, is in determining the ultimate purpose, after assigning the appropriate significance to each presumption and resolving the conflicts among them. Of course, as supreme courts use purposive interpretation more and more, they will develop case law to resolve some of the questions raised by interpretation, thus narrowing judicial discretion. Discretion will always have a place in purposive interpretation, however, because it is impossible to construct a theory of interpretation without interpretive discretion. Interpretive discretion exists within every system of interpretation, whether or not the system admits to it. Nevertheless, discretion should not become the primary element of interpretation. It is a secondary component, confined to particular situations.

Purpose and Language: End and Means

Purposive interpretation pinpoints, along the range of semantic meanings of the legal text, a legal meaning that realizes the purpose of the norm. Purpose is the end, and language is the means. The interpreter learns about the end from the means. Purposive interpretation recognizes the presumption that the language of a norm provides information about its purpose. To be sure, the interpreter learns about the end from other sources as well. He or she may look to any factual or legal source, beyond the text, to find the end. He or she may go beyond the limits of the means (the language) to learn about the end (the purpose). The interpreter may not, however, realize an end that does not have at least a minimal semantic grounding in the means. Purpose must remain within the limits of language. The interpreter need not necessarily learn the purpose from reading the language of the text. The text's language can be general, like language conferring the authority to exercise discretion. It does not always sufficiently clarify the purpose. To satisfy the requirement of semantic grounding, however, the purpose—which the interpreter may have learned from sources external to the language—must be realizable through the textual language. The language, the semantic medium, must be able to bear the purpose of the norm.

Order in Purposive Interpretation

Purposive interpretation has three components: language, purpose, and judicial discretion. There is no order for these components. Each interpreter starts with the component that seems appropriate. Each interpreter acts in accordance with his or her personality and character traits. However, interpreters may not use only some of the components. They must rely on both language and purpose, and, in the hard cases, they must exercise judicial discretion. Purposive interpretation does not take place in separate stages; it is integrative. It does not first turn to language and then to purpose; it does not first turn to one kind of purpose and then to the other. The interpretive conception is holistic. The interpretive presumptions, both subjective and objective, apply immediately with the start of the interpretive process, and they accompany it to its conclusion. Indeed, purposive interpretation is a circular process. The point of departure is irrelevant, so long as interpreters assess all the data and circle back to the starting point. Most importantly, purposive interpretation does not set an order for the use of interpretive and non-interpretive doctrines. Interpreters may begin with non-interpretive doctrines and only later start interpreting.

Purposive Interpretation and the Fundamental Problem in Legal Interpretation

The fundamental problem in legal interpretation is the relationship between text and context, form and substance.[31] Purposive interpretation views purpose as the context in whose light the text should be given meaning. Purpose is the substance that gives meaning to the form. Purposive interpretation takes a stand on each of the three secondary questions at the core of interpretation. *First*, purposive interpretation takes an integrative stance on the dichotomy between the intent of the author and the intent of the legal system. It gives expression to both authorial intent and the "intention" of the legal system by presuming that the purpose of the norm is to realize both kinds of intent. When there is an internal conflict between the two, purposive interpretation establishes criteria for resolving it. These criteria are based on constitutional considerations. In some cases, there is room for discretion.

The *second* secondary question focuses on the intention of the text's au-

---

[31] *Supra* p. 26.

thor. It asks whether to focus on the "true" intention or the "expressed" intention. Purposive interpretation requires attention to be given to the true intention of the text's author, and not just his or her expressed intention. The interpreter can learn about the subjective purpose from any credible source, not just from the language of the text. Having said that, the subjective purpose arising from the language of the text is generally more credible than the subjective purpose derived from sources external to the text. Purposive interpretation expresses this principle as a rebuttable presumption in favor of the intention arising from the text. Furthermore, once the interpreter determines the "true" intention of the author, he or she may only carry it out if the language used by the author allows it.

The *third* secondary question focuses on objective purpose. This purpose reveals the "objective substance" of the text. It is the intention of the legal system, expressed in purposive presumptions that reflect the objective purpose of the system's various features and elements. The interpreter resolves internal conflicts among these presumptions by balancing them according to their relative significance.

The Scope of Purposive Interpretation: Type of Text

Despite the vast literature on interpreting the various legal texts, few scholars have attempted a general interpretive theory that applies to all types of legal texts. Purposive interpretation aspires to that goal. It assumes that there are common elements in the interpretation of all legal texts (constitution, statute, contract, will) while recognizing the individuality of each type of text. It gives each legal text the "breathing room" it needs to convey its individuality, usually expressed in the balance between the text's subjective and objective purpose. Secondary distinctions, tailored to the particular type of text, then shape that balance. These distinctions consider the age of the text (treating old and new texts differently); the scope of the issues that the text regulates (interpreting a code differently from a specific text); the regime and its essence (treating a text created in a totalitarian regime differently than its democratic counterpart); and content-based factors of each text that affect the relationship between the author's intention and the intention of the legal system in constructing the purpose.

Generally—subject to the relevant secondary distinctions—in constitutional interpretation, objective purpose is the determining factor, while subjective purpose (the founders' intent) plays a secondary role. In the interpretation of contracts and wills, subjective purpose is primary. Objective purpose plays a secondary and supplementary role, but it becomes more significant when there is no credible information about the intent of the testator or the joint intent of the parties. In interpreting some kinds of contracts—an adhesion contract, a consumer contract, or a collective agreement, for example—judges should give more weight to objective purpose. In statutory interpretation, the balance between subjective (legislative intent) and objective (the intent of the reasonable legislator or of the legal system) purpose depends on the type of statute. The interpreter of an old statute gives more weight to objective purpose, while subjective purpose is weightier for a new statute; the interpreter of a generally applicable statute (like a code) emphasizes objective purpose, while the interpreter of specific administrative legislation favors subjective purpose. These distinctions allow purposive interpretation to retain its interpretive consistency while preserving the individuality of each text.

Synthesis and Unity

Purposive interpretation is unique for its holistic, universal approach. A judge interpreting a text according to its purpose acts within the context of a legal system. The text is a creature of its environment. The two exist in symbiosis. In interpreting a single statute, a judge interprets all statutes. During the interpretation of a text, there is a continuous flow from the text to its legal system and from the legal system to the text. This flow occurs as the interpreter balances the unique purpose of each text with the legal system's principles, common to all texts, which inform the individual purpose. Varying levels of abstraction facilitate a free flow between the individual and the generic. Purposive interpretation thus seeks to fashion a purpose that creates harmony between the meaning given to a text and the legal system surrounding it. The goal is synthesis and integration between text and legal system. Of course, that is not always possible. Sometimes the language of the text gets in the way. Sometimes subjective purpose—the determining factor for some kinds of texts—prevents synthesis. Sometimes, the system's values themselves contradict each other. Even if the goal is unattainable, however, judges must continue to aspire to synthesis.

Diversity in Purposive Interpretation

The purposive interpretation I discuss in this book creates a general framework for the principles of interpretation. It carves out an interpretive space. I have filled in parts of this space with my own views about purposive interpretation. Other purposive interpreters and other legal systems may fill in the space differently. For example, different purposive interpreters and different legal systems are likely to disagree over the content of the various purposive presumptions and the relationship between them. We should therefore distinguish between the general framework establishing the essence, character, and limits of purposive interpretation, and the reciprocal relationship, within that framework, among its different and nuanced components.

CHAPTER FOUR

The Semantic Component
of Purposive Interpretation

1. INTERPRETIVE THEORY AND SEMANTIC THEORY

A Communicative Text

Every theory of interpretation is based on semantic theory.[1] The object of legal interpretation is a text, whether enacted into law or not, that is expressed through the medium of language. The text is communicative; it is designed to establish a legal norm to which people will conform their behavior. The goal of interpretation is to understand the language of the text. Because the limits of language set the limits of interpretation, we must understand the essence of language and the problems it raises. The difficulty is that there is no one theory for understanding language; each theory evaluates language from its own perspective.[2] Subjective and objective theories diverge on the issue. Objective theories include extensional and intentional theories,[3] each of which incorporates both ontological and epistemological approaches.

Language as a System of Symbols

Language is a system of signs or symbols by which we think and through which we communicate. Natural language is the system of signs or symbols customarily used by members of a given society to communicate with each other. Life experience teaches—and every theory of law or semantics must

[1] See M. Landau, "Hamishpat B'mishpat: Balshanut Mishpatit—Habalshan B'sherut Hamishpatan [Linguistics and Law]," 22 *Iyunei Mishpat* 37 (1999); G.L. Williams, "Language and the Law," 61 *Law Q. Rev.* 71, 179, 293, 384, (1945); 62 *Law Q. Rev.* 387 (1946); P. Goodrich, "The Role of Linguistics in Legal Analysis," 47 *Mod. L. Rev.* 523 (1984); Goodrich, "Law and Language: An Historical and Critical Introduction," 11 *J. Law & Soc.* 173 (1984). Williams discusses the connection between language and interpretation in the fourth article of this series. *See also Law and Linguistics Conference,* 73 *Wash. U. L.Q.* 785 (1995). The end of the issue contains an extensive bibliographic list (p. 1311).

[2] F. Palmer, *Semantics: A New Outline* (1976); D. Taylor, *Explanation and Meaning* (1970).

[3] *The Theory of Meaning* (G. Parkinson ed., 1968) makes this division.

take this into account—that people communicate. Semantic Towers of Babel are the exception. Language has meaning. While the words themselves have no intrinsic meaning, they have an accepted meaning among those who speak the same language.[4] "Words, as mere symbols, are nothing but an empty shell with no meaning."[5]

Language, however, is more than a collection of disembodied symbols; words have meaning in a given language. Saying "automobile" and saying "cigarette" are two different things, in the framework of a linguistic community. The word "automobile" and the word "cigarette" mean different things, even if that meaning is not intrinsic to the words themselves. We could call a four-legged creature that barks "cat." But in a given language, at a given time, and in a given context, words have a given meaning. The meaning comes from the fact that, if we present the symbol (a four-legged creature that barks) and the word (dog), a speaker of English connects the two. When an English speaker hears or reads the word "dog," he or she thinks of that same four-legged animal that barks.[6] This is the power of a language—those who use it, share it, and it allows people to transmit meanings attached to the different symbols. Of course, anyone can express his or her thoughts through a private code. But in order to share those thoughts with someone else, that person will have to provide a key for deciphering the code.

Changes in the Meaning of Language

The meaning that words have in a language is not static.[7] Language changes. Relying on the works of various scholars, Zarfati lists five factors that change language: history, linguistics, social factors, psychological factors, and the influence of foreign languages.[8] When we evaluate the communicative power of language, we take into account a given system of assumptions that are external to the language itself. The key question, of course, is which meaning of the language the interpreter should consult: the meaning it had on the day the text was written, or the meaning it has on the day it is interpreted? Language by itself cannot give an answer. Both meanings together establish the range of semantic possibilities, and the

[4] A. Ross, *On Law and Justice* 112 (M. Dutton trans., 1959).

[5] Sussman, "Miksat Mitaamei Parshanut [Interpretation]," *Sefer Hayovel L'Pinchas Rosen* 148 (1962).

[6] Ogden and Richards, *supra* p. 3, note 3 at 11. For a critique of the plain exposition of this approach, *see* A. Dickerson, "Referentia Meaning: The Static Aspects," 10 *Jurimetrics J.* 58 (1969–70).

[7] See Justice Holmes's comments in *Towne v. Eisner*, 245 U.S. 418, 425 (1918).

[8] G. Zarfati, *Hebrew Semantics* 118 (2d. ed. 1968).

choice between them is guided by the criteria of the system of interpreta-tion.[9] Purposive interpretation gives language the legal meaning that best realizes the purpose of the norm. It may be the meaning of the language at the time the text was created, or the meaning at the time the text is in-terpreted, depending on the particular case at hand.[10]

Limits of Language and the Author's Responsibility

Judge Hand's remark that "Words are such temperamental beings"[11] is as true today as it was when he first said it. Language is temperamental because the agreements people make with each other, based on language, are nei-ther fixed nor precise. Natural language is not mathematics. Language has no single, uncontroversial meaning.[12] Meaning changes with context. As Professor Thayer said at the end of the nineteenth century, we are not in

> Lawyer's Paradise where all words have a fixed, precisely ascertained meaning . . . and where, if the writer has been careful, a lawyer, having a document re-ferred to him, may sit in his chair, inspect the text, and answer all questions without raising his eyes.[13]

Indeed, the best drafter cannot create a text that, when read in any cir-cumstance, will impart the same single meaning to all readers. There is al-ways "maneuvering room" in which understandings about the meaning of language are equivocal. This is especially true of general language referring to people and things not identified in the text. Language does facilitate communication among people, but its limitations prevent the communi-cation from even approaching perfection. Language can mean more than one thing even in a single context; language can be ambiguous; language can be vague. A good drafter can try to limit the ambiguity if he or she chooses. Sometimes there is reason to create an ambiguous text.[14] When

[9] Bennion, *supra* p. 6, note 13 at 698.

[10] Other interpretive methods, of course, reach different conclusions. Subjective interpre-tive methods focus on the meaning the language had at the time the text was created. Ob-jective interpretive methods focus on the meaning of the language at the time of interpreta-tion.

[11] L. Hand, *The Spirit of Liberty* 157 (I. Dilliard ed., 3d ed. 1960). *See also* Z. Chafee, "The Disorderly Conduct of Words," 41 *Colum. L. Rev.* 381 (1941).

[12] B. Bix, *Law, Language, and Legal Determinacy* (1993). *See also* J. Steyn, "Written Con-tracts: To What Extent May Evidence Control Language?" 41 *Current Legal Probs.* 23 (1988); *Slim v. Daily Telegraph Ltd.* [1968] 2 Q.B. 157, 171.

[13] J. Thayer, *A Preliminary Treatise on Evidence at the Common Law* 428 (1898).

[14] On passing legislation that is deliberately ambiguous, see J. Grundfest and A.C. Pritchard, "With Multiple Personality Disorders: The Value of Ambiguity in Statutory De-sign and Interpretation," 54 *Stan. L. Rev.* 627 (2002).

a drafter does not want ambiguity, the best he or she may do is select words that, in particular contexts, give a single meaning for the primary and typical situations that the drafter wishes to address in the text.[15]

Ambiguous Language

Language is ambiguous when a word or sentence has more than one meaning. The ambiguity may be a function of semantics or syntax. Semantic ambiguity occurs when a word in the sentence is ambiguous. A common example is the use of the words "and" and "or." Usually, "and" connects, while "or" separates. But we sometimes use "and" to present alternatives, and "or" to denote combination.[16]

Syntactic ambiguity occurs when the meaning of a sentence is ambiguous because of the structure or order of its words. The phrase "institutions or corporations for public use" is ambiguous because it can mean either of two things: (1) "institutions for public use" or "corporations for public use"; or (2) "institutions" or "corporations for public use."

Ambiguity is unavoidable and natural to natural language. Often, we can resolve the ambiguity by viewing the language in context. There are many potential contexts, however. A theory of interpretation must determine the relevant context. Purposive interpretive establishes the purpose of the norm grounded in the text as the relevant context, but that context does not always resolve the ambiguity. In those cases, judicial discretion is necessary.

Vague Language

Vagueness exists when there is uncertainty about the application of a word or sentence to details.[17] The uncertainty may be of several kinds: *First*, the word or sentence may not include the necessary and sufficient conditions for its application. For example, a reference to a crime with moral turpitude

---

[15] *Seaford Court Estates v. Asher* [1949] 2 All E.R. 155, 164. Friedmann attributes to me the view that there is no such thing as a plain text. D. Friedmann, "Liparshanut Hamunach 'Parshanut' Vihearot Lipsak Din Apropis [Notes on the Apropis Decision]," 7 *Hamishpat* 21 (2002). Indeed, I claim that there is no such thing as a text that is plain under every possible circumstance. However, I naturally think that a text can be plain in most circumstances that the author of the text sought to address. Of course, the determination that the text is plain can be done only after the text has been interpreted. *See supra* p. 12.

[16] A. Dickerson, *The Fundamentals of Legal Drafting* 76 (1965).

[17] J. Waldron, "Vagueness in Law and Language: Some Philosophical Issues," 82 *Cal. L. Rev.* 509 (1994); G. Christie, "Vagueness and Legal Language," 48 *Minn. L. Rev.* 885 (1964); Bix, *supra* p. 9, note 22.

is vague because "moral turpitude" is not self-defining.[18] A *second* kind of vagueness occurs when it is unclear whether a particular condition is necessary for the provision to apply. For example, the word "intent" is vague, because it is not clear if it extends to a situation in which a person does not wish to achieve a particular result by his or her action, but he or she knows, with a reasonable degree of certainty, that his or her action will cause that result. A *third* kind of vagueness occurs when a word or clause applies to the kinds of things that do not have a clearly defined scope or natural end point.[19] For example, words like "day," "night," "far," "near," "forest," "thicket," "mountain," and "hill" are vague. They pose a boundary problem with no semantic solution.[20] Sometimes, but not always, it is clear from the context whether a provision belongs to one or another end of the spectrum of possibilities. The context itself may be vague, however. In any case, a theory of interpretation is needed to decide which context is relevant. According to purposive interpretation, the relevant context is the purpose of the norm in question. Still, in exceptional circumstances, that criterion will not clarify the vagueness, and the interpreter must exercise discretion.

Relevant Context

Context is likely to resolve a text's ambiguity and vagueness.[21] But what counts as "context" for this purpose? The literature distinguishes between intrinsic and extrinsic context.[22] The intrinsic context is the textual context, that is, the other phrases surrounding the phrase being interpreted. It is the chapter that contains the clause being interpreted, or the entire document (constitution, statute, contract, will) containing the chapter. The extrinsic context is broader. It includes every context beyond the textual one. It includes the history of the text, the status of the law before and after the text was written, the general framework of the law in the given legal system, and the legal system's social background and fundamental principles. As Justice Sussman said, referring to the text of a statute, "A word in a statute is a creature of its environment. Its character is a function of its context."[23]

---

[18] W. Alston, *Philosophy of Language* 88 (1964).

[19] Moore, *supra* p. 24, note 67 at 195. Moore calls this "degree-vagueness."

[20] *Hobbs v. London & S.W. Ry. Co.* (1875) L.R. 10 Q.B. 111, 121. *See also Lavery v. Pursell* (1888) 39 Ch. D. 508, 517; *Mayor of Southport Corp. v. Morriss* [1893] 1 Q.B. 359, 361; *Attorney-General v. Brighton & Hove Co-operative Supply Ass'n* [1900] 1 Ch. 276, 282.

[21] For the difference between them, *see* 2 E.A. Farnsworth, *Farnsworth on Contracts* 239 (1990).

[22] *See* Dickerson, *supra* p. 3, note 3 at 103.

[23] H.C. 65/58, *Shalit v. Interior Minister*, 23(2) P.D. 477, 513. *See also Attorney General v. Prince Ernest Augustus of Hanover* [1957] A.C. 436, 461.

The key question regarding context (internal or extrinsic) is: What does the interpreter seek from the context? There are usually many different contexts. We should focus on the context that is relevant to interpretive activity. To find this context, we should evaluate the goal of the interpretation. The purpose of interpretation determines the relevance of the context. For example, if the goal of interpretation were to find the most aesthetically pleasing meaning,[24] the relevant context would be different than if the goal of interpretation were to actualize the values at the core of the text being interpreted. Purposive interpretation is based on the view that the goal of legal interpretation is to realize the purpose of the text being interpreted. Purpose is the relevant context. The internal and extrinsic contexts are just means and devices through which we uncover the purpose at the core of the text. When we study context, we are not looking for beauty. We are looking for purpose. We need to know which of the different contexts the interpreter should use, and what that context means. Interpretive theory is necessary to provide an answer. According to purposive interpretation, the relevant context is that which provides information about the purpose at the core for the text. In choosing among the range of potential contexts, the interpreter in law should focus on the one that provides information about the purpose at the core of the legal text.

Language's "Ability to Bear"

The nature of language is such that a legal text often has more than one semantic meaning. However, the number of semantic meanings is not infinite; people do successfully communicate. Language has a limited ability to bear meaning. It cannot sustain meaning beyond what is accepted in a given legal community or in the parties' private code. A text is not a fortress to be conquered with a dictionary, but it does have walls, beyond whose confines it has no meaning. As Professor Radin noted,

> Words are certainly not crystals, as Mr. Justice Holmes has wisely and properly warned us, but they are after all not portmanteaus. We can not quite put anything we like into them.[25]

The judge must give the language of the text a meaning that will not "tear" the "surface casing"[26] of the words or sentences.[27] Interpretation beyond

---

[24] On aesthetics in law, see P. Schlag, "The Aesthetics of American Law," 115 *Harv. L. Rev.* 1047 (2002).

[25] Radin, *supra* p. 25, note 74 at 866.

[26] C.A. 6339/97, *supra* p. 20, note 54 at 253.

[27] D. Payne, "The Intention of the Legislature in the Interpretation of Statutes," 9 *Cur-*

the language of the text loses its interpretive character and must draw its legitimacy from non-interpretive doctrines.

2. TYPES OF LANGUAGE

Private Code and Public Language

A text in private law expresses the autonomy of the private will.[28] The parties to a contract may formulate the contract as they wish. They may use a private code.[29] They may decide that, in their contract, a horse is a donkey, and a donkey is a horse. Similarly, a testator may formulate his or her will in his or her own private code.[30] He or she may call the wine cellar a "library," and the bottles of wine, "books." In that case, the range of semantic possibilities includes the private meaning as well as the accepted meaning in the given language. A judge applies the relevant interpretive criteria to choose between those meanings. According to purposive interpretation, the decisive factor is the testator's intent (in a will) and the joint intent of the parties (in a contract), so that the meaning they intend will usually trump. Of course, the private code or language cannot remain entirely private. Those who use a private code must give the interpreter a key to understanding it. Once they do, the interpreter should use the key interpret the text according to the intent of the author (for a will) or authors (for a contract).

The process becomes more complicated in the context of a statute or constitution, which are public documents,[31] for use by the public as a whole. A piece of legislation is not a linguistic or logical riddle. It is intended to send a message. It therefore must speak in a language that its target audience understands, that is, in the public language.[32] A legislature that speaks in riddles or in language that is not clear misses the point and the essence of legislation. It tarnishes the rule of law by writing legal instructions that are not understandable to its target audience but neverthe-

---

rent Legal Probs. 96, 104 (1956); G. Williams, "The Meaning of Literal Interpretation," 131 *New L.J.* 1128 (1981).

[28] J.H. Wigmore, *Evidence in Trials at Common Law* 223 (J.H. Chadbourn ed., 4th rev. ed. 1981).

[29] *See* Corbin, *supra* p. 9, note 20 at 155.

[30] *See* Wigmore, *supra* p. 103, note 28 at 231. *See also Re Rowland* [1963] 1 ch. 1, 9; C.A. 1900/96, *supra* p. 61, note 1 at 828.

[31] W.J. Brennan, "Construing the Constitution," 19 *U.C. Davis L. Rev.* 2 (1985).

[32] When the author of a text uses a private code, instead of public language, he must append an additional text that deciphers the code. Such a text is considered an interpretive clause in various statutes, or even an "Interpretive Act" accepted in common law countries.

less impose sanctions on members of that audience who violate those instructions. The legislature—and the legal system—have a basic obligation to formulate statutes in a language that is understandable to members of the given society.[33] Having said that, and subject to constitutional restraints, interpreters must consider language in both its private and its public meaning, the combination of which determines the range of semantic possibilities. The choice between these meanings depends on the relevant interpretive criteria; purposive interpretation makes its selection based on the purpose at the core of the text.

Explicit and Implicit Meaning

The meaning of a text is explicit when it is transmitted to the reader through the dictionary meaning of the language, understood in its relevant (internal and external) textual context.[34] The meaning of a text is implicit when it is transmitted to the reader but is not part of the dictionary meaning of the language.[35] Implicit language is written into the text in invisible ink. It is written between the lines. Dickerson uses the following example[36] to demonstrate implicit meaning: A son asks his mother, "May I go to the pool, and afterward, to the movies?" The mother replies, "You may go to the pool." Implicit in her answer is that the son may not go to the movies (implied negation or "negative arrangement"). Her son arrives at this meaning not from the dictionary meaning of the language, but rather from the use of explicit language, in its extrinsic and internal context. Professor Cross offers another example:[37] Richard tells Simon, "As a present, I'm giving you my apartment in London, my apartment in New York, and the furniture in my apartment in London." Implicit in Richard's words is that he does not give Simon the furniture in his New York apartment. These are obvious examples, but meaning can also be implied in less obvious cases. Consider a constitution whose various provisions establish the authority of the branches of government and protections of human rights. We can say that the constitution implicitly establishes the principles of separation of powers and judicial independence.[38]

The semantic meaning of a text (constitution, statute, contract, and will)

---

[33] *See* L. Fuller, *The Morality of Law* 63 (rev. ed. 1969).

[34] Dickerson, *supra* p. 3, note 3 at 40.

[35] *Id.* at 40.

[36] *Id.* at 41.

[37] Cross, *supra* p. 3, note 3 at 134.

[38] *Reference re Remuneration of Judges of the Provincial Court* [1997] 3 S.C.R. 3.

is both the explicit and implicit meaning. The implicit meaning is also called the ulterior,[39] ellipsis,[40] or tacit[41] meaning. It is part of the range of semantic meanings, just like the explicit meaning. An interpreter learns the implicit meaning through logic, intelligence, and reason. The question is not whether the implicit meaning is critical or necessary, clear or apparent; the question is whether the implicit meaning is reasonable, logical, and warranted.[42]

Readers are likely to disagree over the boundaries of "implication." Do constitutional provisions for democratic and egalitarian elections imply recognition of a constitutional right to freedom of political expression? The Supreme Court of Australia said yes.[43] Is that result implicit? Are we crossing the boundary between "implicit" meaning and a textual gap that the court fills? Whatever the definition, in principle, the text speaks to us explicitly and implicitly. In case of a conflict between the two meanings, the explicit meaning trumps. More precisely, when a text has an explicit meaning relating to a particular issue, there is no room to infer a contradictory implicit meaning relating to the same issue: *expressum facit cessare tacitum*.[44] Indeed, like the explicit meaning, the implicit meaning determines the meaning that the text can bear. It does not determine the legal meaning of the text. An interpreter extracts the text's legal meaning from the range of semantic meanings (explicit and implicit), using the purpose of the norm as the criterion for his or her selection.

Implied Meaning

"Implied meaning" can mean two things. On the one hand, it can be the meaning implicit in the text. On the other hand, implied meaning can fill in a gap in the text.[45] There is a big difference between these two meanings. Implied meaning as implicit meaning does not add "what is" to "what is not." Implied meaning (as implicit meaning) is part of the text: *verba illata est inesse vindentur* (implicit words are considered to be included). Referring to statutory language, Bennion said that

[39] G.L. Williams, "Language of the Law IV," 61 *Law Q. Rev.* 384, 400 (1945).

[40] *See* Bennion, *supra* p. 77, note 64 at 382. *See also* Bennion, *supra* p. 77, note 64 at 250.

[41] *Restatement (Second) of Contracts* §97 (1981).

[42] For a different approach, *see* Lord Westbury's opinion in *Parker v. Tootal* (1865) 11 H.L. 143, 161.

[43] *See supra* p. 70.

[44] *See* Bennion, *supra* p. 77, note 64 at 383, 963.

[45] Williams, *supra* p. 105, note 39 at 14.

It is a fact of language, indeed a fact of life, that every statement consists not only of what is expressed but also of what is implied. Neither portion is more compelling than the other.[46]

Determining the implied meaning (as implicit meaning) of a text is part of interpreting it. On the other hand, an implied meaning (or term) exists when the text contains a gap. The court fills in the gap—adds "what is" to "what isn't"—by adding implied language. According to my theory, this supplementation is part of interpretation in the broad sense, governed by non-interpretive doctrines.

Natural and Ordinary Language, Exceptional and Special Language

The range of semantic possibilities includes the language's totality of meanings. It includes the natural and ordinary meaning and the exceptional and special meaning. Of course, the presumption is that the purpose of a norm is expressed in its natural and ordinary language.[47] This presumption stems from the fact that creating a legal text is a communicative activity. The presumption is, however, rebuttable. Sometimes, the interpreter should give the language of the text an exceptional and special meaning, if that is necessary to achieve the purpose at the core of the text in question. On the semantic level, exceptional and special meanings should be treated like natural and ordinary meanings; the difference is in the rebuttable presumption that the purpose of the norm will be achieved through the natural and ordinary language.

Dictionaries

An interpreter may use a dictionary[48] as a source of the meaning that a text can bear.[49] A dictionary, either general or legal,[50] can help the interpreter (as a linguist) determine the range of semantic possibilities. It does not determine the legal meaning of the text. As Hart and Sachs noted:

A dictionary, it is vital to observe, never says what meaning a word *must* bear in a particular context. Nor does it ever purport to say this. An unabridged

---

[46] Bennion, *supra* p. 77, note 64 at 382.

[47] *See infra* p. 173.

[48] *See* S. Thumma and J. Kirchmeier, "The Lexicon Has Become a Fortress: The United States Supreme Court's Use of Dictionaries," 47 *Buff. L. Rev.* 227 (1999).

[49] *See* Lewison, *supra* p. 42, note 130 at 90.

[50] *See* D. Mellinkoff, "The Myth of Precision and the Law Dictionary," 31 *UCLA L. Rev.* 423 (1983).

dictionary is simply an historical record, not necessarily all-inclusive, of the meanings which words in fact *have* borne, in the judgment of the editors, in the writings of reputable authors.[51]

The dictionary determines what meaning *may* be given to the text; it does not determine what meaning *must* be given to the text. It is a linguistic tool, not a criterion for understanding the legal language of the text. The words of a statute are not fortresses to be conquered with dictionaries.[52] The same is true of all types of legal texts.

3. CANONS OF INTERPRETATION

The Canons Reveal Nonlegal Semantic Meaning

Most legal systems have canons for understanding legal language.[53] For example, it is an accepted canon that the meaning of a word or phrase depends on its environment: *noscitur a sociis*. Legal systems also commonly assume the "no" of the language from the totality of its "yes" (*expressio unius est exclusio alterius*). Similarly, if a legal text contains a string of details followed by a general phrase—like a statute about "trucks, buses, private cars, or other vehicles"—one can assume that the general phrase, "other vehicles," includes additional items of the same type (vehicles that move on land, not ships and airplanes): *ejusdem generis*. What is the legal status of these canons? Some treat them as legal norms that interpreters should use to determine a text's legal meaning. I disagree. The canons reflect semantic rules, not legal rules.[54] They are not unique to law but rather are rules of general applicability for understanding language. They are based on experience, logic, and correct use of language. They are common to all legal systems and systems of interpretation. They belong to the field of language.[55] They help determine the range of a legal text's semantic possibilities. They determine the meaning that the text is capable of bearing.[56] They do not determine the legal meaning that the text bears. As Hart and Sachs said:

[51] Hart and Sachs, *supra* p. 3, note 3 at 1190.

[52] *Cabell v. Markham*, 148 F. 2d 737, 739 (2d. Cir. 1945).

[53] *Infra* p. 170. On the distinction between linguistic canons and textual canons, see W. Eskridge and P. Frickey, "Statutory Interpretation as Practical Reasoning," 42 *Stan. L. Rev.* 321 (1990).

[54] Sunstein, *supra* p. 13, note 31 at 454 ("[T]hey operate as rules of syntax or grammar").

[55] Bennion, *supra* p. 77, note 64 at 897. Justice M. Cheshin distinguishes between "weak" and "strong" rules of interpretation. The former derive from language, logic, and reason. The latter derive from the society's fundamental principles. H.C. 5012/97 *Matach Health, Support, and Welfare Services Ltd. v. Ministry of Health*, 52(1) P.D. 49, 61.

[56] Law Comm. (no. 21), *The Interpretation of Statutes*.

Maxims should not be treated, any more than a dictionary, as saying what meaning a word or group of words *must* have in a given context. They simply answer the question whether a particular meaning is linguistically permissible.[57]

Canons are important because they determine the limits beyond which, in the absence of a private lexicon, interpretation cannot operate. They are tools in the larger project of determining the text's legal meaning.

Some scholars object to linguistic canons on the grounds that they contradict each other, to the point where they become useless.[58] Those scholars are correct to object to attempts to use the canons to determine the legal meaning of a text,[59] but there is nothing wrong with using the canons to understand the semantic meaning of a text.[60] The canons are a compilation of rules of grammar and language.[61] Viewed as tools to help understand the meaning that a text can bear in its language, the canons are of some use.

"No" Derived from the Language of "Yes"

The structure and logic[62] of language allow us to infer the "no" of the text from its "yes": *expressio unius est exclusio alterius.*[63] This canon is an example of implicit semantic meaning, which may be negative or positive. When we can infer a negative meaning from the "yes" of the text, we can rule out the existence of a gap and recognize the existence of a negative arrangement. As Cross writes:

> It is doubtful whether the maxim does any more than draw attention to a fairly obvious linguistic point, *viz.* that in many contexts the mention of some matters warrants an inference that other cognate matters were intentionally excluded.[64]

Of course, logic governs the scope of this canon. If I say that people are mortal, you should not infer that animals live forever. Even when it is pos-

---

[57] Hart and Sachs, *supra* p. 3, note 3 at 1191.

[58] Llewellyn, *supra* p. 54, note 191 at 395.

[59] *See* Frankfurter, *supra* p. 19, note 50 at 544.

[60] W. Lattin, "Legal Maxims and Their Use in Statutory Interpretations," 26 *Geo. L.J.* 1 (1937); G. Miller, "Pragmatics and the Maxims of Interpretation," 1990 *Wis. L. Rev.* 1179, 1202.

[61] The different canons can contradict each other. Resolving the conflict is done according to criteria external to the canons themselves. In purposive interpretation, it is done according to the purpose of the text.

[62] Sutherland, *supra* p. 78, note 70 at 203.

[63] E. Mureinik, "Expressio Unius: Exclusio Alterius," 104 *S.Afr. L.J.* 264 (1987).

[64] Cross, *supra* p. 3, note 3 at 140.

sible to infer "no" from "yes," that choice does not necessarily become the text's legal meaning. Perhaps the "yes" itself is included merely as a precaution, to remove doubt (*ex abundanti cautela*);[65] perhaps it is only as an example; perhaps it reflects sloppy writing.[66]

The General from the Specific

Another accepted canon says that if the text contains a string of specifics followed by a general, supplementary expression, one may understand the general expression to extend to additional specifics of the kind enumerated in the text. For example, if a contract provides that a renter is not liable for rent in case of fire, flood, storm, or other unexpected incident, the phrase "other unexpected incident" may not be understood to include a situation in which it was impossible to use the rental because of construction problems.[67] This linguistic canon says that a list of specifics may restrict an otherwise general supplementary phrase. The canon employs logical deduction, based on common sense and life experience, to arrive at implicit meaning. It is not, however, the criterion for determining the text's legal meaning, which depends on the purpose at the core of the norm.

[65] Bennion, *supra* p. 6, note 13 at 976.

[66] *See* A. Samuels, "The Eiusdem Generis Rule in Statutory Interpretation," [1984] *Statute L. Rev.* 180.

[67] *Saner v. Bilton* (1878) 7 Ch. D. 815.

CHAPTER FIVE

The Purposive Component
of Purposive Interpretation

1. THE ESSENCE OF PURPOSE

A Normative Conception of Purpose

According to purposive interpretation, the purpose of a text is a normative concept. It is a legal construction that helps the interpreter understand a legal text. The author of the text created the text. The purpose of the text is not part of the text itself. The judge formulates the purpose based on information about the intention of the text's author (subjective purpose) and the "intention" of the legal system (objective purpose).

According to purposive interpretation, interpretation is analysis of the text, not psychoanalysis of its author.[1] The judge analyzes the text using interpretive criteria formulated based on both subjective and objective sources. The purpose of a will is not to realize the intent of the testator. The purpose of a will is to distribute the testator's property. The testator's intent is a means of formulating how his or her property will be distributed. The same is true of contracts. The purpose of a contract is not to realize the joint intent of the parties. The purpose of a contract is to achieve the contractual objective. The joint intent of the parties is a means of understanding the contractual objective. Similarly, the purpose of a statute is to bring about a certain kind of social change. The interpreter learns about this change from, among other things, the intentions of the members of the legislative body, but legislative intent is distinct from purpose. Justice Frankfurter expressed this idea well:

> Legislation has an aim; it seeks to obviate some mischief, to supply an inadequacy, to effect a change of policy, to formulate a plan of government. That aim, that policy, is not drawn like nitrogen, out of the air; it is evinced in the language of the statute, as read in the light of other external manifes-

---

[1] *Cf.* H.C. 246/81 *Respect Association v. Broadcast Authority*, 35(4) P.D. 1, 17: "The decision must be made according to the analysis of the statute, not the psychoanalysis of the legislator" (Barak, J.).

tations of purpose. That is what the judge must seek and effectuate, and he ought not to be led off the trail by tests that have overtones of subjective design.[2]

The purpose of a constitution is not to realize the intent of the founders. The purpose of a constitution is to provide a foundation for the social structure and its fundamental values. An interpreter may learn of this purpose from, among other sources, the intent of the founders. The purpose is a goal; the intention (of the author and of the "system") is a source from which the interpreter can learn about the goal. Determining the purpose of a text always combines objective and subjective purpose.

The Purpose of the Text as the Relevant Context

The meaning of a word depends on its context.[3] The context of the language consists of overlapping circles of diverse contexts. The number of contexts is infinite; each context has a context of its own, and so on. Contexts can be semantic, social, historical, and/or value-dependent, to name a few types. A judge must choose the relevant context from this infinite list. What is the relevant context? How does the relevant context of a legal text differ from the relevant context of a literary or musical text? I say that the relevant context of a legal text is the data that provides information about the text's purpose. We look to the language of the text, other texts, the history of the text, and the general values of the system in order to learn about the purpose of the text. The purpose of a legal text is the only relevant context for its interpretation as a normative creation.

Context in legal interpretation does not shed light on the words from the point of view of their beauty or the way they sound.[4] The context of a legal text helps explain the meaning of the words from the point of view of their purpose. The different contexts—the totality of the text's language, similar texts, history, and the legal system's fundamental values—are relevant only insofar as they help the interpreter learn about the purpose of the text. A context that is not connected (directly or indirectly) to the purpose may help interpret a text as a work of literature, but it cannot help interpret the text as a normative construction.

[2] Frankfurter, *supra* p. 19, note 50 at 538.

[3] Wróblewski, *supra* p. 4, note 6 at 91.

[4] On the role of aesthetics in law, see P. Schlag, "The Aesthetics of American Law," 115 *Harv. L. Rev.* 1049 (2002).

Dialogue between the Intention of the Reasonable Author and of the System and the Intention of the Author

Purposive interpretation is a kind of dialogue between the intention of the reasonable author and of the system and the intention of the actual author. Interpreters play a dual role in this dialogue. On the one hand, they live in the present, and their understanding (consciously or unconsciously) is a product of the legal system's contemporary values. On the other hand, interpreters try to understand a text that was created in the past. They seek to discover the intention at the core of the text. Interpreters continuously "move" back and forth between the past and the present. They take into account the historical intent of the text's author and the modern intention of the system. Based on these two kinds of intentions, they formulate the purpose at the core of the text.

"Purpose That the Text Is Designed to Achieve"

It is sometimes said that purposive interpretation is based on the purpose that the norm is "designed" to achieve.[5] The word "designed" may create the mistaken impression that it refers to the (subjective) purpose that the author of the text designated. The purpose that the text is designed to achieve is a normative concept that the judge determines. In order to make this determination, the judge looks to the purpose that the author of the text designated to it (authorial intent; subjective purpose) as well as the purpose that the system designated for that text (systemic intention; objective purpose). This decision is not at the interpreter's absolute discretion. Purposive interpretation sets guidelines for determining the purpose that a text is designed to achieve. These guidelines set the boundaries of subjective purpose and determine the relationship between the two kinds of purposes, to form the ultimate purpose of the text.

The Immediate Application of Purposive Presumptions and the Lack of a Uniform Starting Point

Subjective purpose and objective purpose apply to all legal texts. The purposive presumptions that derive from them—presumptions of subjective and objective purpose—always apply. They apply immediately, regardless of whether or not the text is "plain." Judges presume that the purpose of

[5] Gottlieb, *supra* p. 3, note 1 at 105.

a legal text is both to realize the intent of its author and to realize the intent of the reasonable author and the values of the system (intention of the system). Although these two presumptions may contradict each other, they are simultaneously applicable. Judges resolve the contradiction between them, when such contradiction exists, only at the end of the interpretive process. Judges examine the text and the circumstances surrounding it to learn about the content of subjective purpose and how credible the information about it is. They decide how much weight to give subjective and objective intent according to the type of text. These elements are taken into account in formulating ultimate purpose.

Two principles govern this process. *First*, both subjective purpose and objective purpose accompany the interpretive process from beginning to end. We cannot say that a judge interprets a particular kind of text—like a contract or will—according to the intention of the text's author but interprets another kind of text—like a constitution or statute—according to the intention of the system. There is always the possibility that circumstances will require the judge to accord heavy weight to the intention of the system in the interpretation of a will or contract, or to the intention of the author in the interpretation of a constitution or statute. The judge decides how much weight to give the subjective or objective purpose at the end of the interpretive process. *Second*, there is no principled starting point that gives preference to subjective or objective purpose. Both purposes are immediately applicable. Each judge may choose the starting point that seems best to him or her. In the absence of information to the contrary, the judge may end at this starting point. When the judge discovers information to the contrary, however, he or she must continue with the interpretive process. The judge must evaluate whether the presumption with which he or she began the interpretive process—objective or subjective purpose—remains valid, or whether the new information rebuts the original presumption.

2. MULTIPLE PURPOSES

A Legal Text Has More Than One Purpose

Purposive interpretation assumes that every legal text has multiple objective and subjective purposes.[6] Sometimes, these purposes exist at identical levels of abstraction (horizontal purposes). Usually, however, the different purposes exist at varying levels of abstraction (vertical purposes). Often, the relationship among the purposes is such that the judge can formulate

[6] Sunstein, *supra* p. 13, note 31 at 427.

the ultimate purpose used to determine the text's legal meaning without resorting to judicial discretion. Sometimes, the purposes contradict each other. In those cases, the interpreter must resolve the conflict while achieving synthesis and harmony among the various purposes. At times, he or she will have to exercise discretion.

Multiple Subjective and Objective Purposes

The phenomenon of multiple purposes exists in the context of both subjective and objective purpose. In the context of subjective purpose, the author of a text often seeks to achieve a number of objectives through the text he or she creates. Consider a testator. A number of ideas are likely to cross his or her mind during the writing of a will, beginning with the abstract idea of distributing property and including the details of the division. Or, consider a legislature that seeks to achieve a number of objectives through a piece of legislation. It may pass a tax statute with the aspiration of increasing revenue and readjusting the social distribution of wealth. Sometimes, a statute has a number of purposes because the members of the legislative body could not agree on a single purpose but did agree on a single text.[7] The same is true for objective purpose. It may be the purpose that the author, had he or she acted as a reasonable person, would have aspired to achieve. It may be the purpose that a reasonable author of a text would have envisioned; it may be the purpose natural to a particular kind of norm. It may be the purpose that actualizes the fundamental values of the system, like liberty and public welfare. All the purposes appear before the interpreter as presumptions whose status is determined by the weight assigned to each.

Horizontal Purposes

Purposes are horizontal when they exist at the same level of abstraction. Take a statute that addresses the legal competence of minors. The statute is intended to achieve, *inter alia*, two horizontal purposes: *first*, to protect minors and allow them to act; and *second*, to protect the interests of third parties transacting with minors. Similarly, a rape statute imposing criminal liability for having sexual relations, under certain circumstances, with someone who is mentally disabled, is intended to achieve two horizontal purposes: *first*, to protect a mentally disabled individual from being exploited; and *second*, to allow a mentally disabled individual to have sexual relations and start a family. Legislation requiring a writing in order to com-

---

[7] *See* Grundfest and Pritchard, *supra* p. 99, note 14.

plete a legal act seeks to prevent recklessness and to secure the existence of means of proof (statute of frauds). We can analyze any normative text similarly. A constitution, for example, protects both the reputation of the individual and his or her freedom of speech. These two basic values exist at the same level of abstraction.

Vertical Purposes

Vertical purposes exist at different levels of abstraction. Two parameters determine the levels of abstraction:[8] *first*, the level of particularity or generality of the subject regulated or addressed; and *second*, the extent to which the content at the core of the normative arrangement is value-laden. These parameters create a range of levels of abstraction.

Consider the objective purpose of a contract. At the lowest level of abstraction, the objective purpose focuses on the parties to a contract, trying to determine what intent to attribute to them, as though they had expressed an opinion on the matter. At an intermediate level of abstraction, the focus is not on the parties to the contract but rather on reasonable parties. It asks what objective purpose the parties would have had, had they acted as reasonable people. At this level of abstraction, there is no conjecture as to what the parties' intent would have been, based on the data available, but rather a conjecture as to what reasonable parties would have intended. Interpreters introduce a reasonable person into the circumstances of the contract, but not into the traits and characteristics of the actual parties. At the next level of abstraction, interpreters focus on the purpose typical of that particular kind of contract. They disengage from the specific contract and focus on the purpose that characterizes a category or type of contract. At the highest level of abstraction, interpreters disengage from the category or type of contract and determine an objective purpose of the contract that reflects the legal system's fundamental values. This last inquiry will find the objective purpose of the contract to be the achievement of equality, justice, and other fundamental values.

A similar analysis applies to a piece of legislation at various levels of abstraction. At a low level of abstraction, the statute's purpose is the individual objectives that the statute is designed to achieve. At a higher level, interpreters focus on the objectives that a statute of that particular category or type is designed to achieve. At the highest level are the fundamental values of the system which constitute the general objective purpose shared by all legislation. This last purpose is a kind of "normative umbrella" that extends to all norms in the system.

[8] *See* Charny, *supra* p. 49, note 160.

The Relationship between the Different Purposes: Presumption of Harmony

Usually, the various purposes—and the presumptions that derive from them—are in harmony. The subjective intent of the author of the text, at its various levels, points to a clear subjective purpose that guides interpreters. Usually, the author of the text is a person or entity who acts reasonably, so that the individual's subjective intent is in harmony with the objective intent of the system, and the collective intent of the group that created the text (as in the legislature or the parties to a multi-party contract) is in harmony with the collective intent of society. In these cases, the various purposes blend, and there is no need for interpretive discretion. The overwhelming majority of instances of interpretation belong to this category. The interpretive result is clear, and the issue does not make it to court. In light of the frequency of this kind of situation, we can acknowledge a double presumption: *On the one hand,* we presume that the subjective intent of the author is in harmony with, and seeks to realize, the objective "intention" of the system. *On the other hand,* we presume that the objective intention of the system reflects, and seeks to realize, the subjective intent of the author. This double presumption is, of course, rebuttable. As long as it holds, however, interpreters may ground themselves in either subjective or objective purpose, as they please. At the end of the day, these two purposes, along with the ultimate purpose interpreters infer from them, will lead to the same result.

The Relationship between the Different Purposes: Complementation and Harmony

In most cases, the various purposes—and the presumptions derived from them—complement each other, reinforce each other, and help explain each other. For example, a factual inquiry into the author's intent may raise doubts about the scope of that intent. Even if there is no doubt about the facts, there may be discord among the various levels (horizontal or vertical) of the author's subjective intent. In these cases, objective purpose is likely to help interpreters. Interpreters assume that the author of the text acts as a reasonable person, within the bounds of the legal system and its values, and that he or she seeks to actualize the values of the system. This presumption helps resolve the doubt over subjective purpose: interpreters choose the subjective purpose—from among the various purposes in discord—that is consistent with objective purpose. Similarly, the various levels of objective purpose may, in a given set of facts, lead to different results.

In this case, interpreters choose the objective purpose in accord with the presumption that the norm's purpose is to realize the intent of its creator.

There is continuous back-and-forth between the different purposes, each of which influences the other. Interpreters seek completion and unity, not conflict. Consider a testator who orders her property divided among "my children." Assume that it is not clear whether she bequeaths her property to the children she had on the day she wrote her will, or the children she had on the day she died. Interpreters can resolve this doubt by referring to the intention of the system to guarantee equality among the testator's children. The same is true if the provision about "her children" appears in a statute about succession. When there is doubt about legislative intent, interpreters resolve it based on the system's "intention" to distribute property equally.

Contradiction between Purposes

Usually, the multiplicity of purposes creates no interpretive difficulty, either because all the purposes lead to the same semantic meaning as applied to a given set of facts, or because some of the purposes are so different and distant from the others, that they have no influence on the semantic meanings relevant to a given set of facts. Of course, an interpreter must make every effort to resolve contradictions among the different purposes. That is the uniqueness of purposive interpretation—it takes all the purposes into account and tries to synthesize them.

What happens when these efforts fail?[9] In this case, the interpreter must choose among the conflicting purposes. Purposive interpretation does not give the interpreter discretion in all situations of this kind. It equips the interpreter with presumptions about the purpose of the text and seeks to establish a normative arrangement that determines criteria (in the form of both rules and principles) for resolving the contradiction among these different presumptions. Only in the rare cases in which these criteria do not exist does the interpreter retain discretion. Some of these criteria may be common to every normative text, while others are tailored to specific kinds of normative texts (constitution, statute, contract, will). Legal literature and jurisprudence have yet to develop the subject adequately. We might propose a number of criteria common to all legal texts, something that the common law has yet to recognize. My work here is a proposal for further thought; others may take a different approach.

---

[9] This is most likely to happen when the conflict between the purposes is deliberate, as in the case of a legislative body whose members agreed on a uniform text but not on uniform purposes.

I propose that interpreters should always prefer purpose at a low level of abstraction (either subjective or objective) to purpose at a higher level of abstraction. When choosing between conflicting purposes at a given level of abstraction, interpreters should select the purpose that harmonizes with a purpose at a higher level of abstraction. At a given level of abstraction, a primary purpose should prevail over a subordinate purpose and a specific purpose over a general purpose. In the context of subjective purpose, this ranking assumes that the information about the various purposes is of equal reliability. When the reliability of information about subjective purpose varies, interpreters should prefer the purpose about which the most credible information exists. When the conflict occurs at the (high) level of abstraction engaging the principles of the legal system, the interpreter should resolve the contradiction by balancing (horizontally or vertically) the conflicting values. In doing so, he or she should take into account, *inter alia*, the weight and status of the conflicting values at the point of decision.

Contradictions between Subjective and Objective Purposes

The central question that purposive interpretation resolves is the relationship between subjective and objective purpose. The interpreter should synthesize and harmonize between these purposes, so that one complements the other. But what happens when harmony is impossible? What happens when the presumptions about subjective purpose contradict the presumptions about objective purpose? How is the ultimate purpose determined? In principle, purposive interpretation says that the resolution depends on the kind of text: constitution or statute, or constitution or statute as opposed to will or contract; new or old text; a text defining a specific issue or a text that seeks to regulate an entire field; a text created and interpreted in the same legal system, or a text created in one system but interpreted in another; a text based on rules or a text based on principles. During interpretation, the difference in type of text affects the relationship between authorial intent and the intention of the system.[10] Purposive interpretation is thus sensitive to the essence and type of each text, in an attempt to give expression to the social needs that each text addresses.

No "Early" or "Late" in the Different Purposes

Is there "early" or "late" among the different purposes? Must interpreters start with presumption X, and only after exhausting it, move on to pre-

[10] *Infra* p. 183.

sumption Y? Purposive interpretation says no. The process of interpretation is holistic. Interpreters move in a circle in which the point of departure is irrelevant, so long as they exhaust the entire process by circling back to the starting point. Thus, in interpreting wills, interpreters may start with objective purpose and only then turn to subjective purpose. They may take a "shortcut" by presuming that the intention of the system is also the intent of the testator. However, if this presumption is rebutted, they must continue the interpretive process to its exhaustion.

Lack of Purpose

Are there legal texts that do not contain a purpose relevant to interpreting the text in which the norm is trapped? My answer is no. There is always a purpose to guide the interpreter in pinpointing the legal meaning of a text along the range of its semantic meanings. There may be situations in which the intent of the text's author is not relevant to interpreting the text in a specific factual context. This may happen when the author's intent existed at a low level of abstraction, and it is not relevant to resolving the interpretive problem that the judge faces. Sometimes it is impossible to know the intent of the text's author, as in the case of a referendum. How can we know the intent of all the voters? Similarly, interpreters face special problems in trying to locate the subjective intent at the core of a custom. In these and other cases, the interpreter is faced with a factual situation in which there is no information about the subjective purpose of the text. This is never the case, however, with regard to the objective purpose. It always exists, and it is always relevant. We can always answer the question of what a reasonable author would have envisioned. We can always construct an objective purpose that actualizes the fundamental values of the system. The generality of these values and the high level of abstraction at which they operate always permit a judge to formulate an objective purpose relevant to resolving a concrete legal problem. We will never face a situation of the absence of purpose.

CHAPTER SIX

Subjective Purpose

AUTHORIAL INTENT

1. THE ESSENCE OF SUBJECTIVE PURPOSE

Real Intent

The subjective purpose of a legal text is the subjective intent of its author. When the author is an individual, the subjective purpose is his or her intent. For a will, it is the intent of the testator. When two authors create the text, the subjective intent is the joint intent of the two authors. This is the case for most contracts, where subjective intent is the joint intent of the contracting parties. When the author of the text is a collective body, it is the shared collective intent of that entity (members of a constitutional assembly; members of the legislative body). This intent of the text's author(s) includes the values, objectives, interests, policy, aims, and function that the author(s) sought to actualize. The subjective purpose reflects a true intent of the author at the time the text was created. It is a physical-biological-psychological-historical fact. It is an "archaeological" fact.[1] It is a "genetic" fact.[2] It is a "static" fact. It does not change with time. It is not the intent that the author would have had, had he or she thought about the matter, nor is it the intent of the reasonable person; these types of intent constitute objective purpose. Subjective purpose is the "real" intent of the text's author, the intent the author(s) had, as a matter of fact, at the time he or she (or they) created the text. In contrast to objective intent, which, at a high level of abstraction, is largely the same for all legal texts, subjective intent is specific to each and every text, and it is established at the creation of the text. Interpreting a legal text according to subjective purpose is *ex tunc* interpretation. It brings us back to the meaning that the text would have had, had it been interpreted on the day it was created.

---

[1] For a discussion of "archaeological" in this context, *see* Aleinikoff, *supra* p. 34, note 102.

[2] The German tradition uses the phrase "genetic interpretation" to refer to subjective interpretation. *See* R. Alexy and R. Dreier, "Statutory Interpretation in the Federal Republic of Germany," in *Interpreting Statutes: A Comparative Study* 85 (D.N. MacCormick and R. Summers eds., 1991).

Real Intent, Not Hypothetical Intent

Subjective purpose is the real, not hypothetical, intent of the text's author. The phrase "hypothetical intent" is ambiguous. In *one* sense, it refers to a situation in which true intent is unknown, but the interpreter makes a (hypothetical) assumption about what it is. As long as this assumption is based on the legal community's life experience, it can serve as a presumption about true intent. It becomes one way of proving the author's true intent. A *second* meaning of "hypothetical intent" is an intent that the text's author never had in fact, but that can be attributed to him or her on the assumption that he or she would have had the intent, had he or she thought about the matter. This is individual-hypothetical intent.[3] Because this intent is not real but conjectured, it constitutes part of the objective, not subjective, purpose of the text, at a low level of abstraction. A *third* meaning of "hypothetical intent" is an intent that the author did not really have (not true intent), and that cannot be attributed to him or her, had he or she thought about the issue (not individual-hypothetical intent). However, it is the intent that the text's author would have had as a reasonable person (generic-hypothetical).[4] Because it is not true intent, it does not form part of subjective purpose. It is conjectured intent, operating at a few levels of abstraction, and it constitutes part of the text's objective purpose.

Hidden Intent: Will Theory and Expression Theory

Is hidden intent part of subjective interpretation? That depends on how hidden intent is defined. If hidden intent means an intent to which the author of the text did not give expression, and that remained concealed in his or her heart, then it forms no part of subjective purpose. Such intent, because of its hidden nature, can never be known to the interpreter. The question must then be whether we can take into account a hidden intent that, at some stage of interpretation, is revealed. In this context, intent is hidden if the information about it comes from sources external to the language of the text. Can interpreters ever consider that intent? The question calls up the familiar debate between "will theory" and "expression theory,"[5] namely whether interpreters can consider the true intent of the author if they learn it from sources external to the text (will theory), or whether interpreters should only consider intent that can be learned from the text it-

---

[3] M.L. Fellows, "In Search of Donative Intent," 73 *Iowa L. Rev.* 611, 612 (1992).

[4] *Id.* at 613.

[5] *See, supra,* p. 29.

self (expression theory). Purposive interpretation rejects expression theory. It does not mandate that information about (subjective) intent come from the language of the text alone. The requirement is just that it be possible to realize the intent through the language of the text, even if the information about intent comes from extrinsic sources.

The real question about hidden intent is this: Under what circumstances may an interpreter, in formulating the intent of the text's author, take into account an intent learned from sources external to the text? My answer is that extrinsic information may be used, but its weight should be calculated according to the circumstances of each case. Consider a testator who makes a will. After his or her death, a letter explaining his or her intent surfaces. This information is likely to be of significant weight in formulating the testator's intent. Taking it into consideration will not harm anyone, because no one has a reliance interest. Consider a contract between A and B, for which the relevant intent is the joint intent of the parties. If A knew the hidden intent of B at the time the contract was created, such intent is of great importance, and interpreters should accord it respectable weight.[6] What if B did not know of A's hidden intent?

Interpreters agree that they need not take into account the intent of a person that is unknown to another and that need not be known to the other. It is a concealed intent, which interpreters need not consider, even according to the will theory. Less clear is the following case: A person has an intent that is unknown to the other party, but the other party could learn about such intent by taking reasonable measures. Should an interpreter consider the concealed intent under those circumstances? The question does not arise in a will, because, in the absence of reliance, there is no other party that needs to know. The question does, however, arise in contract law. One party to a contract has an intent unbeknownst to the other, but the other could discover it by taking reasonable measures. In that situation, can the intent of the one party be considered the parties' joint intent? Comparative law sources say yes,[7] and appropriately so.

Presumption of Intent

Subjective intent appears before the interpreter as a presumption that the purpose of the text is to realize the intent of its author. This intent is an issue of fact, to be proven in the way any other fact is proven. The burden of proof generally lies with the one who claims the existence of a certain

[6] J. Murray, "The Realism of Behaviorism under the Uniform Commercial Code," 51 *Or. L. Rev.* 269, 272 (1972).

[7] *Infra* p. 328.

intent, to be proven by a preponderance of the evidence. Presumptions help determine subjective intent, because some of them are factual presumptions (*praesumptio hominis*), based on life experience and common sense. Other presumptions are legal presumptions, like the presumption that the author of the text acts as a reasonable person or that the intent of the author is to realize the intention of the system. The different presumptions that shape objective purpose are likely to provide information about subjective purpose, as well. Both the legal and the factual presumptions of subjective purpose can be rebutted by proof that they do not accord with the intent of the text's author or if they point to an intention that does not appear to have existed, as a historical fact, in the mind of the text's author.

Subjective Purpose and the Reasonable Person

English common law understands the intent of a text's author according to the criteria of the reasonable person.[8] In interpreting a will, therefore, a judge asks what the intent would be of a reasonable person standing in the shoes of the testator.[9] In interpreting a contract, a judge asks what the intent would be of a reasonable person standing in the shoes of each of the parties.[10] For a statute, the question is how a reasonable person would understand legislative intent.[11] Purposive interpretation takes a different view. In considering subjective purpose, that is, authorial intent, it looks for the true intent of the author, not the intent of a reasonable person. It is not clear why we should consider the intent of a reasonable testator, rather than the intent of the actual testator whose will is the subject of interpretation.[12] It is also hard to understand why a court should validate the "objective" intent of contractual parties, that is, the intent that reasonable parties to a con-

---

[8] Steyn, *supra* p. 18, note 49.

[9] O.W. Holmes, "The Theory of Legal Interpretation," 12 *Harv. L. Rev.* 417 (1899). Holmes applied the objective approach to the interpretation of all texts, including wills.

[10] *See* Lord Wilberforce's opinion in *Reardon-Smith, supra* p. 44, note 142 at 789: "When one speaks of the intention of the parties to the contract one is speaking objectively—the parties cannot themselves give direct evidence of what their intention was—and what must be ascertained is what is to be taken as the intention which reasonable people would have had if placed in the situation of the parties." *See also* Lewison, *supra* p. 42, note 130 at 2, 8.

[11] Cross, *supra* p. 3, note 3 at 26.

[12] *See* Justice H. Cohen's comments in C.A. 357/61 *Executor of D. Boger's Estate v. A. Boger*, 16 P.D. 150, 159: "I reject the claim that we should infer the intent of the deceased from what the reasonable person, the "just" person . . . or the person blessed with wisdom . . . would bequeath: this view is taken, perhaps, when there are no clear facts about the intentions and desire to which the deceased gave expression, either in words or deeds; but when the facts prove the intent of the testator, these assumptions are of no use."

tract would have, rather than their joint subjective intent. We may consider objective perspectives on a contract or will in the absence of information about the subjective intent of the testator or in the absence of a joint intent of the contractual parties. Where we can discover these real intents, however, why ignore them? Objective perspectives seek to protect reliance interests, but if two parties have a joint subjective intent, why ignore it and replace it with a reasonable person's intent? The same is true of interpreting statutes. We can reason, as objective systems of interpretation do, that legislative intent is irrelevant, and that the interpretive criterion is the meaning that a reasonable reader would give a statute. If we agree, however, that legislative intent is an appropriate interpretive criterion, why not identify this (subjective) intent? Doesn't it deceive the public to continue to use the terminology of legislative intent, without, in fact, taking it seriously?[13]

Purposive interpretation tells the truth. To the extent that it considers authorial intent—and that extent varies with the type of text being interpreted—it deals with the "real" intent of the author. It is not interested in the intent of a reasonable person standing in the author's shoes. The reasonable person is the subject of objective purpose, which occupies a respectable position in interpretation. The (subjective) intent of the author, however, refers to his or her actual intent, not the hypothetical intent of a reasonable person. Legal scholars have pointed to difficulties in determining this actual intent.[14] However, I am unpersuaded by claims that we can never know what the author of the text sought to accomplish,[15] and that the need for certainty and security in law justifies the objectification of intent.[16] If we can base criminal law—whose consequences are harsh for both the individual and society—on a subjective view of will and intent (*mens rea*), surely we can base a theory of interpretation on this subjective approach. Continental law takes a subjective approach to intent,[17] and it has yet to be proven to enjoy less certainty and security than English law. Indeed, English common law fails to consider authorial intent seriously enough.[18] Purposive interpretation takes subjective intent into account, though it does not always make it the prevailing factor. It considers con-

---

[13] For different explanations, *see* Cross, *supra* p. 3, note 3 at 29.

[14] *See* D.W. McLauchlan, "The New Law of Contract Interpretation," 19 *New Zealand U. L. Rev.* 147 (2000).

[15] Steyn, *supra* p. 18, note 49 at 80.

[16] *See President of India v. Jebsens (UK) Ltd.* [1991] 1 Lloyd's Rep. 1, 9.

[17] *See* sec. 133 of the B.G.B.; sec. 1362 of the Italian Civil Code; sec. 1425 of the Quebec Civil Code.

[18] There have been recent calls to take subjective intent more seriously, particularly in the field of contractual interpretation. *See supra* p. 124, note 14. Now, when one party to a contract knows the other's subjective intent, English law authorizes the subjective approach. *See* J. Steyn, "Contract Law: Fulfilling the Reasonable Expectations of Honest Men," 113 *Law*

jectured and hypothetical intent, too, as part of objective purpose. They are two separate and distinct sources that feed into and help to formulate the (ultimate) purpose.

Subjective Purpose in the Test of Time: Static Purpose

Subjective purpose is an event that occurred at a time and place. The author formulated his or her subjective intent at a point in time in the past. This (subjective) historical intent of the author is fixed in time. It does not change or shift position. It is not a dynamic intent whose character changes over the years. We could construct a system of interpretation that takes into consideration the changing subjective intent of the text's author.[19] Nothing inherent to subjective purpose would bar that. We might, for example, decide that a testator's intent includes intent at the time he or she makes the will as well as afterward. The same could be true of the joint intent of contracting parties. It is for each legal system to decide if it wishes to take these changes in subjective intent into consideration;[20] the theory of subjective purpose takes no position on the issue.[21] Purposive interpretation, however, considers the author's subjective intent at the time he or she created the text, not afterward.

Multiplicity of Subjective Purposes

A legal text generally has a number of subjective purposes. Sometimes the multiplicity is intentional, while at other times, it results from carelessness on the part of the author or the author's lawyer. When the author is a multi-member body, the different purposes are likely to be the produce of compromise between conflicting purposes. Sometimes, the members compromise over the textual language, agreeing not to agree over the purpose that the text is designed to achieve.[22] Rarely, if ever, does a text have a single

---

Q. Rev. 433, 440 (1997). Criticism of the bar against admitting evidence of intent has intensified, id., and now, judges may consult Hansard in interpreting statutes. See Pepper v. Hart [1993] 1 All E.R. 42. On resistance to the change in approach, see J. Steyn, "Pepper v. Hart: A Re-examination," 21 Oxford J. Leg. Stud. 59 (2001).

[19] Supra p. 37.

[20] The general practice is not to take into account the intent a testator has after making the will (post testamentum). T. Kip and H. Coing, Erbrecht 145 (13th ed. 1978).

[21] It would be wrong, however, to say that any intent formed after the creation of the text is part of objective purpose. I define objective purpose not to include this changing subjective purpose. Infra p. 148.

[22] See Grundfest and Pritchard, supra p. 99, note 14.

subjective purpose. We distinguish between the multiplicity of horizontal purposes and some vertical purposes:[23] In addressing horizontal purposes, an author uses the text to achieve a number of purposes at the same level of abstraction. In addressing vertical purposes, an author uses the text to achieve a number of purposes, one of which is more general and more abstract than the others. This multiplicity does not negate the importance of subjective intent. It does, however, indicate that subjective purpose usually does not lead to an unequivocal interpretive conclusion. The different purposes lead to different interpretive results. Subjective purpose alone is an insufficient framework for deciding among them. While subjective purpose is relevant to the interpretive process, by itself it is insufficient to complete the interpretive process.

2. ABSTRACT PURPOSE AND CONCRETE PURPOSE

Concrete Intention ("Consequentialist Intention")

Subjective purpose is the values, objectives, interests, policy, aims, and function that the author of the text sought to actualize. Sometimes, we can identify an intention by the author to reach a particular result in a given situation, through the text he or she created. Following Dworkin, I will call this "concrete intention"[24] (or consequentialist intention). For example, a testator bequeaths her property to "my children." It is proven that she understood "my children" to refer only to the children she had at the time she wrote the will. Similarly, a contract requires that a particular action be taken "soon." It is proven that the parties had an understanding about what "soon" means. A statute imposes strict liability for damage caused by "vehicles." The members of the legislature had an understanding that "vehicles" does not include trains. A constitution establishes "human dignity" as a constitutional right. The members of the constitutional assembly understood that "human dignity" does not include equality. In each of these cases, the author of the text had a concrete or consequentialist intention. Should it be taken into account within the bounds of subjective purpose? Should a judge consider authorial intent only insofar as it influences the meaning of the text (abstract subjective intent)?[25] Or,

---

[23] *Supra* p. 114.

[24] Dworkin, *supra* p. 22, note 63 at 48; R. Dworkin, *Freedom's Law: The Moral Reading of the American Constitution* (1996). It is also called interpretive intention. For a discussion of different kinds of intent, *see* K. Greenawalt, "Are Mental States Relevant for Statutory and Constitutional Interpretation?" 85 *Cornell L. Rev.* 1609 (2000); K. Greenawalt, *Statutory Interpretation: 20 Questions* (1999).

[25] *See* Dworkin, *supra* p. 22, note 63 at 48. Sometimes, Dworkin refers to this as seman-

should a judge also consider authorial intentions about the consequences of such meaning in a given situation (concrete or consequentialist intention; concrete subjective intention)? Should a judge take into account the author's expectations of how the text he or she wrote will be applied in given situations?[26]

Concrete Intention Revealing Abstract Subjective Purpose

Of course, we should take concrete intention into account as a source of information about abstract subjective purpose. Learning the consequentialist intention of the text's author is likely to give a judge information about the author's (abstract) subjective purpose. In that situation, a judge follows the path of the author, but in the reverse direction. The author formulated an abstract purpose which he or she clothed in semantic garb, while drawing conclusions about the results of its interpretation. The judge begins with the results that the author hoped to achieve and infers from it the abstract purpose that guided the author. Purposive interpretation recognizes this retracing of steps as proper judicial activity.

The Weight of Concrete Intention

How much weight should judges give concrete intention in interpreting a legal text? According to the "retracing steps" method, they should give it as much weight as abstract intention. Does purposive interpretation give it additional weight? Can't we say that the authorized interpreter of a text is the author of the text, and thus, judges should give his or her concrete intention a special status in interpretation? In case of a conflict between the interpretation that an interpreter gives a text, taking its (abstract) purpose into account, and the interpretation that the author gave the text (concrete intention), which interpretation trumps?

According to purposive interpretation, the judge—not the author—is the authorized interpreter of a legal text. Therefore, an author's concrete intention weighs in no more heavily than abstract purpose. The concrete (consequentialist) intention may influence the judge as a source of infor-

---

tic intention: *see* his position in R. Dworkin, "Comment," in A. Scalia, *A Matter of Interpretation: Federal Courts and the Law* 117 (1997). Marmor refers to these manifest and supplementary intentions about the meaning of the text as "aims and further intentions." A. Marmor, *Interpretation and Legal Theory* 166 (1992).

[26] Some refer to concrete intent as "intent" and to abstract purpose as "purpose." *See* Manning, *supra* p. 69, note 29 at 6; A. Cox, "Judge Learned Hand and the Interpretation of Statutes," 60 *Harv. L. Rev.* 370 (1947).

mation about abstract purpose—and no more. The weight judges give concrete intention as a determinant of abstract purpose depends on the type of text. Consider a will. In the general spirit of respecting the testator's wishes, the interpreter will accord his or her intent significant weight—and thus will accord significant weight to the testator's concrete intention, as well. Similarly, in the spirit of respecting the autonomy of the private will, a judge will accord significant weight to the joint intent of the parties to a contract. The judge will thus accord significant weight to the parties' joint concrete intention, as well.[27] A party would not be acting in good faith were he or she to claim that the judge should give the contract a different meaning from the very one that he or she, along with the other party, gave it.

When we get to a statute or constitution, however, abstract subjective purpose becomes less influential—meaning that the concrete intention of the legislators and founders becomes less influential, too. This result is consistent with the constitutional principle of separation of powers. The court has the constitutionally assigned task of interpreting statutes and the constitution. The "interpretive intention" of the authors of the statute or constitution cannot bypass this constitutional principle. Consider a statute outlawing escape from lawful custody. A prisoner on furlough for a few hours fails to return on time. According to the information available, the (abstract) purpose of the statute was to safeguard order and discipline in prison and to protect the public welfare. Assume the concrete intention of the legislature (consequentialist intention) was that a prisoner who fails to return from a furlough on time would not be considered to have escaped lawful custody. The interpreter, however, thinks that, in order to achieve the abstract purpose, failure to return from a furlough should be considered escape. How should he or she rule? In my opinion, the interpreter should give preference to the abstract purpose. He or she should recognize that members of the legislature can make mistakes. The interpreter should recognize the obligation to give the statute an interpretation that, as best he or she can tell, achieves the purpose of the statute—even if it contradicts the interpretation of the legislators. The principle of separation of powers mandates this result.[28] The same is true of interpreting a constitution. The

[27] *Restatement (Second) of Contracts* §201(1) (1981); Farnsworth, *supra* p. 101, note 21 at 245.

[28] *See* F.H. 36/84 *Teichner v. Air France French Airlines*, 41(1) P.D. 589, 619: "Referring to preparatory work is justified as a source of information about the general orientation of the statute. Personally, however, I doubt such reference is an appropriate means of finding a specific solution to a concrete problem troubling the interpreter. The judge is required to give that specific solution, not delegate the authority for finding it to someone else. It is important to refer to preparatory work, primarily to learn about the statute's basic orientation, not the interpretation that participants gave to the formulations they created" (Barak, J.);

interpretive intention of the members of the constitutional assembly is relevant only insofar as it teaches about their abstract intention.[29]

3. SUBJECTIVE PURPOSE AND THE PROBLEM OF MULTIPLE AUTHORS

One Author, Two Authors, and Multiple Authors

Legal texts vary by the number of authors and the relationship between them. The simplest text, from this point of view, is a will. It generally has one author, whose intent is the only one to be considered in determining subjective purpose. An exception is when two or more parties formulate a joint intent as to the content of a will. Generally, however, in terms of subjective purpose, a will is the simplest kind of normative text. Like a will, an administrative order or regulation is generally characterized by a single intent, that of the order's author. In this way, the order resembles a will, and in this way, both are distinct from a contract, in which judges must consider the joint intent of the parties.

In a two-party contract, intent is the joint intent of both parties; in a multi-party contract, it is the joint intent of all the contractual parties. In a two-party contract, the parties' intents are in opposition. One wants to sell, and the other wants to buy. The joint intent arises from the clash between these two opposing intents. Sometimes, the various intents in a contract—like a contract among shareholders forming the basis of a company's articles of association—do not clash but rather come together. A similar situation arises with an administrative order created by a number of authors, like a regulation enacted by more than one governmental official. In that case, the subjective purpose is the synthesis of this joint intent. Sometimes, however, the intent belongs to many participants, including those in favor of the text and those opposed, those who participated in the vote and those who abstained. Such is the case with a legislature. How do we determine the subjective intent of such a multi-member body? What is the relationship, in a bicameral legislature, between the respective intents of each house? How do we determine subjective intent in a referendum? Determining an author's (subjective) intent is not as easy at it seemed at first

---

H.C. 142/89, *Laor Movement, One Heart and A New Spirit v. Speaker of Knesset*, 44(3) P.D. 529, 544: "The judge looks to legislative history for information about the purpose of the legislation. He does not use it to research the interpretive viewpoints of members of Knesset [Parliament], how they understood or interpreted a concept or expression, or how they would solve the legal problem faced by the judge" (Barak, J.).

[29] Tribe, *supra* p. 15, note 38 at 54.

glance.[30] The more participants in formulating the text's intent, the more difficult it is to locate that intent. Interpreters sometimes reach the point where they realize that it is impossible to identify the subjective intent of the authors, and that they should abandon the search. Such is the case in interpreting a referendum.

The multiplicity of authors does not necessarily undermine the role of subjective purpose. If interpreters should consider the subjective purpose of a single author, they should also consider that of multiple authors. Additional authors simply make it harder to formulate the collective subjective intent. In extreme examples (like a referendum), it may be too difficult, pragmatically, to take subjective information into account, but the practical difficulty cannot negate the status that subjective intent has, in principle, in interpreting a text written by multiple authors.

The Interpreter's (Present) Ability to Discover (Past) Historical Intent

I reject the argument that it is impossible to discover an intent formulated in the past. That argument eradicates any basis for historical research. The gap in time prevents a contemporary interpreter from entering the shoes of an author who lived (many) years ago. A contemporary judge can, however, still learn about the intent that a text's author had in the past. The judge may not reach the precise intent as formulated on the day the author created the text, but he or she can nevertheless make a real attempt to arrive at the best substitute. A judge may not be a historian, but he or she can still try to discover the historical intent from long ago. We should draw a clear distinction between claims that we can never know an author's historical intent (which I reject) and claims that an author's historical intent is not the only criterion for interpreting a text (which I accept).

Legal Entity as Author

Sometimes the author is not of flesh and blood but rather an (abstract) legal entity, as in, for example, a contract in which one party is a corporation. What is the intent of a legal entity? Corporate law provides the answer: Every legal entity has organs or departments staffed by a person or persons whose intent serves as the intent of the legal entity.[31] The intent of a man-

---

[30] B. Bix, "Questions in Legal Interpretation," in *Law and Interpretation* 137 (A. Marmor ed., 1995).

[31] Marmor calls this "representative intentions." *See* Marmor, *supra* p. 3, note 1 at 159.

ager or director (in his or her official capacity) is the intent of the company. If we use that principle to determine liability in contract and tort law, we can use it for interpretation. This doctrine generally raises no special difficulties for finding the subjective purpose of a legal text's author, nor should it.

The Single Author

The simplest case of a single-author text is a will; other kinds of single-author texts include a regulation enacted by a single governmental agency, like an administrative order issued by an official, or a unilateral legal act by a single author, as when one party to a (two-party or multi-party) contract issues a notice of termination due to a flaw in contract formation. In these and other cases, we are looking for the intent of the single person whose will is at the core of the normative text. There are no special difficulties in this search. It is no different from trying to find out the subjective intent of any actor. Each legal system develops its own rules for proving this intent. Of course, law cannot penetrate the innermost recesses of the author's soul. It can, however, develop different methods of proof for learning about this intent. In this context, wills present real difficulties, because we interpret a will only after the testator has died. We cannot ask him or her about intent. There is no choice but to make do with other means of proof. The situation is easier when the author of the text is alive, and we can pump him or her for information about intent at the time the text was created. In principle, there is no reason not to accept the testimony of the (single) author as to his or her intent at the time the text was created.

Two Joint Authors

The next case examines the joint subjective purpose of two parties, as in a two-party contract, or a unilateral legal action (like a notice of termination due to a defect in the formation of a contract or due to breach) done jointly by two parties to a multi-party contract. The determinative intent is the joint intent of the two parties.[32] The interpreter cannot make do with the intent of one party, but rather must seek the joint intent of both.[33] Each legal system sets its own means of proof. For example, English common law forbids

[32] S.C. Damren, "A 'Meeting of the Minds'—The Greater Illusion," 15 *Law and Phil.* 271 (1996).

[33] Hegel insisted on this. G. Hegel, *Elements of the Philosophy of Right* 105 (A. Wood ed., H.B. Nisbet trans., 1991) (1821).

the parties to a contract containing a patent ambiguity from testifying as to their intent.[34] English courts are suspicious of each party's assertions of his or her intent, viewing them as an attempt by that party to support his or her position.[35] The English position fails to make an effective case against accepting a party's testimony as to his or her intent.[36] Courts should simply examine this type of evidence very carefully and avoid relying on it alone to determine the joint intent of both parties. Courts are presumably capable of distinguishing between facts establishing the unilateral intent of a party to a contract and facts establishing the joint intent of both parties.

Subjective Intent in a Parliament or Other Multi-Member Body

Things get more complicated when the author of a text is a multi-member body.[37] Such is the case for a statute passed by a parliament or a constitution adopted by members of a constitutional assembly. The author of the text is the abstract legal entity (the legislature, the assembly). How can we determine the intent of a multi-member body like a legislature? Some argue that it is impossible.[38] As Professor Curtis expressed, "It is a hallucination, this search for intent. The room is always dark. The hat we are looking for is often black. If it is there at all, it is on our own head."[39] Indeed, identifying the will of a multi-member body like a legislature is a complicated matter. We cannot make do just trying to uncover the intent of the members of the legislative body. Even if this attempt were to succeed, it would not help us formulate the intent of the body itself.

If we are trying to examine the intent of a collective body like a parliament, we should formulate a "theory of legislative organs" that will set rules deciding under which circumstances we should consider the intents of which members of the legislative body to be the intent of the legislature.[40] We might claim that a report by a committee responsible for a bill, to the extent that the members of the legislature were aware of the report, reflects leg-

[34] Lewison, *supra* p. 42, note 130 at 146.

[35] C. Staughton, "How Do the Courts Interpret Commercial Contracts?" 58 *Cam. L.J.* 303, 305 (1999).

[36] K. Keeler, "Direct Evidence of State of Mind: A Philosophical Analysis of How Facts in Evidence Support Conclusions Regarding Mental State," 1985 *Wis. L. Rev.* 435.

[37] Twining and Miers, *supra* p. 87, note 23 at 187. *See also* Greenawalt, *supra* p. 126, note 24.

[38] J. Waldron, *Law and Disagreement* (1999); J. Waldron, *The Dignity of Legislation* (1999); K. Shepsle, "Congress Is a 'They,' Not an 'It': Legislative Intent as Oxymoron," 12 *Int'l Rev. L. & Econ.* 239 (1992); F. Easterbrook, "Statute's Domain," 50 *U. Chi. L. Rev.* 533, 547 (1983) ("Each member [of Congress] may or may not have a design. The body as a whole, however, has only outcomes").

[39] C. Curtis, "A Better Theory of Legal Interpretation," 3 *Vand. L. Rev.* 407, 409 (1950).

[40] Dworkin, *supra* p. 22, note 63 at 48; Marmor, *supra* p. 126, note 25.

islative intent at the time the legislature voted to pass the bill proposed by the committee head. Most democratic countries do not have a rule like this.

We must understand the nature of the body in order to understand its intent. A parliament is composed of a large number of members, each of whom has motivations and intentions of his or her own. A parliament does not have a single intent, like the intent of an individual,[41] but that does not mean that it does not have an intent.[42] The intent of the parliament is the product of negotiation among its different members and of the final agreement they reached. It is the joint intent that brought about passage of the statute. If this intent—which by its nature operates at a high level of abstraction—does not exist, then how was the statute enacted? A parliament enacts statutes. As a matter of fact, there is a vote. The activity is willful and intentional. How could it be impossible to discover that will and intention? We do not want to turn the legislative process into a caricature. Despite the obstacles, the members of parliament managed to arrive at certain agreed-upon objectives,[43] and the statute passed. I concede that these objectives exist at a high level of abstraction; at times, it will be difficult to identify them; even if identified, they may not be responsive to the interpretive problem. The statute may very well have a "multiple personality"—the members of the legislative body agreed on the language of the text but not on its purpose, so that no uniform conception of purpose exists to be discovered.[44] But these facts are a far cry from the dogmatic conclusion that it is impossible to know the subjective intent of any piece of legislation. In a democratic regime with the proper political structure, the members of the legislative body formulate an objective or objectives, and if a majority reaches agreement,[45] it manages to vote and enact a statute designed to achieve these objectives.[46] Sometimes a legislature deliberately creates a multiple personality.[47] Generally, however, it does reach compromise about the purpose (at a high level of abstraction) at the core of the text. Negat-

---

[41] Dickerson, *supra* p. 3, note 3 at 68; J. Willis, "Statutory Interpretation in a Nutshell," 16 *Can. Bar Rev.* 1, 3 (1938).

[42] Greenawalt, *supra* p. 126, note 24; B. Bix, *Law, Language and Legal Determinacy* 183 (1993).

[43] Marmor calls them "shared intentions." Marmor, *supra* p. 3, note 1 at 162.

[44] *See* Grundfest and Pritchard, *supra* p. 99, note 14.

[45] G. MacCallum, "Legislative Intent," 75 *Yale L.J.* 754 (1966).

[46] J. Kernochan, "Statutory Interpretation: An Outline of Method," 3 *Dalhouse L.J.* 333, 335 (1976); Cowen, "The Interpretation of Statutes and the Concept of the Intention of the Legislator," 43 *T.H.R.H. Rev.* 374, 378 (1980); R. Posner, "Legal Formalism, Legal Realism, and the Interpretation of Statutes and the Constitution," 37 *Case W. Res. L. Rev.* 179, 195 (1986) ("Institutions act purposively, therefore they have purposes. A document can manifest a single purpose even though those that drafted and approved it had a variety of private motives and expectations").

[47] *See* Grundfest and Pritchard, *supra* p. 99, note 14.

ing the existence of this abstract and general purpose is like negating the legislation itself. Anyone seeking to reinforce the status of the legislative body and accord it its proper place in the constitutional structure should assume the existence of such purpose as a guiding principle.

The passage of a statute is often the result of negotiations among members of the legislature,[48] such that the reasons and objectives at the core of the statute's passage are diverse. For that reason, an interpreter should not seek the motivations that propelled the members of the legislative body to vote in favor of the statute but rather should focus on the general objectives they sought to achieve. Even if a member of parliament votes in favor of a statute to improve his or her standing with the electorate, that does not mean that the statute, as enacted, can never have an objective that the members of parliament sought to achieve. Some (general) goal usually exists. It is the objective to which most members of parliament agreed. It is their joint intent, even if each member reached it for his or her own reasons.[49] It is usually a general and abstract objective; it is usually one objective among many (multiple purposes); it is often an objective that does not help in the interpretive process, because the interpretive problem that the judge faces was never presented to the members of the legislative body.

Because of the limitations discussed above, we should be cautious in viewing subjective purpose as the end-all and be-all,[50] but we should not pretend that there is no identifiable intent at the core of the statute.[51] To do so would confuse the question of "Should a system of interpretation rely solely on subjective purpose?" (no) with the question of "Does a statute have a subjective purpose?" (yes). Despite the difficulties, subjective purpose—generally at a high level of abstraction—exists, and even if it is sometimes difficult to identify it, it is not impossible. The transition from the intent of a single author to that of a group of authors naturally

[48] Public choice theory points to a diverging system of considerations guiding members of the legislative body. *See* Eskridge, *supra* p. 41, note 126 at 26, 157; J. Macey, "Promoting Public-Regarding Legislation through Statutory Interpretation: An Interest Group Model," 86 *Colum. L. Rev.* 223 (1986); D. Farber and P. Frickey, "The Jurisprudence of Public Choice," 65 *Tex. L. Rev.* 873 (1987); D. Farber and P. Frickey, "Legislative Intent and Public Choice," 74 *Va. L. Rev.* 423 (1988). This literature, however, does not refute the existence of a general purpose at the core of the agreement among the members. Furthermore, the descriptions offered by public choice theorists often fail to reflect reality. *See* A. Mikva, "Foreword," 74 *Va. L. Rev.* 167 (1988).

[49] Marmor, *supra* p. 126, note 25 at 596.

[50] Eskridge, *supra* p. 41, note 126 at 29.

[51] S. Breyer, "On the Use of Legislative History in Interpreting Statutes," 65 *S. Cal. L. Rev.* 845, 866 (1992) ("To refuse to ascribe a 'purpose' to Congress in enacting statutory language simply because one cannot find three or four hundred legislators who have claimed it as a personal purpose, is rather like . . . refusing to believe in the existence of Oxford University because one can find only colleges").

complicates the attempt to identify intent, but the transition is not so dramatic as to negate the existence of any joint intent, the result of the compromise the group reached.[52] It is illogical to attribute intent to a single author while denying that of a group of authors.[53]

4. SOURCES OF SUBJECTIVE PURPOSE

Internal (Textual) Sources and Extrinsic (Contextual) Sources

A judge learns about the subjective purpose (intent, will) of a text from two sources. The *first* is internal—the text itself. There is no source more credible and more appropriate for learning about authorial intent than the text itself. Generally, the author begins with a thought (intent) that he or she seeks to realize through the text. The judge begins with the text and seeks to learn, in a reverse process, about the thought of the author. Both author and judge take the same path. The author starts with the intent that he or she expresses in language, while the judge starts with language as a means of learning about intent.[54] We therefore presume that the language of a text supplies information about its subjective purpose.

The *second* source is external to the text. It is the context in which the text was created. It includes the circumstances up to the creation of the text, and the totality of circumstances related to its creation. It may also include circumstances in existence after the text was created, to the extent that they reflect the intent at the basis of the text's creation. These are the circumstances that brought about the making of the will and the formation of a contract; the legislative history and its place in the legislative pro-

---

[52] Waldron is critical of taking legislative intent into account. He emphasizes that "Legislation is, in my estimation, the product of a multi-member legislature, composed of people with objectives, interests, and backgrounds that differ in purpose. Under these conditions, the special provisions of a particular statute are often the result of compromise reached during the vote or series of votes. The statute very well may in no way reflect the objectives and intentions of those legislators who enacted it together." J. Waldron, "Legislator's Intentions and Unintentional Legislation," in *Essays in Legal Philosophy* 329 (A. Marmor ed., 1995). Even if the conditions are as described above, they do not negate the existence of a joint intent of the legislators.

[53] M. Redish and T. Chung, "Democratic Theory and the Legislative Process: Mourning the Death of Originalism in Statutory Interpretation," 68 *Tul. L. Rev.* 803, 819 (1994) ("The idea that a legislative body aimlessly chooses words for a statute by a mental process equivalent to randomly selecting words from a hat is simply preposterous").

[54] H.C. 7157/97 *Arad v. Speaker of the Knesset*, 50(1) P.D. 573, 611: "The judge takes the reverse path from the legislator: The legislator starts with an idea, interest, purpose—and ends with the text; The judge starts with the text and ends with the text, but also engages the language, idea, interest, and purpose it contains" (Cheshin, J.).

vision; and the background for the creation of the constitution. The interpreter relies on these external sources to find information about the intent of the text's author.

The subjective purpose arising from these two kinds of sources is the subjective purpose of the text. Purposive interpretation uses both text and context to discover the (subjective) intent of the text's author. These two sources differ not by level of acceptability but rather by the weight ascribed to each. Generally, but not always, information from internal sources is more credible than information from external sources. Sometimes, information from the text itself is unreliable, as when the language of the text contains contradictions, while information from external sources may be extremely credible. It depends on the circumstances of each particular issue. It depends, also, on the substance and character of the text. The presumption that subjective purpose arises from the language of the text may be rebutted by information indicating that a more credible expression of the author's intent can be found outside the text itself.

Internal Sources and the Problem of the Hermeneutic Circle

We interpret a text according to its purpose. We learn its purpose, *inter alia*, from the text itself. To do so, we must interpret the text. Does this create a vicious circle (the problem of the hermeneutic circle)? The answer is no. We do not approach the text as blank slates. As Justice M. Cheshin said:

> When we approach a statute of the parliament, we do not come empty-handed. We bring our baggage of language, definitions of language and meanings, social customs and ethics, conventions and axioms, justice and integrity, principles and doctrines.[55]

We read the text as members of a legal community. This membership imparts to us a fore-meaning of the legal text, creating a preliminary understanding of the meaning of the text. From there, we begin to learn about the intent (will) of the author of the text. With the help of this preliminary inference as to the author's intent, we return to the text with a "correction" and "improvement" in our preliminary understanding. This im-

---

[55] H.C. 5503/94 *Segel v. Speaker of Knesset*, 51(4) P.D. 529, 562. *See also* F.C.H. 7325/95 *Yediot Ahronot Ltd. v. Kraus*, 52(3) P.D. 1, 73: "We do our best to interpret, but we are not *tabulae rasae*. Before approaching the statute, we must ask: Who are *we*? The answer is, 'we' are the proper values, principles, ethics, and world order. We begin the interpretive journey—unwittingly and unconsciously, perhaps—with the same values, principles, and doctrines that are the foundation on which the statute is based. We continue from there. We will not 'understand' a statute unless we analyze it with cognitive tools from the quiver [for holding arrows] we wear, and those cognitive tools guide us" (Cheshin, J.).

proved understanding is likely to correct our preliminary impression about the subjective purpose (will, intent) of the text. With this "corrected" intent, we return to the text, then back to intent, and so on. This process ends when, according to Gadamer,[56] the horizon of the author and the horizons of the interpreter fuse (*Horizontverschmelzung*).

Internal Sources: The Text in Its Entirety

Rarely are judges asked to interpret the entire text. Usually, they address one or another part of it. However, the intrinsic context of every part of the text is the text in its entirety. In order to understand one part, one must understand the whole text. The totality of the text is comprised of its explicit and implicit provisions. The structure of the text, its division into parts, and its presentation of matters provide information about the intent of its author. This is the origin of the method—used in all legal systems— that judges must approach each will, contract, statute, and constitution as a complete normative totality. As the Viscount Simonds said, "[T]he elementary rule must be observed that no one should profess to understand any part of a statute or of any other document before he has read the whole of it."[57] Judges must study every provision of the text; they must deal with the text in its entirety. A text is not a federation (or confederation) of provisions, but rather a unified text that must be interpreted as a whole. As the interpretive process progresses, judges learn the internal relationships among the various provisions; the primary provisions and the secondary provisions; the valid provisions and the invalid provisions; the provisions that add to the meaning of the text and the superfluous provisions. They draw these conclusions at the end of the interpretive process. The starting point is an integrative text, the entirety of whose provisions provide information about its subjective purpose. The starting point may shift during the interpretive process. Furthermore, it may become apparent, after analyzing the internal sources, that the document in its entirety does not lead to a subjective purpose that helps resolve a judge's interpretive problem. However, these conclusions are best left for a later stage. Judges should begin the interpretive process by reference to the text as a whole, through an attempt to uncover its subjective purpose.

The need to address the text in its entirety is not limited to cases in which, at the beginning of the interpretive process, the judge has trouble uncovering the subjective purpose. In every case, for every normative text,

---

[56] H.G. Gadamer, *Truth and Method* 238 (G. Barden and J. Cumming, trans., 2d ed. 1986); *See also* Eskridge, *supra* p. 58, note 210.

[57] *Prince Ernest Augustus, supra* p. 101, note 23 at 463.

irrespective of apparent interpretive difficulty, a judge must refer to the entire text. Even in interpreting a text that appears "clear" at first glance, a judge must take the approach that information about its (subjective) purpose comes from the totality of its provisions, understood as a whole and as a unit. The decision as to whether a text is "clear" or not comes at the end of the interpretive process, not at its start. A first reading of a particular provision may create a sense of clarity about its (subjective) purpose and meaning. Only by continuing his or her interpretive work will a judge encounter a different provision that raises doubts and undermines the apparent clarity. Only by reading the entire document as a whole can the judge uncover the subjective purpose of the text.

Semantic Conventions, Logic, and Harmony in Understanding the Text as a Whole

The author of the text envisioned every part of it as a unit within the whole. Judges seeking to uncover the intent of the text's author adopt the same perspective. They give the language of the text its natural and ordinary meaning. They assume that accepted semantic conventions are honored. They employ rules of logic, reasonableness, and common sense. They look for normative harmony within the text's totality. They presume that the text's subjective purpose arises from this accepted and logical inquiry.

Of course, this is just the starting point. In the continuous transition from text to context—from internal to external sources—these assumptions may be rebutted. They may change as the inquiry into subjective purpose continues. Judges may discover that the author of the text used his or her own lexicon;[58] that he or she used language in its special and exceptional sense; that the text he or she created is not internally harmonious, but rather contains disharmony and illogical, unreasonable arrangements; that the text has conflicting and contradictory subjective purposes. These conclusions may develop during the interpretive process. That possibility, however, does not obviate the need to begin with the assumption that language is employed in its natural and accepted use as a means of communication among people. Judges should start with the presumption that the author of the text acted reasonably and logically, with the intention of achieving harmony in the text he or she created; that identical expressions in the text mean the same thing and that different expressions mean different things; that the textual provisions do not contradict each other; that the purposes do not conflict with each other; that harmony infuses the text

---

[58] *Supra* p. 103.

as a whole.[59] Interpreters infer subjective intent from the structure of the text as a whole and the divisions by which the author arranged its parts. They compare different provisions of the text, deriving authorial intent from the comparison. They take the location of each provision into account. They view the text as a living unit operating logically and consistently, whose author designated different parts to fulfill different tasks and functions, in light of which judges infer the text's subjective purpose. I said as much in a case addressing the interpretation of a statute:

> A proper means of interpretation is to view a piece of legislation as a living organism, composed part-by-part, each of which has different tasks that it executes through mutual coordination. The activity of this or that part within the organism should be evaluated against the backdrop of its role and designation within the entire system.[60]

These words apply to every normative text. We assume that the text is an integrative unit, whose parts have different tasks connected to each other, interwoven into a comprehensive pattern. A text is generally not a collection of independent provisions that stand alone. The following image, proposed by Fuller,[61] is helpful: The inventor of a machine dies. He leaves behind an incomplete sketch of the machine he invented. He did not tell anyone which functions the machine was supposed to perform. From the entirety of the sketch, the inventor's son must comprehend the purpose that his father envisioned and complete the work in a way that carries out his father's plan.

Like the inventor's son, interpreters learn the purpose that the author envisioned from the structure of the text as a whole. Of course, as the interpretive process proceeds, these assumptions may change—and judges must be willing to adjust their initial assumptions. They should not cling to assumptions that do not reflect the reality that materializes from reading the text in its entirety. Judges must be realistic; the author of a text does not always behave as a logical and reasonable person, and sometimes the provisions of the text he or she writes are not logically integrated. Judges should take this into account, keeping in mind that they are interpreting a text created by another person. They are not writing a new text for the author. Judges should not, however, go to extremes of dis-integration or

---

[59] *See* H.C. 4031/94, *Bitzedek v. Prime Minister*, 48(5) P.D. 1, 63: "A fundamental rule of interpretation is that the interpreter do his best to interpret a piece of legislation as an orderly, harmonious creation.; as a web of coherent rules whose parts are interlaced and knitted together into a work of art; as a system of norms of consistent direction, at peace with itself and of a single piece; as a well-turned phrase" (Cheshin, J.).

[60] C.A. 503/80 *Zafran v. Mozer*, 34(4) P.D. 831, 835.

[61] Fuller, *supra* p. 89, note 29 at 84.

hyper-integration.[62] A text is sometimes a compromise between different and opposing views, each of which may assume prominence in a different part of the text. No one viewpoint—political, social, sociological, ethical—necessarily governs all parts of the text.

External Sources: The "Circumstances"

External sources such as the circumstances surrounding the text's creation (the context) also provide information about the subjective intent of the text's author. For wills and contracts, it is the data about the will or contract, external to the text, that provide information about the testator's intent or the joint intent of the parties. These circumstances include the factual scenario in place prior to, during, and even after the making of the will or contract, to the extent it provides information about the testator's intent or the joint intent of the parties at the time the will or contract was made. For a statute, the context includes facts that provide information about the intent of the legislature—primarily the history of the statute. This history includes the pre-enactment history (the reasons and factors that led to the statute's passage, including reports of public committees), the parliamentary history (committee and plenum hearings and debates), and the post-enactment history (events taking place after the passage of the statute that point to the intent at its core). For a constitution, the context includes events that brought about the founding of the constitution and that provide information about the intent of its founders. It may include discussions in the constitutional assembly or founding body and later events (like amendments to the constitution) that are likely to provide information about the intent of the authors of the constitution. Comparative law, as it existed at the time the text was written, may be another source of information if the interpreter knows that the authors of the text actually consulted foreign law.[63] Interpreters should assign greater persuasive value to foreign law in situations in which it influences local law.[64] The totality of circumstances helps identify the subjective intent of the text's author.

[62] L. Tribe and M. Dorf, *On Reading the Constitution* 21 (1991).

[63] I. Kisch, "Statutory Construction in a New Key," in *20th Century Comparative and Conflicts Law: Legal Essays in Honor of Hessel E. Yntema* 262 (K. Nadelman, A.T. Von Mehren, J. Hazard eds., 1961).

[64] The influence of foreign law takes place at different levels. An original domestic law is treated differently from a domestic law copied from a foreign system. Discussion of this issue is beyond the scope of this book. *See* Schlesinger et al., *Comparative Law: Cases, Texts, Materials* (5th ed. 1988); K. Zweigert and H. Kötz, *Introduction to Comparative Law* (T. Weir trans., 3rd rev. ed. 1998); A. Watson, "Legal Transplants and Law Reform," 92 *Law Q. Rev.* 79 (1976).

The Problem of Circumstances

A key question in formulating a theory of interpretation is whether the judge may refer to the circumstances of the text's creation as a criterion for interpretation, and if so, what weight those circumstances have. In piecing together the subjective purpose of the author, what is the relationship between information about intent that comes from the text itself (internal sources) and circumstantial information about intent (external sources)? Should an interpreter consider circumstantial evidence, and if so, under what circumstances may he or she do so? We will discuss three possible answers: *First*, under no circumstances may interpreters consider circumstantial evidence; *second*, interpreters may resort to circumstantial evidence only if certain conditions are met; and *third*, interpreters may always consider circumstantial evidence.

OPTION A: CIRCUMSTANTIAL EVIDENCE MAY NEVER BE CONSIDERED (LITERALISM OR EXTREME TEXTUALISM)

Under traditional common law, only the text itself could provide information about the intent of the author. Judges were barred from referring to the circumstances of the drafting of the text to learn about authorial intent. Lord Wensleydale's comments regarding the interpretation of wills exemplify this view:

> The use of the expression that the intention of the testator is to be the guide, unaccompanied with the constant explanation, that it is to be sought in his words, and a rigorous attention to them, is apt to lead the mind insensibly to speculate upon what the testator may be supposed to have intended to do, instead of strictly attending to the true question, which is, *what that which he has written means.* The will must be expressed in writing, and that writing only is to be considered.[65]

In another case from the same year, Justice Coleridge noted, addressing statutory interpretation:

> The sole legitimate inquiry is . . . what intention is to be found in the words of the Act, expressed or implied; unless by words written or words necessarily implied and therefore virtually written, the intention has been declared, we cannot give effect to it.[66]

We can call this literal subjectivism or extreme textualism. The approach is subjective, because the interpretive criterion is the intent of the author

---

[65] *Abbot, supra* p. 32, note 95 at 114.
[66] *Gwynne v. Burnell* (1840) 7 E.R. 1188, 1201.

of the text. The approach is literal or textualist because such intent is derived from within the text. The approach is extreme because the judge learns about intent from the text alone. He or she may not consult circumstantial evidence.

OPTION B: CIRCUMSTANTIAL EVIDENCE MAY BE CONSIDERED IN SPECIAL SITUATIONS (MODERATE TEXTUALISM, OR THE TWO-STAGE THEORY)

According to a *second* approach,[67] a judge may not consult circumstantial evidence if the intent of the author arises from the text itself, as long as the result is not absurd. If, however, an absurdity would result, the judge may go beyond the four corners of the text in order to find another intent of the author of the text that will remove the absurdity. This is the golden rule[68] used in England, the plain meaning rule[69] used in the United States, or the doctrine of *sens clair*[70] used in Continental law. This approach also permits the judge to go beyond the four corners of the text if the language of the text is vague or ambiguous. The judge may consult external sources to resolve the vagueness or ambiguity. Common law countries refer to this exception as the mischief rule.[71]

Even when the judge may consult external sources for authorial intent, he or she is not free to refer to all circumstances. Different legal systems employ different rules. Until recently,[72] for example, English law barred a judge from consulting parliamentary history. A judge in the English system still may not consult information about negotiations prior to contract formation in order to learn about the parties' joint intent.[73] We can call this approach literal subjectivism or moderate textualism. It is subjective because it is based on the view that a text should be interpreted according to the intent of its author. It is literal or textual because the main source of information about intent is the text itself. It is moderate because, in contrast to the extreme version, there are circumstances under which a judge may refer to external sources. He or she may do so to avoid a clear but absurd intention or if the text is too vague or ambiguous to produce a clear

---

[67] Cross, *supra* p. 3, note 3 at 10.

[68] *See* Lord Wensleydale's comments in the *Grey* case, *supra* p. 32, note 96.

[69] J. McBaine, "The Rule against Disturbing Plain Meaning of Writings," 31 *Cal. L. Rev.* 145 (1943).

[70] M. van de Kerchove, "La doctrine du sens clair des textes et la jurisprudence de la Cour de cassation de Belgique," in *L'Interpretation en Droit: Approche Pluridisciplinaire* 13 (M. van de Kerchove ed., 1978).

[71] Cross, *supra* p. 3, note 3 at 10.

[72] The *Pepper* case was the turning point. *Supra* p. 124, note 18.

[73] *See* Steyn, *supra* p. 124, note 18; L.H. Hoffman, *supra* p. 6, note 12.

intention. The process has two stages: First, the judge studies the text alone to find intent. Only if the first attempt fails—because of absurdity or uncertainty—may he or she refer to circumstantial evidence.

OPTION C: REFERENCE TO CIRCUMSTANCES UNDER ALL CIRCUMSTANCES (PURPOSIVE INTERPRETATION)

A *third* option is for a judge to refer to the circumstances under all circumstances, as purposive interpretation permits. A judge may move freely from text to context and back. There is no formal obstacle to consulting circumstantial evidence; there is no need for an initial determination that the language of the text is unclear or ambiguous; there are no "way stations" between the text and the circumstances of its creation; there are no two stages of the interpretive process; there is no sharp distinction between internal and external sources. The interpretive process is continuous. The judge's free movement back and forth between text and context ends only when the interpretive process ends. As I noted in an opinion dealing with the interpretation of a contract:

> A contract is interpreted according to the intent of the parties. This intent is the objectives, aims, interests, and plan that the parties sought to achieve together. The interpreter learns this intent from the contract and the circumstances external to it. Both sources are acceptable. They help the interpreter formulate the joint intent of the parties. The transition from the internal source (the language of the contract) and the external source (the circumstances surrounding its formation) does not depend on fulfilling any initial conditions. There is no need for a preliminary evaluation of whether or not the contractual language is clear. That question is answered only at the end of the interpretive process . . . external circumstances are always considered, not just when the contract itself fails to indicate the parties' intent.[74]

The same is true of other legal texts. An interpreter may move freely between a will and the circumstances of its drafting;[75] between a statute and its history; between a constitution and the circumstances of its founding. The interpreter seeks intention in all of these places. Using this subjective purpose, together with the objective purpose, he or she formulates the ultimate purpose of the text, according to which, at the end of the day, the text receives its legal meaning. This approach is superior because it takes subjective purpose seriously. If interpretation is to take the subjective as-

---

[74] C.A. 4628/93 *State of Israel v. Apropim Housing and Development*, 49(2) P.D. 265, 311, 314.

[75] Israeli case law differs from this approach. C.A. 239/89 *Shorash v. Galili*, 46(1) P.D. 861. This rule was adopted before the *Apropim* case, *id.* at 311.

pect seriously, it should look for it in every available source, without setting formal boundaries to the search. Credibility should be the only standard governing whether or not to consult a source.

References to Sources Early and Late

Purposive interpretation takes the view that there is no early and late in the interpretive process. In his or her free movement from text to context, the judge is not bound by any legally mandated "starting point." Each judge acts according to his or her intuition or natural preference (whether conscious or unconscious; whether under his or her control or not). Some will start with the text and immediately move to the circumstances of its creation. Others will start with the circumstances and move to the text. The only requirement is that the judge close the circle at the end of the interpretive process. Often, one "go-round" will not suffice; the interpreter will refer to the text and the circumstances of its creation according to the timetable he or she feels is best. The interpreter then returns to the text and the circumstances to check whether his or her initial impressions withstand further evaluation. It is a continuous dialogue between the interpreter and the text, the reader and the author, the present and the past.

The Relative Weight of Internal and External Sources

Purposive interpretation allows the interpreter to move freely back and forth between text and context. Both internal and external sources may provide credible information about the subjective purpose of the text. The interpreter does not, however, ascribe the same weight to information from internal and external sources. There is a distinction between admissibility and weight. Interpreters should give greater evidentiary weight to information about intent from the text itself than to circumstantial evidence of intent. As noted above, subjective purpose is presumed to be that arising from the text itself, interpreted according to its ordinary and natural language. This is the "golden presumption."[76] Although it is rebuttable, it is based on the fact that, generally, information about intent arising from the text is more credible than circumstantial evidence of intent. Generally, therefore, when information about intent from the two sources conflicts, interpreters should privilege information from the text itself.

---

[76] In contrast to the common law's "golden rule." *See* Bennion, *supra* p. 6, note 13 at 424, 671.

Language's Dual Role in Subjective Purpose

Language plays two roles in the context of subjective purpose: *First*, language teaches the interpreter about subjective purpose. *Second*, language limits the possibilities of achieving the subjective purpose. An interpreter may not fulfill a subjective purpose that is not grounded in language. Sometimes, studying the language of the text does not produce a relevant subjective purpose, but such purpose becomes apparent after studying the circumstances of the text's creation. This subjective purpose, derived from circumstantial evidence, is acceptable. The interpreter may even accord it significant weight. He or she may not, however, realize that purpose if it is not grounded in the language of the text. This "grounding" means that the subjective purpose, derived from external sources, must be realizable through the language of the text. An interpreter may not take into consideration a subjective purpose that cannot be achieved through the text. The author's attempt to achieve a certain objective must fail if the language he or she chose does not allow it. Again and again, we return to the simple axiom that, while meaning is not limited to just words, the words limit meaning.

5. SUBJECTIVE PURPOSE AS A PRESUMPTION ABOUT THE TEXT'S PURPOSE

Presumption That the (Ultimate) Purpose of the Text Is Its Subjective Purpose

Purposive interpretation is based on a small number of rules and a large number of presumptions about the purpose at the core of the text. These presumptions form the backbone of purposive interpretation. We will discuss them at length in the context of objective purpose.[77] However, the presumptions apply to subjective purpose as well. As we saw,[78] we presume that subjective purpose arises from the text in its entirety. Similarly, we presume that the interpreter learns about subjective purpose from the natural and ordinary meaning of the words in the text.[79] We will now address an additional presumption, of greater significance: *A text's subjective purpose is presumed to determine its ultimate purpose.* This presumption has two major implications for purposive interpretation: *First*, like any presumption, it turns the laws governing the status of subjective purpose (author-

---

[77] *Infra* p. 170.
[78] *Supra* p. 122.
[79] *Supra* p. 106.

ial intent) from rules into presumptions. When the intention of the author and the intention of the system clash, the clash is not between rules, in which one rule is assumed to invalidate the other, but rather between presumptions, in which each presumption can continue to express itself. *Second*, turning subjective purpose into a presumption imbues it with the flexibility demanded by the interpretive process. It gives it "weight" by establishing its relative status among the other presumptions. Such "weight" varies by type of text. Purposive interpretation presumes that the purpose of all legal texts is to realize authorial intent, but the weight of the presumption depends on the type of text in question. In certain situations—as when interpreting an ordinary will or contract—we weight the presumption so heavily that it achieves a rule-like status. In other situations—as when interpreting a constitution—the weight of this presumption is so minimal that we sometimes all but ignore it. In both cases, the proper approach is to view subjective purpose as a presumption about the ultimate purpose of the text. The force of the presumption, however—its power—varies by type of text.

Rebutting the Presumption

There are various kinds of presumptions, each rebuttable by different means. A presumption of fact (*praesumptio hominis*) is rebutted if the challenger proves that it has no basis in fact. This presumption originates in the factual reality, and it is the factual reality that can rebut it. In interpreting a specific contract or will, the court examines the facts and makes presumptions about the joint intent of the parties or the testator's intent. The burden of proof then shifts to the party seeking to rebut that presumption, who must show the intent to be something else. This presumption of fact is a way of establishing the subjective purpose of a specific text. It differs from the presumption of law (*praesumptio juris*) that a text's subjective purpose is its ultimate purpose. The latter derives not from factual assumptions about authorial intent but rather from a normative stance about the interpretive status of such intent in formulating the purpose of a text. A presumption of law is rebutted only by a factual basis showing that the intent of the author is otherwise.

Conflict between the Presumption of Subjective Purpose and the Presumptions of Objective Purpose

The presumption that the ultimate purpose of the text is its subjective purpose is rebuttable. What happens when it clashes with presumptions about objective purpose? The power of a presumption depends on its weight, and the weight of a presumption depends on the weight of the values and principles it reflects. The weight of the presumption of subjective purpose therefore depends on the weight that authorial intent has in formulating the purpose of the text. It varies by type of text. For example, the presumption of subjective purpose prevails in most cases interpreting a will or contract. There are, however, exceptions, such as the case of a mutual will,[80] a relational contract, and an adhesion contract. As for statutes, the weight of the presumption of subjective purpose varies by type of statute. The same holds true for interpreting a constitution, as we will discuss separately.[81]

Justifications for the Presumption of Subjective Purpose

Why recognize the presumption that the (ultimate) purpose of a text is its subjective purpose? Why not just apply the rule that subjective purpose prevails under certain circumstances, as in the interpretation of wills and contracts? There are two reasons. *First*, the "rule" about preferring subjective purpose is not absolute. It is more accurately reflected in the form of a presumption whose weight changes according to the circumstances. Of course, within a given legal system, the status of subjective purpose can be so elevated that a rule requiring a text to be interpreted according to its subjective purpose would accurately reflect the law. If possible, however, it is more accurate to reflect the principle as a presumption. *Second*, the presumption appropriately expresses the idea that subjective purpose—like objective purpose—accompanies the interpretive process from the start. The presumption applies automatically and always. It does not depend on whether or not the text is "clear." It aids interpretation from start to finish. It helps resolve contradictions between presumptions about objective purpose. The presumption also appropriately expresses the idea that there is no early and late in purposive interpretation. Each interpreter may choose his or her point of departure. One may start with the presumption that the (ultimate) purpose of the text is its objective purpose, another with the presumption that the (ultimate) purpose of the text is its subjective purpose. Each interpreter may choose his or her starting point, so long as each interpreter evaluates all the facts, and continues the interpretive process beyond its starting point.

[80] *Infra* p. 308.
[81] *Infra* p. 190. On statutes, see p. 189.

CHAPTER SEVEN

Objective Purpose
(Intent of the Reasonable Author;
Intent of the System)

1. THE ESSENCE OF OBJECTIVE PURPOSE

Objective Test

The objective purpose[1] of a legal text is the intent of the reasonable author. At a high level of abstraction, it is the "intent of the system." The intent of the system is the values, objectives, interests, policy, and function that the text is designed to actualize in a democracy. It is determined by objective criteria. It does not reflect an actual intent, but rather "hypothetical" intent (individual or general). It is not a physical-biological-psychological fact. It does not reflect a historical event. It cannot and need not be proven with evidence. It does not express the "real" intent of the author. It is a legal construction that reflects the needs of society. It is an expression of a social ideal. It reflects, at various levels of abstraction, the purpose that the norm is supposed to achieve within the bounds of a given democracy, at a given time. Like subjective purpose, objective purpose must operate within the limits of the text. Objective purpose is a goal that can be achieved only if the means, the language of the text, permits it. The language of the text must contain an anchor heavy enough to ground the objective purpose.

---

[1] The concept of objectivity is among the most complicated in law. *See* K. Greenawalt, *Law and Objectivity* (1992); N. Stavropoulous, *Objectivity in Law* (1996). Within the phrase "objective purpose," the word "objective" has a double meaning. *First*, it indicates a purpose that is not subjective and that does not belong to the author of the text. *Second*, it indicates a purpose that is not subjective and that does not belong to the interpreter of the text. *See* L. Di-Matteo, "The Counterpoise of Contracts: The Reasonable Person Standard and the Subjectivity of Judgment," 48 *S.C. L. Rev.* 293 (1997). As for the second meaning, suffice it to say that the word "objective" refers to a value judgment external to the judge who adjudicates. Objectivity deals with a search for the values common to members of society, distinct from the judge's personal values.

Individual Objective Purpose and General Objective Purpose ("Normative Umbrella")

Every legal text has its own purpose—the individual objective purpose of the text. Behind every text are objective purposes unique to it or to its type of text ("de facto purpose"; individual purposes; the intent of the reasonable author). The individual objective purpose of a contract or statute dealing with sales is not the same as the individual objective purpose of a contract or statute dealing with leases. Each contract has its own individual purpose, depending on the parties to it and its type.[2] In addition to its individual objective purposes, every legal text contains general objective purposes ("general purposes"; the intention of the system). These are the purposes that every legal text in the system must achieve,[3] the fundamental values—or the proper balance between them when they clash—that every text must express. These general purposes constitute a kind of "normative umbrella" spread over every legal text in the legal system. I noted as much in a case concerning statutory interpretation, but the point is applicable to the interpretation of all legal texts:

> In addition to the particular, unique objective of every specific piece of legislation, there are additional objectives common to all legislation . . . these constitute a kind of 'normative umbrella' spread over all legislation.[4]

While individual purpose is unique to each text, the general purpose is common to all texts. For example, under my theory of purposive interpretation, the general purpose of every normative provision contained in a will, contract, statute, or constitution is to guarantee equality, fairness, and just results. This is an expression of the basic idea that every legal text is a "creature of its environment."[5] In addition to the immediate normative context, this environment includes wider circles of the system's accepted principles, fundamental objectives, and basic standards.

The Objective Purpose's Level of Abstraction

Objective purpose operates at various levels of abstraction, primarily determined by two parameters: *first*, the level of particularity or generality of

---

[2] It is part of the first, second, and third level of abstraction. *See infra* p. 150.

[3] It is determined by the fourth level of abstraction. *Infra* p. 152.

[4] H.C. 953/87, *Poraz v. Mayor of Tel-Aviv-Yafo*, 42(2) P.D. 309, 329 (Barak, J.). The quote within the quote is from C.A. 165/82, *Kibbutz Chatzor v. Tax Assessor of Rehovot*, 39(2) P.D. 70, 75: "These principles need not be repeated in every statute, but rather constitute a kind of 'normative umbrella' spread over all legislation" (Barak, J.).

[5] H.C. 58/68 *Shalit v. Minister of Interior*, 33(2) P.D. 477, 513 (Sussman, J.).

the author of the text; *second,* the degree to which the text is value-laden. Taking these two parameters into account creates a range of levels of abstraction about the objective purpose of a text (will,[6] contract,[7] statute, and constitution[8]). We will discuss four possible levels of abstraction. The lines between the different levels of abstraction are fluid; we could easily articulate additional levels. Also, there is no "timetable" for referring to various levels of abstraction. The interpreter need not start at a low level, and only if it fails to resolve his or her problem, resort to a higher level of abstraction. Each interpreter may start with the level of abstraction that seems fitting to him or her, so long as he or she evaluates all the levels. We will examine these levels of abstraction closely.

LOW LEVEL OF ABSTRACTION: "IMAGINATIVE RECONSTRUCTION"

The *first* and lowest level of abstraction focuses on the author(s) of the text, inquiring into the values, objectives, designs, and function that the authors—the testator, contractual parties, members of the legislature, and members of the constitutional assembly—would have wanted to actualize had they been asked to resolve the legal questions before the judge. This is the hypothetical-individual intent. It does not reflect the "real" intent of a specific author. It reflects a conjecture as to the intent he or she would have had. It is Posner's "imaginative reconstruction."[9] The judge puts himself or herself in the author's shoes, looking for the purpose that the author of the text would have envisioned, had he or she considered the present interpretive issue.[10] The judge tries to find out which purpose would most rationally achieve the social project that the text established. This purpose is not subjective, because it does not reflect what the author really sought to attain. It is an objective purpose at the lowest level of abstraction. The judge tries to enter the shoes of the author of the text,

---

[6] E. Halbach, "Stare Decisis and Rules of Construction in Wills and Trusts," 52 *Cal. L. Rev.* 921, 933 (1964).

[7] Art. 8 of the United Nations Convention on Contracts for the International Sale of Goods; Art. 4.1 of the International Inst. for the Unification of Private Law, *Principles of International Commercial Contracts* (1994).

[8] Greenawalt, *supra* p. 126, note 24 at 1651.

[9] Posner, *supra* p. 27, note 85 at 270, 273. Posner uses the phrase in the context of statutory and constitutional interpretation. I think it can be used in the interpretation of wills and contracts, too.

[10] See Judge Hand's comments in *Borella v. Borden Co.*, 145 F. 2d 63, 64 (2d Cir. 1944): "We can best reach the meaning here, as always, by recourse to the underlying purpose, and, with that as a guide, by trying to project upon the specific occasion how we think persons, actuated by such a purpose, would have dealt with it, if it had been presented to them at the time."

putting himself or herself in the historical reality that existed at the time the text was created. In doing so, the judge does not "discover" subjective intent about which there was no information in the past. He or she is aware that the reconstruction poses questions of the author which, had they in fact been posed at the time the text was written, the author may not have been able to answer, because the author's spiritual world was different from the one that produced the unresolved interpretive questions.[11] Still, the judge uses his or her imagination as best he or she can. The judge does not ask how the author would have interpreted the text in the context of the specific case at hand but rather tries to reconstruct the abstract purpose.

INTERMEDIATE LEVEL OF ABSTRACTION:
THE PURPOSE OF A REASONABLE AUTHOR

The *second* level of abstraction disengages from the individuality of the author and turns to the imaginary figure of the reasonable person.[12] It inquires into the purpose that the author of the text would have envisioned, had he or she behaved as a reasonable person. At this level of abstraction, the judge replaces the specific author with the reasonable person,[13] who stands in the author's shoes. We seek the purpose that a reasonable author in the position of the real author would envision. The term "reasonable person" takes us from the hypothetical intent of the individual author to the hypothetical intent of the ideal author who reflects the proper balance between the system's values and principles, as it exists for someone situated in the position of the real author.

---

[11] Posner, *supra* p. 27, note 85 at 104.

[12] P.C.A. 1185/97, *Heirs and Estate of Milgrim Hinda v. Mishan Center*, 52(4) P.D. 145, 158: "The objective purpose is the hypothetical purpose that the parties would have had, had they behaved as reasonable and fair people" (Barak, J.).

[13] *See* Article 8 of the United Nations Convention on Contracts for the International Sale of Goods:

> **1.** For the purposes of this Convention statements made by and other conduct of a party are to be interpreted according to his intent where the other party knew or could not have been unaware what that intent was.
>
> **2.** If the preceding paragraph is not applicable, statements made by and other conduct of a party are to be interpreted according to the understanding that a reasonable person of the same kind as the other party would have had in the same circumstances.

See, also, Article 4.1 of the *Principles of International Commercial Contracts, supra* p. 150, note 7; J. Honnold, *Uniform Law for International Sales under the 1980 United Nations Convention* 165 (2d ed. 1991) ("The Convention").

HIGH LEVEL OF ABSTRACTION: THE PURPOSE DERIVED FROM THE TYPE AND NATURE OF THE TEXT

The *third* level of abstraction disengages not only from the individual author, but from the individual text, as well. It looks at the type and nature of the text. The judge asks not what (objective) purpose to attribute to the reasonable author of the text, but rather what typical purpose characterizes a certain kind of text. For example, in interpreting a sales contract, a judge looks to the purpose characteristic of a sales contract. Rather than look for the intent of reasonable parties to the specific sales contract that was in fact formed (the second level of abstraction), the judge asks what intent is typical of reasonable parties to this type of contract.[14] Similarly, in statutory interpretation, the judge focuses on the purpose typical of a statute concerned with land taxation or business licensing or any other type of legislation.

THE SUPREME LEVEL OF ABSTRACTION: PURPOSE DERIVED FROM THE SYSTEM'S FUNDAMENTAL PRINCIPLES

At the *fourth* and highest level of abstraction, a judge asks what purpose derives from the fundamental values of the system. The judge consults the legal system's general values, from which he or she tries to derive the legal text's objective purpose. When the text is a will, the judge asks what values and objectives the legal system seeks to actualize through wills. Under my theory of purposive interpretation, at this supreme level of abstraction, the legal system seeks to guarantee equality, justice, and fairness in dividing the testator's property. When the text is a contract, the objective purpose is to actualize the value of equality and bring about just results. The same is true of interpreting a statute.[15] A statute is "a creature of its environment." As I have noted, "In addition to the immediate legislative context, this environment includes wider circles of accepted principles, fundamental objectives, and basic standards."[16] Every piece of legislation is enacted against the backdrop of these fundamental values and principles, which constitute the purpose of all legislation. Fundamental principles fill our legal "universe," serving, among other functions, as the objective purpose of every piece of legislation. As Justice M. Cheshin noted:

[14] P.C.A. 1185/97, *supra* p. 151, note 12 at 156: "In addition to its subjective purpose, a contract has an objective purpose. It is the interests, objectives, and values that a contract of that category or type is designed to actualize . . . this purpose depends on the substance of the deal and the business and economic objective at its core" (Barak, J.).

[15] K.M. Gebbia-Pinetti, "Statutory Interpretation, Democratic Legitimacy and Legal-System Values," 22 *Seton Hall Leg. J.* 233 (1997).

[16] C.A. 165/82, *supra* p. 149, note 4 at 75.

In approaching interpretive work, we are equipped with more than just a dictionary. We carry with us Bible and heritage, love of humanity and our inner quest for freedom . . . all these tenets, values, and principles appear to be extra-legal, but they are the foundation of the statute—of every statute—and no statute can be conceived without them. A statute without that platform is like a house without foundations. . . . We do not come empty-handed. As we read the statute, our robes upon us, we carry on our backs "an interpretive quiver [for holding arrows]." Some will say an "interpretive kit." Inside this quiver are the values, principles, and doctrines without which we would not be who we are: fundamental values of the system, morality, fairness, justice . . . we do our best to interpret, but we are not *tabulae rasae*. Before approaching the statute, we must ask: Who are *we*? The answer is, "we" are the proper values, principles, ethics, and world order. We begin the interpretive journey—unwittingly and unconsciously, perhaps—with the same values, principles, and doctrines that are the foundation on which the statute is based. We continue from there. We will not "understand" a statute unless we analyze it with cognitive tools from the quiver we carry, and those cognitive tools guide us.[17]

The same is true of a constitution. Fundamental values and conceptions surrounding the constitution constitute the objective purpose of the constitution itself. These are the nation's basic conceptions of its values and principles. They express society's basic positions about human rights, separation of powers, and democracy.

Multiple Objective Purposes

Every legal text has a few objective purposes. It could not be otherwise, because (vertical) objective purpose operates at various levels of abstraction. Furthermore, at a given level of abstraction, there may be a few (horizontal) objective purposes. These purposes may or may not be linked. Some complement each other, while others contradict each other. In case of contradiction, no one purpose invalidates another or "expels" it from the legal system. The purposes present themselves to the interpreter as presumptions.[18] They reflect values, and when values clash, a judge does not prefer one value over another but rather balances them appropriately.

[17] F.H.C. 7325/95 *Yediot Ahronot Ltd. v. Kraus* 52(3) P.D. 1, 72, 73, 74 (emphasis in original) (minority opinion).
[18] *Infra* p. 170.

Objective Purposes in the Test of Time

Subjective purpose is static and fixed in time. What of objective purpose? In dealing with objective purpose at the lowest level of abstraction (imaginative reconstruction), we try to get as close as possible to the true intent of the author. The interpreter must return to the time when the text was created, in order to formulate its objective purpose. That is not the case at the other levels of abstraction, where the interpreter disengages from the hypothetical intent of the author in order to engage the intent of the reasonable author, the type of text, or the fundamental values of the system. At these levels of abstraction, the content of the objective purpose depends on the values and principles at the time of interpretation. It is not frozen in time. Like the individual text, fundamental values of the system constitute an organism that lives in its environment. This environment includes the social life in which the system operates—a life that, along with the system's values and principles, is in constant flux. Fundamental values thus have a dynamic meaning that changes with time, depending on when the text is interpreted. Objective purpose changes with time.[19] Hence the view, in statutory interpretation, that "the statute always speaks."[20] Professor Radbruch put it well in saying that the law is wiser than the legislator: "The interpreter may understand the law better than its creators understood it; the law may be wiser than its authors—indeed, it *must* be wiser than its authors."[21] I discussed the issue as well in one of my opinions:

---

[19] See Cr.A. 6696/96, *Kahane v. State of Israel*, 52(1) P.D. 535, 590, in which I referred to objective purpose as "actualizing the fundamental values of the system at the time of the interpretation." This phenomenon can also be seen as a transition from purpose to purpose. *See* S.G. Requadt, "Worlds Apart and Words Apart: Re-examining the Doctrine of Shifting Purpose in Statutory Interpretation," 51 *U. Toronto Fac. L. Rev.* 331 (1993); Sunstein, *supra* p. 13, note 31 at 428 ("Meaning does not remain static across changes in law, policy, and fact").

[20] Bennion, *supra* p. 6, note 13 at 687: "What the original framers intended sinks gradually into history. While their language may endure as law, its current subjects are likely to find that law more and more ill-fitting. The intention of the originators, collected from the Act's legislative history, necessarily becomes less relevant as time rolls by. Yet their words remain law. Viewed like this, the ongoing Act resembles a vessel launched on some one-way voyage from the old world to the new. The vessel is not going to return; nor are its passengers. Having only what they set out with, they cope as best they can. On arrival in the present, they deploy their native endowments under conditions originally unguessed at." *See also R. v. Hammersmith and Fulham London Borough Council, ex p. M* (1997) Times 19 February: "That Act had replaced 350 years of the Poor Law and is a prime example of an Act which is 'always speaking'. Accordingly it should be construed by continuously updating its wording to allow for changes since the Act was written" (Lord Woolf M.R.); *Victor Chandler International v. Customs and Excise Commissioners and Others* [2000] 2 All E.R. 315, 322; *Fitzpatrick v. Sterling Housing Association Ltd* [1999] 4 All E.R. 705, 725.

[21] Radbruch, *supra* p. 53, note 179 at 141.

The statute integrates into its new reality. An old statute speaks to the contemporary person. Hence the interpretive approach that "the statute always speaks" . . . interpretation is a process that renews itself. It puts modern content into old language, narrowing the gap between law and life. . . . England adopts this approach, giving statutes an interpretation that updates and renews . . . the statute is a living organism. Its interpretation must be dynamic. It should be understood in context, so that it advances modern reality.[22]

As Professor Eskridge noted:

Interpretation is not static, but dynamic. Interpretation is not an archeological discovery, but a dialectical creation. Interpretation is not mere exegesis to pinpoint historical meaning, but hermeneutics to apply that meaning to current problems and circumstances.[23]

The same is true of constitutional interpretation. The constitution is a living document.[24] Judges should give the values and liberties grounded in it a contemporary meaning. The question is not what "liberty" or "equality" meant at the time the constitutional text was written, but rather what they mean at the time it is interpreted. Hence the metaphor of the constitution as a living tree.[25] The objective purpose of the constitution reflects contemporary values. It expresses the contemporary national credo and fundamental contemporary constitutional viewpoints.

Does the same hold true for wills and contracts? Do judges determine the objective purpose of the text, at the low level of abstraction, according to the hypothetical intent of the testator or contractual parties at the time the text was written, while at higher levels of abstraction, according to the state of the law at the time of interpretation? I think the answer is yes. At the low level of abstraction, we try to get as close as possible to the actual intent of the testator or contractual parties. It is therefore natural that we would put ourselves in their shoes at the time the text was written. At higher levels of abstraction, however, we disengage from the individual tes-

[22] Cr.A. 2000/97 *Lindorn v. Compensation Fund for Traffic Accident Victims*, 55(1) P.D. 12, 32. *See also* H.C. 680/88 *Shnitzer v. Chief Army Censor*, 42(4) P.D. 617, 629; H.C. 2722/92 *Elamrin v. Gaza Strip I.D.F. Commander*, 46(3) P.D. 693, 705.

[23] W. Eskridge, "Dynamic Statutory Interpretation," 135 *U. Pa. L. Rev.* 1479, 1482 (1987). For its application in Canada, *see* S.G. Requadt, "Worlds Apart on Words Apart: Reexamining the Doctrine of Shifting Purpose in Statutory Interpretation," 51 *U. Toronto Fac. L. Rev.* 331 (1993).

[24] This metaphor is controversial. *See* W. Rehnquist, "The Notion of a Living Constitution," 54 *Tex. L. Rev.* 693 (1976); A.S. Miller, "Notes on the Concept of the 'Living Constitution,'" 31 *Geo. Wash. L. Rev.* 881 (1963); A. Scalia, "Modernity and the Constitution," in *Constitutional Justice under Old Constitutions* 313 (E. Smith, ed., 1995).

[25] *Edwards v. Attorney-General of Canada* [1930] A.C. 124, 136; *Re Motor Vehicle Act (British Columbia)* [1985] 2 S.C.R. 486, 508.

tator or contractual parties. Given this disengagement, there is no reason to focus on the purposes typical to that kind of document (will or contract) or the purposes derived from the fundamental values as they existed at the time the document was written. In a will or contract, as in a statute or constitution, judges determine objective purpose by reference to the basic values and principles in existence at the time of interpretation.

Akhnai's Oven

A wonderful example from ancient Jewish sources clarifies the disconnection between objective purpose and the author of the text and clarifies the dynamic, contemporary meaning of objective purpose: the well-known fifth-century C.E. story of Akhnai's oven.[26] Rabbi Eliezer disagreed with Rabbi Joshua and his colleagues over a matter concerning the oven of a man named Akhnai. The tractate reads as follows:

> It has been taught: On that day R. Eliezer brought forward every imaginable argument, but they did not accept them. [R. Eliezer was disputing with his colleagues and could not get a vote in his favor.] Said he to them: "If the halachah [religious law] agrees with me, let this carob-tree prove it." Thereupon the carob-tree was torn a hundred cubits out of its place. . . . "No proof can be brought from a carob-tree," they retorted. [The majority of the rabbis held that human reason was superior to miraculous proof.] Again he said to them: "If the halachah agrees with me, let this stream of water prove it." Whereupon the stream of water flowed backwards. 'No proof can be brought from a stream of water,' they rejoined. Again he urged: "If the halachah agrees with me, let the walls of the schoolhouse prove it." whereupon the walls inclined to fall. But R. Joshua rebuked the schoolhouse walls saying: "When scholars are engaged in a halachic dispute, what have ye to interfere?" . . . Again he said to them: "If the halachah agrees with me, let it be proved from Heaven." Whereupon a heavenly voice cried out: "Why do ye dispute with R. Eliezer seeing that in all matters the halachah agrees with him?" But R. Joshua arose and exclaimed: "It is not in heaven." What did he mean by this? Said R. Jeremiah: "That the Torah [Bible] had already been given at Mount Sinai; we pay no attention to a Heavenly voice, because thou hast long since written in the Torah at Mount Sinai. After the majority must one incline."[27]

[26] For a discussion of the story, *see* M. Alon, 1 *Hamishpat Haivri [Jewish Law]* 231 (3d revised expanded ed. 1988); Y. Englard, "Tanuro Shel Akhnai—Perusha Shel Haagada [Legend of Akhnai's Oven Interpreted]," 1 *Shnaton Hamishpat Haivri [Yearbook of Jewish Law]* 45 (1974). *See also* M. Silberg, *Kach Darco Shel Talmud [Talmudic Way]* 66, 68 (1964); M. Silberg, "Law and Morals in Jewish Jurisprudence," 75 *Harv. L. Rev.* 356 (1961).

[27] *Baba Mezi'a* 59b, 352–56 (S. Daiches and H. Freedman, trans., Soncino ed. 1935).

This story is a wonderful expression of the distinction between the divine intent of the author and the meaning an interpreter gives to the work, a meaning that is disconnected from the author's intent and may even conflict with it. The legend does not end there:

> R. Nathan met Elijah [the prophet] and asked him: What did the Holy One, blessed be He, do at that time [during the discussion between R. Eliezer and R. Joshua]? Elijah replied: "He smiled, saying: 'My children have bested Me, My children have bested Me.'"[28]

We can interpret the text according to its objective purpose, a purpose that does not seek the intent of the text's author and does not return to the time of the text's creation. Instead, we give a contemporary objective meaning to the work. In a case interpreting a statute, I noted that

> More than once, the legislator, a smile on his lips, will have to say—as the Holy One said while listening to the discussion between Rabbi Eliezer and Rabbi Joshua and his colleagues—"My children have bested me, my children have bested me."[29]

2. SOURCES OF OBJECTIVE PURPOSE: INTERNAL AND EXTERNAL

Like subjective purpose, objective purpose originates in the text and the context. In the subjective context, the judge uses these sources as a means of getting to the intent of the author, while in objective context, the interpreter turns to the sources themselves to discover the (objective) purpose that the text is designed to achieve. Judges may use any source, internal or external, that provides information about the text's concrete or general purpose.

Internal Sources: The Text in Its Entirety

Judges learn objective purpose from the text itself, taking into account both its explicit and implicit language. As is true for subjective purpose, the text plays an important role in objective purpose not just by setting the limits of interpretation but also by determining the content of the text's purpose. Judges use the text to learn about the values, objectives, interests,

---

[28] Qtd. in M. Alon, 1 *Jewish Law* 262 (1988).
[29] H.C. 693/91 *Efrat v. Director of Population Registration at the Interior Ministry*, 47(1) P.D. 749, 764.

policy, designs, and function that a text of that kind is designed to actualize in a democracy. Indeed, the subject of the text, the substance of its normative arrangement, and the types of issues it addresses provide information about its (objective) purpose.[30] The nature of the matter[31] regulated by the text teaches judges about the policy that the text aspires to implement.[32] For example, the substance of a deal laid out in a contract and the economic goal at its core suggest the objective purpose of the contract.[33] Most contracts, from the outset, are identifiable as belonging to one or another well-known category. Each of these categories is characterized by its own trends and objectives. A sales contract differs from a lease, and both are distinct from a service or moving contract. A short-term contract differs from a long-term contract; a discrete contract or "transaction contract" differs from a relational contract. If the object of a text (contract, statute, or constitution) is ownership, for example, we can infer the objective it is designed to achieve from what we know about the nature of the legal institution of ownership. The essence of the issue and the way it is treated in the text shape our understanding of this objective. The internal structure of the text—its divisions into sections and chapters, and their location within the text—may shed light on the objective purpose at its core. Just as studying a machine and its different functions provides information about the task the machine executes,[34] so studying a text in its entirety provides information about the (objective) purpose that the text is designed to achieve. Judges do not seek the intent lodged in the heart of the text's author but the purpose that the text's normative arrangement must achieve. As is the case with subjective purpose,[35] here, too, judges encounter the problem of the hermeneutic circle, and here, too, the foremeanings with which they approach the entire text resolve the problem. In seeking both subjective and objective purpose, judges begin with semantic convention, logic, and the harmony of the text. Logic and reason combined with textual language in its entirety help explain the purpose of the normative arrangement grounded in the text.

---

[30] *Id.* at 765: "The subject of the legislation, the nature of the arrangements, and the reciprocal relationships between them form a basis for inferring the objective of the legislation . . . the methodical structure, the types of issues addressed, the organization of the statute, and the location of its provisions may indicate the aims that the statute is designed to achieve" (Barak, J.).

[31] On the "nature of the matter" *see* Bydlinski, *supra* p. 7, note 14 at 459.

[32] Fuller, *supra* p. 13, note 33 at 86.

[33] H.C. 846/93, *supra* p. 8, note 16 at 10: "By the nature of things, this purpose is determined according to the substance of the issue arranged and the nature and character of the arrangement. This purpose of a contract is determined by the 'substance of the deal' and the 'business and economic objective' at its core" (Barak, J.).

[34] Fuller, *supra* p. 89, note 29 at 86.

[35] *Supra* p. 136.

External Sources

EXTERNAL SOURCES: NEARBY TEXTS ("NATURAL ENVIRONMENT")

Judges may learn the objective purpose of the text from external sources, including related texts. These may be another will of the testator or additional contracts between the same parties; statutes on the same issue as the statute in question, or different parts of a constitution that is composed of multiple documents.[36] The judge tries to infer the purpose of the text from these sources. Beyond that, purposive interpretation tries to understand a text in its "natural environment." This environment includes the immediate normative layout in which the text in question operates. The interpreter aspires to formulate the (objective) purpose of the will and contract in such a way as to integrate it into statutory provisions addressing wills and contracts. Addressing wills, Justice Cheshin noted that

> From a legal point of view, a will is just a legal tool or device for determining the fate of a deceased person's property after his death. As with every legal norm, we must evaluate it in its "natural environment," in other words, in the society of legal norms addressing inheritance, and, we may say, primarily the provisions of the Law of Succession. When we locate the will in its proper context, we will know how to ask the right questions, and those questions will guide our way.[37]

The same is true for interpreting a contract. In formulating its purpose, an interpreter should aspire to harmonize it with contract law. In formulating the purpose of a statute, an interpreter should aspire to the proper integration within legislation addressing similar issues (*in pari materia*). This is what is meant by the text's "natural environment." In understanding a constitutional provision, an interpreter should aspire to harmony and integration with the other constitutional provisions. The individual constitutional provision being interpreted does not stand alone. It constitutes part of the broader constitutional layout. It influences the understanding of the constitution as a whole. The constitutional entirety, in turn, influences the meaning of the individual provision within it. Justice Lamer said as much in a Canadian case interpreting a provision of the Canadian Charter addressing rights and freedoms:

---

[36] Justice Cheshin distinguishes among "three circles of thought": *first*, the expression to be interpreted; *second*, the same expression appearing in different places within the same statute; and *third*, the same expression appearing in statutes of the same family. F.H.C. 4601/95 *Sarosi v. National Labor Court*, 52(4) P.D. 817, 834.

[37] C.A. 1182/90, *Shaham v. Rotman*, 46(4) P.D. 330, 335.

Our constitutional *Charter* must be construed as a system where 'Every component contributes to the meaning as a whole, and the whole gives meaning
to its parts. . . .' The court must interpret each section of the charter in relation to the others.[38]

Hence the perspective that, in formulating the objective purpose at the
core of a constitutional provision, an interpreter should aspire to constitutional harmony through a vision of constitution unity.

EXTERNAL SOURCES: GENERAL LAW ("NORMATIVE HARMONY")

The general system of legislation and case law provides information about
the purpose of a normative text. An author does not create a normative text
in a vacuum or on a desert island. A normative text constitutes part of the
general normative framework from which it derives its power. The individual norm integrates into the generic law, is influenced by it, and influences it.[39] I noted as much in a case addressing statutory purpose:

> A piece of legislation does not stand alone. It constitutes part of the legisla-
> tive alignment. It integrates into it, aspiring to legislative harmony. "No
> statute stands alone . . . all statutes constitute a single project, integrating into
> each other in legislative harmony." He who interprets one statute interprets
> all statutes. The lone statute integrates as a tool into the legislative alignment.
> The legislative alignment as a whole influences the legislative purpose of a sin-
> gle statute. A prior statute influences the purpose of a later statute. A later
> statute influences the purpose of a prior statute.[40]

The same is true of normative texts that are not statutes. An interpreter
should formulate the (objective) purpose of a will or contract[41] so that they
integrate into general law. Terms and expressions in a will or contract are
influenced by similar terms in statutes addressing wills or contracts. A judge
should aspire to achieve harmony among legal texts. We might imagine
legal texts as interconnected beakers in a chemistry lab; the level of fluid in
the beakers becomes aligned, irrespective of the initial level of fluid in each.
Legal texts strive for normative harmony. Of course, that goal is not always
attainable. It is an aspiration to be balanced against additional considerations that may work in the opposite direction. Achieving normative harmony is just an aspiration. Its importance should not be exaggerated, but
neither should it be understated. Neither hyper-harmony nor disharmony
is desirable.

[38] *Dubois v. R.* [1985] 2 S.C.R. 350, 365.
[39] Gebbia-Pinetti, *supra* p. 152, note 15.
[40] H.C. 693/91, *supra* p. 157, note 29 at 765 (internal citations omitted).
[41] Lewison, *supra* p. 42, note 130 at 73.

EXTERNAL SOURCES: THE HISTORY OF THE TEXT'S CREATION

An author writes a text at a specific place and time. A text is not just a creature that lives in its environment; it is also a creature that draws life from its environment. An interpreter deepens his or her understanding of the text and its objective purpose by studying the history and environment that created the text. History should not control us, but neither should we try to escape it. In addition to examining history for authorial intent, in the context of subjective purpose, we examine history to see what it can teach us about the role the text should play in the present.

EXTERNAL SOURCES: GENERAL SOCIAL AND HISTORICAL BACKGROUND

An author creates a legal text within a society whose social and historical background influences the purpose of the text. This is particularly true of statutes and constitutions; social needs motivated people to enact them, and examining those needs helps us understand the purpose of the text. We noted that a legal norm is a creature of its environment. This environment includes not just the immediate needs, but also the distant environment, like the social and historical background of the society that produced the text. It is the fundamental social and cultural assumptions framing the text; the social and intellectual history in which the text operates; the culture and the intellectual conventions surrounding the text's conception; and the "national way of life." Justice Agranat put it well with the rhetorical question, "Is it not axiomatic, that one learns the law of a nation through the looking glass of its national way of life?"[42] This "national way of life" provides information about the purpose of a legal text. As Justice Holmes noted, "A page of history is worth a volume of logic."[43] The history of a system, including its social and cultural history, helps formulate the purpose of a normative text.

EXTERNAL SOURCES: CASE LAW

Judicial case law provides a treasure trove of information about values and principles that help teach about the objective purpose of a text. This is true of judicial case law that forms common law and judicial case law interpreting a normative text.[44] Contemporary judges do not operate in a case law

[42] H.C. 73/53 *Kol Haam Ltd. v. Interior Minister*, 7 P.D. 871, 884.

[43] *New York Trust Co. v. Eisner*, 256 U.S. 345, 349 (1921).

[44] For a discussion of the issue in constitutional interpretation, *see* Tribe, *supra* p. 15, note 38 at 78. *See also* D. Strauss, "Common Law Constitutional Interpretation," 63 *U. Chi. L. Rev.* 877 (1996); H.P. Monagham, "Stare Decisis and Constitutional Adjudication," *88 Colum. L. Rev.* 723 (1988).

vacuum. Each judge is a link in a continuous chain of case law[45] begun long before the era of the modern judge. Continuity, historical commitment,[46] respect for the present and past, rational consideration of the legal tradition,[47] and the need to guarantee security and certainty all justify judges' consulting case law—either as an option or as an obligation—as a source of information about the various levels of every text's objective purpose.

EXTERNAL SOURCES: JURISPRUDENCE AND LEGAL CULTURE

Every legal system has its own jurisprudence, derived from its culture and legal tradition, that establishes first-order ideas and concepts. Jurisprudence is the wellspring from which the laws draw their strength. It fosters a common legal experience. When expressions like "void," "authority," "legal action," "intent," "public order," and similar key jurisprudential concepts appear in a normative text—particularly in a statute or constitution—they reflect a legal culture and legal tradition. These expressions are not empty vessels awaiting content. They reflect fundamental legal conceptions, derived from the legal "family" (tradition) to which the system belongs and from the legal culture[48] that gives these expressions their system-specific, culture-specific, and family-specific jurisprudential meaning.

Every text is created within a legal community. The fundamental conceptions of the legal culture and its jurisprudence influence the formation of the text's purpose. An interpreter of the text must assume these conceptions as the basis for the meaning of the text. As Justice Frankfurter noted,

> An enactment is an organism in its environment. And the environment is not merely the immediate political or social context in which it is to be placed, but the whole traditional system of law and law enforcement, of recognized remedies and procedures which are the presuppositions of . . . law.[49]

Interpreters understand and interpret a statute regulating land use or commercial transactions against the backdrop of the fundamental jurisprudential conceptions of property rights, ownership, and possession; pro-

[45] This is Dworkin's image. *See* Dworkin, "Law As Literature," 60 *Tex. L. Rev.* 527 (1982).

[46] On the principle of historical commitment, *see* J. Rubenfeld, "Reading the Constitution as Spoken," 104 *Yale L.J.* 1119 (1995).

[47] Strauss, *supra* p. 161, note 44 at 891.

[48] Zweigert and Kötz, *supra* p. 140, note 64 at 63; R. David and J. Brierley, *Major Legal Systems in the World Today: An Introduction to the Comparative Study of Law* (1978); M. Glendon, M. Gordon, C. Osakwe, *Comparative Legal Traditions* 14 (1985).

[49] Frankfurter, *supra* p. 19, note 50 at 367.

cedural regulations against the backdrop of the legal system's distinctions between procedure and substance; a statute granting a remedy against the backdrop of the fundamental distinctions between right and remedy; a crime against the backdrop of fundamental conceptions of criminal responsibility; administrative legislation against the backdrop of fundamental conceptions about separation of powers and the role of the executive branch. The purpose of a legal text is closely tied to the law's jurisprudential infrastructure. The law's concepts establish a point of departure. They are background and infrastructure. They are a servant and not a master. They "reflect wisdom and generations of experience. They guarantee stability and certainty. Hence their importance. They refine our thought."[50] They should not, however, become a mandatory ending point in the interpretive process. We should not return to the jurisprudence of concepts (the *Begriffenjurisprudenz*) that supplants the centrality of values and interests. As I noted in the past,

> We should distance ourselves from the jurisprudence of concepts according to which the theoretical concept imposes itself on the interests and values that require a normative arrangement. We must aspire to a jurisprudence of values, according to which a theoretical concept is the product of balance and the normative arrangements of interests and values . . . legal concepts (like ownership, right, offense) are not a reality that we must accept as given. Legal concepts are constructions that are there to assist people.[51]

These constructions are an important external source for understanding the objective purpose of a text. We need not always start with a blank slate. We can use jurisprudence as the background for our formulation of the objective purpose of the text.

EXTERNAL SOURCES: BASIC VALUES OF THE SYSTEM

The basic values of the system fill our normative universe. They justify legal rules and are the reason for the changes we make to them. We derive rights and responsibilities from them. They are the substance that gives meaning to the form (the text). They are the foundation on which the entire house is built.[52] They serve as the general purpose of every single text.[53] This is true not just of statutes and constitutions, but also of private law texts like

[50] F.H.C. 4601/95, *supra* p. 159, note 36 at 826 (Barak, J.).

[51] F.Cr.H. 4603/97 *Meshulam v. State of Israel*, 51(3) P.D. 160, 182 (Barak, P.). F.Cr.H. 4601/95, *supra* p. 159, note 36 at 827: "Law is not a Paradise of concepts, but rather daily life of needs, interests, and values that a given society seeks to actualize at a given time" (Barak, P.).

[52] *See* W. Eskridge, "Public Values in Statutory Interpretation," 137 *U. Pa. L. Rev.* 1007 (1989); D. Oliver, *Common Values and the Public Private Divide* (1999).

[53] *See* Gebbia-Pinetti, *supra* p. 152, note 15.

wills and contracts. Law's basic values are not limited to public law, like constitutional and public administrative law. They apply both to relationships between the individual and the state and to relationships between individuals. As I noted in one case,

> The basic principles of the system in general, and fundamental human rights in particular, are not limited to public law. The distinction between public and private law is not so sharp. A legal system is not a confederation of legal fields, but rather a unity of law and system. The basic principles are the principles of the entire system, not just of public law. Basic human rights do not just exist against the state, they are also infused in relationships between individuals.[54]

Fundamental principles apply to private law indirectly, through various legal doctrines,[55] like the doctrine that we interpret every text, including every private law text, such that its objective purpose is to actualize the fundamental values of the system. Actualizing the system's fundamental values is therefore the objective purpose of every will and contract. Those fundamental values serve as the general objective purpose of every text, not because they express the intention of its author, but rather because the text operates within a system from which it draws life and on which it relies for enforcement. An interpreter refers to the fundamental values of the system not because they arise from the language of the text but rather because the language of the text permits it, and the legal system in which the text operates demands it.

What Are the Basic Values?

A legal system generally does not come with an instruction booklet listing its basic values and principles.[56] They are sprinkled throughout the state's constitution and statutes, and they concentrate in the legal system's judicial opinions. Sometimes, judicial opinions contain a list of basic values accepted at the time. In the following case, I discussed basic values:

> These general principles include equality, justice, and morality. They extend to societal objectives of separation of powers, rule of law, freedom of speech, of assembly, of religion, and of occupation, human dignity, the integrity of the judicial system, public peace and security, the democratic values of the nation, and its very existence. These principles include good faith, natural justice, fairness, and reasonableness.[57]

---

[54] C.A. 294/91 *Jerusalem Community Burial Society v. Kestenbaum*, 46(2) P.D. 464, 530.

[55] These doctrines include "reasonableness," "negligence," "public order," and others.

[56] I do not distinguish between principles and values. For the distinction between them, *see* Peczenik, *supra* p. 16, note 44 at 74.

[57] Cr.A. 677/83 *Borochov v. Yafet*, 39(3) P.D. 205, 218.

The list is not exhaustive. It varies, of course, from legal system to legal system and from era to era. At its core are three kinds of basic principles: ethical principles (like justice, morality, fairness, good faith, human rights); societal objectives (like the preservation of the state and its democratic character, public peace and security, separation of powers, rule of law, judicial independence, consistency and harmony in law, certainty and security in interpersonal arrangements, realization of reasonable expectations, human rights); and patterns of behavior (like reasonableness, fairness, good faith). The categories are fluid; human rights, for example, can be seen as both an ethical value and a societal goal. I see them as both.

These basic values are the general principles about which Professor Dworkin wrote, noting that they can exist even if a particular rule in the system contradicts them.[58] In addressing judicial discretion, Dworkin distinguishes between principles and policy,[59] a distinction that has been criticized.[60] I believe that in interpreting a text, a judge may consider both policy and principles. Both serve as the generic objective purpose of every legal text. Once courts recognize them, they become part of the law itself.[61] Similarly, I do not distinguish between values and standards.[62]

How Are Basic Values Determined?

How do judges arrive at basic values? Judges may certainly not impose on society their own subjective perspectives about the basic values.[63] Judicial rulings should reflect not judges' own values but rather those they believe are warranted by the nature of their legal system and the ethos that characterizes it. "The question is not what the judge wants, but what the society needs."[64] As Cardozo writes,

---

[58] Dworkin, *supra* p. 48, note 157 at 26.

[59] *Id*. at 22.

[60] J. Raz, "Legal Principles and the Limits of Law," 81 *Yale L.J.* 823 (1972); G. Hughes, "Rules, Policy and Decision Making," 77 *Yale L.J.* 411 (1968); D.N. MacCormick, *Legal Reasoning and Legal Theory* (1978).

[61] Therefore, there is no contradiction between recognizing these values and Hart's rule of recognition. *See* Hart, *supra* p. 26, note 78 at 263. *See also*, M.S. Moore, "Legal Principles Revisited," 82 *Iowa L. Rev.* 867 (1997).

[62] For this distinction, *see* L. Alexander and K. Kress, "Against Legal Principle," in *Law and Interpretation: Essays in Legal Philosophy* 279 (A. Marmor ed., 1995); reprinted in 82 *Iowa L. Rev.* 739 (1997).

[63] H.C. 58/68, *supra* p. 149, note 5 at 580: "That does not mean that the court can rule according to the judge's private perspective on what is good and effective for these principled views, but he must be a reliable interpreter of the accepted views of the enlightened public within which he sits" (Landau, J.). In the same case, Court President Agranat said: "Doesn't the principle of rule of law mean that the judge must distance himself, as much as possible, from privileging his private opinions about what justice demands?"

[64] Cr.A. 696/81 *Azulai v. State of Israel*, 36(2) P.D. 565, 574 (Barak, J.).

Their standard must be an objective one. In such matters, the thing that counts is not what I believe to be right. It is what I may reasonably believe that some other man of normal intellect and conscience might reasonably look upon as right. . . . [A] judge, I think, would err if he were to impose upon the community as a rule of life his own idiosyncrasies of conduct or belief . . . he would be under a duty to conform to the accepted standards of the community, the mores of the times.[65]

I discussed this approach in a case before me:

The judge does not impose his subjective values on the society in which he operates. He must balance the different interests according to what appear to him to be the needs of the society in which he lives. He must exercise his discretion, to the best of his ability and the best of his objective recognition, as to what reflects the needs of society.[66]

The nature of the basic values and the proper balance between them when they clash depend on society's basic viewpoints and positions at the time of interpretation. In determining those values, judges must exercise as much objectivity as possible. They draw information about the basic values from society's core documents (the constitution;[67] the declaration of independence). They derive the basic values (like human rights, separation of powers, rule of law, judicial independence) from the nation's democratic character itself. Indeed, our legal system derives from the "political system of governance that we desire,"[68] and our basic values derive from the legal system. "The very fact that the regime is democratic"[69] warrants certain values. Nevertheless, each legal system has its own basic values, as does each era. In declaring a given basic value, judges express the social consensus that has crystallized in their systems. Judges should integrate into the legal system only the values that have gone through the pressure cooker of social recognition.[70] As Justice Holmes noted,

As law embodies beliefs that have triumphed in the battle of ideas and then have translated themselves into action, while there still is doubt, while opposite convictions still keep a battle front against each other, a time for law has not come; the notion destined to prevail is not yet entitled to the field. It is a misfortune if a judge reads his conscious or unconscious sympathy with one

---

[65] B. Cardozo, *The Nature of the Judicial Process* 89, 108 (1921).

[66] C.A. 243/83 *Municipality of Jerusalem v. Gordon*, 39(1) P.D. 113, 131.

[67] Sunstein, *supra* p. 13, note 31 at 466, 468.

[68] C.A. 723/74 *Haaretz Newspaper Publications v. Israeli Electric Co.*, 31(2) P.D. 281, 195 (Shamgar, J.).

[69] H.C. 953/87, *supra* p. 149, note 4 at 330 (Barak, J.).

[70] H.C. 58/68, *supra* p. 149, note 5 at 602.

side or the other prematurely into the law, and forgets that what seems to him to be first principles are believed by half his fellow men to be wrong.[71]

Judges will, on occasion, find themselves in situations in which a certain value seems basic and proper. That is not a good enough reason to recognize the value as basic to the system. Judges should recognize values that society views as basic. Social consensus around fundamental and basic viewpoints should guide judges in their judicial work, both in infusing new basic values into the system, and in removing basic values that have become obsolete. This principle of canonizing values over which there is consensus is itself a basic value of the legal system.

Judges should operate within society's established central framework, not the occasional temporary structures it may build. They need not give expression to the passing trends of a society that is not being true to itself. Judges should resist those trends and give expression to the social consensus that reflects the basic principles, "deep" values, and national credo of their society. The fact that the modern majority thinks that a certain kind of behavior is not worthy of protection does not affect the basic perspective of that same modern society on the behavior in question. For example, the fact that most of the public does not want to hear certain kinds of verbal attacks does not mean that they should no longer enjoy constitutional protections of freedom of speech.[72] The goal of the constitution is, *inter alia*, to protect the individual (or the minority) against the power of the majority. Modern consideration of basic values need not become a device for granting the majority powers that the constitution denies. Judges must refer to society's "deep" values and the basic principles of a mature democratic society.[73] I noted as much in a case before me:

> We act according to constitutional criteria and fundamental legal principles that reflect the credo of our national life. We are guided by basic national perspectives on our existence as a democratic country, not by the dictates of passing trends.[74]

The "basic and principled" values that judges must reflect are the product of the modern present. They grow in the soil of the past and remain connected to it,[75] but their horizons are not limited to the horizons of the past. Each generation creates its own horizons.[76] This approach to basic

---

[71] O.W. Holmes, *Collected Legal Papers* 294 (1921).

[72] See Justice Black's opinion in *Chambers v. Florida*, 309 U.S. 227, 241 (1940).

[73] See Chief Justice Warren's opinion in *Trop v. Dulles*, 356 U.S. 86, 101 (1958).

[74] H.C. 428/86 *Barzilai v. State of Israel*, 40(3) P.D. 505, 585.

[75] See Justice Holmes's opinion in *Gompers v. United States*, 233 U.S. 604, 610 (1914) and Justice Powell's opinion in *Moore v. City of East Cleveland*, 431 U.S. 494, 503 (1977).

[76] T. Sandalow, "Constitutional Interpretation," 79 *Mich. L. Rev.* 1033, 1061 (1981).

values—emphasizing deep perspectives, not passing trends; history, and not hysteria—is also an appropriate response to the claim that interpretation according to original understanding is necessary to protect the constitution, particularly constitutional protections for human rights, from the power of the majority. According to that claim, interpretation according to "objective" basic values of the present contradicts the very idea of protecting the minority from the tyranny of the majority.[77] Part of the reply to this claim is that the basic values of the present are not necessarily the values that today's majority accepts. They are the deep values of society as it moves through history. They are not just the results of public opinion surveys; they are not populism that envelops society. They are basic social perspectives that change their shape but withstand the test of time. Judges, who enjoy independence and who do not, in most systems, stand for periodic reelection, are well placed to ignore passing trends and to express society's deep values.[78] The nonaccountability of judges is their most important asset.[79] It is the judge—who neither seeks power nor hungers to rule—who is capable of expressing society's basic values.

Basic Principles: "Weight" and "Gravity"

Basic principles reflect values or ideals. Principles and ideals are unique in that they can be realized at various levels of intensity.[80] When principles clash, one does not invalidate the other. The clash limits the applicability of the principle that does not prevail, but it does not absolutely destroy it. The two conflicting values continue to apply in the legal system, existing in proper balance. An important trait of principles is that they have a "weight" that reflects their relative social importance,[81] and that we can resolve conflicts between them by balancing them according to that weight. We can also think of basic principles as exercising a "gravitational pull" whose strength depends on the essence of the principles, their sources, and their importance.[82] Basic principles grounded in the constitution are "heavier" than basic values grounded in a statute. In assigning weight to basic values, a judge considers the weight they had in the past and the weight that the system's case law assigns them in addressing other

[77] A. Scalia, "Originalism: The Lesser Evil," 57 *U. Cin. L. Rev.* 849 (1989).

[78] A. Bickel, *The Least Dangerous Branch* 24 (1962).

[79] P.S. Atiyah, "Judges and Policy," 15 *Isr. L. Rev.* 346 (1980).

[80] Dworkin, *supra* p. 48, note 157.

[81] *Id.* at 26. Raz thinks that rules have weight, too. *See* Raz, *supra* p. 165, note 60 at 830. *See also* F. Schauer, "Prescriptions in Three Dimensions," 82 *Iowa L. Rev.* 911, 919 (1997).

[82] W. Eskridge, "Public Values in Statutory Interpretation," 137 *U. Pa. L. Rev.* 1007, 1018 (1989): "Physics suggests a useful metaphor: gravity. Public values have a gravitational force that varies according to their source (the Constitution, statutes, the common law) and the degree of our historical and contemporary commitment to these values."

issues. Judges aspire to unity and harmony. The hard part of their job is determining the weight of values and principles.[83] It is also the most important part of their job as interpreters.

EXTERNAL SOURCES: COMPARATIVE LAW

Comparative law helps a judge understand the objective purpose of a text.[84] You get to know yourself better by comparing yourself to others.[85] Comparative law helps a judge "expand his horizons and interpretive field of vision. Comparative law enriches our options."[86] The same legal institution (like "good faith," for example) may play similar roles in different legal systems.[87] To the extent that is so, comparative literature serves as a source of the objective purpose of a piece of local legislation (micro-comparison[88]). Furthermore, basic democratic principles are common to democratic countries. One democracy may inform or inspire the other (macro-comparison[89]).

Still, the technique has its limits. Comparative law is not just about comparing laws. Comparative interpretation can take place only among legal systems that share a common ideological basis. An interpreter must be sensitive to the uniqueness of each legal system. Sometimes, comparison is im-

---

[83] W. Murphy, "The Art of Constitutional Interpretation," in *Essays on the Constitution of the United States* 130, 147 (H. Abrams et al. eds., 1978).

[84] For a discussion of the role of comparative law in interpretation, see K. Zweigert and H. Kötz, *An Introduction to Comparative Law* (1987); Schlesinger et al., *supra* p. 140, note 64; R. Sacco, "Legal Formants: A Dynamic Approach to Comparative Law," 39 *Am. J. Comp. L.* 1 (1991); H. Smith, "Interpretation in English and Continental Law," 9 *J.C.L.* (*3d Ser.*) 11 (1927); A.A. Schiller, "Roman Interpretation and Anglo-American Interpretation and Construction," 27 *Va. L. Rev.* 733 (1941); A. Lenhoff, "On Interpretative Theories: A Comparative Study in Legislation," 27 *Tex. L. Rev.* 312 (1949); A. Lenhoff, *Comments, Cases and Materials on Legislation* 590 (1949); M. Franklin, "A Study of Interpretation in the Civil Law," 3 *Vand. L. Rev.* 557 (1950); S. Strömholm, "Legislation Material and Construction of Statutes: Notes on the Continental Approach," 10 *Scan. Studies in Law* 175 (1966); J.H. Merryman, "The Italian Style III: Interpretation," 18 *Stan. L. Rev.* 583 (1966); K. Zweigert and H.J. Puttfarken, "Statutory Interpretation—Civilian Style," 44 *Tul. L. Rev.* 704 (1970); S. Herman, "*Quot Judices tot sententiae*: A Study of the English Reaction to Continental Interpretive Techniques," 1 *Leg. Stud.* 165 (1981); S. Abrahamson and M. Fischer, "All the World's a Courtroom: Judging in the New Millennium," 26 *Hofstra L. Rev.* 273 (1997); J. Nofziger, "International and Foreign Law Right Here in the City," 34 *Willamette L. Rev.* 4 (1998); *The Use of Comparative Law by Courts* (U. Drobnig and S. Van Erp eds., 1999); J. Dammann, "General Issue: The Role of Comparative Law in Statutory and Constitutional Interpretation," 14 *St. Thomas L. Rev.* 513 (2002).

[85] *See* Sacco, *supra* p. 169, note 84.

[86] Cr.A. 295/81 *Estate of Sharon Gabriel v. Gabriel*, 36(4) P.D. 533, 542 (Barak, J.).

[87] Zweigert and Kötz, *supra* p. 169, note 84 at 31.

[88] *Id*. at 4.

[89] *Id*. at 4.

possible. When an interpreter is persuaded, however, that the social, historical, and religious circumstances create a common ideological base, he or she may use a foreign legal system to formulate the objective purpose of the text.

Above all, comparative law is important for its ability to expand the interpreter's horizons. It offers the judge guidance about the text's latent interpretive potential. It shows the interpreter what may and may not be accomplished through the text. It gives the judge information about the successes and failures of the different possibilities latent in the text. It makes the interpreter aware of links between a solution to the interpretive problem he or she faces and other legal problems. Comparative law serves as an experienced friend. Of course, judges have no obligation to resort to comparative law, and even when they do, the final adjudication must always be "local." The primary importance of comparative law is its ability to expand an interpreter's horizons about the types of potential normative arrangements, trends, and legal structures. Comparative law does not provide an answer to the specific problem troubling the judge; the judge consults comparative law at a higher level of abstraction, in order to expand his or her interpretive horizons. Judges should be careful, however, not to let intellectual curiosity lead them to imitate at the cost of self-denial. The purpose of consulting comparative law is to understand the local text better. The comparison must not interfere with the normative harmony of local law.

3. PRESUMPTIONS OF OBJECTIVE PURPOSE

Presumptions of General Applicability

A text has numerous objective purposes operating at different (vertical and horizontal) levels of abstraction. How do these different purposes operate? Professor Sunstein sees them as "background norms" that assist the interpreter.[90] I believe that they are part of the objective purpose that the text is designed to achieve. Judges translate them into presumptions about that purpose.[91] These presumptions reflect the essence of the legal system, its aspirations and aims,[92] and its constitutional viewpoint. Because they apply within every legal text, we can call them presumptions of general applica-

---

[90] Sunstein, *supra* p. 13, note 31 at 460. *See also* J. Siegel, "Textualism and Contextualism in Administrative Law," 78 *B.U. L. Rev.* 1023 (1998).

[91] *See* C. Diver, "Statutory Interpretation in the Administrative State," 133 *U. Pa. L. Rev.* 549 (1985).

[92] They reflect what Gebbia-Pinetti calls "legal-system values." *Supra* p. 152, note 15.

bility.[93] They are presumptions about the objective purpose of every will, and they behave—in Atkinson's words—"like rebuttable presumptions in the law of evidence."[94] They constitute, similarly, rebuttable presumptions about the objective purpose of every contract, as I noted in one case: "In the context of objective purpose, we proceed on the presumption (*prae-sumptio juris*)—and it is a rebuttable presumption—that the parties seek to achieve a purpose that is just, efficient, reasonable, and fair."[95] Addressing statutory interpretation, I noted in another case:

> The fundamental values of the system and fundamental human rights determine the purpose of a piece of legislation. It is presumed that the purpose of a piece of legislation is to actualize the principles of the system and advance human rights within it . . . they penetrate every piece of legislation and constitute its purpose.[96]

In a similar spirit, addressing the role of presumptions of purpose in statutory interpretation, Du Plessis wrote that "Their proper application serves to relate to the provisions of a particular statute . . . to the legal order in general, and the precepts, principles and premises upon which it is based."[97] Professor Cross expressed a similar idea:

> These presumptions of general application . . . operate at a higher level as expressions of fundamental principles governing both civil liberties and the relations between Parliament, the executive and the courts. They operate here as constitutional principles which are not easily displaced by a statutory text.[98]

Professor Côté discussed this principle in reference to the situation in Canada:

> The meaning of a new statute is also likely to be moulded by principles associated with the legal system (for example, the principle of non retroactivity) and by the contemporary values of society (for example, what is considered just or unjust, reasonable or unreasonable). Such principles and values, this system of values, find their place within the process of statutory interpretation in the form of presumptions of legislative intent: the legislator is deemed to respect the values and the principles of the society for which he is legislating.[99]

---

[93] Cross, *supra* p. 3, note 3 at 165.
[94] T. Atkinson, *Handbook of the Law of Wills and Other Principles of Succession, Including Intestacy and Administration of Decedent's Estates* 814 (2d ed. 1953).
[95] C.A. 4869/96 *Maliline Ltd. v. The Harper Group*, 52(1) P.D. 845, 856.
[96] H.C. 693/91, *supra* p. 157, note 29 at 763.
[97] L. Du Plessis, *The Interpretation of Statutes* 54 (1986).
[98] Cross, *supra* p. 3, note 3 at 166.
[99] Côté, *supra* p. 77, note 65 at 396.

Presumptions of purpose reflect the fundamental values of the system. They are a mirror image of these values. They express the constitutional perspectives at the core of the legal system. I noted as much in a case before me: "At the core of 'presumptions of general applicability' are constitutional assumptions about the essence of the democratic regime, separation of powers, rule of law, and human rights."[100] Generally, a system first recognizes fundamental values, either in official documents or in case law, and only then does it derive the presumptions about objective purpose from them. Sometimes, however, the primary pipeline through which a fundamental principle penetrates the legal system is through a presumption about the objective purpose of a text. Only later does the principle assume a life beyond the text and become a source of rights and responsibilities. Many fundamental rights, not written in the pages of any book, developed through judicial application of general presumptions about the purpose of legal texts. This is one way in which the presumptions of purpose, reflecting fundamental principles, help develop law.

The Importance of Purposive Presumptions

Presumptions of purpose are the foundation of purposive interpretation. They constitute—to borrow the words of Du Plessis on statutory interpretation—the ABC and XYZ of interpretation.[101] They are the heart of legal interpretation. Presumptions about the meaning of a legal text are increasingly replacing rules of legal interpretation.[102] With their help, legal interpretation has lost its technical character. It no longer depends on intersecting rules that multiply into conflicting dyads.[103] Presumptions replace these rigid rules, reflecting values and policies that the legal system seeks to actualize. Values and policies, characteristically, exist in perpetual internal conflict, as do the presumptions derived from them. This conflict does not reflect any weakness on the part of the presumptions of purpose,

---

[100] H.C. 953/87, *supra* p. 149, note 4 at 329.

[101] Du Plessis, *supra* p. 171, note 97 at 52.

[102] For a discussion of the interpretive "canons," *see* Sunstein, *supra* p. 13, note 31; K. Llewellyn, "Remarks on the Theory of Appellate Decision and the Rules or Canon about How Statutes Are to Be Construed," 3 *Vand. L. Rev.* 395 (1950); D. Harris, "The Politics of Statutory Construction," [1985] *B.Y.U. L. Rev.* 745 (1985); Rodriguez, "The Presumption of Reviewability: A Study in Canonical Construction and its Consequences," 45 *Vand. L. Rev.* 743 (1992); J. Macey and G. Miller, "The Canons of Statutory Construction and Judicial Preference," 45 *Vand. L. Rev.* 647 (1992); W. Eskridge and P. Frickey, "Quasi-Constitutional Law: Clear Statement Rules as Constitutional Lawmaking," 45 *Vand. L. Rev.* 593 (1992); S.F. Ross, "Statutory Interpretation in the Courtroom, the Classroom, and Canadian Legal Literature," 31 *Ottawa L. Rev.* 39 (1999–2000).

[103] Llewellyn describes them as such. *Supra* p. 172, note 102.

but rather is a natural outgrowth of the fact that they reflect values and policies. The more developed the legal system, the more presumptions of objective purpose it will have. The number of purposive presumptions changes from system to system and changes within a single system, as new values are introduced and obsolete values exit the system. Presumptions of purpose are not rigid, set, or static. They change as the fundamental values change. There is no exhaustive list of purposive presumptions. Their categories are always open. Every generation may derive new purposive presumptions from old and new values.

Categories of Purposive Presumptions

There are different categories of presumptions of purpose, but the distinctions are largely artificial and may change over time and between different legal systems. There is no exhaustive list of categories of purposive presumptions; they vary with the type of text being interpreted. Any particular presumption may fit a few categories. For convenience, I outline six primary groups of presumptions accepted in Israeli law:

1. *Purposive presumptions based on the need to guarantee security, certainty, consistency, and normative harmony.* This category includes presumptions that guarantee normative harmony, like preventing contradiction between parts of a text, integrating textual provisions into generic law, and the presumption that a text is valid ("presumption of validity"). It is also presumed that the purpose of a text arises from its natural and ordinary language, that the text does not casually make changes to prior general law, that the author of the text does not use words unnecessarily, and that the text has a dynamic meaning. Of particular importance to this category is the presumption that all norms accommodate the provisions of the constitution.

2. *Purposive presumptions that reflect ethical values*, like the presumption that the purpose of a text is to achieve justice, morality, and fairness; that the purpose of a text is to prevent a wrongdoer from profiting from his or her misdeeds; that the text is designed to realize the rules of natural justice; that the text is designed to prevent conflicts of interests.

3. *Presumptions that reflect social objectives*, like purposive presumptions about the existence of the state, its democratic character, and the achievement of public interest. Presumptions of the separation of powers, judicial independence, and the maintenance of judicial authority are included, too. This category can also include the presumption that the text advances the public interest.

4. *Presumptions that reflect proper forms of behavior*, like the presumption that a text leads to results that are fair, reasonable, and proportional. A text is

presumed not to lead to absurd results; to guarantee fairness and good faith; to increase efficiency. Also included in this category, within contract law, is the presumption of *contra proferentem*, that textual ambiguities should be interpreted in favor of the non-drafting party.

5. *Presumptions that reflect human rights*, like the presumption that a text is designed to guarantee human dignity and freedom, achieve an egalitarian result, and refrain from harming political rights and freedoms (freedom of speech, freedom of movement, freedom of religion, property rights, freedom of occupation, and so forth) and social rights (the right to strike, the right to education, the right to work, and other social rights).

6. *Presumptions that reflect the rule of law.* These include presumptions against vigilantism and of judicial adherence to the law, and the presumption that a text will be interpreted according to its purpose. Also included are the presumption that legal norms should not be bypassed, the presumption that domestic law conforms to public international law, and the presumption of the territorial jurisdiction of local law. A particularly important member of this category is the presumption against retroactive application of a text.

Purposive Presumptions Are Legal Norms Immediately and Always Applicable

Presumptions about the (general) objective purpose of a text are legal norms that the judge must take into account. The fact that they are only presumptions, and that they are rebuttable, does not negate their legal character. Purposive presumptions are matters of law, not fact (*praesumptio juris*). They are not assumptions about the subjective purpose that the text's author envisioned. They are not specific to this or that text. They reflect general values and interests applicable to every will, contract, statute, and constitution. As presumptions of law, they need not be proven. The burden is on the party adversely affected by the presumption to rebut it.

Purposive presumptions apply immediately and always. An interpreter may refer to them at any stage of the interpretive process. They apply regardless of whether or not a text appears "clear"; even if a judge has an initial sense that a text is "clear," he or she must nevertheless refer to the presumptions of purpose. This initial sense of clarity may disappear after the interpreter studies the purposive presumptions and discovers that what seemed clear at first glance is really not at all so. A presumption of purpose is a legal norm of independent applicability. As Cowen wrote, in the context of statutory interpretation,

> Presumptions should be taken into account by the interpreter, *right from the outset*, no matter how wide and general, and no matter how seemingly clear,

the words of the enactment may seem *when considered* in isolation. Furthermore, when all relevant contextual considerations have been duly weighed, the interpreter should *again* test his conclusions in light of the presumptions.[104]

The presumptions are similarly applicable to wills and contracts. The presumptions reflect the natural and ordinary state of affairs. They apply until and unless rebutted, irrespective of the text's apparent clarity.

The Weight of Purposive Presumptions

Every purposive presumption has a "weight" that varies with the weight of the fundamental value from which the presumption is derived. The "heavier" a fundamental value, the heavier the purposive presumption derived from it. Such weight finds expression when purposive presumptions contradict each other.

Purposive Presumptions and the Language of the Text

There are numerous and diverse purposive presumptions that reflect the fullness of a legal system's values and interests. Does every one apply to every text? The answer is no. A purposive presumption operates within the limits of the language of a text. If the language of a text cannot bear the purposive presumption, it does not apply to that text. A purposive presumption applies only if it can, in fact, be realized through the language of the text. That brings us to one of the hard cases presented by the hermeneutic circle. We want to understand the language of the text. In order to do so, we consult a presumption of purpose. We cannot do that, however, unless the presumption can be grounded in the language of the text.

The principle of fore-meaning resolves this dilemma. We approach the text with a fore-meaning that establishes our point of departure. It constitutes—to use Gadamer's term—the interpreter's horizon.[105] From there, we move to the presumption of purpose and back to the text, until we find the ultimate balance and the ultimate understanding of the text, according to its purpose. We need not learn the presumption from within the text. We need not seek a "hint" of the presumption in the language of the text. We learn about the presumption from general law. The text, however, is still the means for actualizing the presumption. If the text cannot bear it, the presumption does not apply to the text.

---

[104] Cowen, *supra* p. 133, note 46 at 391 (emphasis in original).
[105] *Supra* p. 55, note 198.

The Future of Purposive Presumptions

Purposive presumptions are central to purposive interpretation. In most cases, judges resolve interpretive problems by identifying the presumptions of purpose that need to be taken into account and determining the proper relationship between them. One might claim that purposive presumptions simply rationalize interpretive activity that has already taken place. Indeed, one might argue that every presumption has a contradictory counterpart, and that the presumptions march together in opposing pairs. On this claim, relying too heavily on the presumptions reflects a mechanical view of interpretation.

Anyone who thinks that presumptions of purpose constitute rules that determine the single unique legal meaning of a normative text will quickly be disappointed. Purposive presumptions do not lead the interpreter always to a single, unique solution. They sometimes contradict each other. Such contradiction is an expression of their strength, not weakness. They do not reflect rules; they are not intended to determine a unique meaning. They originate in values and principles, and they indicate a direction and trend. They clash with each other, not because they have lost their way, but rather because they reflect the complexity of human experience and the existence of opposing values and principles in law. Purposive presumptions are critical to interpretive activity. They are the basis for interpretive thought. Unfortunately, the law has yet to recognize their importance. Legal science has neglected them, and courts have not sufficiently developed them. Purposive interpretation seeks to change this state of affairs. It offers a mature theory of purposive presumptions, their essence, scope, and weight, and the resolution of contradictions among them. Purposive interpretation transforms the conflicting interpretive rules that create contradictions in other systems of interpretation into clashes between purposive presumptions that reflect clashes between values and principles.

4. CONTRADICTIONS BETWEEN PURPOSIVE PRESUMPTIONS

Contradictions between Values and Principles and the Purposive Presumptions Derived from Them

The presumptions of purpose reflect values and principles, and values and principles relevant to solving a given interpretive problem often contradict each other.[106] The free speech of one person infringes on another's right

---

[106] Sunstein, *supra* p. 13, note 31 at 497.

to his or her reputation. One person's freedom of movement conflicts with the need to protect the public interest. The purposive presumptions that derive from those values and principles often conflict, as well. How do we resolve the contradiction? The answer is, through the proper balance between the conflicting presumptions.[107] As Lord Reid noted, in discussing the purposive presumptions,

> They are aids to construction, presumptions or pointers. Not infrequently one "rule" points in one direction, another in a different direction. In each case we must look at all relevant circumstances and decide as a matter of judgment what weight to attach to any particular "rule."[108]

Purposive presumptions have "weight." A judge balances the conflicting information on a "scale."[109] As Professor Hart has said, we are interested in "the 'weighing' and 'balancing' characteristic of the effort to do justice between competing interests."[110] How does the judge determine weight and conduct the balance?

"Balance," "Weight," "Scales": Metaphors

Of course, there are no physical scales in interpretation. Material weight and balance do not exist, either. The values and principles do not appear

---

[107] Pildes criticizes the theory of balancing, claiming that the judges interpret texts, not orchestrate a balance. He proposes replacing balancing with interpretation. R. Pildes, "Against Balancing: The Role of Exclusionary Reasons in Constitutional Law," 45 *Hastings L.J.* 711 (1994); R. Pildes, "The Structural Concept of Rights and Judicial Balancing," 6 *Rev. Const. Stud.* 179 (2002). I agree with Pildes that the normative framework is interpretation, but I think that in order to interpret—in order to formulate the objective purpose at the core of the text—a judge must orchestrate a balance between conflicting values and principles.

[108] *Maunsell v. Olins* [1975] 1 All E.R. 16, 18. The "rule" mentioned is that conflicting principles should be balanced.

[109] *See* A. Aleinikoff, "Constitutional Law in the Age of Balancing," 96 *Yale L.J.* 943 (1987); P. Kahn, "The Court, the Community and the Judicial Balance: The Jurisprudence of Justice Powell," 97 *Yale L.J.* 1 (1987); F. Coffin, "Judicial Balancing: The Protean Scales of Justice," 63 *N.Y.U. L. Rev.* 16 (1988); K. Sullivan, "Post-Liberal Judging: The Role of Categorization and Balancing," 63 *U. Colo. L. Rev.* 293 (1992); R. Nagel, "Liberals and Balancing," 63 *U. Colo. L. Rev.* 319 (1992); S. Gottlieb, "Introduction: Overriding Public Values," in S. Gottlieb (ed.), *Public Values in Constitutional Law* 1 (1993); N. Strossen, "The Fourth Amendment in the Balance: Accurately Setting the Scales through the Least Intrusive Alternative Analysis," 63 *N.Y.U. L. Rev.* 1173 (1988); L. Henkin, "Infallibility under Law: Constitutional Balancing," 78 *Colum. L. Rev.* 1022 (1978); C. Fried, "Two Concepts of Interests: Some Reflections on the Supreme Court's Balancing Test," 76 *Harv. L. Rev.* 755 (1963); L. Frantz, "The First Amendment in the Balance," 71 *Yale L.J.* 1424 (1962); W. Mendelson, "The First Amendment and the Judicial Process: A Reply to Mr. Frantz," 17 *Vand. L. Rev.* 479 (1964).

[110] H.L.A. Hart, *The Concept of Law* 205 (2d ed. 1994).

before the judge with labels revealing their weights. Nor is there a list of values, arranged by importance and weight. I doubt such a list could be compiled.[111] The interpretive process of resolving contradictions among values and principles—and among the presumptions derived from them—is normative, not physical. Discussion of balance, weight, and weighing is metaphorical.[112] I noted as much in one case:

> These expressions—balance, weight—are just metaphors. Behind them is the view that not all principles are of equal importance to society, and that, in the absence of constitutional guidance, the court must assess the relative social importance of the different values. Just as there is no person without a shadow, so there is no principle without weight. Deciding the balance on the basis of such weight means making a social assessment of the relative importance of the different principles.[113]

Values and principles have weight.[114] We can rank them according to their relative social importance. The "weighing" process is a normative process designed to locate the values and principles—and the purposive presumptions derived from them—within the legal system, and to assign them their relative social values. When there is a contradiction among the values and principles—and the purposive presumptions derived from them—judges resolve the conflict by taking their relative social importance into account. A value with a lighter weight is neither expelled from the legal system nor invalidated. It remains part of the legal system, but the system limits its application or the scope of protection it is afforded for the issue in which a rival value prevailed. In the context of other issues, judges may assign the value a different weight, and the value continues to vie for supremacy. In this respect, values, principles, and their derivative purposive presumptions differ from legal rules. For the latter, conflict ends in life or death. Values and principles, on the other hand, remain in existence, accommodating themselves to the conflict as necessary. Again, the balancing and weighing are not scientific and do not negate the existence of judicial discretion.[115] They do, however, limit it to circumstances in which the legal system ceases to provide the judge with guidance as to the relative social status of the conflicting values and principles. Moderation is necessary. The balance nei-

---

[111] *But see* Murphy, *supra* p. 169, note 83. On the balance of values in German constitutional law, see Hassold, *supra* p. 12, note 29 at 31. On the balance of values in Canadian constitutional law, *see* G. La Forest, "The Balancing of Interests under the Charter," 2 *Nat'l J. Const. L* 133 (1992); B. Wilson, "Decision-Making in the Supreme Court," 36 *U. Toronto L.J.* 227 (1986).

[112] On the benefits and drawbacks of the "balance" metaphor, *see* W. Winslade, "Adjudication and the Balancing Metaphor," in *Legal Reasoning* 403 (H. Hubien ed., 1971).

[113] H.C. 14/86, *Laor v. Council for Review of Films and Plays*, 41(1) P.D. 421, 434.

[114] Dworkin discusses this extensively in R. Dworkin, *Taking Rights Seriously* (1977).

[115] Raz, *supra* p. 165, note 60 at 848.

ther negates the existence of judicial discretion nor leaves an open invitation for judicial discretion in all cases.[116]

Balancing and weighing constitute the internal foundation of the interpretation of a legal text.[117] Consider the *Kol Ha'am* case.[118] An administrative order dating back to the period of the British Mandate authorized the High Commissioner—today, the Minister of Interior—to close any newspaper (temporarily or permanently) if, in his opinion, "any matter appearing in a newspaper is likely to endanger the public peace."[119] The *Kol Ha'am* (*Voice of the People*) newspaper published an article criticizing the Israeli government's position expressing readiness to send troops to the Korean War. The Minister of Interior decided to close the newspaper for a few days. The newspaper petitioned the High Court, raising the question of how the court should interpret the order authorizing the minister to shut down a newspaper. The oral arguments focused on the causal relationship that the word "likely" requires between the article published in the newspaper and the danger to the public peace. Justice Agranat held that the necessary causal connection depends on the balance between the need to safeguard the public peace and the need to protect freedom of expression. Conducting the balance, the court concluded that the causal connection must be one of near certainty (or nearly certain). Thus, the minister may shut down a newspaper if it is nearly certain that something the newspaper published will cause serious harm to the public peace.

Principled and Ad Hoc Balancing

The balance between values and principles—and purposive presumptions—may be principled or ad hoc. A principled balance determines normative weight, which in turn creates a legal standard that can be applied to future cases. In Israel, for example, the principled balance between freedom of expression and public peace is that a public body may restrict freedom of expression only if it is nearly certain that, if the expression is not restricted, the public peace will suffer severe damage. Ad hoc balancing, on the other hand, has no general formula that can be applied in similar situations, except for the general notion that judges should balance competing values and principles according to the circumstances of each case. It is generally preferable to use principled rather than ad hoc balancing. A judge should formulate a "rational principle"[120] that reflects "a standard in-

---

[116] *See* Kelsen, *supra* p. 3, note 4.

[117] *See* Pildes, *supra* p. 177, note 107.

[118] H.C. 73/53 *Kol Ha'am Ltd. v. Minister of Interior*, 7 P.D. 871.

[119] Newspaper Ordinance, Art. 19(2)(a), L.S.I.

[120] H.C. 73/53, *supra* p. 179, note 118 at 881 (Agranat, J.).

formed by values" and not "a random, paternalistic standard whose nature and direction cannot be predicted."[121]

Vertical and Horizontal Balancing

There is no single "balancing formula" for principled balance between competing values and principles. The diversity of situations mandates a diversity of balancing formulas.[122] These include two primary types: horizontal balancing and vertical balancing. Horizontal balancing occurs between values and principles of equal status, as when freedom of speech clashes with the right to privacy, the right to reputation, or freedom of movement. Horizontal balancing expresses the mutual concessions that each value or principle must make in cases of conflict. I noted in one case:

> "Horizontal" balancing occurs between two conflicting values of equal status. The balancing formula evaluates the level of mutual concession of each right. For example, the right to free movement and the right to procession [free assembly] are of equal status. The balancing formula depends on conditions of time, place, and scope, to allow the two rights to co-exist.[123]

In balancing horizontally, judges try to preserve the core of the conflicting values and principles by making mutual concessions on the margins. They try, also, to achieve proportionality in the different concessions and to give each value or principle "breathing room." They should not give one value full expression to the complete frustration of the other. They should establish restrictions of time, place, and manner that will give each of the competing values real and substantial existence. Demonstrations in main thoroughfares should therefore be permitted, even if they interfere with traffic, subject to restrictions of time and manner of demonstration. Sometimes the horizontal balancing sets limits on the conflicting rights.

Vertical balancing is different. Vertical balancing formulas set the conditions under which certain values or principles prevail over others. In Israel, for example, national security or public safety may restrict freedom of speech or freedom of worship and religion if it is likely, on the level of near certainty, that exercising the freedom of speech or freedom of worship and religion will actually and severely damage national security or public safety.

---

[121] F.H. 9/77 *Israeli Electric Company v. Haaretz Newspaper Publications*, 32(3) P.D. 337, 361 (Shamgar, J.). *See also* Aleinikoff, *supra* p. 177, note 109 at 948; T. Emerson, *The System of Freedom of Expression* 16 (1970).

[122] *See* Kahn, *supra* p. 177, note 109 at 3.

[123] H.C. 2481/93 *Dayan v. Jerusalem Regional Commander*, 48(2) P.D. 456, 476.

Similarly, the freedom to leave the country can be limited for reasons of national security only if there is a genuine and serious concern that exercising the freedom of movement will harm national security. Vertical balancing according to different formulas—formulas that reflect the relative status of the conflicting values and principles—does not determine the limits of the right that is restricted. It determines the level of realization and protection that the legal system affords it. The distinction between horizontal and vertical balancing is fuzzy, and in complicated situations, the two kinds of balancing work together.

CHAPTER EIGHT

The Purposive Component:

ULTIMATE PURPOSE

1. THE WEIGHT OF SUBJECTIVE AND OBJECTIVE PURPOSE IN DETERMINING ULTIMATE PURPOSE

The Decisive Stage: Formulating Ultimate Purpose

We arrive at the decisive stage of the interpretive process. It is the stage that distinguishes purposive interpretation from other systems of interpretation. At this stage, judges must formulate the ultimate purpose of the text. They use that purpose to pinpoint the legal meaning of the text along the range of its semantic meanings. This stage is unique to purposive interpretation. It tries to synthesize and integrate subjective and objective purpose. This attempt raises two separate sets of questions: *First,* how do judges achieve the integration, and on what is it based? And *second,* what justifies the integration, what are its benefits and drawbacks, and why prefer it over other systems of interpretation? This chapter and the next will discuss the "how." Chapter 10 will discuss the "why."

Data Constituting the Ultimate Purpose

In formulating the ultimate purpose of a text, judges examine the various relevant data in their kits. *On one hand,* they lay the information about subjective purpose on the table. They study what the author of the text tried to achieve through the text. They consider authorial intent on various levels. Judges do all this through the presumption that the ultimate purpose of the text is to realize the intent of its author. *On the other hand,* they consider the information about objective purpose (intent of the reasonable author; intent of the system). They study what the text is designed to achieve in its society. They take objective purpose into consideration on various levels. Judges do all this through the presumptions of objective purpose. They then reach the stage at which they must formulate the ultimate purpose of the text from all the information. Generally, this task is simple and easy. Usually, all the information about purpose points in the same direction, because the presumptions of subjective and objective purpose are identical in their content. Sometimes, however, there is conflict. Presumptions of subjective purpose contradict each other; presumptions of objective purpose contradict each other; presumptions of subjective purpose contradict presumptions of objective purpose. How should interpreters respond?

Synthesis and Integration

Purposive interpreters seek to reconcile the different presumptions. They aspire to synthesis and integration, not opposition. They do whatever they can to reduce conflict. They seek the ultimate purpose that accords with both subjective and objective purpose. Purposive interpreters look at the life of the text from its conception (and even before that) until the moment of interpretation. They try to formulate an ultimate purpose that takes the fullness of the text's complexity into account. To do so, they make every effort to consider both subjective and objective purpose. If two subjective purposes contradict each other, they choose the subjective purpose that accommodates objective purpose. Similarly, in a contradiction between objective purposes, they try to choose the objective purpose that accommodates the subjective purpose. Purposive interpretation rejects a one-dimensional view—either subjective or objective—of the interpretive process. It views the interpretation of a text—of any text—as a complex process involving both authorial intent and the intention of the system. Having said that, however, this approach will not always bring the interpretive process to its conclusion. Sometimes, interpreters have no choice but to decide which prevails: subjective purpose or objective purpose. How does purposive interpretation respond to this critical situation?

Determining Ultimate Purpose According to the Type of Text

Purposive interpretation has no simple answer to these difficult questions. The answer depends on the substance of the text being interpreted. Purposive interpretation is not based on a single, clear criterion for resolving these questions. Its tool kit contains no clear and sharp "rule of adjudication" or meta-rule. Neither the intent of the historical author nor the intent of the reasonable author or system always trumps. Purposive interpretation distinguishes among different types of texts and determines the relative weight assigned to presumptions of subjective and objective purpose for each of these different types.[1] What types of legal texts does pur-

---

[1] *See* Popkin, *supra* p. 85, note 1 at 221.

posive interpretation address, and what is the relationship between subjective and objective purpose for each type?

The Different Types of Texts

In formulating ultimate purpose, purposive interpretation distinguishes between different types of legal texts. These distinctions derive from the theoretical basis of interpretation—the philosophical, hermeneutic, and constitutional justifications at the core of purposive interpretation. The *first* distinction considers the legal character of the text. The main distinction here is between wills, contracts, statutes, and constitutions. Legal texts exist on a continuum, with wills at one end, constitutions at the other, and, between them, contracts, statutes, and other texts with traits common to these four primary texts. A mutual will, for example, lies on the boundary between a will and contract. An adhesion contract or collective agreement is on the boundary between a contract and statute. On the other side of the boundary are administrative orders, administrative regulations, and judicial decisions. A codification lies at the boundary between a statute and constitution. The *second* distinction is by age of the text. Here, the distinction is between "young" and "old" texts, though, again, this is measured along a continuum, not by discrete stages. The *third* distinction considers the scope of issues arranged in the text and the text's aspirations for completeness. Here, we can distinguish between a specific text that regulates a narrow band of issues and a comprehensive text that seeks to regulate a broad range of issues—for example, a statute that regulates a specific issue versus a codification that regulates a comprehensive system of law, or a specific contract versus an umbrella agreement. The *fourth* distinction considers the character of the regime, the basic assumptions of the society that created the text, and changes in that character and those assumptions. The distinction is important for all texts, but it is particularly relevant to statutes and constitutions. *Fifth* is the design—whether the text is organized through rules, principles, or standards. *Sixth* is the content of the issue regulated. An ordinary will is distinct from a mutual will; an ordinary contract is distinct from an adhesion or consumer contract; "civil" texts are distinct from "criminal" texts.

The above list is not exhaustive. As purposive interpretation develops, we will be able to identify distinctions among additional kinds of texts that are relevant to determining ultimate purpose. Furthermore, the categories often overlap, and we can categorize texts along a myriad of axes. We could place the same text in different categories, and of course, the different classifications may lead to conflicting results.

2. TYPE OF TEXT: WILL, CONTRACT, STATUTE, AND CONSTITUTION

Unity and Diversity in a Text's Ultimate Purpose

The type of text—will, contract, statute, constitution—influences the way we understand it. We interpret a constitution differently from a will. Freund appropriately noted that courts must be careful "not to read the provisions of the Constitution like a last will and testament, lest indeed they become one."[2]

Every kind of text has its own character and role; every kind of text creates its own expectations. These factors influence a text's meaning, but all too often, systems of interpretation ignore them. Purposive interpretation applies to the interpretation of all legal texts, but it treats each type of text specially, according to its nature, allowing texts to develop and express themselves. It is the concept of purpose that facilitates this development and expression. Purpose is a normative concept, shaped by the given legal system, and it extends to both subjective and objective purpose. In the ultimate formulation of this concept ("ultimate purpose"), an interpreter takes the kind of text into account, ensuring the consistent application of the system of interpretation and the interpretive viewpoint to all texts, while expressing the individuality of each kind of text and any special problems it may pose. Presumptions create the flexibility necessary to achieve this goal. Subjective purpose and objective purpose appear before the judge as presumptions, the balance between which gives rise to ultimate purpose. Purposive interpretation is based on legal unity and harmony within the legal system, on the one hand, and on focal points of flexibility at whose center is the purpose of the text, on the other.

Purposive interpretation is holistic. The intent of the author and the intention of the system apply immediately and always, just as the presumptions apply immediately and always, influencing each other and being influenced by each other. An interpreter must decide between them only when they conflict. I will now discuss purposive interpretation's basic perspectives on formulating the ultimate purpose of legal texts according to their types (will, contract, statute, constitution).

The Ultimate Purpose of a Will

A will, like any other text, is interpreted according to its purpose. That includes the interests, objectives, values, and social function that the will is

---

[2] Freund, "The Supreme Law of the United States," 29 *Can. Bar Rev.* 1080, 1086 (1951).

designed to achieve. It is the "platform" at the foundation of the will. It is the will's "plan" for dividing the testator's property. The purpose of a will, like the purpose of any legal text, is a normative concept. It is a legal construction. It is composed of the subjective purpose (testator's intent) and the objective purpose (intent of the reasonable author; intention of the system). These two kinds of purpose appear before the interpreter as presumptions about the ultimate purpose. What is the relationship between these two purposes and the presumptions that derive from them, in case of contradiction? The relationship derives from the unique character of a will. A will expresses the autonomy of an individual's private wishes. It is a unilateral legal act done in contemplation of death (*mortis causa*). Its formation does not depend on acceptance by another person. The testator may amend or terminate it. There is no reliance interest. Heirs may have expectations, but the law does not protect those expectations while the testator is alive. A will is based on a single intent—the intent of the testator.

In formulating the final purpose of a will, therefore, interpreters give prevailing weight to the intent of the legator (subjective purpose). Interpreters learn about this intent from the will in its entirety and the circumstances surrounding its drafting. They may move freely and without restriction from the text to the circumstances and back. The intent of the testator is the primary and central purpose of a will. It is the North Star that guides the interpreter. The presumption that the ultimate purpose of a will is its subjective purpose is decisive.

The presumptions of objective purposes are secondary and supplementary. Nevertheless, they always exist and always apply. Judges should evaluate them at every phase of interpretation. They are particularly important when there is no credible information about the intent of the testator, or when the intent of the testator is known, but it does not solve the problem before the interpreter. This is the case when, between the time the will was made and the time it is interpreted, changes occur that the testator did not anticipate. In these and other circumstances, judges consult objective purpose—the intent of the reasonable testator and of the system. Such purpose reflects, at varying levels of abstraction, the values of the legal system. In this context, the purpose of a will is to divide property reasonably and logically, according to principles of equality and justice, and through achieving the public good. A testator does not make a will on a desert island. A will is part of the legal system. It integrates into that system. It draws life from the system, and in return, it gives life back to the system.

Take a legator who made a will dividing her property among her children without specifying what each child was to get. There is no information about her intent in the matter. In this state of affairs, judges accord significant weight to the objective purpose of the will. They first ask themselves (at a low level of abstraction) if there is enough information to indicate what the testator would have said, at the time she made the will, had she been asked how much each heir would get. In the absence of such information, judges turn to the next and higher level of abstraction—how a reasonable testator would respond. In a democratic society founded on equality, the answer would be that each child gets an equal share. In case of a contradiction between the values of the system, interpreters balance between them. At every level of abstraction, the values and principles appear before judges as presumptions that apply to all wills and that assist in formulating their ultimate purpose. However, these presumptions would not apply if judges could identify a credible and contradictory intent of the testator arising from either internal sources (the will in its entirety) or external sources (the circumstances surrounding its drafting). Credible intent arising from the circumstances—like credible testimony that the testator intended to discriminate among her heirs—is sufficient to render the objective purpose of equality among heirs inapplicable.

The Ultimate Purpose of a Contract

A contract is interpreted according to its purpose. The purpose of a contract is the interests, objectives, values, policy, and social function that the contract is designed to actualize. The purpose of a contract is a normative concept. It comprises subjective purpose (joint intent of the parties) and objective purpose (intent of reasonable parties; intention of the system). What is the relationship between these purposes when, during the interpretation of a contract, they conflict? The answer lies in the nature of a contract. A contract expresses the autonomy of the contractual parties' private will. A contract creates reasonable, legally protected expectations between the parties and reliance on its results. A contract may also create a reliance interest among third parties. Consistent with the character of purposive interpretation, judges determine the ultimate purpose of a contract primarily by the joint intent of the parties at the time the contract was formed. Hence the presumption—which has decisive weight in Israel—that the ultimate purpose of a contract is its subjective purpose. It is not the intent of a single party; it is the joint intent of both parties, or at least the intent of one side that is known to the other. It is not the joint intent as a reasonable person would understand it; it is the "real" joint intent of the parties, as it arises from the entirety of the contract and the circumstances surrounding its formation. A judge moves between the text and the external circumstances freely and without formal restrictions.

What does an interpreter do when he or she cannot know what the parties' joint intent was? What about a contract in which the joint intent of the parties cannot resolve the interpretive question facing the judge? How should the judge interpret a contract if, between its formation and its interpretation, developments take place that the parties did not consider? What meaning should the judge give a contract as it relates to a third party who is unaware of the joint intent of the parties? In these and other cases—and they arise frequently in everyday practice—the judge should consult objective purpose. The judge assumes that the parties to the contract are reasonable persons who seek to achieve reasonable results, fairness, and efficiency. The judge further assumes that the contract is intended to actualize the fundamental values of the system as they exist at the time of interpretation, like justice, the public good, and human rights. These objective purposes—like the subjective purposes—appear before the judge as presumptions. They apply immediately and perpetually. They cease to apply, however, if the joint intent of the parties contradicts them. In a conflict between the joint intent of the parties and the intent of the reasonable person, joint intent trumps, and the judge should interpret the contract accordingly. A party who claims otherwise violates the principle of good faith.

Reliable information about the parties' joint intent, gleaned from sources external to the contract, prevails over the contract's objective purpose. In determining that objective purpose, an interpreter should resolve conflicts among different presumptions of objective purpose according to the respective weights of each systemic value and principle that the presumptions reflect. In contractual interpretation, however, subjective purpose dominates. Objective purpose is decisive only when the interpreter cannot know the subjective purpose. This general preference for subjective purpose may change according to the nature of the contract.[3] The more a contract deviates from the ordinary two-party paradigm, the less influential subjective purpose and its presumptions become, and the greater the role of objective purpose and its derivative presumptions.

The Ultimate Purpose of a Statute

Judges interpret a statute according to the purpose it is designed to achieve. The purpose of a statute is the interests, objectives, values, policy, and social function that the statute is designed to actualize. It is the social change that the statute visits on existing law. It is the *ratio legis*. The purpose of a statute—like the purpose of every other legal text—is a legal construction, composed of subjective and objective components. Subjective purpose in the case of a statute is the intention of the legislature at the time of enactment. It is abstract (not concrete) intention, operating at a high level of abstraction.[4] It indicates the general policy direction that the legislature

---

[3] *Infra* p. 337.
[4] *Infra* p. 341.

seeks to achieve. It reflects the desired social change. Judges learn about it from the language of the text and from the circumstances surrounding its creation. Judges may always consult those circumstances and may take them into account as long as the information about them is certain, credible, and clear. Judges consider this subjective purpose in the form of a presumption that a statute's ultimate purpose is its subjective purpose.

A statute's objective purpose is the special goals that a statute on the subject in question is designed to achieve in a democracy, at the time of interpretation. It appears before the judge in the form of specific presumptions about the purpose of the legislation. At a high level of abstraction, these presumptions are the fundamental values, principles, and aspirations of the system that serve as a normative umbrella over all statutes.

The key issue in formulating a statute's ultimate purpose is the relationship between subjective and objective purpose and the internal relationship among various objective purposes. What happens when these purposes conflict? Resolving the conflict requires a more theoretical inquiry into the type of legislation in question. Democracy itself mandates such inquiry, because legislative supremacy is integral to the concept of democracy.[5] For this reason, a judge interpreting a statute seeks to realize the (abstract) intent of the legislature, as it arises from the statute itself and from the circumstances surrounding its creation. A statute is not, however, just a command that the legislature gives to an individual. It is also a normative arrangement that determines what is permitted and what is forbidden. This normative arrangement operates within the limits of a democratic system of law. Democracy requires—in addition to legislative supremacy—maintaining the system's fundamental values, including human rights.[6] A judge's interpretation must actualize the system's fundamental values, expressed as different presumptions about the legislation's (objective) purpose. When the messages the judge receives about purpose conflict, he or she must achieve the subjective goal of the legislature while actualizing the system's fundamental values. Under certain circumstances, the type of text—its age, the type of issues it addresses, the way it regulates those issues, and the content of the regulation—justifies disregarding legislative intent. Interpreting legislation presents the interpreter with difficulties particular to statutes. He or she must tailor his or her approach. There is no magical formula for determining the relationship between (abstract) subjective purpose and (individual or general) objective purpose. The relationship depends on the type of text, as we shall see when we focus on statutory interpretation.[7]

[5] *Infra* p. 238.
[6] *Infra* p. 239.
[7] *Infra* p. 339.

The Ultimate Purpose of a Constitution

Judges interpret a constitution according to its purpose—the objectives, values, and principles that the constitutional text is designed to actualize. As is the case for any legal text, such purpose is composed of both subjective and objective purpose. The subjective component is the goals, values, and principles that the constitutional assembly sought to achieve through it, at the time it enacted the constitution. It is the original intent of the founding fathers. Purposive interpretation translates such intent into a presumption about subjective purpose, that is, that the ultimate purpose of the text is to achieve the (abstract) intent of its authors. There is also, however, the objective purpose of the text—the goals, values, and principles that the constitutional text is designed to achieve in a modern democracy at the time of interpretation. Purposive interpretation translates this purpose into the presumption that the ultimate purpose of the constitution is its objective purpose.

The key question in formulating a constitution's ultimate purpose is the relationship between subjective and objective purpose and the internal relationship between various objective purposes. Purposive interpretation answers this question according to the character and unique features of the constitutional text.[8] A constitution is at the top of a normative pyramid. It is designed to guide human behavior for a long period of time.[9] It is not easily amendable. It uses many open-ended expressions.[10] It is designed to shape the character of the state for the long term. It lays the foundation for the state's social values and aspirations. In giving expression to this constitutional uniqueness, a judge interpreting a constitution must accord significant weight to its objective purpose and derivative presumptions. Constitutional provisions should be interpreted according to society's basic normative positions at the time of interpretation.

The intent of the constitutional founders (abstract subjective intent) remains important. We need the past to understand the present. Subjective purpose confers historical depth, honoring the past and its importance. In purposive interpretation, it takes the form of a presumption of purpose that applies immediately, throughout the process of interpreting a constitution. It is not, however, decisive. Its weight is substantial immediately following

---

[8] *Infra* p. 370.

[9] W. Douglas, *We the Judges: Studies in American and Indian Constitutional Law from Marshall to Mukherjea* 429 (1956) (noting that a constitution "is a compendium, not a code; a declaration of articles of faith, not a compilation of laws"). For a discussion of the time element of constitutions, see Rubenfeld, *supra* p. 162, note 46; J. Rubenfeld, *Freedom and Time: A Theory of Constitutional Self-Government* (2001).

[10] W.J. Brennan, "Construing the Constitution," 19 *U.C. Davis L. Rev.* 2 (1985).

the founding, but as time elapses, its influence diminishes. It cannot freeze the future development of the constitutional provision. Although the roots of the constitutional provision are in the past, its purpose is determined by the needs of the present, in order to solve problems in the future. In a clash between subjective and objective purposes, the objective purpose of a constitution prevails. It prevails even when it is possible to prove subjective purpose through reliable, certain, and clear evidence. Subjective purpose remains relevant, however, in resolving contradictions between conflicting objective purposes.[11]

3. TYPE OF TEXT: EFFECT OF A TEXT'S AGE ON ITS ULTIMATE PURPOSE

Age As a Factor in Formulating Ultimate Purpose

The age of a text affects the way we understand it.[12] Judges may interpret a newly created legal text according to the intent of its author but, as time passes, interpret the same text according to the intention of the system. Obviously, an author may clarify that he or she wishes the text, as it ages, to be interpreted more and more according to objective purpose, and less and less according to subjective purpose. Perhaps the author intended that, when the text was young, judges would interpret it according to the author's intent, but as the text aged, they would interpret it according to the intention of the system. Honoring that intention is unproblematic. As a text ages, it becomes harder and harder for the interpreter to enter the shoes of the author, to receive reliable information about his or her intent, and to interpret the text as it would have been interpreted on the day it was written.[13] Resorting to objective purpose helps avoid these obstacles.

Indeed, that principle holds true even if the author of the text wished his or her intent to prevail throughout the life of the text, and even if, despite the passage of time, there is credible information about the intent of the author, and judges could interpret the text according to that intent. Even though the text could be interpreted according to its subjective purpose, the passage of time requires us to understand the text according to its objective purpose. A legal text, by its nature, is intended to regulate human relations in the future. It sets rules that will apply for years—sometimes many years—after their enactment. As a text ages, the law, by its nature, weakens the con-

---

[11] For a discussion of this approach, see *infra* p. 204.

[12] Marmor and Raz make this argument based on their idea of authority. *Infra* p. 261.

[13] R. Posner, "Past-Dependency, Pragmatism, and Critique of History in Adjudication and Legal Scholarship," 67 *U. Chi. L. Rev.* 573 (2000).

trol of the author over the text he or she created, and strengthens the control of the legal system—which tries to bridge the gap between law and society's changing needs—in the form of objective purpose. Obsolete social perspectives should not hold contemporary society hostage. As time passes, for example, society changes the way it views women and their role, the best interest of a child and how to achieve it, and numerous other issues. These changes warrant giving a text a meaning—within the limits of its original language—that fits society's contemporary fundamental values. As I noted in one case, "As Israeli judges, it is our responsibility to give the word 'spouse' the meaning it has in Israeli society, not in mid-nineteenth-century British Victorian society."[14] A judge does this by ascribing significant weight to objective purpose in interpreting an "old" text. This is certainly the case for an old constitution, whose claim to validity relies in part on its expression of modern needs.[15] Below I will discuss how judges weight objective purpose for old texts in interpreting contracts and statutes.

The Effect of Age on the Ultimate Purpose of a Contract

Judges interpret a contract according to its purpose. Because judges generally give a contract's subjective purpose more weight, subjective purpose usually prevails over an opposing objective purpose. However, that may not be the case in long-term contracts based on ongoing relations between the parties (a relational contract). These contracts bind the parties in a long-term relationship, whose parameters they establish through the contract.[16] Judges interpreting a newly created relational contract should accord significant weight to the joint intent of the parties. As time passes, however, and the relationship between the parties develops and moves farther away from its point of departure, objective purpose should grow in strength, until it dominates the interpretation of the contract and determines its ultimate purpose.

The Effect of Age on the Ultimate Purpose of a Statute

The presumption of subjective purpose weakens with the passage of time between the enactment of a statute and its interpretation.[17] At a certain

---

[14] Cr. A. 2000/97, *supra* p. 155, note 22.

[15] Raz, *supra* p. 41, note 124 at 164.

[16] Ample literature exists on relational contracts, including a clear summary in R. Hillman, *The Richness of Contract Law* 259 (1997).

[17] Marmor agrees with this position, basing it on his approach to legislative expertise. *See*

point, the weight of subjective purpose disappears entirely, and objective purpose finds full expression. The argument is not that the legislature intended the statute, as it ages, to be interpreted according to the intention of the system. Nor is it that, as time passes, it is impossible to know what the legislature intended. The passage of time does, however, weaken the presumption of subjective purpose and strengthen objective purpose, until eventually, the latter alone determines ultimate purpose.[18] Bennion expressed this idea, as well:

> Each generation lives under the law it inherits. Constant formal updating is not practicable, so an Act takes on a life of its own. What the original framers intended sinks gradually into history. While their language may endure as law, its current subjects are likely to find that law more and more ill-fitting. The intention of the originators, collected from an Act's legislative history, necessarily becomes less relevant as time rolls by.[19]

In no way do I adopt an objective approach to interpretation, which discards legislative intent even in interpreting a young statute. My approach views the age of the text as a continuum, along which the influence of subjective purpose diminishes as the text ages.[20]

4. TYPE OF TEXT: DISTINGUISHING TEXTS BY SCOPE OF ISSUES REGULATED

Scope of Issues Regulated by the Text

Legal texts vary in the scope of issues they regulate, ranging from a narrow slice of human relations to broad and comprehensive fields. Contracts, for example, range from specific agreements to framework agreements covering a number of specific contracts and addressing a number of issues to be

---

A. Marmor, "Kavanat Hamichokek Visamchut Hachok [Legislative Intent and Statutory Authority]," 16 Iyunei Mishpat 593 (1991). Raz agrees, too. *See* J. Raz, "Intention in Interpretation," in *The Autonomy of Law: Essays on Legal Positivism* 249, 277 (R. George ed., 1995).

[18] *See* Dworkin, *supra* p. 13, note 33 at 350. *See also* Zweigert and Puttfarken, *supra* p. 169, note 84 at 712: "[T]here is a proportion between the age of the rule and the weight of its legislative intention: as for a recent statute, there is a presumption that its meaning as intended by its draftsman in the legislature should be its actual meaning; however, the older a statute, the more legitimate is a method of interpretation which frees itself from the ideas of the historic legislator and attempts to find its meaning from different criteria based on the conditions of today."

[19] Bennion, *supra* p. 6, note 13 at 687.

[20] *See* G. Calabresi, *A Common Law for the Age of Statutes* (1982).

regulated in the future between the parties. Statutes, too, range from specific statutes to codifications of the entire body of civil law or a large portion thereof. This distinction is relevant because the more specific a text, the more weight judges should give to the subjective purpose that its author sought to achieve and to the resulting presumptions. The more general and comprehensive a text, the more weight judges should give to its objective purpose and resulting presumptions. The author of a specific text, as opposed to a general text, can better describe the human behavior he or she seeks to regulate; can anticipate future developments more accurately and provide for them; can more easily find precise language to describe the human behavior that is the subject of the text. The interpreter of a specific text is more justified in resorting to authorial intent as a source of information about the details of the arrangement, and has less need to resort to the system's general values.[21] In contrast, for a general text that regulates a broad range of human activity, it is harder to accurately describe the human behavior in question and harder to anticipate future developments. This latter kind of text must use general language and vague descriptions of social behavior. An interpreter has more need to resort to the system's general values to penetrate the text's obscure concepts, and less need to consult authorial intent, which quickly ceases to be helpful.[22]

Interpreting a Codification

A codification is a good example of the way the scope of a statute affects its interpretation. A code is a comprehensive piece of legislation that regulates a broad swath of human relations. It aspires to be whole, methodical, abstract, and innovative.[23] It must rely on open-ended concepts (like good faith, reasonableness, fairness). The interpreter of this kind of legislation—which, to a certain extent, resembles a constitution—should ascribe limited weight to the intent of its authors and heavy weight to the

---

[21] On this point, my views coincide with those of Marmor (*supra* p. 261) to some extent. According to Marmor, the narrower the scope of the statute, and the more it addresses professional or technical issues, the greater consideration should be given to the expertise of its author, including in interpreting the text. My views are not based on the idea of expertise, but they converge with it here.

[22] P.M. Tiersma, "A Message in a Bottle: Text, Autonomy, and Statutory Interpretation," 76 *Tul. L. Rev.* 431 (2001).

[23] S.A. Bayitch, "Codification in Modern Times," in *Civil Law in the Modern World* 161, 162 (A.N. Yiannopoulos ed., 1965); F.F. Stone, "A Primer on Codification," 29 *Tul. L. Rev.* 303 (1955); A. Levasseur, "On the Structure of a Civil Code," 44 *Tul. L. Rev.* 693 (1970); *The Code Napoleon and the Common Law World* (B. Schwartz ed., 1956); K. Zweigert and H. Kötz, *An Introduction to Comparative Laws* 85 (T. Weir trans., 3d rev. ed. 1998).

code's objective purpose.[24] The values and principles that the system seeks to actualize play a prominent role. The interpreter should harmonize the legislative arrangements with each other and with the general legal structure. He or she should give the code's provisions an interpretation that accords with the values and fundamental perspectives in effect on the day of interpretation. Even if the authors of the code did not envision those goals, such that they are not part of the code's subjective purpose, the interpreter should realize them as part of the code's objective purpose. The meaning of the code, therefore, may change over the years. Every generation will read and understand it differently. This is the source of the code's power and its ability to withstand the test of time, continuing to address society's changing needs.

An interpreter learns a code's objective purpose primarily from its language, the nature of its arrangements, and the essence of the issue being regulated. Civil code provisions about contracts, sales, agency, security, guarantee, assignment, gift, leasing, and other topics are legal "institutions" that take on the objective characteristics of each subject regulated. These provisions reflect not the subjective perspectives of the members of the legislative body but rather the modern legal community's fundamental perspectives on the role that these legal institutions should play in modern society. The objective purposes of the various legal institutions and the reciprocal relationships between them indicate the fundamental objective perspectives at the core of the codification.

5. TYPE OF TEXT: CHANGES IN REGIME CHARACTER AND SOCIETY'S FUNDAMENTAL ASSUMPTIONS

When Fundamental Social and Legal Assumptions Change

Every legal text is a creature of its environment, influencing its environment and being influenced by it in return. This environment is not limited to the immediate circumstances of the text's creation but rather overlapping circles of normative and social data and fundamental social and legal assumptions that nourish the text and are nourished by it. They include, among other things, accepted principles, fundamental objectives, and basic standards. An author does not create a text—will, contract, statute, con-

---

[24] J. McDonnell, "Purposive Interpretation of the Uniform Commercial Code: Some Implications for Jurisprudence," 126 *U. Pa. L. Rev.* 795 (1978); S. Herman, "Legislative Management of History: Notes on the Philosophical Foundations of the Civil Code," 53 *Tul L. Rev.* 380, 394 (1979); J. White and R. Summers, *Uniform Commercial Code* (5th ed. 2000); B. Frier, "Interpreting Codes," 89 *Mich. L.* Rev. 2201 (1991).

stitution—in a vacuum,[25] but rather against the backdrop of a social and legal reality, predicated on fundamental social and legal assumptions based in social and legal history and dynamic intellectual conventions that rejuvenate the text. Changes in these fundamental assumptions affect the way we understand a text. Often, these changes occur over time, and the very passage of time affects the way we understand the text. Even when these changes occur quickly, however, they still affect the interpretation of the text.

How does this influence find expression? In my opinion, changes in the character of the regime and in fundamental values express themselves in the formulation of the text's ultimate purpose. Specifically, an interpreter ascribes less weight to the author's intent (subjective purpose and its derivative purposive presumptions) and more weight to the "intention" of the reasonable author and of the legal system (objective purpose and its derivative purposive presumptions). As the fundamental assumptions on which authorial intent was formulated undergo substantial change, there is less and less reason to take that intent into consideration. At the same time, there is greater reason to take the new social and legal data into consideration.

Change in Regime Structure: Transition to Democracy

An example of a change in the character of the regime—which affects the internal relationship between subjective and objective purpose—is the case of a society that undergoes a transition to democracy.[26] In interpreting statutes enacted during the nondemocratic era, an interpreter should give only limited weight to the intent of the nondemocratic legislature. Instead, the interpreter of those statutes should accord significant weight to the contemporary fundamental democratic values which, at the time of interpretation, constitute the framework for the old legislation. In Israel, for example, contemporary judges are called upon to interpret legislation enacted during the pre-state British mandate period. A long line of precedents requires the legislation to be interpreted according to the fundamental values of the new state, not the intent of the nondemocratic legislature. As I noted in one case,

[25] *See* Lord Edmund-Davies's comments in *Morris v. Beardmore* [1981] A.C. 446, 459 ("A statute does not exist in limbo. It has a background, it rests on an assumption that it will operate only in a certain climate and that circumstances of a certain sort will prevail").

[26] An example is the Eastern bloc countries that became democracies. *See* B. Ackerman, *The Future of Liberal Revolution* (1992); R. Teitel, *Transitional Justice* (2000); H. Schwartz, *The Struggle for Constitutional Justice in Post-Communist Europe* (2000).

The interpretation given to defense regulations in the State of Israel differs from the interpretation they may have had during the Mandate period. The defense regulations today are part of the laws of a democratic country. They must be interpreted against the backdrop of the Israeli legal system's fundamental principles.[27]

Interpreters should take a similar approach in the converse situation, where the general values are democratic, but an undemocratic regime takes power. To the extent that the general values of the system continue to operate, judges should use them to interpret legislation passed by the undemocratic regime. They should not consider the intent of the undemocratic legislature. Dyzenhaus discussed the intent of the undemocratic legislature in the context of statutory interpretation in apartheid South Africa:

> [T]he legitimacy of that approach depends on a democratic theory which says that the people speak through their elected parliamentary representatives, and thus the statutes enacted by the legislature must be applied by judges so as best to approximate what those representatives actually intended. In other words, the legitimacy of an approach which requires judges to ignore in their interpretation of the law their substantive convictions about what the law should be requires a substantive commitment at a deeper level to the intrinsic legitimacy of that law. However, the Parliament whose statutes they interpreted was illegitimate by the criteria of any democratic theory and so the subjective justification for their approach was absent.[28]

Purposive interpretation dictates this approach by according significant weight to objective purpose, not subjective purpose, in statutory interpretation. Some judges in South Africa adopted this approach in the era of apartheid.[29]

6. TYPE OF TEXT: TEXTS BASED ON RULES AND TEXTS BASED ON STANDARDS

Rules and Principles in Formulating Ultimate Purpose

There is an accepted distinction between normative arrangements expressed as rules and normative arrangements expressed as principles or

---

[27] H.C. 680/88, *supra* p. 155, note 22 at 628. *See also* H.C. 2722/92 *Alamrin v. IDF Commander in the Gaza Strip*, 46(3) P.D. 693, 705.

[28] D. Dyzenhaus, *Judging the Judges, Judging Ourselves: Truth, Reconciliation and the Apartheid Legal Order* 166 (1998).

[29] D. Dyzenhaus, *Hard Cases in Wicked Legal Systems: South African Law in the Perspective of Legal Philosophy* (1991).

standards.[30] A rule details a set of facts that, if it materializes, mandates a normative conclusion. For example, the prohibition against driving faster than 55 miles per hour is a rule. A principle or standard, in contrast, establishes background values that, if they materialize, mandate a normative conclusion. For example, the prohibition against driving at an unreasonable speed is a principle. Of course, both a rule and a principle or standard are based on fundamental values. The difference is that the fundamental values on which a rule is based are external to the rule. The author of the text derives a normative conclusion from the fundamental value or principle and gives it independent normative status as a rule. On the other hand, the fundamental values shaping a normative arrangement formulated as a principle or standard are part of the normative conditions of that principle or standard.

This distinction between texts that ground rules and texts that ground principles or standards becomes important in formulating ultimate purpose. The interpreter of a rule-based text should give greater weight to the intent of the author (subjective purpose). The interpreter of a principle- or standard-based text should give greater weight to the intention of the system (objective purpose). The justification for this distinction is not that the author of a principle- or standard-based text intended for it to be interpreted according to objective purpose. Nor is it that rules generally establish specific arrangements, while principles generally regulate a broad scope of human activities. The reason for distinguishing between rule-based and standard-based texts goes to the heart of purposive interpretation: A text formulating a rule makes a precise decision about what is permitted and what is forbidden. In understanding the objective at the core of the prohibition and permission, judges should ascribe significant weight to the intent of the author at the time the text was written. Because the author made specific decisions about what is allowed and what is forbidden, judges should inquire into the objective he or she sought to achieve. In contrast, a text formulating a principle or standard sets an ideal to be attained. The ideal operates within a legal system, is shaped by it, and influences it. Judges should therefore ascribe significant weight to the system's fundamental values, in order to learn how a member of society understands the ideal at the time it is given meaning.

A Statute Providing for "Reasonable" Behavior

A statute sometimes provides for certain results if behavior is reasonable. Judges must formulate the scope and extent of the word "reasonable."

---

[30] M. Bayles, *Principles of Law: A Normative Analysis* 11 (1987); K. Sullivan, "Foreword: The Justices of Rules and Standards," 106 *Harv. L. Rev.* 22, 38 (1992).

How do they do so? In my opinion, legislative intent is of little assistance. Again, the question is not what the legislature understood by the word "reasonable" at the time of enactment but rather what a member of contemporary society, to whom the provision is addressed, understands it to mean at the time of interpretation. We tend to say that a decision is reasonable if it is made by a reasonable person. Of course, that only reframes and personifies the problem. We must ask how a reasonable person would behave in contemporary society. The reply that the court is the reasonable person, or that reasonableness depends on the circumstances, does not take us very far, either. "Reasonableness" is a vague concept often used circularly to avoid giving it any real content. We should recognize that reasonableness is not a physical or metaphysical concept, but rather a normative concept. Reasonableness means identifying the relevant considerations and balancing them according to their weight. It is evaluative, not descriptive. Reasonableness is not just rationality. As MacCormick noted,

> [W]hat justifies resort to the requirement of reasonableness is the existence of a *plurality* of factors requiring to be *evaluated* in respect of their *relevance* to a common *focus of concern* (in this case a decision). Unreasonableness consists in ignoring some relevant factor or factors, in treating as relevant what ought to be ignored. Alternatively, it may involve some *gross* distortion of the relative values of different factors even though different people can come to different evaluations each of which falls within the range of reasonable opinions in the matter in hand.[31]

A decision is reasonable if it is reached after giving the proper weight to the different values that need to be taken into account. Nothing is reasonable in itself.

How, then, do we determine how much weight to give each of the relevant values? Perlman thinks judges should give the different values the weight to which an audience would agree after listening to a debate on the subject, conducted with the tools of legal rhetoric.[32] That approach does not seem to take us very far. Germany has developed the theory of *topoi*,[33] which details each alternative, weighing its advantages and disadvantages, in a discussion and exchange of ideas that leads to the optimal solution. Under the *topoi* theory, judges should avoid exaggeration and take a proportional approach to determining the proper balance between competing considerations of principle. MacCormick uses the metaphor of the reason-

---

[31] D.N. MacCormick, "On Reasonableness," in *Les Notions à Contenu Variable en Droit* 136 (Ch. Perelman and R. Vander Elst eds., 1984). *See also* M. Atienza, "On the Reasonable in Law," 3 *Ratio Juris* 148 (1990).

[32] Ch. Perelman, *Legal Logic* 144 (1984).

[33] Larenz, *supra* p. 3, note 5 at 14.

able person who, to his mind, represents Aristotelian wisdom. According to MacCormick, the reasonable person represents a continuing attempt to find a foothold for objective evaluation, free of subjectivity. He believes that the reasonable person represents "our common desire to find common criteria of moral and practical judgment which have at least inter-subjective, if not absolutely objective, validity within a given social milieu."[34] We must appraise and evaluate this attempt to find a common standard. We do not seek to uncover what is already there, but rather to find something new. MacCormick continues: "The point is indeed one of *constructing* rather than discovering an order of relative priority among competing values, and yet of doing so in such a way as could command the assent of all interested parties if they could but abstract from their personal engagement in the contested issue."[35]

MacCormick concludes that judges should accord the different values the weight to which a universal audience of listeners would agree. But how do we know to what a universal audience of listeners would agree? We seem to have returned to the "interpretive community"[36] that reflects social agreement in a given society at a given point in time. A decision or activity would be reasonable if it gives the different values the weight that the legal community gives them. That is why we need objective purpose to give content to the phrase "reasonableness." The weight that the legal community ascribes to different values changes with time, and it is determined not by the views of the text's author, but rather by the views of society at the time of interpretation.

7. TYPE OF TEXT: CONTENT OF THE PROVISION

Content of the Provision and Its Effect on Ultimate Purpose

Although the framework may be identical—will, contract, statute, constitution—legal texts make provisions that differ in content. In the fields of wills and contracts, purposive interpretation distinguishes between ordinary situations (the paradigm) and special and exceptional situations. In wills, the exception is the joint and mutual will. In contracts, exceptions include contracts that reflect unequal bargaining positions (like a consumer contract or adhesion contract), contracts in which one party represents the public interest (government contracts), and contracts that affect third parties (collective agreements). In the field of legislation, we should take into

---

[34] MacCormick, *supra* p. 199, note 31 at 153.
[35] *Id.*
[36] *Supra* p. 38.

consideration special kinds of legislation, like criminal legislation,[37] the understanding of which affects public expectations.

Do these distinctions within each kind of legal text affect the relationship between authorial intent and the intent of the reasonable author or of the system (i.e., the relationship between subjective and objective purpose) in formulating the ultimate purpose of a legal text? The answer is far from simple. In theory, there is no reason not to draw distinctions of content. Purposive interpretation is flexible enough—in the stage of determining how to formulate ultimate purpose—to give expression to the different kinds of content. However, legal traditions have yet to address the issue satisfactorily. Below, I raise a number of ideas for consideration in this area.

Ultimate Purpose in a Joint and Mutual Will

The interpreter of an "ordinary" will gives decisive weight to the intent of the testator. What of a joint and mutual will? A will is joint if two or more parties reached a joint decision about the content of the will that will be executed in a single physical document, signed by both testators. A will is mutual if the arrangements of one testator are based on the arrangements of the other in a set of reciprocal or identical provisions for the disposition of each testator's property. An example is a joint decision (joint will) made by a couple about the will they will make, in a single document. If the document provides that when one dies, the other inherits the property, and then when the other dies, the property is divided equally among their children from previous marriages, the will is both joint and mutual. A joint and mutual will differs from an ordinary will, in which judges accord decisive weight to the intent of the testator. In a joint and mutual will, judges must consider the joint intent of both testators. In this respect, a joint and mutual will resembles a contract.[38] The judge should consider the intent of both testators, and if the intent of one is unknown, the judge should replace the missing intent with the objective purpose of the will, giving it the same weight as the (known) intent of the other testator.

Ultimate Purpose in an Adhesion Contract

An adhesion contract[39] is subject to the laws of interpretation, just like any other contract. In principle, significant weight should be ascribed to the

---

[37] P.M. Tiersma, "A Message in a Bottle: Text, Autonomy, and Statutory Interpretation," 76 *Tul. L. Rev.* 431 (2001).

[38] H. Brox, *Erbrecht* 152 (15th rev. ed., 1994).

[39] For a discussion of adhesion contracts, *see* F. Kessler, "Contracts of Adhesion—Some

joint intent of the parties. Joint intent is generally created when, during contractual negotiations, parties have exchanged ideas that crystallize into a joint intent as to the purpose of the contract. The parties to an adhesion contract (supplier and customer), however, rarely conduct negotiations and formulate their own joint intent. The burden of proof rests with the person who contends that such negotiations took place. Ordinarily, the supplier prepares a draft adhesion contract, and the customer accepts it as-is, without formulating a joint intent beyond the intent to form a contract. In the absence of joint intent, judges should not interpret an adhesion contract according to the intent of either the customer or the supplier, but rather according to its objective purpose. Objective purpose is the central purpose at its core or the rationale for creating an adhesion contract. I noted as much in a case before me: "The purpose of an adhesion contract is primarily its objective purpose. An adhesion contract does have a subjective purpose . . . but it is generally difficult to prove. Only rarely can the joint intent of the parties be revealed."[40]

The text of an adhesion contract does not result from negotiations between the parties. It reflects the objective interests, values, and principles at the core of the deal. It does not vary from party to party. The objective purpose of an adhesion contract is therefore uniform, despite the differences between the parties. This uniformity has the advantage of reducing transaction costs and guaranteeing security and certainty in the legal relationship. To some extent, the uniformity mitigates the disadvantages of an adhesion contract to the non-drafting party by detaching objective purpose from the particularities of each party and each deal. In contrast to the outfit sewn by a tailor, an adhesion contract is a mass-produced garment. It is neither personal nor special. Only a subjective intent common to both parties and contradicting objective purpose can justify deviating from objective purpose.

Ultimate Purpose in a Consumer Contract

A consumer contract is unique for its own reasons. It requires a special balance between the consumer and those who are parties to the contract as part of the course of their business. The rules of interpretation help achieve

---

Thoughts about Freedom of Contract," 43 *Colum. L. Rev.* 629 (1943); R. Dugan, "Standardized Form Contracts—An Introduction," 24 *Wayne L. Rev.* 1307 (1978); W.D. Slawson, "The New Meaning of Contract: The Transformation of Contract Law by Standard Forms," 46 *U. Pitt. L. Rev.* 21 (1984); T. Rakoff, "Contracts of Adhesion: An Essay in Reconstruction," 96 *Harv. L. Rev.* 1174 (1983).

[40] P.C.A. 1185/97, *supra* p. 151, note 12 at 158. *See also* C.A. 779/89 *Shalev v. Sela Insurance Company,* 48(1) P.D. 1 221, 228.

this balance in the way they do for any other contract. Purposive interpretation, however, does this by giving expression to the consumer nature of the contract through its objective purpose. We might develop a rule requiring judges, in interpreting a consumer contract, to accord significant weight to the contract's objective purpose.

Ultimate Purpose in a Criminal Statute

Purposive interpretation applies to criminal statutes just as it applies to any other legal text. The interpreter of a criminal statute, therefore, balances between its subjective and objective purpose. Does the criminal character of the statute have special significance? Shouldn't we say that, because of the criminal nature of the statutory arrangements, we should give greater weight to the natural and ordinary meaning of the statutory language, even if such meaning does not achieve the statute's purpose?[41] I think not. I do not think that a criminal statute is unique in this respect. An interpreter may give the language of the statute an unnatural and non-ordinary meaning, within the range of its semantic possibilities, as long as such meaning achieves the purpose of the provision. However, because of the harm such extraordinary meaning may inflict on the liberty of the individual who misunderstands it, judges should accord significant weight to the civil rights of the accused in balancing the purposes to arrive at ultimate purpose.

8. THE EFFECT OF TYPE OF TEXT ON ULTIMATE PURPOSE

The Purposive Approach to Determining Ultimate Purpose

The type of text affects the relative weight given to authorial intent, on the one hand, and the intent of the reasonable author and the values of the system, on the other hand, in determining ultimate purpose. True, subjective and objective purposes, and the presumptions that derive from each, play a role in the interpretation of all texts. The presumptions apply immediately and always. There is no fixed point of departure. One interpreter will start with the presumption of subjective purpose, while another will start with the presumption of objective purpose. The picture becomes clear as the interpretive process continues. This is particularly true as the purposive interpreter seeks to overcome conflicts between objective and subjective purpose to

---

[41] For this approach, see M. Kremnitzer, *Interpretation in Criminal Law*, 21 *Isr. L. Rev.* 358 (1988); D. Kahan, "Lenity and Federal Common Law Crime," 1994 *Sup. Ct. Rev.* 345; J. Hall, *General Principles of Criminal Law* 19, 32 (1947).

achieve synthesis. Conflict exists, however, and the interpreter must deal with it. In interpreting a will or contract, he or she generally resolves the conflict in favor of subjective purpose, though certain kinds of wills and contracts warrant an exception. Objective purpose may also trump when significant time has elapsed between the creation of the will or contract and its interpretation (an "old text"); if the text addresses a broad scope of issues ("framework agreement"); if the structure of the regime and the values of the society have undergone significant change; if the text is based on principles and not rules; or if the communication in question deviates from the ordinary paradigm of a will (like a joint, mutual will) or of a two-party contract (like an adhesion contract or consumer contract). In interpreting a statute, a judge gives significant weight to subjective purpose if there is reliable, certain, and clear evidence—sometimes from the explicit language of the text itself, and sometimes from the circumstances surrounding its creation—about legislative intent ("abstract" intent, not "concrete" intent). Judges do not give significant weight to legislative intent if the statute is "old"; if it regulates a comprehensive and broad scope of issues (a codification, for example); if the regime and its fundamental values have undergone deep and comprehensive changes (like a transition to democracy or deep changes in fundamental values); if the text of the statute establishes principles and not rules (like "reasonableness"); or if the content of the statute (like a statute addressing human rights) justifies according significant weight to objective purpose. In interpreting a constitution, significant weight is accorded to objective purpose. Having said that, however, the interpreter of certain kinds of constitutional texts, such as a young constitutional text, ascribes significant weight to the abstract intent of the authors of the constitution.

Should We Give Up on Authorial Intent?

Does the normative picture I have sketched lead us to give up entirely on the presumptions of subjective purpose? Shouldn't we say that judges interpret legal texts according to their objective purpose, with a few particular exceptions? My answer to both these questions is no. Subjective purpose continues to be an important factor in interpreting all legal texts. The presumptions of subjective purpose apply immediately and always, and they accompany the interpretive process from the start. In interpreting wills and contracts, those presumptions retain their footing so long as they are not contradicted by the text, by circumstances surrounding its creation, or by considerations particular to certain kinds of wills and contracts. Ordinarily, subjective purpose occupies a central position at every stage of the interpretive process. What of interpreting a statute? Shouldn't we say that the many cases in which the type of text requires us to accord heavy weight to objective purpose justify a general principle of interpreting statutes according to their objective purpose, except for exceptional cases in which subjective purpose applies? Again, I respond in the negative. We must evaluate each kind of text individually. We can say that generally, in interpreting legislation, the scales are balanced between subjective and objective purpose, and that we must start the interpretive process from there. The same is not true of a constitution, in which objective purpose is particularly weighty, though subjective purpose still applies immediately and always.

9. FORMULATING ULTIMATE PURPOSE

"Easy," "Medium," and "Hard" Cases

An interpreter sits down to the different presumptions about authorial intent (subjective purpose) and the intent of the reasonable author or of the system (objective purpose). When all those presumptions point in the same direction, there is no real interpretive problem. The interpreter has an "easy case." He or she gathers the different presumptions and formulates the text's ultimate purpose. This is the principle by which the interpreter extracts the text's single, unique, legal meaning from the range of its semantic possibilities.

Sometimes, however, the different presumptions point in opposite directions. Some data argue in favor of authorial intent (the text is young; it regulates a specific issue). Other data point in the direction of objective purpose (the text is formulated in terms of standards; it addresses human rights). The interpreter must place the different presumptions on the scale, accord the proper weight to the different data, and adjudicate the dispute accordingly. Sometimes, placing those competing values on the scale resolves the dispute. The balance tips in one or another direction, giving us a "medium case." The interpreter collects the data and formulates ultimate purpose according to the heavier weight accorded to either subjective or objective purpose.

What does an interpreter do, however, when the balance does not resolve the dispute? There may be two reasons for this failure. *First*, the interpreter may not have access to enough information to ascribe weight to the various considerations. *Second*, the weight he or she does ascribe to the various considerations may result in an even balance. What is the interpreter to do in these "hard cases"? The legal system fails to give sufficient guidance. The interpreter must formulate ultimate purpose—subjective or objective—at his or her own discretion. We will discuss how this discretion operates separately.[42]

---

[42] *Infra* p. 212.

Shortcut: The Purpose Arising from the Text as Ultimate Purpose

The search for ultimate purpose may seem complicated. Judges need a lot of information from a wide range of sources. They must balance the competing presumptions. Indeed, purposive interpretation contains a degree of complication, but only in special cases. Generally, purposive interpretation operates simply and easily. Judges study a text. This initial examination produces, according to the judges' fore-meanings, a certain purpose. Judges presume that such purpose accords with the intention of the reasonable author and of the system and with the intent of the author of the text. No data contradict this presumption. The interpretive process ends there—in these situations, judges may make do with the purpose that arises from the language of the text, shaped by the presumption about the text's purpose. In the absence of warning signs to the contrary, judges may assume that the purpose arising from their fore-meanings is also the purpose that will arise at the end of the interpretive process. The initial presumption becomes the final presumption.

Interpretation usually follows this path. The sources of information do not produce conflicting presumptions of purpose; the parties appearing in court do not raise conflicting purposes; the interpretive process is simple and quick. Judges take a shortcut and arrive directly at their final destination. Only in special cases must judges raise questions and seek additional answers. Only when the purpose arising from the language of the text raises the specter of conflict with the intent of the reasonable author, the values of the system, or the abstract intent of the text's author, must judges pause and begin the more complicated interpretive process described above.

CHAPTER NINE

Discretion as a Component
in Purposive Interpretation

1. THE ESSENCE OF JUDICIAL DISCRETION

Language, Purpose, and Judicial Discretion

Purposive interpretation is based on language, purpose, and discretion.[1] Language sets the limits of interpretation.[2] Purpose determines the choice of legal meanings, within the boundaries of language. Discretion operates when the purpose of the text does not point to a single, unique legal meaning. I noted as much in a case, saying that, in interpretation, there is

> an entire set of situations in which the interpreter of a legal text (whether it be contract, will, legislation, or constitution) encounters a number of potential purposes, and he cannot formulate the ultimate purpose of the norm grounded in the text. In ordinary cases, the interpreter should use discretion to formulate, as objectively as possible, the purpose at the core of the legal text.[3]

Discretion is a critical component of purposive interpretation. I think it is a critical component of every system of interpretation. It is a myth to think we can build any system of interpretation without it. Purposive interpretation openly acknowledges that. Without judicial discretion, interpretation could not fulfill its aim in law (condition of efficacy[4]). However, interpretation must not become entirely a question of interpretive discretion. Discretion should be confined to special situations. Interpretive discretion is a necessary condition for any system of interpretation, but it is not a sufficient condition. Various systems of interpretation, primarily subjective and textualist, justify their approaches by claiming to avoid the use of judicial discretion. They base their claim of superiority over other sys-

---

[1] For a discussion of discretion, see *The Uses of Discretion* (K. Hawkins ed., 1992); D. Galligan, *Discretionary Powers: A Legal Study of Official Discretion* (1986); R. Pattenden, *Judicial Discretion and Criminal Litigation* (2d ed. 1990); M. Iglesias Vila, *Facing Judicial Discretion: Legal Knowledge and Right Answers Revisited* (2001).

[2] Judicial discretion also exists, of course, in non-interpretive activities. On the general theory of judicial discretion, see *supra* p. 54, note 189.

[3] C.A. 779/89 *Shalev v. Sela Insurance Co.*, 48(1) P.D. 221, 230.

[4] *Infra* p. 219.

tems of interpretation on the argument that they either eliminate or restrict the use of judicial discretion. They ignore the fact that every system of interpretation, by virtue of the nature of law and of interpretation in law, must base itself on a component of judicial discretion. The only question is how broad or narrow such discretion should be. Without judicial discretion, there can be no interpretation in law.

The Essence of Judicial Discretion

Judicial discretion is a normative concept, not a psychological concept. It does not just reflect thought, consideration, and deliberation. It reflects a state of affairs in which a judge must choose among a number of options, none of which the legal system has determined to be the right choice. It is as though law says to the judge: "Up to now, I determined the content of the norm and its results in the circumstances of a particular case. From now on, you, the judge, must decide." It is as though the law stops walking at an intersection, and the judge must decide—without a clear and precise standard—which direction to take.[5] Discretion is the freedom to choose between multiple legal solutions.[6] Each alternative before the judge must be legal. The legality, not the effectiveness, of the choice is what creates discretion.[7] Again, an alternative is not legal because the judge chooses it; the judge may choose it only because it is legal.

Judicial Discretion and the Legal Community

Judicial discretion exists because there are legal problems that do not have a single legal solution;[8] because law contains uncertainty;[9] because there are situations with more than one legal resolution. In these situations, judges have "the sovereign prerogative of choice,"[10] informed by the legal community's fundamental viewpoints,[11] that is, the professional views of

[5] H.C. 267/88 *Reshet Kolelei Haidra, Nonprofit v. Local Affairs Court*, 43(3) P.D. 728, 745 (Barak, J.).

[6] Hart and Sachs, *supra* p. 3, note 3 at 144. Professor Iglesias calls this "strong discretion": M. Iglesias Vila, *Facing Judicial Discretion: Legal Knowledge and Right Answers Revisited* 8 (2001).

[7] Professor Davis takes a different approach, basing (administrative) discretion on the efficacy of the choice. *See* K. Davis, *Discretionary Justice: A Preliminary Inquiry* 4 (1969).

[8] Barak, *supra* p. 54, note 189.

[9] Bix, *supra* p. 133, note 42; K. Greenawalt, "How Law Can Be Determinate," 38 *UCLA L. Rev.* 1 (1990); J. Moreso, *Legal Indeterminacy and Constitutional Interpretation* (1998).

[10] O.W. Holmes, *Collected Legal Papers* 239 (1952).

[11] O. Fiss, "Objectivity and Interpretation," 34 *Stan. L. Rev.* 739 (1982). *See also* K. Greenawalt, "Discretion and Judicial Decision: The Elusive Quest for the Fetters That Bind

the legal public. The concept of "the legal community" is imprecise by its nature. It is not clear what position the "community" takes on borderlines cases. This concept is important, however, because it provides criteria for determining the legality of alternatives that span the range of judicial discretion.

Does Judicial Discretion Exist?

Dworkin claimed that judicial discretion does not exist, and that every legal problem has a single legal solution.[12] Even in hard cases, the text guides the judge, requiring him or her to choose only one option. According to Dworkin, "hard cases" are not "hard," and judicial "discretion" does not exist as I have described it. "Hard cases" are complicated. They require study and consideration. At the end of the day, however, they have a single legal solution. In his later writings, Dworkin maintained his basic view that judicial discretion does not exist.[13] He did, however, note that "It would make no difference to my thesis if instead of saying that there was a single 'true' answer in controversial cases I said that there was a single 'most reasonable' answer."[14] There, Dworkin appears to concede that there is more than one single, legal solution because, within a "range of reasonableness," there are likely to be a few alternatives that are reasonable and legal. Reasonableness does not provide a single, legal solution to every case.[15]

I maintain that two judges may reach two opposing, reasonable results. From a systemic point of view—and this is the proper point of view—there is no single, unique solution. Even from the point of view of the individual judge, until ruling on a matter, he or she retains choice. Only upon adjudication does a single legal possibility exist. Judicial discretion exists.[16] It

---

Judges," 75 *Colum. L. Rev.* 359 (1975); J. Bell, *Policy Arguments in Judicial Decisions* 24 (1983); R. Posner, *The Federal Courts: Crisis and Reform* 205 (1985); S.J. Burton, *An Introduction to Law and Legal Reasoning* 136 (1985); M. Krygier, "The Traditionality of Statutes," 1 *Ratio Juris* 20 (1988); W. Blatt, "Interpretive Communities: The Missing Element in Statutory Interpretation," 95 *Nw. U. L. Rev* 629 (2001).

[12] R. Dworkin, "Judicial Discretion," 60 *J. Phil.* 624, 631 (1963); Dworkin, *supra* p. 178, note 114 at 81; R. Dworkin, "No Right Answer?" 53 *N.Y.U. L. Rev.* 1 (1978). Dworkin is not the only one to express this view. *See also* Shapira, "Biayat Shikul Hadaat Hashiputi [Problem of Judicial Discretion]" 2 *Mishpatim* 57 (1970); R. Sartorius, "The Justification of the Judicial Decision," 78 *Ethics* 171 (1968); R. Sartorius, "Social Policy and Judicial Legislation," 8 *Am. Phil. Q.* 151 (1971).

[13] R. Dworkin, "Pragmatism, Right Answers, and True Banality," in *Pragmatism in Law and Society* 135 (M. Brint and W. Weaver eds., 1991).

[14] *Id.* at 367.

[15] *Supra* p. 198.

[16] For a critique of Dworkin's view, see W.J. Waluchow, "Strong Discretion," 33 *Phil. Q.* 321 (1983); B. Hoffmaster, "Understanding Judicial Discretion," 1 *Law and Philosophy* 21 (1982).

does not reflect judicial imperialism but rather uncertainty in law. Law is not mathematics. It is a normative framework. Until we can predict the future; until semantic generalizations can extend to every relevant detail; until we can overcome human limitations—judicial discretion will exist. Judicial discretion is natural to law. Without it, law is a form with no substance. Raz noted as much:

> [P]roblems of interpretation are rarely problems of the meaning of one term or phrase. They are more often than not questions of the interpretation of sentences, or of articles in statutes or in constitutions, or of moral and political doctrine. And they can arise in unexpected places. No set of explicitly articulated rules of interpretation can deal with all of them. The same is true of rules of interpretation implied in a legal culture, rather than explicitly articulated in its laws. Such rules cannot settle all possible issues of interpretation. All too often interpretation is just a matter of reasoning to a reasonable view on the basis of a variety of considerations, some reinforcing each other, some clashing. There is no way of reducing such reasoning to the application of rules, or other norms, nor is there any way of eliminating the need and desirability of interpretation that consists in and results from such reasoning.[17]

In other words: We cannot avoid using judicial discretion.

Scope of Judicial Discretion

Judicial discretion is forever limited.[18] It is not absolute.[19] Cardozo put it well in saying:

> Given freedom of choice how shall the choice be guided? Complete freedom—unfettered and undirected—there never is. A thousand limitations—the product some of statute, some of precedent, some of vague tradition or of an immemorial technique—encompass and hedge us even when we think of ourselves as ranging freely and at large. The inscrutable force of professional opinion presses upon us like the atmosphere, though we are heedless of its weight. Narrow at best is any freedom that is allotted to us.[20]

Discretion is subject to both procedural and substantive restrictions. Procedural restrictions require the exercise of judicial discretion to be fair. Judges must act without bias. They must treat the parties equally. They must make decisions based on the evidence presented. They must explain

---

[17] Raz, *supra* p. 41, note 124 at 179.
[18] Cappelletti, *supra* p. 53, note 182 at 15.
[19] Barak, *supra* p. 54, note 189 at 44. *See also* Hart, *supra* p. 26, note 78 at 252.
[20] B. Cardozo, *The Growth of the Law* 60–61 (1924).

their decisions. They must act objectively.[21] Substantive restrictions require the exercise of judicial discretion to be rational, consistent, and coherent.[22] Judges must act reasonably.[23] They must take into account the existence of the system[24] and the need for a solution that integrates into it. They must consider institutional limitations.[25] They must be aware that the information and available means of processing it are limited[26] and that they cannot predict all developments and all the considerations of policy. As former Israeli Supreme Court President Meir Shamgar said,

> We are interested in the discretion that Dworkin called discretion in the "strong" sense. He meant discretion that has no specific criteria to instruct the decision-maker how he must decide. The lack of criteria, however, does not mean total freedom. The concept of "discretion," by its nature, is conferred by an authority, for a particular purpose, and it is limited by a particular type of consideration that can be taken into account.[27]

Judges never have absolute freedom of choice. The scope of their freedom varies from issue to issue, but it is always bounded. Most cases have a sin-

---

[21] Barak, *supra* p. 54, note 189 at 187; H.C. 6163/92 *Eisenberg v. Minister of Construction and Housing*, 47(2) P.D. 229, 265; H.C. 693/91, *supra* p. 157, note 29 at 782; C. Clark, "The Limits of Judicial Objectivity," 12 *Am. U. L. Rev.* 1 (1963); G. Christie, "Objectivity in the Law," 78 *Yale L.J.* 1311 (1969); R. Nagel, The Limits of Objectivity," in 1 *The Tanner Lectures on Human Values* 77 (1980); O. Fiss, "Objectivity and Interpretation," 34 *Stan. L. Rev.* 739 (1982); H. Edwards, "The Judicial Function and the Elusive Goal of Principled Decisionmaking," 1991 *Wis. L. Rev.* 837; K. Greenawalt, *Law and Objectivity* (1992); H. Feldman, "Objectivity in Legal Judgment," 92 *Mich L. Rev.* 1187 (1994); J. Coleman and B. Leiter, "Determinacy, Objectivity, and Authority," in *Law and Interpretation* 203 (A. Marmor ed., 1995); A. Marmor, "Three Concepts of Objectivity," in *Law and Interpretation* 177 (A. Marmor ed., 1995); N. Stavropoulos, *Objectivity in Law* (1996); A. Marmor, "An Essay on the Objectivity of Law," in *Analyzing Law* 3 (B. Bix ed., 1998).

[22] Barak, *supra* p. 54, note 189 at 227; Peczenik, *supra* p. 16, note 44. *See also* R. Alexy and A. Peczenik, "The Concept of Coherence and Its Significance for Discursive Rationality," 3 *Ratio Juris* 130 (1990); K. Kress, "Coherence," in *A Companion to the Philosophy of Law and Legal Theory* 533 (D. Patterson ed., 1996); D.N. MacCormick, "Coherence in Legal Justification," in *Theory of Legal Science* 235 (A. Peczenik, L. Lindahl, B. Roermund eds., 1984); A. Peczenik, "Coherence, Truth and Rightness in the Law," in *Law, Interpretation and Reality: Essays in Epistemology, Hermeneutics and Jurisprudence* (P. Nerhot ed., 1990); Raz, "The Relevance of Coherence," 72 *B.U. L. Rev.* 273 (1992).

[23] H.C. 547/84 *Chicken of the Valley, Registered Cooperative Agricultural Association v. Ramat-Yishai Municipality*, 40(1) P.D. 113, 141: "A judge may not toss a coin. He may not consider any factor that he chooses. He must consider reasonably" (Barak, J.). *See also* F. Pollock, "Judicial Caution and Valour," 45 *Law Q. Rev.* 293, 294 (1929); D. Lloyd, "Reason and Logic in the Common Law," 64 *Law Q. Rev.* 468, 475 (1948); Posner, *supra* p. 27, note 85 at 130. Popkin argues for "ordinary judging": *see* Popkin, *supra* p. 85, note 1 at 207.

[24] L. Fuller, *Anatomy of the Law* 94 (1968).

[25] Barak, *supra* p. 54, note 189 at 241.

[26] *Id.* at 246.

[27] C.A. 915/91, *State of Israel v. Levy*, 48(3) P.D. 45, 82.

gle, unique solution, so that judicial discretion does not exist at all. The few cases in which judicial discretion does exist, however, introduce an element of flexibility into the legal system. They allow the proper balance between past and present; between security and certainty, on the one hand, and progress and change, on the other.

Judicial discretion is bounded by what we might call a "zone of reasonableness." Judges may not act according to their personal predilections[28] or individual values, when those are inconsistent with the values of the system. Judges must make the best decision they can, taking into account objective considerations. They cannot remake the system of values from square one. They must move forward, seeking the best solution they can find, within the constraints of the legal system. They exercise choice, but they remain within the confines of a society, a legal system, and a judicial tradition.

How Do Judges Exercise Discretion?

The nature of judicial discretion defies the formulation of rules regulating its use. A judge's interpretation is the product of his or her personality and life experience; the product of the balance he or she strikes between certainty and experimentation, security and change, reason and emotion.[29] Judges make choices informed by their judicial philosophy, their constitutional views, and the way they understand their role and the relationship of the judiciary to the other branches of government. Judicial choice is the product of the delicate balance in the judge's soul between the particular and the general, the individual and society, the human being and his or her environment. This kind of discretion forces judges to make difficult decisions. They are subject to psychological pressure. They wonder, did they choose the right path? Did they reach the proper solution? How will the resolution influence future legal developments? How will their decisions affect public confidence in the judiciary? In these moments, the judge's personal responsibility reaches its peak.[30]

A judge must choose the solution that seems best to him or her.[31] In my opinion, that solution is the one that the judge thinks is just.[32] Law and

[28] S. Breyer, "Judicial Review: A Practising Judge's Perspective," 19 *Oxf. J.L. Stud.* 153, 158 (1999).

[29] W.J. Brennan, "Reason, Passion and 'The Progress of Law,'" 10 *Cardozo L. Rev.* 3 (1988).

[30] W.J. Brennan, "The Constitution of the United States: Contemporary Ratification," 27 *S. Tex. L. Rev.* 433, 434 (1986).

[31] J. Raz, *The Authority of Law* 197 (1979); H.J. Friendly, "Reactions of a Lawyer—Newly Become Judge," 71 *Yale L. J.* 218, 229 (1961).

[32] *See* G. Tedeschi, *Masot B'Mishpat* [*Essays in Law*] 23 (1978), who refers the judge to the "wisdom" "that for us is no different from justice."

justice converge. My advice, at this stage of interpretation, is for the judge to aspire to achieve justice—justice for the parties before the judge; justice in law itself. Justice accompanies the interpretive process from start to finish. It is one of the values of the legal system. Justice becomes a "residual" value that decides the hard cases.

Of course, it is natural that different judges will have different ideas about justice. Justice is a complicated concept.[33] Jewish thought[34] and Greek thought[35] contributed a great deal to understanding it. Nevertheless, each of us has an instinctive sense of the just solution. That feeling must accompany us throughout the interpretive process. It must guide our decisions when we face a situation of judicial discretion. Professor Tedeschi noted:

> The rules alone will never suffice to decide the issue the interpreter faces. He must, therefore, be graced with wisdom, as well . . . wisdom that, for us, is no different than justice, meaning true justice, in terms of facts and results; taking into account all the factual foundations, the interests affected by the question discussed, the results the decision is likely to cause for the parties and for the public.[36]

Wisdom is a component of discretion in interpretation. Like Professor Tedeschi, I think judges should use their wisdom to find justice. Others disagree. In the absence of rules, each interpreter may use his or her discretion on the matter.

Judicial Discretion and Pragmatism

Like all systems of interpretation, purposive interpretation contains junctions of judicial discretion. Purposive interpretation establishes an exhaustive list of the components of purpose that the judge should consider in formulating ultimate purpose and the weight to accord each component—which in turn governs the balance of the components in determining ultimate purpose. As we saw, these determinations sometimes take place at junctions of judicial discretion, at which purposive interpretation—in its current form—cannot direct the interpreter about how much weight to accord the components of (ultimate) purpose. At these points, interpreters

[33] Ch. Perelman, *Al Hatzedek* [*On Justice*] (1981); H. Cohen, *Hamishpat* [*Law*] (updated ed. 1996); J. Rawls, *A Theory of Justice* (1972).

[34] Y. Englard, *Mavo Litorat Hamishpat* [*Introduction to Jurisprudence*] 42 (1990).

[35] Primarily Plato and Aristotle. Aristotle distinguished between corrective justice and distributive justice. *See* E. Weinrib, "Aristotle's Forms of Justice," in *Justice, Law and Method in Plato and Aristotle* 133 (S. Panagiotou ed., 1987); J. Finnis, *Natural Law and Natural Rights* (1980).

[36] Tedeschi, *supra* p. 212, note 32 at 23.

may (and indeed, are likely to) weigh the pragmatic consequences of the weights they assign. They will assign weight to the components of purpose in order to bring about the best interpretive result. Purposive interpretation therefore shares some commonalities with pragmatism at those junctions at which judges exercise discretion. The pragmatic judge is, of course, freer to determine the weight of the various components, because he or she is unfettered by the need to balance subjective and objective purpose. Where purposive interpretation does, however, provide for judicial discretion, the judge takes pragmatic considerations into account, looking for the best and most reasonable solution. I personally look for the most just solution.

2. SITUATIONS OF JUDICIAL DISCRETION

Establishing the Range of Semantic Meanings

Judicial discretion accompanies the interpreter throughout the interpretive process.[37] An interpreter who starts with the language of the text will need to exercise discretion in the field of language. This is because, *inter alia*, an interpreter often acts as a linguist, and the rules of linguistics often give the linguist discretion. Linguistic discretion becomes legal discretion. It is naïve to think that a textualist approach to interpretation will eliminate judicial discretion. Textualism leaves ample opportunity for judges to use discretion. To the extent that semantic meaning is based on a "sense of language," different linguists may have different senses. In the field of interpretation, the linguistic dispute becomes an interpretive dispute, the resolution of which requires discretion. Often, two linguists disagree over whether a text can bear a certain meaning in its language. This dispute enters the field of law and may become the basis for judicial discretion. Sometimes, the interpreter has discretion in inferring the implicit meaning of a text, or distinguishing between its natural and ordinary language and its special and extraordinary language. The distinction is important because of the presumption that the purpose of the text is that arising from its natural and ordinary language. In addition, the linguistic canons that reveal the text's semantic meaning sometimes require an interpreter to exercise discretion. Can the interpreter infer the positive from the negative? What is the generality, and is the individual item included therein? Sometimes, there is no single, unique answer to these questions. Sometimes, we need discretion to answer them.

---

[37] W.H. Charles, "Extrinsic Evidence in Statutory Interpretation: Judicial Discretion in Context," 7 *Dalhousie L.J.* 7 (1983).

Determining Subjective Purpose

Judges will sometimes need to use discretion to determining the subjective purpose at the core of the text. Judicial discretion comes into play when the language is ambiguous or vague and can lead to multiple subjective purposes; when the circumstances surrounding the text's creation point to multiple subjective purposes; when the subjective purpose arising from the language of the text is out of sync with the subjective purpose arising from the circumstances. Furthermore, subjective purpose generally exists at various (vertical) levels of abstraction. Within a given level of abstraction, there may be multiple (horizontal) purposes. Selecting the proper level of abstraction may be a matter of discretion.

Determining Objective Purpose

Objective purpose operates at various levels of abstraction, each of which implicates its own kind of discretion. Consider a contract whose objective purpose is the purpose that reasonable parties would have sought to achieve. Reasonable interpreters may arrive at different results. Or, consider a text whose objective purpose is determined by the system's fundamental values. An interpreter must use discretion to locate the values and derive objective purpose from them. Discretion is inherent to values,[38] which are based on worldviews over which people naturally disagree. We have yet to succeed—and I think we would err to succeed—in formulating a theory of values that negates judicial discretion.

Consider the concepts of "balance" and "weight," necessary to engage the fundamental values of a legal system. The technique of balance always leaves room for judicial discretion.[39] Words like "balance" and "weight" are metaphorical. A judge engaging them does not do so mechanically. He or she engages in normative activity.[40] Assigning weight to competing values and balancing them accordingly "describes the interpretive starting point, but it is insufficient to establish criteria or scales of value to assist in the interpretive

[38] B. Cardozo, *The Paradoxes of Legal Science* 62 (1928); J. Dickinson, "The Law behind Law," 29 *Colum. L. Rev.* 113 (1929); H. Jones, "An Invitation to Jurisprudence," 74 *Colum. L. Rev.* 1023 (1974); J.M. Steiner, "Judicial Discretion and the Concept of Law," 35 *Camb. L.J.* 135 (1976); J. Raz, "Legal Principles and the Limits of Law," 81 *Yale L.J.* 823 (1972).

[39] H.L.A. Hart, *The Concept of Law* (2d ed. 1994); R. Pound, "A Survey of Social Interests," 57 *Harv. L. Rev.* 1 (1944); B. Cardozo, *The Nature of the Judicial Process* (1921); G. MacCallum, "Comments on Ronald Dworkin's 'Judicial Discretion,'" 60 *J. Ph.* 638 (1963).

[40] H.C. 6163/92, *supra* p. 211, note 21 at 264.

project."[41] In order to take a stance regarding the social importance of a value, a judge must sometimes exercise discretion. Kelsen made this point:

> The principle called "weighing of interests" (Interessenabwägung) is merely a formulation of the problem, not a solution. It does not supply the objective measure or standard for comparing conflicting interests with each other and does not make it possible to solve, on this basis, the conflict. . . . The need for an "interpretation" results precisely from the fact that the norm to be applied or the system of norms leaves open several possibilities—and this means that it contains no decision as to which of the interests in question has a higher value than the other, but leaves this decision to an act of norm creation to be performed, for example in rendering a judicial decision.[42]

Kelsen's words are too extreme. It is possible to "weigh" and "balance" without exercising judicial discretion, but not in every case.

Determining Ultimate Purpose

All the purposes—subjective and objective, vertical and horizontal—appear before the judge. When they do not point in the same direction, the judge must decide between them. In its current state, interpretive science cannot resolve every conflict between different purposes. Judges retain discretion over many questions.[43] I said as much in a case before me:

> This situation of uncertainty and murkiness . . . is not unique to the case before us . . . it is a subset of an entire class of situations in which the interpreter of a legal text (contract or will, legislation or constitution) encounters a number of potential purposes, without being able to formulate the ultimate purpose of the norm grounded in the text. Ordinarily, the interpreter must exercise his discretion to formulate, as objectively as possible, the purpose at the core of the legal text.[44]

Of course, as purposive interpretation develops, legal norms governing the choice between conflicting purposes will supplant more and more areas of judicial discretion. Those norms, however, will create new situations of

---

[41] F.H.C. 9/77, *supra* p. 180, note 121 at 361 (Shamgar, J.).

[42] Kelsen, *supra* p. 3, note 4 at 352.

[43] N. Isaacs, "The Limits of Judicial Discretion," 32 *Yale L.J.* 339 (1923); F.E. Horack, "In the Name of Legislative Intention," 38 *W. Va. L.Q.* 119, 126 (1932); H.W. Jones, "Statutory Doubts and Legislative Intention," 40 *Colum. L. Rev.* 957 (1940); J. Sneed, "The Art of Statutory Interpretation," 62 *Tex. L. Rev.* 665 (1983); J. Landis, "A Note on 'Statutory Interpretation,'" 43 *Harv. L. Rev.* 886, 893 (1930); F.E. Horack, "Cooperative Action for Improved Statutory Interpretation," 3 *Vand. L. Rev.* 382, 383 (1950).

[44] C.A. 779/89, *supra* p. 202, note 40 at 230.

judicial discretion. We cannot predict how judicial discretion will develop, but we do know that it will never disappear entirely. Interpretation without discretion is a myth.[45] Indeed, the very norms that govern the resolution of conflicts among the different purposes are themselves legal norms grounded in a text that must be interpreted.[46] Interpretation is based on the existence of numerous components whose weight cannot be determined in advance. MacDougal, Laswell, and Miller put it well in noting that

> There can be no arbitrary weighing or fixed hierarchies of signification that, when chosen by the interpreter in advance, remove ambiguity from the contents of communication. This follows implacably from the contextual principle that each detail in the whole of an act of communication is affected by, and in turn affects, all other details.[47]

In any case, we would want to leave some room for judicial discretion in order to guarantee change and renewal in the legal system. Every legal system contains a normative system that provides a clear and known resolution of some disputes, namely the easy and medium cases. They form a static, skeletal structure to ensure security and stability. However, the legal system also has a method of resolving hard cases, a dynamic method that guarantees renewal and change. Both kinds of methods are critical to any legal system. The one could not exist without the other. Stability without change breeds sedimentation. Change without stability is anarchy. It is a mistake to see only stability in law. It is a mistake to think that every problem has only one legal solution. By the same token, however, it is a mistake to see only change in law. It is a mistake to think that all problems are open, and that none has a unique solution. The reality is far more complicated.

---

[45] J. Dickinson, "Legal Rules: Their Function in the Process of Decision," 79 *U. Pa. L. Rev.* 833, 835 (1931); I. Kaufman, "The Anatomy of Decisionmaking," 53 *Fordham L. Rev.* 1, 6 (1984); M. Cappelletti, "The Law-Making Power of the Judge and Its Limits: A Comparative Analysis," 8 *Monash U. L. Rev.* 14, 17 (1981).

[46] Raz, *supra* p. 215, note 38 at 846.

[47] M.S. McDougal, H.D. Laswell, J.C. Miller, *The Interpretation of Agreements and World Public Order: Principles of Content and Procedure* xvi (1967).

CHAPTER TEN

The Theoretical Basis for Purposive Interpretation

1. THE NEED TO JUSTIFY A SYSTEM OF INTERPRETATION

"Creation" and Not "Discovery":
The Range of Interpretive Legitimacy

There is no "true" interpretation.[1] The text cannot establish what the best system of interpretation is for understanding it, because we understand the text itself only through its interpretation. Interpretation is not just discovery. It is also creation. The question is what "creation" is best.

The fact that there is no true interpretation does not mean that every interpretation is good or "correct." Every legal community develops a legal tradition and legal culture over the course of years. That development includes establishing which systems of interpretation are legitimate and which are illegitimate. It establishes the range of interpretive legitimacy. But which system of interpretation within that range is best? Is every interpreter free to choose the "legitimate" system that seems best to him or her? Is it enough to toss a coin? I think not. The proposition that there is no true interpretation, and that interpretation is the product of social consensus, does not mean that all systems on which members of society agree are equally good. One should choose the best from among the accepted viewpoints. This choice should not reflect the subjectivity of the judge. We should try to articulate criteria for choosing the proper interpretation. We should justify our choice of a proper system of interpretation.[2] In this chapter, I present the justifications and criteria for choosing the system of interpretation I find proper. I will try to show why, according to these justifications and criteria, the purposive system of interpretation is best.

Justifications for the Proper System of Interpretation:
Efficacy of the Interpretation

Proper interpretation must meet two conditions: *First*, it must be able, in all situations, to extract the legal meaning from the range of semantic

---

[1] *Supra*, p. 9.
[2] C. Sunstein, "Five Theses on Originalism," 19 *Harv. J.L. & Pub. Pol'y* 311 (1996).

meanings of the text ("condition of efficacy"). *Second*, it must be able to give the text the meaning that best achieves the goal of interpretation in law ("condition of the goal"). We will first discuss the condition of efficacy.[3] A system of interpretation that arrives at a few semantic meanings, without deciding which one is the legal meaning, does not fulfill its role. A system of interpretation is proper only if it projects itself onto the normative text, clarifying it so that the text takes on a single, unique legal meaning. True, in order to fulfill the condition of efficacy, a system of interpretation will have to recognize the existence of judicial discretion. That is no cause for concern. As long as it is not the exclusive or central component of a system of interpretation, judicial discretion can be an integral part of a system of interpretation. In my opinion, it is a necessary component of every system of interpretation, because no system of interpretation can resolve every case presented to the interpreter (the condition of efficacy) without some exercise—broad or narrow—of judicial discretion.

Purposive interpretation meets the condition of efficacy. Unlike some systems of interpretation, like textualist systems, it has the power to resolve every interpretive problem presented to it. True, the interpreter sometimes must exercise judicial discretion, but that discretion is a legitimate—but neither exclusive nor primary—component of purposive interpretation. I reject the contention that a system of interpretation must give a solution, known in advance, to every interpretive problem, without resorting to judicial discretion.[4] Every system of interpretation—like law itself—contains elements of uncertainty. Judicial discretion resolves them. It is a critical component of any system of interpretation.

Justifications for the Proper System of Interpretation: Goal of Interpretation

The condition of efficacy is necessary but not sufficient. Tossing a coin is a highly efficacious system that can resolve every interpretive problem. Similarly, interpretation based on the decision of an anonymous party (say, the judge's spouse) can also meet the condition of efficacy. That is insufficient. We cannot answer the question of what the best system of interpretation is without addressing what goal we seek in interpretation. It is not enough to say that the goal of interpretation is to determine the normative message arising from a legal text. We must decide, not just what interpretation

---

[3] J. Wróblewski, *The Judicial Application of Law* 108 (1992). The author discusses "a normative theory of interpretation" as a theory that gives a solution to every interpretive problem.

[4] *See* Eskridge and Frickey, *supra* p. 107, note 53 at 325.

is, but also why we do it. The reason that we interpret shapes the system of interpretation.[5] For example, if the goal of interpretation were to give the text its most aesthetically pleasing meaning, we might choose a different interpretive system than if the goal of interpretation were to realize the intent of the text's author. Moreover, the text alone, without external information, cannot tell us the goals of interpretation.[6] As Posner noted, "[I]nterpretation is always relative to a purpose that is not given by the interpretive process itself but that is brought in from the outside and guides the process."[7] What, then, is the goal of interpretation in law?

The Goal of Interpretation Is to Achieve the Objective of the Legal Norm

At some point, we need to find an Archimedean foothold, external to the text, from which to answer that question. My answer is this: The goal of interpretation in law is to achieve the objective—in other words, the purpose—of law.[8] The role of a system of interpretation in law is to choose, from among the semantic options for a given text, the meaning that best achieves the purpose of the text. Each legal text—will, contract, statute, and constitution—was chosen to achieve a social objective. Achieving this objective, achieving this purpose, is the goal of interpretation. The system of interpretation is the device and the means. It is a tool through which law achieves self-realization. In interpreting a given text, which is, after all, what interpretation in law does, a system of interpretation must guarantee that the purpose of the norm trapped in the text—in our terminology, the purpose of the text—will be achieved in the best way. Hence the requirement that the system of interpretation be a rational activity. A coin toss will not do. This is also the rationale—which is at the core of my own views— for the belief that purposive interpretation is the most proper system of interpretation. This system is proper because it guarantees the achievement of the purpose of law. There is social, jurisprudential, hermeneutical, and

---

[5] D. Hermann, "Phenomenology, Structuralism, Hermeneutics, and Legal Study: Applications of Contemporary Continental Thought to Legal Phenomena," 36 *U. Miami L. Rev.* 379, 402 (1982).

[6] Texts sometimes contain a statement of purpose listing the goals of the text. But even that provision requires interpretation.

[7] R. Posner, *Law and Literature* 209 (revised and enlarged ed. 1998). *See also* A. Vermeule, "Interpretive Choice," 75 *N.Y.U. L. Rev.* 74, 82 (2000) ("Interpreters must hold some conception, stated or implied, of the ends, aims, or goals of statutory interpretation").

[8] D. Brink, "Legal Theory, Legal Interpretation, and Judicial Review," 17 *Phil. and Pub. Aff.* 105, 125 (1988).

constitutional support for my claim that the proper criterion for interpretation is the search for law's purpose, and that purposive interpretation best fulfills that criterion. A comparative look at the law supports it, as well. I will discuss each element of that support below.

2. SOCIAL SUPPORT FOR PURPOSIVE INTERPRETATION

Law Has a Social Aim

Law is a device.[9] It is designed to achieve the social aim[10] that lies at the core of the legal system. Such aim creates the legal system. It develops it.[11] It interprets it. I noted as much in a case before me: "Law is a social device. Legal concepts were designed to achieve social objectives. They are an instrument to achieve social aims. They express the proper balance among conflicting values and interests."[12] In the same case, Justice Cheshin made a similar point: "Law is not a purpose in itself. It is a tool to achieve non-legal objectives and purposes: discovering truth, doing justice, achieving social and economic purposes. 'Doing law' (Micah 7, 8) means 'Doing justice with the tool of law.'"[13]

There is disagreement over the content of this aim.[14] Some say the aim is to guarantee human beings' natural rights. Others apply utilitarian theories of law, like maximizing wealth as efficiently as possible.[15] Some emphasize historical[16] or sociological foundations. I have always found ac-

---

[9] This approach is consistent with the sociological view of law. See R. Pound, "Mechanical Jurisprudence," 8 Colum. L. Rev. 605 (1908); R. Pound, "A Survey of Social Interests," 57 Harv. L. Rev. 1 (1943). However, the approach is not unique to the sociological view of law. Most philosophical jurisprudences assume that law has a role, though they differ as to the location of that role. See J. Harris, Legal Philosophies 237 (1980); W. Friedmann, Law in a Changing Society (2d ed. 1972); R. Summers, Law: Its Nature, Functions and Limits 440 (2d ed. 1972); R. Summers, Instrumentalism and American Legal Theory (1982); J. Stone, The Province and Function of Law (1946).

[10] J. Raz, The Authority of Law 163 (1979); R. Wasserstrom, The Judicial Decision 10 (1961); S.J. Burton, An Introduction to Law and Legal Reasoning 107 (1985).

[11] This view is Jhering's central contribution to jurisprudence. See R. Jhering, The Law as a Means to an End (Husik trans., 1914).

[12] F.H.C. 4601/95, supra p. 159, note 36 at 826.

[13] Id. at 836.

[14] R. Summers, "Pragmatic Instrumentalism in Twentieth Century American Legal Thought—A Synthesis and Critique of Our Dominant General Theory about Law and Its Use," 66 Cornell L. Rev. 861 (1981).

[15] For a discussion of utilitarian theories of law, see Harris, supra p. 221, note 9 at 36. See also R. Posner, Economic Analysis of Law (5th ed. 1998).

[16] On the historical movement in law, see Harris, supra p. 221, note 9 at 219.

ceptable foundations in each of the different theories about the purpose of law, without being able to embrace any one theory in its entirety. My approach is eclectic.[17] Human experience seems too rich for me to bind myself to one or another theory. In my view, the naturalists, positivists, realists, neorealists, and members of the historical or sociological tradition, all reflect, from different perspectives, the wealth of accumulated human experience. Each has his or her own truth. I can agree with each of them in principle, so long as I maintain the need to balance the different worldviews. In my opinion, no single theory contains the proper solution. We should borrow certain foundations from each of the major theories, while striking the proper balance among them. None can remain unadulterated. I find myself agreeing with Patterson's approach: "My own philosophy of law is eclectic because I recognize that each of the major philosophers has begun his or her system with several appealing self-evident principles, and I cannot reject it as wholly wrong."[18]

Law is designed to guarantee orderly social life. It therefore contains order and security. It is designed to guarantee human rights, equality, and justice. It therefore contains justice and ethics. The history of law is the search for the proper balance between individual and collective; between preserving the social framework and guaranteeing the rights of the individual. My pluralistic approach tells me there is disagreement over the relative weight of these purposes. My approach to tolerance tells me that, in formulating the relative weight of these purposes, we should consider the different worldviews of the public, of both the majority and the minority. Tolerance must have limits, in order to maintain orderly social life. Those charged with setting those limits need room, within constraints, to exercise discretion. Interpretation in law is designed to give law the meaning that allows it to achieve optimal self-realization;[19] it is designed to give law its social meaning; it is designed to determine the proper balance between the conflicting considerations that allow society to exist and allow the individual to achieve optimal self-realization.[20]

[17] Perhaps the eclectic approach itself constitutes a philosophical movement? *See* J. Hall, "Integrative Jurisprudence," in *Interpretation of Modern Legal Philosophies: Essays in Honor of Roscoe Pound* 313 (P. Sayre ed., 1947); H. Berman, "Toward an Integrative Jurisprudence: Politics, Morality, History," 76 *Cal. L. Rev.* 779 (1988).

[18] E. Patterson, *Jurisprudence: Men and Ideas of the Law* 556, 557 (1953).

[19] For a discussion of the various ways in which law is used to achieve purpose (as in providing a remedy, imposing punishment, creating administrative arrangements), see H. Kelsen, "The Law as a Specific Social Technique," 9 *U. Chi. L. Rev.* 75 (1941); R. Summers, "The Technique Element in Law," 59 *Cal. L. Rev.* 733 (1971).

[20] J. Kohler, "Judicial Interpretation of Enacted Law," in *Science of Legal Method* 187 (E. Bruncken and L. Register trans., 1917).

Particular Legal Texts Have Social Purposes

Interpretation in law does not span the entire scope of law. It examines the meaning of particular texts. It gives meaning to a constitutional provision or to a clause or chapter in a statute, contract, or will. The goal of interpretation is to achieve the purpose of the particular text, within the framework of the entire system. If law as a social device has a purpose, then every individual text has a purpose within the system.[21] A will is a social device. It is designed to allow a person to divide his or her property as he or she chooses. It reflects the view that "the power to bequeath stems directly from a person's ownership of his property."[22] When a testator makes a will, he or she seeks to achieve a certain purpose. There is no will without a purpose. A will expresses the aims of the testator, and its interpretation must therefore achieve those aims. Similarly, a contract is a device to achieve co-operation in society. A proper system of interpreting a contract must give it the meaning that allows a contract to fulfill its role as a device for cooperation. Hence the conclusion that proper interpretation imparts to a contract a meaning that fulfills its purpose. The same is true in legislation. A piece of legislation is an expression of policy. The legislation is designed to achieve a social aim. It has a purpose.[23] It constitutes a tool through which society changes and articulates its aims. A piece of legislation with no purpose is a piece of nonsense.[24] If legislation is a device to achieve a social purpose, then the interpretation of the statute must be undertaken in such a way as to achieve that social purpose. Interpretation should express, as best as possible, the objective of the statute. The social view that a statute is a purposive creation leads to the interpretive conclusion that the statute should be interpreted to achieve its purpose. The same is true of a constitution, which is the most important social device. It establishes patterns of social behavior for generations. It has an objective and a purpose which vary from constitution to constitution.[25]

Whatever its content, a constitution is a super-norm designed to achieve social aims. Jurists disagree over the content of those aims, but there is no

---

[21] Gottlieb, *supra* p. 3, note 1 at 106; Hassold, *supra* p. 12, note 29 at 232.

[22] G. Tedeschi, "Al Hadin Hadispositivi [On Dispositive Law]," 15 *Iyunei Mishpat* 5, 8 (1990).

[23] Hart and Sachs, *supra* p. 3, note 3 at 1124.

[24] Llewellyn, *supra* p. 172, note 102 at 400: "A statute merely declaring a rule, without purpose or objective, is nonsense."

[25] As Justice Dixon wrote, "I begin with the obvious. The *Canadian Charter of Rights and Freedoms* is a purposive document. Its purpose is to guarantee and to protect, within the limits of reason, the enjoyment of the rights and freedoms it enshrines." *Hunter v. Southern, Inc.* [1984] 2 S.C.R. 145, 156.

disputing the existence of those aims. A constitution with no purpose is like a person with no shadow. The proper interpretation of a constitution gives the constitutional text a meaning that achieves the social aims that the constitution is designed to achieve.

Every norm has a purpose. Peczenik rightly pointed out that "[t]he point of a norm is incomprehensible without a thought of a will or a purpose it expresses."[26] Achievement of this purpose is the point of interpreting every legal text. Furthermore, we must understand the individual text against the backdrop of the tapestry of the system. In one sense, we can say that the interpreter of one legal text interprets all legal texts within a given legal system.

Purposive interpretation gives full expression to these social considerations about the objective of law and the objective of the individual text. Purposive interpretation is built around the central idea that every text has an objective and a purpose, and that the goal of interpretation is to achieve that objective and that purpose. The social aims of law are diverse. An individual text may have a number of social objectives. Purposive interpretation accords with this reality because it is based on a multiplicity of purposes, both horizontal and vertical. We rely on constitutional considerations, however, for guidance about the relationship between the intent of the author and the intention of the system in determining ultimate purpose.

3. JURISPRUDENTIAL SUPPORT FOR PURPOSIVE INTERPRETATION

Philosophical Theories Regarding Purpose

A theoretical examination of a few theories of law suggests that, in the main, they accept the purpose of the text as a critical component of a proper system of interpretation. They do not dispute the importance of the purpose at the core of the text as a criterion for understanding it. They differ, however, over the essence of that purpose—whether it is subjective purpose (authorial intent), objective purpose (intent of the reasonable author or of the system), or some combination of the two—and how to discover it. I will briefly discuss a few of these philosophical theories. I do not suggest that these theories agree with my definition of purpose or with purposive interpretation as I develop it. I claim only that each contains an element of purpose as the core of the interpretive theory derived from it. These philosophical theories provide one important layer in the founda-

---

[26] Peczenik, *supra* p. 16, note 44 at 406.

tion of a theory of interpretation—the recognition that the purpose of a text affects its interpretation. Some of these theories also take a position on the content of the purpose at the core of the text.

The American Realists

The founders of the American realist movement argued that "legislative intent" is not an appropriate criterion for interpreting a statute. They vigorously attacked those who supported using the subjective intent of the author of the statute to reach a particular interpretive conclusion, calling that attempt an "absurd fiction."[27] They limited their criticism to "concrete intention" or "consequentialist intention,"[28] however, not "abstract intention" or the purpose derived from it.[29] Indeed, the American realists viewed the abstract purpose of the statute as imperative to interpreting the enacted norm.[30] Radin had this to say on the issue:

> The use of the "purpose" of the law as a means of interpreting it is duly listed as one of the methods of doing so in every discussion of interpretation. What I should like to insist upon is not that it is legitimate to inquire into the purpose of the statute, but that it is imperative to do so first and principally.[31]

Llewellyn took a similar stance.[32] He noted that a statute should be interpreted according to its purpose, and that a statute creating a purposeless rule is nonsense. Every statute has a purpose or objective it is designed to achieve.

Positivism

Does positivism, as a philosophical movement in law,[33] have its own system of interpretation? Professor Kelsen, as a founder of legal positivism,

[27] M. Radin, "Statutory Interpretation," 43 *Harv. L. Rev.* 863, 870 (1930).

[28] *See supra* p. 126, for a discussion of these concepts.

[29] *See, e.g.,* J. Frank, "Words and Music: Some Remarks on Statutory Interpretation," 47 *Colum. L. Rev.* 1259 (1947). For an analysis of this article, see K. Greenawalt, "Variation on Some Themes of a 'Disporting Gazelle' and His Friend: Statutory Interpretation As Seen by Jerome Frank and Felix Frankfurter," 100 *Colum. L. Rev.* 176 (2000).

[30] *See* Popkin, *supra* p. 85, note 1 at 145.

[31] Radin, *supra* p. 85, note 1, at 400 n. 20.

[32] Llewellyn, *supra* p. 172, note 102 at 400. *See also* J. Breen, "Statutory Interpretation and the Lessons of Llewellyn," 33 *Loy. L.A. L. Rev.* 263 (2000) ("Llewellyn believed that both the articulation and the interpretation of legal language was always done with a purpose in mind").

[33] For a discussion of positivism as jurisprudence, see B. Bix, *Jurisprudence* 31 (2d ed. 1999).

had no preference for any particular system of interpretation. He thought that the Pure Theory of Law[34] took no stance on selecting a system of interpretation. According to him, legal science should limit itself to establishing the different meanings that a text can sustain—the frame of the picture—and leave it to legal policy to select the meaning that the text should bear.[35] In his view, every text has an element of uncertainty (*Unbestimmtheit*), inevitable because a text is general, but language is brief. An interpreter, therefore, has discretion in determining the meaning of the text, without jurisprudence guiding his or her selection. Every text is a frame for the interpreter to fill, unencumbered by jurisprudential direction.

Professor H.L.A. Hart continued Kelsen's line of thinking, assuming the existence of uncertainty in a text (open texture) and discretion for the interpreter. Hart, however, did not assume that all texts contain uncertainty and require the use of discretion. Hart distinguished between situations falling into the core of the "open" text and situations falling into the gray area or penumbra of the text. The second instance requires the interpreter to exercise discretion in order to interpret the text according to the purpose or aim of its author,[36] while balancing conflicting values and principles.[37] Hart used the now-classic example[38] of the "No vehicles in the park" rule to illustrate his point. In his view, there are cases that are clearly included in the prohibition. There are also, however, borderline cases in which purpose or aim determines the meaning of the rule.[39] In later writings, Hart emphasized—in response to criticism[40]—that the "core" cases are decided according to context.[41] He did not, however, develop his theory of interpretation.[42] He did not discuss the concept of purpose or aim, although for him, they seem to reflect the subjective purpose of the author.

---

[34] H. Kelsen, *Pure Theory of Law* 348 (Knight trans., 1967) (1934).

[35] S. Paulson, "Kelsen on Legal Interpretation," 10 *Leg. Stud.* 136 (1990); C. Luzzati, "Discretion and 'Indeterminacy' in Kelsen's Theory of Legal Interpretation," in *Hans Kelsen's Legal Theory: A Diachronic Point of View* 123 (L. Gianformaggio ed., 1990); P. Chiassoni, "Legal Science and Legal Interpretation in the Pure Theory of Law," in *Hans Kelsen's Legal Theory* 63 (L. Gianformaggio ed. 1990).

[36] Hart, *supra* p. 26, note 78 at 124.

[37] *Id.* at 124.

[38] P. Schlag, "No Vehicles in the Park," 23 *Seattle U. L. Rev.* 381 (1999).

[39] Hart, *supra* p. 26, note 78 at 127, 129, 204; H.L.A. Hart, "Positivism and the Separation of Law and Morals," 71 *Harv. L. Rev.* 593 (1958).

[40] L. Fuller, "Positivism and Fidelity to Law—A Reply to Professor Hart," 71 *Harv. L. Rev.* 630 (1958).

[41] H.L.A. Hart, *Essays in Jurisprudence and Philosophy* 8 (1983).

[42] MacCormick's approach is similar to Hart's. *See* D.N. MacCormick, *Legal Reasoning and Legal Theory* 202 (1978); D.N. MacCormick and O. Weinberger, *An Institutional Theory of Law* 201 (1986); D.N. MacCormick, "On 'Open Texture' in Law," in *Controversies about Law's Ontology* 72 (P. Amselek and D.N. MacCormick ed. 1991).

Professor Raz has developed Hart's idea of aim as reflecting subjective purpose,[43] arguing that a statute should be interpreted according to the intent of its author. However, he defined intent narrowly, limiting it to the intent to enact a statute. Marmor gives a more operative meaning to intent, but he limits its relevance to statutes whose authority derives from the legislator's expertise;[44] in other cases, according to Marmor, the practice accepted in the legal system should be followed, without the need for input from theories of philosophy. Both Raz and Marmor limit their intentionalist theories to legislation, excluding, among other things, constitutions.[45]

Legal Process

The legal process movement held sway in American jurisprudence in the 1950s and 1960s. Professors Henry Hart and Albert Sacks were at the vanguard.[46] Legal process scholars paid special attention to interpretation in law, particularly statutory interpretation. Hart and Sacks began with the idea that law is designed to achieve social purposes,[47] and that interpretation must realize those purposes of law. Interpretation is a process of giving meaning to an enacted norm, not of expressing the concrete or consequentialist intention of the legislature.[48] In interpreting statutory language, a judge must give it a meaning that achieves the purpose of the legislation.[49] At the core of the approach taken by Hart and Sacks is the presumption—which they claim is non-rebuttable—that legislation is a purposive activity. Statutes are enacted to achieve social objectives. Legislation without purpose is foreign to the concept of law: "Every statute must be conclusively presumed to be a purposive act. The idea of a statute without an intelligible purpose is foreign to the idea of law and inadmissible."[50] In another place, they note:

[43] J. Raz, "Intention in Interpretation," in *The Autonomy of Law: Essays on Legal Positivism* 249 (R.P. Georg ed. 1996).

[44] A. Marmor, "Kavanat Hamichokek Visamchut Hachok [Legislative Intent and Statutory Authority]," 16 *Iyunei Mishpat* 593 (1991); A. Marmor, *Interpretation and Legal Theory* (1992).

[45] On Raz's theory of constitutional interpretation, see Raz, *supra* p. 41, note 124 at 152.

[46] Hart and Sachs, *supra* p. 3, note 3. Professor Fuller has also influenced this movement tremendously. *See* L. Fuller, *The Law in Quest of Itself* (1940); L. Fuller, "The Case of the Speluncean Explorers," 62 *Harv. L. Rev.* 616 (1949); L. Fuller, "The Forms and Limits of Adjudication," 92 *Harv. L. Rev.* 353 (1978).

[47] Hart and Sacks, *supra* p. 3, note 3 at 148 ("Law is a doing of something, a purposive activity, a continuous striving to solve the basic problems of social living").

[48] *See supra* p. 126 for a discussion of these concepts.

[49] For a discussion of the movement's purposive approach to judicial process, *see* Popkin, *supra* p. 85, note 1 at 147. For Greenawalt's analysis of this article, see Greenawalt, *supra* p. 225, note 29.

[50] Hart and Sachs, *supra* p. 3, note 3 at 1124.

Law is a doing of something, a purposive activity, a continuous striving to solve the basic problems of social living. . . . Legal arrangements (laws) are provisions for the future in aid of this effort. Sane people do not make provisions for the future which are purposeless. It can be accepted as a fixed premise, therefore, that every statute and every doctrine of unwritten law developed by the decisional process has some kind of purpose or objective, however difficult it may be on occasion to ascertain it or to agree exactly how it should be phrased.[51]

The text alone does not suffice. The text cannot be clear until it achieves the purpose at its core. Hart and Sacks recognized the complexity of determining purpose, and that a piece of legislation may have multiple purposes. It is not clear from their writing if they favored achieving a subjective or objective purpose. Their assumption that the legislature is reasonable seems to recognize an element of objective purpose, in addition to the subjective.[52]

Dworkin

Dworkin has developed a general theory of interpretation that accords significance to the purpose at the core of a text. Like the American realists, Dworkin discounts considering the concrete intention of the authors of the statute. Instead, Dworkin accords great significance to the abstract intention of the author of the statute and the founders of the constitution, that is, what the legislature sought to achieve through the legislation (linguistic or semantic intention)[53] and what the founders sought to achieve through the constitution.[54] Addressing the distinction, Dworkin writes:

This is the crucial distinction between what some officials intended to *say* in enacting the language they used, and what they intended—or expected or hoped—would be the *consequence* of their saying it. . . . Any reader of anything must attend to semantic intention, because the same sounds or even words can be used with the intention of saying different things.[55]

[51] *Id.* at 148.

[52] V. Wellman, "Dworkin and the Legal Process Tradition: The Legacy of Hart and Sacks," 29 *Ariz. L. Rev.* 443, 462 (1987).

[53] R. Dworkin, *Freedom's Law: The Moral Reading of the American Constitution* 291 (1996). Dworkin distinguishes between the concept of the legislature, with which the interpreter is concerned, and the conceptions of the legislature, which do not concern the interpreter. *See* R. Dworkin, *A Matter of Principle* 39 (1985).

[54] R. Dworkin, *Freedom's Law: The Moral Reading of the American Constitution* 10 (1996).

[55] R. Dworkin, "Comment," in A. Scalia, *A Matter of Interpretation: Federal Courts and*

He goes on to stress the decisive importance of the distinction "between the question of what a legislature intended to say in the laws it enacted, which judges applying those laws must answer, and the question of what the various legislators as individuals expected or hoped the consequences of those laws would be, which is a very different matter."[56] Achieving the (abstract) intent at the core of the text is a primary, if not exclusive, component of Dworkin's system of interpretation.

Law and Economics

We now turn to the law and economics movement. Law and economics values efficiency and sets wealth maximization as the goal of law. Scholars of law and economics, however, do not have a uniform position on interpretation. In contractual interpretation,[57] some favor considering the joint intent of the parties, because the parties are the best judges of their own interests.[58] Others prefer objective interpretation that takes market failures and the parties' limited rationality into account, to achieve a more efficient result.[59] A similar dispute exists in statutory interpretation. Some scholars, led by Posner, think that the purpose at the core of the legislation—according to the method of "imaginative reconstruction"[60]—is the proper criterion for interpretation, to be determined using pragmatic considerations, common sense, and the interpreter's personal views on reasonableness. Others favor an "objective textualist" approach ("new textualism") that discounts any consideration of the statute's purpose in its interpretation. The legislature is thus encouraged to formulate laws clearly.[61] Addressing the rules of interpretation, Easterbrook wrote that "Rules are desirable not because legislators in fact know or use them in passing laws but because rules serve as off-the-rack provisions that spare legislators the costs of anticipating all possible interpretative problems and legislating solutions

---

the Law 116–17 (1997). *See also* R. Dworkin, "The Arduous Virtue of Fidelity: Originalism, Scalia, Tribe, and Nerve," 65 *Fordham L. Rev.* 1249 (1997).

[56] Dworkin, "Comment," *supra* p. 228, note 55 at 118.

[57] L. Kaplow and S. Shavell, "Economic Analysis of Law," in A.J. Auerbach and M. Feldstein, *Handbook of Public Economics* (1985); A. Katz, "Contract Formation and Interpretation," in 1 *The New Palgrave Dictionary of Economics and the Law* 425 (P. Newman ed. 1998).

[58] Zamir, *supra* p. 15, note 39 at 1789; Posner, *supra* p. 221, note 15 at 93. *See also* A. Schwartz, "Justice and the Law of Contract: A Case for the Traditional Approach," 9 *Harv. J.L. & Pub. Pol'y* 107 (1986).

[59] Zamir, *supra* p. 15, note 39 at 1789–90.

[60] *Supra* p. 36.

[61] Popkin, *supra* p. 85, note 1 at 159.

for them."[62] His is the clearest law-and-economics stance on the interpretation of legal texts. However, some of the most prominent scholars of law and economics—Posner foremost among them—use the purpose of the legislation and the joint intent of the parties as the proper criteria for interpreting legal texts.

4. HERMENEUTIC CONSIDERATIONS IN FAVOR OF PURPOSIVE INTERPRETATION

Combining the Horizons of the Text and the Interpreter

Purposive interpretation stems from hermeneutic study. It is based on a kind of dialogue between interpreter and text. The interpreter does not try to enter the shoes of the text's author, a task made impossible by the gap in time. The interpreter and the text's author live in different time periods. Each has his or her own pre-understanding. The interpreter therefore does not try to relive the experience of creating the text. He or she tries to combine his or her modern understanding with the understanding at the core of the text. This blending of horizons, central to purposive interpretation,[63] expresses the proper hermeneutic perspective. The contemporary interpreter is not stuck in his or her (contemporary) pre-understanding, but rather reconsiders the text and the understanding at its core. The interpreter studies the intent of the text's author and the way the text would have been understood by the author's contemporaries.[64] Aided by pre-understanding, the interpreter tries to learn the purpose at the core of the text. He or she does consult the understanding in the background of the text's creation, but only to create a modern understanding of the text that combines his or her pre-understanding in the present with the understanding that lay at the core of the text in the past. This blending of horizons expresses the activity of interpretation. It also allows the interpreter to understand a particular textual provision against the backdrop of his or her pre-understanding of the text as a whole. The interpreter thus overcomes the problem of the hermeneutic circle.[65] This process occurs within the bounds of a legal community that restrains the interpreter. It determines the expanse of his or her pre-understanding. It constitutes the social consensus in which the interpreter operates. The pre-understanding in-

---

[62] F. Easterbrook, "Statute's Domain," 50 *U. Chi. L. Rev.* 533, 540 (1983).

[63] Based on Gadamer's hermeneutic perspective. *See also* Eskridge, *supra* p. 58, note 210.

[64] In this sense, purposive interpretation takes originalism into consideration. *See infra* p. 277.

[65] *Supra* p. 136.

cludes, *inter alia*, the legal system's interpretive rules that guide the interpreter toward the proper interpretation.[66] It also includes society's view on the role of the judge and the way he or she should exercise discretion.

Holistic Approach

Hermeneutics teaches us to take a holistic approach to the text, treating a will, contract, statute, or constitution singularly and as a whole. We raze the barriers between interpreter and text to allow free movement from text to interpreter and back again. We eliminate barriers of time. There is no early or late. There is no threshold of admissibility. All credible evidence— whether internal or external to the text—is admissible. There is no distinction between a clear and an unclear text. No text is clear until the conclusion of the interpretive process. And every text is clear—for the purposes of the interpretive problem to be adjudicated—once the interpretive process concludes. The text cannot be understood without the context, whose boundaries are not limited in advance. The interpreter may consult any and all circumstances. He or she formulates the purpose of the text, based on his or her comprehensive understanding. This interpretive activity, characteristic of purposive interpretation, is a fitting expression of modern hermeneutic views on the essence of proper interpretation. These views emphasize understanding the text as a whole, against the background of the interpreter's pre-understanding, which is itself a product of time and place. Interpretation is seen as a dialogue between interpreter and text, as part of an attempt to create a link between past and present. Purposive interpretation reflects all of the above principles.

Hermeneutic Considerations in All Kinds of Texts

Because they deal with texts created in the past, interpreters of all legal texts engage in some form of hermeneutic consideration. Interpreters of wills and contracts should related to the text holistically, understanding the life and circumstances of a testator and the circumstances under which a contract was formed. They should accord significant weight to the intent of the testator or the joint intent of the contractual parties. They should also give expression to hypothetical intent, which is the "will" of the system, at various levels of abstraction. Interpreters take a similar approach to statutes and constitutions, although in that context, the emphasis on subjective and

---

[66] O. Fiss, "Objectivity and Interpretation," 34 *Stan. L. Rev.* 739 (1982); O. Fiss, "Conventionalism," 58 *S. Cal. L. Rev.* 177 (1985).

objective purpose shifts. Interpreters seek not to respond to questions asked at the time the statute was enacted, but rather to respond to questions that their contemporaries ask. After all, the statute regulates contemporary life. The past, however, cannot be ignored. Statutory interpretation should be regarded as an ongoing process.[67] Statutory interpretation is not just uncovering the intent of the historical author. It is a modern interpretation of a text created in the past. It requires us to deal with the element of time. At the same time, it cannot ignore the intent of the author. Purposive interpretation of legislation expresses these principles.

The same is true for constitutional interpretation. The interpreter cannot penetrate the minds of the authors of the constitution, nor is there a need to do so. The authors of the constitution lived in the past. Their world was different from ours, and it contained different problems, although we can use their world to understand our own. Constitutional interpretation must reflect the connection between the two worlds. The horizons of the historical constitutional text must blend with the horizons of the modern interpreter. Such blending—central to purposive interpretation—fully expresses the proper hermeneutic perspective. Understanding of the constitution changes as it moves through history. It is a modern understanding that does not ignore the past, but seeks to synthesize the past with the present.

Limitations of Hermeneutic Considerations

Hermeneutic considerations advance our understanding of interpretation in law. They do not, however, resolve the fundamental problems of legal interpretation. The central problem in legal interpretation is what role to assign the intent of the creator when interpreting the creation. Hermeneutics has no clear answer to this problem. Its scholars differ over the issue of whether hermeneutics requires authorial intent to be the primary goal of interpretation.[68] Hermeneutics expresses the holistic aspect of legal interpretation and allows it to deal with the element of time. It is limited, however, because it does not help the interpreter assume a stance with respect to the relationship between authorial intent and the intention of the system. Non-hermeneutic considerations—specifically, constitutional considerations[69]—help resolve the latter issue.

---

[67] W. Eskridge, "Dynamic Statutory Interpretation," 135 *U. Pa. L. Rev.* 1479, 1482 (1987).

[68] *Supra* p. 56.

[69] *Supra* p. 60.

Semantic Considerations

Language may be communicative, but its limitations prevent it from always transmitting a single, unique meaning. Rather, it creates a range of semantic possibilities. Such range varies in breadth from issue to issue, and also looks different, depending on our angle of approach, but it is not unlimited. An interpreter cannot give a text any meaning he or she chooses. Semantic theory teaches us that every text requires interpretation, and that interpretation requires the interpreter to consider both intrinsic and extrinsic context.[70] Understanding is an ongoing dialogue between reader and text. There should be no artificial restraints on that conversation. What does the interpreter seek in these sources of (external and internal) context? Context is just a vessel for understanding the text. The content of that vessel depends on an element external to language. As Patterson noted, "Theories of meaning have no gospel that will save lawyers the pain of thinking."[71] Semantic theory teaches that, as crucial as the semantic component is to interpretation, it can never be the sole component. Textualist systems of interpretation that focus on language must be supplemented with additional components of interpretation. The text does not ask questions; the interpreter does, learning the answers from the text, with the help of the context. The central problem in interpretation is: What questions should the interpreter ask? Systems of interpretation that are not sensitive to this semantic lesson are doomed to fail. Purposive interpretation, on the other hand, is aware of the interpreter's need to ask questions, and those questions are connected to the purpose of the text and the aim it is designed to achieve.

5. CONSTITUTIONAL CONSIDERATIONS IN FAVOR OF PURPOSIVE INTERPRETATION

The Need for Constitutional Theory

Semantic theory teaches us that language limits meaning, but meaning is not limited to language. Various social and jurisprudential theories about the nature of law agree that the appropriate context for understanding the text is its purpose. They disagree, however, over the essence of that purpose. We said that the purpose of legal interpretation is to achieve the purpose of a legal text. The fundamental questions about legal interpretation,

[70] Hoffman, *supra* p. 6, note 12.
[71] Patterson, *supra* p. 222, note 18 at 29–30.

however, raise doubt about the weight to give authorial intent in formulating ultimate purpose, and how to balance it with the objective intention
of the system and the internal relationships between the components of objective purpose. We must answer the question of whether the intent of the
framers and the members of the legislature are decisive in interpreting constitutions and statutes. We must address the claim that the judge's task is
to interpret the text, not create it. We must weigh the autonomy of the private will in interpreting texts in private law. We must know what sources
external to the text the interpreter may use. We must know how to balance
the different kinds of objective purpose.

These questions and the responses to them are not foreign to law. They
exist in constitutional law in every legal system. Semantic or hermeneutic
theories are not what determine which system of interpretation we choose.
Constitutional law is the locus for this decision, and the considerations to
be taken into account are constitutional. Interpretive theory must derive
from a constitutional perspective.[72] As Professor Mashaw noted, "Any theory of statutory interpretation is at base a theory about constitutional law.
It must at the very least assume a set of legitimate institutional roles and
legitimate institutional procedures that inform interpretation."[73] The same
is true of interpreting wills and contracts.

I do not contend that constitutional law provides a clear answer to every
question troubling an interpreter. I claim only that the different factors that
must be considered and balanced are of a constitutional nature. Different
interpreters have different views about what constitutional law requires,
but regardless of their views, they must consider constitutional factors, not
merely social, jurisprudential, or hermeneutic elements. Those who claim
that a statute should be interpreted according to legislative intent do so
based on a constitutional perspective about the role of the legislative
branch in the triad of powers. Those who oppose interpreting a statute according to legislative intent also base their views on a constitutional stance
about the role of the legislature. Similarly, those who favor (and those who
oppose) interpreting a legal text to actualize fundamental values, such as
equality and fairness, base their views on a constitutional theory.

We cannot formulate an interpretive viewpoint about the meaning of a
legal text that does not rest on a constitutional theory about the power and
role of the author, his or her control over the text created, and the values

[72] See Rubenfeld, *supra* p. 162, note 46.

[73] J. Mashaw, "As If Republican Interpretation," 97 *Yale L.J.* 1685, 1686 (1988). *See also*
J. Schacter, "Metademocracy: The Changing Structure of Legitimacy in Statutory Interpretation," 108 *Harv. L. Rev.* 593 (1995); J. Corry, "Administrative Law and Interpretation of
Statutes," 1 *U. Toronto L.J.* 286 (1935–36). *See also* Redish and Chung, *supra* p. 135, note
53 at 847.

and principles that judges should safeguard in interpreting the author's creation. That constitutional theory must also address the role of the interpreter and the limits of the discretion he or she may exercise. Because the
court's interpretation is binding, the key question is really: What is a
judge's role in interpreting a legal text?[74] The answer lies in constitutional
law. In the process of answering the question, we express the fundamental
constitutional perspectives that shape the regime and society. We express
fundamental perspectives on democracy, separation of powers, faith in the
judiciary, constitutional and systemic structure, fundamental constitutional
principles, and human rights.

Naturally, these perspectives have great force in constitutional and statutory interpretation. They also exist, however—if in diminished force—in
the interpretation of contracts and wills. Contracts and wills also implicate
democracy and separation of powers. A constitutional theory that views the
judge as the legislature's junior partner in statutory interpretation also
views the judge as a junior partner to the testator or contractual parties in
interpreting a will or contract. Human rights are prominent in interpreting private law texts, too, because contracts and wills are based on the autonomy of the private will. The need to maintain public confidence in the
judiciary and actualize fundamental principles is common to the interpretation of all legal texts. Below, I discuss the various constitutional considerations that should be taken into account in order to show that, taken together, those considerations point toward purposive interpretation as the
most proper system of interpretation.[75]

Constitutional Theory and Democracy

All constitutional theories have a common point of departure: a democratic
regime. I am aware of the various disputes over what democracy is. However, we can agree on two core assumptions:[76] *First*, democracy cannot
exist without recognizing the sovereignty of the people and its right to
choose representatives in regular and free elections;[77] and *second*, proper
democracy cannot exist without recognizing fundamental constitutional
values (separation of powers, rule of law, judicial independence), central to

---

[74] On the role of a judge in a democracy, see A. Barak, "Foreword: The Role of a Supreme
Court in a Democracy," 116 *Harv. L. Rev.* 16 (2002).

[75] I do not claim that other systems of interpretation are unconstitutional. If a statute were
to establish one of them as the way to interpret legislation, that statute would be constitutional. *See* Rosenkranz, *supra* p. 49, note 159. I make the narrower claim that constitutional
arguments weigh in favor of purposive interpretation.

[76] R. Fallon, How to Choose a Constitutional Theory," 87 *Cal. L. Rev.* 537 (1999).

[77] R.A. Dahl, *On Democracy* (1998).

which are human rights.[78] A proper democracy has its own morality, based on human dignity and equality of persons. These two assumptions are at the core of my constitutional theory. They are the source of my conclusions about purposive interpretation. I would not adopt a purposive system of interpretation without the core assumption of a proper democratic regime. Purposive interpretation is not appropriate for those seeking to oppose a totalitarian regime. When a dictator writes the constitution, we should not encourage a judge to interpret it in a way that achieves its purpose; when the fundamental values of the system do not respect human rights, a legal text should not be interpreted to actualize those values. Textualism may be the appropriate system of interpretation for totalitarian systems.

Constitutional Theory and the Role of the Judge

The judiciary plays a central role in every democratic structure. As we shall see,[79] it is the junior partner in interpreting all legal texts. This partnership has two aspects: *First,* the role of the judge is to help bridge the gap between law and society's changing needs; *second*—and this is central to interpretation—the judge must preserve democracy and defend the constitution. Democracy cannot exist unless we fight for it. It should not be taken for granted. Unless we protect democracy, democracy will not protect us. All branches of government and all individuals, of course, are responsible for preserving democracy. But judges—particularly supreme court justices—have a special responsibility to protect democracy.[80] A legal system's approach to interpretation should therefore maximize the achievement of these twin goals. In my view, only purposive interpretation achieves these goals. Its dynamic approach allows it to bridge the gap between law and society's changing needs. The weight it accords to legislative supremacy (as part of subjective purpose) and the system's fundamental values and human rights (as part of objective purpose) protects democracy.

Constitutional Theory and the Uniqueness of the Constitution

A constitution shapes the character of society. It is based on the will of the people, which is different from the will of the people at the core of ordinary

---

[78] R. Dworkin, *A Bill of Rights for Britain* 33, 35 (1990).

[79] *Infra* p. 249.

[80] B. McLachlin, "The Role of the Supreme Court in a New Democracy" (unpub. 2001); M. Kirby, "Australian Law—After 11 September 2001," 21 *Austl. Bar Rev.* 21 (2001); A. Mason, "A Bill of Rights for Australia?" 5 *Austl. Bar Rev.* 79 (1989).

legislation.[81] The will of the people at the core of the constitution is the "deep" will that justifies the constitutional character of the democratic regime. This "deep" will establishes the branches of government and expresses the basic values and principles of the people. Human rights are paramount among them. These components of the constitutional structure—the branches of government and basic values, in general, and human rights in particular—are the basis for judicial review of the constitutionality of statutes. They are also the basis for interpreting the constitution.[82] In engaging in this interpretation, a judge should express the basic constitutional values that constitute the "normative umbrella"[83] spread over the constitution.

A constitution does not operate in a normative vacuum. Outside and around the constitution are values and principles that the constitution must actualize. These are not a judge's personal values but rather the national values of the country. "It is axiomatic that the law of a nation is learned from the looking glass of its national way of life."[84] The values and principles that the constitution seeks to actualize stem from this way of life. They reflect the social consensus at the core of the legal system. They ground basic social views. They are derived in part from the constitutional text and its history, and in part from the history of the people,[85] its social and religious worldviews, tradition, and heritage.[86] The constitution does not (explicitly or implicitly) mention all the values and principles that constitute the normative umbrella. Interpreters should avoid artificially introducing into the constitution values that are not (explicitly or implicitly) mentioned in it. These unmentioned values, however, are a point of engagement for understanding the values and principles that are mentioned in the constitution. They form part of the "unwritten constitution" that in turn serves as an interpretive criterion for understanding the written constitution. Because of this unique aspect of the constitution, a judge should accord significant weight to objective purpose in its interpretation. Only then can the constitution fulfill its aim in law.[87]

---

[81] B. Ackerman, "Constitutional Politics/Constitutional Law," 99 *Yale L.J.* 453 (1989).

[82] For the connection between judicial review and constitutional interpretation, see Rubenfeld, *supra* p. 162, note 46.

[83] C.A. 165/82, *supra* p. 149, note 4.

[84] H.C. 73/53, *supra* p. 179, note 118 at 884 (Agranat, J.).

[85] T. Sandalow, "Constitutional Interpretation," 79 *Mich. L. Rev.* 1033 (1981).

[86] *Poe v. Ullman*, 367 U.S. 497, 542 (1961). Justice Harlan notes that a source of constitutional values is "The tradition from which [this country] developed as well as the traditions from which it broke."

[87] *Infra* p. 371.

Democracy and Purposive Statutory Interpretation

The sovereignty of the people is the starting point for a discussion of constitutional democracy. It is the source of authority for the founding of the constitution, based on separation of powers.[88] The principle has a double meaning: *First*, it means distinguishing among different branches of government, giving each branch a central and primary function. *Second*, it means that the different branches have a reciprocal relationship in which each checks and balances the other branches.[89] The powers are separated not to maximize efficiency but rather to maximize freedom.[90] On this view of separation of powers, the primary and central function of the legislative branch is to create general legal norms that are "laws" in the functional sense. These laws are subordinate to the constitution. They are binding on everyone. A court may not void them if it doesn't like them. Its job is to interpret. Hence the principle of legislative supremacy.[91]

What can be inferred from the role of the legislative branch in enacting statutes to be interpreted by the judicial branch? I see three conclusions: *First*, judges may not interpret a statute in order to achieve their own policies or the policies of those who selected them for the judiciary. Judges are not subject to the standard electoral process. They do not receive their position in order to implement the political platform of those who appointed them. Judges are not accountable to the people in the way that politicians are. That is their independence. In interpreting a piece of legislation, judges should realize neither their own intentions nor those of their political backers.[92]

Second, in their interpretive work, judges should give weight to a statute's subjective purpose as an expression of legislative supremacy. The legislature enacts a statute in order to achieve a certain purpose. The goal of interpretation is to achieve this purpose. True, the subjective purpose is not part of the statute, but it is the goal that the statute is designed to achieve, and thus it should serve as a criterion for understanding the statute.[93] The legislative branch uses legislation to establish social policy,

---

[88] E. Levi, "Some Aspects of Separation of Powers," 76 *Colum. L. Rev.* 371 (1976).

[89] H.C. 306/81 *Sharon v. Knesset Committee*, 35(4) P.D. 118, 144–45. *See also* A. Feld, "Separation of Political Powers: Boundaries or Balance," 21 *Ga. L. Rev.* 171 (1986).

[90] *Myers v. United States*, 272 U.S. 52, 293 (1926). Montesquieu put freedom at the core of separation of powers. *See* C. Montesquieu, 11 *The Spirit of Laws* 209 (Eng. trans., 1977).

[91] Farber, *supra* p. 25, note 73; W. Eskridge, "Spinning Legislative Supremacy," 78 *Geo. L.J.* 319 (1989); E. Maltz, "Rhetoric and Reality in the Theory of Statutory Interpretation: Underenforcement, Overenforcement, and the Problem of Legislative Supremacy," 71 *B.U. L. Rev.* 767 (1991).

[92] C.A. 481/73, *Rosenberg v. Stasel*, 29(1) P.D. 505, 516.

[93] S. Smith, "Law without Mind," 88 *Mich. L. Rev.* 104, 122 (1989).

allocate national resources, and set the national agenda. The statute is a tool for achieving policy goals. Further, it does not suffice—contrary to Raz's claim[94]—for the judge merely to validate the intent of the legislature to legislate, ignoring the legislature's intentions about the content of the statute. A legislature does not enact statutes for the sake of legislating— it does so to achieve a particular social goal. Legislative supremacy requires an interpreter to validate the legislature's (abstract[95]) intention about that goal. True, there is sometimes no available information about a statute's subjective purpose, or the information is not credible or certain enough. Sometimes, an interpreter knows the purpose of legislation at a level so abstract, it is of no assistance in resolving his or her interpretive problem. Sometimes, the interpreter encounters conflicting subjective purposes. Sometimes, there are good reasons to stray from the purpose that the legislature envisioned because of the type of statute being interpreted. These are the reasons that subjective purpose is not the sole criterion for interpreting a statute. They do not, however, justify completely ignoring subjective intent in statutory interpretation. Where there is sure and credible evidence about the abstract intent of the legislature (subjective purpose), and that intent is relevant to resolving the problem facing the interpreter, it should be given weight in interpreting the statute.

Third, in statutory interpretation, objective purpose should be considered in addition to subjective purpose. This conclusion is also inherent to democracy. Democracy is not just about legislative supremacy—it requires actualizing the values and principles at its core.[96] There can be no true democracy without protecting human rights, rule of law, and the independence of the judiciary. Democracy is not just rule by the majority. It is also rule by fundamental values, in general, and human rights, in particular. Democracy is not just formal democracy (concerned with the electoral process governed by the majority and expressed in legislative supremacy). Democracy is also substantive democracy (concerned with fundamental values and human rights). As Dworkin writes:

> True democracy is not just *statistical* democracy, in which anything a majority or plurality wants is legitimate for that reason, but *communal* democracy, in which majority decision is legitimate only if it is a majority within a community of equals. That means not only that everyone must be allowed to participate in politics as an equal, through the vote and through freedom of speech and protest, but that political decisions must treat everyone with equal concern and respect, that each individual person must be guaranteed funda-

---

[94] J. Raz, "Intention in Interpretation," in *The Autonomy of Law: Essays on Legal Positivism* 249 (R. George ed., 1996).

[95] See *supra* p. 126 for the distinction between concrete and abstract intention.

[96] Peczenik, *supra* p. 16, note 44 at 350; Gebbia-Pinetti, *supra* p. 152, note 15 at 256.

mental civil and political rights no combination of other citizens can take away, no matter how numerous they are or how much they despise his or her race or morals or way of life.[97]

Democracy should not be understood one-dimensionally, extending only to majority rule and legislative supremacy. Democracy is a multi-dimensional concept. It requires rule of fundamental values, too, central to which are human rights. Hence the democratic justification for judicial review of the constitutionality of legislation. Hence, also, the democratic justification for interpreting legislation in a way that actualizes the system's fundamental values, particularly human rights. There is a close link between the justification for judicial review of the constitutionality of legislation and the justification for purposive interpretation of it (and of all other legal texts). Both stem from a view of democracy based on rule of law and rule of values and human rights.[98] In his or her interpretation, therefore, a judge must give expression to the system's fundamental values. The purpose of a statute is presumed to be the actualization of the system's fundamental values and of human rights—the objective purpose at the core of the statute. In achieving this purpose, the judge does not violate democracy but rather actualizes its values. Interpreting a statute to actualize the system's fundamental values is democratic in the same way that reviewing a statute for conformity with the constitution is democratic. In both instances, judges express democracy's multidimensional character. They thus fulfill their role in a democracy.[99]

Democracy and the Image of the Legislature

Modern literature on statutory interpretation focuses on the judge and his or her means of interpretation.[100] Little attention is paid to the legislature and legislation.[101] Waldron does not exaggerate when he notes that "Legislation and legislatures have a bad name in legal and political philosophy, a name sufficiently disreputable to cast doubt on their credentials as respectable sources of law."[102] Modern public choice theories[103] have con-

---

[97] R. Dworkin, *supra* p. 236, note 78 at 35.

[98] Mashaw, *supra* p. 234, note 73 at 1690 ("Judicial interpretation and judicial review are largely congruent if not identical. In both, courts police legislative activity to avoid antirepublican results"). For a critique of this approach, see Redish and Chung, *supra* p. 135, note 53 at 871.

[99] *Supra* p. 236.

[100] J. Brudny, "Congressional Commentary on Judicial Interpretations of Statutes: Idle Chatter or Telling Response?" 93 *Mich. L. Rev.* 1, 3 (1994).

[101] J. Waldron, *Law and Disagreement* (1999).

[102] J. Waldron, *The Dignity of Legislation* 1 (1999).

[103] *Supra* p. 134, note 48.

tributed to this skepticism by revealing the considerations that members of the legislature take into account when voting on legislation. By presenting the voting members of the legislature as acting out of personal motivations, public choice theories refuse to credit legislators with an abstract intention to advance social interests.

Certain aspects of law and economics[104] also undermine the credibility of legislative intent. Scholars of law and economics argue that legislation is just a deal or an agreement between different interest groups and the members of the legislative body. In other words, many branches of law and economics argue, members of the legislature are motivated by the desire for reelection, not the public good. As part of this deal, the legislature makes certain assets available for use by interest groups. Judges cannot know what stands behind the deal or what its "purpose" is.[105] All they have is the language of the agreement, and they must give effect to that language.[106] Legislative intent should not play a role in statutory interpretation, nor should legislative history be a source for understanding the statute. On this approach, the legislature is a political body, motivated by political considerations, that seeks to achieve political results.

There is some truth to this approach, but it is not the whole truth. The view that members of the legislative body are a group of egoists interested only in reelection is distorted. The legislature is composed of human beings like you and me. Of course they have personal ambitions, but they also try to achieve proper social objectives. They act rationally and in good faith to actualize the values and interests in which they believe. If the values conflict with each other, they try to balance them to the best of their ability. Sometimes their work earns them reelection. Sometimes it doesn't. We need not take a cynical approach to the legislature, nor, for that matter, to democracy itself. We should assume a viewpoint of respect, appreciation, and faith that the legislature is properly playing its constitutional role. We should assume that members of the legislature act rationally and seek to advance the public good, as they see it, through mutual persuasion and consideration of social interests.[107] Hart and Sacks put it well in noting that a judge

---

[104] Other aspects of law and economics emphasize the importance of the legislature as the institution best equipped to distribute society's wealth. R. Posner, *Economic Analysis of Law* 569 (5th ed. 1998).

[105] Posner, *supra* p. 27, note 85 at 277.

[106] *See* Easterbrook, *supra* p. 132, note 38 at 547 ("Although legislators have individual lists of desires, priorities, and preferences, it turns out to be difficult, sometimes impossible, to aggregate these lists into a coherent collective choice"). *See also* F. Easterbrook, "The Supreme Court, 1983 Term—Foreword: The Court and the Economic System," 98 *Harv. L. Rev.* 4 (1984).

[107] C. Sunstein, "The Republican Civic Tradition: Beyond the Republic Revival," 97 *Yale L.J.* 1539 (1988).

should assume, unless the contrary unmistakably appears, that the legislature was made up of reasonable persons pursuing reasonable purposes reasonably. It should presume conclusively that these persons, whether or not entertaining concepts of reasonableness shared by the court, were trying responsibly and in good faith to discharge their constitutional powers and duties.[108]

This approach establishes the proper role of the legislature in the constitutional structure and properly articulates the relationship between the legislative and judicial branches. It influences the formulation of a proper system of interpretation.[109] It lays the foundation for purposive interpretation to interpret legislation according to both the (abstract) intent of the legislators and the intent of the reasonable legislature and of the system.

Rule of Law

Purposive interpretation takes rule of law[110] into account. Rule of law is a complicated concept.[111] Rubinstein correctly noted that "Few concepts are so often used and so little understood as the concept of rule of law."[112] To understand this concept, we should distinguish three of its primary aspects: formal rule of law, jurisprudential rule of law, and substantive rule of law. There is significant overlap among these aspects of rule of law. There are, however, substantial differences among them that are relevant in formulating a system of interpretation. Formal rule of law means that

> everyone in the country—individuals, corporations, and arms of the state—must act according to law, and unlawful activity must meet with the organized sanction of society. Rule of law, in this sense, has a double meaning, extending to both the legality of the rule and the rule of the law. It is a formal principle that addresses not the content of the law but rather the need for it to reign supreme, irrespective of content. Rule of law in this sense is not related to the quality of the regime but rather the principle of public order.[113]

This aspect of rule of law does not help us formulate a proper system of in-

[108] Hart and Sachs, *supra* p. 3, note 3 at 1378.
[109] W. Blatt, "Interpretive Communities: The Missing Element in Statutory Interpretation," 95 *Nw. U. L. Rev.* 629 (2000).
[110] R. Cass, *The Rule of Law in America* (2001); P. Craig, "Formal and Substantive Conceptions of the Rule of Law: An Analytical Framework," [1997] *Pub. L.* 467.
[111] R. Fallon, "'The Rule of Law' as a Concept in Constitutional Discourse," 97 *Colum. L. Rev.* 1 (1997).
[112] A. Rubinstein, *Constitutional Law of Israel* 227 (5th ed. 1996).
[113] H.C. 428/86, *supra* p. 167, note 74 at 621 (Barak, J.). *See also* A. Scalia, "The Rule of Law as a Law of Rules," 56 *U. Chi. L. Rev.* 1175 (1989).

terpretation. Every system of interpretation, once adopted and respected, helps impose law as it is understood after being interpreted.

Rule of Law: Jurisprudential Aspect

Legal philosophers (including Rawls,[114] Fuller,[115] and Raz[116]) have given the principle of rule of law a jurisprudential meaning. They have said that the rule of law sets the minimum requirements that a legal system needs in order to exist. These requirements are critical to ensuring a system of the rule of law and not the rule of man. It is what Rawls called "formal justice." Fuller called it the internal morality of law, adding that

> With all its subtleties, the problem of interpretation occupies a sensitive, central position in the internal morality of the law. It reveals, as no other problem can, the cooperative nature of the task of maintaining legality. If the interpreting agent is to preserve a sense of useful mission, the legislature must not impose on him senseless tasks.[117]

The theoretical aspect of rule of law focuses on the role of the social framework in the legal system. What factors distinguish the legal system from a gang controlled by a leader who imposes his or her will on everyone?

The leading scholars disagree over the answer to this question.[118] Fuller suggested an interesting list: law must be general, known, and publicized; law must be clear and understandable; law must be stable; law cannot be retroactive; laws must not contradict each other; law must not demand physically impossible tasks; there must be a system of enforcement by the responsible governing bodies. Rawls's list is no shorter: *First*, prohibitions imposed by law must be implementable and must be the product of action by the legislative, executive, and judicial branches, operating in good faith, and perceived as such by the public. *Second*, the principle of equality must be achieved. The system must treat similar situations similarly so that a person can maintain his or her actions within societal limits. *Third*, there can be no sanctions for a crime undefined by law. The law must be public and known, clear and understandable. There can be no retroactive legislation. *Fourth*, the rules of natural justice must be observed. Raz also has a list: Laws must be prospective, public, clear, and relatively stable; the judiciary must be independent; rules of natural justice must be observed; courts

[114] Rawls, *supra* p. 213, note 33 at 235.
[115] L. Fuller, *The Morality of Law* 33 (rev. ed. 1969).
[116] J. Raz, "The Rule of Law and Its Virtue," 93 *Law Q. Rev.* 195 (1977).
[117] Fuller, *supra* p. 243, note 115 at 91.
[118] C.R. Sunstein, *Legal Reasoning and Political Conflict* 101 (1996).

must have oversight authority, and they must be easily accessible. In his book on constitutional law, Rubinstein articulates "three useful principles that are an integral part of rule of law: equality of all before the law; certainty of the law; publicity of the law."[119]

In developing a system of interpretation, we would do well to pause at the requirement of certainty of the law, stability of the law, and security in interpersonal relationships. This means that the law should be clear and readable. A person must be able to understand what is forbidden and what is permitted by reading the law, if with the help of a legal professional. A statute is not a riddle. Similarly, there can be no retroactive statutes, particularly not in criminal law. Ultimately, law must be stable. We cannot periodically introduce changes as they suit us.

Purposive interpretation uses the presumptions of purpose to translate these requirements, derived from the jurisprudential aspect of rule of law, into the field of interpretation. Hence the presumptions that the purpose of a statute arises from its ordinary language; that legislation does not seek to introduce substantial changes casually; that a statute does not use words needlessly, that identical words have identical meanings, and that different words have different meanings; the presumption against retrospective application of legislation; and the presumption of interpretive and normative harmony between a statute and other statutes and between a statute and the laws of the system. The jurisprudential aspect of rule of law also warrants a number of presumptions about the judiciary, like the presumption that the purpose of legislation is to grant judicial powers to the judicial branch and the presumption against negating the powers of the court and against infringing on judicial independence.

The Jurisprudential Aspect and the Problem of Publicity: Considering External Circumstances

The jurisprudential aspect of rule of law requires laws to be public. Legal texts must be publicized and known. There can be no secret legislation. Not all publicized legislation, however, fulfills the rule of law's requirements of publicity. The principle of publicity requires, in addition to the publication itself, that the public be able to know, by reading the text, what is permitted and what is forbidden, to plan its activities accordingly, and to have its expectations of legality met. What does this mean for interpreting a legal text? Some have claimed that considering sources external to the text in order to learn about the text's subjective purpose violates the principle of publicity. This contention certainly has no place in the interpreta-

[119] Rubinstein, *supra* p. 242, note 112 at 262.

tion of wills. There is no reliance interest worthy of protection, so there is therefore no room to require publicity. As for contractual interpretation, the external circumstances do not provide information about the intent of one party but rather about the parties' joint intent. What claim of publicity can a party raise in this context? Generally, requirements of publicity apply to public documents like statutes and constitutions. In this latter context, the requirement of publicity is more persuasive. As Lord Oliver writes:

> every legislative enactment constitutes a *diktat* by the state to the citizen which he is not only expected but obliged to observe in the regulation of his daily life, and it is the judge and the judge alone who stands between the citizen and the state's own interpretation of its own rules. That is why it is so vitally important that legislation should be expressed in language that can be clearly understood and why it should be in a form that makes it readily accessible.[120]

As important as this argument is, it does not justify ignoring extrinsic sources of purpose. Understanding the statute by reading it assumes professional assistance, certainly in the case of complicated economic or social legislation. Using professional assistance and modern technology that affords ready access to primary legislative materials, one can consult legislative history easily and without excessive cost.[121]

Substantive Rule of Law and Purposive Legislative Interpretation

If rule of law were limited to its formal and jurisprudential meanings, it could include corrupt law (*lex corrupta*), as well. Why glorify and protect a piece of legislation that—publicly, certainly, generally, and prospectively—gives the regime authority to violate human rights? Former Israeli Supreme Court Vice President Haim Cohen correctly pointed out that rule of law

> does not just mean that the regime and those in power act according to law: totalitarian governments also act according to the laws of their countries, laws they themselves enacted for their own plans and purposes. The Nazi rulers came to power according to law, and they committed most of their crimes under legal authorization they hammered together for that very purpose. No one would say that "rule of law" prevailed in Nazi Germany. No one would disagree that a rule of outlaws prevailed.[122]

---

[120] P.R. Oliver, "A Judicial View of Modern Legislation," 14 *Stat. L. Rev.* 1, 2 (1993).

[121] For a different approach, see the minority opinion of Lord Mackay L.C. in *Pepper v. Hart* [1993] All E.R. 42. Lord Mackay notes that the need to consult parliamentary debate (the Hansard) increases legal costs.

[122] Cohen, *supra* p. 213, note 33 at 143.

It is a mistake to equate the principle of rule of law with the principle of the legality of the regime, supplemented by jurisprudential requirements. Dworkin's "rule-book conception" of the rule of law is not enough.[123] Rule of law must include an aspect that Dworkin calls the "right conception" of rule of law.[124] There is no general agreement over the scope of this concept. I think it derives from the very concept of democracy. Rule of law mandates both formal and substantive democracy. For our purposes, rule of law requires both majority rule (legislative supremacy) and human rights (guaranteeing the system's fundamental values). This is the origin of my belief that rule of law means the proper balance between the individual and the collective. Rule of law is not just public order. It is social justice based on social order. Its formal and substantive aspects cannot be separated; there is a necessary connection between the two. Law exists to guarantee normal social life, but social life is not a goal in itself. Rather, it is a means to enable the individual to develop himself or herself. Society exists for the good of its members, not for itself. Substantive rule of law is the rule of law that constitutes the proper balance between, on the one hand, society's need for political independence, social equality, economic development, and domestic order, and, on the other hand, the needs of the individual, his or her personal liberty, and his or her human dignity.

With this rich and complex view of rule of law in mind, we return to the constitutional considerations in statutory interpretation. We saw that democracy requires legislative supremacy and recognition of fundamental values and human rights. Rule of law considerations lead us to a similar result. Purposive interpretation thus balances legislative supremacy with "proper law" that takes human rights and the system's fundamental values into account. No harm is thereby done to rule of law. Indeed, the balance fully realizes it. Thus, our need to understand the statutory purpose not just in its subjective sense (legislative intent) but also in its objective sense (intent of the reasonable author and of the system) is consistent with the principle of rule of law. We do no harm to the rule of law by preventing subjective purpose from applying fully in every case in which there is highly credible information about it. Purposive interpretation actualizes the rule of law by taking both subjective and objective purpose into account in statutory interpretation.

The Role of the Judge in the Separation of Powers and in Purposive Interpretation

A central constitutional principle in any democratic regime is the principle of separation of powers. According to this principle, the primary function

---

[123] Dworkin, *supra* p. 236, note 78 at 9, 11.

[124] *Id.* at 9, 11. *See also* Fallon, *supra* p. 242, note 111 at 21, discussing the "substantive ideal type."

of the judiciary is to adjudicate disputes. In order to do so, it must give meaning to the legal text at the center of the dispute. Interpretation is therefore a judicial activity. It binds the other branches of government and individuals within the legal system. This constitutional status of the judge in interpretation leads to the following conclusion: The author of the text cannot determine its meaning. Determining the meaning of the text is the task of the judge within the triad of powers. Of course, the author of the text can create rules for its interpretation. The legislature, for example, may set rules for interpreting statutes, contracts, and wills. Contractual parties or a testator may set rules for themselves for interpreting the texts they write. The individual act of interpretation, however, must leave the judge with the independence to determine the meaning of the text according to accepted rules of interpretation. Of course, the author of the text may change the text if he or she is unhappy with the interpretation that the judge gave it. But this change, even if it consists of a declaration, is the creation of a new text, not an interpretation of the old one. Even when a judge interprets a text according to the intent of its author, that intent belongs to the purpose that the text must achieve (including abstract intent), not the interpretation that its author gives it (in other words, not according to concrete or interpretive intent).[125] Hence my claim that the interpretation that the executive branch gives to a statutory provision does not determine a judge's interpretation of the provision.[126] The role of the judge is not to evaluate whether the executive branch's interpretation is reasonable. The judge must evaluate whether it is the proper interpretation. It is the judiciary that has constitutional responsibility for the content of the interpretation. It cannot delegate that responsibility.[127]

There is no such thing as authentic statutory interpretation. The legislature legislates, and the judge judges. Subsequent legislation does not interpret prior legislation, although it may affect the way a judge interprets the earlier legislation. A prior statute may influence the interpretation of a subsequent statute; a subsequent statute may influence the interpretation of a prior statute. A statute does not stand alone. It is part of an ongoing process of legislation. That does not, however, lead us to authentic inter-

[125] *Supra* p. 126.
[126] *Supra* p. 51.
[127] H.C. 3648/97, *Stamaka v. Minister of Interior*, 53(2) P.D. 728, 743: "Authority to interpret a statute is given to the court. With that authority granted to the court comes the responsibility to interpret the statute. This is the principle of separation of powers. We don't call it dispersal of powers among the different branches. And here is the division among them: the legislator legislates; the executive executes; and the judge judges, interprets, and establishes the areas to which the law extends. Thus, as soon as the legislator passes a law, the authority to interpret it is the authority of the court, and the court's authority alone" (Cheshin, J.).

pretation. The legislature's interpretive assumption at the time it enacts a new statute does not bind the judge.

What does this teach us about the proper system of interpretation? Does it answer the questions of whether legislation should be interpreted according to its purpose, and what the relationship is between subjective and objective purpose? These questions—arising in the context of a discussion of the role of legislation in the separation of powers—recur in the context of a discussion of the role of the judge in the separation of powers. Two models compete to answer the questions. The first is the agency model, and the second is the partnership model. I will discuss each and then evaluate what each has to teach about the role of the judge as an interpreter.

THE AGENCY MODEL AND ITS INFLUENCE ON INTERPRETATION

According to the agency model's view of the separation of powers, the judge acts as the agent of the legislature.[128] He or she must follow the legislature's instructions.[129] The legislature sets policy that the judge must implement. Posner analogized the position of the judge to the position of a subordinate officer who must execute his or her superior's orders.[130] This model supports a subjective system of interpretation—based on legislative supremacy—that seeks to interpret the text of the statute according to the intent of its author. When that intent is unknown, the model supports an objective approach, in which the judge asks himself or herself what interpretation the author of the statute would have wanted, had he or she thought about the issue. This is the system of "imaginative reconstruction."

I do not think the above model appropriately reflects the role of the judge as interpreter. The model is inappropriate for three reasons: *First*, a judge is certainly not the agent of the legislature.[131] Both judge and legislature are organs of the state. There is no agency relationship between judge and legislature or between judge and state. Organ theory—not

---

[128] Easterbrook, "Supreme Court," *supra* p. 241, note 106 at 60; Manning, *supra* p. 69, note 29; R. Posner, *The Federal Courts: Crisis and Reform* 286 (1985); E. Maltz, "Statutory Interpretation and Legislative Power: The Case for a Modified Intentionalist Approach," 63 *Tul. L. Rev.* 1 (1988); J. Manning, "Deriving Rules of Statutory Interpretation from the Constitution," 101 *Colum. L. Rev.* 1648 (2001). For an historical critique of the agency model in U.S. law, see W. Eskridge, "All about Words: Early Understanding of the 'Judicial Power' in Statutory Interpretation," 101 *Colum. L. Rev.* 1 990 (2001).

[129] On the agency model in informal relations, see K. Greenawalt, "From the Bottom Up," 82 *Cornell L. Rev.* 994 (1997).

[130] Posner, *supra* p. 27, note 85 at 269.

[131] Farber, *supra* p. 25, note 73 at 284; R.J. Pierce, "The Role of the Judiciary in Implementing an Agency Theory of Government," 64 *N.Y.U. L. Rev.* 1239 (1989).

agency theory—best explains these relationships. *Second*, legislation is not to be understood as the command of a sovereign. Our understanding of law and jurisprudence has developed beyond Austin's scholarship[132] advocating the command model. Legal norms are complicated and elude the simple image of command.[133] *Third*, the agency model expresses one aspect of democracy, namely legislative supremacy. It does not express other crucial aspects of democracy, like fundamental values in general, and human rights in particular.[134] The agency model reflects a formal view of democracy and rule of law. It does not express the richness of substantive democracy and substantive rule of law. It therefore cannot reflect the full complexity and scope of the judicial role in statutory interpretation. Such role is not limited to fulfilling the commands of the legislature. It is much broader, concerned with understanding the statute as part of the legal system by integrating it into the law and understanding the judicial role in statutory interpretation as part of the judge's role in creating law and protecting democracy. The partnership model expresses these principles more appropriately.

THE PARTNERSHIP MODEL AND PURPOSIVE INTERPRETATION

If the judge is not an agent who must obey the orders of his or her principal (the legislature), what does the principle of separation of powers teach us about the role of the judge in interpreting legislation? I favor viewing the judge as a partner[135] in the legislative project.[136] Dworkin said as much in noting that a judge:

> will treat Congress as an author earlier than himself in the chain of law, though an author with special powers and responsibilities different from his own, and he will see his own role as fundamentally the creative one of a partner continuing to develop, in what he believes is the best way, the statutory scheme Congress began.[137]

[132] J. Austin, *The Province of Jurisprudence Determined and the Use of the Study of Jurisprudence* 1 (H.L.A. Hart ed., 1954).

[133] J. Raz, *The Concept of a Legal System: An Introduction to the Theory of Legal System* (1970).

[134] C. Sunstein, *supra* p. 13, note 31 at 423, 438.

[135] The agency model does not authorize consultations between judge and legislature. The metaphor of "partnership" should not lead to any kind of contact. In the context of a dispute awaiting adjudication, the partnership model does not infringe on the independence of the judiciary and its status as the authorized interpreter of the statute.

[136] Eskridge, *supra* p. 238, note 91 at 330. *See also* M. Dorf, "Foreword: The Limits of Social Deliberation," 112 *Harv. L. Rev.* 4, 19 (1998).

[137] Dworkin, *supra* p. 13, note 33 at 313. *See also* R. Dworkin, *Freedom's Law: The Moral Reading of the American Constitution* 1–38 (1996).

While I do not accept every detail of his approach, Dworkin accurately describes the judge's role in statutory interpretation, reflecting a more comprehensive view of the role of the judge in creating law. In my view, both legislature and judge must bridge the gap between law and society, and protect democracy. To do so, they create law. For the legislature, it is a primary task. The legislature directly creates law. The judge's primary task is to adjudicate disputes. Creating law ("judicial lawmaking") and protecting democracy are incidental side effects of adjudicating a dispute.[138] Judicial lawmaking stems from the act of judging, and it has no existence independent of that act. The judge and legislature are partners in creating law. The partnership changes according to the kind of the judicial lawmaking. Within the common law project, the judge is the senior partner.[139] The legislature's role is secondary, mostly expressed in making corrections, via legislation, to the common law project. In statutory interpretation, the legislature is the senior partner, and the judge is the junior partner.[140] Payne made a similar point:

> The proper office of a judge in statutory interpretation is not, I suggest, the lowly mechanical one implied by orthodox doctrine, but that of a junior partner in the legislative process, a partner empowered and expected within certain limits to exercise a proper discretion as to what the detailed law should be.[141]

In both cases, the judge fulfills his or her role in a democracy—a role that obligates him or her to bridge the gap between law and society and to preserve and realize democracy.

There is a lot of similarity between these two tasks—interpretation and creating common law.[142] In both tasks, the judge creates law using limited judicial discretion. No credible legal theory clings to the claim that judicial activity is merely declarative.[143] Montesquieu's view that the judge is the "mouth" of the legislator is no longer accepted. Similarly discredited is Blackstone's view that common law is about uncovering and declaring laws hidden in the recesses of the system.[144] In creating law, in both senses, a

---

[138] Barak, *supra* p. 54, note 189 at 242. *See also* Hart and Sachs, *supra* p. 3, note 3 at 342.

[139] *See* D.N. MacCormick and R.S. Summers (eds.), *Interpreting Precedents: A Comparative Study* (1997).

[140] See Popkin, *supra* p. 85, note 1 at 155, who sees judges as "collaborators in the interpretive process, albeit as junior partners."

[141] D. Payne, "The Intention of the Legislature in the Interpretation of Statutes," 9 *Current Legal Probs.* 96, 105 (1956). Continental law takes a similar approach. *See* S. Herman and D. Hoskins, "Perspectives on Code Structure: Historical Experience, Modern Formats and Policy Considerations," 54 *Tul. L. Rev.* 987 (1980).

[142] *See* Strauss, *supra* p. 161, note 44.

[143] Barak, *supra* p. 54, note 189 at 166.

[144] Lord Reid, "The Judge as Law Maker," *J. Soc'y Pub. Teachs. L.* 22 (1972). *See also* M. Cohen, "The Process of Judicial Legislation," *Law and the Soc. Ord.* 12 (1933).

judge must mediate between law and society. In engaging in this "judicial lawmaking"—in both common law and interpretation—a judge must preserve democracy, maintaining and developing human rights, and actualizing the rule of law. Of course, the judicial act of creating law differs substantially between common law and statutory interpretation. In interpretation, a judge does not create the normative text but rather gives it meaning. The legislature creates the message; the judge adds the final touches. The judge is therefore the junior partner. But the judge is not an agent following orders. He or she does not simply carry the statutory provisions into practice; the judge must ensure—just as when developing common law—that he or she gives the legislation a meaning that accords with the fundamental views of society and of law. The judge must guarantee that there is no conflict between the provisions of the statute being interpreted and its immediate and distant environment, and that there is normative harmony within the system.

Of course, the relative freedom given to judges in statutory interpretation is far more limited than the freedom they enjoy in developing common law.[145] Judges cannot give the text of a statute a meaning that its language cannot bear. This restriction does not exist in developing common law. In addition, judges must give the text a meaning that realizes the (abstract) intent of the legislature. A similar restriction—as in realizing the (abstract) intent of the judges who adjudicated in the past—does not exist in the common law. Even within this limited creative activity—in which the judge acts as the legislature's junior partner "interstitially"[146]—the judge must maintain loyalty to the system as a whole. Judges must, to the extent possible, make sure that the meaning they give the language of the statute integrates into the system's general structure and basic values and viewpoints. Judges therefore give expression, in statutory interpretation, to the objective purpose of the statute. The partnership model recognizes both legislative intent and the intent of the system as appropriate interpretive criteria; the junior partner must take both into consideration in interpreting a statute.

This holds true for texts in both public and private law. The judge is the "junior partner" of the testator and of the contractual parties. Making the will and forming the contract are private matters. Interpreting the text created is a public matter for the judge. It is his or her part in the "project of the will" and the "project of the contract." Judges do not create the will or contract, but they interpret what private actors create. This is their role in the "separation of powers" between the judiciary and private individu-

---

[145] Barak, *supra* p. 54, note 189 at 308.
[146] Holmes's phrase in *Southern Pacific Co. v. Jensen*, 244 U.S. 205, 221 (1917). *See* J. Bell, *Policy Arguments in Judicial Decisions* 9 (1983).

als. The individual is the legislator. The will is the law according to which the testator's property will be distributed after his or her death. The contract is the law that the parties created to regulate their relationship.[147] They are the authors of the text. They set the policy. The judge interprets their text. The agency model, however, misstates the junior nature of the judge's role. The judge is not the agent of the testator or the parties to a contract. The judicial role is far more complicated. As is the case for public law texts, in interpreting private law texts, judges must ensure that the text takes on a meaning that accords with the fundamental views of law and society and protects democracy. The testator made a will so that the legal system would enforce it. The parties to a contract formed the contract to obtain the assistance of the legal system in enforcing it. Judges are the long arm of the law. In interpreting wills and contracts, they should give expression to the relationship between the individual text and the system as a whole. In other words, they should give expression to the objective purpose of wills and contracts.

The Role of the Judge and Public Confidence in the Judiciary

Public confidence in the judiciary is an important constitutional consideration for any system of interpretation.[148] Such confidence is crucial to any democracy. De Tocqueville is credited with saying that without public confidence, judges are impotent.[149] De Balzac correctly noted that the lack of public confidence in the judiciary is the beginning of the end of society.[150] Without public confidence, there can be no independent, objective judiciary. Justice Frankfurter made this point with the following comment: "The Courts' authority—possessed of neither the purse nor the sword—ultimately rests on sustained public confidence in its moral sanction."[151] I also noted the importance of public confidence in a case before me:

> Public confidence is a necessary condition for the existence of an independent judiciary. It is public confidence that the judiciary is doing justice according to law. It is public confidence that judging is done fairly and neutrally, treat-

---

[147] Article 1134 of the French Code Civile establishes that "Les conventions lègalement formées tiennent lieu de loi à ceux qui les ont faites."

[148] Barak, *supra* p. 54, note 189 at 291; H. Cohen, *Hirhurei Kfira B'Imun Hatzibor [Musings of Denial in Public Confidence], Mivchar Katavim: Katzir Haesor Haacharon [Selected Articles of the Last Decade]* 367 (2001). *See also* A.S. Miller, "Public Confidence in the Judiciary: Some Notes and Reflections," 35 *Law and Contemp. Probs.* 69 (1970).

[149] P. Kurland, "Toward a Political Supreme Court," 37 *U. Chi. L. Rev.* 19, 21 (1969).

[150] De Balzac, qtd. in O. Kirchheimer, *Political Justice* 175 (1961).

[151] *Baker v. Carr,* 369 U.S. 186, 267 (1961).

ing parties equally and without the hint of personal interest in the result. It is
public confidence that the judiciary operates with a high level of morality.
Without public confidence, the judiciary cannot act . . . public confidence in
the judiciary is the most valuable asset the judiciary has. It is also one of the
most valuable assets the nation has.[152]

The need to ensure confidence does not mean the need to ensure popu-
larity. The need for public confidence is the need to create a feeling among
the public that judges act objectively, applying the laws neutrally, according to the system's fundamental values; that judicial activity advances the
national credo and not judges' own personal credos; that judges are not
party to the state's power struggles, and that they do not fight for their
own power but rather to keep democracy intact. Public confidence does
not require public agreement with judicial decisions, but rather public confidence in the integrity of those decisions. When judges do law, not just the
parties, not just the law, but judges themselves stand on trial.[153] In their
judicial opinions, judges account for their own actions. As I said in one
case, "When we [judges] sit at trial, we also stand on trial."[154]

Public Confidence in the Judiciary and Purposive Interpretation

A system of interpretation that allows judges to realize their own intent
would undermine public confidence in the judiciary. A public that believes
judges follow their own personal credos will lose confidence in the judiciary.[155] Public confidence in the judiciary will increase, however, if judges
achieve the purpose at the core of a statute. That purpose is not subjective
to judges. It is not a judicial creation. It is not "like nitrogen out of the
air."[156] It is a legal construction done according to interpretive rules and
principles that bind judges. The subjective and objective understandings of
purpose are also binding legal constructions. When judges bridge the gap
between law and society and protect democracy, they increase public confidence in the judiciary. Further, public recognition that interpretive activity is not mechanical, and that it can answer contemporary problems, will
increase public confidence in the courts.

Law, then, avoids the danger of obsolescence, and the gap between it

---

[152] H.C. 732/84, *Tzavan v. Minister of Religious Affairs*, 40(4) P.D. 141, 148.

[153] H. Stone, "The Common Law in the United States," 50 *Harv. L. Rev.* 4, 10 (1936).

[154] H.C. 5100/94 *Public Committee against Torture in Israel v. Government of Israel*, 53(4) P.D. 817, 845.

[155] A. Cox, "Judge Learned Hand and the Interpretation of Statutes," 60 *Harv. L. Rev.* 370, 373 (1947).

[156] Frankfurter, *supra* p. 19, note 50 at 539.

and society narrows. A system of interpretation that freezes legal development, allows the past to dominate the present, and undermines the delicate balance at the foundation of democracy, will undermine public confidence in both judging and law. This is true of interpreting texts in both public and private law. It is important that the public feel that the judge's interpretation of a will or contract is done according to law, not according to his or her subjective views on what is appropriate and desirable. The testator made a will, believing that his or her property would be divided according to his or her intent. The public will have confidence in judging if the judge interprets the will according to the intent of the testator. The same is true of contractual parties, who expect an interpretation according to their joint intent. In the absence of information about authorial intent, judges interpret texts according to the intent of the reasonable author and of the system. In the latter case, judges will strengthen public confidence in judging if they achieve justice, fairness, and integrity.

Constitutional and Systemic Structure and Purposive Interpretation

A legal norm does not stand alone—it integrates into the existing legal framework, becoming part of the systemic and constitutional structure. It is important for interpretation to make sure that the norm extracted from the text integrates into the constitutional and systemic structure as best as possible. Interpretation should aspire to normative harmony within the system, so that the system's parts work in harmony and prevent internal conflict between different norms. In that way, the system can achieve its constitutional objectives. This aspiration applies to the interpretation of all legal texts. It is less pronounced in the interpretation of private law texts, but it is present nonetheless. A will and a contract—like a statute and a constitution—are legal norms. They must be woven into the general constitutional and systemic fabric. They draw life from the statutes that regulate their activity. Their objective purpose helps them integrate into these statutes and into the general law. Purposive interpretation's consideration of the intention of the system allows private law texts to integrate into the general systemic framework.

The need for such integration—and thus the need to consider the constitutional and systemic structure—is particularly acute in the interpretation of a statute or constitution. A piece of legislation is not the one-time act of a temporary legislature. It is one brick in the structure being built by a permanent legislature. A statute is woven into the legislative fabric. Legislation as a whole is woven into the systemic fabric. Understanding a statute or constitution must take place against the background of legislation, law, and the legal system as a whole. Interpreting a statute or constitution requires consideration of the character and structure of the system and the structure of the regime. Interpreters cannot limit themselves to just the text being interpreted. They must look at the system as a whole. Their "horizon" is not just the statute or constitutional provision being interpreted, but the system as a whole—its understandings, perspectives, and constitutional foundations. Hence the view that a judge interpreting a single provision in a statute interprets legislation as a whole, and a judge interpreting a single constitutional provision interprets the constitution as a whole. The norms in the system and the system itself are integrated tools. As Fuller noted,

> Those responsible for creating and administrating a body of legal rules will always be confronted by a *problem of system*. The rules applied to the decision of individual controversies cannot simply be isolated exercises of judicial wisdom. They must be brought into, and maintained in, some systematic interrelationship; they must display some coherent internal structure.[157]

I noted that a statute is a creature of its environment. The environment of a statute or constitution includes the structure of the entire system and regime and the totality of its basic constitutional assumptions.[158] True, a legislature may seek to change direction and disentangle from the fabric of the system. This desire, of course, raises questions about the constitutionality of the resulting statute, but it also raises questions of meaning. A legislature that tries to make such a change—even if it is constitutional—must say so clearly and unequivocally. An interpreter need not take for granted that such change is the purpose of the statute. The natural assumption, expressed in the presumptions about the objective purpose of every statute, is that the legal system grows organically and develops gradually. We assume evolutionary, not revolutionary, development.[159] Legal development is continuous, preserving the thread running through the past, present, and future. In interpreting every statute or constitution, judges should view themselves as continuing the tradition of an existing system. That is Dworkin's apt image of each judge writing a chapter in the infinite book of law, a chapter that must integrate into the story as a whole.[160]

---

[157] L. Fuller, *Anatomy of the Law* 94 (1968).

[158] F. Frankfurter, "Foreword to a Symposium on Statutory Construction," 3 *Vand. L. Rev.* 365, 367 (1950).

[159] Barak, *supra* p. 54, note 189 at 227. *See also* R. Traynor, "The Limits of Judicial Creativity," 29 *Hastings L.J.* 1025, 1031 (1978).

[160] R. Dworkin, "Law as Interpretation," 60 *Tex. L. Rev.* 527 (1982).

Fundamental Constitutional Values and Purposive Interpretation

The interpreter of any legal text must integrate it into the constitutional structure of the democracy and the system's fundamental values. These values reflect the constitution's democratic character, the basic values and aspirations of the legal system, and its constitutional law. They constitute its credo and the environment of every legal norm. They are the normative umbrella spread over every piece of legislation. Sometimes, these values are part of the intent of the author of the text (subjective purpose). They are always part of the intent of the reasonable author and of the system (objective purpose). They reflect the pre-understanding with which the interpreter approaches his or her work. They express the background assumptions at the base of the legal system.[161] This approach plays a central role in interpreting constitutions and statutes, but it applies to the interpretation of every legal text. We assume, based on the various presumptions of purpose, that a statute actualizes constitutional values. A specific legislature that wants to deviate from this fundamental system must express that desire explicitly and unequivocally, in the language of the statute. An interpreter should not assume that a particular text seeks to deviate from fundamental constitutional principles. To the contrary, the interpretive assumption—and it is the objective purpose of every text, expressed in the presumptions of objective purpose—is that the text of a statute is designed to realize democracy and the fundamental principles of the system, not to deviate from them.

A statute should thus be interpreted against the background of institutional principles, justice, and human rights. When fundamental constitutional principles clash, as they inevitably do sometimes, a judge resolves the conflict through a balance that constitutes the normative environment for interpretation. Purposive interpretation fulfils this task by its view of the system's fundamental values as a central component.

Fundamental Constitutional Values and the Purposive Interpretation of Private Law Texts

Fundamental constitutional values do not just apply to the interpretation of public law texts. They are generally applicable, including to the interpretation of wills and contracts. Wills and contracts are not created on a

---

[161] W. Eskridge, "Public Values in Statutory Interpretation," 137 *U. Pa. L. Rev.* 1007 (1989); C. Sunstein, "Interpreting Statutes in the Regulatory State," 103 *Harv. L. Rev.* 405 (1989).

desert island. They assume the existence of a society. They are part of a complicated system of relationships which influences them and which they influence. They assume the existence of a legal system of which they are an integral part. Wills and contracts do not just express the autonomy of the private will. They are legal norms that activate the power of the state through the court system. They activate the court system in dividing property upon the death of the testator or in providing remedies for breach of contract. Professor Cohen outlined the process in the 1930s, in a well-known article.[162] Professor Zamir described Cohen's approach:

> The role of contract law is not to let the parties do as they wish, but to put the legal enforcement mechanism of the state—judges, court officers, and the police—at the service of one party against the other. This enforcement power need not be exercised in each and every case. It suffices that there are some cases in which it is exercised for its potential threat to be taken into account by the parties. Put differently, contract law puts the sovereign power of the state at the disposal of one party, thereby giving that party limited sovereignty over the other party.[163]

Zamir's description emphasizes the social nature of the contract, exposing the need to weave it into the fabric of the legal system's values. The testator and contractual parties are not satisfied with just the text they have created. They seek to involve the state in the text's chronicles and development. They seek to involve the courts in the execution of the will and the enforcement of the agreement or the award of damages for its breach. Hence the need to connect these texts to the values and principles of the system.

The interpretation of a will or contract must take into consideration the legal system in which it was created. Contracts and wills are creatures of their environment. This environment includes not just the circumstances of the text's creation, but also the "normative circumstances." The normative circumstances are "wider circles of accepted values, fundamental objectives, and basic standards."[164] They are circles of statutes, beginning with the statutes "close" to the will (statute of succession) and the type of contract (like leasing statutes for a lease) and including the system's fundamental values. Those values permeate every will and contract. That is why we must interpret a will or contract according to principles of reason-

---

[162] M. Cohen, "The Basis of Contract," 46 *Harv. L. Rev.* 553 (1933).

[163] E. Zamir, "The Inverted Hierarchy of Contract Interpretation and Supplementation," 97 *Colum. L. Rev.* 1710, 1777 (1997).

[164] C.A. 165/82 *Kibbutz Chatzor v. Tax Assessor of Rehovot*, 39(2) P.D. 70, 75. This case refers to statutory interpretation, but its principles extend to the interpretation of private law texts.

ableness, fairness, justice, and equality. In interpreting these texts, we must aspire to integrate them into the general law of the democratic legal system, to achieve normative harmony. We must give them a meaning consistent with the public interest. Subjective purpose and the presumptions derived from it are inadequate to the task; we must also resort to objective purpose and its presumptions, which apply so long as the intent of the author does not contradict them. Purposive interpretation achieves this goal.

Autonomy of the Private Will and Purposive Interpretation

The individual's right to free will is both a central human right and one of the most important fundamental values. An individual's right to "breathing space" to express himself or herself, without being hindered by the state or by other individuals, is at the core of human rights. All democratic legal systems make the autonomy of the private will a central constitutional value. It derives from human dignity and property rights. It finds expression in the interpretation of all legal texts. Its position in the interpretation of public law texts (constitutions and statutes) is, however, somewhat compromised. We do not justify the need to consider the intent of the constitutional framers or of the legislature with the need to realize the autonomy of their will but rather with arguments about the structure of government and fundamental values.

In wills and contracts, however, the autonomy of the private will plays a central role. A will is the ultimate expression of that autonomy. Within the bounds outlined by law, the individual is his or her own master, the "legislator." Individuals—and not the state—determine what to do with their own property after their death. The state's job is to ensure that the testator's intent is within the bounds of the law, and that it is expressed as required. Beyond that, the state leaves individuals to order the division of their property as they choose. These characteristics of wills teach us that actualizing the intent of the testator (subjective intent) is the central aim in interpreting a will. No other parties have legally protected interests. There is no reliance interest. Hence the centrality of the testator's intent in interpreting a will.

Nevertheless, it is not the only factor to be considered. If it were, how would we interpret a will when the testator's intent is unknown or does not help us understand the will? Like every legal text, a will is a creature of its environment. The constitutional and systemic structure and the fundamental values apply in its interpretation, too. I therefore claim that the goal of interpreting a will is not to realize the intent of the testator. The goal is to achieve the purpose at the core of the will. The primary—but not exclusive—determinant of this purpose is the testator's intent. The will's objective purpose, however, plays a secondary but nonetheless important role. Purposive interpretation takes these factors into account.

The same is true of contractual interpretation. The individual's freedom to enter into a contract and to determine the content of the contract derive from the autonomy of the private will. Some legal systems consider these two freedoms—two aspects of freedom of contract—to be constitutional rights. They derive from human dignity and property rights. Realizing freedom of contract is central to contractual interpretation. The goal of contractual interpretation is therefore to actualize the joint intent of the parties. It is pointless to view realizing the real intent of the parties as the basis for a contract, only to ignore it in giving meaning to the agreement they create. As in a will, however, the joint intent of the parties is not the be-all and end-all. Such intent cannot always be identified; it is not always relevant to resolving the judge's interpretive problem. Sometimes, a third party's reliance interest must be considered. Above all, however, a contract, too, is a creature of its environment. The constitutional considerations I mentioned apply to contractual interpretation, too. These considerations find expression in the application of objective purpose to the interpretation of every will—and hence the importance of purposive interpretation in law.

CHAPTER ELEVEN

Purposive Interpretation and Its Critique of Other Systems of Interpretation

1. PURPOSIVE INTERPRETATION AND SUBJECTIVE SYSTEMS OF INTERPRETATION

Subjective Systems of Interpretation (Intentionalism)

Subjective systems of interpretation tell an interpreter to give a text the meaning that actualizes the intent of its author. These systems accord well with similar theories from the field of literature. According to Hirsh's theory, for example, there is only one valid interpretation, the one that uncovers the meaning that the author of the work sought to give it. Such meaning is fixed and static.[1] Intentionalist systems in law take a similar approach.[2] They differ over the level of abstraction at which they consider the historic intent of the text's author. They also disagree over the sources from which authorial intent should be learned, and the preconditions that must exist before resorting to those sources. The rhetoric of both common law and civil law systems often refers to intentionalism, debating the admissibility of the original intent of the founding fathers, the intent of the legislature, the intent of the contractual parties, and the intent of the testator as criteria for interpreting constitutions, statutes, contracts, and wills. Subjective systems of interpretation would seem to prevail over objective systems, at least, in the rhetoric.

Critics of these systems contend that there is no intent, or that it cannot be identified, and that the search for it is a fiction.[3] I reject this criticism. Certainly, there are instances in which we can identify a person's intent. Courts do it all the time in most branches of law (like criminal law, for example, which imposes sanctions based on the perpetrator's *mens rea*).

---

[1] E.D. Hirsh, *Validity in Interpretation* (1967); E.D. Hirsh, *The Aims of Interpretation* (1978).

[2] Intentionalism is distinct from originalism. According to the former, a text should be interpreted according to the subjective intention of its author. According to the latter, a text should be interpreted according to the (objective) understanding that readers had of it at the time it was written. This is a substantial difference that is not always noted. Scalia, for example, is an originalist, not an intentionalist.

[3] *Supra* p. 130.

There is no particular problem in identifying the intent of a testator, the joint intent of parties to a contract, or the intent of a government official who enacts a regulatory order. In the context of interpreting contracts and wills, courts have been identifying this intent for centuries. The criticism is reduced to the problem in identifying the intention of a collective body (like a constitutional assembly or legislature).[4] The problem is legitimate but not fatal. It is not true that we can never pinpoint the intent—or, more precisely, the joint intent, based on compromise—of a collective body. True, it is sometimes difficult and even impossible to identify intent, but that does not mean that subjective systems of interpretation never apply.

Hermeneutics, primarily literary hermeneutics, provides another source of criticism of subjective interpretation. Some hermeneutic scholars claim that authorial intent is not an interpretive criterion. They talk of the "failure of intent." I reject this critique, too.[5] For every hermeneutic scholar who opposes considering intent, there is a hermeneutic scholar who says interpretation consists precisely of understanding a text according to authorial intent. Hermeneutic analyses of literary or musical interpretation should not determine what kind of system of interpretation is proper in law. Hermeneutic studies do play a role in formulating a system of legal interpretation, but they cannot determine what system is appropriate. The answer to that question lies in the field of law itself—specifically, in the appropriate constitutional considerations.[6] We begin with the theories of Raz and Marmor, and the critique of them. We will then turn to flaws in subjective systems of interpretation and the reasons to prefer purposive interpretation.

The Intentionalist Theory of Raz and Marmor, and the Idea of Authority

Raz argues that a statutory legal text should be given the meaning that realizes the intent of its creator.[7] The basis of the theory is inherent to the

---

[4] *Supra* p. 132.

[5] For the relationship between legal interpretation and literary interpretation, see S. Almog, *Law and Literature* (2000); R. Posner, *Law and Literature: A Misunderstood Relation* (1988). For the relationship between legal interpretation and musical interpretation, see J. Frank, "Words and Music: Some Remarks on Statutory Interpretation," 47 *Colum L. Rev.* 1259 (1947); S. Levinson and J. Balkin, "Law, Music and Other Performing Arts," 139 *U. Pa. L. Rev.* 1597 (1991); J. Balkin and S. Levinson, "Interpreting Law and Music: Performance Notes on 'The Banjo Serenader' and 'The Lying Crowd of Jews,'" 20 *Cardozo L. Rev.* 1513 (1999).

[6] *Supra* p. 234.

[7] Raz, *supra* p. 239, note 94. Raz's theory has been developed primarily through statu-

idea of authority. An interpreter should consider the intent of the text's author because people are subject to that author's authority. The justification
for taking the intent of the author into account derives from the justification for the author's authority over others. Raz writes:

> To give a person or an institution law-making powers is to entrust them with
> the power to make law by acts intended to make law, or at least undertaken
> in the knowledge that they make law. It makes no sense to give any person or
> body law-making power unless it is assumed that the law they make is the law
> they intended to make.[8]

Raz calls this the authoritative intention thesis. According to him, a collective body (like a legislature) has intentions, and the constitution determines whose intentions should be taken into account. From Raz's perspective, the importance of intention finds expression in the fact that an act
can be considered legislative only if it was intended to be so. Legislation,
furthermore, requires not just the intent to legislate but also awareness of
the content of the legislation. It is both necessary and sufficient for a legislature to intend for the content of a bill to become law. Raz writes:

> A person is legislating (voting for a Bill, etc.) by expressing an intention that
> the text of a Bill on which he is voting will—when understood as such texts,
> when promulgated in the circumstances in which this one is promulgated, are
> understood in the legal culture of this country—be law.[9]

Raz is aware that the requirement is minimal. It does not require a legislature to understand the content of the statute; it only requires awareness of
the act of legislation and the ability to know, after consulting the conventions of the legal culture, the meaning of the legislation. Of course, a legal
system can add to these requirements, mandating further intentions. For
example, a statute may be given a meaning that does not accord with the
original intention, once it becomes clear that the statute has not produced
the results expected of it. There is sometimes no choice but to stray from
these minimum requirements, as when the authority is based on the principle of coordination, or when the statute is old. Summarizing this view,
Raz writes:

> While the theory of authority shows that the legitimacy of legislated—that is,
> authority-based—law depends on it being interpreted in accordance with its
> author's intentions, the guide to interpretation which the theory of authority
> indicates is reliance on the conventions for interpreting legislative texts of the

---

tory interpretation. On his approach to constitutional interpretation, *see* Raz, *supra* p. 41,
note 124.

[8] Raz, *supra* p. 239, note 94 at 258.

[9] *Id.* at 267.

kind in question prevailing in the legal culture when the legislation in question was promulgated. Intention legitimates, but conventions interpret.[10]

In my view, Raz's intentionalist approach is too minimalist. Legislative supremacy requires us to consider legislative intent. This requirement is not satisfied by considering merely the intention to pass a statute. It also requires us to try to achieve the policies and objectives at the core of the statute. Raz's approach does not provide a strong enough basis for considering intent in statutory interpretation.

Marmor, who bases his own work on Raz's concept of authority,[11] provides a stronger foundation—if within narrower bounds—for the importance of authorial intent in interpreting a work. Marmor continues along Raz's line of thought,[12] which is limited to statutory interpretation.[13] He outlines two ways of understanding the legitimacy of authority. The *first* is inherent to the concept of expertise. We assume that those who wield authority are experts in the fields in which they make decisions. The *second* is inherent to the concept of coordination. We assume that wielders of authority take positions that allow them to solve problems of coordination. Marmor justifies using authorial intent for the first reason:

> Suppose one acknowledges the authority of one's doctor, considering him the best available expert on the relevant medical problems. Now, suppose further that the doctor's medical prescription is ambiguous, as there happen to be two different medicines which fit it. Under normal circumstances, attempting to clarify the doctor's intention would be the most sensible thing to do.[14]

Marmor, however, does not recognize the authority inherent to the concept of coordination. He sees no reason to consult the intent of the wielder of authority because "the person in authority was not presumed to have a better access [*sic*] than the subjects themselves to the reasons on which they should act."[15] Marmor adds that even where the authority figure is an expert, his or her intentions do not carry absolute weight.[16] In this context, one should consider the level of expertise. Marmor notes that sometimes other factors outweigh the intent of the authority figure as the right standard for making the decision:

---

[10] *Id.* at 280.

[11] J. Raz, *The Morality of Freedom* 1 (1986).

[12] J. Raz, "Facing Up: A Reply," 62 *So. Cal. L. Rev.* 1153 (1989).

[13] A. Marmor, *Interpretation and Legal Theory* (1992).

[14] *Id.* at 178. Consider the following additional example: Richard gives Simon directions on how to get to his house. Where the instructions are open-ended, what Richard intended is obviously the right standard for understanding them. *See* P.M. Tiersma, *Legal Language* 126 (1999).

[15] Marmor, *supra* p. 263, note 13 at 178. Raz agrees. *See* Raz, *supra* p. 239, note 94 at 273.

[16] Marmor, *supra* p. 263, note 13 at 179.

One's reasons for complying with the judgements of one's physician are confined to those considerations which apply to the questions of the most appropriate medical treatment. They should not include reasons which are not based on expertise, like, for instance, the reasons involved in a decision to commit suicide instead of taking the treatment.[17]

Marmor argues that as more time elapses between the decision of the person in authority and the time of interpretation, the justifications for considering the intent of the authority figure, based on his or her expertise, weaken. "The more ancient a law is the more suspicious one has to be of the relevance of the legislators' intentions."[18]

WALDRON'S CRITIQUE AND THE COUNTER-CRITIQUE

Waldron has criticized Raz's early work and Marmor's approach.[19] He emphasizes, *inter alia*, that the model that Raz and Marmor suggest is suitable for an individual who holds power. It is appropriate for a statute created by a single author. However, the model is not at all suitable for modern legislation:

[M]odern statutes are not the products of single expert authors. They are produced by the deliberations of large multi-member assemblies whose claim to authority in Raz's sense (if indeed they can make any such claim at all) consists in their ability to integrate a diversity of purposes, interests, and aims among their members into the text of a single legislative product.[20]

Waldron believes that while each member of the legislative body has an intent, the collective body does not necessarily have a similar intent for the product it has created. All that the collective body produced is the statute itself: "Beyond the meanings embodied conventionally in the text of the statute, there is no state or condition corresponding to 'the intention of the legislature' to which anything else—such as what particular individuals or groups of legislators said, wrote, or did—could possibly provide a clue."[21] Only the language of the statute is canonized—not the shared worldviews of the members of the legislative body or their sense of a common goal.

This critique is well placed, but it does not delegitimate considering legislative intent in at least some cases.[22] I agree that a collective body like a

---

[17] *Id.* at 179.

[18] *Id.* at 182.

[19] J. Waldron, *Legislators' Intentions and Unintentional Legislation* in *Essays in Legal Philosophy* 329 (A. Marmor ed., 1995).

[20] *Id.* at 331.

[21] *Id.* at 353.

[22] J. Goldsworthy, "Legislation, Interpretation, and Judicial Review," 51 *U. Toronto L.J.*

legislature does not possess intent in the way that an individual does. Instead of individual intent, an interpreter should look for the goals, social changes, and aims upon which members of the legislative body agreed. Such agreement exists and can be identified.[23] Farber put it well in noting that "Individual members of Congress may have had inconsistent motives for favoring the adoption of certain statutory language, but the adoption of that language itself generally indicates a purpose to enact a statute specifying a certain domain in policy space."[24] This agreement may not be part of the statute, but it constitutes a criterion for understanding the statute. Again, intent is not the only criterion, and it is not always decisive, but Waldron's critique cannot delegitimate considering joint intent, when it can be identified. In any case, Waldron—perhaps intentionally[25]—fails to propose a proper system of understanding a statute.[26] I think Waldron's critique of considering authorial intent in interpreting a work misses the mark.

PURPOSIVE CRITIQUE OF INTENTIONALISM

I will now suggest a critique of the intentionalist approach from another direction, with three primary components: *First*, I claim that most subjective systems are not really "subjective" at all because they do not investigate the actual will of the author; *second*, I claim that no subjective system of interpretation can serve as the sole criterion for interpreting a statute; *third*, I claim that the perspective that all subjective theories—and their critics—adopt toward the text is too narrow. We should consider a text as part of the totality of the system.

Intentionalism Is Not Really Subjective

"True" subjectivity focuses on the true intent of the author.[27] Only the text itself (according to extreme literal-subjective systems) or the text and the circumstances surrounding its creation (according to other subjective systems) can provide information about this intent. In contrast, "pseudo"-subjectivity or "unreal" subjectivity employs the rhetoric of authorial in-

---

77, 83 (2001) ("Simple common sense tells us what the lawmaker was attempting to achieve, and it would be absurd to interpret the law without taking that into account").

[23] *See* Greenawalt, *supra* p. 126, note 24.

[24] D. Farber, "The Inevitability of Practical Reason: Statutes, Formalism, and the Rule of Law," 45 *Vand. L. Rev.* 533, 551–52 (1992).

[25] J. Waldron, *The Law* 130 (1990).

[26] W. Eskridge, "The Circumstances of Politics and the Application of Statutes," 100 *Colum. L. Rev.* 558, 566 (2000).

[27] Raz, *supra* p. 239, note 94 at 256: "Unless real intentions are involved, talk of hypothetical intentions of fictitious people is rarely of any real significance. It does not advance our understanding in any way."

tent, but in practice looks for how a reasonable reader would understand the intent of the author.

Since the nineteenth century, English law has adopted a "pseudo"-subjective approach to interpreting all legal texts. Courts use the rhetoric of the intent of the text's author, but by this they mean the intent of the reasonable author. Describing the English approach, Steyn said that "It cannot aim to discover what the parties to a contract or the collective body of individuals constituting the legislature subjectively intended."[28]

American law uses both real and pseudo-subjective approaches in interpreting contracts,[29] although the trend favors "real" subjective intent, as expressed by the *Restatement (Second) of Contracts*.[30] The picture is no clearer in the field of statutory interpretation, although there is evidence of a search for the true intent of the legislature, including permission and even a requirement to consult legislative history. There are also opposing arguments that favor looking for the intent that can be reasonably attributed to the legislature. Expressing the latter view, Scalia writes, "The evidence suggests that, despite frequent statements to the contrary, we do not really look for subjective legislative intent. We look for a sort of 'objectified' intent."[31] It is not easy to pin down the American approach. I will examine subjective systems that are only pseudo-subjective in the context of objective systems of interpretation. The rhetoric of these systems is misleading. They are subjective in words but objective in practice.

My theory leaves room for considering the real intent of the author of a text (subjective purpose). This is the actual, "true" intent.[32] It is not pseudo-intent; it is not hypothetical intent; it is not the intent of a reasonable person. The hypothetical intent—the intent of the reasonable author—is another component, in addition to, and not instead of, the subjective component.

Intentionalism Does Not Solve All Interpretive Problems

The *second* flaw of intentionalism is that it does not provide a solution to all the interpretive problems that the judge faces. It does not meet the condition of efficacy.[33] Often, it is impossible to know what the intent of the

[28] Steyn, *supra* p. 18, note 49 at 80. *See also* J. Steyn, "Written Contracts: To What Extent May Evidence Control Language?" 41 *Current Legal Probs.* 23 (1988); Lord Wilberforce's comments in *Reardon-Smith, supra* p. 44, note 142 at 574.

[29] J. Perillo, "The Origins of the Objective Theory of Contract Formation and Interpretation," 69 *Fordham L. Rev.* 427 (2000).

[30] 2 *Restatement (Second) of Contracts* art. 201(1). *See also* E.A. Farnsworth, *Contracts* 245 (1990).

[31] Scalia, *supra* p. 34, note 103 at 17.

[32] Raz, *supra* p. 239, note 94 at 263.

[33] *Supra* p. 218.

author(s) was. Studying the work does not reveal the intent of the author, and the external circumstances do not point to a credible, certain, and clear intent. Sometimes, even when intent can be identified, it is not relevant to resolving the interpretive problem before the judge. Sometimes, the interpreter finds a few intentions, at various levels of abstraction, that are inconsistent with each other. This latter case may be an inadvertent result of sloppy drafting, or it may be deliberate. In each of these cases and in many others, the criterion of "authorial intent" is inadequate to complete the interpretation.

This flaw originates in the nature of natural language, on the one hand, and the limits of human thought, on the other. The author of the text cannot—and usually does not want to—supply a detailed list of situations to which the legal norm extends. He or she chooses a generalization, which will inevitably be ambiguous or vague. To resolve the interpretive problem inherent to language, subjective interpretation refers an interpreter to the intent of the author. However, because of human limitations, such intent cannot extend to all future situations. Even if we project the intent at a high level of abstraction, looking for the generalization to which the author aspired, we cannot always use it to solve the interpretive problem. Sometimes the author did not aspire to an abstract level of generalization, envisioning only the cases that had surfaced at the time he or she created the text. Sometimes, the author envisioned a general purpose, but life is too complex to be captured by a generalization, and the interpretive problem may be beyond the limits of the generalization. In these and other cases, intentionalism falls short, leaving the interpreter without a solution to his or her interpretive problem. In these situations, the interpreter must abandon the true intent of the author and move on—consciously or unconsciously—to hypothetical intent.

Intentionalism Fails to View the Text as Part of the System

The *third* flaw in intentionalism is that it fails to view the text being interpreted as a creature of a changing environment. It is insensitive to the existence of a legal system and democratic regime in whose framework the text operates. It views the text being interpreted as a fossilized creature, standing alone. If a legal system's law began and ended with a single statute, we could justify intentionalism. But a legal system contains a panoply of legal norms that influence each other. Interpreting statute X according to the intent of its author at the time of enactment, while interpreting statute Y according to the intent of another author, at a different time, would create disharmony. It would freeze the meaning of each statute to the four corners of its text, without reflecting the system as a whole. Intentionalism does not and cannot integrate the individual text into the legal system as a whole. It does not allow the meaning of the text to develop as the legal system develops. It fails to view the text as one of the units comprising the legal system. It freezes the meaning of the text to the historical point in time of its creation, sometimes rendering it irrelevant to the meaning of the text in a modern democracy. The legal text ceases to fulfill its aim. The judge becomes historian and archaeologist,[34] ceasing to fulfill his or her own aim in society as a bridge between law and society's changing needs and as a defender of democracy. Instead of looking forward, he or she looks backward. The judge becomes sterile and frozen.[35] Stasis[36] replaces dynamism.[37] Law solves the problems of the past but is helpless before the problems of the future. It ceases to deal with life's needs. It becomes distant from the system's fundamental values and democratic principles. Instead of partnership between author and interpreter, the interpreter becomes subordinate to the historical author—a subordination incompatible with the principles of separation of powers and proper democracy.

Purposive Interpretation's Satisfaction of the Conditions for Proper Interpretation

Purposive interpretation avoids the three flaws discussed above. The components of purposive interpretation—language, purpose, discretion—allow it to give a legal text a meaning in every circumstance. The influence of authorial intent varies by circumstance, but it always plays some role in interpreting the work. The intent of the author must project—with varying levels of force, depending on the type of text—onto the meaning of the text. Interpretive approaches that ignore this intent neglect an important aspect that should be considered.

Authorial intent is not, however, the be-all and end-all. The goal of interpretation must be to achieve the purpose at the core of the text. Authorial intent is just one means among many—whose significance varies according to the type of text—to arrive at the purpose of the text. The possibility of considering other means (which constitute objective purpose)—most prominently, the system's fundamental values and human rights—gives interpretation the depth it requires. It facilitates viewing the text as part of the totality of the system as a whole and helps the text and its interpreter fulfill their roles in a democracy. This multifaceted approach satisfies the social, jurisprudential, hermeneutic, and constitutional requirements discussed above.

---

[34] A. Aleinikoff, *Updating Statutory Interpretation*, 87 *Mich. L. Rev.* 20 (1988).
[35] A. Rieg, "Judicial Interpretation of Written Rules," 40 *La. L. Rev.* 49 (1979).
[36] K. Engisch, *Einführung in das Juristische Denken* 90 (7th ed. 1977).
[37] *See* Eskridge, *supra* p. 41, note 126.

2. PURPOSIVE INTERPRETATION AND OBJECTIVE SYSTEMS OF INTERPRETATION: TEXTUALISM, "OLD" AND "NEW"

Objective Systems of Interpretation

There are multiple objective systems of interpretation, and the variation among them is sometimes greater than that among subjective systems. While authorial intent is the common thread running through subjective systems of interpretation, the understanding of the reasonable reader is what unites objective systems of interpretation. That understanding, however, is a slacker common thread than authorial intent. We will begin by discussing objective systems of interpretation that focus on the text, an approach known as textualism. Later, we will examine objective systems that go beyond the text.

The Historic Development of Textualism

Textualism is the view that the understanding of a reasonable reader determines the meaning of a text. It is not a new idea. Many ancient legal systems employed formal textualism.[38] The textualist interpreter is not concerned with what the author of the text wanted, but rather with what he or she wrote. A text has a meaning "of its own." Its author cannot change this (objective) meaning. The different systems of interpretation moved from formal textualism to subjective textualism. The more "modern" the system, the further interpretation has moved from the "ossified" meaning of the language of the text. As Wigmore wrote, "The history of the law of interpretation is the history of a progress from a stiff and superstitious formalism to a flexible rationalism."[39] In their purest form, subjective systems of interpretation seek to actualize the intent of the text's author, focusing on finding his or her "true" intent.[40] In its next phase, textualism involved the objectification of interpretation.[41] Interpretation continued its subjective rhetoric, claiming to seek the interpretation that actualizes authorial intent, but it looked for that intent in the author's external, objective, ex-

---

[38] R. Zimmerman, *The Law of Obligations: Roman Foundations of the Civilian Tradition* 621 (1990) ("Archaic legal systems are usually dominated by a very literal, word-oriented (i.e. objective) approach").

[39] J.H. Wigmore, 9 *Evidence in Trials at Common Law* 193 (Chadbourn ed., 1981).

[40] W. Blackstone, *Commentaries on the Laws of England* 59 (facsimile of 1st ed. of 1765, 1979).

[41] D.J. Davies, "The Interpretation of Statutes in the Light of Their Policy by the English Courts," 35 *Colum. L. Rev.* 519, 522 (1935).

pression. Hence the view that an interpreter should understand authorial intent as a reasonable reader would.[42] This is what is now referred to as "old" textualism. The new version is a breed that has developed in recent years, but whose seeds were sown in the nineteenth century.[43] New textualism abandons the rhetoric of authorial intent altogether, requiring the interpreter to confer on the text the meaning that a reasonable reader would give it at the time of the enactment. New textualism has made inroads into American law. There are a few kinds of (new and old) textualist systems and they are still used today. I will first discuss old textualism, then the new version.

Old Textualism

Old textualism adopts the interpretive goal of realizing the intent of the text's author, as expressed in the text itself, according to the understanding of the reasonable reader (plain meaning rule; literal rule). That is the only intent that is certain enough, and therefore the only intent to be considered. Where this objective understanding of the text leads to an absurd result, however, one may go beyond the four corners of the text to remove the absurdity.[44] One may also exceed the text if no plain meaning arises from a reasonable reader's reading of it. In that case, in order to resolve the lack of clarity, one may go beyond the four corners of the text to consider authorial intent as a means of clarification (the golden rule).[45] These textualist systems use two stages in the interpretive process: *First*, the interpreter determines if the text is plain and if it leads to a non-absurd result. If the answer is yes, the first stage is also the last stage. If the answer is no—if the meaning of the text is not plain, or it is plain but the result is absurd—the interpreter moves to the second stage. At the *second* stage, the interpreter tries to clarify the vagueness and prevent the absurdity.

I have six criticisms of old textualist systems, which I will discuss below: *First*, they do not take authorial intent seriously. *Second*, they ignore credible information about intent from sources external to the text. *Third*, they are based on a false distinction between a plain and unclear text. *Fourth*, they fail to achieve the rationale at their core—security and certainty in law. *Fifth*, old textualism fosters judicial superficiality and encourages judges to avoid dealing with the policy that the author of the text tried to actualize. *Sixth*, old textualism lacks hermeneutic and social support. It does not draw

---

[42] *See* Perillo, *supra* p. 266, note 29.

[43] Holmes, for example, discussed it. *See* O.W. Holmes, "The Theory of Legal Interpretation," 12 *Harv. L. Rev.* 417 (1899).

[44] *Supra* p. 80.

[45] *See* Cross, *supra* p. 3, note 3.

its legitimacy from constitutional considerations. It does not allow the text to connect to the system as a whole.

OLD TEXTUALISM FAILS TO TAKE AUTHORIAL INTENT SERIOUSLY

Old textualism exists in internal tension. *On the one hand*, it claims that the goal of interpretation is to confer on the text a meaning that actualizes the intent of its author. *On the other hand*, it restricts the sources from which an interpreter may learn about authorial intent to the text itself, allowing the interpreter to go beyond the four corners of the text only in the special cases of an absurdity or an unclear text. As such, it does not take authorial intent seriously.[46] If old textualism really puts the intent of the author at the center of its attention, why not allow an interpreter to learn about authorial intent from any credible source? Of course, an intent that cannot be realized through the language of the text—that does not lie within the range of semantic possibilities—cannot be considered. But why not consider data about authorial intent that exist beyond the text itself, when such intent can be realized through the text?

Consider a will. The testator bequeathed his property to "Mother." The testator has a biological mother. The will is "plain." Upon his death, his mother will inherit his property. But what if the testator had an idiosyncratic habit? What if he called his wife "Mother"? Why not validate his intent? If the goal of interpretation is to realize the intent of the testator, why not learn about this intent from any credible source? If judges are indeed to give expression to the intent of the testator, not their own intent, why should they stop at their initial sense of what the text warrants, without confirming that sense with information arising from the circumstances? The same is true of contractual interpretation. Richard and Simon agreed on a deal involving a horse. That is the word they use to refer to Richard's tractor. A reasonable person unfamiliar with the pair's semantic habits would say that the deal involves an animal (a horse). But the parties have a different joint intent. They want to execute a deal involving the tractor. Why not give the deal a meaning in accord with their joint intent? Similar criticism arises in statutory interpretation. If the goal of interpretation really is—as the old textualists claim—to realize the intent of the legislature, why not, in all cases, resort to credible information about intent that exists beyond the four corners of the text?

[46] H.W. Jones, "The Plain Meaning Rule and Extrinsic Aids in the Interpretation of Federal Statutes," 25 *Wash. U. L.Q.* 2, 6 (1940); C. Nutting, "The Ambiguity of Unambiguous Statutes," 24 *Minn. L. Rev.* 509 (1940); A. Murphy, "Old Maxims Never Die: The 'Plain Meaning Rule' and Statutory Interpretation in the 'Modern' Federal Courts," 75 *Colum. L. Rev.* 1299 (1975); M. Merz, "The Meaninglessness of the Plain Meaning Rule," 4 *Dayton L. Rev.* 31 (1979).

Old textualism offers three answers to this set of questions.[47] *First,* the text itself is the only sure source of information about the intent of the author. No intent gleaned from sources external to the text can be certain enough.[48] *Second,* considering sources external to the text damages the rule of law (in its jurisprudential sense).[49] Publicity requires that an individual be able to plan his or her actions through reading the text itself, without needing to resort to external sources that are generally not available to him or her. *Third,* giving the judge permission to consult external sources will expand the judge's discretion, undermining certainty and security and impairing the judge's role in the separation of powers. I will discuss the last two claims at another point.[50] I now turn to the first claim.

OLD TEXTUALISM AND THE CREDIBILITY OF INFORMATION ABOUT INTENT FROM DATA EXTERNAL TO THE TEXT

The claim that only the text can provide credible information about intent is out of sync with our life experience. Often, the most credible evidence about the intent of an author originates in sources external to the text in question. Letters written by a testator can indicate his or her intent with a high level of reliability. Verbal exchanges between contracting parties can provide credible information about their joint intent. Legislative history may indicate, with a high degree of reliability, the joint (abstract) intent of members of the legislative body.

Of course, I accept that information about the intent of the author gleaned from the text itself is generally—if not always—more credible than information derived from external sources. We should therefore recognize—as purposive interpretation does—a (rebuttable) presumption that the intent of an author is that arising from the language of the work. I further accept that, sometimes, information from external sources is unreliable and even manipulative.[51] We should evaluate external information cautiously. But such caution is a far cry from a hard-and-fast rule rendering the information inadmissible. A judge is trained to distinguish between what is and is not credible. We do so in various branches of law. Why not trust a judge to do so in interpreting a legal text? Old textualism permits a judge to consult external sources only when a clear text leads to an absurdity or when a text is "unclear." If these external sources are credible

[47] *See* Steyn, *supra* p. 99, note 12.
[48] Cross, *supra* p. 3, note 3 at 31.
[49] *Supra* p. 244.
[50] *Infra* pp. 274 and 303.
[51] Cross, *supra* p. 3, note 3 at 158; A. Dickerson, "Statutory Interpretation: Dipping into Legislative History," 11 *Hofstra L. Rev.* 1125 (1983).

enough to consult when the text leads to an absurdity or when it is unclear, why impose a blanket ban on consulting them when the text is "plain" or does not lead to an absurdity? Old textualism provides no satisfying answer to these questions.

OLD TEXTUALISM IS BASED ON A FALSE DISTINCTION BETWEEN A PLAIN AND AN UNCLEAR TEXT

Old textualism distinguishes between a plain text and an unclear text. In the first instance, the interpreter realizes the intent of the author, as expressed in the plain text, by giving the language of the text its natural meaning. In the second instance, the interpreter may go beyond the four corners of the text to find the intent of the author. When the interpreter finds it, he or she gives the language of the text a meaning that realizes this intent. This aspect of old textualism is cousin to the approach that a clear text needs no interpretation.[52] Only when the text is unclear does the interpretive process begin.

Both these perspectives are mistaken.[53] The text becomes clear, for purposes of the interpretive problem before the judge, only at the conclusion of the interpretive process. As long as the author's intent is not realized, the text remains unclear. As Hart and Sachs noted,

> *The meaning of a statute is never plain unless it fits with some intelligible purpose.* Any judicial opinion . . . which finds a plain meaning in a statute without consideration of its purpose, condemns itself on its face. The opinion is linguistically, philosophically, legally and generally ignorant. It is deserving of nothing but contempt.[54]

The clarity that old textualism grasps is initial clarity, the product of a semantic "sense." It must be evaluated and checked against the totality of information about the intent of the author. As Justice Frankfurter noted,

---

[52] *Supra* p. 12.

[53] For literature on this issue, *see* F. Schauer, "Statutory Construction and the Coordinating Function of Plain Meaning," 1990 *S. Ct. Rev.* 231; A. Aleinikoff and T. Shaw, "The Costs Incoherence: A Comment on Plain Meaning, *West Virginia University Hospitals, Inc. v. Casey,* and Due Process of Statutory Interpretation," 45 *Vand. L. Rev.* 687 (1992); F. Schauer, "The Practice and Problems of Plain Meaning: A Response to Aleinikoff and Shaw," 45 *Vand. L. Rev.* 715 (1992); B. Karkkainen, "'Plain Meaning': Justices Scalia's Jurisprudence of Strict Statutory Construction," 17 *Harv. J.L. & Pub. Pol'y* 401 (1994); S.F. Ross, "The Limited Relevance of Plain Meaning," 73 *Wash. U. L.Q.* 1057 (1995); M.S. Moore, "Plain Meaning and Linguistics—A Case Study," 73 *Wash U. L. Rev.* 1253 (1995); D. Strauss, "Why Plain Meaning?" 72 *Notre Dame L. Rev.* 1565 (1997).

[54] Hart and Sachs, *supra* p. 3, note 3 at 1124 (emphasis in the original).

Of course one begins with the words of a statute to ascertain its meaning, but one does not end with them. The notion that the plain meaning of the words of a statute defines the meaning of the statute reminds one of T.H. Huxley's gay observation that at times "a theory survives long after its brains are knocked out."[55]

Take the will in which the testator bequeaths his property to "Mother."[56] The text is clear only if you do not look at the true intent of the testator. When credible information on the matter comes to your attention, it becomes apparent that the word "Mother" in its textual context is not at all clear but rather has two meanings: "Mother" in its biological meaning and "Mother" in the special language of the testator. Indeed, old textualism is based on a mistaken view of semantic theory and jurisprudence, namely that a text can be clear without examining the context.[57] Judge Learned Hand rightly noted that "There is no surer way to misread any document than to read it literally."[58] Justice Cohen similarly noted that "the same simple meaning of words that so many judges so often take to be the foundation of statutory interpretation is, in actuality, just a delusion."[59] It is illogical to claim that the interpretive test is the clarity of the text, while at the same time preventing the judge from consulting credible evidence that the text is not clear.[60]

OLD TEXTUALISM DOES NOT FOSTER SECURITY AND CERTAINTY

A central claim in favor of old textualism is that it fosters certainty and security in the meaning given a text. The interpretive result is expected, because the meaning of the text is plain. Government entities and individuals can plan their behavior according to that meaning.[61] Such claim is fundamentally mistaken. Whether a text is plain—and what it "plainly" says—depends on the subjective feeling of each judge. This personalized

---

[55] *Massachusetts Bonding & Insurance Co. v. U.S.*, 352 U.S. 128, 138 (1956) (Frankfurter, J., dissenting). Also see Justice Frankfurter's comments in *United States v. Monia*, 317 U.S. 424, 431 (1943) (Frankfurter, J., dissenting) ("The notion that because the words of a statute are plain, its meaning is also plain, is merely pernicious oversimplification"); R. Traynor, "No Magic Words Could Do It Justice," 49 *Calif. L. Rev.* 615, 618 (1961) ("Plain words, like plain people, are not always so plain as they seem").

[56] *Supra* p. 271.

[57] E. Lasky, Note, "Perplexing Problems with Plain Meaning," 27 *Hofstra L. Rev.* 891 (1999).

[58] *Guiseppi v. Walling*, 144 F. 2d 608, 624 (2d Cir. 1944) (Hand, J., concurring).

[59] Cohen, *supra* p. 257, note 162 at 7.

[60] H.J. Friendly, *Benchmarks* 206 (1967).

[61] Lord Simon of Glaisdale's comments in *Stock v. Frank Jones (Tipton) Ltd.* [1978] ICR 347, 354. *See also* Steyn, *supra* p. 99, note 12 at 30.

approach fails to achieve security and certainty.[62] The same is true of the question, whether a plain text leads to absurdity. One judge's absurdity is another's reasonable result.[63] How can we decide that a particular interpretation leads to absurdity, if we do not examine it in context of the objective that the text is designed to achieve? Furthermore, old textualism's focus on the plain language of the text prevents it from developing clear rules about the sources that judges may consult when they are allowed to go beyond the four corners of the text. May they study legislative history? May judges consult the system's fundamental values? Old textualism trades law for emotion; it trades the intent of the legislature for the intent of the interpreter. The rhetoric of authorial intent often masks the intent of judges who lie to themselves in order to insulate themselves from criticism.

OLD TEXTUALISM FOSTERS JUDICIAL SUPERFICIALITY

One justification for old textualism is that it frees judges from the need to examine the objectives at the core of the text. As such, it conserves the court's time. It also prevents disagreement among judges who "unite" around the plain language of the text.[64] The result is often judicial superficiality and avoidance of any attempt to understand the text in depth. The following comments by Zander are harsh, but there is truth to them. They were made in reference to statutory interpretation, but are true of the interpretation of any legal text:

> A final criticism of the literal approach to interpretation is that it is defeatist and lazy. The judge gives up the attempt to understand the document at the first attempt. Instead of struggling to discover what it means, he simply adopts the most straightforward interpretation of the words in question—without regard to whether this interpretation makes sense in the particular context. It

---

[62] Cowen, "The Interpretation of Statutes and the Concept of the Intention of the Legislator," 43 *T.H.R.H. Rev.* 374, 388 (1980) (discussing the "unprincipled exercise of choice").

[63] J. Willis, "Statutory Interpretation in a Nutshell," 16 *Can. Bar Rev.* 1, 13 (1938) ("Absurdity is a concept no less vague and indefinite than 'plain meaning' . . . It is infinitely more a matter of personal opinion and infinitely more susceptible to the influence of personal prejudice").

[64] J.W. Hurst, *Dealing with Statutes* 51 (1982); F. Schauer, "Statutory Construction and the Coordinating Function of Plain Meaning," 1990 *Sup. Ct. Rev.* 231; J. Macey and G. Miller, "The Canons of Statutory Construction and Judicial Preferences," 45 *Vand. L. Rev.* 647, 649 (1992); J. Polich, "The Ambiguity of Plain Meaning: *Smith v. United States* and the New Textualism," 68 *S. Cal. L. Rev.* 259, 262 (1994); G.H. Taylor, "Structural Textualism," 75 *B.U. L. Rev.* 321, 356 (1995); E. Lam, "The Limit and Inconsistency of Application of the Plain Meaning Rule to Selected Provisions of the Bankruptcy Reform Act of 1994," 20 *Hamline L. Rev.* 111 (1996); E. Lasky, Note, "Perplexing Problems with Plain Meaning," 27 *Hofstra L. Rev.* 891 (1999).

is not that the literal approach necessarily gives the wrong result but rather that the result is purely accidental. It is the intellectual equivalent of deciding the case by tossing a coin. The literal *interpretation* in a particular case may in fact be the best and wisest of the various alternatives, but the literal *approach* is always wrong because it amounts to an abdication of responsibility by the judge. Instead of decisions being based on reason and principle, the literalist bases his decision on one meaning arbitrarily preferred.[65]

Judges wash their hands of the matter. They duck out of judicial responsibility. They find an alternative to tossing a coin.

OLD TEXTUALISM IS UNSUPPORTED BY HERMENEUTIC, SOCIAL, OR CONSTITUTIONAL THEORY

Old textualism makes authorial intent the primary test for interpreting a legal text. However, it understands this intent in objective terms, effectively abandoning it as a real criterion. The understanding of the reasonable person replaces it. Such understanding could give content to old textualism, if reasonableness were grasped in its full sense, and if judges were permitted to access all external sources of understanding, including the system's fundamental values. Old textualism, however, narrows the interpreter's horizons, requiring him or her to focus on the text itself. Judges can go beyond the text only under certain preconditions (absurdity; lack of clarity), and even then, they may consult only defined sources, like additional texts by the same author and the circumstances surrounding the creation of the text in question. They may not refer to the system's values and principles. Authorial intent seems to cast its shadow, restricting the sources that judges may consult, and preventing the judge from finding an interpretive resolution to every interpretive problem he or she may face. The result is a system of interpretation that lacks hermeneutic, social, and constitutional grounding. Old textualism is also subject to the same criticism as subjective systems of interpretation.[66] Interpretation freezes the text being interpreted in the day of its creation. The text ceases to fulfill its aim, and judges cease to fulfill their roles as bridges between law and society and defenders of democracy.

Purposive interpretation avoids these problems. It employs old textualism as a source of the text's objective purpose, at a low level of abstraction. Old textualism is just one means of understanding the text. Purposive interpretation, on the other hand, considers both subjective textualism (in the form of subjective purpose) and old textualism (in the form of objective purpose). The weight of old textualism in purposive interpretation de-

---

[65] M. Zander, *The Law-Making Process* 125 (5th ed. 1999).
[66] *Supra* p. 265.

pends on the type of text. Purposive interpretation therefore achieves the objective of interpretation: giving the text a meaning that achieves the goal for which the text was designed.

New American Textualism in Statutory and Constitutional Interpretation

In recent years, American law has seen the development of a "new" breed of textualism, mostly in the fields of statutory and constitutional interpretation. Surprisingly, it applies very minimally to the interpretation of private law texts.[67] If new textualism is good and appropriate for legislation and the Constitution, why is it inappropriate for wills and contracts? The underlying justification for using new textualism—that the author created the text and not the intent—is appropriate and applicable to wills and contracts, too. Like the legislature or constitutional assembly, the author of a will or contract created only the text. On the flip side, if American law is ready to consult authorial intent in contracts and wills, why is it unwilling to do so for statutes and for the Constitution? I have not found a satisfactory answer from supporters of new textualism.

New textualism is an objective textualist system. It favors understanding the text the way a reasonable reader would have read it at the time it was enacted.[68] According to new textualism, the goal of interpretation is not to discover the intent of the legislature; the question is not what the legislature wanted, but rather what it said. As Scalia writes:

> It is the *law* that governs, not the intent of the lawgiver. . . . [T]he objective indication of the words, rather than the intent of the legislature, is what constitutes the law. . . . I object to the use of legislative history on principle, since I reject intent of the legislature as the proper criterion of the law.[69]

New textualism's approach to constitutional interpretation is similar. It does not seek to realize the intent of the framers, but rather to understand the Constitution as a reasonable reader would understand it at the time of its founding. Scalia notes, "What I look for in the Constitution is precisely what I look for in a statute: the original meaning of the text, not what the original draftsmen intended."[70]

---

[67] R. Scott, *The Case of Formalism in Relational Contracts*, 94 *Nw. U. L. Rev.* 847 (2000).

[68] *See* K.E. Whittington, *Constitutional Interpretation: Textual Meaning, Original Intent, and Judicial Review* (1999).

[69] A. Scalia, *A Matter of Interpretation: Federal Courts and the Law* 17, 29, 31 (1997). *See also* F. Easterbrook, "The Role of Original Intent in Statutory Interpretation," 11 *Harv. J.L. & Pub. Pol'y* 59 (1987).

[70] Scalia, *supra* p. 277, note 69 at 38. *See also* C. Fried, "Sonnet LXV and the 'Black Ink'

This "new" system is anything but new. Holmes employed a version of it at the end of the nineteenth century:

> We ask, not what this man meant, but what those words would mean in the mouth of a normal speaker of English, using them in the circumstances in which they were used. . . . We do not inquire what the legislature meant; we ask only what the statutes mean. So in the case of a will . . . his words must be sufficient for the purpose when taken in the sense in which they would be used by the normal speaker of English under his circumstances.[71]

Some of the American realists adopted this approach,[72] although it is not unique to American law. It exists as an exception in English law. Lord Reid used it in a 1975 case, noting that "We often say that we are looking for the intention of Parliament, but that is not quite accurate. We are seeking the meaning of the words which Parliament used. We are seeking not what Parliament meant but the true meaning of what they said."[73]

New textualism is honest about intent. If, as the old textualists claim, we seek not the "real" intent of the legislature but rather its intent as a reasonable person would understand it, why not take the additional step of giving up altogether on the need to realize legislative intent? A reasonable person's understanding should suffice. In this regard, new textualism tells the truth. Its rhetoric matches its practice. Of course, the question remains of how a reasonable person would understand the text.[74] On this issue, all new textualists agree that judges must study the language of the text as a whole, and if the statute is plain, they should give it its plain meaning. They may also consult dictionaries and linguistic aids to equip themselves with information about how readers understood the statute at the time of its enactment. They may consult interpretive maxims in effect at the time of enactment—like *expressio unius est exclusio alterius* (inferring the "no" of one matter from the "yes" of another), *ejusdem generis* (learning about the specific from the general enumeration), and the rule that an unclear criminal law should be interpreted in favor of the accused. Referring to these maxims is permissible because they indicate the way in which a reasonable reader understood the legislation at the time of enactment. Further, new textualists realize that a text cannot be understood out of context. They therefore permit interpreters to consult other statutes passed by the legis-

---

of the Framer's Intention," in *Interpreting Law and Literature: A Hermeneutic Reader* 45 (S. Levinson et al. eds., 1988).

[71] O.W. Holmes, "The Theory of Legal Interpretation," 12 *Harv. L. Rev.* 417 (1899).

[72] *Supra* p. 225.

[73] *Black-Clawson International Ltd. v. Papierwerke Waldhof-Auschaffenburg A.G.* [1975] 1 All E.R. 810, 814.

[74] For an internal examination of new textualism, see G.H. Taylor, "Structural Textualism," 75 *B.U. L. Rev.* 321 (1995).

lature, in order to draw inferences from the legislature's use of similar language. New textualists do not, however, under any circumstances, allow interpreters to consult legislative history or the system's fundamental values, as they existed at the time of interpretation. Even when the plain language leads to absurdity, or when the language is unclear, interpreters may not consult legislative history or fundamental values. In these latter situations, interpreters have no choice but to say that the issue lies beyond the reach of the statute.

To its credit, new textualism speaks the truth. Does it have additional advantages? What are its core justifications?[75]

THE CORE JUSTIFICATIONS FOR NEW TEXTUALISM

New textualism disentangles itself from the view that the goal of interpretation is to advance the intent of the legislature. It relies on three justifications. *First*, it is claimed that a collective body like a legislature has no intent of its own, or if it does, that intent is manipulative and cannot be trusted. We discussed this issue in our criticism of intentionalism. We saw[76] that these claims have some truth, but they do not prove that we can never attribute joint intent to a collective body like a legislature, or that such joint intent—when it can be inferred—will always be too speculative to be credible. A *second* justification—unique to new textualism—is the argument that, whether or not the legislature has an intent, it is not relevant to interpreting the statute. The legislature enacted the statute—not the intent. We should not rely on legislative intent because it did not go through the legislative process. Using it as an interpretive criterion is harmful to democracy. As Scalia writes:

> [I]t is simply incompatible with democratic government, or indeed, even with fair government, to have the meaning of a law determined by what the lawgiver meant, rather than by what the lawgiver promulgated. . . . Government by unexpressed intent is similarly tyrannical. It is the *law* that governs, not the intent of the lawgiver.[77]

---

[75] *See* R. Barnett, "On Originalism for Nonoriginalists," 45 *Loy. L. Rev.* 611 (1999); Manning, *supra* p. 69, note 29.

[76] *Supra* p. 264.

[77] Scalia, *supra* p. 277, note 69 at 17. Not all new textualists seem to accept this approach. Some believe that legislative intent is relevant in its objective sense, not in the sense of what the legislature (subjectively) thought. *See* Manning, *supra* p. 69, note 29 at 16 ("Textualists deny that anyone can meaningfully determine 'actual' legislative intent. . . . They do not, however, believe that the concept of 'intent' is irrelevant to interpretation. Nor could they"). If this is the case, what is the difference between old and new textualism? And if "reasonable" intent is relevant, why isn't "actual" intent relevant? I wonder.

A *third* justification is the argument that, when the judge considers the legislature's intentions, he or she focuses, in fact, on the intentions attributable to a reasonable legislature. The meaning the statute must bear becomes the meaning that the judge wants it to bear. The decisive intent is really the intent of the judge. Scalia argues that "It is simply not compatible with democratic theory that laws mean whatever they ought to mean, and that unelected judges decide what that is."[78] The need to restrict judicial discretion—and thus to guarantee rule of law (security and certainty)—justifies new textualism.[79] Defenders of new textualism claim it protects the individual from a potentially tyrannical collectivity. They say that interpreting constitutional language according to modern worldviews would ultimately exchange civil rights for the changing worldviews of the majority.[80]

CRITIQUE OF NEW TEXTUALISM AND ITS UNDERSTANDING OF DEMOCRACY

New textualism is not new, and it makes no new contribution. In many ways, it is a repetition of old textualism. Most of the criticism we discussed of old textualism applies to the new version. The distinction between a "plain" and an unclear text is baseless and not clear at all.[81] New textualism does not achieve the security and certainty to which it aspires.[82] Textualism—old and new—fosters judicial superficiality.[83] New textualism relies on inadequate justifications. As I noted, a collective body does have a joint intent at the core of its normative activity, usually at a high level of abstraction. True, such intent is not always helpful to interpretation. But there is no reason to declare, as a matter of principle, that a legislature never has an intent. New textualism correctly points out that the legislature enacted the statute and not the intent. However, that does not mean that we cannot take the intent into consideration, in order to understand the statute. We might as well say that the legislature enacted the statute and not the dictionary, and thus we cannot take the dictionary into consideration in understanding the statute. We should distinguish between the text

[78] Scalia, *supra* p. 277, note 69 at 22.

[79] Some argue that there is an internal connection between new textualism and the judicial process movement we discussed on p. 227. *See* N. Zeppos, "Justice Scalia's Textualism: The 'New' New Legal Process," 12 *Cardozo L. Rev.* 1597 (1991). I reject this argument. Judicial process is based on the purpose of the statute and, apparently, on its subjective aspect. *See supra* p. 228. New textualism takes a different approach.

[80] A. Scalia, "Originalism: The Lesser Evil," 57 *U. Chi. L. Rev.* 849 (1989).

[81] *Supra* p. 12.

[82] *Supra* p. 274.

[83] *Supra* p. 275.

and the tools we need to understand it. The legislature enacted the text, and the interpreter does not try to change it. It is not clear, however, why the interpreter cannot use information external to the text, in order to understand it. New textualism itself recognizes that, in order to understand a text, one must take the context into consideration. Why not view the intent of the legislature as part of the context to be considered? Again, I do not claim that the intent of the legislature is the only context to be considered. I also do not favor giving it decisive weight in every situation. But why ignore it completely? Why not consider the values and principles of the legal system that encompasses the statute?

I cannot accept the claim of new textualism that taking legislative intent and the system's fundamental values in consideration is anti-democratic. Taking legislative intent into account gives the legislature's text a meaning in accord with its intent. Doing so visits no harm on democracy.[84] To the contrary: new textualism's technique harms democracy, both formal and substantive.

New textualism harms formal democracy by treating a piece of legislation—which expresses the decision of the majority—as a decision made with no goal. It would treat the interpretation of a statute enacted in parliament through the accepted legislative process the same as the interpretation of a statute enacted in a parliament whose members sleepwalked through the legislative process.[85] In both cases, new textualism treats the text, and only the text, as decisive. It is a caricature of legislation. A legislature passing a statute seeks to enact a policy. That policy requires us to consider the meaning of the statute.[86] Formal democracy does not require absolute severance of the statute from its author. Such severance is not only impossible, in light of the organic relationship between legislature and statute—it is also undesirable.[87] Even the American realists, who proclaimed the virtues of severing statute from legislature,[88] emphasized that, while a statute should not be interpreted according to the legislature's concrete intention (i.e., interpretive or consequential intention), it should be interpreted according to

---

[84] C. Sunstein, "Justice Scalia's Democratic Formalism," 107 *Yale L.J.* 529 (1997); W. Eskridge, "Textualism, The Unknown Ideal?" 96 *Mich. L. Rev.* 1509 (1998).

[85] Some new textualists seek to overcome this criticism by minimally recognizing "objective" intent (according to Raz). *See* Manning, *supra* p. 69, note 29 at 16 n.65. For Raz's view, *see supra* p. 261. In doing so, these scholars eradicate the basis of new textualism, converting it back to old textualism with all its drawbacks.

[86] Redish and Chung, *supra* p. 135, note 53 at 828.

[87] In H.C. 4031/94, *supra* p. 139, note 59, Justices Goldberg and Cheshin adopted the metaphor of severing the creation from the creator, but both emphasized that the creation or work must achieve its purpose.

[88] Radin argued that, once it enacts the statute, the legislature is *"functus officia." See* M. Radin, "Statutory Interpretation," 43 *Harv. L. Rev.* 863, 871 (1930).

the legislature's general intention. If we take legislative supremacy seriously, we must take legislative intent into consideration.

New textualism harms substantive democracy as well. The textualist interpretation severs the statute from society's fundamental values in general, and from human rights in particular. Democracy is more than just the formally democratic passage of a statute. A corrupt statute (*lex corrupta*) is not democratic. New textualism's formalistic approach fails to achieve substantive democracy. Nor is it necessary to protect the individual from the modern views of the collectivity. An interpreter need give expression not to the passing trends of the majority, but rather to society's deeply held views. Interpretation should reflect history and not hysteria.[89]

CRITIQUE OF NEW TEXTUALISM AND ITS VIEW OF THE JUDICIAL ROLE

At the core of new textualism is the suspicion that considering legislative intent will ultimately replace the intent of the legislature with that of the judge, expanding judicial discretion and impairing the rule of law (security and certainty). To avoid this unhappy state of affairs, new textualism completely ignores legislative intent, focusing on the understanding of the reasonable reader. But who is this reasonable reader, if not the judge? And why assume—in the absence of proof—that the discretion of a judge as a reasonable reader is narrower than the discretion of a judge taking into account legislative intent and the system's fundamental values? The logical conclusion would seem to be the opposite of what new textualism claims it to be.[90] The discretion of the judge who must consider legislative intent and the system's fundamental values becomes narrower than that of the judge who is free to focus on language alone. A judge should adhere to legislative intent and the intent of the reasonable legislature or of the system, not just to his or her sense of language. Indeed, new textualism may very well expand judicial discretion. It also fails to advance the rule-of-law values of security and certainty, because it determines that the meaning of a text is "plain" by sense, outside any normative framework.[91] Judges ex-

---

[89] *Supra* p. 168.

[90] Sunstein, *supra* p. 13, note 31 at 430; W. Eskridge, "The New Textualism," 37 *UCLA L. Rev.* 621 (1990); N. Zeppos, "Legislative History and the Interpretation of Statutes: Toward a Fact-Finding Model of Statutory Interpretation," 76 *Va. L. Rev.* 1295 (1990); D. Farber and P. Frickey, *Law and Public Choice: A Critical Introduction* 92 (1991); M. Redish and T. Chung, "Democratic Theory and the Legislative Process: Mourning the Death of Originalism in Statutory Interpretation," 68 *Tul. L. Rev.* 803, 819 (1994) ("Rather than disciplining judicial behaviour, the theory may, by its terms, indirectly condone the use of an unduly broad judicial policymaking prerogative").

[91] *Supra* p. 273.

ercise their discretion to the fullest extent, thwarting the twin goals of security and certainty.[92]

Beyond that, however, what position does new textualism adopt about the role of the judge? New textualism correctly asserts that judges are not agents taking orders from their principal (the legislature).[93] But why not view judges as faithful junior partners in the legislative process? There is no point in suspecting, every hour of every day, that judges will abuse their offices, because if that were true, new textualism would not be able to restrain even those judges who adopt it. And, if new textualism rejects the agency model, what model does it endorse? Is it the model of the judge as linguist? Would it matter to new textualism if, instead of judges, linguists or reasonable people off the street engaged in statutory interpretation? New textualism carves out a narrow, formalistic role for judges. Judges do not create law in their interpretation. They simply declare existing law. Law, then, is static. In effect, we have returned to the formalistic view[94] of the judge as the "mouth" of the legislator. On this view, judges do not bridge the gap between law and society;[95] it is not their job to protect democracy.

CRITIQUE OF NEW TEXTUALISM AND ITS HERMENEUTIC AND SOCIAL VIEWS

New textualism relies on the understanding of the reasonable reader. This understanding cannot be entirely passive, however. A text does not initiate a conversation. It responds to the questions the reader asks of it. What does new textualism ask the text? What does it seek to learn from it? New textualism agrees that a text cannot be understood out of context.[96] It accepts dictionaries, other statutes of the same legislature, and interpretive canons as valid sources of context, but, inexplicably, it stops there. Why not consider legislative history as a factor that shapes context?[97] Why not consider the values of the system in general, and human rights in particular, as part of the context framing our understanding of the text?[98] In any case, de-

[92] Popkin, *supra* p. 85, note 1 at 176.

[93] Some scholars do reconcile new textualism with the agency model. *See* Manning, *supra* p. 69, note 29 at 15. He relies on F. Easterbrook, "Text, History, and Structure in Statutory Interpretation," 17 *Harv. J. L. & Pub. Pol'y* 61, 63 (1994); F. Easterbrook, "Foreword: The Court and the Economic System," 98 *Harv. L. Rev.* 4, 60 (1984). Does Scalia adopt this position, too?

[94] On the relationship between formalism and new textualism, see the symposium on formalism published in 66 *U. Chi. L. Rev.* 527 (1999), particularly C. Sunstein, "Must Formalism Be Defended Empirically?" 66 *U. Chi. L. Rev.* 636 (1999).

[95] Zeppos, *supra* p. 282, note 90 at 1369.

[96] Scalia, *supra* p. 277, note 69 at 37. *See also* Easterbrook, *supra* p. 283, note 93 at 64.

[97] Taylor, *supra* p. 278, note 74 at 378.

[98] Siegel, *supra* p. 170, note 90 at 1031.

termining the understanding of the reasonable person means balancing—whether consciously or unconsciously—the values and principles relevant to resolving the interpretive problem. The reasonable reader (the judge) is part of a legal community, acting within the framework of shared values and principles. The proper balance between them determines what constitutes a reasonable reading. Why is new textualism unwilling to recognize this? Why allow—generally, unconsciously—interpretive intuition and a sense of language to suffice? Values and principles framed the text's creation, and they frame its interpretation. Why not consciously recognize them as an indispensable device for understanding the text?

I have said that we cannot know how to interpret without knowing why we interpret.[99] Why does new textualism interpret, and what does it do when the meaning of the text is not plain, and dictionaries and other statutes fail to clarify it? By limiting the context that a new textualist may consult, new textualism fails the condition of efficacy;[100] it cannot solve all interpretive problems and must rely on judicial discretion. It does, not, however, admit to it.

THE ORIGINALISM OF NEW TEXTUALISM

New textualism is generally considered to adopt originalism as its constitutional outlook. New textualism seeks to understand the text as a reasonable reader would have understood it at the time it was written.[101] Why restrict itself to this historic understanding? A public law text guides human behavior for many years—in the case of the American constitution, for hundreds of years—after it is written. Why must we freeze our understanding of the text to its historic understanding? I do not claim that we can never access such historic understanding. A contemporary reader may try to insert himself or herself into the time the text was created, in an attempt to understand it as it was understood then. I ask, however, what constitutional theory justifies originalism? True, formal democracy teaches us that the legislature enacted a statute and not legislative intent or the intent of the system, but we may consider either or both of these without claiming that they are the legislature's text. There is a difference between the text that the legislature enacted and criteria for understanding it. Furthermore, substantive democracy—which requires maintaining not just majority rule but also fundamental values and views—certainly does not comport with new textualism.

---

[99] *Supra* p. 219.
[100] For the condition of efficacy, *see* p. 218.
[101] *See* Scalia, *supra* p. 277, note 69.

New textualism is also at odds with the principles of separation of powers and proper judicial role, according to which the judge is a junior partner in the legislative project who should integrate the statute being interpreted into the framework of the system as a whole. To achieve this integration, the interpreter should consider contemporary, as well as original, understanding. As a partner, the judge should give a statute the meaning that responds to society's needs and protects democracy. The originalism of new textualism prevents the judge from doing so.

IMPROVED AND CORRECTED NEW TEXTUALISM

New textualism may not itself constitute a proper system of interpretation, but it may serve as the basis for a proper system of interpretation. Its insistence on the text as the basis of interpretation is appropriate. A statute barring dogs from a particular location cannot be interpreted to bar cats from the same place. Language limits interpretation. There are also positive aspects to new textualism's skepticism toward legislative intent and legislative history. Sometimes we cannot know the intent of the legislature; sometimes the information about intent is not reliable; sometimes there is no credible intent that can help the interpretive process. Sometimes a statute (intentionally or unintentionally) reflects conflicting intentions. These are important lessons to deduce from new textualism's insistence that the legislature enacted the statute and not its own intent. We should also encourage new textualism's consideration of legislation as a whole, as a source for understanding a single statute. However, we need to expand the interpreter's horizons from the time of enactment to the time of interpretation. The context of a statute—whose importance new textualism recognizes—need not be limited to other statutes, but can also include society's principles, values, and fundamental views, at the time of enactment and at the time of interpretation. An interpreter may consult them, as well.[102] With these corrections,[103] new textualism would become a proper system of interpretation; but then it would cease to be new textualism, and it would become purposive interpretation.

---

[102] Scalia himself admits that "We look for a sort of 'objectified' intent—the intent that a reasonable person would gather from the text of the law, placed alongside the remainder of the *corpus juris.*" Scalia, *supra* p. 277, note 69 at 17. Apparently, the *corpus juris* includes the fundamental values.

[103] Manning has introduced some of them. *See* Manning, *supra* p. 69, note 29 at 105.

3. PURPOSIVE INTERPRETATION AND PRAGMATISM

Pragmatism

Pragmatism is a well-known philosophical school[104] that has legal applications in the form of legal pragmatism.[105] Pragmatism in legal interpretation[106] is a secondary branch that includes a few pragmatic systems of interpretation. These systems generally deal with interpreting public law texts

---

[104] For a survey of pragmatism, see R. Rorty, "Pragmatism," in 7 *Routledge Encyclopedia of Philosophy* 633 (E. Craig ed., 1998).

[105] *See, generally,* Popkin, *supra* p. 3, note 1 at 219; D.A. Farber and S. Sherry, *Desperately Seeking Certainty: The Misguided Quest for Constitutional Foundations* (2002); P.S. Atiyah, "From Principles to Pragmatism: Changes in the Function of the Judicial Process and the Law," 65 *Iowa L. Rev.* 1249 (1980); V. Wellman, "Practical Reasoning and Judicial Justification: Toward an Adequate Theory," 57 *U. Colo. L. Rev.* 45 (1985); P.S. Atiyah, *Pragmatism and Theory in English Law* (1987); C.W. Hantzis, "Legal Innovation within the Wider Intellectual Tradition: The Pragmatism of Oliver Wendell Holmes, Jr.," 82 *Nw. U. L. Rev.* 541 (1988); T. Grey, "Holmes and Legal Pragmatism," 41 *Stan. L. Rev.* 787 (1989); S.J. Burton, "The Works of Joseph Raz: Law as Practical Reason," 62 *S. Cal. L. Rev.* 747 (1989); D. Patterson, "Law's Pragmatism: Law as Practice and Narrative," 76 *Va. L. Rev.* 937 (1990); S. Smith, "The Pursuit of Pragmatism," 100 *Yale L.J.* 409 (1990); Posner, *supra* p. 27, note 85; D. Van Zandt, "An Alternative Theory of Practical Reason in Judicial Decisions," 65 *Tul. L. Rev.* 775 (1991); M. Brint and W. Weaver (eds.), *Pragmatism in Law and Society* (1991); R. Westmoreland, "Dworkin and Legal Pragmatism," 11 *Oxford J. Legal Stud.* 174 (1991); R.J. Lipkin, "Kibitzers, Fuzzies, and Apes without Tails: Pragmatism and the Art of Conversation in Legal Theory," 66 *Tul. L. Rev.* 69 (1991); L. Baker, "'Just Do It': Pragmatism and Progressive Social Change," 78 *Va. L. Rev.* 697 (1992); M. Nussbaum, "Skepticism about Practical Reason in Literature and the Law," 107 *Harv. L. Rev.* 714 (1994); *The Revival of Pragmatism: New Essay on Social Thought, Law and Culture* (M. Dickstein ed., 1998); R. Posner, "Past-Dependency, Pragmatism and Critique of History in Adjudication and Legal Scholarship," 67 *U. Chi. L. Rev.* 573 (2000); B. Bix, "Law, Social Science and Pragmatism: Conceptual Jurisprudence and Socio-Legal Studies," 32 *Rutgers L.J.* 227 (2000); M. Jenkins, "Can Pragmatism Overcome the Impasse in Contemporary Legal Theory?" 15 *Can. J.L. & Juris.* 85 (2002); D.A. Farber and S. Sherry, *Desperately Seeking Certainty: The Misguided Quest for Constitutional Foundations* (2002).

[106] *See, generally,* M.B.W. Sinclair, "Law and Language: The Role of Pragmatics in Statutory Interpretation," 46 *U. Pitt. L. Rev.* 373 (1985); D. Farber and P. Frickey, "Practical Reason and the First Amendment," 34 *UCLA L. Rev.* 1615 (1987); D. Farber, "Legal Pragmatism and the Constitution," 72 *Minn. L. Rev.* 1331 (1988); P. Halewood, "Performance and Pragmatism in Constitutional Interpretation," 3 *Can. J.L. and Juris.* 91 (1990); G. Miller, "Pragmatics and the Maxims of Interpretation," 1990 *Wis. L. Rev.* 1179; W. Eskridge and P. Frickey, "Statutory Interpretation as Practical Reasoning," 42 *Stan. L. Rev.* 321 (1990); D. Farber, "The Inevitability of Practical Reason: Statutes, Formalism and the Rule of Law," 45 *Vand. L. Rev.* 533 (1992); L. Alexander, "Practical Reason and Statutory Interpretation," 12 *Law & Phil.* 319 (1993); M. Dorf, "Create Your Own Constitutional Theory," 87 *Calif. L. Rev.* 593 (1999); R. Posner, "Pragmatism versus Purposivism in First Amendment Analysis," 54 *Stan. L. Rev.* 737 (2002).

(statutes, constitutions), and resist formalism in favor of substance. Pragmatists consider both text and context. They read the text as a whole; they study the intent of the author, the way understanding of the text has developed, and the system's fundamental values. They adopt a commonsensical approach to finding the best solution. As Eskridge and Frickey note:

> Our model holds that an interpreter will look at a broad range of evidence—text, historical evidence, and the text's evolution—and thus form a preliminary view of the statute. The interpreter then develops that preliminary view by testing various possible interpretations against the multiple criteria of fidelity to the text, historical accuracy, and conformity to contemporary circumstances and values. Each criterion is relevant, yet none necessarily trumps the others.[107]

Similarly, Posner writes that "Maybe the best thing to do when a statute is invoked is to examine the consequences of giving the invoker what he wants and then estimate whether those consequences will on the whole be good ones."[108] Judges retain discretion in this search, to be exercised according to their accumulated life experience.

Pragmatism and Dynamic Interpretation

Pragmatism leads to an important result, a result that can be reached in other systems of interpretation,[109] including purposive interpretation: the dynamic interpretation[110] of statutes and constitutions. The legislator or framer does not control statutory or constitutional interpretation. An interpreter must also consider changes in language, in legislation, in the fundamental views of the public, and in the fundamental values of the system, changes that occur between the creation of the text and its interpretation. Using all these components, the interpreter gives the best possible interpretation to the text. It is a dynamic, not a static, meaning. Indeed, dynamic interpretation—like liberal or conservative interpretation, expansive or restrictive interpretation—is not a system of interpretation. It is an interpretive product of pragmatic interpretation. Other systems of interpretation may also give rise to dynamic interpretation.[111] Purposive interpre-

---

[107] Eskridge and Frickey, *supra* p. 286, note 106 at 352.

[108] Posner, *supra* p. 286, note 105 at 300.

[109] Radbruch, *supra* p. 53, note 179 at 266; Popkin, *supra* p. 61, note 1 at 207.

[110] Eskridge, *supra* p. 41, note 126 at 107. Eskridge tries to prove that dynamic interpretation is compatible with most modern jurisprudences.

[111] Côté, *supra* p. 77, note 65 at 10; Driedger, *supra* p. 69, note 31 at 137. *See also* P. Hogg, *Constitutional Law of Canada* 815 (4th ed., 1997).

tation, for example, is also based on dynamic interpretation. Dynamic interpretation addresses the problem of time, but time is not the only problem that interpretation must address. The central issue of interpretation is the relationship between the form of the text and its substance, between text and context. Dynamic interpretation is important to this inquiry, but it is not decisive. It is certainly not unique to pragmatic interpretation.

Pragmatism and Purposive Interpretation

Pragmatic systems of interpretation share many similarities with purposive interpretation. Both kinds of systems consider the totality of components—text, authorial intent, and the intent of the reasonable author and of the system—through the interpreter's free movement from one component to another. Both kinds of systems lead to dynamic results. Both rely on hermeneutic perspectives that emphasize the interaction between interpreter and text in an attempt to blend the horizons of the text with those of the interpreter. Both systems recognize the interpreter's discretion, which at the end of the day he or she uses to find the solution that seems best. In this sense, purposive interpretation is pragmatic.

The two systems also diverge substantially. Purposive interpretation asks, first and foremost: What is the goal of interpretation? Its answer is that the goal of interpretation is to achieve the objective of the text. Even when the purposive interpreter faces two legitimate alternatives, with discretion to choose the proper option, such discretion is not absolute. In pragmatic interpretation, however, the guidance of purposive interpretation, directing the interpreter to search for and achieve the goal of the text, does not exist—or exists to a diminished extent.[112] From the beginning of the interpretive process until its conclusion—at least when there is no information about the (actual or reconstructed) intent of the author—the pragmatic interpreter is left to himself or herself, free to select the meaning that produces the pragmatic results that seem best.

Consider a statute interpreted according to its purpose. Imagine that the type of statute warrants assigning significant weight to subjective purpose. The purposive interpreter does not ask whether the (pragmatic) consequences are desirable, but realizes the (abstract) intent of the legislature, whether or not the results are desirable, and leave it to the legislature to make any necessary changes. On the other hand, when faced with a statute that, according to purposive interpretation, should be interpreted accord-

---

[112] Posner is a pragmatist, but he begins with the (actual or reconstructed) intent of the author, and only if it is unknown does he adopt a pragmatic approach. *See* Posner, *supra* p. 286, note 105 at 263.

ing to the system's fundamental values, the purposive interpreter will do so even when the results are out of step with the trends currently popular with the majority. The purposive interpreter achieves a balance between basic values, when pragmatism would lead him or her to ignore those values in favor of contemporary trends. Pragmatism balances the various components of purpose according to the pragmatism of the result. Purposive interpretation assigns weights to those same components according to purposive considerations grounded in constitutional law. The systems do, however, converge on the issue of judicial discretion, exercised to achieve the most desirable results. In the circumstances in which purposive interpretation recognizes judicial discretion, like pragmatism, it takes a commonsense approach. As I noted, I think that, in exercising discretion, the interpreter should choose the meaning that best achieves justice.

Critique of Pragmatism as a System of Interpretation

It is not surprising that pragmatic interpretation, like other systems, encounters piercing criticism.[113] Subjective systems of interpretation criticize pragmatic interpretation for failing to make authorial intent the decisive factor. Objective systems of interpretation criticize pragmatism for taking authorial intent into consideration at all. These systems have similar criticisms of purposive interpretation,[114] which also incorporates subjective and objective elements.

What is my critique of pragmatic interpretation, from the perspective of purposive interpretation? It is not that pragmatism imparts the judge with discretion. Every system of interpretation—including both old and new textualism—must be based on at least a modicum of discretion. My critique is this: You cannot know what the best (pragmatic) solution is without first establishing the objective that interpretation is to achieve. Posner correctly pointed out that "Practical reason involves setting a goal—pleasure, the good life, whatever—and choosing the means best suited to reaching it."[115] Pragmatism, however, fails to establish a goal beyond achieving the most practical solution.[116] Pragmatic interpretation rightly considers the different building blocks of the interpretive process—text, authorial intent, the intent of the system, discretion—but it does not set a

---

[113] For an analysis of the critique and responses to it, *see* D. Farber, "The Inevitability of Practical Reason: Statutes, Formalism, and the Rule of Law," 45 *Vand. L. Rev.* 533 (1992).

[114] *Infra* p. 301.

[115] Posner, *supra* p. 27, note 85 at 71.

[116] N. Levit, "Practically Unreasonable: A Critique of Practical Reason," 85 *Nw. U. L. Rev.* 494 (1991).

goal to which the interpreter must aspire in assembling these building blocks. All that is left is the interpreter's subjective will as to what seems good. This is not enough for the interpretive process,[117] which is more than just interpretive subjectivity. Commonsensical pragmatism needs a goal, for the sake of whose achievement it selects the most practical and best means. Purposive interpretation, on the other hand, sets a goal before the interpreter: Achieve the purpose at the core of the text.

A purposive interpreter does act as a pragmatist at the many junctures of interpretation in which judicial discretion exists. In the absence of sufficient guidance from purposive interpretation itself, the interpreter chooses the "best" purpose, which is simply the most pragmatic. Even in exercising discretion pragmatically, however, the purposive interpreter remains bound by the commandment of purposive interpretation to achieve the purpose at the core of the text.

4. PURPOSIVE INTERPRETATION AND DWORKIN'S SYSTEM OF INTERPRETATION

Law as Integrity

Dworkin is one of the leading contemporary philosophers of law. His views on the essence of law and the scientific model that explains law are key to understanding the modern view of law. Just as we cannot understand law without understanding the positive theory of law—from the schools of Austin, Kelsen, Hart, and Raz—we cannot understand law without understanding Dworkin's theory of it.[118] In his books and articles, Dworkin has created a whole structure of the essence of law, its relationship to other sciences, and its connections to social reality. We are especially interested in Dworkin's theory about the interpretation of legal texts (enacted, as in a statute or constitution, as well as case law), which he calls "constructive interpretation."[119] We should not, however, separate Dworkin's view on law from his view on interpretation in law. The reason for this close link is Dworkin's own view that law itself is the result of an interpretive process.

Dworkin's point of departure is that law is based on integrity. In explaining this view, he notes that "According to law as integrity, proposi-

---

[117] Hart, *supra* p. 215, note 39 at 138. *See also* Farber *supra* p. 289, note 113 at 547; R. Dworkin, "Pragmatism, Right Answers, and True Banality," in *Pragmatism in Law and Society* 359, 371 (M. Brint and W. Weaver eds., 1991).

[118] S. Honeyball and J. Walter, *Integrity, Community, and Interpretation: A Critical Analysis of Ronald Dworkin's Theory of Law* (1998).

[119] Dworkin, *supra* p. 13, note 33 at 53.

tions of law are true if they figure in or follow from principles of justice, fairness and procedural due process that provide the best constructive interpretation of the community's legal practice."[120] To further explain the components of his view, Dworkin says:

> The integrity of a community's conception of fairness requires that the political principles necessary to justify the legislature's assumed authority be given full effect in deciding what a statute it has enacted means. The integrity of a community's conception of justice demands that the moral principles necessary to justify the substance of its legislature's decisions be recognized in the rest of the law. The integrity of its conception of procedural due process insists that trial procedures that are counted as striking the right balance between accuracy and efficiency in enforcing some part of the law be recognized throughout, taking into account differences in the kind and degree of moral harm an inaccurate verdict imposes. These several claims justify a commitment to consistency in principle valued for its own sake. They suggest what I shall argue: that integrity rather than some superstition of elegance is the life of law as we know it.[121]

Dworkin applies his claim of integrity to both legislation (integrity of legislation) and case law (integrity of adjudication). Integrity in legislation means preserving coherence in principles. Integrity in judging means that those responsible for establishing "what law is" do so coherently. The judge should identify rights and responsibilities with the assumption that they were created by an author—the community as an entity—expressing a coherent view of justice and fairness.

The Meaning That Gives the Statute the Best Political Justification

In statutory interpretation, the judge should treat the statute with integrity. He or she must give the piece of legislation the meaning that shows its political history in the best light.[122] As Dworkin writes of the judge, "He will ask himself which reading of the act . . . shows the political history including and surrounding that statute in the better light."[123] The judge should ask not what meaning seems best to him or her, but rather what meaning would give the piece of legislation the best justification, against the background of its enactment. Considering the judge as interpreter and using the image of Judge Hercules, Dworkin writes:

[120] *Id.* at 225.
[121] *Id.* at 166.
[122] *Supra* p. 290.
[123] Dworkin, *supra* p. 13, note 33 at 313.

He tries to show a piece of social history—the story of a democratically elected legislature enacting a particular text in particular circumstances—in the best light overall, and this means his account must justify the story as a whole, not just its ending. His interpretation must be sensitive, that is, not only to his convictions about justice and . . . policy . . . but also to his convictions about the ideals of political integrity and fairness and procedural due process as these apply specifically to legislation in a democracy.[124]

The interpreter must select, from among the potential semantic meanings, the meaning that advances the principles and policies that give the statute its best political justification.

Legislative History and the Intent of Members of the Legislature

How should a judge choose the meaning that gives a statute its best political justification? The judge should consider the abstract intent of the members of the legislature. Abstract purpose derives from the principle of integrity. In contrast, concrete intent is a subjective concept that the interpreter need not consider. Referring to the judge, Dworkin says that "He understands the idea of a statute's purpose or intention, not as some combination of the purposes or intentions of particular legislators, but as the upshot of integrity, of taking the interpretive attitude toward the political events that include the statute's enactment."[125]

Legislative history is one source of information about abstract intention. To the extent that such history testifies to the policy of the legislative institution—as distinct from the policy of a single member of the legislative body—it is a formal declaration that should be taken into consideration. Dworkin writes:

Official statements of purpose, made in the canonical form established by the practice of legislative history, should be treated as themselves acts of the state personified. They are themselves political decisions, so the chief command of integrity, that the state act in a principled way, embraces them as well as the more discrete decisions captured in statutes. Hercules aims to make the legislative story as a whole as good as it can be; he would make the story worse if his interpretation showed the state saying one thing while doing another.[126]

---

[124] *Id.* at 338.
[125] *Id.* at 316.
[126] *Id.* at 343.

Dynamic Interpretation

According to Dworkin, the judge's interpretation does not focus on an historical point in time. Instead, referring to the judge, Dworkin writes that "The history he interprets begins before a statute is enacted and continues to the moment when he must decide what it now declares."[127] The meaning of a piece of legislation is therefore likely to change according to events taking place after its enactment. According to Dworkin, the judge (as Hercules) has the following task:

> Hercules' method . . . rejects the assumption of a canonical moment at which a statute is born and has all and only the meaning it will ever have. Hercules interprets not just the statute's text but its life, the process that begins before it becomes law and extends far beyond that moment. He aims to make the best he can of this continuing story, and his interpretation therefore changes as the story develops.[128]

A judge must therefore consider other statutes passed following the enactment of the statute being interpreted. He or she must consider attempts—whether or not successful—to change the statute being interpreted. He or she must also consider the interpretation given to the various provisions and the development of case law.

Interpretation as Writing in a Chain

Dworkin's point of departure is the present. The goal of interpretation is to give a statute enacted in the past the best present political justification, in order to regulate social life in the future. Dworkin writes:

> Law as integrity, then, begins in the present and pursues the past only so far as and in the way its contemporary focus dictates. It does not aim to recapture, even for present law, the ideals or practical purposes of the politicians who first created it. It aims rather to justify what they did . . . in an overall story worth telling now, a story with a complex claim: that present practice can be organized by and justified in principles sufficiently attractive to provide an honorable future.[129]

According to Dworkin, the activity of the judge—whether in interpretation or in developing common law—is like writing a chapter in a book

[127] *Id.* at 316.
[128] *Id.* at 348.
[129] *Id.* at 227.

whose previous chapters were written by previous authors.[130] In Dworkin's image, the book is written by "chain writing." Each author in the chain interprets the chapters written by his or her predecessors, in order to write his or her own chapter. The job of each author in the chain is to write his or her chapter, based on his or her interpretation, so that the work as a whole will be interpreted in the most favorable light. All participants in the writing have a common goal, to create the best unified work they can. In bringing this literary image to the field of statutory interpretation, Dworkin argues that the judge is like the contemporary author in the chain. The legislature is like the previous author who wrote a prior chapter in the common work. The judge, according to Dworkin,

> will treat Congress as an author earlier than himself in the chain of law, though an author with special powers and responsibilities different from his own, and he will see his own role as fundamentally the creative one of a partner continuing to develop, in what he believes is the best way, the statutory scheme Congress began.[131]

In considering the content of the "chapter" the judge writes by interpreting the statute, the judge must make two decisions. The *first* deals with how the new chapter fits into the work as a whole. The judge must be aware of the role of the legislature in the legal system and his or her own limitations as a judge. He or she must recognize the system's fundamental principles. The *second* decision addresses the justification for the new chapter in the chain of prior chapters. The judge must choose a suitable possibility that shows society's institutions and decisions in the best light vis-à-vis the political message. The judge is likely to encounter a misfit between two ways of presenting the institutions and decisions, from the point of view of their political ethics. In these situations, judges should adjudicate the conflict by expressing their worldviews of how to balance contradictory ideals. Referring to the judge, Dworkin writes that "He must choose between eligible interpretations by asking which shows the community's structure of institutions and decisions—its public standards as a whole—in a better light from the standpoint of political morality."[132] Judges adjudicate according to their worldviews of justice and fairness and of how to balance these ideals when they clash. Different judges will arrive at different results.[133]

---

[130] R. Dworkin, "Law as Interpretation," 60 *Tex. L. Rev.* 527, 542–43 (1982).
[131] *Id.* at 313.
[132] *Id.* at 256.
[133] *Id.* at 256.

Constitutional Interpretation

Dworkin interprets a constitution in the same way he interprets a statute. He does, however, consider the special nature of the constitution as a foundational document of the legal system:

> The Constitution is foundational of other law, so Hercules' interpretation of the document as a whole, and of its abstract clauses, must be foundational as well. It must fit and justify the most basic arrangements of political power in the community, which means it must be a justification drawn from the most philosophical reaches of political theory.[134]

Dworkin, of course, takes the constitutional text as the starting point for constitutional interpretation. To the extent that such text is based on language articulating a political institution of human rights and values (like equality), judges should give the text a meaning that accords with the abstract intent of its authors, as opposed to their interpretive intent:

> We turn to history to answer the question of what they intended to *say*, not the different question of what *other* intentions they had. . . . We are governed by what our lawmakers said—by the principle they laid down—not by any information we might have about how they themselves would have interpreted those principles or applied them in concrete cases.[135]

Judges learn about the abstract intent from the language and history of the text, as well as from the meaning that courts have given the text since its founding. In giving meaning to the constitutional text, judges should treat it with integrity ("constitutional integrity"). They should give the constitution the interpretation that shows its political history in the best light. Referring to a judge interpreting a constitution, Dworkin writes:

> His arguments embrace popular conviction and national tradition whenever these are pertinent to the sovereign question, which reading of constitutional history shows that history overall in its best light. For the same reason and toward the same end, they draw on his own convictions about justice and fairness and the right relation between them.[136]

---

[134] *Id.* at 380.

[135] R. Dworkin, *Freedom's Law: The Moral Reading of the American Constitution* 10 (1996).

[136] *Id.* at 389.

Purposive Interpretation and Dworkin's
System of Interpretation: Similarities

There are many similarities between purposive interpretation and Dworkin's system of interpretation.[137] Like Dworkin, I see interpretation as an ongoing process in which author and judge are partners in a creative chain. The judge should interpret society's values, not impose his or her subjective values on society. Like Dworkin, I see legislation as continuous activity, not a one-time act. The interpreter of a statute should aspire to a solution that treats legislation as a totality whose parts exist in harmony. Purposive interpretation, like Dworkin's system of interpretation, uses the present as its point of departure. It looks both forward and backward and, like Dworkin's system, avoids freezing the interpretive process at a fixed point in the past. Interpretation is dynamic, developing, and changing. Both systems use the abstract intent of members of the legislature, learned from legislative history, as an interpretive criterion—not their concrete subjective intent. Both systems take language into account, rejecting the nihilism of giving the text any meaning the judge desires. Neither system stops at language, however, relying also on general values common to members of society. Both fit the system of interpretation into a general framework of values. Both balance internally contradictory values by privileging the value most in accord with the system's general structure and the way it balances similar cases.

Purposive Interpretation and Dworkin's
System of Interpretation: Differences

Dworkin begins with the idea that law is based on integrity. To me, law is much more complex. It reflects society, and society is multifaceted. No one magic word like integrity (according to Dworkin) or efficiency (according to scholars of law and economics) or justice can capture law as a social phenomenon. My view is eclectic, with pragmatic foundations. In any event, I doubt that integrity alone can describe the development of law in every democratic legal system.[138] I am not convinced that the common law developed based on integrity. I certainly do not think that legislation reflects an overall conception of integrity. Dworkin argues that integrity aims at justice, fairness, and procedural due process. I see no reason to privilege these principles over the totality of society's fundamental democratic val-

---

[137] *Id.* at 398.
[138] P. Soper, "Dworkin's Domain," 100 *Harv. L. Rev.* 1166, 1182 (1987).

ues. Dworkin also fails to recognize the existence of judicial discretion, an important component of purposive interpretation. He does, however, recognize an exercise of judicial choice that resembles judicial discretion. According to Dworkin, judges sometimes face a number of interpretive options, guided only by the mandate to choose the most reasonable alternative.[139]

DWORKIN AND THE ABSTRACT INTENT OF THE AUTHOR

The abstract intent of the legislature and the constitutional author is central to Dworkin's system. He gives that intent full expression through the concept of integrity, which mandates giving a text the meaning that casts its political history in the best light. Purposive interpretation does not give the abstract intent of the text's author such a central role. When the type of text warrants it, the purposive interpreter gives abstract intent very little weight, even when the result fails to cast the political history of the text in its most favorable light. To the extent that it does seek to actualize the fundamental values of the system, purposive interpretation, like Dworkin's system, adopts a moral-political approach. It differs from Dworkin's system, however, in its treatment of those fundamental values. Purposive interpretation treats the fundamental values of the system as a purpose that coexists with—and sometimes supplants—subjective purpose. Dworkin, on the other hand, views the system's fundamental values as an extension of the abstract intent of the legislature. Such intent develops according to the principle of integrity.

5. PURPOSIVE INTERPRETATION AND FREE INTERPRETATION

Free Interpretation

According to free interpretation, there are no interpretive rules to guide judges. Instead, judges give texts a meaning that actualizes the values they think are desirable. Such values originate in the interpreter's conception of the good, not in the text and not in the mind of the author.[140] In essence, the free approach is not interpretive at all—it negates the guiding power of interpretive rules. Because the rules of interpretation have no ability to

---

[139] *Supra* p. 209.

[140] C. Curtis, "A Better Theory of Legal Interpretation," 3 *Vand. L. Rev.* 407, 415 (1950). *See also* W. Lucy, *Understanding and Explaining Adjudication* (1999) (referring to free interpretation as "heresy" in contrast to the "orthodoxy" of the other systems of interpretation we discussed).

guide, judges are free to formulate the content of the norm as they choose. The subjectivity of the interpreter replaces the subjectivity of the author. Free scholars made use of this approach in late-nineteenth-century and early-twentieth-century Europe.[141] The American realists imported their principles into the United States,[142] and critical legal studies scholars made use of them in the last quarter of the twentieth century.[143]

Free interpretation teaches that the language of the text is always vague and ambiguous. Understanding is a function of context, but the context itself is vague and ambiguous. Language does not restrain the interpreter. According to free interpretation, the language of the text is flexible enough to bear most of the aims that the interpreter seeks to reach by using it. There is almost no aim that the free interpreter cannot achieve through the language of the text.[144] The rules of interpretation do not restrain the interpreter, because they themselves must be interpreted. Law is politics,[145] and legal interpretation is a form of political activity. According to this "free" approach, it is impossible to formulate objective criteria to guide the judge. Any attempt to do so is just an attempt to obscure the reality that the judge interprets a text according to his or her political views. Free interpretation says we should openly admit that interpretation is the politics of law, and that the only real interpretive rule is the rule that a judge interprets a legal text according to his or her conception of the good and the just.

Critique of Free Interpretation

Free interpretation is not a system of interpretation. Interpretive freedom is not the product of a proper view of interpretation, but rather reflects the

---

[141] This is France's *Libre recherche scientifique* and Germany's *Freirechtslehre. See* J. Stone, *The Province and Function of Law; Law as Logic, Justice and Social Control; A Study in Jurisprudence* 152 (1946); F. Geny, *Methode d'Interpretation et Sources en Droit Privé Positif* (J. Mayda trans., Louisiana State Law Institute 2d ed. 1963) (1954).

[142] J. Gray, *The Nature and Sources of the Law* 128 (2d ed. 1927). Note that some American realists viewed the purpose of the statute as the criterion for interpreting it. *See supra* p. 225.

[143] P. Brest, "The Misconceived Quest for the Original Understanding," 60 *B.U. L. Rev.* 204 (1980); S. Levinson, "Law as Literature," 60 *Tex. L. Rev.* 373 (1982); M. Tushnet, "Following the Rules Laid Down: A Critique of Interpretivism and Neutral Principles," 96 *Harv. L. Rev.* 781 (1983); D. Kennedy, "The Turn to Interpretation," 58 *S. Cal. L. Rev.* 251 (1985); D. Kennedy, *A Critique of Adjudication* (1997). *See also* M. Kelman, *A Guide to Critical Legal Studies* (1987); R.W. Bauman, *Critical Legal Studies: A Guide to the Literature* (1996).

[144] Even the American constitutional provision mandating that the president be at least 35 years of age seems, under certain circumstances, to permit electing an 18-year-old president. *See* D'Amato, *supra* p. 25, note 73.

[145] D. Kairys, "Law and Politics," 52 *Geo. Wash. L. Rev.* 243 (1984); J.W. Singer, "The

deconstruction of law and of the possibility of interpreting it. Interpretation under the free approach is a political act not because it expresses constitutional considerations, but rather because it has no rules, and every "interpreter" does politics, not law. The deconstructionist movement in literary criticism has influenced these approaches to law.[146]

It is generally true that law is a tool for achieving social aims, and thus constitutes a political tool. Law is a normative system, with its own rules and its own coherence. It exists not for its own sake, but to achieve certain aims that are social, not "legal." We could call them "political aims," but to do so would create an erroneous impression of division and conflict. It would confuse the means (politics) with the goal (social and principled aims). I believe that the legal system—as coherent and autonomous as it may be in its formal conceptions—operates in order to achieve social goals. Law's formal structure includes "air valves" or open-ended terms whose social goal is to connect law, as a normative device, to social reality. If the judge is an engine, society is the fuel that allows him or her to operate. Social reality and social forces drive law and determine the aims of legal discipline. To this extent, we can accept some precepts of the free approach.[147]

My main quarrel with free interpretation is not over the essence of law (at the macro level), but rather over positive law, in general, and the interpretation of texts (at the micro level), in particular. Even at the micro level, I recognize the existence of hard cases in which the interpreter's subjective decision ultimately determines the interpretation. I disagree, however, about how frequently such cases occur. Free interpretation says that every case is "difficult." I cannot accept that. Law inevitably contains uncertainty,[148] but uncertainty does not surround every legal text, in every circumstance. Most legal texts, in most circumstances created by life's practical exigencies, have a single, unique meaning. For law to fulfill its general aim, it must recognize that the language of an individual text sets limits

---

Player and the Cards: Nihilism and Legal Theory," 94 *Yale L.J.* 1 (1984); G. Peller, "The Metaphysics of American Law," 73 *Cal. L. Rev.* 1151 (1985); A. D'Amato, "Can Any Legal Theory Constrain Any Judicial Decision?" 43 *U. Miami L. Rev.* 513 (1989); *The Politics of Law: A Progressive Critique* (D. Kairys ed., 3d ed. 1998).

[146] Symposium, "Deconstruction and the Possibility of Justice," 11 *Cardozo L. Rev.* 919 (1990). *See also Deconstruction and the Possibility of Justice* (D. Cornell, M. Rosenfeld, D.G. Carlson eds., 1992); J. Culler, *On Deconstruction: Theory and Criticism after Structuralism* 123 (1982).

[147] *See, generally,* Kennedy, *supra* p. 298, note 143. For an excellent analysis claiming that free interpretation is not so far apart from the orthodox approaches, see Lucy, *supra* p. 297, note 140 at 135.

[148] L. Solum, "On the Indeterminacy Crisis: Critiquing Critical Dogma," 54 *U. Chi. L. Rev.* 462 (1987); K. Greenawalt, "How Law Can Be Determinate," 38 *UCLA L. Rev.* 1 (1990).

for the operation of the norm trapped within it. A judge's power to insert content into a text exists, but it is not completely free, and it is not unlimited. Recognizing the existence of law means recognizing rules for its interpretation.

That is my primary criticism of the free approach. It is inappropriate because it ignores the independent existence of a legal text. It fails to distinguish between an existing text and the creation of a new text. It does not actualize proper constitutional values. If words can bear *any* meaning at all, then the text has no meaning at all, and its author is of no importance. Indeed, if a text has no "objective" meaning, it is hard to understand how scholars of free interpretation expect the reader to understand their own writing. If every text can be given any desired meaning, why can't I decide that the free approach is not free? So long as communication among human beings is possible, and people rely on language as a device for understanding, the free approach to language cannot be valid. Interpretation with no semantic boundaries is not interpretation.

Free interpretation claims that law is based on values and goals. According to the free approach, however, interpreters are not guided by these values and goals, but act according to their political aims. To this, I counter that law is a device for achieving social aims and values, expressed by judges. They may enjoy a certain degree of freedom to balance those aims, but they are not free to create them. Even where uncertainty in law gives judges discretion, that discretion is far from absolute.[149] Constitutional requirements act as a de facto restraint on complete interpretive freedom. Principles of democracy and separation of powers bar such freedom, which would undermine the rule of law and public confidence in the judiciary. Society's elected officials, not judges, play the primary role in determining social aims (consideration of democracy). The judge is a junior partner in the interpretive project (consideration of separation of powers). Interpretation that reflects the judge's subjectivity harms security, certainty, and the reasonable expectations of individuals (rule of law considerations). Under a free system of interpretation, the public would view judges as politicians and lose trust in them (consideration of public faith in the judiciary). A judge's personal views will sometimes diverge from society's fundamental perspectives and from its constitutional and systemic structure. Giving expression to those views may undermine important societal principles (considerations of constitutional and systemic structure). A judge's personal views may also infringe on the autonomy of individuals who use private law texts to create norms for themselves (considerations of autonomy and the private will).

---

[149] O. Fiss, "The Death of the Law," 72 *Cornell L. Rev.* 1, 10 (1986). *See also* O. Fiss, "The Law Regained," 74 *Cornell L. Rev.* 245 (1989).

Judges have discretion, but they must use it to formulate and achieve social aims. Judicial discretion is limited, in accordance with the status of the judge as a junior partner in the interpretive project. If the text being interpreted is a constitution, the constitutional assembly is the senior partner. In the case of a statute, the legislature is the senior partner. For a contract, the contractual parties are the senior partners. For a will, the senior partner is the testator. I do not claim that judges are absolutely bound, but neither are they completely free. The interpreter may—and sometimes must—formulate social policy, but only in the interstices created by the senior partner.[150] If the judge were to become the sole actor in the interpretive project, the constitutional structure of both law and society would change. Law would become a tool for achieving the aims of an unelected minority. Any attempt to recognize cooperation and reciprocal relationships between the branches of government and between them and the individual would become bankrupt, and the interpretive project would lose its legitimacy.[151] Western legal communities do not see law this way. Absent a revolutionary change in the way we view law, the judiciary, and interpretation, free interpretation is unacceptable.

6. CRITIQUE OF PURPOSIVE INTERPRETATION AND SOME RESPONSES

Critique from Subjective and Objective Systems

Because purposive interpretation is neither purely objective nor purely subjective, it is subject to criticism from both subjective and objective systems of interpretation. I addressed this criticism in my analysis of the various systems of interpretation.[152] But what is the critique of purposive interpretation as an independent system? I identify three primary criticisms: *First*, purposive interpretation tries to achieve the impossible by formulating a theory of interpretation that applies to all legal texts; *second*, purposive interpretation confers overly broad interpretive discretion to the interpreting judge; *third*, purposive interpretation is too complicated. I discuss these objections and respond to them below.

---

[150] R. Pound, "Mechanical Jurisprudence," 8 *Colum. L. Rev.* 605 (1908). Justice Holmes uses the phrase "interstitially" in his opinion in *Southern Pacific, supra* p. 251, note 146 at 221: "I recognize without hesitation that judges do and must legislate, but they can do so only interstitially; they are confined from molar to molecular motions."

[151] S. Carter, "Constitutional Adjudication and the Indeterminate Text: A Preliminary Defense of an Imperfect Muddle," 94 *Yale L.J.* 821 (1985).

[152] *Supra* p. 260.

A COMPREHENSIVE SYSTEM OF INTERPRETATION IS OVERLY AMBITIOUS

The first objection is this: No comprehensive theory of interpretation can answer every interpretive problem without relying on judicial discretion.[153] This criticism is particularly strong where the interpretive theory does not restrict itself to a particular kind of legal text, like a constitution or statute, but rather seeks an interpretive solution for all legal texts. Purposive interpretation, however, readily acknowledges the need for judicial discretion in a system that provides answers to all interpretive problems. What remains, then, is the claim that it is overly ambitious to create a system of interpretation that applies to all legal texts,[154] that each type of legal text has its own unique characteristics, and that it would be artificial to try to lump them all together.[155]

I acknowledge that there is no divine or hermeneutic decree mandating a uniform system of interpretation for all legal texts. I claim only that legal texts contain more similarities than differences, and that purposive interpretation expresses these similarities by giving every legal text a meaning, within the limits of language, that realizes the (subjective and objective) purpose of the text. That element is common to all legal texts, and it supersedes what is different about them. Furthermore, purposive interpretation does not ignore or suppress the elements that divide texts. To the contrary: It takes the differences into consideration and gives them full expression by tailoring the internal balance between subjective and objective purpose accordingly. It gives each text full range to express its individuality. Such expression does not lead to a separate, independent system of interpretation for each text but rather takes place within purposive interpretation.

Purposive interpretation is built on the internal tension between the forces that unify its different components under the banner of "the purpose of the text" and the centrifugal forces that seek to recognize each text as its own interpretive unit. I think the unifying forces are stronger than those that divide. It is therefore possible to construct a comprehensive theory of interpretation that unifies all legal texts, while recognizing the individuality of each text. I think purposive interpretation overcomes the in-

---

[153] *See* Farber and Sherry, *supra* p. 286, note 105.

[154] Betti tried this in the past. *See* E. Betti, *Teoria Generale della Interpretazione* (1955). His book has been translated into German (E. Betti, *Allgemeine Auslegungslehre als Methodik der Geisteswissenschaften* [J. Mohr trans., 1967]), but not into English. For a discussion of Betti's theory, see Levi, *supra* p. 238, note 88 at 100; J. Buttigieg, "The Growing Labors of the Lengthened Way: The Hermeneutics of Emilio Betti," 34 *Union Seminary Q. Rev.* 97 (issue 2 1979); G. Wright, "On a General Theory of Interpretation: The Betti-Gadamer Dispute in Legal Hermeneutics," 32 *Am. J. Juris.* 191 (1987).

[155] For a criticism of the trend of analogizing statutory interpretation from contractual interpretation, see M.L. Movsesian, "Are Statutes Really 'Legislative Bargains'? The Failure of the Contract Analogy in Statutory Interpretation," 76 *N. Carolina L. Rev.* 1145 (1998).

ternal tension in which it exists. It does not splinter into separate interpretive theories for wills, contracts, statutes, and constitutions, and it facilitates cross-fertilization of interpretive viewpoints. By adopting purposive interpretation, we overcome the phenomenon in which the interpreter of a statute or constitution ignores the interpretation of a contract or will, and the interpreter of a contract or will ignores statutory and constitutional interpretation. By taking all texts into account comprehensively, we strengthen the different components of purposive interpretation and made progress toward developing a unitary theory that recognizes the individuality of its components.

PURPOSIVE INTERPRETATION DICTATES OVERLY BROAD DISCRETION FOR THE JUDGE

The second objection is that purposive interpretation gives the judge overly broad discretion. The need to balance between subjective and objective purpose and the multiplicity of presumptions of objective purpose expand a judge's discretion without providing enough limiting rules. This expansion of discretion undermines security and certainty in law and, eventually, undermines public faith in its judges.

It is true that purposive interpretation is based on a component of judicial discretion, but that is necessarily true of any system of interpretation that aspires to provide a solution to every interpretive problem.[156] The question is a matter of degree. I do not think purposive interpretation gives judges broader discretion than other systems of interpretation; to the contrary, I think that purposive interpretation restricts judicial discretion more than other systems. Unlike many systems of interpretation, purposive interpretation adopts a normative stance on the relationship between the different presumptions (subjective and objective). Whereas other systems leave some decisions buried in the intuition of the interpreter, purposive interpretation pushes those issues to the surface and forces the interpreter to adopt a normative stance, dictated by rules and principles, with respect to those issues. Other systems create a gap between rhetoric and practice, for example, by paying lip service to legislative intent but defining it as the intent of the reasonable legislature, which in turn becomes the intent of the court. Purposive interpretation, on the other hand, tells the truth. It acknowledges the need to give expression to the real intent of the author, but notes that when there is no credible information about that intent, or such intent is not relevant to resolving the interpretive problem, then the interpreter abandons legislative intent in favor of the fundamental values of the system. It acknowledges that the ultimate purpose of a text is a legal

[156] *Supra* p. 207.

construction based on the balance between different purposes. It acknowledges the existence of judicial discretion, limited judicial subjectivity, and judicial creativity. It lays its cards on the table, demanding complete transparency of the judicial work of interpretation. It subjects judges to ongoing professional review, strengthening confidence in the judiciary. Above all, however, purposive interpretation allows interpretation to fulfill its aim. Purposive interpretation achieves the goal of law; it realizes the role of the judge in a democracy; its dynamic approach allows judges to bridge the gap between law and society; its constitutional approach gives full expression to formal and substantive democracy.

PURPOSIVE INTERPRETATION IS TOO COMPLICATED

The third objection is that purposive interpretation is too complicated. While the second objection claims there is too much judicial discretion based in too few rules and principles, the third objection claims there are too many rules and principles that burden the interpreter.

At first glance, there is something to this claim, but only at first glance. Any system of interpretation appears complicated or even threatening until it becomes familiar. Once an interpreter becomes schooled in purposive interpretation and begins to understand it, the complication disappears. Indeed, in most cases, particularly at the trial level, there is no real dispute over the purpose of the text. In those instances, a judge may take a shortcut.[157] Whether starting with objective or subjective purpose, usually the judge will immediately reach the ultimate purpose. That purpose—without resort to judicial discretion—will resolve the interpretive problem. Only in a minority of cases will the interpreter need to exhaust every avenue of purposive interpretation. In these few instances, there are no easy solutions, and the interpreter will have to go through the entire interpretive process. There is no reason to assume, however, that that process is longer or more complicated in purposive interpretation than in the other systems of interpretation.

Up to this point, I have discussed the general doctrines that characterize purposive interpretation. I emphasized the commonalities among legal texts and the way in which purposive interpretation takes the particular character of each text into consideration. I will now address the different legal texts and their treatment within purposive interpretation. Having dealt with purposive interpretation as a unitary system that applies to different legal texts, I will use Part 3 to focus on the various legal texts (will, contract, statute, and constitution) and their purposive interpretation.

[157] *Supra* p. 206.

Part Three

INTERPRETATION IN LAW

CHAPTER TWELVE

The Interpretation of Wills

1. THE UNIQUENESS OF A WILL AND HOW IT AFFECTS INTERPRETATION

The Uniqueness of a Will

Three traits characterize a will:[1] *First*, a will is the product of the testator's intent. Testators may express their intent in any language, lexicon, or sign they choose. They may call black, white, and white, black. Language is their raw material. That is the difference between a will and a public law document, addressed to the public and therefore obligated to speak in a language that the public understands. A will reflects the testator's thoughts and intent. He or she therefore may choose to express it any way he or she likes. Wills share this linguistic flexibility with contracts. *Second*, the testator must formulate the will in a particular format. While a contract may take any form, a will can only assume one of a finite number of forms. *Third*, a will is a unilateral legal act. It enters into force upon the testator's writing or speaking it, without further legal process.[2] It is an ambulatory norm.[3] It does not create a reliance interest.[4] True, sometimes heirs expect to inherit from their loved one, but the law does not protect such expectations while the testator is alive.[5] These particular traits of wills influence their interpretation, as we shall see.

Uniqueness in Interpretation: Superior Role of Testator's Intent

Purposive interpretation ascribes tremendous weight to the intent of the legator as an expression of the unique character of a will. The "commandment to honor the wishes of the dead"[6] is a common thread running

---

[1] Barak, *supra* p. 15, note 40 at 48.

[2] P. Piotet, *Erbrecht* 205 (1978).

[3] T. Atkinson, *Law of Wills* (2d ed., 1953). A will is "completed" when written, but it confers rights only upon the death of the testator. In the interim period, it is revocable.

[4] W.H. Page, 4 *Page on the Law of Wills* 2 (W. Bowet & D.H. Parker eds., rev. ed. 1961).

[5] A. Corbin, 3 *Corbin on Contracts: A Comprehensive Treaty on the Roles of Contract Law* 4 (1960).

[6] Rabbi Meir is credited with this phrase. *Babylonian Talmud*, Tractate Gitin, 14:72 (3d to 5th centuries C.E.). *See also* A. Golack, 3 *Foundations of Jewish Law* 126 (1999).

through all legal systems,[7] dating back to ancient Jewish law. The intent of the testator—an expression of his or her constitutional right to dignity and property—is the "polar star" of will interpretation.[8] Where subjective purpose (the intent of the testator) clashes with objective purpose (the intent of the reasonable testator or of the system), subjective purpose prevails.[9] The testator's intent is his or her historical, psychological intent as formulated at the time the will was made.[10]

The Meaning of a Will and Its Objective Purpose

While subjective purpose occupies a senior position in the interpretation of wills, it is not the only factor. Objective purpose and the presumptions derived from it continue to apply, immediately and always. They are the background for understanding the subjective purpose. They may be decisive in choosing between contradictory subjective purposes. They apply in the absence of a relevant subjective purpose. Objective purpose occupies a secondary but more than marginal place in the interpretation of wills. Usually, when courts interpret wills, they do so without knowing the (subjective) intent of the testator. They must make their decision based on objective purpose. This is certainly the case in a joint and mutual will, for which a court must consider the joint intent of both testators. From the point of view of each of the testators, the court considers a fact external to his or her intent. We should openly acknowledge this objective aspect of will interpretation.[11] We should not falsely claim adherence to subjectivity,[12] employing the rhetoric of subjective intent but the practice of ob-

[7] *See* Art. 133 of the B.G.B. applicable to the interpretation of wills. French and Italian law include the interpretation of wills in their code provisions on contractual interpretation, requiring contracts to be interpreted according to the intent of the parties (and thus, a will, according to the intent of the testator). *See Leçons de Droit Civil, Successions Liberalités*, vol. 4 (3d ed. 1980); C. Grosetti, "Interpretazione de Negozi Giuridici, 'Mortis Cousa,'" 8 *Novissimo Digesto Italiano* 907 (1962). On American law, see Restatement of the Law, *Property (Donative Transfers) Tentative Draft No. 1* (1995) (hereinafter: *Tentative Draft*). On English law, see H.S. Theobald, *The Law of Wills* (15th ed. 1993).

[8] *Smith v. Coffin* (1795) 126 E.R. 641, 644 ("The question always must be, what was the intention of the testator? This is the polar star by which we must be guided") (Buller, J.). Other scholars refer to such intention as "the queen of the will" (H. Swinburne, *A Brief Treatise of Testaments and Wills* 9 (1590 4 Photo, reprint 1978)).

[9] Feeney, *Canadian Law of Wills, supra* p. 79, note 74 at 1.

[10] *In Re Rowland* [1963] 1 ch. 1, 10 ("True it is that you must discover his intention from the words he used: but you must put upon his words the meaning which they bore to him . . . not the meaning which a philologist would put upon them") (Denning, J.).

[11] Atkinson, *supra* p. 307, note 3 at 813. *See also Boai v. Metropolitan Museum of Art*, 292 F. 303, 304 (S.D.N.Y 1923).

[12] L. Sims, *Handbook of the Law of Future Interests* 183 (2d ed. 1966).

jective approach. If intent does not exist, or if we have no information about it, we should acknowledge as much. Purposive interpretation does so. It fully acknowledges the role of the intent of the reasonable author and of the system (objective purpose) as a secondary but important criterion for interpreting a will.

2. THE LANGUAGE OF A WILL

A statute is a means of communication between the legislature and the public. It therefore must use language that the public understands. A will, on the other hand, expresses the intent of the testator. Testators may express themselves any way they choose. Of course, a will is a form of communication with the legal system, as represented by the judge who interprets the will. The judge must therefore understand the will. If the testator drafts the will in a language that the judge does not understand, the judge may interpret the will in a way that does not realize the testator's intent. The judge may even invalidate a provision of the will because the language is too vague. A testator willing to run that risk may use his or her own private language or code. He may bequeath his property to "Mother," meaning his wife, whom he calls "Mother." A testator may bequeath her "books" to X, when by "books," she means her bottles of wine. Central to "honoring the wishes of the dead" is allowing the testator to create his or her own private lexicon. I do not claim that this lexicon determines the legal meaning of the will. The legal meaning of the will depends on its purpose. I mean only that a judge must include both the private and public meanings of the language of a will as part of the will's range of semantic possibilities. Many legal systems take this approach.[13]

3. THE PURPOSE OF A WILL

The Essence of the Purpose of a Will

The purpose of a will is the interest, goals, values, aims, policies, and function that the will is designed to achieve. It is the platform at the foundation of the will. It is the will's "plan" for distributing the testator's prop-

---

[13] On the situation in Germany, see Münchener Kommentar, 9 *Bürgerliches Gesetzbuch* 941 vol. 3 (3d ed. 1997); On England, see H.S. Theobald, *Theobald on Wills* 216 (15th ed. 1993). Canada, Australia, and New Zealand take a similar approach. *See* Feeney, *supra* p. 79, note 74 at 52; I.J. Hardingham, M.A. Neave, H.A.J. Ford, *Wills and Intestacy in Australia and New Zealand* 287 (2d ed. 1989). On the situation in the United States, see the *Tentative Draft, supra* p. 308, note 7 at 31.

erty. Such purpose—like the purpose of a contract, statute, and constitution—is a normative concept. It is a legal construction, composed of objective and subjective purpose. Subjective purpose is the intention of the testator, an expression of his or her actual will. It can be proven through any evidence used to prove a person's intent. Objective purpose is the concrete intent the testator would have had, had he or she behaved as a reasonable person. If that intent is unknown, then it is the intent of the reasonable testator. At the highest level of abstraction, it reflects the fundamental values of the system. Subjective intent occupies a central position in determining the purpose of a will, but the purpose of a will is not synonymous with the testator's intent. The intent of the testator is a primary source for determining purpose, but it is not the only source. The purpose of a will is an abstract, normative concept containing both actual and hypothetical aspects. Every will has a number of purposes (subjective and objective). In a tiny minority of cases, these purposes conflict. Judges must resolve those conflicts in determining the will's ultimate purpose.[14]

Subjective Purpose of a Will

The subjective purpose of a will is the interests, goals, values, aims, policies, and function that the testator seeks to achieve through the will. It is real intent. It is the images that in fact went through the testator's mind. It is composed of biological-psychological-historical facts that took place in the past. Once a testator has revealed his or her intent and made a will, the judge should interpret it according to the testator's actual intent. Such intent may be reasonable or unreasonable; it may be just or unjust; it may be balanced by the standards of the system or it may be capricious and absurd. We need not assume that every testator is unreasonable, malicious, or capricious. To the contrary: We may assume that every testator exercises reason, fairness, and integrity. We may assume that every testator uses his or her will to actualize the fundamental values of the system. Hence, purposive interpretation's presumption that a will's subjective purpose is consistent with its objective purpose. However, that presumption is rebuttable. It is rebutted if the intent of the testator proves to be inconsistent with the intent of the system. It is rebutted if the circumstances surrounding the making of the will show the testator's subjective purpose to diverge from the objective purpose. It is rebutted by proof that the testator could not have conceived of the content of the presumption of objective purpose.

---

[14] *Infra* p. 316.

Subjective purpose tells the truth. It reflects true intent. It applies, however, only when there is reliable information about that intent.[15]

SOURCES OF SUBJECTIVE PURPOSE

An interpreter learns about the subjective purpose of a will from two sources: *first*, the will itself, and *second*, the circumstances surrounding its making. The first source is intrinsic (textual context), while the second source is extrinsic (external context).

The first (internal) source treats the will, like all legal texts, as a whole. All legal systems adopt that approach to a will.[16] An interpreter treats the will as a whole regardless of whether or not its language is "plain." Of course, here we encounter the problem of the hermeneutic circle: To understand any provision of a will, we must understand the will as a whole; but to understand the will as a whole, we must understand its parts. Pre-understanding rescues us from this dilemma.[17] We approach a will with the totality of our assumptions, perspectives, and points of departure. Using this pre-understanding, we formulate an understanding of part of the will, which helps us develop a preliminary understanding of the whole thing. We then move back and forth from the part to the whole.

The other source of information about subjective purpose is the circumstances surrounding the making of the will. These are the ever-expanding circles of reality framing the making of the will. They are the "story" at the core of the will.[18] The interpreter consults the circumstances in order to formulate the testator's intent. The most immediate circumstances—the innermost circle—are the circumstances under which the will was made. The next closest circle is the events and facts occurring before and after the making of the will.[19] The circumstances surrounding the making of the will are probative of subjective purpose only if the testator was aware of them. If they were not in his or her consciousness, even if a reasonable testator would have known about them, they have no probative value. The standard of proof for demonstrating these circumstances is the civil standard of a preponderance of the evidence.

English law does not admit direct evidence of a testator's intent as part

[15] Z. Chafee, "The Disorderly Conduct of Words," 41 *Colum. L. Rev.* 381, 398 (1941).

[16] Feeney, *supra* p. 79, note 74 at 18; Page, *supra* p. 307, note 4 at 42.

[17] *Supra* p. 57.

[18] On "storytelling" in law, *see* J. Baron, "The Many Promises of Storytelling in Law," 23 *Rutgers L.J.* 79 (1991). For an application of this approach to the interpretation of wills, *see* J. Baron, "Intention, Interpretation and Stories," 42 *Duke L.J.* 630 (1992).

[19] Feeney, *supra* p. 79, note 74 at 16; E.A. Kellaway, *Principles of Legal Interpretation of Statutes, Contracts and Wills* 571 (1995).

of the extrinsic evidence demonstrating the circumstances of his or her will.[20] The English Law Reform Committee split over the issue,[21] but the English Parliament has adopted its majority opinion barring the introduction of direct evidence.[22] American law has no uniform opinion on the matter, but the modern trend is to admit direct extrinsic evidence.[23] Israeli law rejects the English approach.[24] Indeed, the English rule is puzzling. If we take the testator's intent seriously, why not admit information about it from all reliable sources?

WHEN MAY AN INTERPRETER CONSULT THE CIRCUMSTANCES OF THE WILL'S CREATION?

Purposive interpretation's general rule permitting an interpreter to refer to the circumstances surrounding the creation of a legal text in every circumstance[25] applies to wills. This is also the traditional approach of Continental law,[26] and American law is coming into conformity. In the nineteenth century, the prevailing American doctrine permitted an interpreter to consult the circumstances surrounding a will's creation only if the meaning of the will or its language was unclear. If the meaning of the will (or contract) was plain, an interpreter could not consult the circumstances. Wigmore criticized that approach: "The . . . 'plain meaning' is simply the meaning of the people who did *not* write the document."[27] Wigmore applied this criticism to the interpretation of wills, contracts, and statutes. Gradually, the American doctrine changed. The 1940 *Restatement of Property* registered the change, allowing judges to consult the circumstances always.[28] The *Restatement*'s approach took root,[29] although the older doctrine did not completely die out. The *Tentative Draft* adopted the view that an interpreter may always consult the circumstances.[30]

---

[20] Feeney, *supra* p. 79, note 74 at 66; Page, *supra* p. 307, note 4 at 221; Note, "Admissibility of Testator's Declarations of Intention," 17 *S. Cal. L. Rev.* 276 (1965).

[21] The minority opinion in the committee report supported admitting such evidence. Law Reform Committee, *Interpretation of Wills* 19 (Cmnd 5301 1973).

[22] Art. 21 of the Administration of Justice Act, 1982.

[23] *Tentative Draft, supra* p. 308, note 7 at 14.

[24] C.A. 45/62 *Holon v. Executors of the Estate of Aryeh Shenker*, 16 P.D. 1707, 1710.

[25] *Supra* p. 143.

[26] E. Schanze, "Interpretation of Wills—An Essay Critical and Comparative," *Comparative and Historical Essays in Scots Law* 104 (D.L.C. Miller and D.W. Miers eds., 1992). *See also* J. von Staudinger, *Kommentar zum Bürgerlichen Gesetz mit Einführungsgesetz und Nebengesetzen* 769 (vol. 5, 1996); P. Malaurie and L. Aynes, *Droit Civil, les Successions, les Libéralités* 288 (3d ed. 1995).

[27] J.H. Wigmore, 9 *Evidence in Trials at Common Law* 198 (Chadbourne rev. ed., 1981).

[28] 3 *Restatement of Property (Future Interests)* 1198 (1940).

[29] W. Page, 2 *Page on the Law of Wills* 819 (1941).

[30] *Tentative Draft, supra* p. 308, note 7 at 6, 19.

English law underwent similar developments. From the nineteenth century until the 1980s, English judges were permitted to consult the circumstances only if the language of the will was not plain. That literal rule applied to the interpretation of all legal texts. Change came with the 1982 Administration of Justice Act that liberalized the possibility of consulting the circumstances.[31] Free access, however, is still barred.[32]

A Will's Objective Purpose

The objective purpose of a will is the purpose that the testator, as a reasonable person, would have placed at its core. In the absence of more specific information, it is the purpose that a reasonable person would have sought to achieve through the will. It is the will that actualizes the fundamental values of the system ("intention of the system"), including equality, justice, reasonableness, and fairness in distributing the testator's property.[33] It also takes the public interest into account, for example by preventing a situation in which heirs can profit from their misdeeds.[34] A will may be unilateral, but it is not made on a desert island. The judiciary sustains and implements a will. A will draws life from the system and fertilizes the system in return—introducing an element of objectivity into the purpose of the will.

At a low level of abstraction, the judge learns about objective purpose from the will and the circumstances of its creation. At a higher level of abstraction, the judge learns about objective purpose from the law. Such purpose should not, however, be considered if it cannot be achieved through the language of the will. Purposive interpretation's position that "interpretive work is not limited to the words, but the words limit the interpretation"[35] applies to objective purpose as well. There must be a linguistic

[31] *See* Art. 21 of the statute. The relevant provision is in subsection (c), permitting an interpreter to consult the circumstances: "in so far as evidence, other than evidence of the testator's intention, shows that the language used in any part of it is ambiguous in the light of surrounding circumstances."

[32] But see legislation from the Australian state of Victoria, Art. 22A(1) of the Wills Act. The need for reform has been noted in New Zealand. J.K. Maxton, "Construction of Wills: A Need for Reform" [1983] *New Zealand L.J.* 69. Ireland takes a different stance, permitting free access to the circumstances. See article 90 of the 1965 Irish Law of Succession.

[33] E. Halbach, "Stare Decisis and Rules of Construction in Wills and Trusts," 52 *Cal. L. Rev.* 921 (1964).

[34] For a history of the "murderous heir," see A. Reppy, "The Slayer's Bounty—History of Problem in Anglo-American Law," 19 *N.Y.U. L. Rev.* 229 (1942). *See also* M.L. Fellows, "The Slayer Rule: Not Solely a Matter of Equity," 71 *Iowa L. Rev.* 489, 538 (1986). For Dworkin's position, *see supra* p. 63. Dworkin resolves the problem through the doctrine of filling in a lacuna in the statute.

[35] F.H. 40/80 *Koenig v. Cohen*, 36(3) P.D. 701, 703.

hook—an Archimedean foothold in the text of the will—through which objective purpose can be achieved.

One might ask whether the objective purpose of a will is established at the time the will is made or at the time it is interpreted. I tend to think that, in looking at objective purpose at a low level of abstraction ("What would the testator, as a reasonable person, have wanted?"), the relevant time is the time the will was made. At higher levels of abstraction ("the intention of the system"), the relevant time frame is the moment of interpretation.

Presumptions to Identify Objective Purpose

Objective purpose appears before the judge in the form of presumptions of purpose.[36] These presumptions always apply, irrespective of the apparent clarity of the text or the given phase of interpretation. Presumptions of purpose, as the name indicates, are not absolute. A contradictory subjective purpose of the testator, as learned from the will and circumstances, rebuts them. The mere fact that an individual testator could not have intended the objective purpose is not enough to rebut the presumption, however. The presumption of objective purpose is rebutted only when inconsistent with the actual will of the testator.

What are these presumptions of purpose? They vary with each legal system. The following is a partial list of presumptions of objective purpose accepted in most legal systems:

> **1.** The presumption that the subjective purpose of the will arises from its natural and ordinary language,[37] referred to in case law and in the literature as "the golden rule."[38] Purposive interpretation replaces the golden rule with the "golden presumption," reflecting a desire to guarantee stability and certainty.[39]
>
> **2.** The presumption that the provisions of the will do not contradict each other; that the will is consistent with a previous will; that identical phrases in the will have the same meaning, and that different phrases have different meanings.
>
> **3.** The presumption that the will is valid. This is the "rule of validity" that purposive interpretation turns into the presumption of validity.

---

[36] Barak, *supra* p. 15, note 40 at 287.

[37] Theobold, *supra* p. 309, note 13 at 200.

[38] *Supra* p. 34.

[39] We can supplement it with an additional presumption, that subjective purpose arises from the plain and unequivocal language of the will. *See* C.A. 239/89 *Shoresh v. Galili*, 46(1) P.D. 861, 867.

4. The presumption that the will integrates into the relevant law of succession. This presumption has implications in a number of different fields. For example, there is a presumption against legally dispossessing an heir from inheritance.[40] When a legator's will refers to "my heirs," he or she is presumed to mean the order of succession prescribed by law.[41] When a legator bequeaths property to two heirs, one instead of the other, he or she is presumed to do so according to the relevant law of succession's provisions for substituting one heir for another. When the legator bequeaths property to two heirs, one after the other, he or she is presumed to do so according to the law of succession's provisions for inheritance by one heir after another.

5. The presumption that the will integrates into the general law.[42] A will's property provisions are presumed to integrate into the law of property; its provisions for obligation into the law of obligations; its tax provisions into tax law.[43]

6. The presumption that the will applies to assets and people as they exist on the day of the testator's death. This expresses the approach that "the will speaks from the day of death."[44]

7. The presumption that the will applies to all of a testator's estate, not just part of it.[45]

8. The presumption that the will justly divides the testator's property.[46] This presumption reflects the legal system's fundamental values. These values guide us toward just results; they bind us to do what is good and right; they aim to prevent malice and injustice. A will is therefore interpreted to prevent an unfit heir (such as the heir who murders his or her legator) from inheriting.

9. The presumption of egalitarian distribution of the testator's property. The testator is presumed to have sought to guarantee equality among heirs of the same level of relationship to the legator. This is consistent with the spirit of modern legal systems. It sometimes takes the form of a legal rule. I favor treating it as a presumption.

10. The presumption that the will advances the public interest. The interpreter of a will should assume that the reasonable testator sought to advance the public interest.[47] Hence, it is presumed that expensive paintings should

---

[40] Page, *supra* p. 307, note 4 at 111; Feeney, *supra* p. 79, note 74 at 27.

[41] Piotet, *supra* p. 307, note 2 at 211.

[42] Page, *supra* p. 307, note 4 at 92; Feeney, *supra* p. 79, note 74 at 22.

[43] *Tentative Draft, supra* p. 308, note 7 at 48.

[44] Kellaway, *supra* p. 311, note 19 at 530.

[45] Feeney, *supra* p. 79, note 74 at 24; Kellaway, *supra* p. 311, note 19 at 599; Page, *supra* p. 307, note 4 at 98.

[46] Feeney, *supra* p. 79, note 74 at 21. *See also* C.H. Sherrin, "The Words of Change in the Law of Wills," 40 *The Conveyancer and Property Lawyer* 66 (1976).

[47] *Tentative Draft, supra* p. 308, note 7 at 82.

not be destroyed, manuscripts should not be ruined, and antiques should not disappear.[48]

11. The presumption that the will does not bar access to the courts for arbitration of serious claims made in good faith.

12. The presumption that the will achieves reasonable, fair, non-absurd results acceptable in interpersonal relationships. This presumption is an expression of the legal system's fundamental values.

13. The presumption that the will meets reasonable expectations. This leads to the presumption of egalitarian distribution among heirs and the presumption that the will is not designed to infringe on the freedom or autonomy of an heir in, for example, matters of marriage and adoption. The purpose of the will is presumed to be the distribution of property in a way that is customary and acceptable in the testator's community.

14. The presumption that the will prefers family members over strangers. Intact families reflect the preferred way of the world. Within that presumption, "close" family members are to be preferred over "distant" relatives.[49] The will is presumed to preserve the order of family relationships.[50]

15. The presumption that the will preserves human rights. Hence the presumption that the testator sought an egalitarian distribution among heirs at the same level, as well as the presumption that the testator did not intend to discriminate based on religion, race, or gender.

The Ultimate Purpose of a Will

We have now reached the final stage. The interpreter studies the different pieces of information—in the form of presumptions—about the purpose of the will. When all the information points in the same direction, the work is easy. The interpreter determines the ultimate purpose of the will according to the information. He or she determines the legal meaning of the will's language.

Sometimes, however, the data about the purpose of the will point in different directions. Then, the interpreter must decide which data to privilege. Because of a will's unique character, the interpreter accords decisive weight to subjective purpose. In case of contradiction among data about the subjective purpose, information pointing to a primary purpose prevails over information pointing to a subordinate purpose, and a specific purpose

---

[48] *See, e.g., Eyerman v. Mercantile Trust Co.*, 524 S.W.2d 210 (Mo. App. 1975) (refusing to enforce a provision in will directing the demolition of testatrix's house because it would harm neighboring property owners, in violation of public policy).

[49] *Tentative Draft, supra* p. 308, note 7 at 81.

[50] *Id.* at 81.

prevails over a general purpose. Similarly, in deciding between data at the same (subjective) level, an interpreter should give preference to data that is consistent with the will's objective purpose.

What does the interpreter do if there is no relevant information about subjective purpose? In that case, ultimate purpose depends on the data about objective purpose. When those pieces of information contradict each other, the lower level of abstraction (how the testator would have decided, had he or she considered the matter) prevails over a higher level of abstraction (how a reasonable testator would decide). When the presumptions of objective purpose contradict each other, an interpreter should balance them according to the weight of the values they represent.[51] If the scale is balanced, the interpreter must exercise discretion to come to a decision.[52] In my opinion, the interpreter should choose the purpose that best achieves justice. Other purposive interpreters may use different criteria. It is a question of judicial discretion,[53] exercised pragmatically.

[51] *Supra* p. 178.
[52] *Supra* p. 207.
[53] *Supra* p. 211.

CHAPTER THIRTEEN

The Interpretation of Contracts

1. THE UNIQUENESS OF A CONTRACT AND HOW IT AFFECTS INTERPRETATION

The Uniqueness of a Contract

A contract expresses the autonomy of the contractual parties' private will, which is a constitutional right that derives from the right to human dignity and the right to property. The right to human dignity safeguards the right to decide whether to communicate through a contract and with whom to communicate, and the freedom to formulate the content of the contract. In contrast to a will—which also expresses private autonomy—a contract creates reasonable expectations among the parties to it. It creates reliance on itself and on its results. It can also create a reliance interest in third parties.

Uniqueness in Interpretation: Superior Role of the Joint Intent of the Parties

The uniqueness of a contract influences its interpretation. Because a contract is an expression of the private will of the parties, judges should interpret it to express that will. We saw[1] that the key question in interpreting a legal text is, "Interpretation for what?" The "what" is to achieve the purpose of the text. Because the primary purpose of a contract is to realize the joint intent of its parties, judges should interpret contracts according to that intent.

The emphasis on the joint intent of the parties runs as a common thread through Continental systems of law.[2] Article 1156 of the French Civil Code is typical, proclaiming that "On doit dans les conventions rechercher quelle a été la commune intention des parties contractantes, plutôt que de s'arreter au sens littéral des termes."[3] International "legislation"—such as

---

[1] *Supra* p. 219.

[2] K. Zweigert and H. Kötz, *Introduction to Comparative Law* 400 (T. Weir trans., 1998); Art. 133 of the B.G.B.; Art. 18 of the Swiss Law of Obligations; Art. 1362 of the Italian Civil Code; Art. 1425 of the Quebec Civil Code.

[3] "In interpreting a contract, one should seek the joint intent of the parties communicating through the contract, and not stop at the literal meaning of the terms."

the Unidroit principles of international commercial contracts,[4] the United Nations Convention on Contracts for the International Sale of Goods,[5] and the Principles of European Contract Law[6]—adopts the same stance. The American Restatement of Contracts has also followed suit,[7] marking the end of an interesting development in American law.[8]

English common law, on the other hand, takes an exceptional stance, interpreting contracts according to the intention attributable to reasonable parties. The following comments by Lord Wilberforce typify the English doctrine:

> When one speaks of the intention of the parties to the contract, one is speaking objectively—the parties cannot themselves give direct evidence of what their intention was—and what must be ascertained is what is to be taken as the intention which reasonable people would have had if placed in the situation of the parties.[9]

In recent years, the English have relaxed this approach, now construing the understanding of the reasonable person against the background of the circumstances that one can reasonably assume were known to the parties at the time the contract was formed.[10] English law does, however, continue

---

[4] Article 4.1 of Unidroit states that "(1) A contract shall be interpreted according to the common intention of the parties; (2) If such intention cannot be established, the contract shall be interpreted according to the meaning that reasonable persons of the same kind as the parties would give to it in the same circumstances."

[5] *See* Article 8 of the Convention, which constitutes an addition to the law of sales (sale of international goods), 1999—"(1) For the purposes of this Convention statements made by and other conduct of a party are to be interpreted according to his intent where the other party knew or could not have been unaware what that intent was; (2) If the preceding paragraph is not applicable, statements made by and other conduct of a party are to be interpreted according to the understanding that a reasonable person of the same kind as the other party would have had in the same circumstances."

[6] Chapter 5.101 of the Principles states that "(1) A contract is to be interpreted according to the common intention of the parties even if this differs from the literal meaning of the words. (2) If it is established that one party intended the contract to have a particular meaning, and at the time of the conclusion of the contract the other party could not have been unaware of the first party's intention, the contract is to be interpreted in the way intended by the first party. (3) if the intention cannot be established according to (1) or (2), the contract is to interpreted according to the meaning that reasonable persons of the same kind as the parties would give to it in the same circumstances." *Principles of European Contract Law* (O. Lando and H. Beale eds., 2000).

[7] *Restatement (Second) of Contracts* §201 (1981).

[8] J. Perillo, "The Origins of the Objective Theory of Contract Formation and Interpretation," 69 *Fordham L. Rev.* 427 (2000).

[9] *Reardon-Smith Line Ltd. v. Hansen-Tangen* [1976] 1 W.L.R. 989, 996.

[10] *Mannai Investment Co. Ltd. v. Eagle Star Life Assurance Co Ltd* [1997] A.C. 749, 774; *Investors Compensation Scheme Ltd v. West Bromwich Bldg. Soc'y* [1998] 1 W.L.R. 896, 912. *See also* J. Steyn, "Contract Law: Fulfilling the Reasonable Expectations of Honest Men," 113 *Law Q. Rev.* 433 (1997).

to reject the parties' joint (subjective) intent—their "real" intent, as opposed to that of a reasonable person—as an interpretive criterion. The English justify their approach in two ways:[11] *First*, they say, we cannot know the joint intent of the parties, when the parties themselves disagree over it; and *second*, we need an objective approach to guarantee stability and certainty in law.[12]

These explanations are not persuasive.[13] Investigating the joint intent of the parties is no different than any other legal investigation into facts. Direct testimony from a party about his or her intent should be admissible. It would not impair security and certainty in law. To the contrary: It would assure more security and certainty than the current situation, in which everything depends on a judge's sense of the contractual language.[14] Of course, when a judge cannot ascertain joint intent, he or she should resort to objective purpose. But why not try to find the subjective purpose shared by the parties? A contract expresses the autonomy of the contractual parties' private will—the actual will at the core of the contract, not a hypothetical will.[15] Indeed, if the real intent diverges too far from the hypothetical intent, the contract is likely to be voided on grounds of mistake.[16] It is therefore difficult to understand the objection to using actual, not hypothetical, intent, as the basis for contractual interpretation. Of course, we might say—in the spirit of new textualism[17]—that the intent of the author of the text is irrelevant to its interpretation. But English common law does not adopt that view. So long as it continues to accept the intent of the parties as a proper interpretive criterion, there is no reason for it to ignore real intent when it can be discovered. If we take seriously the idea that the parties' joint intent is at the core of a contract—whether or not they behave reasonably—then we should interpret a contract to realize that intent, without assuming its reasonability.

[11] *President of India v. Jebsens (UK) Ltd* [1991] 1 Lloyd's Rep. 1, 9 (Goff, L.); J. Steyn, "Interpretation Legal Texts and Their Landscape," in *The Coming Together of the Common Law and the Civil Law* 79 (B. Markensinis ed., 2000).

[12] J. Steyn, "Written Contracts: To What Extent May Evidence Control Language?" 41 *Current Legal Probs.* 23 (1988).

[13] D.W. McLauchlan, "The New Law of Contract Interpretation," 19 *New Zealand U.L. Rev.* 147 (2000).

[14] *Supra* p. 264; D.W. McLauchlan, "A Contract Contradiction," (1999) 30 *VUWLR* 175, 189.

[15] *See* D. Friedman and N. Cohen, *Chozim [Contracts]* 32 (vol. 11, 1991).

[16] There is an important connection between the laws of contractual interpretation and the laws about mistake in contract formation. The two fields should be harmonized; what is the point of giving a contract an "objective" interpretation, if that interpretation will void the contract? *See* P.S. Atiyah and F.A.R. Bennion, "Mistake in the Construction of Contracts," 24 *Mod. L. Rev.* 421 (1961); R. Zimmerman, *The Law of Obligations: Roman Foundations of the Civilian Tradition* 621 (1990).

[17] *Supra* p. 277.

The Meaning of a Contract and Objective Purpose

The investigation into the parties' joint intent does not supplant a contract's objective purpose, which applies immediately and always. Objective purpose constitutes the background for understanding subjective purpose. It may resolve contradictions among conflicting subjective purposes. Most importantly, objective purpose applies to situations in which there is no subjective purpose that can resolve the judge's interpretive problem. It is then that objective purpose is decisive. Purposive interpretation thus maintains consistency between rhetoric and practice. It openly seeks and achieves subjective purpose when possible and efficacious, and admits as much. Otherwise, it openly adopts the rhetoric and practice of objective purpose—and admits as much.

2. CONTRACT THEORY AND CONTRACTUAL INTERPRETATION

The Importance of Contract Theory to Contractual Interpretation

At the core of contract law is contract theory,[18] which seeks to account for the essence of a contract and its role in society. It tries to answer the question of why we put the resources of the state at the disposal of the parties to enforce their obligations, and why we give the parties a remedy in case of breach. Contract theory helps explain contract law, but it also affects the way we interpret contracts.[19] Despite their connection, I have not found significant treatment[20] of the relationship between contract theory and contractual interpretation. I will now briefly discuss a few basic theories of contracts and evaluate their relationship to the theory of interpretation.

"CLASSICAL" THEORY: AUTONOMY OF THE PRIVATE WILL

The "classical" theory of contracts[21] views freedom of contract as an expression of the autonomy of the private will. A contract is binding because

---

[18] For an analysis of the various theories, see R. Hillman, *The Richness of Contract Law: An Analysis and Critique of Contemporary Theories of Contract Law* (1997).

[19] Charny, *supra* p. 49, note 160 at 1815; C. McCracken, Note, "Hegel and the Autonomy of Contract Law," 77 *Tex. L. Rev.* 719, 721 (1999).

[20] Professor Zamir is a noteworthy exception. *See* E. Zamir, "The Inverted Hierarchy of Contract Interpretation and Supplementation," 97 *Colum. L. Rev.* 1710 (1997).

[21] Neoclassical theory takes a similar view. *See* I. Macneil, "Contracts: Adjustment of Long Term Economic Relations under Classical, Neoclassical and Relational Contract Law," 72 *Nw. U. L. Rev.* 854, 855 (1978).

people have a moral obligation to keep their promises,[22] because they have consented to transfer their rights to another party,[23] or because they communicated to another person their intention to be obligated to him or her.[24] It would seem, on those theories, that contractual interpretation should seek the real intent of the parties to the contract.[25] A proper theory of interpretation would then be subjective. Judges would refer to objective aspects only in the absence of information about joint intent, or when it can be assumed that the parties to a particular contract behaved as reasonable people. Such a theory would cut in favor of beginning with objective interpretation at a low level of abstraction, and only moving up to a higher level if necessary.[26]

ACTUALIZING SOCIAL VALUES

Another movement in contract theory emphasizes social values like fairness, justice, and equality.[27] According to these theories, contract law can legitimately achieve social values beyond the intent of the parties alone, such as solidarity, corrective justice,[28] or distributive justice.[29] These approaches lay the groundwork for objective theories of interpretation. They would seem to cut in favor of a higher level of abstraction that seeks to actualize social values. The question is not what the parties to a contract would have sought to achieve, had they considered the matter, but rather what reasonable parties, envisioning the total picture and considering all social values, would have sought to achieve.

EFFICIENCY TO MAXIMIZE GAIN

Law and economics[30] is a movement that affects every branch of law, with particularly important implications for contract law.[31] Law and economics

---

[22] C. Fried, *Contract as Promise: A Theory of Contractual Obligations* 17 (1981).

[23] R. Barnett, "A Consent Theory of Contract," 86 *Colum. L. Rev.* 269 (1986).

[24] J. Raz, "Promises and Obligations," in *Law, Morality and Society* 210 (P. Hacker and J. Raz eds., 1977); J. Raz, "Promises in Morality and Law", 95 *Harv. L. Rev.* 916 (1982).

[25] H. Collins, *The Law of Contract* 212 (3d ed. 1997).

[26] Charny, *supra* p. 49, note 160 at 1825.

[27] J. Beatson, "Public Law Influences in Contract Law," in *Good Faith and Fault in Contract Law* 263 (J. Beatson and D. Friedmann eds., 1995).

[28] S. Henderson, "Promises Grounded in the Past: The Idea of Unjust Enrichment and the Law of Contracts," 57 *Va. L. Rev.* 1115 (1971); E. Weinrib, *The Idea of Private Law* (1995). Note that Weinrib does not see corrective justice as a social value for contract law to actualize. Rather, he sees corrective justice as a basis for the rationality of private law.

[29] A. Kronman, "Contract Law and Distributive Justice," 89 *Yale L.J.* 472 (1980); H. Collins, "Distributive Justice through Contracts," 45 *Current Legal Probs.* 49 (1992).

[30] R. Posner, *Economic Analysis of Law* (5th ed. 1998).

[31] A. Kronman and R. Posner, *The Economics of Contract Law* (1979); D. Farber, "Contract Law and Modern Economic Theory," 78 *Nw. U. L. Rev.* 303 (1983).

takes wealth maximization to be the goal of law. In the context of a contract, it means that at least one of the parties to a contract should be in a better position after the contractual transaction, without worsening the position of the other party. Law and economics requires a cost-benefit analysis, taking into account the transaction costs of the deal itself. There is sparse literature discussing what theory of interpretation law and economics favors. Some say that law and economics favors subjective interpretation,[32] because the parties are the best judges of their own interests.[33] Others say law and economics cuts in favor of objective interpretation, which takes market failures and limited rationality into account in order to reach a more efficient outcome than that emerging from the joint intent of the parties.[34]

RELATIONAL CONTRACTS

In recent years, jurists have developed a theory of relational contracts[35] concerning long-term contracts establishing a protracted relationship between the parties. These relationships are typically complex and uncertain. Parties to relational contracts—employment contracts, distribution contracts, nursing home contracts—have different considerations than parties to a business contract. Relational contracts by their nature require flexibility and semantic adaptability. They require trust, solidarity, and reciprocity. It is difficult to determine all the terms in advance, because the contracts extend over a long period of time, during which the relationship between the parties changes. A relational contract develops with time.

What system of interpretation do relational contracts warrant? There is no easy answer. We might say that a subjective system is appropriate because the subjective intent of the parties to a relational contract is to guarantee mutual consideration and flexibility over a protracted contractual relationship. We might even take it further and claim that the subjective purpose of the contract is to achieve objective purpose at its low level of abstraction, that is, what the parties to a relational contract would have wanted, had they considered the matter. On the other hand, we might argue that a theory of relational contracts should focus on the intent of the parties at the time the dispute arises between them, rather than at the time they formed the contract. If the latter is true, the "relational" interpreter should heavily weight values such as trust, solidarity, and reciprocity—the objective purpose of the contract.

[32] Posner, *supra* p. 322, note 30 at 93.

[33] Zamir discusses this rationale. *See* Zamir, *supra* p. 321, note 20 at 1789; A. Schwartz, "Justice and the Law of Contracts: A Case for the Traditional Approach," 9 *Harv. J.L. & Pub. Pol'y* 107 (1986).

[34] Zamir, *supra* p. 321, note 20, 1789–90.

[35] For a description of this theory—central to which is Professor Macneil—see Hillman, *supra* p. 321, note 18 at 255.

FEMINISM AND CONTRACT THEORY

Feminist theory is constantly evolving across disciplines,[36] including in the field of law in general,[37] and in contract law[38] in particular. Feminist theory, or at least a branch of it, claims that conventional contract theory reflects a masculine bias. Traditional contract theory is abstract and rigid, and it claims to be objective. The feminist approach, on the other hand, emphasizes subjectivity and contextuality, moving from abstraction to the particular circumstances of the case. The (conventional) masculine view emphasizes opposition and conflict. The feminist view emphasizes commonality and compromise. At a superficial glance, the feminist approach to interpretation would appear to favor subjective purpose and the joint intent of the parties in contractual interpretation. On the other hand, we might say that, when it is impossible to locate a joint intent of the parties, feminist theory argues in favor of the objective purpose that reflects balance and compromise among social values.

What Does Contract Theory Teach about Contractual Interpretation?

The various contract theories reflect the complexity of the contract as a fundamental social phenomenon. The contract expresses the autonomy of the private will, on the one hand, and the values, principles, and goals of organized society, on the other. It encompasses individuality and communitarianism; self-expression and paternalism; egoism and solidarity. Each theory reflects a different aspect of the contract. None by itself expresses the full complexity of the contract,[39] but considered together, the theories express its uniqueness.[40] A contract is a private device, the product of the creativity of the parties to it. But it is also a public device in the form of the enforcement that the legal system makes available to the parties. A contract is part of the legal system. The system's fundamental values, including jus-

[36] C. Gilligan, *In a Different Voice: Psychological Theory and Women's Development* (1982).

[37] K. Bartett and R. Kennedy, *Feminist Legal Theory: Readings in Law Gender* (1991); Scales, "The Emergence of Feminist Jurisprudence: An Essay," 95 *Yale L.J.* 1373 (1986); S. Sherry, "Civic Virtue and the Feminine Voice in Constitutional Adjudication," 72 *Va. L. Rev.* 543 (1986); R. West, "Jurisprudence and Gender," 55 *U. Chi. L. Rev.* 1 (1988); C. MacKinnon, *Toward a Feminist Theory of the State* (1989).

[38] Hillman, *supra* p. 321, note 18; D. Threedy, "Feminists and Contract Doctrine," 32 *Ind. L. Rev.* 1247 (1999).

[39] Hillman, *supra* p. 321, note 18 at 267.

[40] M.A. Eisenberg, "The Responsive Model of Contract Law," 36 *Stan. L. Rev.* 1107, 1109 (1984) ("[L]aw generally, and contract law specifically, have too many rooms to unlock with one key").

tice, equality, reasonableness, fairness, and human rights, permeate the contract and shape its character. They do not supplant the autonomy of the parties but rather accompany it. This is the complex dialectic of the contract in law.[41]

Purposive interpretation expresses this dialectic. It makes achieving the purpose of the contract the goal of contractual interpretation. The purpose—as a normative concept—reflects the complicated dialectic. Most theories of the contract appear to share this starting point. Subjective purpose gives expression to the autonomy of the private will and individualistic views. Objective purpose gives expression to the needs of the collectivity and communitarian views. The various theories are likely to disagree over the balance between these purposes. As is the case in jurisprudence in general, in contract jurisprudence the general theory helps make the purpose of the contract an interpretive criterion. It does not, however, offer a clear resolution to the internal relationship between subjective and objective purpose. To resolve that issue, we evaluate each of the theories of contracts. The classical theory of contracts, (at least one branch of) law and economics, certain aspects of relational contract theory, and some branches of feminist theory favor giving preference to subjective purpose when it conflicts with objective purpose. On the other hand, contract theories that take social values into consideration, as well as some branches of law and economics and of feminism, favor objective purpose. The purposive interpretation of contracts that I advocate privileges subjective purpose, although objective purpose continues to apply. This approach expresses the complex nature of the contract and the need to regard it from both subjective and objective viewpoints.

3. THE PURPOSE OF A CONTRACT

The Essence of the Purpose of a Contract

The purpose of a contract—like the purpose of a will, statute, and constitution—is the interests, goals, values, aims, policies, and function that the contract is designed to accomplish. It is a normative concept. It is a legal construction.[42] It is a legal institution—like the right to a legal personality—that the judge shapes. It comprises subjective and objective purpose.[43] Subjective purpose reflects the actual intent of the parties: the in-

---

[41] Eisenberg, *supra* p. 324, note 40 at 1111.

[42] C.A. 4628/93 *State of Israel v. Guardian of Housing and Initiative (1991) Ltd.*, 49(2) P.D. 265, 312.

[43] *Id.* at 312; C.A. 4869/96 *Meleline Ltd. v. The Harper Group*, 52(1) P.D. 845, 856.

terests, values, aims, policies, and function that the parties (subjectively) sought to accomplish. Objective purpose is the interests, values, aims, policies, and function that a contract of that type is (objectively) designed to accomplish. It reflects hypothetical, not actual, intent.

Comparative Law

Legal systems from other parts of the world consider both the objective and subjective components of contractual purpose.[44] That is the view of the United Nations Convention on Contracts for the Sale of International Goods.[45] It is the foundation for the principles of Unidroit.[46] It is the basis for the Principles of European Contract Law.[47] The comments explaining the European Principles note that

> Following the majority of laws in EU Member States, the general rules on interpretation combine the subjective method, according to which pre-eminence is given to the common intention of the parties, and the objective method which takes an external view by reference to objective criteria such as reasonableness, good faith, etc.[48]

Judges determine the ultimate purpose of a contract. They must consider both subjective and objective purpose,[49] ruling on any contradiction between them. Purposive interpretation privileges subjective purpose without negating the immediate and continuous application of objective purpose.

4. THE SUBJECTIVE PURPOSE OF A CONTRACT

Its Essence

The subjective purpose of a contract is the interests, goals, values, aims, policies, and function that the parties to a contract (subjectively) sought to achieve. It is the true intent that the parties actually had at the time they formed the contract. A judge formulating this (abstract) intent should accord significant weight to the concrete (or interpretive) intent of the contracting parties.[50] Farnsworth explained it as follows: "[I]f one party shows

---

[44] Zweigert and Kötz, *supra* p. 318, note 2 at 400; H. Kötz and A. Flessner, *European Contract Law* 106 (T. Weir trans. 1997).

[45] Article 8 of the Convention, *supra* p. 151, note 13.

[46] Article 4.1 of the Principles, *supra* p 319, note 6.

[47] Chapter 101.5 of the Principles, *supra* p. 319, note 6.

[48] Lando and Beale, *supra* p. 46, note 149 at 288.

[49] C.A. 4628/93, *supra* p. 325, note 42 at 313.

[50] This approach is particular to contracts and wills, in contrast to statutes and constitu-

that the other party attached the same meaning that the first party did, the other party should not be able to avoid that meaning by showing that a reasonable person would have attached a different one."[51] Nevertheless, purposive interpretation seeks the purpose of the contract, not the meaning that the parties attach to its language.

Joint Subjective Intent

Western legal systems agree that subjective intent is the subjective intent shared by both parties.[52] Israeli law,[53] American law,[54] the principles of Unidroit,[55] and the Principles of European Contract Law[56] reflect that view, as do Germany,[57] France,[58] and Italy.[59] The basic principles of contract law, expressing the autonomy of private will, warrant that view. It does not infringe on the principle of reliance, because we assume that the intent is shared by both parties. It is therefore difficult to justify the English legal focus on objective meaning, at the expense of expressing the joint subjective intent of the parties.[60] Why privilege an objective expression, if both parties do not share it? A party's request to replace his or her understanding with that of the reasonable person is not a good faith argument. Good faith requires that a contract be interpreted according to the joint (subjective) intent of the parties.

---

tions. In interpreting a statute or constitution, we are concerned with the role of the legislature (or constitutional assembly) in the separation of powers, which is to legislate, not to interpret. In interpreting a contract, we are primarily concerned with the autonomy of the private will and the power of interpretation that the parties to a contract have. The principle of good faith also cuts in favor of considering concrete intention. We should not allow a party to escape contractual obligation by claiming that he or she, together with the other party, gave the contract an unreasonable meaning. A. Corbin, 3 *Corbin on Contracts: A Comprehensive Treaty on the Roles of Contract Law* 58 (1960).

[51] E.A. Farnsworth, 2 *Contracts* 245 (vol. 2, 1990).

[52] Hegel noted as much early on. *See* G. Hegel, *Elements of the Philosophy of Right* 105 (A. Wood ed., H.B. Nisbet trans., 1991) (1821). The joint intent of the parties as a central criterion for interpreting international contracts (conventions) is at the core of the interpretive viewpoint of M.S. McDougal, H.D. Lasswell, J.C. Miller, *The Interpretation of Agreements and World Public Order: Principles of Content and Procedure* 40 (1967).

[53] C.A. 554/83 *"Ata" Textile Co. v. Estate of Zolotolov*, 41(1) P.D. 282, 305. *See also* C.A. 4869/96. *Mililine Ltd. v. Harper Group*, 52(1) P.D. 845.

[54] Article 201(1) of the *Restatement (Second) of Contracts*.

[55] Article 4.1(1) of the Principles, *supra* p. 319, note 6.

[56] Chapter 101.5 of the Principles of European Contract Law, *supra* p. 319, note 6.

[57] Articles 133 and 157 of the B.G.B.

[58] Article 1156 of the French Civil Code.

[59] Article 1362 of the Italian Civil Code.

[60] *Supra* p. 319.

Subjective Intent of One Party Known to the Other

What happens when each party has his or her own intent, and one party knows of the other's intent[61] but has managed to keep his or her own intent undisclosed to the other party? Comparative law[62] suggests that, if one party knows of the other's (mistaken) intent, and continues to form the contract with him or her, without correcting the mistake, then the (mistaken) intent of the first party becomes the joint intent of both parties. Consider a case in which Richard offers to sell Simon an animal, and Simon accepts. Richard intends to sell a horse. Simon knows that. The deal that takes place is then the sale of a horse. It is the basis for forming the contract. It is also the basis for its interpretation. In a situation like this, it makes no difference how a reasonable person would understand the word "animal."

Subjective Purpose and Third Parties

What of a third party? Consider a case in which Richard and Simon form a contract for the sale of a horse. In their private code, and according to their joint intent, the animal in question is a tractor. The reasonable observer would understand a horse to be a horse. Larry, a third party, relies on the objective meaning and enters into a contract with Richard for the acquisition of the tractor. Simon sues Larry for tortious interference with a contractual relationship.[63] The suit should fail. From Larry's point of view, the contract should be interpreted according to his understanding of it.[64] Larry did not intend to interfere with the contract to sell a horse.[65]

---

[61] What happens when one party does not know but should have known of the other's intent? See Article 201(2) of the *Restatement (Second) of Contracts*, determining that the contract should be interpreted according to the intent of the one party. The Principles of Unidroit prescribe a similar approach: Article 4.2 of the Principles, *supra* p. 73, note 54. The United Nations Convention on Contracts for the International Sale of Goods takes the same approach: Article 8(a), *supra* p. 151, note 13.

[62] Art. 201(2) of the *Restatement (Second) of Contracts*; Article 4.2(1) of the Principles of Unidroit ("The statements and other conduct of a party shall be interpreted according to that party's intention if the other party knew or could not have been unaware of that intention"). *See also* Article 8(1) of the United Nations Convention on Contracts for the International Sale of Goods, *supra* p. 151, note 13; chapter 101.5(2) of The Principles of European Contract Law, *supra* p. 319, note 6.

[63] Torts Ordinance, Art. 62., 1968, L.S.I.

[64] Wigmore, *supra* p. 312, note 27 at 215: "Where a *third person* has become a party to the transaction or has been induced to rely upon it, *without knowledge of the special sense* of terms used therein, the special sense of the original parties should not be enforced against him" (emphasis in original).

[65] The law governing claims for tortious interference with contractual relations leads to

The same contract should be given two different meanings: one meaning, for purposes of the relationship between the parties, that reflects their joint intent, and another meaning, for purposes of the effect of the contract on a third party, reflecting the contract's objective purpose.

5. SOURCES OF SUBJECTIVE PURPOSE

Subjective Purpose Derived from Within the Contract and the Problem of the Hermeneutic Circle

First and foremost, a judge learns about the subjective purpose of a contract from the contract itself. The contract is the internal or textual context. Using the contract itself as a source of objective purpose raises the problem of the hermeneutic circle.[66] We can resolve this problem by approaching the contract with our pre-understanding, as discussed in Part 2.[67]

Treating the Contract as a Whole

In seeking the purpose of a contract, judges should treat the contract as a whole. They learn its subjective purpose from the totality of contractual provisions.[68] No one provision is the source of subjective purpose. The various parts of a contract are entwined and connected with each other. As I noted in one case:

> A contract is an integrative framework. Its different parts are entwined and in-termingled. Its various branches influence each other. In interpreting a con-tract, a judge should, on the one hand, view it holistically, as a whole, but on the other hand, evaluate the connections between its various provisions, as part of the attempt to formulate the parties' joint intent.[69]

This interpretive view is not limited to cases in which the interpreter experiences initial difficulty in finding the purpose of the contract. This view applies to every contract, regardless of whether it is difficult to interpret. Even when interpreting a contract whose meaning appears "plain" at first glance, a judge should study the totality of its provisions, taking them as a whole and considering them separately.

---

the same result. To be liable, a party must have knowingly interfered with the contractual re-lations. Torts Ordinance, Art. 62a, 1968, LS.I.

[66] *Supra* p. 136.

[67] *Supra* p. 57.

[68] For extensive case law on the issue, see A. Barak, *Parshanut Bimishpat* [Interpretation in Law] 450 (vol. 4, 2001).

[69] C.A. 554/83 *"Ata" Textile Co. v. Estate of Zolotov*, 41(1) P.D. 282, 305.

Learning Intent of the Parties from the Circumstances: What Are the Circumstances?

The "circumstances" include all facts beyond the four corners of the contract that can provide information about the parties' intent. The relevant time frame is the time of the contract formation, although circumstances that existed before and after may also shed light on the intent that existed at the time of formation. Of course, the most immediate circle of events is the circumstances at the time of formation—the behavior of the parties and what they said to each other at the time they formed the contract. A less immediate circle includes the contract negotiations and any compromises the parties reached. A third, more distant circle includes circumstances following the contract formation that can project backward onto the joint intent of the parties at the time the contract was formed. An interpreter may also use previous contractual relationships between the parties and the customs they established between them, projecting forward to understand their intent at the time they formed the contract in question.

Judges may use the circumstances to learn about subjective intent in the same way they evaluate evidence of any other factual proposition. The English legal system[70] errs in forbidding parties to a contract from testifying about their intent in order to resolve a patent ambiguity.[71] Courts should admit all oral testimony to prove the intent of the parties from the circumstances, including direct testimony from the parties.

When May an Interpreter Consult the Circumstances?

Continental law permits an interpreter to consult the circumstances surrounding contract formation in all circumstances, moving freely from the text of the contract to its circumstantial context.[72] Israeli law,[73] the Principles of Unidroit,[74] the United Nations Convention on Contracts for the International Sale of Goods,[75] and the Principles of European Contract

---

[70] Levison, *supra* p. 42, note 130 at 196; C. Staughton, "How Do the Courts Interpret Commercial Contracts?" 58 *Cam. L.J.* 303 (1999).

[71] K. Keeler, "Direct Evidence of State of Mind: A Philosophical Analysis of How Facts in Evidence Support Conclusions Regarding Mental State," 1985 *Wis. L. Rev.* 435.

[72] Art. 133 of the B.G.B.; Art. 1156 of the French Code Civile; Art. 1362 of the Italian Civil Code.

[73] C.A. 4628/93 *State of Israel v. Guardian of Housing and Initiatives (1991) Ltd.*, 49(2) P.D. 265.

[74] Unidroit, *Principles of International Commercial Contracts* 284 (1994).

[75] Article 8(3) of the Convention states that "In determining the intent of a party or the understanding a reasonable person would have had, due consideration is to be given to all

Law[76] also adopt this approach. The United States takes a more complicated view. Until the nineteenth century, American law did not permit a judge to refer to the circumstances if the language of the contract was plain and unambiguous. Only when the language of the contract was not plain could a judge consult extrinsic circumstances for information about the intent of the parties and the meaning of the words in the contract.[77] This is the plain meaning rule,[78] which in turn is the basis for the parole evidence rule. There has been some relaxing of this approach to allow a judge to consider extrinsic evidence about the circumstances under which the contract was formed, even if the language of a contract is plain.[79] Under the influence of Professors Corbin and Llewellyn, the United States has changed its approach. Corbin helped shape the Restatement (Second),[80] and Llewellyn is the spiritual father of the Uniform Commercial Code (UCC).[81] According to the UCC[82] and the Restatement (Second),[83] the meaning of the words depends on their context, including the circumstances surrounding contract formation. A court must put itself in the position of the parties at the time the contract was formed. It may always consult the circumstances.[84]

This is not to say that all legal systems adopt this approach. Some courts reject the view of the Restatement (Second) and retain the plain meaning rule.[85] English law permits a judge to consult the circumstances only when

---

relevant circumstances of the case including the negotiations, any practices which the parties have established between themselves, usages and any subsequent conduct of the parties." *See also* J. Honnold, *Uniform Law for International Sales under the 1980 United Nations Convention* 115 (3d ed. 1999).

[76] Art. 1, ch. 102 of the Principles of European Contract Law, European Union (1998).

[77] Article 230 of the *Restatement of Contracts*, published in 1932, reflects this view.

[78] J. McBaine, "The Rule against Disturbing Plain Meaning of Writings," 31 *Cal. L. Rev.* 145 (1942); E.W. Patterson, "The Interpretation and Construction of Contracts," 64 *Colum. L. Rev.* 833, 838 (1964).

[79] Patterson, *supra* p. 331, note 78 at 843.

[80] R. Braucher, "Interpretation and Legal Effect in the *Second Restatement of Contracts*," 81 *Colum. L. Rev.* 13, 14 (1981).

[81] E. Mooney, "Old Kontract Principles and Karl's New Kode: An Essay on the Jurisprudence of Our New Commercial Law," 11 *Vill. L. Rev.* 213 (1966); A. Kamp, "Between-the-Wars Social Thought: Karl Llewellyn, Legal Realism, and the Uniform Commercial Code in Context," 59 *Alb. L. Rev.* 325 (1995); W. Twining, *Karl Llewellyn and the Realist Movement* (1973).

[82] Art. 2-202 of the UCC.

[83] Art. 202(1) of the *Restatement (Second) of Contracts*.

[84] E.A. Farnsworth, 1 *Farnsworth on Contracts* 225 (1990); M. Van Alstine, "Of Textualism, Party Autonomy, and Good Faith," 40 *Wm & Mary L. Rev.* 1223, 1273 (1999).

[85] Zamir notes—based on his empirical investigation—that resort to the plain meaning rule is usually merely rhetorical. *See* E. Zamir, "The Inverted Hierarchy of Contract Interpretation and Supplementation," 97 *Colum. L. Rev.* 1710, 1728 (1997).

the language of the contract is not plain and creates ambiguity. This is the mischief rule.[86] Even then, a judge cannot consider evidence about the parties' negotiations and their interpretation of the contract as reflected in their behavior subsequent to formation. English jurisprudence on this point is evolving, however, and a judge may now put himself or herself in the shoes of the parties and consider the matrix of fact, even for a plain contract.[87] Nevertheless, the parties still may not testify about their intent—a situation that I hope will change as English law continues to develop.[88]

6. THE OBJECTIVE PURPOSE OF A CONTRACT

Its Essence

The objective purpose of a contract is the interests, goals, values, aims, policies, and function that a contract of the type in question is designed to achieve. It is a legal construction, determined by an objective test.[89] It reflects values of reasonableness, fairness, and economic, business, and commercial rationality. It reflects business efficiency and the nature and substance of the deal. It reflects the hypothetical intent of the parties to the contract. It is not an attributed intent. It is not based on fiction. It reflects the values of the legal system. We can therefore call it the "intention of the system." Often, but not always, the objective purpose of a contract is also its subjective purpose. Of course, regardless of how we learn about it, objective purpose does not apply if it cannot be achieved within the language of the contract.

Ranking Levels of Abstraction of Objective Purpose

Objective purpose appears before the judge at various levels of abstraction.[90] At the lowest level of abstraction, it is the purpose that the parties would have envisioned, had they thought about the matter. At an inter-

---

[86] Lewison, *supra* p. 42, note 130 at 201.

[87] *Id.* at 56. *See also Prenn v. Simmonds* [1971] 1 W.L.R. 1381, 1384; *Reardon-Smith Line Ltd. v. Hansen-Tangen* [1976] 1 W.L.R. 989, 995; *Mannai Investments Co. Ltd. v. Eagle Star Life Assurance Co. Ltd.* [1997] A.C. 749; *Investors Compensation Scheme Ltd. v. West Bromwich Bldg. Soc'y* [1998] 1 W.L.R. 896.

[88] *See* McLauchlan, *supra* p. 320, notes 13 and 14.

[89] Art. 8(2) of the United Nations Convention on Contracts for the International Sale of Goods, *supra* p. 319, note 6; Art. 4.1(1) of the Principles of Unidroit, *supra* p. 330, note 74; Art. 5, ch. 101(3) of the Principles of European Contract Law, *supra* p. 319, note 6.

[90] *Supra* p. 149.

mediate level, it is the purpose that the parties would have had, had they behaved as reasonable people. At the next higher level, it is the purpose typical of the type of contract in question. At the highest level of abstraction, the fundamental values of the system determine objective purpose. To which level of abstraction should the interpreter aspire? The answer depends on contract theory. No dominant trend emerges from the current state of contract law development. I think it is best to begin with a low level of abstraction and work upward. We should start with the hypothetical intent that is closest to the subjective intent of the parties to the contract. This is the intent we may assume the parties would have had, had they behaved as reasonable people. Only when that assumption does not help resolve the legal problem should we turn to a higher level of abstraction. This ranking does not derive from purposive interpretation per se; it derives from the significant weight I attach to the autonomy of the private will in formulating a theory of contracts. Those who take a different approach to contracts may decide on a different ranking. Purposive interpretation is flexible enough to allow for variation on this ranking, depending on one's approach to contract law.

OBJECTIVE PURPOSE REFLECTING REASONABLENESS, LOGIC, AND EFFICIENCY

Subjective purpose reflects the actual intent of the parties. It may be devoid of reasonableness, logic, and/or efficiency. Objective purpose, on the other hand, as a reflection of the reasonable person, is based on reasonableness, logic, and efficiency. As Justice Cheshin noted, "In approaching the meaning of a business contract, we can assume the common sense of rational, fair businesspeople."[91] Our understanding of the reasonable person takes the principles of fairness, efficiency, and common sense into consideration.

OBJECTIVE PURPOSE REFLECTING FUNDAMENTAL VALUES

At the highest level of abstraction, objective purpose is the system's fundamental values. These values apply to the relationship between individual and regime and to relationships between individuals. I noted in one case that

> The fundamental values of the system as a whole, and fundamental human rights in particular, are not limited to public law. The distinction between public and private law is not so sharp. A legal system is not a confederation of areas

[91] C.A. 5795/90, *Scully v. Dor'an Ltd.*, 46(5) P.D. 811, 819.

of law. It is a unity of system and law. Fundamental principles are principles of the system as a whole, not just of public law. Fundamental human rights are not just the rights of an individual against the regime, but include protections for individuals in their relationships with each other.[92]

The legal system's fundamental values permeate private law through the ordinary doctrines of private law.[93] These values include interpretive rules.[94] The objective purpose of a contract is therefore to promote justice and the public interest.[95] Because human rights are central among fundamental values, the objective purpose of a contract is also to promote equality, free speech,[96] and freedom of occupation.[97] I discussed what values are fundamental to a system, and how they came to be so, in my general discussion of objective purpose.[98]

7. PRESUMPTIONS FOR IDENTIFYING OBJECTIVE PURPOSE

The Essence of the Presumptions of Objective Purpose

Presumptions of purpose are a central component of purposive interpretation.[99] They apply to the interpretation of all legal texts, including contracts. The process of interpreting contracts must begin and end by relying on the various presumptions. Sometimes, the presumptions of purpose contradict each other. "Second order"[100] presumptions may help resolve the conflict. For example, one second order presumption is the doctrine of *contra proferentem*, that ambiguities in determining the purpose of a contract should be construed against the drafter. Each legal system has its own presumptions of purpose. For convenience, I will group them into cate-

---

[92] C.A. 294/91 *Jerusalem Community Burial Society v. Kastenbaum*, 46(2) P.D. 464, 530.

[93] Fundamental values apply "indirectly." The *Drittwirkung* theory discusses their influence on third parties, such as the individual in his relationships with other individuals. For a discussion of this issue, see Barak, *supra* p. 329, note 68 at 649; A. Barak, "Constitutional Human Rights and Private Law," in D. Friedmann and D. Barak-Erez (eds.), *Human Rights in Private Law* 13 (2001).

[94] C.A. 294/91, *supra* p. 334, note 92 at 530 (public law rules find expression in private law in the form of various interpretive principles, applied to legal activities in private law") (Barak, P.).

[95] *Restatement (Second) of Contracts* §207; Farnsworth, *supra* p. 331, note 84 at 269.

[96] A. Garfield, "Promises of Silence: Contract Law and Freedom of Speech," 83 *Cornell L. Rev.* 261 (1998).

[97] The laws governing restraint of trade are based on the view that freedom of occupation applies to the relations between parties to a contract.

[98] *Supra* p. 164.

[99] *Supra* p. 170.

[100] C.A. 4869/96, *supra* p. 327, note 53 at 856.

gories and briefly discuss the presumptions accepted in most legal systems.[101]

Presumptions of Purpose Reflecting Security, Certainty, Satisfaction of Reasonable Expectations, and Normative Harmony

The *first* group of purposive presumptions expresses the need to guarantee security and certainty, to meet reasonable expectations,[102] and to achieve harmony in interpersonal relations. It includes the presumption that the purpose of a contract arises from its natural and ordinary language, that the provisions of a contract are not designed to contradict each other, and that multiple contracts between the same parties do not contradict each other. It is presumed that the same phrases mean the same thing, and different phrases mean different things. It is also presumed that a contract is valid. In order to guarantee normative harmony, a contract is presumed to be designed to integrate into the general law, by custom and practice. Included in this group, too, is the presumption that the purpose of a contract is to satisfy the reasonable expectations of the weaker party, for example, the insured in an insurance agreement.

Presumptions of Purpose Reflecting Ethical Values

A *second* group of purposive presumptions concerns ethical values. A contract is presumed to achieve just results; to prevent a wrongdoer from profiting from his or her misdeeds; to give effect to the rules of natural justice.

Presumptions of Purpose Reflecting Social Goals

A *third* group of purposive presumptions reflects social goals. For example, a contract is presumed to promote the public interest.[103] A contract is presumed to be designed not to hinder access to the courts.

---

[101] For a detailed analysis of these presumptions, see Barak, *supra* p. 329, note 68 at 563.

[102] A. Corbin, 1 *Contracts: A Comprehensive Treaty on the Rules of Contract Law* 1 (1963); B. Reiter and J. Swan, "Contracts and the Protection of Reasonable Expectations," in B. Reiter and J. Swan (eds.), *Studies in Contract Law* 1 (1980); J. Steyn, "Contract Law: Fulfilling the Reasonable Expectations of Honest Men," 113 *Law Q. Rev.* 433 (1997); S.M. Waddams, "Good Faith, Unconscionability and Reasonable Expectations," 9 *J. Con. Law* 55, 59 (1995).

[103] Restatement (Second) of Contracts §207.

Presumptions of Purpose Reflecting Proper Modes of Behavior

A *fourth* group of purposive presumptions deals with proper modes of behavior like reasonableness, rationality, fairness, efficiency, and good faith.
These presumptions of purpose are not based in altruism. They do not require a person to sacrifice his or her personal interests for the sake of the
interests of another. They do not expect people, in their interpersonal relationships, to behave like angels. They expect people, in their interpersonal
relationships, to behave like people. A contract is presumed to achieve reasonable and rational results;[104] to avoid absurdity; to achieve results consistent with efficiency and good faith; and to be construed against the
drafter.

Presumptions of Purpose That Realize Human Rights

Constitutional protections for human rights enter private law in general,
and contract law in particular, in the form of rebuttable presumptions of
purpose. The right to equality translates into a presumption that the purpose of a contract is to achieve equality; the right to freedom of speech
translates into a presumption that the purpose of a contract is to guarantee free speech.

8. THE ULTIMATE PURPOSE OF A CONTRACT

Not Everything Is Subject to Judicial Discretion

Presented with information about subjective and objective purpose, how
does a judge determine the ultimate purpose that becomes the criterion for
pinpointing the legal meaning along the spectrum of semantic possibilities?
The difficulty arises, of course, only in cases in which the different presumptions point in different directions. Some pragmatists say that the decision should be left to the discretion of the judge, perhaps with an ad-
monishment to exercise such discretion reasonably.[105] In my opinion, a
theory of interpretation should do more to narrow a judge's discretion.
Purposive interpretation sets rules for assigning weights to the various presumptions and deciding among them.

[104] Restatement (Second) of Contracts §203(a).
[105] *Supra* p. 287.

Determining Subjective Purpose

Judges may have a lot of information about subjective purpose. Where the information conflicts, they should prefer information about a primary purpose over that dealing with a subordinate purpose. They should move from the specific to the general. Most of all, in deciding between two conflicting subjective purposes, they should privilege the subjective purpose that is consistent with objective purpose.

Determining Objective Purpose

In cases of contradiction among presumptions of objective purpose, judges should move from the specific to the general. They should prefer information about purpose at a lower level of abstraction, because the lower the level of abstraction, the closer objective purpose will be to subjective purpose (intent of the parties). Within a given level of abstraction, they should prefer the presumptions that reflect society's higher order values and principles.

Contradiction between Subjective and Objective Purpose

Contractual parties generally behave as reasonable people. The objective purpose of a contract is therefore presumed to be its subjective purpose. That presumption is rebuttable, however, and in rare instances, the two kinds of purpose will conflict. Purposive interpretation does not leave resolution of that conflict to the judge's discretion. It guides him or her with the general principle that the subjective purpose of a contract prevails. That principle stems from the unique character of a contract, whose point of departure is the autonomy of the private will. A judge should therefore interpret a contract according to the joint intent of the parties, even if such interpretation leads to an unreasonable result that conflicts with the fundamental values of the system. Sometimes, after interpreting the contract in this way, a judge may be forced to void it as contrary to public policy. A judge should preserve the integrity of the interpretative process, even if it forces him or her to void the contract. The meaning of a contract is distinct from its validity.

Thus, judges give subjective purpose significant weight, so long as the contract reflects the autonomy of the private will. When the contract does not reflect the autonomy of the private will, or does so to a diminished extent, judges should assign less weight to subjective purpose. For example, judges interpreting adhesion contracts or consumer contracts weight subjective purpose less heavily. Also, in certain kinds of contracts, like long-term contracts, including relational contracts, judges should give less weight to historic intent as time passes. The contract must tackle new problems, and to allow it to do so, judges may privilege objective purpose. They thus give expression to different views about the contract and to its complexity as a social phenomenon of both public and private dimensions. Only when the presumptions of purpose are evenly balanced may judges exercise discretion, using pragmatism to choose the best solution within the parameters (subjective and objective) we discussed. I personally recommend—and each judge may accept or reject this recommendation—that in exercising discretion, a judge should aspire to the purpose that best achieves justice.

CHAPTER FOURTEEN

Statutory Interpretation

1. THE UNIQUENESS OF A STATUTE AND HOW IT AFFECTS INTERPRETATION

Legislature and Judge in a Democracy

In a democracy predicated on the separation of powers, the job of the legislature is to pass statutes. The statutes are subject to the constitution, which reflects legislative supremacy, the supremacy of human rights, and the social values grounded in the constitution.[1] The legislature uses statutes to make social policy. Every statute integrates into the legislative system; the legislative system integrates into the legal system as a whole, which is comprised of values, principles, and rights. The role of the judge is to protect democracy and to bridge the gap between law and society's needs, giving expression to legislative supremacy and to the supremacy of constitutional values. Judges should therefore give statutory provisions a meaning that bridges the inevitable gap between the legal norm and social reality.

How does this schematic description of legislation affect its interpretation? *First*, the legislature passes legislation in order to achieve a certain purpose. Judges should therefore use the subjective purpose of the legislation as a criterion for interpreting it. True, once the legislature passes a statute, the statute becomes severed from the legislature, but that need not negate the role of subjective purpose in interpretation. To ignore subjective purpose in interpretation is to interpret based on words, as opposed to goals.

Second, a statute is not a one-time creation of a transient legislature acting within the confines of a randomly assembled society. A statute is part of the ongoing creation of a permanent legislature, acting within a democratic society. The basic values of the legal system are more than just the background for a legislative act; they are also the purpose that the legislation is designed to achieve. That is the justification for interpreting every piece of legislation in a way that actualizes the basic values of the system. It is only fitting, then, that a statute's objective purpose—reflecting the system's fundamental values in general, and human rights in particular—is a criterion for interpreting that legislation.

---

[1] *Supra* p. 238.

These two derivative principles lead to the same conclusion: A statute should be interpreted according to its subjective and objective purpose. This type of interpretation expresses democracy in its full sense, including majority rule (reflected in legislative supremacy) and recognition of fundamental values (reflected in constitutional supremacy). Judges play a role in giving democracy its full expression. Within the triumvirate of powers, the role of the judge is to adjudicate disputes. In order to adjudicate, a judge should interpret statutes, acting as the legislature's junior partner—not as its agent. Judges should realize the intent of the legislature by giving expression to the statute's subjective purpose, but they also should integrate the statute into the legislative system as a whole by giving expression to the fundamental values of the system.

Purposive Interpretation of Statutes

The purpose of a statute is the interests, goals, values, aims, policies, and function that the statute is designed to accomplish. It is the *ratio legis*. It is a normative concept. It is a legal "institution," composed of subjective and objective purpose. What, then, is the relationship between subjective and objective purpose in determining the ultimate purpose of a statute? When the two are inconsistent, which prevails? In private law texts, we gave preference to subjective purpose. Is the same true of statutory interpretation?

Comparative Law

Purposive interpretation is well established in comparative legal systems.[2] Continental law refers to it as teleological interpretation (subjective and objective).[3] Common law systems call it purposive interpretation, and English law explicitly applies it.[4] As Lord Diplock noted, "If one looks back

---

[2] The literature on purposive interpretation in comparative law is sparse. *See* A. Lenhoff, "On Interpretative Theories: A Comparative Study in Legislation," 27 *Tex. L. Rev.* 312 (1949). *See also* A.A. Schiller, "Roman Interpretation and Anglo-American Interpretation and Construction," 27 *Va. L. Rev.* (1941) 733; H.C. Gutteridge, "A Comparative View of the Interpretation of Statute Law," 8 *Tul. L. Rev.* 1 (1933).

[3] MacCormick and Summers, *supra* p. 250, note 139 at 88. *See also* Zweigert and Puttfarken, *supra* p. 169, note 84. On teleological interpretation in German law, see Larenz, *supra* p. 3, note 5; K. Engisch, *Einführung in das Juristische Denken* (7th ed. 1977). On teleological interpretation in Scandinavia, see P.O. Ekelof, "Teleological Construction of Statutes," 2 *Scan. Stud. L.* 757 (1958). On teleological interpretation in Italy, see J.H. Merryman, "The Italian Style III: Interpretation," 18 *Stan. L. Rev.* 582 (1966).

[4] Bennion, *supra* p. 6, note 13 at 731.

to the actual decisions of this House on questions of statutory construction over the past thirty years one cannot fail to be struck by the evidence of a trend away from the purely literal towards the purposive construction of statutory provisions."[5] Lord Denning made a similar point, noting that "The literal method is now completely out of date. It has been replaced by the approach which Lord Diplock described as the 'purposive approach' . . . In all cases now in the interpretation of statutes we adopt such a construction as will 'promote the general legislative purpose' underlying the provision."[6] Canadian,[7] Australian,[8] and New Zealand[9] case law express similar positions. American jurisprudence engages the purpose guiding statutory interpretation, using, to some extent, the phrase "purposive interpretation."[10] Of course, "purposive interpretation" may have different meanings. I do not claim that all these legal systems have adopted the model of interpretation set forth in this book, but I do note that the modern trend favors acceptance of purposive statutory interpretation. I will now discuss the components of legislative purpose, beginning with subjective purpose.

2. THE SUBJECTIVE PURPOSE OF A STATUTE

Its Essence

The subjective purpose of a statute is the subjective intent at its core. It is the abstract purpose of the statute's creators. Within the separation of powers, the subjective purpose of a statute expresses the actual will of the au-

---

[5] *Carter v. Bradbeer* [1975] 3 All E.R. 158, 161. *See also Kammins Ballrooms Co. Ltd v. Zenith Investments (Torquay) Ltd* [1971] A.C. 850, 879.

[6] *Nothmam v. Barnet Council* [1978] 1 W.L.R. 220, 228. *See also Buchanan v. Babco Forwarding and Shipping (UK) Ltd.* [1977] 1 All E.R. 518, 522 (referring to the Continental practice of teleological interpretation) (Denning, L.).

[7] Driedger, *supra* p. 69, note 31 at 35.

[8] H. Mayo, "The Interpretation of Statutes," 29 *Austl. L.J.* 204 (1955–56); G. Barwick, "Divining the Legislative Intent," 35 *Austl. L.J.* 204 (1961–62); D.C. Pearce and R.S. Geddes, *Statutory Interpretation in Australia* 23 (3d ed. 1988).

[9] J. Evans, *Statutory Interpretation: Problems of Communication* 50 (1988) ("Judges nowadays are keen to interpret statutes in the light of their purpose: 'purposive interpretation' has become the modern slogan"); D.A.S. Ward, "Trends in the Interpretation of Statutes," 2 *Victoria U. L. Rev.* 155 (1956–58); D.A.S. Ward, "A Criticism of the Interpretation of Statutes in New Zealand Courts," [1963] *New Zealand L.J.* 293; J.F. Burrows, "The Cardinal Rule of Statutory Interpretation in New Zealand," [1969] *New Zealand U. L. Rev.* 253; J.F. Burrows, "Statutory Interpretation in New Zealand," 11 *New Zealand U. L. Rev.* 1 (1984).

[10] *Supra* p. 85.

thors of the legislation. Legal literature contains extensive discussions of whether a multi-member legislative body has a subjective intent (like the intent of an individual) and if so, how one can identify it. My discussion of this issue[11] leads me to conclude that the legislature, as a collective body, does have a subjective will. It is the goals, social changes, and aims to which the members of the legislative body have agreed.[12] An interpreter learns this intent from the language of the statute and the circumstances surrounding its passage.

Objectivization of Subjective Purpose?

The subjective purpose of a statute is the purpose that the legislative body actually had. It is not the purpose of a reasonable legislature, or the purpose that a reasonable person would understand.[13] There is no objectivization of subjective purpose. It remains distinct from objective purpose, which is an independent factor in interpretation. Of course, we may recognize (factual) presumptions about the actual intent of the legislature, and those presumptions may indeed be based on the approach of the reasonable legislature. However, proof that the legislature in fact had a different intent will rebut these presumptions. When judges do not have reliable data about subjective purpose, they should say so openly, and resort to objective purpose.

3. SUBJECTIVE PURPOSE LEARNED FROM THE LANGUAGE OF THE STATUTE

The Statute as a Source of Its Own Purpose

The language of the statute is a primary source for understanding its subjective purpose. In most cases, the legislature succeeds in achieving the goals of the statute through the statutory language. The interpreter, then, learns the purpose from the language, and the purpose in turn helps him or her determine the legal meaning of the statute's language. Sometimes, the legislature helps the interpreter by writing a preamble or statement of purpose to help the interpreter formulate purpose. That statement itself, however, requires interpretation. In any case, a preamble or statement of

---

[11] *Supra* p. 129.
[12] *See* Greenawalt, *supra* p. 126, note 24.
[13] A. Scalia, *A Matter of Interpretation: Federal Courts and the Law* 17 (1997).

purpose does not constitute an exhaustive list of purposes but rather emphasizes those that are primary and central.

The Statute as a Whole

The interpretive process general begins with a "legislative unit" requiring interpretation. Interpretation does not, however, end with that unit. The judge must study the statute as whole.[14] In order to find the legal meaning of a word, an interpreter must read the paragraph framing the word, the article of the statute framing the paragraph, the chapter framing the article, and the entire piece of legislation framing the chapter.[15] The same phrase may have different meanings in two different statutes, because they aspire to different purposes. Generally, the same phrase has the same meaning everywhere it appears in a single statute, because it is designed to achieve the same purpose.

One should not assume, however, that the legislature's work is flawless. Members of a legislative body—and the aides drafting versions of bills—are as fallible as any other human beings. The interpreter should adopt a skeptical attitude toward the statute. The legislature may have passed the statute under a tight deadline; the drafters may have made political compromises at the last minute; the legislature may have deliberately left some provisions vague, leaving it to courts to give them their legal meaning. A judge's approach to interpretation should reflect the reality of the legislative process.

Legislative "Accessories"

Every piece of legislation has its own "accessories." By that I mean the name of the statute, the names of its chapters, its headings and subhead-

---

[14] *See* Judge Learned Hand's comments in *Helvering v. Gregory*, 69 F.2d 809, 810 (1934): "The meaning of a sentence may be more than that of the separate words, as a melody is more than the notes, and no degree of particularity can ever obviate recourse to the setting in which all appear, and which all collectively create." Justice Frankfurter is said to have named the following as the three rules of statutory interpretation: "Read the statute, read the statute, read the statute." Qtd. in H. Friendly, *Benchmarks* 202 (1967). *See also* J.P. Stevens, "The Shakespeare Canon of Statutory Construction," 140 *U. Pa. L. Rev.* 1373, 1376 (1992).

[15] See Celsus's comments in *Digeste* 1, 3, 24: "In civile est nisi tota lege perspecta una aliqua particula eius proposita indicare vel respondere" (it is unethical to respond to a single question without adopting the perspective of the statute as a whole). *See also* G. Devenish, "Interpretation 'From the Bowels of the Act'—An Essential Methodology for Unqualified Contextual Interpretation," 106 *S.A. L.J.* 68 (1989).

ings, and its punctuation. To the extent that these accessories underwent the legislative process, they serve as a tool for uncovering the statute's subjective purpose. We can always consult them, whether or not a statute seems "plain" at first glance. Generally, however, the intent arising from the body of the statute's provisions is more reliable than the intent arising from its accessories, because members of the legislature usually devote more attention to the body of the provisions than to their accessories.

Subjective Purpose Learned from the Natural and Ordinary Language

Judges learn the purpose of a statute from its natural and ordinary language. They employ the rebuttable presumption that the legislature expressed its purpose using natural and ordinary language. Of course, sometimes judges can achieve the purpose of a statute only by giving its language an unusual and exceptional meaning.

4. SUBJECTIVE PURPOSE LEARNED FROM SOURCES EXTERNAL TO THE STATUTE: LEGISLATIVE HISTORY

A legislature does not pass statutes in a vacuum. It acts against the backdrop of a dynamic social and legal reality. A judge interpreting legislation must recognize the context framing the legislative act. That social and legal reality is a source of information about the subjective purpose of a statute. Legislation is not just a creature of its environment; it is a creature that draws life from its environment. An interpreter should therefore take an interest in legislative history as a source of background and depth on a piece of legislation. I do not know if Justice Holmes was right to say that "a page of history is worth a volume of logic,"[16] but the history of a statute plays an important role in its interpretation. There is no question that judges should consider legislative history. The question is how to balance the need to be free of the past with the need to learn from it. We should find the proper balance between past and future, information about what was with information about what should be. When properly used, legislative history strikes the right balance, helping the judge ascertain subjective purpose.

---

[16] *New York Trust Co. v. Eisner*, 256 U.S. 345, 349 (1921).

Legislative History, Comparatively

LEGISLATIVE HISTORY IN AMERICAN LAW

Legislative history in the United States as a criterion for interpretation is highly controversial.[17] The intentionalists,[18] on the one hand, advocate

---

[17] The literature is extensive, to say the least. *See* F.E. Horack, "In the Name of Legislative Intention," 38 *Va. U. L.Q.* 119 (1932); H.W. Jones, "Statutory Doubts and Legislative Intention," 40 *Colum. L. Rev.* 957 (1940); F. Frankfurter, "Some Reflections on the Reading of Statutes," 47 *Colum. L. Rev.* 527 (1947); G. MacCallum, "Legislative Intent," 75 *Yale L.J.* 754 (1966); R. Pildes, Note, "Intent, Clear Statements, and the Common Law: Statutory Interpretation in the Supreme Court," 95 *Harv. L. Rev.* 892 (1982); O. Fiss, "Objectivity and Interpretation," 34 *Stan. L. Rev.* 739 (1982); N. Zeppos, "Judicial Candor and Statutory Interpretation," 78 *Geo. L.J.* 353 (1989); P. Wald, "Some Observations on the Use of Legislative History in the 1981 Supreme Court Term," 68 *Iowa L. Rev.* 195 (1983); R. Posner, "Statutory Interpretation—in the Classroom and in the Courtroom," 50 *U. Chi. L. Rev.* 800 (1983); E. Maltz, "Statutory Interpretation and Legislative Power: The Case for a Modified Intentionalist Approach," 63 *Tul. L. Rev.* 1 (1988); A. Aleinikoff, "Updating Statutory Interpretation," 87 *Mich. L. Rev.* 20 (1988); W. Popkin, "The Collaborative Model of Statutory Interpretation," 61 *S. Cal. L. Rev.* 541 (1988); P. Schanck, "The Only Game in Town: An Introduction to Interpretive Theory, Statutory Construction, and Legislative Histories," 38 *U. Kan. L. Rev.* 815 (1990); C. Sunstein, "Interpreting Statutes in the Regulatory State," 103 *Harv. L. Rev.* 405 (1989); N. Zeppos, "Legislative History and the Interpretation of Statutes: Toward a Fact-Finding Model of Statutory Interpretation," 76 *Va. L. Rev.* 1295 (1990); W. Eskridge, "Legislative History Values," 66 *Chi. Kent L. Rev.* 365 (1990); W. Eskridge, "The New Textualism," 37 *UCLA L. Rev.* 621 (1990); A. Stock, "Justice Scalia's Use of Sources in Statutory and Constitutional Interpretation: How Congress Always Loses," 1990 *Duke L.J.* 160; E. Maltz, "Rhetoric and Reality in the Theory of Statutory Interpretation: Underenforcement, Overenforcement, and the Problem of Legislative Supremacy," 71 *B.U. L. Rev.* 767 (1991); N. Zeppos, "Justice Scalia's Textualism: The 'New' New Legal Process," 12 *Cardozo L. Rev.* 1597 (1991); W. Popkin, "An 'Internal' Critique of Justice Scalia's Theory of Statutory Interpretation," 76 *Minn. L. Rev.* 1133 (1992); S. Breyer, "On the Uses of Legislative History in Interpreting Statutes," 65 *S. Cal. L. Rev.* 845 (1992); M. McCubbins et al., "Legislative Intent: The Use of Positive Political Theory in Statutory Interpretation," 57 *Law & Contemp. Probs.* 3 (1994); M. Redish and T. Chung, "Democratic Theory and the Legislative Process: Mourning the Death of Originalism in Statutory Interpretation," 68 *Tul. L. Rev.* 803 (1994); J. Schacter, "Metademocracy: The Changing Structure of Legitimacy in Statutory Interpretation," 108 *Harv. L. Rev.* 593 (1995); G.H. Taylor, "Structural Textualism," 75 *B.U. L. Rev.* 321 (1995); R.J. Pierce, "The Supreme Court's New Hypertextualism: An Invitation to Cacophony and Incoherence in the Administrative State," 95 *Colum. L. Rev.* 749 (1995); M.A. Eisenberg, "Strict Textualism," 29 *Loy. L.A. L. Rev.* 13 (1995); J. Manning, "Textualism as a Nondelegation Doctrine," 97 *Colum. L. Rev.* 673 (1997); J. Schacter, "The Confounding Common Law Originalism in Recent Supreme Court Statutory Interpretation: Implications for the Legislative History Debate and Beyond," 51 *Stan. L. Rev.* 1 (1998); A. Vermeule, "Legislative History and the Limits of Judicial Competence: The Untold Story of Holy Trinity Church," 50 *Stan. L. Rev.* 1833 (1998); M.H. Koby, "The Supreme Court's Declining Reliance on Legislative History: The Impact of Justice Scalia's Critique," 36 *Harv. J. on Leg.* 369 (1999); M. Healy, "Legislative Intent and Statutory Interpretation in England and

using legislative history to understand legislative intent (subjective purpose), while the new textualists[19] negate any consideration of legislative intent as a criterion for statutory interpretation and consider any use of legislative history to be inappropriate. Both views are too extreme. We cannot construct a theory of interpretation based solely on authorial intent. Sometimes we cannot know what the intent was; sometimes it does not help resolve the question at issue; sometimes it is inappropriate to take intent into consideration. However, completely ignoring legislative intent is harmful to democracy[20] and to the role of the judge.[21] In interpreting statutes, judges should consider both subjective and objective intent.[22] The question is then, how much weight should we accord legislative intent, and to what extent can we learn about it from legislative history?[23] We ask, when legislative intent arising from legislative history conflicts with the intent of the reasonable legislature or the intent of the system, which prevails?

LEGISLATIVE HISTORY IN ENGLISH LAW

English common law permits an interpreter to consult legislative history. The courts took the right step in *Pepper v. Hart*,[24] when they removed the prohibition against consulting *Hansard* (the protocols of parliamentary debate) in order to find legislative intent.[25] It is clear that if, as the new textualists claim, legislative intent is an inappropriate criterion for statutory interpretation, then interpreters should not consult legislative debates (although it is unclear why legislative debates cannot be used as a source of information about the original understanding of the statute). However, if legislative intent is relevant to understanding a statute—as common law rhetoric claims—then it seems natural to consult legislative history as an important source of information about legislative intent. The problem is that, while English common law employs the rhetoric of using legislative intent as a source of information about subjective purpose, in practice, it seeks the understanding of the reasonable person—in other words, objective purpose.[26] The English system now correctly perceives the relevance

---

the United States: An Assessment of the Impact of *Pepper v. Hart*," 35 *Stan. J. Int'l L.* 231 (1999); J. Siegel, "The Use of Legislative History in a System of Separated Powers," 53 *Vand. L. Rev.* 1457 (2000); K. Greenawalt, "Are Mental States Relevant for Statutory and Constitutional Interpretation?" 85 *Cornell L. Rev.* 1609 (2000); J. Manning, "Textualism and the Equity of the Statute," 101 *Colum. L. Rev.* 1 (2001).

[18] *Supra* p. 260. [19] *Supra* p. 277. [20] *Supra* p. 238. [21] *Supra* p. 247. [22] *Supra* p. 239.
[23] Sunstein, *supra* p. 345, note 17 at 413. [24] *Pepper v. Hart* [1993] 1 All E.R. 42.
[25] For an analysis of the decision, see Bennion, *supra* p. 6, note 13 at 472. *See also* S. Beaulac, "Parliamentary Debates in Statutory Interpretation: A Question of Admissibility or of Weight?" 43 *McGill L.J.* 287 (1998); J. Steyn, "*Pepper v. Hart*, A Re-examination," 21 *Oxford J. Leg. Stud.* 59 (2001).
[26] D. Payne, "The Intention of the Legislature in the Interpretation of Statutes," 9 *Current Legal Probs.* 96 (1956).

of legislative history in general, and legislative debate in particular, as a source of information not only about legislative intent, but also about the role of the statute. At this stage, however, it is not clear whether English common law will draw a clear distinction between subjective and objective purpose, recognizing the admissibility of legislative history and understanding its role in the interpretive process. Legislative history plays a dual role: It is a source of information about the actual intent of the legislature, but it also provides information about the objective role of the statute.

Stages of Legislative History

PRE-LEGISLATIVE HISTORY

The social and legal background of a statute can be a useful source of information about the intent at its core. The reasons and circumstances that created the need for legislation may reveal the purpose that lawmakers sought to achieve. English common law recognized the importance of this history as far back as the sixteenth century, with the articulation of the "mischief rule" in the *Heydon* case (1584):

> For the sure and true interpretation of all statutes in general (be they penal or beneficial, restrictive or enlarging by the common law), four things are to be discerned and considered: 1st. What was the common law before the making of the Act, 2nd. What was the mischief and defect for which the common law did not provide, 3rd. What remedy the Parliament hath resolved and appointed to cure the disease of the Commonwealth, and 4th. The true reason of the remedy; and then the office of all the judges is always to make such construction as shall suppress the mischief, and advance the remedy, and to suppress subtle inventions and evasions for continuance of the mischief, *pro privato commodo*, and to add force and life to the cure and remedy, according to the true intent of the makers of the Act, *pro bono publico*.[27]

These words, pronounced in England more than 400 years ago, are still valid today. They justify studying reports of public committees that recommended changes in the legal status quo, if those reports were available to the legislature. They also justify resort to the general legal situation that existed prior to the act of legislation.

HISTORY OF THE STATUTE'S PASSAGE

Legislative history itself—the chronicles of the statute from the time it was presented as a bill in the legislature to its passage—is also a source of information about legislative intent. It includes the bill and accompanying

---

[27] *Heydon's Case* (1584) 3 Co. Rep. 7a.

notes and comments; comments by legislators debating the bill in the plenary; hearings in legislative committees; and the relevant legislative committee's recommendation to the legislature. Judges may use all these sources to determine the abstract purpose[28]—as opposed to the concrete purpose—of the legislation. Judges do not ask what solution members of the legislative body envisioned for the interpretive problem they face, but rather what is the abstract (general) purpose of the statute; in other words, what compromise did the legislators reach? Based on this purpose, the judge—and the judge alone—decides the solution to the interpretive problem in question. He or she seeks the legislature's concept of the goal of the statute, not its concept of the solution to the specific dispute before the court.[29] The judge should make an effort to distinguish between what legislators said in legislative debates in order to achieve the compromise necessary to pass the statute, and what legislators said in legislative debates for the purpose of entering it into the record so that it would influence how judges interpret the statute. The judge should take only the former into consideration.

POST-LEGISLATIVE HISTORY

Because legislation is an ongoing process, subsequent legislation[30] can shed light on the purpose of earlier legislation. True, subsequent legislation[31] cannot interpret earlier legislation. The legislature legislates; it does not interpret.[32] Subsequent legislation may, however, help the interpreter find the meaning of the earlier legislation. This occurs, *inter alia*, when subsequent legislation is used as a source of information about the original purpose at the core of the earlier legislation.

A judge should exercise caution. Sometimes the new legislation can only

---

[28] See *supra* p. 126 for a discussion of this terminology.

[29] *See* K.G. Wurzel, "Methods of Juridical Thinking," *Science of Legal Method* 345 (E. Bruncken and L. Register trans., 1917). On the distinction between concept and conception, *see* R. Dworkin, "Forum of Principle," 56 *N.Y.U. L. Rev.* 469 (1981).

[30] Subsequent legislation is treated differently than comments by members of the legislative body made subsequent to the statute's passage. The latter—while it may be admissible—is of almost negligible weight. *See* P. Wald, "Some Observations on the Use of Legislative History in the 1981 Supreme Court Term," 68 *Iowa L. Rev.* 195, 205 (1983).

[31] Judges should infer nothing, however, from legislative silence, i.e., inaction in the face of a court's interpretation of earlier legislation. *See* A. Barak, 2 *Interpretation in Law* 123 (1993) at 785; Hart and Sachs, *supra* p. 3, note 3 at 1385.

[32] Declaratory Acts or Interpretive Acts that go beyond being simply cautionary, have a retroactive character. *See* Note, "Declaratory Legislation," 49 *Harv. L. Rev.* 137 (1935–1936). Common law countries sometimes pass Interpretation Acts. Because these acts define terms within a statute, they do not constitute interpretive statutes, although they do sometimes contain provisions about the proper system of interpretation.

clarify or reinforce the existing interpretation (*ex abundanti cautela*); sometimes it is based on a misguided understanding of the earlier legislation. Sometimes, however, it can shed light on the original legislation.

Admissibility of Legislative History

Judges admit information about legislative purpose from pre-legislative, legislative, and post-legislative history. The history helps them understand the purpose that the legislature envisioned. As I noted in one case:

> Every interpretive question begins with the statute, but it does not end there. The human mind must absorb all relevant information and assign it weight according to its reliability. In the words of Chief Justice Marshall of the United States Supreme Court, "Where the mind labours to discover the design of the legislature, it seizes every thing from which aid can be derived." Judges can therefore use legislative history to learn about the goal and purpose of a statute.[33]

Legislative history is admissible whether or not the statute seems clear on a first reading. The plain meaning rule does not bar a judge from consulting the legislative history of a statute and possibly determining that its "plain-ness" was only a mistaken first impression. Of course, legislative history must not substitute for the statute itself. Justice Frankfurter wisely warned against exaggerating to the point where only when the legislative history is vague do judges consult the statute itself.[34] Judges should investigate legislative history for the abstract, not concrete, purpose of the legislation, keeping in mind that subjective purpose arising from legislative history is valid only if it can be achieved through the language of the statute.[35] In the words of Justice Cheshin,

> We must be cautious lest we see things in the statute that it does not contain; lest our innermost thoughts and wisdom, acquired in extra-statutory realms, take us outside the limits of the statute; lest we impose upon the statute a "pur-

---

[33] H.C. 47/83 *Air Tours (Israel) Ltd. v. Chair of Antitrust Council*, 39(1) P.D. 169, 175, quoting *United States v. Fisher*, 6 U.S. 358 (1805).

[34] Frankfurter, "Some Reflections on the Reading of Statutes," 47 *Colum. L. Rev.* 527, 543 (1989). See also *Greenwood v. United States*, 350 U.S. 366, 374 (1955) (Frankfurter, J.).

[35] In addressing the interpretation of private law texts, I discussed the private code of the author of the text. *Supra* p. 103. Such a code has no place in public law texts. If a statute creates a normative regulation whose object is a horse, a judge cannot interpret the regulation to apply to a car, based on the claim that the legislators used their own private code. A public law text is addressed to the public, using public language. It creates a reliance interest. If the legislature wants to use the word "horse" to denote a car, it must say so in the statute's definitional clauses.

pose" that we find outside the statute, thinking it is the right thing to do. We must not forget that the language of the legislature is paramount, and it is what informs our activities.[36]

Weight of Legislative History

In assigning weight to legislative history for purposes of determining subjective purpose, we should remember that it is the statute that underwent the legislative process, not its history. Legislative history is not part of the statute, but rather a source of information about the statute's subjective purpose. Judges should assign weight to the information commensurate with its reliability. Often, it is not very reliable at all. Legislative history is fragmentary. It is subjective to one or another member of the legislature. It is subject to manipulation. For these and other reasons, legislative history does not provide a lot of information about subjective purpose. It is certainly less persuasive than information about subjective purpose that originates in the statute itself. Under some circumstances, however, judges should heavily weight legislative history in determining subjective purpose. This happens, for example, when no clear picture emerges from the language of the statute, while legislative history provides credible information.

5. THE OBJECTIVE PURPOSE OF A STATUTE

Its Essence

The objective purpose of a statute is the interests, goals, values, aims, policies, and function that the statute is designed to actualize in a democracy. This purpose, as the name suggests, depends on objective criteria—in other words, criteria external to the subjective intent of the legislature. Objective purpose is not a conjecture or presumption about the subjective purpose of the legislature. It exists independently, even when it is clear that the legislature did not envision it as a purpose. While it does not depend on facts that can be proven historically, it is nonetheless tightly bound to the language of the statute in two ways: *First*, the language of the statute often provides information about its objective purpose. *Second*, an interpreter cannot use a statute to achieve a purpose that the statute cannot bear in its language. Indeed, sometimes reading the language of the statute provides no information about objective purpose. The interpreter is free to

---

[36] H.C. 5503/94, *Segel v. Speaker of Knesset*, 51(4) P.D. 529, 562.

learn about the purpose of a statute from sources external to the statutory language, so long as the language of the statute can bear that external purpose.

Levels of Abstraction of Objective Purpose

The objective purpose of a statute exists at four levels of abstraction. At the lowest level, we seek the abstract purpose that the legislators who passed the statute would have wanted to achieve, had they faced the interpretive problem in question. At this level of abstraction, the judge engages in what Posner called "imaginative reconstruction" of the intent of the legislature.[37] At the next level of abstraction, we replace the specific legislature that passed the statute with a reasonable legislature. At a higher level of abstraction, we focus on the nature of the matter regulated by the statute, deriving objective purpose from the type of statute in question.[38] The essence of the legal "institution" provides information about its purpose. For example, for a statute regulating guarantees, the essence of the legal institution of guarantees guides the judge toward the goal of the regulation. Finally, at the highest level of abstraction, the objective purpose of the statute derives from the fundamental principles of the legal system. It is not specific to one or another statute but rather constitutes a normative umbrella covering all statutes. Purposive interpretation translates this general purpose into general presumptions about the purpose of the legislation.[39]

Objective Purpose in the Test of Time: Dynamic Interpretation

We have not yet addressed whether judges should evaluate the objective purpose of a statute as it existed at the time the statute was enacted, or at the time they interpret it. In my opinion, when judges refer to the objective purpose of a statute at the lowest level (imaginative reconstruction or "what the legislators would have envisioned as the purpose, had they considered the matter"), they should put themselves in the shoes of the legislators at the time of enactment. However, when judges consult objective purpose at higher levels of abstraction, they deal with values and principles that change over time. At these levels, objective purpose should reflect the reasonable legislature, the essence of the legal institution under regulation, and the fundamental values of the system as they exist at the time of inter-

[37] Posner, *supra* p. 27, note 85 at 270, 273.
[38] Larenz, *supra* p. 3, note 5 at 291.
[39] *Infra* p. 358.

pretation. At these higher levels of abstraction, interpretation is dynamic. The statute speaks always, and it is wiser than the legislature that passed it.

6. SOURCES OF OBJECTIVE PURPOSE

Internal and External Sources

The interpreter leans about the objective purpose of the statute from two primary sources: the statute itself (internal source) and its surroundings (external source). Judges use their pre-understanding to circumvent the problem of the hermeneutic circle and access the language of the statute.[40] They also derive objective purpose from other statutes and from the values and principles of the legal system of which the statute is a part and without which the statute could not exist. Sources external to the legislation itself, including the legal situation that existed prior to the statute's enactment, provide useful information about the objective purpose of the statute.

Internal Sources: The Statute as a Whole

The issue that a statute addresses and the nature of its arrangements provide the judge with information about its objective purpose. When a statute addresses a well-known legal institution (sale, guaranty, right, power, cancellation, licensing) the judge can infer the goal of the statute from the essence of the legal institution itself. For example, when a statute addresses a particular type of tax, it carries in its wake the objective purpose characteristic of that type of tax. The subject of the legislation and the way the statute treats that subject provide information about the purpose at the core of the legislation. Just as studying a machine and the way it performs provides information about the task that the machine is designed to execute, so studying a statute and its arrangements provides information about the objective purpose that the statute is designed to achieve.[41] The scope of the issues that the legislation addresses suggests the scope of its purpose. The form of the arrangement (procedural or substantial), the way the issue is regulated (sharp deviation or gradual evolution), and the measures employed (criminalizing behavior, creating civil liability, or establishing a licensing regime) all guide judges toward objective purpose. Judges engage in a logical process, searching the data set arising from the language of the

---

[40] *Supra* p. 136.
[41] L. Fuller, *The Morality of Law* 86 (rev. ed. 1969).

statute and external to it for the generalization that reflects the statute's aims and goals. They infer objective purpose from the structure of a statute as a whole, its division into chapters, and a comparison of its different provisions. They may take into consideration the location of a statutory provision in order to understand its purpose. They should view the statute in its entirety as an integrated unit. Each part performs one of the micro-functions that together perform the function of the statute.

Of course, judges should not exaggerate the integrated nature of a statute. Sometimes, a statute represents a compromise between conflicting worldviews. One view may prevail in one part of the statute, while its rival trumps in another part. A single, uniform view—political, societal, or so-cial—does not always dominate all parts of the statute. Judges should keep that in mind as they navigate their way among the statutory provisions.

External Sources: Other Statutes ("Legislative Harmony")

A statute is not the one-time act of a transient legislature operating in a leg-islative vacuum. A statute is a single link in the legislative chain of a per-manent legislature. The statutes taken together create the legal system's legislative project. This project is the environment surrounding every statute. The interpreter learns the purpose of a statute through a holistic examination of the legislative project,[42] whether it consists of prior or sub-sequent legislation. The interpreter should assume harmony within the leg-islative project and should avoid severing a statutory provision from the to-tality of legislation. Whoever applies a single statute, applies the entirety of legislation.[43] The boundaries of the statute being interpreted are not lim-ited by the horizon of the interpreter. They extend to the horizon of the system as a whole, including all legislation. The various statutes in a system exist as integrated tools, like different limbs of a single body. The way the body as a whole functions indicates the tasks designated to each statute. For example, the role designated to a legal institution (like a commercial document) in private law tends to influence the purpose at the core of the protection of that institution in criminal law. The purposes behind the statute of frauds, the consideration requirement, protections of the rights of third parties, remedies, and other legal arrangements determined by var-ious statutes are likely to be similar—hence the utility of comparing vari-ous pieces of legislation. "Thousands of chords run between the general and specific law, such that the specific law interacts with the general. That interaction creates legislative harmony in civil law as a whole, guaranteeing

---

[42] 2A Sutherland, *Statutes and Statutory Construction* 549 (Sands ed., 4th ed. 1984).
[43] R. Stammler, *Theorie der Rechtswissenschaft* 24 (1911).

the coordinated and controlled operation of each specific provision within the framework of the general project."[44]

Consistent with the harmony of legislation, judges should adopt the same balancing formula for the same values at the core of conflicting rights. In other words, they should maintain consistency in balancing value X and value Y, even when the rights those values underpin are different. When a statute provides a particular kind of protection, given a particular set of facts (like protecting a third party who acquired an asset knowing that a competing claim existed), then legislative harmony requires providing at least that level of protection, when the minimum set of facts exists to justify the protection. Furthermore, legislative harmony requires providing broader protection when additional factors are present to justify it (like protecting a third party who acquired an asset *without* knowing about the existence of a competing claim).[45] If the law protects certain values and expresses them through the legal tools at its disposal (like criminal law), then legislative harmony justifies providing similar protection to the same values through the use of less drastic legal tools at its disposal (like civil and public law).

Legislation takes place against the background of fundamental jurisprudential viewpoints, legal concepts, and general laws. Legislative harmony requires an interpreter to consider those viewpoints, in order to formulate a legislative purpose consistent with them. For example, judges should assume that phrases in private legislation, like "sale" and "lease," when used in public law (as in tax law or penal law), retain the meaning designated to them in private law. Legislative harmony assumes that different statutes have different roles that interconnect and facilitate the proper functioning of legislation as a whole. Because conflicting statutory provisions undermine legislative harmony, interpretation should try to avoid internal conflict between different pieces of legislation. The assumption is that the purpose of the various statutes is to create internal harmony and prevent a frontal conflict that would implicitly rob one statute of its validity. By the same principle, interpretation should not give a statute a meaning that renders another statute completely superfluous.

Of course, normative harmony is not always possible. Sometimes statutes contradict each other; sometimes a judge has no choice but to determine that a statutory provision is superfluous; sometimes disharmony reigns. One should not compel harmony where disharmony exists. Legislative harmony is a relative concept. It is an aspiration, a rebuttable presumption. It applies regardless of the apparent clarity of the statute. Legislative harmony

[44] F.H. 20/82 *Adras Building Materials Ltd. v. Harlow and Jones*, 42(1) P.D. 221, 263 (Barak, J.).

[45] Bydlinsky, *supra* p. 7, note 14 at 458.

is a means of formulating the purpose of legislation. The presumption of harmony applies not just to statutes of the same subject matter (*in pari materia*) but to all statutes, regardless of their subject matter. The judge is responsible for maintaining normative harmony. Mindful of the internal relationships between different statutes, he or she should view the legislative system as a whole. The magnitude of the responsibility might make it seem as though only a Herculean judge[46]—a figment of Professor Dworkin's imagination—could accomplish the task. The truth, however, is that every judge can do it, and every judge should try.

External Sources: Legislative History

The originalists, who negate the role of subjective purpose in interpretation,[47] discount legislative history in the mistaken belief that it is useful only to determine legislative intent. Legislative history is valuable irrespective of subjective purpose, particularly for the originalists who want to know how a reasonable reader would have understood the statute at the time it passed. The understanding of the legislators at the time they enacted the statute naturally helps an interpreter formulate the "original" understanding of the statute. But one need be neither an originalist nor an intentionalist (concerned with legislative intent) to be interested in the history of a statute (pre-legislative, legislative, and post-legislative). History teaches us about the "social background or the circumstances that made the legislation necessary."[48] A statute without history is like a tree without roots. History teaches us about the objective and subjective purposes of the statute and should always be consulted as part of the process of interpretation.

External Sources: Social Background and General History

The passage of every statute takes place against a social and legal background.[49] The socio-historical background of a statute constantly projects itself onto the legislation, helping shape its purpose. What can we understand about Israel's Law of Return, which makes Israeli citizenship available to Jews and their descendants, without understanding the history of

---

[46] R. Dworkin, *Taking Rights Seriously* 81 (1977); R. Dworkin, *Law's Empire* 239 (1986).
[47] *Supra* p. 277.
[48] A.L.A. 593/86 *Putshenik v. Shlissel*, 41(4) P.D. 533, 539 (Bejsky, J.).
[49] *Morris v. Beardmore* [1981] A.C. 446, 459. *See also* Krygier, "The Traditionality of Statutes," 1 *Ratio Juris* 20 (1988).

the founding of the State of Israel? What can we understand about the legislation passed on the heels of the 1967 Six-Day War in the Middle East, without knowing the history of the war? In addition to considering history, judges should consider the social and cultural assumptions prevalent at the time the statute was passed. Legislation is based on a shared viewpoint of language and culture, and it assumes a particular social and cultural system.[50]

External Sources: The General Law

A piece of legislation is a sapling in the field of law. Its cultivation and development depend on a given framework of laws (statutory, case law, customary). Of course, a legislature often passes a statute in order to change the existing law. In doing so, however, it does not seek to change all existing laws. Legislation is a process of evolution, not revolution. It seeks to make a particular change while maintaining the existence of all the other laws, in the context of a system of law and society. We assume that a law—be it a statute or judge-made case law—does not casually seek to disrupt the fundamental viewpoints of a legal system. Indeed, judge-made case law, forming part of the general law, provides information about the individual objective purpose of a statute, as well as the general objective purpose of the system as a whole.

External Sources: Case Law

Case law is an important external source of information about the objective purpose of a statute. This is true of both individual and general objective purpose.

External Sources: The Fundamental Values of the System

Judges interpreting any statute must take the fundamental values of the legal system into consideration.[51] They derive those values from the core documents of the legal system, the democratic nature of the regime, the status of the individual as a free person, the social consensus, and the case law of courts. The list of fundamental values and principles is in constant

---

[50] Kohler, *supra* p. 59, note 216 at 188.
[51] W. Eskridge, "Public Values in Statutory Interpretation," 137 *U. Pa. L. Rev.* 1007 (1989).

flux, as new ones are added and obsolete ones are dropped.[52] Judges must exercise great caution in handling these values and principles, lest they mistake their own subjective values and principles for those of the legal system and its credo.

External Sources: Comparative Law

Comparative law is an important and valid source of information for a judge seeking to determine the objective purpose of a piece of legislation.[53] It is useful for both specific purpose (micro-comparison)[54] and general purpose (macro-comparison).[55] A similar statute in the democratic legal system of another nation may provide inspiration in understanding specific purpose. The same is true of attempts to understand the purpose at the core of legislation regulating a legal institution, like agency or leasing. Rather than analyze the minute details of a foreign piece of legislation, judges examine the function that the legal institution performs in the two systems. To the extent that the functions are similar, the foreign example may provide interpretive inspiration for understanding the purpose of the domestic legislation.

Consider, for example, the principle of good faith in negotiations to form a contract and in contractual performance. To the extent that the principle fulfills similar roles in two legal systems, the foreign system may help the judge formulate the purpose at the core of the domestic principle of good faith. Comparative law also helps determine the general purpose that expresses the system's fundamental principles and values. This can only occur when the two systems share a common ideological basis.

Comparative law can play an important role in formulating the purpose of legislation, but judges should use it cautiously.[56] Interpretive inspiration is appropriate only when the two systems share similar functions, similar basic assumptions, and similar goals. When that condition is met, a judge

---

[52] *Supra* p. 166.

[53] G. Zaphiriou, "Use of Comparative Law by the Legislature," 30 *Am. J. Comp. L.* 71 (1982); D.N. MacCormick and R. Summers (eds.), *Interpreting Statutes: A Comparative Study* (1991); M. Healy, "Legislative Intent and Statutory Interpretation in England and the United States: An Assessment of the Impact of *Pepper v. Hart*," 35 *Stan. J. Int'l Law* 231 (1999); U. Drobnig and van Erp (eds.), *The Use of Comparative Law by Courts* (1994); H.P. Glenn, "Centennial World Congress on Comparative Law: Comparative Law and Legal Practice: On Removing the Borders," 75 *Tul. L. Rev.* 977 (2001).

[54] On this term, see Zweigert and Kötz, *supra* p. 318, note 2 at 5.

[55] *Id.* at 4.

[56] For arguments against using comparative law, see G. Frankenberg, "Critical Comparisons: Re-thinking Comparative Law," 26 *Harv. Int'l L.J.* 411 (1985).

may use comparison even if it is clear that when passing the statute, the legislature did not consider the foreign law.

7. PRESUMPTIONS OF OBJECTIVE PURPOSE

Presumptions about the General Purpose of Legislation

Purposive interpretation translates the legal system's fundamental values into presumptions about the general purpose of every statute.[57] Those presumptions apply whether or not a statute explicitly declares or repeats them. A statute designed to deviate from them, however, must state as much explicitly. The general presumptions of purpose are rooted in the constitutional law[58] specific to each legal system. Even within a legal system, those viewpoints change over time. I will discuss just a few presumptions of purpose valid in most legal systems.

Presumptions of Purpose Reflecting Security, Certainty, Harmony, and Consistency in Law

Every modern democratic legal system recognizes security and certainty in interpersonal relations as fundamental values.[59] All legal systems aspire to legislative harmony and legislative consistency,[60] although their absolute realization is impossible and perhaps undesirable. Legal systems thus presume security, certainty, consistency, and harmony in legislation. They presume that the purpose of a statute arises from its natural and ordinary language and that it does not conflict with other pieces of legislation. They presume that statutes do not conflict with the constitution, that implementing legislation does not conflict with primary statutes, that different provisions of a statute do not conflict with each other, and that a statute integrates into the general law.[61] Every piece of legislation assumes the existence and validity of the fundamental doctrines of public and private law,

[57] Du Plessis, *supra* p. 171, note 97 at 54.

[58] J. Kernochan, "Statutory Interpretation: An Outline of Method," 3 *Dalhousie L.J.* 333 (1976).

[59] L. Fuller, *Anatomy of the Law* 94 (1988). *See also* K. Diplock, *The Courts as Legislators* 16 (1965). Hence the basis for the principle of binding precedent. *See Burnet v. Coronado Oil & K. Gas Co.*, 285 U.S. 393, 406; *Sheddon v. Goodrich*, 32 E.R. 441, 447 (1803).

[60] Peczenik, *supra* p. 16, note 44; J. Raz, "The Relevance of Coherence," 72 *B.U. L. Rev.* 273 (1992); J. Coons, "Consistency," 75 *Cal. L. Rev.* 59 (1987).

[61] Additional presumptions derive from this last presumption. *See* A. Vermeule, "Saving Constructions," 85 *Ga. L.J.* 1945 (1997).

the system's jurisprudential infrastructure, and its operative legal theory. Legal systems presume that every statute is based on fundamental distinctions between might and right; right and remedy; validity and voidability; voidability and voidness; substance and procedure; adult and minor; natural persons and legal entities; authority and discretion; and the admissibility of evidence and its probative value. They presume that a statute that uses terms of general meaning intends the meaning of the terms in general law; they presume that a public law statute (like a tax or criminal statute) uses terms from private law (like ownership and property) in their private law meanings. A particularly important presumption is that statutes are not designed to effect substantial change in the law casually or coincidentally,[62] and that the legislature does not waste its breath.

The presumption of normative harmony means legal systems assume that every statutory provision has a role in the general project, that no provision is superfluous, and that there is no legislation for the sake of legislation. They presume that a new statute is designed to achieve a purpose, either to change existing law or declare and reinforce it. They presume that legislation aims to create a valid provision, to give identical words identical meaning, and to give different words, different meanings. Of course, these presumptions are rebuttable.

Presumptions of Purpose Reflecting Ethical Values

Democracy rests on a foundation of ethics. The purpose of every statute is therefore presumed to be to achieve justice. As Justice Silberg said,

> I am aware that I am not a lawmaker, nor the child of a lawmaker, but rather a judge of flesh-and-blood, sworn and ready to do as the law commands. I think, however, that when the scales are balanced, and a statute could be interpreted this way or that, my obligation is to give it a meaning consistent with the commandment to do good and right, not a meaning offensive to a feeling of natural justice.[63]

I would add only that looking to justice as a source of interpretation is not limited to a case in which "the scales are balanced." Judges must always keep justice in mind. It is not the only value to be considered, and its weight is not decisive, but we presume that the purpose of a statute is to achieve the rules of natural justice and avoid a conflict of interests.

---

[62] Bennion, *supra* p. 6, note 13 at 626.
[63] C.A. 260/57 *Padva v. Friedman*, 14 P.D. 427, 436.

Presumptions of Purpose Reflecting Social Goals

The social goals of a democratic regime constitute part of the objective purpose of every piece of legislation. The objective purpose of every statute is presumed to be to ensure the continued existence of the state.[64] The purpose of every statute is also presumed to be the preservation and development of democracy and the advancement of the public interest, including public order, public welfare, and public security. These conditions are necessary for the existence of all the other values of the state or legal system. Human rights cannot exist in a state of anarchy. There can be no freedom without order. "Democracy need not commit suicide in order to prove its vitality."[65]

One of the most important social goals is the principle of the separation of powers. Purposive interpretation translates that goal into the presumption that the objective purpose of every statute is to preserve and advance the separation of powers. Hence the presumption that the purpose of legislation is to leave legislative authority in the hands of the legislature,[66] executive authority in the hands of the executive,[67] and judicial authority in the hands of the judiciary. The separation-of-powers presumption means we also presume that a statute does not undermine the authority of the courts to judge and interpret.[68] An additional, important presumption is that statutes seek to guarantee judicial independence and public confidence in the judiciary. Every statute is presumed to preserve the rule of law in its formal, theoretical, and substantive sense; to apply both to individuals and to public agencies; to be enforced against everyone in an equal manner; to prevent people from taking the law into their own hands; and to avoid allowing people to bypass it.

In addition, the theoretical principle of rule of law leads to a number of presumptions already discussed. These include the substantive aspect of rule of law, the need to ensure rule of law on the international plane by making sure domestic law is compatible with public international law,[69] and the territorial application of local law.

---

[64] This is a "constitutional given." E.A. 1/65 *Yardor v. Chair of the Central Election Committee of the Sixth Knesset,* 19(3) P.D. 365, 384 (Agranat, P.). *See also* E.A. 2/84 *Neemon v. Chair of Knesset Elections Committee,* 38(3) P.D. 85.

[65] E.A. 2/84, *supra* p. 360, note 64 at 315 (Barak, J.).

[66] Hence the bar against recognizing the power of the executive to legislate in the absence of explicit statutory permission, i.e., the non-delegation doctrine. *See* Sunstein, *supra* p. 13, note 31.

[67] This is the basis of the theory of the "zone of reasonableness" in administrative law.

[68] *See* Du Plessis, *supra* p. 171, note 97.

[69] M. Hunt, *Using Human Rights Law in English Courts* (1997).

Presumptions of Purpose Reflecting Proper Modes of Behavior

Legal norms regulate interpersonal relations, permitting and forbidding different types of interpersonal behavior. Each society sets for itself the proper level of behavior among its members. It generally does so by regulating the control that people may exercise over the interests of others. Law sets a level of ordinary, accepted behavior that is somewhere between the ideal to which human behavior aspires and behavior bad enough to warrant legal sanction. "Ordinary" behavior is based on reasonableness, rationality, proportionality, fairness, and good faith. This level of behavior is at the core of social order. It allows members of society to engage in communal life. It depends on the balance of values and interests at stake for any particular matter.

Against this backdrop, the legislature enacts statutes with the objective purpose of achieving these proper modes of behavior. Hence the presumption that legislation seeks to achieve reasonable results, logically, avoiding anything that is needlessly contrary to common sense. The purpose of a statute is presumed not to be the performance of a useless activity, not to make unrealistic demands, and not to mandate something that is impossible (*lex non cogit ad impossibilia*). Legislation is also presumed to avoid the unexpected or the illegal and to avoid frustrating its own application. Legislation is presumed to avoid fictions, superfluity, unnecessary complications, and creating loopholes or unnecessary, valueless tools. A statute is presumed to aspire to harmony with the constitution and other statutes while retaining its validity (*ut res magis valeat ereat*), and the administrative body in charge of it is presumed to act reasonably. Hence, the presumption that the purpose of legislation is to achieve proportional, fair results. A particularly important presumption is the presumption of good faith, an objective concept that reflects a proper level of behavior. In most legal systems, good faith is a fundamental principle that permeates the objective purpose of every statute.

Presumptions of Purpose Reflecting Human Rights

In a democracy, judges interpret every piece of legislation with the basic assumption that human rights are protected. As I noted in one case:

> The constitutional point of departure is the existence and preservation of fundamental democratic rights. We assume that, in enacting a piece of legislation, the legislature (or agency enacting regulations) seeks to maintain and preserve fundamental rights. Hence the purpose of every piece of legislation is to preserve, not harm, fundamental rights.[70]

[70] C.A. 524/88 *Pri Haemek Cooperative Agricultural Association v. Sde Yaakov Workers Collective*, 45(4) P.D. 529, 561.

Legislation is presumed to aim at the protection of at least one of the human rights recognized in the legal system and in international law.[71] These rights vary by legal system, but every democracy presumes human rights protections. There is also a presumption that improper infringement on constitutionally protected human rights can render a statute unconstitutional. Extensive case law in Israel has recognized this presumption of purpose in broad areas of life. The logical inference is that, if someone or something infringes on a human right, the law is presumed to compensate the victim.

Presumptions of Purpose against Retroactive Application of Statutes

Most democracies—including the United Kingdom,[72] the United States,[73] Canada,[74] South Africa,[75] France,[76] and Israel[77]—accept the presumption that legislation does not apply retroactively. Legislation is designed to guide human behavior, to tell people what is permitted and what is forbidden, which actions have legal repercussions, and which do not. Statutes inherently guide future action. It is meaningless, today, to issue a directive about an action that occurred yesterday.[78] Still, not every retroactive statute is unconstitutional. Consider a new statute decriminalizing what had been a violation of a prior criminal law. Is there any real reason not to apply the new statute, retrospectively? Why oppose a statute rectifying the unjust results of a prior statute? Not all retrospective legislation is negative. We must balance the negative with the positive. Nevertheless, the general presumption is against giving legislation retrospective applicability. It is difficult, however, to define what is retrospective. The literature on the subject is extensive[79] and beyond the scope of this book. I note only that the follow-

---

[71] *See* Hunt, *supra* p. 360, note 69.

[72] Cross, *supra* p. 3, note 3 at 187; Bennion, *supra* p. 6, note 13 at 235.

[73] Sutherland, *supra* p. 69, note 31, vol. II at 348.

[74] Driedger, *supra* p. 69, note 31 at 508; Côté, *supra* p. 77, note 65 at 99.

[75] Du Plessis, *supra* p. 171, note 97 at 98.

[76] 1 H. Mazeaud, J. Mazeaud, F. Chabas, *Leçons de Droit Civil* 191 (1989); 1 J. Ghestin, *Traité de Droit Civil* 262 (2d ed. 1983).

[77] Barak, *supra* p. 348, note 31 at 609.

[78] Fuller, *supra* p. 352, note 41 at 53.

[79] W.D. Slawson, "Constitutional and Legislative Considerations in Retroactive Lawmaking," 48 *Cal. L. Rev.* 216 (1960); S. Munzer, "Retroactive Law," 6 *J. Leg. Stud.* 373 (1977); E. Driedger, "Statutes: Retroactive Retrospective Reflections," 61 *Can. Bar Rev.* 264 (1978); S. Munzer, "A Theory of Retroactive Legislation," 61 *Tex. L. Rev.* 425 (1982); G. De Mars, "Retrospectivity and Retroactivity of Civil Litigation Reconsidered," 10 *Ohio N.U. L. Rev.* 253 (1983); P. Côté, "La Position Temporelle des Faits Juridiques et L'application de la Loi dans le Temps," 22 *R.J.T.* 207 (1988); P. Côté, "Contribution a la theorie de la rétroactivite

ing definition of retrospective[80] legislation is appropriate for our purposes: "Legislation is retrospective if it changes, for future purposes, the legal status, characteristics, or results of situations that have ended or activities or events (acts or omissions) that were done or took place before the statute became applicable."[81]

We should avoid defining retrospectivity in terms of rights that have been granted. True, it is presumed that statutes do not violate rights already granted. We are concerned with a different presumption, however, against the retrospective application of statutes. The presumption does not apply to retrospective laws that confer a benefit.[82] It does, however, apply to statutes creating substantive and procedural law. Not all new procedural laws are retrospective. Not everything that occurs subsequent to the vesting of a substantive right or after the commencement of a judicial procedure is retrospective with respect to that right or procedure. Whether a new statute is retrospective depends on how it affects activities completed under the auspices of the old statute. Not every new procedural provision changes the legal character of activities conducted according to the old procedural rule. Applying a new procedural norm to a pending procedure does not constitute retrospective application but rather concurrent application. However, if the new procedural provision changes the legal effect of procedural activities completed in the past, it does constitute retrospective application, and the presumption against retrospective application of legislation should apply.[83]

8. THE ULTIMATE PURPOSE OF A STATUTE

Contradictory Information about Subjective and Objective Purpose

Many systems of interpretation, including those prevalent in Continental[84] and common law systems, allow judges to resolve contradictions between subjective and objective purpose through the unfettered exercise of discretion. At this stage of interpretation, the pragmatists, for example, tell

---

des lois," 68 *Can. Bar Rev.* 60 (1989); D. Shaviro, *When Rules Change: An Economic and Political Analysis of Transition Relief and Retroactivity* (2000).

[80] There is a distinction between retrospectivity and retroactivity. A retroactive statute works backward in time to change a law that had been in effect prior to its passage. A retrospective statute works in the future but looks back to change the future results of activities that took place in the past. *See* Driedger, *supra* p. 69, note 31 at 511.

[81] P.C.A. 1613/91 *Arviv v. State of Israel*, 46(2) P.D. 765, 777 (Barak, J.).

[82] Bennion, *supra* p. 6, note 13 at 237.

[83] P.C.A. 1613/91, *supra* p. 363, note 81 at 786.

[84] Larenz, *supra* p. 3, note 5; Bydlinski, *supra* p. 7, note 14.

judges to consider all information (subjective and objective) but provide no additional guidance.[85] Purposive interpretation takes a different approach, providing criteria to guide the exercise of discretion. We will first discuss this guidance in the context of internal contradictions within a statute's subjective purpose, and then discuss internal contradictions within its objective purpose. We will close with a discussion of how to resolve conflicting data about subjective and objective purpose.

Determining a Statute's Subjective Purpose

In cases of contradictory information about the (abstract) subjective purpose of a statute, judges should begin by according significant weight to the abstract subjective purpose arising from the natural and ordinary language of the statute. That purpose is presumed to be the purpose of the statute. The legislature is presumed to have succeeded in expressing its purpose through its language. Therefore, when that purpose contradicts the purpose arising from external sources (like legislative history), judges should give priority to the subjective purpose arising from the language of the statute itself. Only when that purpose is not clear enough, or does not provide enough assistance, should the abstract subjective purpose arising from external sources prevail. The weight of this latter source of purpose depends on its reliability. Judges should not make assumptions of reasonableness. If credible information about the abstract subjective purpose that the legislators actually envisioned is available, then judges should take it into consideration, even if it contradicts the presumption that subjective purpose is that arising from the language of the legislature. If no such information is available, then judges should end their inquiry into subjective purpose, and turn to objective purpose.

Sometimes, a clear picture of legislative intent emerges, but it is self-contradictory. To resolve those contradictions, purposive interpretation prefers a specific purpose to a general purpose and a primary subjective purpose to a subordinate subjective purpose. If the scales remain balanced, judges will take information about objective purpose into account, in order to resolve the deadlock. Indeed, as judges determine subjective purpose, they remain aware of objective purpose. When the "subjective" scales are even, judges should weigh competing pieces of information about both objective and subjective purpose, at the final stage of determining the statute's ultimate purpose.

---

[85] Eskridge and Frickey, *supra* p. 286, note 106 at 352.

Determining a Statute's Objective Purpose: Conflict between Individual and General Purpose

In a minority of cases, the various pieces of information about objective purpose conflict. We begin with a possible conflict between individual objective purpose and general objective purpose, that is to say, presumptions of objective purpose derived from the system's fundamental principles. The former is unique to each statute, while the latter is common to all statutes (the normative umbrella). In principle, purposive interpretation prefers individual purpose to general purpose.

A purposive interpreter does not lightly decide that an individual purpose conflicts with the general purpose, in part because he or she presumes the constitutionality of every piece of legislation. He or she will make every effort to avoid recognizing a contradiction, because a contradiction would place the validity of the statute in question. Meaning and validity, however, are two separate things, and sometimes, an interpreter has no choice but to conclude that the individual objective purpose contradicts the general purpose. The individual objective purpose will generally, but not always, prevail. An exception would be the case of an individual purpose that clashes with the general purpose of human rights. Because a democracy puts such tremendous emphasis on human rights, an interpreter may decide that the general purpose prevails, particularly if the individual purpose is not explicitly, clearly, and unequivocally stated in the language of the statute.[86] Israeli law has developed this approach,[87] as articulated by then-acting Court President Meir Shamgar: "A fundamental right cannot be denied or restricted except by an explicit piece of legislation by the primary [non-administrative] legislature."[88] I established a similar holding: "A piece of legislation should not be interpreted to authorize the violation of fundamental rights unless the authorization is clear, unequivocal, and explicit."[89]

This approach has developed primarily in the context of a contradiction between individual purpose and presumptions of purpose relating to human rights, but it has expanded over time to include additional, general presumptions of purpose, like the presumption that the purpose of a statute is to achieve natural justice. In the context of the right to a hearing, for example, the Israeli Supreme Court has held that "a statutory provision is necessary not to recognize the right to a hearing but rather to deny it. Such de-

---

[86] C. Sunstein, "Nondelegation Canons," 67 *U. Chi. L. Rev.* 315 (2000). Sunstein views the different canons he discusses—which in our terms would be presumptions of purpose—as an expression of the nondelegation doctrine.

[87] Barak, *supra* p. 348, note 31 at 493.

[88] H.C. 337/81 *Mitrani v. Minister of Transportation*, 36(3) P.D. 337, 358.

[89] H.C. 333/85 *Aviel v. Minister of Labor and Welfare*, 45(4) P.D. 581, 600.

nial must be done through clear and explicit language."[90] Similarly, "only the legislature's clear and explicit instruction can provide exemption from the rule against a conflict of interests."[91] The same high bar is required to rebut the presumption that the purpose of legislation is to give judicial authority to the judiciary.[92] Clear and explicit language is not necessary to rebut every general presumption. Presumptions of purpose reflecting security, certainty, and harmony in law[93] may be rebutted by the implicit language of a statute.[94] However, the heavier the weight of the values and principles at the core of a general purpose, the greater the tendency to require clear, explicit, and unequivocal language in order to rebut a presumption derived from that general purpose. In borderline cases, where the scales are balanced between individual and general objective purpose, the interpreter takes the (abstract) subjective purposes into account, as we shall discuss.

Determining a Statute's Objective Purpose: Conflict between Presumptions of General Purpose

We have discussed situations of conflict between various presumptions about the general purpose of all legislation.[95] We saw that judges resolve the contradiction by assigning weight to the various presumptions and conducting a principled balance (horizontal and vertical) between them. The weight of the presumptions depends on the relative importance of the values and principles for which they stand. The balance generally yields a clear and unequivocal resolution. In cases where the scales are even, however, judges should use subjective purpose to help resolve the contradiction, as we shall discuss.

Conflict between the (Abstract) Subjective Purpose of a Statute and Its Objective Purpose

We have reached the decisive and most difficult stage—a situation of conflict between the (abstract) subjective purpose and objective purpose of a

[90] H.C. 654/78 *Gingold v. National Labor Court*, 35(2) P.D. 649, 657 (Barak, J.).

[91] H.C. 531/79 *Likud Party in Petach Tikvah v. Petach Tikvah Municipal Council* 34(2) P.D. 566, 574.

[92] H.C. 403/71 *Alcourdi v. National Labor Court*, 26(2) P.D. 66, 72; H.C. 222/68 *Chugim Leumiim, Nonprofit v. Minister of Police*, 24(2) P.D. 141, 172; H.C. 294/89 *National Insurance Institute v. Appeals Committee*, 45(5) P.D. 445, 451.

[93] *Supra* p. 358.

[94] In Israel, there is some ambiguity over whether this applies to the presumption against the retrospective application of a statute. *See* Barak, *supra* p. 348, note 31 at 644.

[95] *Supra* p. 176.

statute. We assume, of course, that the subjective purpose has arisen from the language of the statute or its external sources. We assume that the interpreter has not engaged in guesswork or conjecture, but rather has uncovered a clear, certain, and credible subjective purpose. The interpreter considers both subjective and objective purpose, understanding one in the context of his or her awareness of the other. He or she uses objective purpose to choose among competing subjective purposes; he or she uses subjective purpose to choose among competing objective purposes. If, however, after the interpreter clarifies and articulates both kinds of purposes, the contradiction between them remains unresolved, one or the other will have to prevail.

Purposive interpretation does not create "rules of adjudication" in which one or the other kind of purpose always prevails. Instead, it takes a differential approach. It regards a contradiction between a statute's (abstract) subjective purpose and its individual objective purpose differently from the contradiction between a statute's (abstract) subjective purpose and its general objective purpose. In the *first* instance, purposive interpretation tends to prefer subjective purpose. When there is clear information about what the legislature wanted to achieve through the statute, preliminarily, it will trump information about what *could be* achieved through the statute. This approach validates the principle of legislative supremacy, so long as it does not conflict with the system's fundamental democratic values. In the *second* instance, purposive interpretation has no generalized preference, because it confronts internal tension within democracy itself. Legislative supremacy (and the subjective purpose derived from it) conflicts with the system's fundamental values (and the general objective purpose derived from it). We can minimize this tension by recognizing a "real" conflict only when the (abstract) subjective purpose has arisen from the explicit language of the statute. If we have derived subjective purpose from sources external to the statute, we can discount the probative value of those sources in the face of a contradictory objective purpose. We may justify this tendency to disregard an (abstract) subjective purpose that does not arise clearly and explicitly from the language of the statute itself with considerations of democracy.[96] In cases like these, however, there are no rigid rules. The tendencies we identify are only preliminary, because the type of statute and its essence play a significant role in resolving these contradictions, as we discuss below.

---

[96] We took a similar approach in dealing with a conflict between individual objective purpose and the fundamental values of the system. *Supra* p. 176.

Taking the Type of Statute into Consideration

Purposive interpretation's differential approach to conflict distinguishes between different types of legislation, for purposes of determining the relationship between subjective and objective purpose. We discussed a preliminary approach to resolving contradictions between the (abstract) subjective purpose of a statute and its individual objective purpose. That approach may change, once we take the type of statute into consideration. Where (abstract) subjective purpose contradicts general objective purpose, the type of statute is the decisive factor. We made a partial list of the different categories of statutes[97] that influence the way we resolve contradictions between the two kinds of purpose. In interpreting an old text, we ascribe significant weight to objective purpose (individual or general), even when it comes at the expense of subjective purpose arising from the explicit language of the statute. The same is true of texts that extend to broad areas of human relationships, texts that effect fundamental changes in the character of the regime and in the foundation of society, and texts based on standards rather than rules. In contrast, we validate our preliminary approach and ascribe significant weight to (abstract) subjective purpose, even at the expense of (individual or general) objective purpose, for young texts, technical texts, texts that address a narrow slice of human relationships, and texts based on rules rather than standards.

Is There a General Rule of Preferring Subjective or Objective Purpose?

Can we make a generalization about which type of purpose trumps? Can we say that, as a general rule, we should prefer subjective purpose, while recognizing exceptions derived from the type of text? Or, should objective purpose trump as a matter of policy, subject to enumerated exceptions? Should we just eliminate the exceptions and allow one or the other purpose to prevail?

My answer is no. A general principle, with or without exceptions, would offend the constitutional understanding at the core of purposive interpretation—namely that democracy is a delicate balance between legislative supremacy and the supremacy of fundamental values, central to which are human rights. The delicate balance between subjective purpose, derived from legislative supremacy, and objective purpose, derived from the sys-

---

[97] *Supra* p. 191.

tem's fundamental values, mirrors this understanding. So long as we understand democracy to be based on this balance, we should not disturb the delicate relationship between the different kinds of purpose.

Judicial Discretion in Determining the Ultimate Purpose of a Statute

Even after exhausting these guiding principles, the judge sometimes finds that the scales remain balanced. This may occur for statutes that straddle different categories of legislation reflecting competing preferences for subjective or objective purpose. Consider a statute of medium age, whose clear and explicit language gives rise to a subjective purpose. Since its enactment, the system's fundamental values have not changed in any way relevant to its interpretation. The statute addresses a broad issue of human experience. It employs a terminology of rules. Judges have no choice but to use discretion to make a decision about the conflicting elements of the statute. I believe that justice should serve as the decisive criterion for resolving this conflict, but I concede that other purposive interpreters may disagree.

CHAPTER FIFTEEN

Constitutional Interpretation

1. THE UNIQUENESS OF A CONSTITUTION AND HOW IT AFFECTS INTERPRETATION

A Constitution as a Super-Norm

A constitution is a legal text[1] that grounds a legal norm. As such, it should be interpreted like any other legal text. However, a constitution sits at the top of the normative pyramid. It shapes the character of society and its aspirations[2] throughout history. It establishes a nation's basic political points of view. It lays the foundation for social values, setting goals, obligations,[3] and trends. It is designed to guide human behavior over an extended period of time, establishing the framework for enacting legislation[4] and managing the national government.[5] It reflects the events of the past, lays a foundation for the present, and shapes the future. It is at once philosophy, politics, society, and law. The unique characteristics of a constitution warrant a special interpretive approach to its interpretation,[6] because "it is a constitution we are expounding."[7] Chief Justice Dickson of the Canadian Supreme Court said as much in one of the first decisions interpreting the Canadian Charter of Rights and Freedoms:

> The task of expounding a constitution is crucially different from that of construing a statute. A statute defines present rights and obligations. It is easily enacted and as easily repealed. A constitution, by contrast, is drafted with an eye to the future. Its function is to provide a continuing framework for the legitimate exercise of governmental power and, when joined by a Bill or a Char-

---

[1] *See* Rubenfeld, *supra* p. 162, note 46; T. Grey, "The Constitution as Scripture," 37 *Stan. L. Rev.* 1, 14 (1985).

[2] *See* Brennan, *supra* p. 59, note 218.

[3] *See* Rubenfeld, *supra* p. 162, note 46.

[4] *Attorney General (NSW) v. Brewery Employees Union of NSW (Union Label)* (1908) 6 C.L.R. 469, 612 ("It is a constitution, a mechanism under which laws are to be made, not a mere act which declares what the law is to be") (Higgins, J.).

[5] A. Mason, "Trends in Constitutional Interpretation," 18 *UNSW L.J.* 237, 283 (1995).

[6] L. Tribe and M.C. Dorf, *On Reading the Constitution* (1991); 1 Bruce Ackerman, *We the People: Foundations* 90 (1991).

[7] *McCulloch v. Maryland*, 17 U.S. 316, 407 (1819) (Marshall, C.J.).

ter of rights, for the unremitting protection of individual rights and liberties. Once enacted, its provisions cannot easily be repealed or amended. It must, therefore, be capable of growth and development over time to meet new social, political and historical realities often unimagined by its framers. The judiciary is the guardian of the Constitution and must, in interpreting its provisions, bear these considerations in mind.[8]

A constitution occupies a special status in the legal system. It plays a role that no other legal text can fill.[9]

The Uniqueness of a Constitution and Purposive Interpretation

In its treatment of constitutions, purposive interpretation maintains the integrity of its interpretive approach to all legal texts while expressing the uniqueness of the constitutional text. Purposive interpretation demonstrates its sensitivity to the uniqueness of a constitution in the balance it strikes between subjective purpose (the intent of the authors of the constitution) and objective purpose (the intent of the system). As is the case for other legal texts, the purposive interpreter learns these purposes from the language of the text and from external sources. Without negating the applicability of subjective purpose, purposive interpretation favors objective purpose in constitutional interpretation.

Purposive Interpretation of a Constitution: Comparative Law

Legal systems in different countries recognize that a constitution should be interpreted according to its purpose.[10] Chief Justice Dickson of Canada expressed this principle in an opinion holding that courts should give Canada's constitution—most notably its Charter of Rights and Free-

---

[8] *Hunter v. Southam Inc* [1984] 2 S.C.R. 145, 156.

[9] D. Farber, "The Originalism Debate: A Guide for the Perplexed," 49 *Ohio St. L.J.* 1085, 1101 (1989).

[10] *See, e.g.,* the literature on Australian constitutional interpretation: Tucker, "Textualism: An Australian Evaluation of the Debate between Professor Ronald Dworkin and Justice Antonin Scalia," 21 *Syd. L. Rev.* 567 (1991); A. Mason, "Trends in Constitutional Interpretation," 18 *U.N.S.W. L. J.* 237 (1995); A. Mason, "The Interpretation of the Constitution in a Modern Liberal Democracy," in *Interpreting Constitutions: Theories, Principles and Institutions* 13 (C. Samford and K. Preston eds., 1996); Goldworthy, "Originalism in Constitutional Interpretations," 25 *Fed. L. Rev.* 1 (1997); Lloyns, "Original Intent and Legal Interpretation," 24 *Aus. J. Leg. Phil.* 1 (1999); J. Kirk, "Constitutional Interpretation and a Theory of Evolutionary Originalism," 27 *Fed. L. Rev.* 323 (1999); M. Kirby, "Constitutional Interpretation and Original Intent: A form of Ancestor Worship?" 24 *Melb. U. L. Rev.* 1 (2000).

doms—a purposive interpretation: "The proper approach to the definition of the rights and freedoms guaranteed by the *Charter* was a purposive one. The meaning of a right or freedom guaranteed by the *Charter* was to be ascertained by an analysis of the *purpose* of such guarantee."[11] In other words, in interpreting the language of the constitution, Canadian courts should evaluate the interest that the constitution was designed to protect.[12] The German Constitutional Court takes a similar approach, according decisive weight to the *telos* of the constitutional provision and the function it is designed to fulfill, at the time of interpretation.[13]

2. THE LANGUAGE OF A CONSTITUTION

"Majestic Generalizations"

Constitutional language is no different than any other kind of language. It is the natural language used by a given society, at a given point in time. Constitutions, however, contain more "opaque" expressions than other legal texts.[14] They include many terms that could be interpreted in a number of ways, and many constitutional provisions are "open-textured"[15] and opaque. Of course, all language can be open-textured and opaque for some sets of facts, but constitutional language is open-textured and opaque for many, if not most, sets of facts. Three primary reasons explain this state of affairs: *First*, a constitutional text expresses national agreement. In order to reach agreement, nations generally must confine themselves to opaque and open-ended terms, reflecting their ability to reach consensus only at a high level of abstraction. *Second*, a constitutional text seeks to establish the nation's fundamental values, covenants, and social viewpoints. We tend to express those concepts in value-laden language, conveying a message that is

---

[11] *R. v. Big M Drug Mart Ltd* [1985] 1 S.C.R. 295, 34 (emphasis in original). *See also Re B.C. Motor Vehicle Act* [1985] 2 S.C.R. 486, 499 (Lamer, J.).

[12] P. Hogg, *Constitutional Law of Canada* 819 (4th ed. 1997).

[13] K.H. Friauf, "Techniques for the Interpretation of Constitutions in German Law," in *Proceedings of the Fifth International Symposium on Comparative Law* 12 (1968): "The *teleological* method is today probably the most important technique of interpretation in German constitutional law. . . . The teleological method might also be characterized as 'functional,' because it asks for the function which a certain rule has to accomplish within the context of the Constitution. . . . Today the teleological method asks for the *present* purpose and the present meaning of a rule."

[14] S. Magiera, "The Interpretation of the Basic Law," in *Main Principles of the German Basic Law* 89 (Starck ed., 1983).

[15] B. McLachlin, "The Charter: A New Role for the Judiciary," 29 *Alb. L. Rev.* 540, 545 (1990); W.J. Brennan, "The Constitution of the United States: Contemporary Ratification," 27 *S. Tex. L. Rev.* 433 (1986).

rarely clear or unequivocal. *Third*, a constitutional text is designed to regulate human behavior for future generations. It takes a long-term view, assuming that viewpoints, positions, and social behavior will change. It must adopt language flexible enough to include the new viewpoints, positions, and modes of behavior that cannot be predicted at the time it is written. Otherwise, the constitutional text would be obsolete the day it is enacted. At the same time, a constitutional text must be definitive enough to bind the branches of government and prevent them from behaving, in the future, in a way that is contrary to the viewpoints, positions, and social behavior that the text seeks to preserve. The language of a constitutional text must be both rigid and flexible. "Air valves" or open-ended terms that can be interpreted in a number of ways serve this purpose. Constitutions define human rights in open-textured terms, using "majestic generalities."[16] Along with those generalities, however, constitutions include "closed-textured" provisions, of rules instead of standards. Note that open-textured or opaque language does not mean incomplete language. This is important because, when faced with a gap or incompletion, a judge must use non-interpretive doctrines to fill the gap.[17] Within the bounds of interpretation, however, the judge must respect the limits of the constitutional language.

Constitutional Language and Constitutional Structure

Constitutional language includes both explicit and implicit language.[18] The implications are as much a part of the constitutional text as its explicit provisions. They are written into the constitution between the lines, in invisible ink. The interpreter discerns them from the structure of the text as a whole.[19] As Professor Tribe noted,

> The Constitution's "structure" is (borrowing Wittgenstein's famous distinction) that which the text *shows* but does not directly *say*. Diction, word repetitions, and documentary organizing forms (e.g., the division of the text into articles, or the separate status of the preamble and the amendments), for example, all contribute to a sense of what the Constitution is about that is as obviously "constitutional" as are the Constitution's words as such.[20]

Thus, we infer the principle of the separation of powers and the independence of the judiciary from constitutional provisions establishing the pow-

---

[16] *Fay v. New York* 332 U.S. 261, 282 (1947) (Jackson, J.).

[17] *Supra* p. 66.

[18] *See supra* p. 104, for a definition of implicit language.

[19] C.L. Black, Jr., *Structure and Relationship in Constitutional Law* (1969).

[20] Tribe, *supra* p. 15, note 38 at 40–41.

ers of each of the three branches of government—legislative, executive, and judiciary—and from constitutional provisions protecting human rights. What else can be inferred? Can we recognize an implicit constitutional right to freedom of political expression from a constitutional provision establishing a democratic regime? The Australian Supreme Court said yes.[21] Similarly, Justice Douglas recognized human rights established by the United States Constitution in its penumbras, including the right to privacy.[22] The structure of the constitution can give implicit meaning to what is written between the lines of the text, but it cannot add lines to the text. To do so would be to fill in a gap or lacuna,[23] using non-interpretive doctrines. Tribe is right to claim that the text of the constitution is not just its words but also "spaces which structures fill and whose patterns structures define,"[24] but we must nevertheless be careful to preserve the limits of a constitution's (implicit) language.

The Dual Role of Language in Constitutional Interpretation

Constitutional language—like the language of any legal text—plays a dual role.[25] *On the one hand*, it sets the limits of interpretation. The language of the constitution is not clay in the hands of the interpreter, to be molded as he or she sees fit.[26] A constitution is neither a metaphor[27] nor a nonbinding recommendation.[28] *On the other hand*, the language of the constitution is a source of its purpose. There are other sources, to be sure, but constitutional language is an important and highly credible source of information. The fact that we may learn the purpose of a constitution from

---

[21] This is the "implied bill of rights" recognized in Australia. *Supra* p. 70.

[22] *Griswold v. Connecticut*, 381 U.S. 479 (1965). For an analysis of the opinion, see P. Kauper, "Penumbras, Peripheries, Emanations, Things Fundamental and Things Forgotten: The *Griswold* Case," 64 *Mich. L. Rev.* 235 (1965); L. Henkin, "Privacy and Autonomy," 74 *Colum. L. Rev.* 1410 (1974); R. Posner, "The Uncertain Protection of Privacy by the Supreme Court," 1979 *Sup. Ct. Rev.* 173; B. Henly, "'Penumbra': The Roots of a Legal Metaphor," 15 *Hast. Const. L.Q.* 81 (1987).

[23] I doubt that the term "gap" as I use it (*supra* p. 66) means the same as it does in the literature on the United States Constitution (like, for example, Justice Douglas's words in *Baker v. Carr*, 369 U.S. 186, 242 (1987), referring to "large gaps in the Constitution").

[24] Tribe, *supra* p. 15, note 38 at 47.

[25] S. Munzer and J. Nickel, "Does the Constitution Mean What It Always Meant?" 77 *Colum. L. Rev.* 1029 (1977); L. Alexander, "Modern Equal Protection Theories: A Metatheoretical Taxonomy and Critique," 42 *Ohio St. L.J.* 3 (1981).

[26] D. Laycock, "Constitutional Theory Matters," 56 *Tex. L. Rev.* 767, 773 (1987).

[27] F. Schauer, "An Essay on Constitutional Language," 29 *U.C.L.A. L. Rev.* 797, 801 (1982).

[28] P. Brest, "The Misconceived Quest for the Original Understanding," 60 *B.U. L. Rev.* 204 (1980).

sources external to it does not mean that we can give a constitution a meaning that is inconsistent with its explicit or implicit language. Interpretation cannot create a new constitutional text. Talk of judges amending the constitution through their interpretation of the constitution is just a metaphor.[29] The claim that a constitutional text limits but does not command[30] is true only for the limited number of cases in which, after exhausting all interpretive tools, we can still extract more than one legal meaning from the constitutional language and must therefore leave the final decision to judicial discretion. In these exceptional cases, language provides a general direction but does not draw a precise map of how to reach the destination.[31] Usually, however, constitutional language sets not only the limits of interpretation, but also its specific content.

3. THE SUBJECTIVE PURPOSE OF A CONSTITUTION

Its Essence

The subjective purpose of a constitution is the goals, interests, values, aims, policies, and function that the founders of the constitution sought to actualize. Despite literature arguing the contrary,[32] I believe that a constitution has a subjective purpose that judges can identify. Without such intention, the founders could not have enacted the constitution. If credible historical information about it exists, then it can be identified.[33] Recall that we are interested in abstract, not concrete or interpretive, intention. We are not interested in how the authors of the constitution envisioned that a particular right would apply to a given set of facts (concrete intention).[34] Their abstract subjective intention exists at various levels of abstraction,[35] and the purposive interpreter considers all of them. Where the constitu-

---

[29] S. Levinson (ed.), *Responding to Imperfection: The Theory and Practice of Constitutional Amendment* (1995).

[30] Schauer, *supra* p. 374, note 27 at 830.

[31] W. Harris, "Bonding Word and Polity: The Logic of American Constitutionalism," 76 *Am. Pol. Sci. Rev.* 34 (1982).

[32] *See supra* p. 264; K. Greenawalt, "Are Mental States Relevant for Statutory and Constitutional Interpretation?" 85 *Cornell L. Rev.* 1609 (2000).

[33] On the problem that passage of time poses, see H.J. Powell, "Rules for Originalists," 73 *Va. L. Rev.* 659 (1987).

[34] Dworkin, *supra* p. 126, note 24 at 131; Brest, *supra* p. 374, note 28; M. Perry, "The Legitimacy of Particular Conceptions of Constitutional Interpretation," 77 *Va. L. Rev.* 669, 681 (1991). *See also* Brennan's critique of taking the concrete (interpretive) intention of the founders of the constitution into account: W.J. Brennan, "The Constitution of the United States: Contemporary Ratification," 27 *S. Tex. L. Rev.* 433 (1986).

[35] T. Sandalow, "Constitutional Interpretation," 79 *Mich. L. Rev.* 1033 (1981).

tional text says that elections should be egalitarian, for example, the interpreter asks how its authors viewed equality. Did they focus on "one person, one vote," or did they also consider equal opportunity? The interpreter will not ask whether the authors of a constitutional text considered a specific elections statute to be egalitarian. The constitutionality of a particular statute is an interpretive decision that belongs to the judiciary. No interpretive decision by the constitutional founders is binding.

Of course, judges should take subjective purpose into account only if it can be achieved through the language of the constitution. If we learn from external sources that the founders intended something that cannot be achieved through the language of the constitution, we must conclude that while they wanted to achieve a particular purpose, they failed to agree on a text that would make it possible. Unfortunately, they missed the mark.

Its Sources: The Text as a Whole

Because we presume that the founders of a constitution expressed their intentions through the language of the constitution, the text remains a highly credible source of subjective purpose. We approach the constitution with our pre-understanding, including our values and our interpretive approach. This pre-understanding allows us to understand the essence of the intent itself from the language that we interpret according to abstract intent. We read the text as a whole, paying attention to its structure and its division into different provisions that play different roles. The founders' use of identical or different provisions provides information about their intent.[36] The interpreter investigates subjective purpose from the constitution's natural and ordinary language as well as its technical or extraordinary language.

Its Sources: Constitutional History

A constitution is the product of the history of a people and a nation. We can therefore derive its subjective purpose from its history, including its pre-enactment history—the social and legal background that gave birth to the constitution. Constitutional history includes the history of the procedures by which the constitution was founded, including the constitutional

---

[36] A. Amar, "Intratextualism," 112 *Harv. L. Rev.* 747 (1999); A. Amar, "Foreword: The Document and the Doctrine," 114 *Harv. L. Rev.* 26 (2000). Amar identifies two levels of interest—the text and the doctrine (or, in my terms, the purpose). In my opinion, we are interested in just one level, accessible through the free movement from text to doctrine (purpose). For a critique of Amar's approach, see A. Vermeule and E. Young, "Hercules, Herbert, and Amar: The Trouble with *Intratextualism*," 113 *Harv. L. Rev.* 730 (2000).

assembly that created it and the process by which the nation ratified it. The protocols of debates in the founding assembly (in the plenary and in committees) reveal the (manifest) intent of the authors of the text. Judges can also infer authorial intent from post-enactment developments, such as constitutional amendments that provide information about original intent.[37]

4. THE OBJECTIVE PURPOSE OF A CONSTITUTION

Its Essence

The objective purpose of a constitution is the interests, goals, values, aims, policies, and function that the constitutional text is designed to actualize in a democracy. A democratic legal system's values and principles shape the objective purpose of its constitution. The constitutional text tightly binds its objective purpose in two ways: *One*, the essence of a constitution's objective purpose may arise from its language; and *two*, we cannot use the constitution to achieve a purpose that its language cannot bear.

The Levels of Abstraction of Objective Purpose

The objective purpose of a constitution exists at various levels of abstraction. At the lowest level, it is imaginative reconstruction, the purpose that the authors of the constitution would have envisioned, had they considered the matter. The next level asks what purpose reasonable authors of the constitution would have envisioned. At a higher level of abstraction, the interpreter seeks the purpose at the core of a constitutional arrangement of the type and nature in question, in other words, the purpose of a particular constitutional right or fundamental political structure. At the highest level of abstraction, objective purpose consists of the fundamental values of the system that form the normative umbrella spread over all legal texts in the system, including the constitutional text.

5. SOURCES OF OBJECTIVE PURPOSE

Internal Sources: The Constitution as a Whole and the Search for Constitutional Consistency

The structure of the constitution and the relationship between its different parts provide information about the function, values, and principles

---

[37] Tribe, *supra* p. 15, note 38 at 67.

that it is (objectively) designed to realize.[38] Justice Lamer of Canada expressed this well in noting that "Our constitutional *Charter* must be construed as a system where every component contributes to the meaning as a whole, and the whole gives meaning to its parts. . . . The court must interpret each section of the Charter in relation to the other."[39] We assume constitutional unity.[40] A constitutional norm is part of a larger constitutional project. A specific constitutional provision affects our understanding of the constitution as a whole, and vice versa. In formulating the purpose of a constitutional text, the interpreter should seek the purpose that best advances constitutional unity and harmony. He or she should avoid an objective constitutional purpose that dissolves constitutional unity or divides its provisions into disconnected parts.

We should not exaggerate constitutional unity, however. Social life is not perfect, and neither is a constitutional text. Interpretation should not dissolve constitutional unity, but neither should it artificially impose unity where none exists. We want neither disintegration nor hyper-integration.[41] The founders of a constitution blend political, philosophical, social, and legal views that do not always reflect a coherent approach. Justice Holmes correctly noted that a constitution generally does not reflect a single social or philosophical viewpoint: "The Fourteenth Amendment does not enact Mr. Herbert Spencer's Social Statics. . . . [A] constitution is not intended to embody a particular economic theory, whether of paternalism and the organic relation of the citizen to the State or of *laissez faire*."[42] I made a similar point in a case addressing the scope of the right to dignity: "Human dignity is a complicated principle. In formulating it, an interpreter should not try to adopt one or another moral or philosophical world view. Nor should he or she turn human dignity into a Kantian concept, or an expression of natural law views." A constitution is the totality of national experience, united around a common nucleus. We can never achieve a perfect constitution, but we should continue to aspire to constitutional unity, subject to what we know about the constitution and the limits of the national compromise it reflects. We do not just seek the semantic meaning of the constitutional provisions and the intratextualism of the constitution.[43] We are interested in their legal meaning as a reflection of constitutional purpose ("intrapurposivism").

[38] Black, *supra* p. 373, note 19; Tribe, *supra* p. 15, note 38 at 40.

[39] *Dubois, supra* p. 160, note 38 at 356.

[40] Friauf, *supra* p. 372, note 13 at 18. *See also* K. Hesse, *Grundzüge des Verfassungsrechts der Bundesrepublik Deutschland* 28 (8th ed., 1975); W. Murphy, "An Ordering of Constitutional Values," 53 *S. Cal. L. Rev.* 703, 746 (1980).

[41] Tribe and Dorf, *supra* p. 370, note 6 at 19.

[42] *Lochner v. New York*, 198 U.S. 45, 75 (1905).

[43] *See* Amar, *supra* p. 376, note 36.

External Sources: Other Constitutional Provisions

A constitution is sometimes "scattered" among different documents en-acted at different times. That is true of Israel's Basic Laws, passed over the course of five decades, which make up its constitution. That is also true of constitutions that have been amended over the years. Purposive interpretation views all parts of the constitution as a unity.[44] It derives the purpose of one constitutional provision from that of others found in separate constitutional texts or in later amendments to a single docu-ment. A constitutional norm does not exist in isolation. It is part of a con-stitutional project that may span multiple constitutional texts. All consti-tutional texts constitute one complete totality from which the interpreter learns the purpose of each part. A later constitutional text may influence the understanding of an earlier one,[45] as judges interpret the earlier pro-vision to avoid internal contradictions in the text. There is a rebuttable (objective) presumption that the various provisions of a national consti-tution do not contradict each other. Judges may have to revise their view of an old constitutional text, in order to maintain its consistency with a new constitutional text.

External Sources: Post-Enactment History

The post-enactment history of a constitution is important to formulat-ing its objective purpose. Understanding a constitution requires under-standing the historical continuity of which it is a part, or the break in con-tinuity and beginning of something new. As Justice Holmes said, "The case before us must be considered in the light of our whole experience and not merely in that of what was said a hundred years ago."[46] An in-terpreter learns the objective purpose of the constitution from its histor-ical continuity.[47] We understand ourselves by understanding where we came from. We look to history not for answers to modern questions, but rather for guidance in formulating the objective and modern purpose of the constitution.

---

[44] On interpreting the constitutional amendments that make up the American Bill of Rights, see A. Amar, *The Bill of Rights: Creation and Reconstruction* (1998).

[45] Tribe, *supra* p. 15, note 38 at 67.

[46] *Missouri v. Holland*, 252 U.S. 416, 433 (1920). *See also* Justice Frankfurter's comments in *Rochin v. California*, 342 U.S. 165, 171 (1952).

[47] T. Sandalow, "Constitutional Interpretation," 79 *Mich. L. Rev.* 1033, 1050 (1981).

External Sources: Judicial Constitutional Case Law

Another important external source of objective purpose is case law. A judicial opinion interpreting the constitution is more than just an operational directive about the meaning of a specific constitutional text. A judicial opinion includes a general component that provides explanations for its operational result. These explanations include value-laden generalizations about the objective purpose of the constitutional text.[48] The modern interpreter does not work in a precedential vacuum. He or she is just one link in a common law chain[49] that directly and indirectly affects his or her work.[50] The direct impact comes in the form of *stare decisis*; a modern judge is not free to ignore prior judicial holdings on the purpose of the constitutional provision, whether or not he or she agrees with them. Even when not absolutely binding, precedent always influences the modern judge's decision, if only as one more datum for the judge to take into account. Precedent affects the judge's work indirectly by the burden it imposes on the judge to maintain constitutional unity. A judicial holding determining the purpose of a constitutional provision affects the interpretation of similar constitutional provisions.[51] Prior judicial interpretation of the constitution creates a continuity of case law that affects (directly or indirectly) the constitutional purpose to be determined in the present. This influence is particularly strong when the judge considers a question implicating the objective purpose of the constitution, at the relevant level of abstraction. A prior holding establishing the level of abstraction at which a judge should treat a constitutional provision may affect the level of abstraction at which a judge should treat that constitutional provision being interpreted in the present.[52] A judicial determination about the proper level of abstraction at which to interpret a constitutional provision affects the interpretation of another provision indirectly related to the first.

Different constitutional provisions are often based on a common principle. When judges ascribe purposes to individual constitutional provisions,

---

[48] *See* Strauss, *supra* p. 161, note 44; R. Fallon, "A Constructive Coherence Theory of Constitutional Interpretation," 100 *Harv. L. Rev.* 1189, 1202 (1987).

[49] Dworkin, "Law as Literature," 60 *Tex. L. Rev.* 527 (1982).

[50] *See* Strauss, *supra* p. 161, note 44; Rubenfeld, *supra* p. 162, note 46; Monagham, *supra* p. 161, note 44.

[51] J. Balkin, "The Rule of Law as a Source of Constitutional Change," 6 *Const. Comm.* 21 (1989).

[52] For example, a level of abstraction established for the interpretation of a free speech provision is likely to affect the level of abstraction used to interpret a provision about freedom of movement. American law recognizes different levels of constitutional scrutiny. A decision interpreting one constitutional provision may be relevant to the examination of another constitutional provision that imposes the same level of constitutional scrutiny.

the decisions they write shape the principle at the core of those provisions. That constitutional principle, in turn, shapes the purposes of those provisions. Law is a system whose components work together. Case law interpreting constitutional provisions plays a central role[53] in the work of modern judges adjudicating constitutional purpose.[54]

External Sources: Fundamental Values

A constitution draws life from fundamental values that in turn are an important tool for determining its objective purpose.[55] Fundamental values reflect a society's deeply held viewpoints.[56] They express a society's national ethos, its cultural legacy, its social tradition, and the entirety of its historical experience. Fundamental values like freedom, human dignity, privacy, and equality saturate constitutional texts. These fundamental values are embodied in the words of the constitution that require interpretation as well as the objective purpose guiding the interpretation. Additional fundamental values, external to the constitution,[57] encompass the constitution and form part of its objective purpose. These values may include the separation of powers, judicial independence, rule of law, the preservation of the state and its security, justice, fairness, security in interpersonal relationships, and many others. The interpreter learns them from fundamental documents like the declaration of independence, from case law, and from the totality of the national experience.

I wish to make three points about fundamental values: *First*, whether or not they receive explicit mention in the constitution, fundamental values should be interpreted according to their meaning at the time of interpretation. They reflect contemporary needs.[58] The question is not how the founders of the constitution understood liberty, but rather what it means in our modern understanding. *Second*, fundamental values should be understood by the contemporary interpreter as the fundamental views en-

[53] Subject, of course, to the principles of straying from precedent. *See* Monagham, *supra* p. 161, note 44; S. Reinhardt, "The Conflict between Text and Precedent in Constitutional Adjudication," 73 *Cornell L. Rev.* 434 (1988).

[54] L. Pollak, "'Original Intention' and the Crucible of Litigation," 57 *U. Cin. L. Rev.* 867, 870 (1989); H. Wellington, *Interpreting the Constitution* (1990).

[55] Tribe, *supra* p. 15, note 38 at 70; Walton, *supra* p. 85, note 4. *See also* R. Post, *Constitutional Domains* 23 (1995).

[56] In Australia, this influence takes the form of "community values" considered in constitutional interpretation. *See* A. Mason, "The Role of a Constitutional Court in a Federation: A Comparison of the Australian and the United States Experience," 16 *Fed. L. Rev.* 1 (1986); H. Patapan, "Politics of Interpretation," 22 *Syd. L. Rev.* 247 (2000).

[57] T. Grey, "Do We Have an Unwritten Constitution?" 27 *Stan. L. Rev.* 983 (1975).

[58] W.J. Brennan, "Construing the Constitution," 19 *U.C. Davis L. Rev.* 2 (1985).

trenched in society's values, not its passing trends. The interpreter seeks "society's long-term covenants."[59] He or she should "uncover what is basic and value-laden, rejecting what is fleeting."[60] Modern generations use constitutional interpretation to give expression to their fundamental views, even when those views differ from those of the constitutional founders or of previous generations.[61] *Third*, the interpreter should only take into account fundamental values that can be achieved through the constitutional text. A constitutional text is not an empty frame to be filled with every new value, regardless of how important it may be. The basic principle that language restricts interpretation, and that the limits of interpretation are the limits of language, applies to constitutional interpretation.

External Sources: Comparative Law

Comparative law is a source of information about the objective purpose of a constitutional text. Democratic countries share fundamental values, and legal institutions fulfill similar roles across systems. The meaning that one legal system gives to a constitutional arrangement may provide insight into the purpose that the same arrangement fulfills in another legal system.[62] Comparative constitutional law helps widen horizons and share information across systems.[63] This is obviously the case when the constitutional

[59] H.C. 693/91, *supra* p. 157, note 29 at 781 (Barak, J.).

[60] C.A. 105/92, *Re'em Engineers and Contractors Ltd. v. City of Nazareth Ilit*, 47(5) P.D. 189, 206.

[61] Sandalow, *supra* p. 167, note 76 at 1061.

[62] In *Stanford v. Kentucky*, 492 U.S. 361 (1989), the United States Supreme Court interpreted the Eighth Amendment to the United States Constitution, which prohibits "cruel and unusual punishment," in light of, *inter alia*, "standards of decency that mark the progress of a maturing society." *See Trop v. Dulles*, 356 U.S. 86, 101 (1958). Justice Scalia noted, in footnote 1 of the decision, that "[I]t is *American* conceptions of decency that are dispositive, rejecting the contention . . . that the sentencing practice of other countries are relevant." Yes, the decision is "American," but in order to make it, judges should—as the dissenting opinion in *Stanford* said (at 389)—accept interpretive inspiration from other countries whose approach to the sanctity of human life and to human rights in general is similar to that of the United States. *See also Thompson v. Oklahoma*, 487 U.S. 815 (1988); *Prinz v. United States*, 521 U.S. 898 (1997).

[63] A. Slaughter, "A Typology of Transjudicial Communication," 29 *U. Rich. L. Rev.* 99 (1994); G. Fletcher, "Comparative Law as a Subversive Discipline," 46 *Am. J. Comp. L.* 683 (1998); C. McCrudden, "A Common Law of Human Rights? Transnational Judicial Conversations on Constitutional Rights," in K. O'Donovan and G. Rubbine (eds.), *Human Rights and Legal History* (1999); V.C. Jackson and M. Tushnet, *Comparative Constitutional Law* (1999); Choudhry, "Globalization in Search of Justification: Toward a Theory of Comparative Constitutional Interpretation," 74 *Ind. L.J.* 819 (1999); K. Perales, "It Works Fine in Europe, So Why Not Here? Comparative Law and Constitutional Federalism," 23 *Vt. L.*

text of one country influences the constitutional text of another.[64] But interpretive inspiration has a place even in the absence of direct or indirect influence of one constitutional text on another. This is certainly true when a constitution makes reference to democratic values[65] or democratic societies.[66] Even when the constitution does not refer to values common to all democracies, however, judges may consult comparative law,[67] so long as the two countries share a common ideological basis and common fundamental values. I noted in one case:

> From the founding of the State, we drew extensive interpretive inspiration from the wellsprings of American and English constitutional law. The views of those countries in many areas, like human rights, often serve as an example for us. However, we must limit the nourishment we seek from them. Inspiration can occur only if there is a common foundation. We can only compare institutions, procedures, and views that have a common basis.[68]

A common foundation of democracy is a necessary but insufficient condition. A judge should study the foreign system's historical development and social fabric for differences that would render interpretive inspiration un-

---

Rev. 885 (1999); M. Tushnet, "The Possibilities of Comparative Constitutional Law," 108 *Yale L.J.* 1225 (1999); C. McCrudden, "A Part of the Main? The Physician-Assisted Suicide Cases and Comparative Law Methodology in the United States Supreme Court," in C. Schneider (ed.), *Law at the End of Life* (2000); E. Weinrib, "Constitutional Conceptions and Constitutional Comparativism," in V. Jackson and M. Tushnet (eds.), *Defining the Field of Comparative Constitutional Law* 23 (2002).

[64] One example is the influence of the United States Constitution on the constitutions of a number of countries, including Japan and Argentina. These are instances of "migrating laws." Judge Calabresi noted that "Wise parents do not hesitate to learn from their children." *United States v. Then*, 56 F. 3d 464, 469 (1995) (Calabresi, J. concurring). One should exercise caution, however, in applying this principle. *See* Jackson and Tushnet, *supra* p. 382, note 63 at 169.

[65] *See* Art. 1 of Israel's Basic Law: Human Dignity and Freedom, establishing that "The goal of this Basic Law is to protect human dignity and freedom, in order to ground, in this Basic Law, the values of the state of Israel as a Jewish and Democratic state."

[66] *See* Art. 1 of the Canadian Charter, establishing that "The Canadian Charter of Rights and Freedoms guarantees the rights and freedoms set out in it subject only to such reasonable limits prescribed by law as can be demonstrably justified in a free and democratic society." *See also* D. Beatty, "The Forms and Limits of Constitutional Interpretation," 49 *Am. J. Comp. L.* 79 (2001).

[67] D.P. Kommers, "The Value of Comparative Constitutional Law," 9 *Marshall J. of Practices & Procedures* 685 (1976).

[68] H.C. 428/86, *supra* p. 167, note 74 at 600 (Barak, J., dissenting). In a dissenting opinion in that case, on the issue of the authority of the president to issue a pretrial pardon, I refused to seek interpretive inspiration from the pardon power of the English king or the United States president. I stressed the differences in how the role and status of the Israeli president is viewed, contrasted with the English king or United States president.

helpful or inappropriate.[69] When the two systems share a common foundation, the judge may derive interpretive inspiration from foreign and international law, particularly from international covenants that ground constitutional values.[70] Those covenants influence the way courts formulate the objective purpose of a national constitutional text. Case law from international and foreign tribunals, interpreting those covenants, is also a good source of inspiration for the interpretation of a national constitution.

6. THE ULTIMATE PURPOSE OF A CONSTITUTION

How Is Ultimate Purpose Determined?

Judges assemble the different kinds of data about purpose, including information about (abstract) subjective purpose and information about objective purpose gleaned from other constitutional provisions, constitutional history, case law, fundamental values, and comparative law. When all the information points in the same direction, it is not difficult to determine the ultimate purpose of the constitutional text. That is generally what happens.[71] Occasionally, however, the data contradict each other. What should judges do in those cases?[72] Is the determination of ultimate purpose at their discretion, or can we guide their determination of ultimate purpose? If so, what guidance can we offer?

Because we have no pre-interpretive understanding to compare with the post-interpretive understanding, there is no "true" ultimate purpose. That does not, however, leave the understanding of a constitutional text to the whim of each interpreter. Just because there are a number of ways we can interpret a constitutional text[73] does not mean there are a number of ways we *should* interpret a constitutional text.[74] We seek to develop a system that gives priority to one understanding over another—without claiming that

---

[69] *R. v. Rahay* [1987] 1 S.C.R. 588, 639 (La Forest, J.); *R. v. Keegstra* [1990] 3 S.C.R. 697, 740 (Dickson, C.J.). For an analysis of the situation in Canada, see Betti, *supra* p. 46, note 151; P. Hogg, *Constitutional Law of Canada* 827 (4th ed. 1997).

[70] The most central of which are the Universal Declaration of Human Rights (1953); the European Convention for the Protection of Human Rights and Fundamental Freedoms (1950); the International Covenant for the Elimination of All Forms of Racial Discrimination (1966); the International Covenant on Civil and Political Rights (1966); the International Covenant on Economic, Social, and Cultural Rights (1966); the American Convention on Human Rights (1969).

[71] Fallon, *supra* p. 380, note 48.

[72] Post, *supra* p. 381, note 55 at 39.

[73] S. Levinson, "Law as Literature," 60 *Tex. L. Rev.* 373, 391 (1982).

[74] W. Kaplin, "The Process of Constitutional Interpretation: A Synthesis of the Present and a Guide to the Future," 42 *Rutgers L. Rev.* 983 (1990).

one understanding is truer than another.[75] Tribe was right to note that no criteria external to a constitution can determine how to prioritize the various interpretive considerations.[76] Still, the absence of a "true" meaning does not bar the search for a proper meaning.[77] Such meaning lies not in the text of the constitution itself but rather in a constitutional interpretation based on a particular constitutional and interpretive perspective.[78] We return, now, to our original question: In its quest to find ultimate purpose, how does purposive interpretation formulate the proper (not the true) relationship between the different kinds of data about subjective and objective purpose?

Purposive Interpretation's Approach

Purposive interpretation asks the interpreter to examine all data about the purpose of the constitutional text. There are no phases of transition from one kind of datum to another, no *a priori* ranking of data. While the interpreter cannot understand a constitutional text without considering the intent of its authors, he or she does not limit his or her understanding of the constitutional text to the intent of its authors alone.[79] The purposive interpreter aspires to synthesis and coordination between the various pieces of information, resolving any lack of coordination between the different levels of abstraction of subjective purpose by choosing the level of abstraction that accords with objective purpose. In the same kind of process, the interpreter chooses the level of abstraction for objective purpose that is consistent with subjective purpose. What does a judge do, however, when the data on the subjective and objective purpose of a constitution are inconsistent?

Purposive interpretation gives decisive weight to objective purpose in constitutional interpretation. Only then can the constitution fulfill its aim; only then can it guide human behavior over generations of social change; only then can the constitution respond to modern needs; only then can it

---

[75] R. Dworkin, "The Arduous Virtue of Fidelity: Originalism, Scalia, Tribe and Nerve," 65 *Fordham L. Rev.* 1249, 1258 (1997).

[76] Tribe, *supra* p. 15, note 38 at 88. *See also* P. Bobbitt, *Constitutional Interpretation* 178 (1991).

[77] M. Dorf, "Integrating Normative and Descriptive Constitutional Theory: A Case of Original Meaning," 85 *Geo. L.J.* 1765 (1997).

[78] M. Tushnet, "Justification in Constitutional Adjudication: A Comment on Constitutional Interpretation," 72 *Tex. L. Rev.* 1707 (1994); S. Winter, "The Constitution of Conscience," 72 *Tex. L. Rev.* 1805 (1994); D. Patterson, "Wittgenstein and Constitutional Theory," 72 *Tex. L. Rev.* 1837 (1994); P. Bobbitt, "Reflections Inspired by My Critics," 72 *Tex. L. Rev.* 1869 (1994).

[79] Dorf, *supra* p. 385, note 77 at 1788.

balance the past, present, and future. The past guides the present, but it does not enslave it. Fundamental social perspectives—which draw life from the past and are interwoven into socio-legal history—find modern expression in the old constitutional text.[80] Justice Brennan expressed this idea eloquently in the following comments:

> We current Justices read the Constitution in the only way that we can: as Twentieth Century Americans. We look to the history of the time of framing and to the intervening history of Interpretation. But the ultimate question must be, what do the words of the text mean in our time. For the genius of the Constitution rests not in any static meaning it might have had in a world that is dead and gone, but in the adaptability of its great principles to cope with current problems and current needs. What the Constitutional fundamentals meant to the wisdom of other times cannot be their measure to the vision of our times. Similarly, what those fundamentals mean for us, our descendants will learn, cannot be the measure to the vision of their time.[81]

In a similar vein, Justice Kirby of Australia's Supreme Court said:

> [I]n the kind of democracy which a constitution such as ours establishes, judges should make their choices by giving meaning to the words in a way that protects and advances the essential character of the polity established by the constitution. In Australia, this function is to be performed without the need constantly to look over one's shoulder and to refer to understandings of the text that were common in 1900 when the society which the Constitution addresses was so different. It is today's understanding that counts. Reference to 1900, if made at all, should be in the minor key and largely for historical interest. Not for establishing legal limitations. In my opinion, a consistent application of the view that the Constitution was set free from its founders in 1900 is the rule that we should apply. That our Constitution belongs to succeeding generations of the Australian people. That it is bound to be read in changing ways as time passes and circumstances change. That it should be read so as to achieve the purposes of good government which the Constitution was designed to promote and secure. Our Constitution belongs to the 21st century, not to the 19th.[82]

The Subjective Purpose of a Constitution Is Not Decisive

Subjective purpose is not decisive. Judges should not ignore it, but nor should they give it a central role in their formulation of ultimate consti-

---

[80] B. Wilson, "Decision-Making in the Supreme Court," 36 *U. Toronto L.J.* 227, 247 (1986).

[81] Brennan, *supra* p. 381, note 58.

[82] Kirby, *supra* p. 371, note 10 at 14. *See also Re Wakin* (1999) 73 *A.J.L.R.* 839, 878 (Kirby,

tutional purpose. Legal systems in many countries adopt this approach. Canada's Supreme Court, for example, accords only minimal weight to the intent of the constitutional authors in its interpretation of the constitution.[83] In a case discussing a provision of the Canadian Charter providing that every person has a right to life, liberty, and security, and that these rights cannot be denied, "except in accordance with the principles of fundamental justice,"[84] a question arose as to whether "fundamental justice" is procedural (natural justice) or substantive. The court heard arguments that the subjective intent was procedural—that the authors of the Charter, aware of the controversy over "due process" in the United States, intentionally avoided using the American phrase to signal their reference to procedural, not substantive, justice. The Canadian court decided not to accord significant weight to subjective intent, holding, in an opinion by Justice Lamer, that

> Another danger with casting the interpretation of s. 7 in terms of the comments made by those heard at the Special Joint Committee Proceedings is that, in so doing, the rights, freedoms and values embodied in the *Charter* in effect become frozen in time to the moment of adoption with little or no possibility of growth, development and adjustment to changing social needs. . . . If the newly planted 'living tree' which is the *Charter* is to have the possibility of growth and adjustment over time, care must be taken to ensure that historical materials . . . do not stunt its growth.[85]

The Australian Supreme Court has taken a similar view in a number of opinions,[86] warning against leaving decisions in the dead hands of the au-

---

J.); M. Kirby, "Australian Law—After 11 September 2001," 21 *A.B.R.* 1, 9 (2001) ("Given the great difficulty of securing formal constitutional change, it is just as well that the High Court has looked creatively at the document put in its charge. Had this not been done, our Constitution would have remained an instrument for giving effect to no more than the aspirations of rich white males of the nineteenth century. Fortunately, we have done better than this").

[83] P. Hogg, *Constitutional Law of Canada* 1393 (4th ed. 1997).

[84] Art. 7 of the Canadian Charter.

[85] *Re B.C. Motor Vehicle Act* [1985] 2 S.C.R. 486, 504. *See also R v. Therens* (1985) 18 D.L.R. (4th) 655, 675; *Mahe v. Alta* [1990] 1 S.C.R. 342, 369.

[86] H. Patapan, "The Dead Hand of the Founders? Original Intent and the Constitutional Protection of Rights and Freedoms in Australia," 25 *Fed. L. Rev.* 211 (1997). *See also Theophenous v. Herald Weekly Time Ltd.* (1995) 182 C.L.R. 104, 171 (Deane, J.) ("[E]ven if it could be established that it was the unexpressed intention of the framers of the Constitution that the failure to follow the United States model should preclude or impede the implication of constitutional rights, their intention in that regard would be simply irrelevant to the construction of provisions whose legitimacy lay in their acceptance by the people. Moreover, to construe the Constitution on the basis that the dead hands of those who framed it reached from their graves to negate or constrict the natural implications of its express provisions or fundamental doctrines would deprive what was intended to be a living instrument of its vitality and adaptability to serve succeeding generations").

thors of the constitution who, from their graves, obstruct or limit what is implicit in constitutional provisions and doctrines. The German Constitutional Court has also adopted this view, notably in a case holding that a mandatory life sentence without possibility of release is inconsistent with "human dignity." The court ruled against denying a prisoner any spark of hope for freedom, rejecting arguments that the authors of the constitution intended to impose life imprisonment as a mandatory sentence, in place of the death penalty:

> Neither original history nor the ideas and intentions of the framers are of decisive importance in interpreting particular provisions of the Basic Law. Since the adoption of the Basic Law, our understanding of the content, function, and effect of basic rights has deepened. Additionally, the medical, psychological, and sociological effects of life imprisonment have become better known. Current attitudes are important in assessing the constitutionality of life imprisonment. New insights can influence and even change the evaluation of this punishment in terms of human dignity and the principles of a constitutional state.[87]

Summarizing the German approach to constitutional interpretation, Kommers said:

> [I]n Germany, original history—that is, the intentions of the framers—is seldom dispositive in resolving the meaning of the Basic Law. The Court has declared that "the original history of a particular provision of the Basic Law has no decisive importance" in constitutional interpretation. Original history performs, at best, the auxiliary function of lending support to a result already arrived at by other interpretive methods. When there is conflict, however, arguments based on text, structure, or teleology will prevail over those based on history.[88]

These legal systems (Canadian, Australian, German) do not expend significant judicial resources on considerations of subjective purpose.[89] They do not ignore it, but neither do they make it a primary factor—unlike the American legal system, whose judges and legal scholars engage in extensive discussions of the original intent of the founding fathers.[90] The United

---

[87] In *Re Life Imprisonment*, 45 BVerfGE 187 (1977). Kommers has translated it into English: D.P. Kommers, *The Constitutional Jurisprudence of the Federal Republic of Germany* 307 (2d ed. 1977).

[88] Kommers, *supra* p. 388, note 87 at 42. *See also* Friauf, *supra* p. 372, note 13.

[89] C. L'Heureux-Dube, "The Importance of Dialogue: Globalization, the Rehnquist Court and Human Rights," in *The Rehnquist Court: A Retrospective* 234 (M. Belskey ed., 2002).

[90] The literature on this issue is expansive. For an analysis of the problematic nature of the issue, see Tribe, *supra* p. 15, note 38 at 47 and citations therein. *See also* M. Perry, "The Le-

States Supreme Court has divided over this question.[91] American constitutional law is in crisis because of the American legal community's failure to reach consensus over the relationship between the intent of the founders of the Constitution,[92] the original understanding of the Constitution at the time of its founding, and the modern view of understanding the Constitution through its interpretation. Canada and Germany have avoided this conflict, and I hope that other legal systems will do the same.

Purposive interpretation does not ignore subjective purpose in constitutional interpretation, but it does not give it a prominent role. Instead, it favors objective purpose, which reflects modern, deep perspectives in the movement of the legal system through history. Through objective purpose, the constitution remains a living, not fossilized, norm. Resort to objective purpose rescues the present from being enslaved to the past. Constitutional interpretation is a process in which every generation expresses its fundamental views, as they are formulated against the backdrop of its past.[93] This process is not free. An interpreter who interprets a constitutional provision operates in a given socio-historical framework. He or she may sometimes have discretion, but such discretion operates within a given system of values, tradition, history, and text. A modern interpreter must respect the past. He or she formulates modern constitutional purpose while forging a

---

gitimacy of Particular Conceptions of Constitutional Interpretation," 77 *Va. L. Rev.* 669 (1991); W. Kaplin, "The Process of Constitutional Interpretation: A Synthesis of the Present and a Guide to the Future," 42 *Rutgers L. Rev.* 983 (1990). For a survey of this history, *see* R.R. Kelso, "Styles of Constitutional Interpretation and the Four Main Approaches to Constitutional Interpretation in American Legal History," 29 *Valparaiso U. L. Rev.* 121 (1994).

[91] See Justice Stevens's comments in *W. Va. Univ. Hosps. Inc. v. Casey*, 499 U.S. 83, 112 (1991); M. Dorf, "Foreword: The Limits of Socratic Deliberation," 112 *Harv. L. Rev.* 4, 4 (1998). Compare Justice Brennan's comments, *supra* p. 386, with the following words of Justice Scalia: "I do not worry about my old Constitution 'obstructing modernity', since I take that to be its whole purpose. The very objective of a basic law, it seems to me, is to place certain matters beyond risk of change, except through the extraordinary democratic majorities that constitutional amendment requires. . . . The whole *purpose* of a constitution—old or new—is to impede change, or, pejoratively put, to 'abstract modernity.'" A. Scalia, "Modernity and the Constitution," in *Constitutional Justice under Old Constitutions* 313, 315 (E. Smith ed., 1995).

[92] Including the approach that the authors of the Constitution intended it to be interpreted according to its objective purpose. *See* H.J. Powell, "The Original Understanding of Original Intent," 98 *Harv. L. Rev.* 883 (1985); S. Sherry, "The Founders' Unwritten Constitution," 54 *U. Chi. L. Rev.* 1127 (1994); C. Lofgren, "The Original Understanding of Original Intent," 5 *Const. Commentary* 77 (1988); P. Finkelman, "The Constitution and the Intention of the Framers: The Limits of Historical Analysis," 50 *U. Pitt. L. Rev.* 349 (1989); H. Baade, "'Original Intent' in Historical Perspective: Some Critical Glosses," 69 *Tex. L. Rev.* 1001 (1991); R.N. Clinton, "Original Understanding, Legal Realism, and the Interpretation of 'This Constitution,'" 72 *Iowa L. Rev.* 1177 (1987); W.J. Michael, "The Original Understanding of Original Intent: A Textual Analysis," 26 *Ohio North. U. L. Rev.* 201 (2000).

[93] Sandalow, *supra* p. 167, note 76 at 1068.

connection with the past and remaining enmeshed in it. The ultimate constitutional purpose is modern, but its roots are in the past.

Objective Purpose and Protections of the Individual

Scalia argues that giving the language of the constitution a modern meaning cripples the constitution as a source of protection of the individual from the collectivity.[94] In his opinion, if judges interpret the constitution according to modern worldviews, the constitution will reflect the perspectives of the majority, at the expense of the rights of the minority. One response to this claim is that a modern perspective on human rights does not necessarily mean the perspective that the majority favors. As we have seen, the purposive approach interprets the constitution according to basic, fundamental values that reflect modern society's deep perspectives, not passing trends.[95] True, it is not always easy for a judge to ignore popular trends and give expression to society's deep perspectives; it is not easy to reflect history and not hysteria. Judges play this role throughout their judicial activity, however. They will know how to avoid the tyranny of the majority in the interpretation they give the constitution.

"Living Constitution" and "Living Tree"

Resort to the ultimate purpose of a constitution allows the constitution to address life's changing realities. At the founding of the constitution, its authors lay a basis for the document that is intended to exercise control over the future. This control—lest it become mastery—must be flexible enough to allow development. That is the meaning of the metaphor, "a living constitution." Its life is not expressed in imposing old constitutional principles on new circumstances.[96] The aliveness of a constitution means giving modern content to old constitutional principles.[97] That is also the meaning behind the metaphor comparing a constitution to a living tree.[98] Note that the tree is rooted. The aliveness of the fundamental values is not license for

---

[94] A. Scalia, "Originalism: The Lesser Evil," 57 *U. Chi. L. Rev.* 849 (1989).

[95] *Supra* p. 381.

[96] W. Rehnquist, "The Notion of a Living Constitution," 54 *Tex. L. Rev.* 693 (1976); Robert Bork, *The Tempting of America: The Political Seduction of the Law* 163 (1990).

[97] *See* Justice Deane's comments, quoted in note 86.

[98] Lord Sankey's words in *Edwards v. A.G. of Canada* [1930] A.C. 124, 136 (P.C.) (comparing a constitution to "a living tree capable of growth and expansion within its natural limits"). *See also* Walton, *supra* p. 85, note 4.

a judge to do with them as he or she pleases. We must not replace the subjectivity of the authors of the constitution with the subjectivity of those who interpret it. The evolving content of the fundamental values reflects change in society's fundamental perspectives on its national credo. These changes reflect history, tradition, and the web of the nation's shared life. They should not reflect the individuality of the judge.

Interpretation with a Broad View

Judges should adopt a broad perspective on constitutional interpretation. Their interpretation should be generous,[99] not legalistic or pedantic.[100] A constitution establishes a structure for the government, regime, and protections of the individual. Its interpretation should reflect the broad scope of its role. As Justice Agranat said, "When the issue relates to a document that sets a framework for the state's authority, the court should take a 'spacious view' of the powers it enumerates."[101] I echoed his words in another case, noting that

We are interested in the interpretation of a fundamental constitutional provision. We should take a "spacious view" of interpreting a fundamental provision . . . with the understanding that we are interested in a provision that determines ways of life . . . we are interested in human experience that must adapt itself to life's changing realities.[102]

In another case, I noted that

The constitutional proposition is that constitutional provisions should be interpreted in accordance with their senior status and as befits their tendency to determine ways of life. A fundamental provision does not freeze an existing situation. It guides human experience. Therefore, it should be interpreted with a broad view, not just technically.[103]

[99] See Lord Wilberforce's opinion in *Minister of Home Affairs v. Fisher* [1979] 3 All E.R. 21, 25 ("a generous interpretation avoiding what has been called 'the austerity of tabulated legalism' suitable to give to individuals the full measure of the fundamental rights and freedoms referred to"). *See also* Justice Dickson's opinion in *R v. Big M Drug Mart* [1985] 1 S.C.R. 295, 344 ("The interpretation should be . . . a generous rather than a legalistic one, aimed at fulfilling the purpose of the guarantee and securing for the individual the full benefit of the *Charter*'s protection").

[100] *See* Justice Dixon's opinion in *Australian National Airways Pty Ltd v. Commonwealth* (1945) 71 C.L.R. 29, 81 ("[W]e should avoid pedantic and narrow construction in dealing with [such] an instrument of government").

[101] F.H. 13/60, *Attorney General v. Matana*, 16 P.D. 430, 442.

[102] E.A. 2/84 *supra* p. 360, note 64 at 306.

[103] H.C. 428/86, *supra* p. 167, note 74 at 618.

Taking a broad view of interpretation does not mean interpreting in a manner that exceeds the meaning of the language. A judge taking a broad view of interpretation would give the constitution a meaning that achieves its (ultimate) purpose—a purpose that reflects historical continuity and fundamental modern perspectives. It means an interpretation that aspires to constitutional unity and harmony. A broad view of interpretation goes beyond the meaning of words in the literal-historical context that created them. It gives the language of the constitution meaning in its historical context, in the framework of modern fundamental perspectives. Justice Holmes wrote that

> The provisions of the Constitution are not mathematical formulas having their essence in their form; they are organic living institutions transplanted from English soil. Their significance is vital, not formal; it is to be gathered, not simply by taking the words and a dictionary, but by considering their origin and the line of their growth.[104]

Constitutional interpretation from a broad view is purposive interpretation. A judge taking a broad view looks at the past, present, and future to see what he or she can learn from language, history, culture, and fundamental modern principles. He or she adopts a comprehensive perspective on law at a given time, in a given society. A broad view of interpretation is not expansive (or liberal) interpretation. A broad view means that judges take a purposive approach to constitutional interpretation but do not prejudge the results of that approach. A broad view of interpretation may lead to a constrictive or expansive interpretive outcome. A broad view of interpretation regards the constitutional provision in its entire context, as part of the life of the nation, through the course of its history.

Judicial Discretion in Determining the Ultimate Purpose of a Constitution

Constitutional-interpretive thought has come a long way since the naïve proclamation of Justice Roberts that all a judge does is "To lay the article of the Constitution which is invoked beside the statute which is challenged and to decide whether the latter squares with the former."[105] The interpretive role is much more complicated. In constitutional interpretation—as in the interpretation of every legal text—judges should have room to exercise judicial discretion.[106] This room is always lim-

---

[104] *Gompers v. United States*, 233 U.S. 604, 610 (1914).

[105] *United States v. Butler*, 297 U.S. 61, 62 (1936).

[106] B. McLachlin, "The Charter: A New Role for the Judiciary," 29 *Alb. L. Rev.* 540, 546 (1990).

ited.[107] Judges may not read their personal worldviews into the constitutional text.[108] They should interpret the provisions of a constitution objectively.[109] The result of their interpretation should not determine constitutional principles; constitutional principles must determine the result of their interpretation. That is the meaning of the requirement that judges exercise their discretion neutrally.[110] Neutrality requires the judge to arrive at the interpretive result by applying constitutional principles, regardless of whether he or she approves of the outcome. We must recognize, however, that sometimes there is no choice but to resort to judicial discretion.[111] Justice Frankfurter expressed this idea well in saying that "The words of the Constitution . . . are so unrestricted by their intrinsic meaning or by their history or by tradition or by prior decisions that they leave the individual justice free, if indeed they do not compel him or her, to gather meaning not from reading the Constitution but from reading life."[112] In exercising discretion, an interpreter can only choose the solution that appears best to him or her, taking pragmatic considerations into account. Different interpreters will arrive at different results. My suggestion is to aspire to the constitutional solution that is most just. Law and justice thus meet. Could there be a better meeting?

[107] *Cf.* M. Tushnet, "Following the Rules Laid Down: A Critique of Interpretation and Natural Principle," 96 *Harv. L. Rev.* 781 (1983); M. Tushnet, "Critical Legal Studies and Constitutional Law: An Essay in Deconstruction," 36 *Stan. L. Rev.* 623 (1984).

[108] B. Cardozo, *The Nature of the Judicial Process* 141 (1921).

[109] *Planned Parenthood of Southeastern Pennsylvania v. Casey*, 505 U.S. 833 (1992). *See also* D. Millon, "Objectivity and Democracy," 67 *N.Y.U. L. Rev.* 1 (1992); R. Bennett, "Objectivity in Constitutional Law," 132 *U. Pa. L. Rev.* 445 (1984).

[110] H. Wechsler, "Toward Neutral Principles of Constitutional Law," 73 *Harv. L. Rev.* 1 (1959).

[111] C.A. 294/91, *supra* p. 334, note 92 at 514; J.J. Moreso, *Legal Indeterminacy and Constitutional Interpretation* (1998).

[112] F. Frankfurter, *Felix Frankfurter on the Supreme Court: Extrajudicial Essays on the Court and the Constitution* 464 (1970).

Appendix 1

The Structure of Legal Interpretation

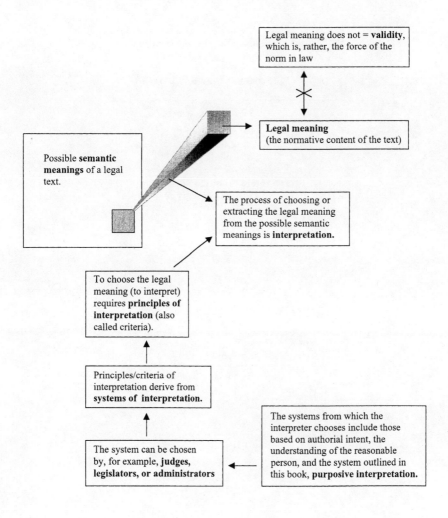

Legal meaning does not = **validity**, which is, rather, the force of the norm in law

Legal meaning
(the normative content of the text)

Possible **semantic meanings** of a legal text.

The process of choosing or extracting the legal meaning from the possible semantic meanings is **interpretation.**

To choose the legal meaning (to interpret) requires **principles of interpretation** (also called criteria).

Principles/criteria of interpretation derive from **systems of interpretation.**

The system can be chosen by, for example, **judges, legislators, or administrators**

The systems from which the interpreter chooses include those based on authorial intent, the understanding of the reasonable person, and the system outlined in this book, **purposive interpretation.**

Purposive Interpretation

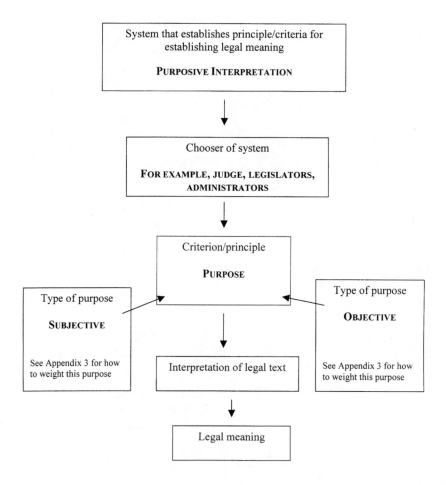

Appendix 3

Weighting Subjective
and Objective Purposes

PURPOSE	TEXT		
	Contracts and wills	*Statutes*	*Constitutions*
Subjective The intention of the author of the text:	Prevails in most cases	Is given special weight with a young statute, a specific statute, and a statute expressed in the form of rules	Is relevant mainly when there are conflicting objective purposes
Objective Goals, interests, and values that a text each type is designed to actualize:	Are relevant when information is lacking about the subjective purpose	Are given special weight with an old statute, a general statute or codification, and a statute expressed in the form of standards	Prevails in most cases

Index

Abbot case, 141
Abraham, K., 56
Abrahamson, S., 169
abstract intent: Dworkin on, 297; legislative history in interpreting, 292; subjective, 126–127; —, of constitutional founders, 190–191
abstract purposes, 126–129; conflicting with objective purpose, 366–367; of constitutions, 375–376; of statutes, 348
abstraction levels: of constitution's objective purpose, 377; different, purposes at, 114–115; high, 152; —, intent at, 267; intermediate, 151; for interpretation of free speech, 380n.52; low, 150–151; low versus high, 118; objective purpose at, 149–153, 154, 351; in objective purpose of contract, 332–334; of purposes of will, 186–187; same, purposes at, 115; supreme, 152–153
absurdity: avoidance of, 80; circumstantial evidence in removing, 142–143; presumptions of purpose avoiding, 336; prevention of, 270; vagueness of, 275n.63
Ackerman, Bruce, 196, 237, 370
ad hoc balance, 179–180
adhesion contract, 184; content of, 200–201; objective purpose in interpreting, 95; ultimate purpose in, 201–202
adjudication: integrity of, 291; rules of, 367
Administration of Justice Act of 1982, 313; Art. 21 of, 313n.31
administrative orders, 184
administrative regulations, 184
Adras Building Materials Ltd. v. Harlow and Jones, 353–354
aesthetics, 111
agency model, 248–249
Agranat, Justice, 161, 165n.63, 179, 391
Air Tours (Israel) Ltd. v. Chair of Antitrust Council, 349
Akhnai's oven, 156–157
Aleinikoff, A., 34, 120, 177, 180n.121, 268, 273, 345n.17
Alexander, L., 51, 52, 71, 165, 286n.106
Alexy, R., 38, 120n.2, 211n.22

Allan, J., 85
Almog, S., 261n.5
Alon, M., 156, 157
Alston, W., 101
Amar, A., 21, 376n.36, 378, 379
ambiguity: in communication, 217; in free interpretation, 298; in joint contract, 131–132; in legal texts, 99–100
American Convention on Human Rights, 384n.70
American law: contractual, 319; —, circumstances in, 331; correcting mistakes in statutes in, 78; on interpreting wills, 312; on joint subjective intent, 327; legal process movement in, 227–228; legislative history in, 345–346; new textualism in, 277–285; plain meaning rule in, 142–143; pseudo-subjective approach in, 266; purposive interpretation in, 85–86; —, statutory, 341
American realist movement, 225, 298
Anglo-American legal system: contradictory texts in, 64–65; norms of equal status in, 11; purposive interpretation in, 85–86
Anglo-Saxon legal system: on judicial authority to fill in gaps, 69; sources of interpretative laws in, 49–50
antinomic contradiction, 74
apartheid system: legal interpretation in, 11n.28; statutory interpretation in, 197
approximation, doctrine of, 65
Arad v. Speaker of the Knesset, 135n.54
archaeological fact, 120
argument, rules of, 40–41
Aristotle, 26, 213n.35
Atiyah, P.S., 70, 168, 286n.105; on correcting contracts, 15; on legal development, 42; on mistake in contract construction, 320n.16
Atkinson, T., 80–81n.20, 171, 307, 308
Atria, F., 67n.18
Attorney General (NSW) v. Brewery Employees Union of HSA (Union Label), 370
Attorney General v. Matana, 391
Aubert, J.F., 70
Auerbach, A.J., 229

in, 73; on interpreting wills, 312; on
joint subjective intent, 327; on judicial
authority to fill in gaps, 69–70; non-
interpretive doctrine in, 62; purposive interpretation in, 86, 340–341; sens clair
doctrine in, 142–143; statutory interpretation in, 340–341; subjective approach
of, 124–125; subjective-objective interpretation in, 36; teleological interpretation in, 87. *See also specific countries*
contra proferentem doctrine, 334–335; presumption of, 174
contracts, 184; age of text in ultimate purpose of, 192; categories of, 158; in comparative law, 326; conflicting interpretation of, 44; construction versus language
of, 65; content of, 200–201; contradiction between subjective and objective
purposes of, 337–338; correcting mistakes in, 79; correcting or filling gap in,
15, 67; creating new versus interpreting,
19–20; dynamic interpretation of, 155–
156; essence of purpose of, 325–326;
freedoms of, 259; fundamental constitutional values in interpreting, 256–258;
gaps in, 72–74; implied term in, 6; interest in, xii; international, 318–319;
interpretation of, xvii–xviii, 318–338;
interpretive rules in developing, 41–42;
in Jewish law, 27n.84; joint authors in,
131–132; judge's partnership in interpreting, 251–252; liability in, 130–131;
long-term, 337–338; mistakes in formation of, 320n.16; multi-party, 129–130;
natural environment of, 159; negotiations for, 330; normative harmony of,
160; objective intent of, 123–124; objective interpretation in, 44; objective purpose of, 94–95, 332–334; —, meaning
and, 321; —, presumptions of identifying, 334–336; plain versus ambiguous
language in, 331–332; publicity principle
and, 244–245; silence as gaps in, 68; social context of, 195–196; subjective purpose of, 32–33, 124–125n.18, 326–
329; —, sources of, 329–332; as texts
and norms, 12; theory of, 321–325; —,
classical, 321–322; —, in contractual interpretation, 324–325; —, feminism
and, 324; —, neoclassical, 321n.21;
treating as whole, 329; two-party, 129–

130; ultimate purpose of, 187–188,
201–203, 336–338; uniqueness of,
318–321; weighting subjective and objective purposes in, 397
contractual parties, 326–327n.50
contradictions: normative resolution of,
74–77; between norms in single text, 75;
between norms of same status, 75–76;
between purposes, 117–118; real versus
imaginary, 74–75; resolving, 5, 64, 65;
between subjective and objective purposes, 118; between superior and inferior
norms, 76–77
Coons, J., 358
Corbin, A., 9, 65, 103, 326–327n.50, 331,
335
corporate laws, legal entities in, 130–131
corrected intent, 136–137
corrupt statutes, 282
Corry, J., 51, 85, 234
cost-benefit analysis, 323
Côté, P.A., 77, 171, 287, 362
courts, interpretive responsibility of, 51
Cowen, 133, 174–175, 275
Cox, A., 253
Craig, P., 242
creation: versus declaring law, 52–53; interpretation as, 218
creativity, judicial, 304
credibility standard, 143–144
criminal statutes: interpretation versus filling gaps in, 17; ultimate purpose in, 203
criminal texts, 184
critical hermeneutics, 55
Cross, R., 3, 70, 80, 104, 123, 142, 171,
272, 362; on logic and structure of language, 108; on purposive interpretation,
87
Culler, J., 299n.146
Curtis, C., 33, 53, 132, 297
custom, as source of interpretive laws, 49
cy pres performance, 80–81

Dahl, R.A., 235
Damaska, M., 71
D'Amato, A., 25, 298–299n.145
Dammann, J., 169
Damren, S.C., 131
data, constituting ultimate purpose, 182–183
David, R., 162
Davies, D.J., 269

Feeney, T., 79, 308, 309n.13, 311, 312, 315
Feld, A., 238
Feldman, H., 211n.21
Feldstein, M., 229
Fellows, M.L., 121, 313n.34
feminism, contract theory and, 324
Fessler, F., 201
Fifth Amendment, 70–71
Finkelman, P., 389n.92
Finnis, J., 213n.35
First Amendment, 70–71
Fisch, E., 80
Fischer, M., 169
Fish, S., 9–10, 17, 48
Fiss, O., 38, 39, 54, 59, 208, 211n.21, 231, 345n.17
Fletcher, G., 382n.63
Ford, H.A.J., 309n.13
foreign law, influence of, 140n.64
fore-meanings, 57
formalism, 27; new textualism and, 283n.94
form-substance relationship, 26–28, 31
Fourteenth Amendment, 70–71, 378
Fourth Amendment, 70–71
Frank, J., 54, 225, 225n.29, 261n.5
Frankenberg, G., 357
Frankfurter, F., 19, 85n.1, 225n.29, 252, 253, 255, 345n.17; on admissibility of legislative history, 349; on constitutional interpretation, 379n.46, 393; on legal environment, 162; in *Massachusetts Bonding & Insurance Co. v. U.S.*, 274; on normative purpose, 110–111; on statutory interpretation rules, 343n.14
Franklin, M., 169
Frantz, L., 177
free interpretation, 297–298; critique of, 298–301
free speech provision, 380n.52
freedom(s): balancing of, 180–181; maximizing, 238
French Civil Code: Article 1134 of, 252n.147; Article 1156 of, 318–319, 327, 330
French law, 77; on interpreting wills, 308n.7
Freund, 185
Friauf, K.H., 372n.13, 378
Frickey, P., 58, 107, 134n.48, 172, 219,

282, 286n.106; on pragmatism, 287; on purposive statutory interpretation, 364
Fried, C., 177, 277, 322
Friedmann, D., 100n.15, 320; on drafters of texts, 14
Friedmann, W., 54, 221n.9
Friendly, H.J., 39, 212, 274
frustration doctrine, 42
Fry, E., 80
Fuller, L., 104, 139, 158, 211, 226, 243, 255, 352, 358
fundamental assumptions, changing, 195–197
fundamental values: actualization of, 154n.19; constitutional, 235, 256–258; in constitutional interpretation, 377, 381–382; in contractual interpretation, 324–325; determining, 164–169; in determining statute's ultimate purpose, 368–369; flux of, 154–155; of legal system, 339; objective purpose reflecting, 333–334; presumptions of purpose reflecting, 335; purposive interpretation and, 256; rule of law in guaranteeing, 246; severance of statutes from, 282; in statutory interpretation, 189, 288–289, 356–357; in will, 310. *See also* principles, fundamental; values

Gadamer, H.G., 55, 137, 230
gain, maximizing, 322–323
Galligan, D., 207n.1
Gant, S., 51
gaps, filling in, 66–74, 72–74; ban on, 69n.30; criteria for, 71–74
Garfield, A., 334
Gebbia-Pinetti, K.M., 152, 160, 163, 170, 239
general, from specific, 109
general purposes, 149
generalia specialibus non derogant, 76
generalization: level of, 267; majestic, 372–373
generic-hypothetical intent, 121
genetic fact, 120
genetic interpretation, 120n.2
Gerhards, A., 70
German Constitutional Court, 372, 388
German judges, Nazi regime, 11n.28
German law: constitutional interpretation in, 387–389; on judicial authority to fill